Maple Programming Guide

L. Bernardin
P. Chin
P. DeMarco
K. O. Geddes
D. E. G. Hare
K. M. Heal
G. Labahn
J. P. May
J. McCarron
M. B. Monagan
D. Ohashi
S. M. Vorkoetter

Copyright © Maplesoft, a division of Waterloo Maple Inc.
2012

Maple Programming Guide

by L. Bernardin, P. Chin, P. DeMarco, K. O. Geddes, D. E. G. Hare, K. M. Heal, G. Labahn, J. P. May, J. McCarron, M. B. Monagan, D. Ohashi, and S. M. Vorkoetter

Copyright

Maplesoft, Maple, MapleNet, MaplePrimes, Maplet, Maple T.A., and OpenMaple are all trademarks of Waterloo Maple Inc.

© Maplesoft, a division of Waterloo Maple Inc. 1996-2012. All rights reserved.

No part of this book may be reproduced, stored in a retrieval system, or transcribed, in any form or by any means — electronic, mechanical, photocopying, recording, or otherwise. Information in this document is subject to change without notice and does not represent a commitment on the part of the vendor. The software described in this document is furnished under a license agreement and may be used or copied only in accordance with the agreement. It is against the law to copy the software on any medium except as specifically allowed in the agreement.

Adobe and Acrobat are either registered trademarks or trademarks of Adobe Systems Incorporated in the United States and/or other countries.

Java is a registered trademarks of Oracle and/or its affiliates.

MATLAB is a registered trademark of The MathWorks, Inc.

Microsoft and Windows are registered trademarks of Microsoft Corporation.

NAG is a registered trademark of The Numerical Algorithms Group Ltd.

All other trademarks are the property of their respective owners.

This document was produced using Maple and DocBook.

Printed in Canada.

ISBN 978-1-926902-25-8

Contents

Preface xxiii
1 Introduction to Programming in Maple 1
   1.1 In This Chapter 1
   1.2 The Maple Software 1
      The User Interface 1
      The Computation Engine 1
   1.3 Maple Statements 2
      Getting Help 2
      Displaying a Text String 2
      Performing an Arithmetic Operation 3
      Assigning to a Name 3
      Using Maple Library Commands 3
   1.4 Procedures 4
      Defining a Simple Procedure 4
      Entering a Procedure Definition 4
      Adding Comments to a Procedure 7
      Calling a Procedure 8
      Maple Library Commands, Built-In Commands, and User-Defined Procedures 8
      Full Evaluation and Last Name Evaluation 9
      Viewing Procedure Definitions and Maple Library Code 10
   1.5 Interrupting Computations and Clearing the Internal Memory 11
      Interrupting a Maple Computation 11
      Clearing the Maple Internal Memory 12
   1.6 Avoiding Common Problems 12
      Unexpected End of Statement 12
      Missing Operator 13
      Invalid, Wrong Number or Type of Arguments 14
      Unbalanced Parentheses 14
      Assignment Versus Equality 14
   1.7 Exercises 15
2 Maple Language Elements 17
   2.1 In This Chapter 17
   2.2 Character Set 17
   2.3 Tokens 18
      Reserved Words 18
      Programming-Language Operators 19
      Names 22
   2.4 Natural Integers 23
   2.5 Strings 24
      Length of a String 24

Substrings 24
Searching a String 25
String Concatenation 25
Mutability of Strings 26
Special Characters in Strings 26
Parsing Strings 27
Converting Expressions to Strings 28
2.6 Using Special Characters 28
Token Separators 28
Blank Spaces, New Lines, Comments, and Continuation 28
Punctuation Marks 30
Escape Characters 33
2.7 Types and Operands 33
DAGs 33
Maple Types 34
Operands and op 36
2.8 Avoiding Common Problems 39
Attempting to Assign to a Protected Name 39
Invalid Left-Hand Assignment 40
Incorrect Syntax in Parse 40
White Space Characters within a Token 40
Incorrect Use of Double and Single Quotes 40
Avoid Using Maple Keywords as Names 41
2.9 Exercises 42
3 Maple Expressions 43
3.1 In This Chapter 43
3.2 Introduction 43
Expressions and Statements 43
Automatic Simplification and Evaluation 43
Syntax and Constructors 43
3.3 Names 44
Creating Names: Lexical Conventions 45
3.4 Unevaluated Expressions 48
Protecting Names and Options 49
Generic Expressions 50
Pass by Reference 50
Displaying the Original Command 51
Unassigning Names 51
Evaluation and Automatic Simplification 51
Example: Defining a Procedure that Is Returned Unevaluated 53
3.5 Numbers 55
Integers 55
Fractions 55

Floats	56
Complex Numbers	60
3.6 Indexed Expressions	64
3.7 Member Selection	69
3.8 Functions	70
Calls to Procedures	71
3.9 Arithmetic Expressions	72
Arithmetic Operators	72
Noncommutative Multiplication	85
Factorials	87
Forming Sums and Products	88
3.10 Boolean and Relational Expressions	89
Boolean Constants	89
Boolean Operators	89
Relational Operators	92
Efficient Boolean Iteration	96
3.11 Expressions for Data Structures	97
Sequences	97
Lists	99
Sets	101
Tables	102
Rectangular Tables	103
3.12 Set-Theoretic Expressions	104
Membership	104
Set Inclusion	104
Other Binary Operators for Sets	105
3.13 Other Expressions	107
Functional Operators	107
Composition	108
Neutral Operators	109
Ranges	110
The Concatenation Operator	112
The Double Colon Operator	114
Series	115
3.14 Attributes	117
3.15 Using Expressions	119
Evaluating and Simplifying Expressions	119
Substituting Subexpressions	120
Structured Types	123
3.16 Exercises	127
4 Basic Data Structures	**129**
4.1 In This Chapter	129
4.2 Introduction	129

- 4.3 Immutable Data Structures ... 129
  - Lists ... 130
  - Sets ... 136
- 4.4 Mutable Data Structures ... 141
  - Tables ... 141
  - Arrays ... 148
- 4.5 Other Data Structure Operations ... 158
  - Filtering Data Structure Elements ... 158
  - Converting Data Structures ... 158
- 4.6 Other Data Structures ... 159
  - Records ... 159
  - Stacks ... 161
  - Queues ... 164
- 4.7 Data Coercion ... 167
- 4.8 Data Structure Performance Comparisons ... 167
  - Indexing ... 167
  - Membership ... 167
  - Building a Collection of Data ... 168
- 4.9 Avoiding Common Problems ... 169
  - Passing Sequences into Functions ... 169
  - Incorrect Index Values ... 170
  - Do Not Treat Lists and Sets as Mutable ... 171
- 4.10 Exercises ... 171

5 Maple Statements ... 173

- 5.1 In This Chapter ... 173
- 5.2 Introduction ... 173
- 5.3 Statement Separators ... 173
- 5.4 Expression Statements ... 174
- 5.5 Assignments ... 174
  - Multiple Assignment ... 175
- 5.6 Flow Control ... 177
  - Sequencing ... 177
  - Branching ... 177
  - Loops ... 181
  - Looping Commands ... 186
  - Non-Local Flow Control ... 188
- 5.7 The use Statement ... 192
- 5.8 Other Statements ... 196
  - The quit Statement ... 196
  - The save Statement ... 197
  - The read Statement ... 197
- 5.9 Exercises ... 198

6 Procedures ... 199

6.1 Terminology 199
6.2 Defining and Executing Procedures 200
6.3 Parameter Declarations 201
 Required Positional Parameters 201
 Optional Ordered Parameters 202
 Expected Ordered Parameters 204
 Keyword Parameters 204
 The End-of-Parameters Marker 206
 Default Value Dependencies 207
 Parameter Modifiers 208
 Procedures without Declared Parameters 212
6.4 Return Type 213
6.5 The Procedure Body 213
 Description 214
 Options 214
 Variables in Procedures 221
 Non-Variable Name Bindings 224
 The Statement Sequence 224
 Referring to Parameters within the Procedure Body 224
6.6 How Procedures Are Executed 231
 Binding of Arguments to Parameters 232
 Statement Sequence Interpretation 236
6.7 Using Data Structures with Procedures 244
 Passing Data Structures to Procedures 244
 Returning Data Structures from Procedures 245
 Example: Computing an Average 246
 Example: Binary Search 247
 Example: Plotting the Roots of a Polynomial 248
6.8 Writing Usable and Maintainable Procedures 252
 Formatting Procedures for Readability 252
 Commenting Your Code 253
6.9 Other Methods for Creating Procedures 255
 Functional Operators: Mapping Notation 255
 The unapply Function 256
 Anonymous Procedures 258
6.10 Recursion 259
6.11 Procedures that Return Procedures 261
 Example: Creating a Newton Iteration 261
 Example: A Shift Operator 264
6.12 The Procedure Object 265
 The procedure Type 265
 Procedure Operands 266
6.13 Exercises 269

7 Numerical Programming in Maple ... 271
7.1 In This Chapter ... 271
7.2 Numeric Types in Maple ... 271
- Integers ... 271
- Rationals ... 273
- Floating-Point Numbers ... 274
- Hardware Floating-Point Numbers ... 276
- Extended Numeric Types ... 277
- Complex Numbers ... 278
- Non-numeric Constants ... 279

7.3 More about Floating-Point Numbers in Maple ... 279
- Representation of Floating-Point Numbers in Maple ... 280
- Precision and Accuracy ... 282
- Floating-Point Contagion ... 283
- More on the Floating-Point Model ... 286

7.4 Maple Commands for Numerical Computing ... 287
- The evalf Command ... 287
- Numeric Solvers ... 290
- The evalhf Command ... 291
- Numerical Linear Algebra ... 294

7.5 Writing Efficient Numerical Programs ... 297
- Writing Flexible Numerical Procedures ... 297
- Example: Newton Iteration ... 299
- Example: Jacobi Iteration ... 303

8 Programming with Modules ... 309
8.1 In This Chapter ... 309
8.2 Introduction ... 309
- Encapsulation ... 309
- Creating a Custom Maple Package ... 309
- Creating Objects ... 309
- Creating Generic Programs ... 310

8.3 A Simple Example ... 310
8.4 Syntax and Semantics ... 311
- The Module Definition ... 311
- The Module Body ... 311
- Module Parameters ... 311
- Named Modules ... 312
- Declarations ... 314
- Exported Local Variables ... 316
- Module Options ... 320
- Special Exports ... 320
- Implicit Scoping Rules ... 325
- Lexical Scoping Rules ... 326

| Modules and Types 328
| 8.5   Records 330
| Creating Records 330
| Record Types 332
| Using Records to Represent Quaternions 332
| Object Inheritance 333
| 8.6   Modules and use Statements 335
| Operator Rebinding 336
| 8.7   Interfaces and Implementations 340
| Generic Programming as a Good Software Engineering Practice 340
| Distinction between Local and Exported Variables 341
| Interfaces 341
| A Package for Manipulating Interfaces 342
| The load Option 346

9 Object Oriented Programming 347
| 9.1   In This Chapter 347
| 9.2   Introduction To Object Oriented Programming 347
| Terminology 347
| Benefits of Object Oriented Programming 347
| 9.3   Objects in Maple 348
| Creating a New Class of Objects 348
| Creating More Objects 348
| Objects and Types 349
| 9.4   Methods 349
| Methods Can Access Object Locals 349
| Method Names Should Be Declared static 349
| Methods Are Passed the Objects They Manipulate 349
| Calling Methods 349
| Objects in Indexed Function Calls 350
| Special Methods 350
| 9.5   Overloading Operators 350
| Supported Operators 351
| Implementing Operators 351
| 9.6   Overloading Built-in Routines 351
| Overridable Built-in Routines 351
| 9.7   Examples 352
| 9.8   Avoiding Common Mistakes 357
| Overloaded Operators and Built-in Routines Must Handle All Possibilities 357
| Make Sure to Access the Correct Routine 358
| Be Aware of NULL 358
| Lexical Scoping Does Not Circumvent local 359

10 Input and Output 361
| 10.1 In This Chapter 361

- 10.2 Introduction ... 361
- 10.3 Input and Output in the Worksheet ... 362
  - Interfaces ... 363
  - Interactive Output ... 364
  - Interactive Input ... 366
  - Customization ... 366
- 10.4 Input and Output with Files ... 366
  - Introduction ... 366
  - Working with General Files ... 367
  - Importing and Exporting Numerical Data ... 372
  - Files Used by Maple ... 374
- 10.5 Reading and Writing Formatted Data ... 375
  - The scanf and printf Commands ... 375
  - Format Strings ... 377
  - Related Commands ... 378
- 10.6 Useful Utilities ... 378
  - The StringTools Package ... 378
  - Conversion Commands ... 379
- 10.7 2-D Math ... 379
  - Introduction ... 379
  - The Typesetting Package ... 380
  - Additional Tips ... 380
- 10.8 Exercises ... 381

11 Writing Packages ... 383
- 11.1 In This Chapter ... 383
- 11.2 What Is a Package ... 383
  - Packages in the Standard Library ... 383
  - Packages Are Modules ... 383
  - Package Exports ... 384
  - Using Packages Interactively ... 384
- 11.3 Writing Maple Packages By Using Modules ... 385
  - A Simple Example ... 385
  - Custom Libraries ... 387
- 11.4 A Larger Example ... 389
  - ModuleLoad ... 389
  - The Preprocessor and Structured Source Files ... 390
  - Subpackages ... 392
- 11.5 Example: A Shapes Package ... 392
  - Source Code Organization ... 393
  - Package Architecture ... 394
  - The Package API ... 395
  - The make Procedure ... 395
  - The area Procedure ... 395

  The circumference Procedure 395
  Shape Representation 396
  Procedure Dispatching 396
  Dispatching on Submodule Exports 396
  Conditional Dispatching 397
  Table-based Dispatching 398
  Shape-specific Submodules 399
  The point Submodule 399
  The circle Submodule 399

12 Graphics 401
12.1 In This Chapter 401
12.2 Introduction 401
  Plots in Maple 401
  Generating a Plot 402
12.3 The Plot Library 403
  Generating 2-D and 3-D Plots 404
  Plotting Points, Polygons, and Text 415
  Combining Plots 421
  Specialty Plots 423
  Other Packages 429
12.4 Programming with Plots 432
  A 2-D Example 432
  A 3-D Example 437
12.5 Data Structures 441
  Types of Data Structures 442
  Creating Plot Structures 446
  Altering Plot Structures 447
12.6 Customizing Plots 449
  Controlling the Sampling 449
  Colors 452
  View 458
  Typesetting 461
  Axes and Gridlines 462
  Coordinate Systems 464
  Setting Options 468
12.7 Animations 470
  Building an Animation with plots:-display 470
  The plots:-animate command 471
  3-D Animations with the viewpoint Option 473
  Other Animation Commands 475
  Displaying an Animation as an Array of Plots 475
12.8 Miscellaneous Topics 478
  Efficiency in Plotting 478

xii • Contents

Interfaces and Devices 479
12.9 Avoiding Common Problems 479
    Mixing Expression and Operator Forms 479
    Generating Non-numeric Data 482
13 Programming Interactive Elements 487
    13.1 In This Chapter 487
    13.2 Programming Embedded Components 487
        Adding Embedded Components to a Document 487
        Editing Component Properties 488
        Example: Creating a Tic-Tac-Toe Game 489
        Retrieving and Updating Component Properties 491
        Using the GetProperty Command to Retrieve Properties 491
        Using the SetProperty Command to Update Properties 492
        Using the Do Command to Retrieve and Update Component Properties 492
    13.3 Programming Maplets 493
        Layout Managers 493
        Box Layout 494
        Grid Layout 496
        Border Layout 498
14 Advanced Connectivity 503
    14.1 In This Chapter 503
        Connecting to the Maple Engine 503
        Using External Libraries in Maple 503
        Connecting Maple to Another Program 503
        Code Generation 504
    14.2 MapleNet 504
        Computation on Demand 504
        Embedding a Maple Application in a Web Application 505
    14.3 OpenMaple 506
        Runtime Environment Prerequisites 507
        Interface Overview 507
        C/C++ Example 509
        C# Example 511
        Java Example 512
        Visual Basic 6 Example 514
        Visual Basic .NET Example 515
        Memory Usage 516
    14.4 The Maple Command-line Interface 516
        Batch Files 517
        Directing Input to a Pipeline 517
        Specifying Start-up Commands 517
    14.5 External Calling: Using Compiled Code in Maple 518
        Calling a Function in a Dynamic-link Library 518

Contents • xiii

    Specifying Parameter Types for Function Specifications 521
    Scalar Data Formats 521
    Structured Data Formats 522
    External Function Interface 523
    Specifying Parameter Passing Conventions 526
    Generating Wrappers Automatically 526
    Passing Arguments by Reference 528
    External API 529
    System Integrity 529
14.6 Accessing Data over a Network with TCP/IP Sockets 530
    Socket Server 530
    Socket Client 531
14.7 Code Generation 531
    Calling CodeGeneration Commands 531
    Notes on Code Translation 532
    Translation Process 532
    Example 1: Translating a Procedure to Java 533
    Example 2: Translating a Procedure to C 533
    Example 3: Translating a Procedure to Fortran 534
    Example 4: Translating an Expression to MATLAB 534
    Example 5: Translating a Procedure to Visual Basic 535
    Example 6: Using the defaulttype and deducetypes Options 535
    Example 7: Using the declare Option 536
    The Intermediate Code 536
    Extending the CodeGeneration Translation Facilities 537
    The Printing Phase 537
    Defining a Custom Translator 537
    Using a Printer Module 538
    Language Translator Definition 539
    Using the Define Command 539
    Creating a Language Definition Module 540
    Using a New Translator 541
14.8 CAD Connectivity 541
14.9 Maple Plug-in for Excel 542
14.10 Connecting MATLAB and Maple 543
    Accessing the MATLAB Computation Engine from Maple 544
    Accessing the Maple Computational Engine from MATLAB 544
15 Parallel Programming 547
15.1 In This Chapter 547
15.2 Introduction 547
15.3 Introduction to Parallel Programming with Tasks 548
    Parallel Execution 548
    Controlling Parallel Execution 552

15.4 Task Programming Model ... 556
- Tasks ... 556
- The Task Tree ... 557
- Starting Tasks ... 557
- Task Management ... 559

15.5 Examples ... 564
- The N Queens Problem ... 564

15.6 Limitations of Parallel Programming ... 567
- Library Code ... 567
- Maple Interpreter ... 567

15.7 Avoiding Common Problems ... 567
- Every Execution Order Will Happen ... 567
- Lock around All Accesses ... 567
- Debugging Parallel Code ... 568

15.8 Introduction to Grid Programming ... 568
- Starting a Grid-Based Computation ... 568
- Communicating between Nodes ... 569

15.9 Grid Examples ... 571
- Computing a Mandelbrot Set ... 571

15.10 The Grid Computing Toolbox ... 578

15.11 Limitations ... 578
- Memory Usage ... 578
- Cost of Communication ... 579
- Load Balancing ... 579

15.12 Troubleshooting ... 579
- Deadlocking ... 579
- 'libname' and Other Engine Variables ... 579
- Missing Functions ... 579

16 Testing, Debugging, and Efficiency ... 581

16.1 In This Chapter ... 581

16.2 The Maple Debugger: A Tutorial Example ... 581
- Example ... 582
- Numbering the Procedure Statements I ... 583
- Invoking the Debugger I ... 584
- Setting a Breakpoint ... 584
- Controlling the Execution of a Procedure during Debugging I ... 585
- Invoking the Debugger II ... 589
- Setting a Watchpoint ... 589

16.3 Maple Debugger Commands ... 593
- Numbering the Procedure Statements II ... 593
- Invoking the Debugger III ... 594
- Controlling the Execution of a Procedure during Debugging II ... 601
- Changing the State of a Procedure during Debugging ... 601

  Examining the State of a Procedure during Debugging 604
  Using Top-Level Commands at the Debugger Prompt 608
  Restrictions 608
 16.4 Detecting Errors 609
  Tracing a Procedure 609
  Using Assertions 612
  Handling Exceptions 615
  Checking Syntax 617
 16.5 Creating Efficient Programs 618
  Displaying Time and Memory Statistics 618
  Profiling a Procedure 620
 16.6 Managing Resources 624
  Setting a Time Limit on Computations 625
  Garbage Collection 626
  Other Kernel Options for Managing Resources 626
 16.7 Testing Your Code 627
  Verifying Results with verify 627
  A Simple Test Harness 628
  Writing Good Tests 629
  Test Coverage 629
 16.8 Exercises 630
A Internal Representation 633
 A.1 Internal Functions 633
  Evaluators 633
  Algebraic Functions 634
  Algebraic Service Functions 634
  Data Structure Manipulation Functions 634
  General Service Functions 634
 A.2 Flow of Control 634
 A.3 Internal Representations of Data Types 635
  AND: Logical AND 635
  ASSIGN: Assignment Statement 636
  BINARY: Binary Object 636
  BREAK: Break Statement 636
  CATENATE: Name Concatenation 636
  COMPLEX: Complex Value 637
  CONTROL: Communications Control Structure 637
  DCOLON: Type Specification or Test 637
  DEBUG: Debug 637
  EQUATION: Equation or Test for Equality 638
  ERROR: Error Statement 638
  EXPSEQ: Expression Sequence 638
  FLOAT: Software Floating-Point Number 639

FOR: For/While Loop Statement 639
FOREIGN: Foreign Data 640
FUNCTION: Function Call 640
GARBAGE: Garbage 640
HFLOAT: Hardware Float 641
IF: If Statement 641
IMPLIES: Logical IMPLIES 641
INEQUAT: Not Equal or Test for Inequality 642
INTNEG: Negative Integer 642
INTPOS: Positive Integer 642
LESSEQ: Less Than or Equal 643
LESSTHAN: Less Than 643
LEXICAL: Lexically Scoped Variable within an Expression 643
LIST: List 644
LOCAL: Local Variable within an Expression 644
MEMBER: Module Member 644
MODDEF: Module Definition 644
MODULE: Module Instance 646
NAME: Identifier 647
NEXT: Next Statement 647
NOT: Logical NOT 647
OR: Logical OR 647
PARAM: Procedure Parameter in an Expression 647
POLY: Multivariate Polynomials with Integer Coefficients 649
POWER: Power 650
PROC: Procedure Definition 650
PROD: Product, Quotient, Power 651
RANGE: Range 652
RATIONAL: Rational 652
READ: Read Statement 652
RETURN: Return Statement 652
RTABLE: Rectangular Table 653
SAVE: Save Statement 654
SDPOLY: Sparse Distributed Multivariate Polynomial 654
SERIES: Series 655
SET: Set 655
STATSEQ: Statement Sequence 655
STOP: Quit Statement 656
STRING: Character String 656
SUM: Sum, Difference 656
TABLE: Table 657
TABLEREF: Table Reference 657
TRY: Try Statement 657

UNEVAL: Unevaluated Expression 658
USE: Use Statement 658
XOR: Logical Exclusive-Or 658
ZPPOLY: Polynomials with Integer Coefficients modulo n 658
A.4 Hashing in Maple 659
  Basic Hash Tables 660
  Dynamic Hash Tables 660
  Cache Hash Tables 661
  The Simplification Table 662
  The Name Table 663
  Remember Tables 663
  Maple Language Arrays and Tables 664
  Maple Language Rectangular Tables 664
  Portability 664
Index 667

List of Figures

Figure 1.1: Maple Toolbar 12
Figure 2.1: Expression Tree 37
Figure 2.2: Expression DAG 38
Figure 2.3: Actual Expression DAG 39
Figure 3.1: expr DAG 83
Figure 3.2: subsop Example DAGs 121
Figure 11.1: Organization of Package Source Files 393
Figure 11.2: Design of Package 394
Figure 13.1: Code Region for an Embedded Component 489
Figure 13.2: Border Layout Diagram 499
Figure 14.1: Maple in Excel 543
Figure 16.1: The Maple Debugger in the Standard Interface 582

List of Figures

List of Tables

Table 2.1: Special Characters 17
Table 2.2: Reserved Keywords 18
Table 2.3: Binary Operators 19
Table 2.4: Unary Operators 20
Table 2.5: Element-wise Operators 21
Table 2.6: Token Separators 30
Table 2.7: Subtype 35
Table 3.1: Initially Known Names 46
Table 5.1: Operators That Can Be Rebound 196
Table 6.1: Procedure Operands 266
Table 7.1: Floating-Point Contagion Rules 286
Table 11.1: RandomnessTests 390
Table 14.1: Basic Data Types 521
Table 14.2: Compound Data Types 522
Table 14.3: Printer Commands 538
Table 16.1: sieveTest.mpl 628
Table 16.2: sieveTest2.mpl 629
Table 16.3: Modified sieveTest2.mpl 630
Table A.1: Maple Structures 633

Preface

Technical computation forms the heart of problem solving in mathematics, engineering, and science. To help you, Maple™ offers a vast repository of mathematical algorithms covering a wide range of applications.

At the core of Maple, the symbolic computation engine is second to none in terms of scalability and performance. Indeed, symbolics was the core focus when Maple was first conceived at the University of Waterloo in 1980 and to this day Maple continues to be the benchmark software for symbolic computing.

Together with a large repository of numeric functionality, including industry-standard libraries such as the Intel® Math Kernel Library (MKL), Automatically Tuned Linear Algebra Software (ATLAS), and the C Linear Algebra PACKage (CLAPACK), as well as a broad selection of routines from the Numerical Algorithms Group (NAG®) libraries, you can rely on Maple to support you a across many domains and applications. Using its unique hybrid technology, Maple integrates the symbolic and numeric worlds to solve diverse problems more efficiently and with higher accuracy.

The Maple user interface allows you to harness all this computational power by using context-sensitive menus, task templates, and interactive assistants. The first steps are intuitively easy to use and quickly lead you into the captivating, creative, and dynamic world of Maple.

As you get more proficient, you will want to explore more deeply and directly access all of the computational power available to you. You can accomplish this through the Maple programming language. Combining elements from procedural languages (such as Pascal), functional languages (such as Lisp) and object-oriented languages (such as Java™), Maple provides you with an exceptionally simple yet powerful language to write your own programs. High-level constructs such as map allow you to express in a single statement what would take ten lines of code in a language like C.

Maple allows you to quickly focus and reliably solve problems with easy access to over 5000 algorithms and functions developed over 30 years of cutting-edge research and development.

Maple's user community is now over two million people. Together we have built large collections of Maple worksheets and Maple programs, much of which is freely available on the web for you to reuse or learn from. The majority of the mathematical algorithms you find in Maple today are written in the Maple Programming Language. As a Maple user, you write programs using the same basic tools that the Maple developers themselves use. Moreover you can easily view most of the code in the Maple library and you can even extend the Maple system, tying your programs in with existing functionality.

This guide will lead you from your first steps in Maple programming to writing sophisticated routines and packages, allowing you to tackle problems in mathematics, engineering, and science effectively and efficiently. You will quickly progress towards proficiency in Maple programming, allowing you to harness the full power of Maple.

Have fun!

Audience

This guide provides information for users who are new to Maple programming, as well as experienced Maple programmers. Before reading this guide, you should be familiar with the following.

- The Maple help system
- How to use Maple interactively
- The **Maple User Manual**

Maple User Interfaces

You can access Maple functionality through several *user interfaces*. Maple interfaces accept user input, communicate with the Maple computational engine, and display solutions to mathematical problems.

The Standard Interface

The standard interface facilitates the performance of computations and lets you manipulate mathematical expressions. It also provides layout and document processing features that you can use to annotate your problem-solving process. The standard interface will be the focus of this guide.

To display the standard interface, double-click your **Maple** desktop icon (Windows® and Macintosh®) or run the **xmaple** command (UNIX®).

Other Maple Interfaces

- **MapleNet**™ lets you publish your interactive Maple documents on the web. Users with an Internet connection can then view and manipulate your published documents in a web browser. MapleNet also provides a web service interface that allows connected applications to pass data to Maple, run a program, and retrieve results. It also lets you create custom JavaServer™ Pages (JSP) applications and Java applets. For more information about MapleNet, see *MapleNet (page 504)*.

- **OpenMaple**™ is the Maple application programming interface (API) that lets you build custom user interfaces or embed Maple in an existing application. OpenMaple can be used with a variety of languages including C, C++, Java, Fortran, Visual Basic®, and C#. For more information about OpenMaple, see *OpenMaple (page 506)*.

- The **Maple command-line interface** is a console-based application that can be used for batch processing Maple command files. For more information, see *The Maple Command-line Interface (page 516)*.
- **Maplet**™ applications are custom interfaces that are created using the Maple programming language. For more information, see *Programming Interactive Elements (page 487)*.

For more information about the Maple user interfaces, refer to the *Maple User Manual* or the **versions** help page.

Programming in the Standard Interface

Most of the time, you will enter Maple code directly in a worksheet or document. The standard interface also provides other functionality for entering Maple code. For example, you can enter your code in a *startup code region* if you want to run certain commands or procedures automatically when a Maple document is opened. You can also enter your code in a *code edit region* if you want to keep a set of Maple commands or procedures in a confined region within your document. For more information, refer to the **worksheet,documenting,startupcode** and **CodeEditRegion** help pages.

You can also include your code in an external text file to be read by a worksheet or document, or batch processed. For more information, refer to the **file** help page.

Document Mode and Worksheet Mode

Two modes of interactive operation are available in the standard interface: *document mode* and *worksheet mode*.

In document mode, you enter mathematical expressions within document blocks; no Maple input prompt (>) or execution group boundaries are displayed in the document. You can use this mode to create professional reports that combine text and typeset math with plots, images, and other interactive components.

In worksheet mode, you enter mathematical expressions at input prompts, which are displayed at the start of each input line in a Maple document. When you type an expression and press **Enter**, the expression is evaluated and a new input prompt is displayed in the next line. In both modes, the default format for entering mathematical text is 2-D math notation.

Both modes are equally suitable for creating and running programs in Maple. Select the mode that suits your preferences and tasks. For more information about both modes, refer to the **worksheet,help,documentsvsworksheets** help page.

1-D and 2-D Math Notation

When programming in Maple, you must also consider whether to use 2-D math notation or 1-D math notation. In 2-D math notation, typeset mathematical text is displayed in black italicized characters.

$$\int \sin(x)\, dx$$

In 1-D math notation (or Maple input), mathematical text is displayed in a red fixed-width font that is not typeset.

```
> int(sin(x),x):
```

1-D math notation can be used in external text files to write Maple code that can be read by a worksheet or batch processed. You can enter individual statements in 1-D math notation or configure Maple to display mathematical input in 1-D math by default in all future Maple sessions.

> **Note:** While 2-D math is the recommended format for mathematical text and equations and can be used for short command sequences and procedures, it is generally not recommended for long programs and package definitions.

Most input in this guide is shown in 1-D math notation. To clearly distinguish commands and input, this guide uses a leading prompt character (>) and all input is entered in worksheet mode.

For more information on starting Maple, toggling between 1-D and 2-D math notation, and managing your files, refer to the *Maple User Manual* or enter **?managing** at the Maple prompt.

Web Resources

- **Maplesoft Application Center**: The Application Center provides thousands of complete applications that you can download and use in Maple. For more information, visit **http://www.maplesoft.com/applications**.

- **MaplePrimes™**: MaplePrimes is an online forum where you can search for tips and techniques, read blogs, and discuss your work in Maple with an active community. For more information, visit **http://www.mapleprimes.com**.

- **Maplesoft Online Help**: Documentation included with Maple is also posted online. The web version offers the latest updates, Google™-based searching, and an easy way to provide feedback on help documentation. For more information, visit, **http://www.maplesoft.com/support/help**.

- **Teacher Resource Center**: The Teacher Resource Center provides course content, lecture notes, demonstrations, and other resources to help teachers incorporate Maple in their classrooms. For more information, visit **http://www.maplesoft.com/TeacherResource**.
- **Student Resource Center**: The Student Resource Center provides online forums, training videos, and other resources to help students with their work in Maple. For more information, visit **http://www.maplesoft.com/studentcenter**.

For additional resources, visit **http://www.maplesoft.com**.

Conventions

This guide uses the following typographical conventions.

- **bold** font - Maple command, package name, option name, dialog box, menu, or text field
- *italics* - new or important concept
- **Note** - additional information that is relevant to a concept or section
- **Important** - information that must be read and followed

Customer Feedback

Maplesoft welcomes your feedback. For suggestions and comments related to this and other manuals, contact doc@maplesoft.com.

1 Introduction to Programming in Maple

Maple provides an interactive problem-solving environment, complete with procedures for performing symbolic, numeric, and graphical computations. At the core of the Maple computer algebra system is a powerful programming language, upon which the Maple libraries of mathematical commands are built.

1.1 In This Chapter

- Components of the Maple software
- Maple statements
- Procedures and other essential elements of the Maple language

1.2 The Maple Software

The Maple software consists of two distinct parts.

- The user interface
- The computation engine

The User Interface

You can use the Maple *user interface* to enter, manipulate, and analyze mathematical expressions and commands. The user interface communicates with the Maple computation engine to solve mathematical problems and display their solutions.

For more information about the Maple user interface, refer to the *Maple User Manual*.

The Computation Engine

The Maple computation engine is the command processor, which consists of two parts: the kernel and math library.

The *kernel* is the core of the Maple computation engine. It contains the essential facilities required to run and interpret Maple programs, and manage data structures. In this guide, the kernel commands are referred to as *built-in* commands.

The Maple kernel also consists of *kernel extensions*, which are collections of external compiled libraries that are included in Maple to provide low-level programming functionality. These libraries include Basic Linear Algebra Subprograms (BLAS), GNU Multiple Precision (GMP), the NAG® C Library, and the C Linear Algebra PACKage (CLAPACK).

The math *library* contains most of the Maple commands. It includes functionality for numerous mathematical domains, including calculus, linear algebra, number theory, and combinatorics. Also, it contains commands for numerous other tasks, including importing data into Maple, XML processing, graphics, and translating Maple code to other programming languages.

All library commands are implemented in the high-level Maple programming language, so they can be viewed and modified by users. By learning the Maple programming language, you can create custom programs and packages, and extend the Maple library.

1.3 Maple Statements

There are many types of valid statements. Examples include statements that request help on a particular topic, display a text string, perform an arithmetic operation, use a Maple library command, or define a procedure.

Statements in 1-D notation require a trailing semicolon (;) or colon (:). If you enter a statement with a trailing semicolon, for most statements, the result is displayed. If you enter a statement with a trailing colon, the result is computed but *not* displayed.

```
> 2 + 3;
```

$$5 \tag{1.1}$$

```
> 2 + 3:
```

For more information about statements in Maple, see *Maple Statements (page 173)*.

Getting Help

To view a help page for a particular topic, enter a question mark (**?**) followed by the corresponding topic name. For example, **?procedure** displays a help page that describes how to write a Maple procedure.

For more information about getting help in Maple, refer to the **help** and **HelpGuide** help pages.

This type of Maple statement does not have a trailing colon or semicolon.

Displaying a Text String

The following statement returns a *string*. The text that forms the string is enclosed in *double quotes*, and the result (the string itself) is displayed because the statement has a trailing semicolon.

```
> "Hello World";
```

$$\text{"Hello World"} \tag{1.2}$$

Normally, you would create a string as part of another statement, such as an assignment or an argument for a procedure.

For more information about strings in Maple, see *Maple Language Elements (page 17)*.

Performing an Arithmetic Operation

The arithmetic operators in Maple are + (addition), - (subtraction), * (multiplication), / (division), and ^ (exponentiation). A statement can be an arithmetic operation that contains any combination of these operators. The standard rules of precedence apply.

```
> (44*3+13)^2/116;
```

$$\frac{725}{4} \tag{1.3}$$

Maple computes this result as an exact rational number.

Assigning to a Name

By naming a calculated result or complicated expression, you can reference it. To assign to a name, use the assignment operator, :=.

```
> a := 103993/33102;
```

$$a := \frac{103993}{33102} \tag{1.4}$$

```
> 2 * a;
```

$$\frac{103993}{16551} \tag{1.5}$$

For more information about names and assignment, see *Maple Language Elements (page 17)*.

Using Maple Library Commands

After a value is assigned to a name, for example, the value assigned previously to **a**, you can use the name as if it were the assigned object. For example, you can use the Maple library command **evalf** to compute a floating-point (decimal) approximation to **103993/33102** divided by **2** by entering the following statement.

```
> evalf(a/2);
```

$$1.570796326 \tag{1.6}$$

You can use the Maple library of commands, introduced in *The Computation Engine (page 1)*, for many purposes. For example, you can find the derivative of an expression by using the **diff** command.

```
> diff(x^2 + x + 1/x, x);
```

$$2x + 1 - \frac{1}{x^2} \tag{1.7}$$

Note the difference between the names used in these two examples. In the first example, **a** is a variable with an assigned value. In the second example, **x** is a symbol with no assigned value. Maple can represent and compute with symbolic expressions.

For more information about the Maple library commands, refer to the *Maple User Manual* or the help system.

1.4 Procedures

This section introduces the concept of procedures in Maple. For more information about procedures, see *Procedures (page 199)*.

Defining a Simple Procedure

A Maple procedure (a type of program) is a group of statements that are processed together. The easiest way to create a Maple procedure is to enclose a sequence of commands, which can be used to perform a computation interactively, between the **proc(...)** and **end proc** statements.

Entering a Procedure Definition

The following procedure generates the string *"Hello World"*. Enter this procedure in a Maple session by entering its definition on one line.

```
> hello := proc() return "Hello World"; end proc;
```

$$hello := \mathbf{proc}(\ )\ \mathbf{return}\ \text{"Hello World"}\ \mathbf{end\ proc} \tag{1.8}$$

You can also enter a procedure or any Maple statement on multiple lines. To move the cursor to the next line as you are entering a multiline statement, hold the **Shift** key and press **Enter** at the end of each line.

Note: This is necessary in the interactive worksheet environment only. If you enter code in a *code edit region*, you can simply type the text and press **Enter** to move the cursor to next line. For more information on code edit regions, refer to the **CodeEditRegion** help page. For more information about using **Shift+Enter**, see *Unexpected End of Statement (page 12)*.

You can indent lines in a procedure by using the spacebar. After you enter the last line, **end proc;**, press **Enter**.

```
> hello := proc()
          return "Hello World";
  end proc;
```

$$hello := \mathbf{proc}(\ )\ \mathbf{return}\ \text{"Hello World"}\ \mathbf{end\ proc} \qquad (1.9)$$

To run this procedure, enter its name followed by a set of parentheses and a semicolon:

```
> hello();
```

$$\text{"Hello World"} \qquad (1.10)$$

Procedures can also accept arguments. Consider the following example.

```
> half := proc(x)
          evalf(x/2);
  end proc;
```

$$half := \mathbf{proc}(x)\ evalf(1/2*x)\ \mathbf{end\ proc} \qquad (1.11)$$

This procedure requires one input, **x**. The procedure computes the approximation of the value of **x** divided by **2**. When a **return** statement is not specified, a Maple procedure returns the result of the last statement that was run. Since **evalf(x/2)** is the last calculation performed in the procedure **half** (in fact, it is the only calculation), the result of that calculation is returned.

The procedure is named **half** by using the := notation in the same way that you would assign any other object to a name. After you have named a procedure, you can use it as a command in the current Maple session. The syntax to run your procedure is the same syntax used to run a Maple library command: enter the procedure name followed by the input to the procedure enclosed in parentheses.

```
> half(2/3);
```

$$0.3333333333 \qquad (1.12)$$

```
> half(a);
```

$$1.570796326 \qquad (1.13)$$

```
> half(1) + half(2);
```

$$1.500000000 \qquad (1.14)$$

The basic syntax for a procedure is given below.

```
proc( P )
      ...
end proc
```

The letter **P** indicates the parameters. The body of the procedure is between the **proc** and **end proc** keywords.

Consider the following two statements, which calculate the angle in a right triangle given the lengths of two sides.

```
> theta := arcsin(opposite/hypotenuse);
```

$$\theta := \arcsin\left(\frac{opposite}{hypotenuse}\right) \tag{1.15}$$

```
> evalf(180/Pi*theta);
```

$$57.29577950 \arcsin\left(\frac{opposite}{hypotenuse}\right) \tag{1.16}$$

The following example shows a procedure that corresponds to these statements. The procedure definition contains two input parameters for the length of two sides of a right triangle.

```
> GetAngle := proc( opposite, hypotenuse )
       local theta;
       theta := arcsin(opposite/hypotenuse);
       evalf(180/Pi*theta);
  end proc;
```

$$\begin{aligned}&\textit{GetAngle} := \mathbf{proc}(\textit{opposite}, \textit{hypotenuse}) \\ &\quad \mathbf{local}\ \theta; \\ &\quad \theta := \arcsin(\textit{opposite}/\textit{hypotenuse});\ \textit{evalf}\left(180*\theta/\pi\right) \\ &\quad \mathbf{end\ proc}\end{aligned} \tag{1.17}$$

When you run the procedure definition, the output shown is the Maple interpretation of this procedure definition. Examine it carefully and note the following characteristics.

- The *name* of this procedure (program) is **GetAngle**. Note that Maple is case-sensitive, so **GetAngle** is distinct from **getangle**.

- The procedure definition starts with **proc(opposite, hypotenuse)**. The two names in parentheses indicate the parameters, or inputs, of the procedure.

- Semicolons or colons separate the individual commands of the procedure.

- The **local theta;** statement declares **theta** as a local variable. A local variable has meaning in the procedure definition only. Therefore, if you were to declare another variable called **theta** outside of the procedure, that variable would be different from the local variable **theta** declared in the procedure and you could use **theta** as a variable name outside of the procedure **GetAngle** without conflict.

For more information about local variables, see *Variables in Procedures (page 221)*.

- **Pi** is a predefined variable in Maple. Two predefined functions, **evalf** and **arcsin**, are used in the calculation.
- The **end proc** keywords and a colon or semicolon indicate the end of the procedure.
- As you enter the procedure, the commands of the procedure do not display output. The procedure definition is displayed as output only after you complete it with **end proc** and a semicolon.
- There is no explicit **return** statement, so the result of calling the procedure is the result of the last calculation.
- The procedure definition that displays in the output is equivalent to, but not identical to, the procedure definition you enter. When Maple parses the statement, the commands of the procedure may be simplified.

The procedure definition syntax is flexible. You can do the following:

- Enter each statement on one or more lines
- Enter multiple statements on one line, provided they are separated by colons or semicolons
- Place extra semicolons between statements
- Omit the semicolon (or colon) from the statement preceding **end proc**

To hide the output resulting from a complicated procedure definition, use a colon instead of a semicolon at the end of the definition.

Adding Comments to a Procedure

Consider the following example.

```
(* this procedure computes an interior angle of a right
   triangle given the length of the side opposite the angle, and
   the length of the hypotenuse.
*)
GetAngle := proc( opposite, hypotenuse )
       local theta;
       theta := arcsin(opposite/hypotenuse);
       # convert the angle from radians to degrees
       evalf(180/Pi*theta);
end proc:
```

You can include single line comments anywhere in the procedure. They begin with a pound character (#). You can also enter multiline comments between (* and *) symbols as shown in the example above.

Note: Multiline comments cannot be entered in 2-D math notation. As an alternative, in a Maple document, you can enter comments as text by adding a paragraph above or below the Maple statement.

Calling a Procedure

Running a procedure is referred to as an *invocation* or a *procedure call*. When you invoke a procedure, Maple runs the statements that form the procedure body one at a time. The result of the last computed statement within the procedure is returned as the value of the procedure call.

For example, to run the procedure **GetAngle**--that is, to cause the statements that form the procedure to be run in sequence--enter its name followed by parentheses enclosing the inputs, in this case, two numbers delimited (separated) by commas (,). End the statement with a semicolon.

```
> GetAngle(4,5);
```

$$53.13010234 \qquad (1.18)$$

Only the result of the last calculation performed within the procedure **GetAngle** is returned--the result of **evalf(180/Pi*theta)**. The assignment **theta:=arcsin(opposite/hypotenuse);** is performed, but the statement result is not displayed.

Maple Library Commands, Built-In Commands, and User-Defined Procedures

Maple comes with a large collection of commands and packages. Before writing custom procedures, refer to the Maple help system to find out which commands are available. You can easily include complex tasks in your user-defined procedures by using existing Maple commands instead of writing new code.

Maple commands are implemented in one of two formats: those written and compiled in an external language such as **C** and those written in the Maple programming language.

The commands that are compiled as part of the Maple kernel are referred to as *built-in* commands. These are widely used in computations, and are fundamental for implementing other Maple commands.

For more information about built-in kernel commands, see *The Computation Engine (page 1)* and *The builtin Option (page 215)*.

The commands in the Maple library are written in the Maple programming language. These commands exist as individual commands or as packages of commands. They are accessed and interpreted by the Maple system as required. The code for the library commands and the definitions of user-defined procedures can be viewed and modified. However, before exploring library commands, it is important that you learn about evaluation rules to understand the code.

Full Evaluation and Last Name Evaluation

For most expressions assigned to a name, such as **e** defined with the following statement, you can obtain its value by entering its name.

```
> restart;
> e := 3;
```

$$e := 3 \tag{1.19}$$

```
> e;
```

$$3 \tag{1.20}$$

This is called *full evaluation*--each name in the expression is fully evaluated to the last assigned expression in any chain of assignments. The following statements further illustrate how full evaluation works.

```
> c := b;
```

$$c := b \tag{1.21}$$

```
> b := a;
```

$$b := a \tag{1.22}$$

```
> a := 1;
```

$$a := 1 \tag{1.23}$$

```
> c;
```

$$1 \tag{1.24}$$

This group of statements creates the chain of assignments. $c \rightarrow b \rightarrow a \rightarrow 1$, and **c** fully evaluates to **1**.

If you try this approach with a procedure, Maple displays only the *name* of the procedure instead of its value (the procedure definition). For example, in the previous section, **GetAngle** is defined as a procedure. If you try to view the body of procedure **GetAngle** by referring to it by name, the procedure definition is *not* displayed.

```
> GetAngle;
```

$$GetAngle \tag{1.25}$$

This model of evaluation is called *last name evaluation* and it hides the procedure details. There are several reasons for this approach relating to advanced evaluation topics. The most important concept to understand is that you will only see the name of a procedure when you reference it by itself or when it is returned unevaluated; you will not see the full procedure definition. To obtain the value of the name **GetAngle**, use the **eval** command, which forces full evaluation.

Last name evaluation applies to procedures, tables, and modules in Maple. For more information, refer to the **last_name_eval** help page.

```
> eval(GetAngle);
```

$$GetAngle \qquad (1.26)$$

Viewing Procedure Definitions and Maple Library Code

You can learn about programming in Maple by studying the procedure definitions of Maple library commands. To *print* the body of Maple library commands, set the Maple **interface** variable **verboseproc** to **2**, and then use the **print** command.

For example, to view the procedure definition for the Maple *least common multiple* command, **lcm**, enter the following statements.

For more information about **interface** variables, refer to the **interface** help page.

```
> interface(verboseproc = 2):
```

```
> print(lcm);
```
$$\begin{aligned}
&\mathbf{proc}(a, b)\\
&\quad \mathbf{option}\ \textit{remember},\\
&\quad \textit{Copyright (c) 1990 by the University of Waterloo. All rights}\\
&\quad \textit{reserved.};\\
&\quad \mathbf{local}\ q, t;\\
&\quad \mathbf{if}\ \textit{nargs} = 0\ \mathbf{then}\\
&\qquad 1\\
&\quad \mathbf{elif}\ \textit{nargs} = 1\ \mathbf{then}\\
&\qquad t := \textit{expand}(a);\ \textit{sign}(t) * t\\
&\quad \mathbf{elif}\ 2 < \textit{nargs}\ \mathbf{then}\\
&\qquad \textit{foldl}(\textit{procname}, \textit{args})\\
&\quad \mathbf{elif}\ \textit{type}(a, \text{'integer'})\ \mathbf{and}\ \textit{type}(b, \text{'integer'})\ \mathbf{then}\\
&\qquad \textit{ilcm}(a, b)\\
&\quad \mathbf{else}\\
&\qquad \textit{gcd}(a, b, \text{'}q\text{'});\ q*b\\
&\quad \mathbf{end\ if}\\
&\mathbf{end\ proc}
\end{aligned} \quad (1.27)$$

Because the built-in kernel commands are compiled in machine code, and not written in the Maple language, you cannot view their definitions. If you **print** the definition of a built-in procedure, you will see that the procedure has only an **option builtin** statement and no visible body.

```
> print(add);
```
$$\mathbf{proc}(\ )\ \mathbf{option}\ \textit{builtin} = \textit{add};\ \mathbf{end\ proc} \quad (1.28)$$

1.5 Interrupting Computations and Clearing the Internal Memory

Interrupting a Maple Computation

To stop a computation, for example, a lengthy calculation or infinite loop, use one of the following three methods.

Note: Maple may not always respond immediately to an interrupt request if it is performing a complex computation. You may need to wait a few seconds before the computation stops.

- Click the stop icon in the toolbar (in worksheet versions).

- Click the interrupt icon ⊙ in the toolbar (in worksheet versions). See **Figure 1.1**.

Figure 1.1: Maple Toolbar

Note: For more information on the toolbar icons, refer to the **worksheet/reference/WorksheetToolbar** help page.

- Hold the **Ctrl** key and press the **C** key (in UNIX and Windows command-line versions).
- Hold the **Command** key and press the period key (**.**) (in Macintosh command-line and worksheet versions).

To perform a *hard* interrupt, which stops the computation and exits the Maple session, in the Windows command-line interface, hold the **Ctrl** key and press the **Break** key.

Clearing the Maple Internal Memory

Clear the internal memory during a Maple session by entering the **restart** command or clicking the restart icon in the worksheet toolbar. When you enter this command, the Maple session returns to its startup state, that is, all identifiers (including variables and procedures) are reset to their initial values.

```
> restart;
```

For more information on clearing the Maple internal memory and the **restart** command, refer to the **restart** help page. For more information on the toolbar icons, refer to the **worksheet/reference/WorksheetToolbar** help page.

Maple tracks the use of permanent and temporary objects. Its internal garbage collection facility places memory that is no longer in use on free lists so it can be used again efficiently as needed. For more information on garbage collection and the **gc** command, see *Garbage Collection (page 626)*.

1.6 Avoiding Common Problems

This section provides a list of common mistakes, examples, and hints that will help you understand and avoid common errors. Use this section to study the errors that you may encounter when entering the examples from this chapter in a Maple session.

Unexpected End of Statement

Most valid statements in Maple must end in either a colon or a semicolon. An error message is displayed if you press **Enter** in an input region that is incomplete.

Tip: You can use the **parse** command to find errors in statements, and the Maple debugger to find errors in programs. For more information on the debugger, see *The Maple Debugger: A Tutorial Example (page 581)* or refer to the **parse** and **debugger** help pages.

If you press **Enter** to move the cursor to a new line when you are entering a procedure definition on multiple lines, the following error is displayed.

```
> p:=proc()
Warning, premature end of input, use <Shift> + <Enter> to avoid this
message.
```

To prevent this error message from displaying as you enter a procedure definition, hold the **Shift** key and press **Enter** at the end of each line, instead of pressing only **Enter**.

```
> p := proc()
        "Hello World";
  end proc;
```

$$p := \mathbf{proc}(\ ) \text{ "Hello World" } \mathbf{end\ proc} \tag{1.29}$$

In 1-D math notation, if you do not enter a trailing semicolon or colon, Maple inserts a semicolon and displays the following warning message.

```
> 1 + 2
Warning, inserted missing semicolon at end of statement
```

$$3 \tag{1.30}$$

Maple also inserts a semicolon after **end proc** in procedure definitions.

```
> p := proc()
        "Hello World";
  end proc
Warning, inserted missing semicolon at end of statement
```

$$p := \mathbf{proc}(\ ) \text{ "Hello World" } \mathbf{end\ proc} \tag{1.31}$$

Missing Operator

The most common error of this type is omitting the multiplication operator.

```
> 2 a + b;
Error, missing operator or `;`
```

You can avoid this error by entering an asterisk (*) to indicate multiplication.

```
> 2*a + b;
```
$$2a+b \tag{1.32}$$

Implicit multiplication, which can be used in 2-D math input, is not valid syntax in 1-D math input.

Invalid, Wrong Number or Type of Arguments

An error is displayed if the argument(s) to a Maple library command are incorrect or missing.

```
> evalf();
Error, invalid input: evalf expects 1 or 2 arguments, but received 0
> solve(y=3*x+4, 5);
Warning, solving for expressions other than names or functions is not
 recommended.
Error, (in solve) a constant is invalid as a variable, 5
> cos(x, y);
Error, (in cos) expecting 1 argument, got 2
```

If such an error occurs, check the appropriate help page for the correct syntax. Enter **?topic_name** at the Maple prompt.

The same type of error message is displayed if you call a user-defined procedure, such as **GetAngle**, with the wrong number of the arguments.

Unbalanced Parentheses

In complicated expressions or nested commands, it is easy to omit a closing parenthesis.

```
> {[1,0], [0,1};
Error, `}` unexpected
```

In a valid statement, each **(**, **{**, and **[** requires a matching **)**, **}**, and **]**, respectively.

```
> {[1,0], [0,1]};
```
$$\{[0,1],[1,0]\} \tag{1.34}$$

Assignment Versus Equality

When you enter statements in a Maple session, it is important to understand the difference between equality (using =) and assignment (using :=).

The equal sign, =, is used in equality tests or to create *equations*. Creating an equation is a valid Maple statement.

```
> x = y^2+3;
```
$$x = y^2 + 3 \tag{1.35}$$

```
> solve(%,y);
```
$$\sqrt{x-3}, -\sqrt{x-3} \tag{1.36}$$

```
> x;
```
$$x \tag{1.37}$$

In the example above, **%** is a special name that stores the value of the last statement. The **solve** command is used to isolate **y** in the equation defined in the first statement. The first statement is not an assignment; **x** remains a symbol with no assigned value.

You can use the assignment operator, **:=**, to assign **x** the value **y^2+3**. The assignment operator assigns the value of the right-hand side to the left-hand side. After an assignment is made, the left-hand side can be used in place of the value of the right-hand side. The left-hand side cannot be a number; it must be a *name*, indexed name, function call, or sequence of these values.

```
> x := y^2+3;
```
$$x := y^2 + 3 \tag{1.38}$$

```
> solve(x,y);
```
$$I\sqrt{3}, -I\sqrt{3} \tag{1.39}$$

```
> x;
```
$$y^2 + 3 \tag{1.40}$$

For more information about equations and Boolean testing, see *Boolean and Relational Expressions (page 89)* or refer to the **evalb** help page. For more information about names and assignment, see *Names (page 44)* and *Assignments (page 174)*.

1.7 Exercises

1. Assign the integers **12321**, **23432**, and **34543** to the names **a**, **b**, and **c**. Use these names to find the sum and difference of each pair of numbers.

2. Write two procedures. The first requires two inputs and finds their sum. The second requires two inputs and finds their product. Use these procedures to add and multiply pairs of numbers. How could you use these procedures to add and multiply three numbers?

3. Display your procedure definitions. Are they identical to the code you entered to write them?

2 Maple Language Elements

Before programming in Maple, it is important to learn the properties and roles of the basic elements of the Maple language. This chapter introduces some of the main concepts, which will be described in more detail later in this guide.

2.1 In This Chapter

- Basic elements of the Maple language: the character set and tokens
- Maple tokens: reserved words, operators, names, strings, and natural numbers; function types
- Using special characters
- Maple data types related to the tokens

2.2 Character Set

The Maple character set consists of letters, digits, and special characters. These include 26 lowercase letters, 26 uppercase letters, and 10 decimal digits.

a b c d e f g h i j k l m n o p q r s t u v w x y z
A B C D E F G H I J K L M N O P Q R S T U V W X Y Z
0, 1, 2, 3, 4, 5, 6, 7, 8, 9

There are also 33 special characters, which are listed in **Table 2.1**. These characters, or combinations of these characters, have special meanings in the Maple language.

Table 2.1: Special Characters

Character	Meaning	Character	Meaning
	blank	(	left parenthesis
;	semicolon	)	right parenthesis
:	colon	[	left bracket
+	plus	]	right bracket
-	minus	{	left brace
*	asterisk	}	right brace
/	slash	`	left single quote (back quote)
^	caret	'	right single quote (apostrophe)
!	exclamation	"	double quote
=	equal	|	vertical bar
<	less than	&	ampersand

Character	Meaning	Character	Meaning
>	greater than	_	underscore
@	at sign	%	percent
$	dollar	\	backslash
.	period	#	pound sign (sharp)
,	comma	?	question mark
~	tilde		

These are the only characters used in the Maple language. However, all character types can be used in names and strings, including international characters. For more information on how to create names using international characters, see *Names (page 22)*.

Note: When you manipulate a string or determine the length of a string, non-ASCII and international characters may be counted as more than one byte.

Many string manipulation commands interpret multibyte characters as multiple characters.

```
> s := "\xC3\xBC";
```
$$s := "ü" \qquad (2.1)$$

```
> convert(s, bytes);
```
$$[195, 188] \qquad (2.2)$$

2.3 Tokens

The Maple language combines characters into tokens. The set of tokens consists of reserved words (also called *keywords*), programming-language operators, names, strings, and natural integers.

Reserved Words

Maple *keywords* are reserved words that have special meanings. Therefore, you cannot change them or use them as variables in procedures. The keywords are listed in **Table 2.2**. You can find information about specific keywords in later chapters of this guide or the help system.

For more information about reserved words in Maple, refer to the **keyword** help page.

Table 2.2: Reserved Keywords

Keywords	Purpose
break, next	loop control

Keywords	Purpose
if, then, elif, else	**if** statement
for, from, in, by, to, while, do	**for** and **while** loops
proc, local, global, option, error, return, options, description	procedures
export, module, use	modules
end	ends structures
assuming	assume facility
try, catch, finally	exception handling
read, save	**read** and **save** statements
quit, done, stop	ending Maple
union, minus, intersect, subset	set operators
and, or, not, xor	Boolean operators
implies	implication operator
mod	modulus operator

Programming-Language Operators

There are two main types of Maple language operators: *unary* and *binary*. Simply put, a *unary* operator acts on one operand, as in **-a**, where the operator **-** is applied to **a**. A binary operator acts on two operands, as in **a+b**, where **+** is the operator and the operands are **a** and **b**.

The Maple binary and unary operators, and their meanings, are listed in **Table 2.3** and **Table 2.4**. For more information about these operators, refer to the **operators,binary** and **operators,unary** help topics.

For information about the order of precedence of programming-language operators, refer to the **operators/precedence** help page.

Table 2.3: Binary Operators

Operator	Meaning	Operator	Meaning
+	addition	<	less than
-	subtraction	<=	less or equal
*	multiplication	>	greater than
/	division	>=	greater or equal
^	exponentiation	<>	not equal
$	sequence operator	=	equal or equation
@	composition	union	set union
@@	repeated composition	minus	set difference
&*string*	neutral operator	intersect	set intersection

Operator	Meaning	Operator	Meaning
,	expression separator	::	type declaration and pattern binding
||	concatenation	in	membership
.	non-commutative multiplication	and	logical and
->	arrow operator	or	logical or
..	ellipsis	xor	exclusive or
mod	modulo	implies	implication
:=	assignment	subset	subset

Table 2.4: Unary Operators

Operator	Meaning
+	unary plus (prefix)
-	unary minus (prefix)
!	factorial (postfix)
$	sequence operator (prefix)
not	logical not (prefix)
&*string*	neutral operator (prefix)
.	decimal point (prefix or postfix)

Most of the unary and binary operators can also be used in *element-wise* form with objects that have multiple elements. To perform an element-wise operation, add a trailing tilde (~) after an operator that has an element-wise form. An element-wise operation allows you to apply an operation to the elements of a list, set, table, Array, Matrix, or Vector. For example, compare Matrix multiplication with element-wise multiplication of paired entries in a Matrix.

> <1,2;3,4> . <2,2;2,2>;

$$\begin{bmatrix} 6 & 6 \\ 14 & 14 \end{bmatrix} \quad (2.3)$$

> <1,2;3,4> .~ <2,2;2,2>;

$$\begin{bmatrix} 2 & 4 \\ 6 & 8 \end{bmatrix} \quad (2.4)$$

The Maple element-wise operators are listed in **Table 2.5**. For more information about these operators, refer to the **operators,elementwise** help page.

2.3 Tokens • 21

Table 2.5: Element-wise Operators

Element-wise Operator	Meaning	Element-wise Operator	Meaning
+~	addition or unary plus	<~	less than
-~	subtraction or unary minus	<=~	less or equal
*~	multiplication	>~	greater than
/~	division	>=~	greater or equal
^~	exponentiation	<>~	not equal
!~	factorial (unary postfix)	=~	equal or equation
@~	composition	union~	set union
@@~	repeated composition	minus~	set difference
&*name* ~	neutral operator	intersect~	set intersection
&*name* ~	neutral operator (unary prefix)	in~	membership
subset~	subset	or~	logical or
.~	non-commutative multiplication	and~	logical and
||~	concatenation	xor~	exclusive or
mod~	modulo	implies~	implication
funct~	element-wise	not~	logical not (unary prefix)

Also, three special *nullary* operators (also called *ditto* operators) can be used in interactive sessions. These are special Maple names that can be used to refer to previously computed non-NULL expressions.

%	last expression
%%	second-last expression
%%%	third-last expression

While they can be used for simple computations, the ditto operators should be avoided when writing programs. For results that need to be used in subsequent expressions, assign values to variables instead.

Note: In a worksheet, the ditto operators do *not* necessarily reference the results of the lines located above the execution groups in which they are used. They reference the results of the *most recently performed* computations in the Maple session, regardless of the execution group or document in which they are located. Also, in terms of evaluation, the ditto operators are treated differently than local variables in a procedure. They are fully evaluated, which may require more processing than one-level evaluation of local variables. For more information about local variables, see *Local Variables (page 222)*.

For more information about the ditto operators, refer to the **ditto** help page.

Names

A *name* in Maple is a sequence of one or more characters that uniquely identifies a command, file, variable, or other entity.

The simplest instance of a name consists of a letter followed by a sequence of letters, digits, and underscores.

```
> My_Name_1;
```

$$My\_Name\_1 \qquad (2.5)$$

If you need to create a name that includes blank spaces or international characters, use left single quotes (`` ` ``).

```
> `A quoted name`;
```

$$A \ quoted \ name \qquad (2.6)$$

```
> `1. A silly name`;
```

$$1. \ A \ silly \ name \qquad (2.7)$$

In general any name that can be formed without left single quotes is identical to the same name with quotes. For example, **x** and `` `x` `` refer to the same name **x**. Left single quotes are similar to double quotes in that double quotes are used to build strings while left single quotes are used to build names.

Note that the reverse is not true, some names can be formed with left single quotes that are not identical to expressions typed in without quotes. One example is the name `` `2` ``. By putting quotes around the 2 here, a name is formed instead of a number. Another example is a quoted keyword, like `` `**module**` ``. To test if an expression is of type module, check **type(expr,`module`)**. Without the quotes, the Maple parser determines that this is the start of a module definition and the parser will flag a syntax error.

Characters in Maple are case-sensitive. Therefore, for example, the name **Apple** is different from the name **apple**.

```
> Apple := 4;
```

$$Apple := 4 \qquad (2.8)$$

```
> apple := 5;
```

$$apple := 5 \qquad (2.9)$$

```
> Apple + apple;
```

$$9 \qquad (2.10)$$

Other Maple names are used for

- mathematical functions such as **sin** and **cos**
- Maple commands such as **expand** or **simplify**
- type names such as **integer** or **list**
- symbols, for example, **x** and **y** in the expression **x+y**
- variables, or names with assigned values

For example, in the first statement below, **y** is a name that does not have a value. In the second statement, the variable **x** has the value **3**.

```
> 2*y - 1;
```
$$2y - 1 \qquad (2.11)$$

```
> x := 3; x^2 + 1;
```
$$x := 3$$
$$10 \qquad (2.12)$$

You can create an *empty name*, which has no characters in its spelling.

```
> type(``, 'name');
```
$$true \qquad (2.13)$$

Early versions of Maple did not have separate types for names and strings. As a result, many commands for string processing will also accept names and process their characters the same way. It is generally better to use strings for such processing as strings can never have assigned values.

For more more information about names, see *Names (page 44)*.

2.4 Natural Integers

A *natural integer* is a sequence of one or more decimal digits.

```
> 00003141592653589793238462643;
```
$$3141592653589793238462643 \qquad (2.14)$$

For more information about integers, see *Integers (page 55)* and *Numeric Types in Maple (page 271)*.

2.5 Strings

A *string* is a sequence of characters that evaluates to itself. To create a string, enclose any sequence of characters in double quotes.

```
> "This is a string";
```

$$\text{"This is a string"} \qquad (2.15)$$

You *cannot* assign a value to a string.

```
> "hello" := 5;
Error, invalid left hand side of assignment
```

In the following sections, strings and string operations are described. For information on the **StringTools** package, refer to the **StringTools** help page.

Length of a String

Use the **length** command to determine the number of bytes in a string.

```
> length("What is the length of this string?");
```

$$34 \qquad (2.16)$$

All of the characters between, but excluding, the double quotes are counted. Each blank space is counted as one character. Non-ASCII characters may be counted as more than one byte.

The maximum string length is system-dependent and ranges from about 268 million bytes on 32-bit systems to more than 34 billion bytes on 64-bit systems.

Substrings

You can extract a substring of a string by using a subscripted integer range (also called a *selection operation*).

```
> S := "This is a string";
```

$$S := \text{"This is a string"} \qquad (2.17)$$

```
> S[6];
```

$$\text{"i"} \qquad (2.18)$$

```
> S[6..9];
```

$$\text{"is a"} \qquad (2.19)$$

Negative numbers in the range count backwards from the end of the string. -2 is the second last character in the string. Either range endpoint can also be left off to indicate from the beginning, or to the end.

> S[-6..-1];

$$\text{"string"} \qquad (2.20)$$

> S[11..];

$$\text{"string"} \qquad (2.21)$$

Searching a String

To perform case-sensitive and case-insensitive string searching, use the **SearchText** and **searchtext** commands, respectively.

```
SearchText( pattern, exprString, range );
searchtext( pattern, exprString, range );
```

The **SearchText** command searches for exact matches of **pattern** in **exprString**. The **searchtext** command performs the same search, but it is case-insensitive. If **pattern** is found, Maple returns an integer indicating the position of the first character in **pattern** in **exprString**. If the pattern is not found in **exprString**, **0** is returned.

> SearchText("my s", "This is my string.");

$$9 \qquad (2.22)$$

> searchtext("My S", "This is my string.");

$$9 \qquad (2.23)$$

The optional **range** restricts the search to the specified range. It is equivalent to performing a search on a substring, and it is useful when the pattern occurs more than once in the string.

> SearchText("is", "This is my string.", 4..-1);

$$3 \qquad (2.24)$$

String Concatenation

Strings can be formed through concatenation by using the **cat** command.

```
cat( sequence )
```

Here, the **sequence** parameter can contain any number of expressions that are separated by commas.

The **cat** command is commonly used to concatenate strings with names and integers, and the result returned has the type (name or string) of the first argument to **cat**.

```
> i := 5;
```

$$i := 5 \tag{2.25}$$

```
> cat( "The value of i is ", i, "." );
```

$$\text{"The value of i is 5."} \tag{2.26}$$

```
> filename := cat( kernelopts(mapledir), kernelopts(dirsep), "lib"
    );
```

$$\text{"C:\textbackslash Program Files\textbackslash Maple 16\textbackslash lib"} \tag{2.27}$$

Mutability of Strings

Strings are not mutable objects in Maple. This means that appending text to a string is not done in-place, but involves allocating new storage for the result and copying the original text, plus the appended text, into that new space. This is typically not an issue unless you are incrementally processing large amounts of text. In the latter case, the **StringBuffer** command may be useful.

```
> with(StringTools):
> s := StringBuffer();
```

$$s := \text{""} \tag{2.28}$$

```
> s:-append("The quick brown fox"):
> s:-newline():
> s:-append("jumped over the lazy dog"):
> s:-value();
```

$$\begin{array}{c}\text{"The quick brown fox}\\ \text{jumped over the lazy dog"}\end{array} \tag{2.29}$$

For more information, refer to the **StringBuffer** help page.

Special Characters in Strings

To display the double quote character in a string, enter a backslash character (\) followed by a double quote (") where you want the double quote character to appear. For more information, refer to the **backslash** help page.

```
> "a\"b";
```

$$\text{"a\"b"} \tag{2.30}$$

Similarly, to display a backslash character as one of the characters in a string, enter two consecutive backslash characters, \\. You must escape the backslash in this manner because backslash is itself a special character. For more information, see *Blank Spaces, New Lines, Comments, and Continuation (page 28)*.

```
> "a\\b";
```

$$"a\backslash b" \qquad (2.31)$$

The special backslash character mentioned above counts as only one character, as demonstrated by using the **length** command.

```
> length((2.31));
```

$$3 \qquad (2.32)$$

Doubling up backslashes is most notable when entering full path names in Maple. For this situation it is easier to use forward slash instead. Forward slash is recognized as a directory separator on all platforms including Windows.

Parsing Strings

The **parse** command accepts any Maple string and parses the string as if it had been entered or read from a file. This is especially useful when you want to interpret commands typed into text-components inside your Maple document.

```
parse( exprString, option );
```

Without specifying extra options, the string should contain exactly *one* Maple expression. The expression is parsed and returned unevaluated.

```
> parse("a+b");
```

$$a + b \qquad (2.33)$$

```
> parse("a+b;");
```

$$a + b \qquad (2.34)$$

If the string is syntactically incorrect, the **parse** command displays an error message of the form **incorrect syntax in parse: ... (number)**.

The **number** indicates the offset in characters, counted from the beginning of the string, at which the syntax error was detected.

```
> parse("a++b");
Error, incorrect syntax in parse: `+` unexpected (near 3rd character
 of parsed string)
```

If the option **statement** is specified, the string is parsed and evaluated, and then the result is returned.

```
> parse("sin(Pi)");
```
$$\sin(\pi) \tag{2.35}$$

```
> parse("sin(Pi)", 'statement');
```
$$0 \tag{2.36}$$

Partial statements or incomplete expressions cannot be parsed. Multiple statements or expressions can be interpreted via multiple calls to parse using the **lastread** and **offset** options.

For more information, refer to the **parse** help page.

Converting Expressions to Strings

To convert an expression to a string, use the **convert** command.

Maple can convert a variety of expressions. For more information about expressions, see *Maple Expressions (page 43)*. For more information about conversions in Maple, refer to the **convert** help page.

```
> convert(a, 'string');
```
$$\text{"a"} \tag{2.37}$$

```
> convert(a+b-c*d/e, 'string');
```
$$\text{"a+b-c*d/e"} \tag{2.38}$$

```
> convert(42, 'string');
```
$$\text{"42"} \tag{2.39}$$

2.6 Using Special Characters

Token Separators

You can separate tokens by using white space characters or punctuation marks. The separator indicates the end of one token and the beginning of the next.

Blank Spaces, New Lines, Comments, and Continuation

The *white space characters* are space, tab, return, and line-feed. This guide uses the term *new line* to refer to a return or line-feed since the Maple system does not distinguish between these characters. The term *blank* refers to a space or tab.

2.6 Using Special Characters

The white space characters separate tokens, but are *not* themselves tokens. White space characters cannot normally be used within a token.

```
> a: = b;
Error, `=` unexpected
```

However, you can use white space characters between tokens.

```
> a * x + x*y;
```

$$ax + xy \tag{2.40}$$

White space characters can be part of a token in a name or string formed by enclosing a sequence of characters in left single quotes or double quotes respectively. For more information, see *White Space Characters within a Token (page 40)*.

Except in a string, all characters that follow a pound sign "#" on a line are part of a *comment*.

For information about adding comments in Maple procedures, see *Adding Comments to a Procedure (page 7)*.

```
> a := 1 + x + x^2;   #This is a comment
```

$$a := 1 + x + x^2 \tag{2.41}$$

Since white space and new line characters are functionally identical, you can continue *statements* from line to line, as described in *Entering a Procedure Definition (page 4)*.

```
> a:= 1 + x +
  x^2;
```

$$a := 1 + x + x^2 \tag{2.42}$$

Note: Press **Shift+Enter** to continue typing on the next line without evaluating the expression.

To enter a long *number* or *string* on multiple lines, use the backslash character (\) as a line continuation character.

Line continuation functions as follows: if a backslash \ immediately precedes a new line character, the Maple parser ignores both the backslash and the new line. If a backslash is in the middle of a line, Maple usually ignores it. For more information about the backslash character and exceptions to this rule, refer to the **backslash** help page.

You can use the backslash character to break up a long sequence of digits into groups of smaller sequences to enhance readability.

```
> "The input should be either a list of \
  variables or a set of variables";
```

"The input should be either a list of variables or a set of variables" (2.43)

```
> G:= 0.57721566490153286060\
  6512090082402\43104215933593992;
```

$$G :=$$
$$0.5772156649015328606065120900824024310421593359391$$
$$92$$ (2.44)

You can also enter long strings by using a continuation character. Maple automatically concatenates string constants that are on separate lines, so another way to enter a long string is to close one set of double quotes at the end of a line and enter a new double quote at the beginning of the next line.

```
> S:= "This is the start of a long string "
  "and this is part of the same string with no line in between";
```

$$S :=$$
"This is the start of a long string and this is part of the same (2.45)
string with no line in between"

Punctuation Marks

The punctuation marks that act as token separators are listed in **Table 2.6**.

Table 2.6: Token Separators

;	semicolon	(	left parenthesis
:	colon	)	right parenthesis
`	left single quote	[	left bracket
'	right single quote	]	right bracket
|	vertical bar	{	left brace
<	left angle bracket	}	right brace
>	right angle bracket	,	comma

Semicolon (;) and Colon (:)

Use the semicolon and the colon to separate statements. During an interactive session, a semicolon displays the result of the statement while a colon prevents the result of the statement from displaying.

```
> f:=x->x^2;
```

$$f := x \rightarrow x^2 \tag{2.46}$$

```
> p:=plot(f(x), x=0..10):
```

Right Single Quotes (')

Enclosing an expression, or part of an expression, in right single quotes (or *apostrophes*) delays the evaluation of an expression (subexpression) by one level. This is often used to ensure that procedure options are passed correctly as unevaluated names even when they have a value. For more information, see *Unevaluated Expressions (page 48)*.

```
> 'sin'(Pi), sin(Pi);
```

$$\sin(\pi), 0 \tag{2.47}$$

```
> right := 42;
```

$$right := 42 \tag{2.48}$$

```
> limit(1/x, x=0, 'right');
```

$$\infty \tag{2.49}$$

Left Single Quotes (`)

To form a name, enclose an expression in left single quotes.

```
> `My Var` := 4;
```

$$My\ Var := 4 \tag{2.50}$$

Parentheses

The left and right parentheses group terms in an expression, arguments in a function call, and parameters in a procedure definition.

```
> (a+b)*c; cos(Pi);
  proc( x, y, z )
    x+y+z;
  end proc:
```

$$(a+b)\,c$$
$$-1 \tag{2.51}$$

The left and right parentheses are also used to select components from certain data structures (programmer indexing).

Square Brackets

Use the left and right square brackets to form indexed (subscripted) names and to select components from data structures such as Arrays, tables, and lists. For more information on selection, see *Indexed Expressions (page 64)*. For more information on mathematical indexing and programmer indexing, see *Basic Data Access (page 149)*.

```
> a[1]; L:=[2,3,5,7]; L[3];
```

$$a_1$$

$$L := [2, 3, 5, 7]$$

$$5 \tag{2.52}$$

Square Brackets and Braces

Use the left and right square brackets ([]) to form lists, and the left and right braces ({}) to form sets. For more information on sets and lists, see *Immutable Data Structures (page 129)*.

```
> L:=[2,3,5,2]; S:={2,3,5,2};
```

$$L := [2, 3, 5, 2]$$

$$S := \{2, 3, 5\} \tag{2.53}$$

Angle Brackets

The left and right angle brackets (<>) in conjunction with the the comma, semicolon, and/or vertical bar (|) can be used to create Matrices and Vectors. For more information, refer to the **Matrix** and **MVshortcut** help pages.

```
> <1,2,3; 4,5,6>;
```

$$\begin{bmatrix} 1 & 2 & 3 \\ 4 & 5 & 6 \end{bmatrix} \tag{2.54}$$

```
> <1,2,3| 4,5,6>;
```

$$\begin{bmatrix} 1 & 4 \\ 2 & 5 \\ 3 & 6 \end{bmatrix} \tag{2.55}$$

Comma

Use the comma to form an expression sequence. Expression sequences are used to specify the arguments of a function call or the elements of a list or set.

```
> sin(Pi), 0, limit(cos(xi)/xi, xi=infinity);
```
$$0, 0, 0 \qquad (2.56)$$

Escape Characters

An *escape character* indicates that the character that follows the escape character must be handled in a special manner. The escape characters in Maple are **?**, **!**, **#**, and ****.

? - The question mark character, if it appears as the first non-blank character on a line, opens the Maple help system. The words following **?** on the same line determine the terms used to display a help page. Use either "," or "/" to separate the words that follow the question mark character. For more information, refer to the **help** help page.

! - The exclamation mark character, if it appears as the first non-blank character on a line, passes the remainder of the line as a command to the host operating system. For more information, refer to the **system** and **escape** help pages.

and **(*, *)** - The pound sign character indicates that the characters that follow it on the line are a comment. The multiline comment characters, **(***, and ***)** indicate the beginning and end of a comment. For more information, see *Adding Comments to a Procedure (page 7)* or refer to the **comment** help page.

** - The backslash character is used to continue lines, to group characters in a token, and introduce control characters. For more information, refer to the **backslash help page.

2.7 Types and Operands

In most programming languages, data is divided into different classes of information called *data types*. In Maple, there is a logical or mathematical notion of *type* that is related to, but distinct from, the underlying data structure.

DAGs

All data in Maple is stored as a *directed acyclic graph* (DAG). An identifying tag for each DAG indicates what type of data it stores and how it is stored. Names, strings, lists, and positive and negative integers are examples of some DAG types. For a list of DAG types and how they are stored in memory, see *Internal Representation (page 633)*. The **op** command (short for *operand*) can often be used to determine the DAG type of the underlying data by returning the zeroth operand. This only applies to certain data structures where **op(0,e)**, where **e** is an expression, is defined as a special case. For more information, see the particular data structure help page.

```
> op(0, [1,2,3]);
```
$$list \qquad (2.57)$$

```
> op(0, "some text");
```
$$\text{string} \tag{2.58}$$

```
> op(0, `some name`);
```
$$\text{symbol} \tag{2.59}$$

```
> op(0, 123456);
```
$$\text{Integer} \tag{2.60}$$

However, the correspondence is not exact. A notable exception to this is function calls where the zeroth operand is the function name.

```
> op(0, f(x));
```
$$f \tag{2.61}$$

```
> op(0, op(0, f(x)));
```
$$\text{symbol} \tag{2.62}$$

When names are assigned to data, they act as pointers in other languages. However, for most purposes, the Maple evaluation rules are such that you can think of them as variables. If you want to manipulate an assigned name rather than the data assigned to it, you can use right single quotes (also called **unevaluation quotes**), which are described in more detail in *Unevaluated Expressions (page 48)*.

Assigned names that are pointers do not require type declarations as in low-level programming languages. This means that a name **a** may be assigned an integer and then later assigned a list without discretion. This system of *weak typing* means that, when writing robust code, you must verify types since variables may be assigned any value.

Maple Types

The type facility in Maple is accessed by using the **type** command. It is a mathematical type facility; however, some basic types such as **integer** or **list** map directly to the type of DAG. Some types, such as **numeric**, encapsulate a group of many different kinds of structures and structured types, such as **name^integer**, can match a very specific value.

Type checking is important in Maple to decide whether an expression is valid input for procedure calls and Maple commands. You can use the the **type** command or the **::** operator for type checking. The operator form is primarily used to declare the type of a procedure parameter (see *Procedures (page 199)*). The **type** command has the following syntax.

```
type( expression, typeName );
```

If the **expression** is of type **typeName**, the **type** command returns a value of **true**. Otherwise, a value of **false** is returned.

```
> type([1,2,3], 'list');
```
$$true \tag{2.63}$$

```
> type("string", 'list');
```
$$false \tag{2.64}$$

```
> type(123456, 'integer');
```
$$true \tag{2.65}$$

```
> type(f(x), 'function');
```
$$true \tag{2.66}$$

The type of any integer is **integer**. The **type** command can also interpret many subtypes of integers, some of which are listed in **Table 2.7**.

Table 2.7: Subtype

Subtype	Meaning
integer[8]	64-bit sized integer
integer[4]	32-bit sized integer
negint	negative integer
posint	positive integer
nonnegint	non-negative integer
nonposint	non-positive integer
even	even integer
odd	odd integer
prime	prime number

For more information, refer to the **type** help page, which also contains a complete list of types in Maple.

The type facility can also interpret compound or *structured types* such as **list(integer)** for a list of integers or **list({negint,prime})** for a list of negative or prime integers.

```
> type([-1, 2, 11], 'list({negint,prime})');
```
$$true \tag{2.67}$$

```
> type([0, 2, 11], 'list({negint,prime})');
```
$$false \tag{2.68}$$

For more information about structured types, see **type,structure**.

Operands and op

In addition to providing information about the underlying type, the **op** command can provide information about the other operands or parts of a data structure. Most data structures in Maple can be divided into components. For example, an equation of the form **x=y+x** can be divided as follows.

- the operator, =
- the left-hand side, **x**
- the right-hand side, **y+x**

To determine the operands and the number of operands in an expression, use the **op** and **nops** commands respectively. These commands have the following basic syntax.

```
op( i, expression );
nops( expression );
```

If the optional first argument **i** to the **op** command is a positive integer, the **i**th operand of **expression** is returned.

```
> eq := x=y+x:
> nops(eq);
```
$$2 \qquad (2.69)$$

```
> op(0, eq);
```
$$`=` \qquad (2.70)$$

```
> op(1, eq);
```
$$x \qquad (2.71)$$

```
> op(2, eq);
```
$$y + x \qquad (2.72)$$

```
> op(0, eq)(op(1,eq), op(2,eq));
```
$$x = y + x \qquad (2.73)$$

The **op** command can also determine the operands of an expression at various levels of a structure with the following syntax.

```
op( [i1, i2, ...], expression );
```

This syntax is equivalent to and more efficient than a nested call to the **op** command.

> op([2,0], eq);

$$`+`\qquad(2.74)$$

> op(0,op(2, eq));

$$`+`\qquad(2.75)$$

This hierarchical structure of expressions explains the name DAG. The internal representation of $x = y + x$ looks like an infix expression tree. See **Figure 2.1**

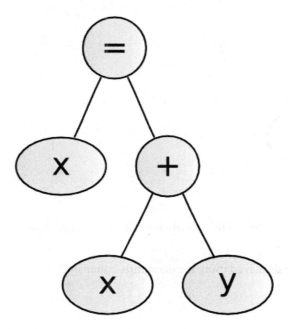

Figure 2.1: Expression Tree

For efficiency, Maple does not store multiple copies of identical objects, so the two **x** nodes in the tree can be represented in a picture like the one in **Figure 2.2**. In **Figure 2.1** you see two "x" nodes in the tree, implying a copy of each "x". **Figure 2.2** shows that the same instance of "x" is referred to in both places.

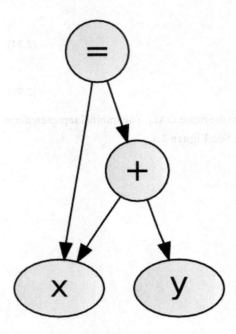

Figure 2.2: Expression DAG

The term *directed acyclic graph* simply refers to this variation of a tree where nodes may have multiple parents.

The tree form of an expression can be displayed using the **dismantle** command.

```
> dismantle(eq);

EQUATION(3)
   NAME(4): x
   SUM(5)
      NAME(4): y
      INTPOS(2): 1
      NAME(4): x
      INTPOS(2): 1
```

This model is not exactly what is used in practice but the principle of uniqueness, with respect to nodes, still applies. Maple uses a more sophisticated internal representation for sums as described in *Internal Representation (page 633)*. The real structure of the DAG shown in **Figure 2.3**.

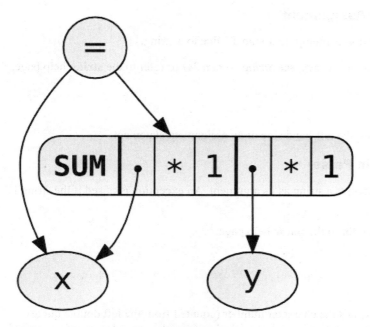

Figure 2.3: Actual Expression DAG

The next three chapters introduce many of the other types in Maple and describe how to create and use them in programs.

2.8 Avoiding Common Problems

This section provides you with a list of common mistakes, examples, and hints that will help you understand and avoid common errors. Use this section to study the errors that you may encounter when entering the examples from this chapter in a Maple session.

Attempting to Assign to a Protected Name

An exception is raised if you attempt to assign a value to a protected name. To resolve this error, specify a different name.

For more information about protected names, see *Protected Names (page 47)* or refer to the **protect** help page.

```
> int := 10;
Error, attempting to assign to `int` which is protected
```

Invalid Left-Hand Assignment

An exception is raised if you attempt to assign a value to a string.

For more information about strings, see *Strings (page 24)* or refer to the **string** help page.

```
> "my string" := 10;
Error, invalid left hand side of assignment
```

Use only valid names on the left-hand side of an assignment statement.

Incorrect Syntax in Parse

The **parse** command accepts a string as its argument. An exception is raised if the string is syntactically incorrect.

For more information, refer to the **parse** help page.

```
> parse("a^2--b");
Error, incorrect syntax in parse: `-` unexpected (near 5th character
 of parsed string)
```

The error message indicates the character number (counted from the left double quote) where the error was detected. In this case, the **6**th character (the second minus sign) caused the error.

White Space Characters within a Token

An exception is normally raised if a white space character occurs in a token.

```
> evalb(2 < = 3);
Error, `=` unexpected
```

The less-than-or-equal operator <= is a token in Maple. Therefore, it cannot contain a space.

```
> evalb(2 <= 3);
```

$$true \tag{2.76}$$

Incorrect Use of Double and Single Quotes

In Maple, double quotes form a string, left single quotes form a name, and right single quotes delay evaluation of an expression. Confusing a string with a name, or a name with delayed evaluation causes errors. Study the following examples to see the different uses of these quotes.

For more information about using quotes, see *Punctuation Marks (page 30)* or refer to the **quotes** help page.

2.8 Avoiding Common Problems

To form a string, enclose the expression in double quotes.

> `"2 + 3";`

$$"2+3" \tag{2.77}$$

> `type((2.77),'string');`

$$true \tag{2.78}$$

To form a name, enclose the expression in left single quotes. Unlike a string, which is displayed with double quotes around it, names are usually printed without quotes. The name in this example only looks like an expression.

> `` `2 + 3`; ``

$$2+3 \tag{2.79}$$

> `type((2.79),'name');`

$$true \tag{2.80}$$

To delay the evaluation of an expression, enclose it in right single quotes.

> `x := 2: y := 3: f := 'x + y';`

$$f := x + y \tag{2.81}$$

> `eval(f);`

$$5 \tag{2.82}$$

Avoid Using Maple Keywords as Names

If you use a Maple keyword in a name, and do not enclose it in left single quotes, an exception is raised.

> `1 + end;`

`Error, reserved word `end` unexpected`

To resolve this issue, select a variable name that is not a Maple keyword.

Note: It is possible to use a Maple keyword as a name by enclosing it in left single quotes. For example,

> `` `end` := 2; ``

$$end := 2 \tag{2.83}$$

> `` 1 + `end`; ``

$$3 \tag{2.84}$$

However, this approach is not recommended, since it makes it very likely that errors will be introduced if, for example, you forget to place back-ticks around keywords. When possible, avoid using keywords as names.

2.9 Exercises

1. Using Maple operators, do the following:
    a Compute the sum of **5434** and **6342**.
    b Compute the product of **92** and **310**.
    c Compute the quotient of the result from a) divided by the result from b).
    d Create a list containing the numbers from a), b), and c).
    e Square each element of the list from d).

2. Create variables named "my quotient" and "my remainder". Use these variables and the **irem** command to find the integer quotient and remainder of **12345** divided by **234**. **Tip**: Because the **irem** command stores extra results by assigning to the third argument you will need to make sure the name is passed and not its assigned value. Do this by using uneval quotes (').

3. Compute **3^(3^98)** modulo **7**.

4. Concatenate the three strings "int", "(x^2,", and "x)". Parse the resulting string. Evaluate the parsed string.

5. Determine a random integer between 40 and 100 using the command **rand(40..100)**. Concatenate this number with the string, "The student's grade is ". Extract the student's grade from the resulting string.

6. Assign the expressions **x^2** and **x*x** to the names **a** and **b**. Find the three operands of **a** and **b**. Compare the results with those returned by using the **dismantle** command, that is, **dismantle(a)** and **dismantle(b)**. The **dismantle** command displays the internal data structure used.

3 Maple Expressions

This chapter introduces Maple expressions associated with *scalar* data structures.

3.1 In This Chapter

- Introduction: automatic simplification and evaluation; syntax and constructors
- Using names, strings, and numbers in expressions
- Unevaluated expressions
- Expression types: arithmetic, Boolean, relational, and set-theoretic expressions; expressions for data structures; indexed expressions; function and member selection expressions
- Assigning attributes
- Classifying, examining, and manipulating expressions

3.2 Introduction

Expressions and Statements

Maple language elements can be classified as either *expressions* or *statements*. An expression is a first-class data element in the Maple language. In other words, expressions can be stored in data structures, passed as arguments to procedures, and manipulated in various ways; they are often used to represent mathematical objects. Statements, on the other hand, are not first-class data elements; they generally describe non-mathematical programming constructs and are used to affect the state of Maple.

This chapter describes expressions associated with *scalar* data structures. For information about non-scalar data structures, see *Basic Data Structures (page 129)*.

For more information about Maple statements, see *Maple Statements (page 173)*.

Automatic Simplification and Evaluation

Maple uses two processes to compute expressions: *automatic simplification* and *evaluation*. Automatic simplification is a process that Maple applies to the input immediately; this process cannot be controlled. Expression evaluation occurs after an initial round of automatic simplification; this process can be controlled in certain ways. For each kind of expression described in this chapter, the rules for both automatic simplification and expression evaluation are described.

Syntax and Constructors

You can create most expressions by entering the appropriate syntax. However, some expressions, such as expressions that include tables or a series, can only be created by calling a *constructor*. A constructor is a command that can be used as an alternative method of creating certain expressions.

For example, a sum that would normally be entered using the syntax for addition

```
> a + b + c + d;
```

$$a + b + c + d \tag{3.1}$$

can also be entered using the constructor `` `+` ``.

```
> `+`( a, b, c, d );
```

$$a + b + c + d \tag{3.2}$$

With some exceptions (for example, series, lists, sets, and procedures), the name of the constructor for an expression can be displayed by using the **op** command with its first argument equal to **0**.

```
> op( 0, a + b + c + d );
```

$$`+` \tag{3.3}$$

The example above shows that the constructor for the expression **a + b + c + d** is the command assigned to the name `` `+` ``.

3.3 Names

Names have several purposes in Maple. They can be used to reference algebraic indeterminates, symbols, and variables in your code.

Names (page 22) provided a basic introduction to Maple names. The following section describes concepts related to names in more detail.

A Maple name can be either *global* or *local*, depending on its *scope*. In this chapter, only global names are used. A global name is created either by referring to it at the top level of your program or by declaring it to be global in either a procedure or module definition. For more information about scope, see *Variables in Procedures (page 221)*.

Two names are the same if they have the same spelling and scope. Maple keeps only one copy of any name in memory, so in a large expression that includes an indeterminate **x**, only one copy of the name **x** is kept in memory. Each occurrence of **x** in the expression refers to the same name **x**.

The polynomial

```
> x^3 - 3*x^2 + 3*x - 1;
```

$$x^3 - 3x^2 + 3x - 1 \tag{3.4}$$

contains three occurrences of the name **x**, but all three point to the same location in memory.

Maple is unique in that names can represent themselves. As a result, you can use names as algebraic indeterminates, for example, to construct polynomials or other algebraic expressions.

Names can also be used to represent variables in your code. When a name is *assigned* a value, that name is associated with another expression and evaluating the name results in its assigned value being returned. When a name is *unassigned*, evaluating the name results in the name itself.

In this example, the name **a** is assigned to the value **2**.

> a := 2;

$$a := 2 \tag{3.5}$$

Before using a name on the left side of an assignment, the name has no assigned value.

> b;

$$b \tag{3.6}$$

When a value is assigned to a name, subsequent evaluation of the name results in its assigned value.

> a;

$$2 \tag{3.7}$$

For more information about assigning values, see *Assignments (page 174)*.

Creating Names: Lexical Conventions

When creating names in Maple, you must be aware of certain lexical conventions.

Environment Variables

Names beginning with an underscore character (_) are reserved for use by the Maple library. You should *not* create names that begin with an underscore.

As a special case, any name beginning with the four character sequence "_Env" is treated as an environment variable.

Environment variables are a special kind of variable in that an assignment to one within a procedure is automatically unassigned when the procedure has finished running. Therefore, environment variables only affect subprocedures called from that procedure, unless they are superseded locally.

The following predefined environment variables do not begin with **_Env**: **Testzero**, **UseHardwareFloats**, **Rounding**, **%**, **%%**, **%%%**, **Digits**, **_ans**, **index/newtable**, **mod**, **Order**, **printlevel**, **Normalizer**, **NumericEventHandlers**.

Environmental Variables Scope

Unlike a local variable, whose scope is restricted to the procedure containing the local variable itself, an environment variable can be referenced globally by all sub procedures called by or deeper than the current procedure, but the environment variable cannot be referenced by procedures above the current procedure.

For more information about environment variables, refer to the **envvar** help page. For more information about procedures, see *Procedures (page 199)* or refer to the **procedure** help page.

Constants

In addition to keywords, as described in *Reserved Words (page 18)*, Maple has several *predefined constants*.

You can display a sequence of all the names that represent *symbolic* constants in Maple by using the global variable **constants**.

> constants;

$$\textit{false}, \gamma, \infty, \textit{true}, \textit{Catalan}, \textit{FAIL}, \pi \tag{3.8}$$

> seq(i=evalf(i), i in constants);

$$\textit{false} = \textit{false}, \gamma = 0.5772156649, \infty = \textit{Float}(\infty), \textit{true} = \textit{true},$$
$$\textit{Catalan} = 0.9159655942, \textit{FAIL} = \textit{FAIL}, \pi = 3.141592654 \tag{3.9}$$

Maple also has several other special constants. **Table 3.1** lists some of them. For more information, refer to the **initialconstants** help page.

Table 3.1: Initially Known Names

Name	Meaning	Name	Meaning
lasterror	the most recent error	constants	initially known symbolic constants
libname	path of the Maple libraries	Digits	number of digits in floating-point computations
NULL	empty expression sequence	FAIL	cannot determine value
Order	truncation order for series	printlevel	control display of information
I	complex number	undefined	undefined numeric quantity

For more information about constants in Maple, refer to the **constant** help page.

Protected Names

A *protected name* has a predefined meaning; you cannot *directly* assign a value to a protected name. For example, the names of built-in commands such as **sin**; utility operations such as **degree**; commands such as **diff**; and type names such as **integer** and **list**, are protected names. An error occurs if you attempt to assign a value to any of these names.

```
> list := [1,2];
Error, attempting to assign to `list` which is protected
```

The Maple system prevents these names from re-assignment. However, even though it is *not* recommended, it is possible to reassign values to these names by first unprotecting them as illustrated by the following statements.

Note: You can unassign values to Maple system names by entering a **restart** command or by ending your Maple session. In general, using the **unprotect** command to modify Maple system names is *not* recommended.

```
> unprotect(sin);
> sin := "a sin indeed";
```

$$sin := \text{"a sin indeed"} \tag{3.10}$$

As a result, Maple components that rely on the sine function may not work as expected.

```
> plot( sin, 0..2*Pi, coords=polar );
Error, invalid input: plot expects its 1st argument, p, to be of type
 {array, list, rtable, set, algebraic, procedure, And(`module`, appli-
 able)}, but received a sin indeed
```

To check whether a name is protected, use the **type** command.

```
> type(sin, protected);
```

$$false \tag{3.11}$$

```
> type(sine, protected);
```

$$false \tag{3.12}$$

To prevent values from being assigned to a name, use the **protect** command.

```
> mysqr := x -> x^2;
```

$$mysqr := x \rightarrow x^2 \tag{3.13}$$

```
> type(mysqr, protected);
```

$$false \tag{3.14}$$

```
> protect( mysqr );
> mysqr := 9;
Error, attempting to assign to `mysqr` which is protected
```

3.4 Unevaluated Expressions

In general, Maple evaluates all expressions immediately. In some situations, it is necessary to delay the evaluation of an expression. An expression enclosed in right single quotes is called an *unevaluated* expression. It takes the general form

```
'expr'
```

where *expr* is an arbitrary expression. All of the expressions contained within the right single quotes are not evaluated.

For example, the **sin** command normally performs the following computations.

```
> sin( 0.5 );
```

$$0.4794255386 \tag{3.15}$$

```
> sin( Pi / 2 );
```

$$1 \tag{3.16}$$

To prevent the evaluation of these computations, you can enclose the expressions in right single quotes (also called *unevaluation quotes*) as follows.

```
> 'sin( 0.5 )';
```

$$\sin(0.5) \tag{3.17}$$

```
> 'sin( Pi / 2 )';
```

$$\sin\left(\frac{1}{2}\pi\right) \tag{3.18}$$

You can enclose expressions of any length or complexity in unevaluation quotes.

```
> 'sin( 0.5 )^2 + cos( 0.5 )^2';
```

$$\sin(0.5)^2 + \cos(0.5)^2 \tag{3.19}$$

Also, you can enclose subexpressions in unevaluation quotes to prevent certain parts of an expression from evaluating.

```
> 'sin( 0.5 )'^2 + cos( 0.5 )^2;
```

$$\sin(0.5)^2 + 0.7701511530 \tag{3.20}$$

The sections below describe cases in which you may want to delay evaluation.

Protecting Names and Options

Unevaluation quotes can be used to prevent the evaluation of names.

```
> a := x^2 + x + 1;
```

$$a := x^2 + x + 1 \qquad (3.21)$$

```
> a;
```

$$x^2 + x + 1 \qquad (3.22)$$

```
> 'a';
```

$$a \qquad (3.23)$$

This is important when you want to use a variable as a name, regardless of whether it has an assigned value.

Also, unevaluation quotes can be used to protect options. Names are often used as options to control the behavior of a command. If the name of that option has been used as a variable, the command that has been called uses the value of the variable and not the option name as expected. Unevaluation quotes can be used around option names to protect against this.

```
> periodic := 4;
```

$$periodic := 4 \qquad (3.24)$$

```
> numtheory:-cfrac(3^(1/2),'periodic');
```

$$1 + \cfrac{1}{1 + \cfrac{1}{2 + \cfrac{1}{1 + \cfrac{1}{2 + ...}}}} \qquad (3.25)$$

In the next example, an exception is raised because the name of a command option is not enclosed in unevaluation quotes.

```
> output := 2:
> CodeGeneration:-C( x^2, output = string );
Error, (in Translate) options [2 = string] not recognized
```

In this example, the best way to use the **output** option is to quote the name, thus preventing its evaluation in case the name **output** has an assigned value.

```
> CodeGeneration:-C( x^2, 'output' = 'string' );
```
$$\text{"cg = x * x;} \tag{3.26}$$

Tip: It is also recommended that you also use unevaluation quotes for the names of types and conversions. For more information, see *Structured Types (page 123)*.

For more information on types and conversions, refer to the **type** and **convert** help pages.

Generic Expressions

Expressions sometimes describe the operation to take place in a generic sense. For example, **B[i]** can be used in certain contexts with unevaluation quotes to denote a generic index into B. If unevaluation quotes are not used, Maple will try to look up the specific **i**th element of B.

```
> B := <1,2,3,4>;
```
$$B := \begin{bmatrix} 1 \\ 2 \\ 3 \\ 4 \end{bmatrix} \tag{3.27}$$

```
> sum(B[i], i = 1..4);
Error, bad index into Vector
> sum('B[i]', i = 1..4);
```
$$10 \tag{3.28}$$

Pass by Reference

Some commands accept a name as an argument, with the intent that it will be used to store a result. Unevaluation quotes ensure that the variable name (and not the value assigned to the variable) is used in the procedure.

```
> remainder := irem(45,3,'quotient'); quotient;
```
$$remainder := 0$$
$$15 \tag{3.29}$$

```
> remainder := irem(44,3,'quotient'); quotient;
```
$$remainder := 2$$
$$14 \tag{3.30}$$

If **quotient** is not enclosed in unevaluation quotes, the second call in the above example raises an exception because 15, the value of **quotient**, is not a valid third argument to the **irem** command.

Displaying the Original Command

For display purposes, it is sometimes useful to show the original command before a solution is computed.

```
> v := 'int(x*y^2, [x=0..1, y=0..1] )';
```

$$v := \int_0^1 \int_0^1 xy^2 \, dx \, dy \tag{3.31}$$

```
> v;
```

$$\frac{1}{6} \tag{3.32}$$

Unassigning Names

To reset the value of a name, assign the unevaluated name (its initial value) to the name. For example,

```
> x := 2+3;
```

$$x := 5 \tag{3.33}$$

```
> x := 'x';
```

$$x := x \tag{3.34}$$

Now, the value of **x** is reset to **x**.

Evaluation and Automatic Simplification

It is important to note the differences between computations that occur during the evaluation process and those that occur during the automatic simplification process. Unevaluation quotes do *not* prevent automatic simplifications from occurring. For example, basic numeric arithmetic is one form of automatic simplification. In the following expression, the unevaluation quotes do *not* prevent the numeric addition from occurring.

```
> '2 +3';
```

$$5 \tag{3.35}$$

In this example, Maple first simplifies the unevaluated sum **'2 + 3'** to the expression **'5'**. During the evaluation process, Maple "removes" the right single quotes and produces the numeric result **5**.

All unevaluated expressions are of the type **uneval**. You can use the **type** command to check whether an expression is an unevaluated expression.

```
> type( ''x'', 'uneval' );
```

$$\mathit{true} \tag{3.36}$$

In the example above, the first argument to the call to the **type** command is the name **x**, which is enclosed in two sets of unevaluation quotes. The result of evaluating the first argument is the unevaluated expression **'x'** because the evaluation process removes one set of unevaluation quotes. The resulting expression is therefore of type **uneval**.

On the other hand, if you enclose the first argument to **type** in only one set of unevaluation quotes, the evaluation process removes the only set of unevaluation quotes, leaving the result as the name **x**, which is not an unevaluated expression.

```
> type( 'x', 'uneval' );
```

$$\mathit{false} \tag{3.37}$$

In other words, the **type** command accesses the name **x**, rather than the unevaluated expression **'x'**, since the **type** command accesses the result of its arguments that have been evaluated.

In the example above quotes were also used around the type name **uneval**. This provides a measure of protection just in case the variable name, **uneval** has an assigned value (which is unlikely because **uneval** is protected). During normal function evaluation, each argument, **x** and **uneval** is evaluated. With quotes, **'x'** becomes **x**, and **'uneval'** becomes **uneval** as seen by the **type** procedure. Without quotes, x would become the value of x (which may be the symbol **x** itself), and **uneval** would become the value of **uneval**, which is usually the symbol **uneval** itself. Unevaluation quotes make the displayed call robust against cases where the variable you are using unexpectedly has a value. It is rarely necessary to use this level of caution in interactive use, but when you write programs, it is a good practice to include unevaluation quotes to make your code as robust as possible.

Another special case of unevaluation arises in function calls.

```
'f'(a)
```

Suppose **f** is not assigned to anything. Since evaluating **f** does not call a procedure, Maple returns the unevaluated function call **f(a)**.

```
> f(a);
```

$$f(x^2 + x + 1) \tag{3.38}$$

Similarly, using **uneval** quotes around a function evaluation will cause Maple to behave as if the named function had no value.

```
> ''sin''(Pi);
```

$$\text{'sin'}(\pi) \tag{3.39}$$

```
> (3.39);
```

$$\sin(\pi) \tag{3.40}$$

```
> (3.40);
```

$$0 \tag{3.41}$$

You will find this facility useful when writing procedures that need to act on the whole original expression, not the evaluated result.

For more examples and information on unevaluated expressions, refer to the **uneval** help page.

Example: Defining a Procedure that Is Returned Unevaluated

You may need to use unevaluation quotes when you are defining a procedure that is returned unevaluated. This is necessary, for example, when you are defining a procedure that evaluates a numeric result for numeric inputs, but does not produce a numeric result otherwise. (The procedure may perform normalizations and apply symmetries, if appropriate.) It is important to write procedures using this method so that they can be plotted, optimized, or numerically integrated, for example.

Consider the following procedure.

```
> f := proc( x )
    if x > 2 then
       x
    else
       2
    end if
  end proc:
```

Using the wrong calling sequence in a call to plot results in an error.

```
> plot( f( x ), x = -10 .. 10 );
Error, (in f) cannot determine if this expression is true or false:
2 < x
```

The correct calling sequence would be either **plot('f'(x), x=-10..10)**, which puts uneval quotes around **f**, or **plot(f, -10..10)**, which avoids computing **f(x)** by omitting the variable altogether. Remember that arguments in a function call are evaluated first before the called procedure sees them.

Here, the precursor evaluation of **f(x)** tries to apply **f** to the unassigned symbol, **x**.

```
> f( x );
Error, (in f) cannot determine if this expression is true or false:
2 < x
```

The procedure could be rewritten so that it returns unevaluated whenever it encounters arguments that cannot be processed. This trick causes **f(x)** to evaluate to itself when non-numeric input is passed in.

```
> f := proc( x )
    if type( x, 'numeric' ) then
      if x > 0 then
        x
      else
        2
      end if
    else
      'procname( _passed )'
    end if
  end proc:
```

The unevaluated expression **'procname(_passed)'** returns the full calling sequence unevaluated.

```
> f( x );
```

$$f(x) \tag{3.42}$$

The expression **procname(_passed)** must be enclosed in unevaluation quotes to prevent an infinite loop.

3.5 Numbers

Maple supports computation with exact numerical quantities, as well as approximate computation to arbitrarily high accuracy with floating-point numbers.

Integers

A *natural integer* is any sequence of one or more decimal digits.

```
> 12345;
```

$$12345 \tag{3.43}$$

The maximum number of digits is system-dependent. To determine the maximum number of digits, use the following command.

```
> kernelopts( 'maxdigits' );
```

$$38654705646 \tag{3.44}$$

A *signed integer* is formed by appending + or - before any natural integer.

```
> -42;
```

$$-42 \tag{3.45}$$

```
> +42;
```

$$42 \tag{3.46}$$

An *integer* is either a natural integer or a signed integer.

You can use the **length** command to determine the number of digits in an integer.

```
> 2^42;
```

$$4398046511104 \tag{3.47}$$

```
> length( 2^42 );
```

$$13 \tag{3.48}$$

Fractions

A rational number (fraction) is the quotient of two integers, where the denominator is always positive.

Use the division operator (forward slash) / to enter a fraction.

```
integer / natural
```

For example,

```
> 2 / 3;
```

$$\frac{2}{3} \qquad (3.49)$$

You can enter a fraction in which the numerator and denominator have a common (integer) factor, but Maple automatically simplifies this to the lowest terms.

```
> 4 / 6;
```

$$\frac{2}{3} \qquad (3.50)$$

In addition, Maple automatically moves a negative sign to the numerator.

```
> 2/(-3);
```

$$-\frac{2}{3} \qquad (3.51)$$

Fractions are automatically simplified to an integer if the denominator is a divisor of the numerator.

```
> 6/3;
```

$$2 \qquad (3.52)$$

You can use the **numer** and **denom** commands to extract the numerator and denominator, respectively, of a fraction.

```
> numer( 2/3 );
```

$$2 \qquad (3.53)$$

```
> denom( 2/3 );
```

$$3 \qquad (3.54)$$

Fractions can also be created by using the **Fraction** constructor with the numerator and denominator as arguments.

```
> Fraction( 2, 3 );
```

$$\frac{2}{3} \qquad (3.55)$$

Floats

Maple supports computation with floating-point numbers to arbitrary precision.

A *float* can be input using a period for the decimal.

```
> 2.3;
```

$$2.3 \tag{3.56}$$

```
> 2.;
```

$$2. \tag{3.57}$$

```
> .7;
```

$$0.7 \tag{3.58}$$

```
> -.567;
```

$$-0.567 \tag{3.59}$$

Or, using exponent form using a suffix containing the letter "**e**" or "**E**" followed by an integer with no spaces between.

```
> 4e3;
```

$$4000. \tag{3.60}$$

```
> 2.3e6;
```

$$2.3 \, 10^6 \tag{3.61}$$

```
> .2E3;
```

$$200. \tag{3.62}$$

Observe that spaces are significant. The first example is a difference rather than a float in exponent form.

```
> .2e -3;
```

$$-2.8 \tag{3.63}$$

```
> .2e-3;
```

$$0.0002 \tag{3.64}$$

Also, the following is invalid.

```
> 3.e4;
Error, missing operator or `;`
```

Floats represent numbers of the form **s*10^e**, where the number **s** is called the *significand* or *mantissa* of the float, and the number **e** is called the *exponent*. The significand is a Maple integer. Therefore, it is restricted to values that have, at most, the number of digits indicated by the **kernelopts('maxdigits')** command.

```
> kernelopts( 'maxdigits' );
```

$$38654705646 \tag{3.65}$$

The maximum value of the exponent is a platform-dependent quantity whose value may be queried by using the **Maple_floats** command.

```
> Maple_floats( 'MAX_EXP' );
```

$$9223372036854775806 \tag{3.66}$$

Similarly, the minimum value of the exponent is given by the value

```
> Maple_floats( 'MIN_EXP' );
```

$$-9223372036854775806 \tag{3.67}$$

returned by the **Maple_floats** command. For more information, refer to the **Maple_floats** help page.

You can also create software floats by using the constructor **SFloat**. This constructor accepts the significand and exponent as arguments, and has the general form

```
SFloat( m, e )
```

```
> SFloat( 23, -1 );
```

$$2.3 \tag{3.68}$$

To extract the significand and exponent of a software float, use the **SFloatMantissa** and **SFloatExponent** commands.

```
> SFloatMantissa( 2.3 );
```

$$23 \tag{3.69}$$

```
> SFloatExponent( 2.3 );
```

$$-1 \tag{3.70}$$

The significand and exponent are also the operands of a software float.

```
> op( 2.3 );
```

$$23, -1 \tag{3.71}$$

Two software floats are equal if they represent the same number. However, equal floats by themselves do not need to be the same object in memory.

```
> evalb( 2.3 = 2.30 );
```

$$true \tag{3.72}$$

> `addressof( 2.3 ); addressof( 2.30 );`

$$18446884532539008510$$

$$18446884532539009726 \tag{3.73}$$

Observe that the significands (and therefore, also, the exponents) differ in this example.

> `SFloatMantissa( 2.3 );`

$$23 \tag{3.74}$$

> `SFloatMantissa( 2.30 );`

$$230 \tag{3.75}$$

Note that equal floats with different significands inside of two otherwise identical objects will require something stronger than **evalb** for comparison. **evalb** is the implicit comparison used when evaluating conditionals in **if** statements.

> `evalb( 2.3 + x = 2.30 + x );`

$$\textit{false} \tag{3.76}$$

> `evalb(<2.3,4.5> = <2.30,4.50>);`

$$\textit{false} \tag{3.77}$$

Testing the difference of the two expressions, or calling a command to do a deeper comparison may be necessary.

> `evalb( (2.3 + x) - (2.30 + x) = 0 );`

$$\textit{true} \tag{3.78}$$

> `EqualEntries(<2.3,4.5>, <2.30,4.50>);`

$$\textit{true} \tag{3.79}$$

The names of the constructor **SFloat** and accessors **SFloatMantissa** and **SFloatExponent** all begin with the letter **S**. The **S** stands for "software" because these floating-point numbers are implemented in software. Maple also supports the floating-point numbers supported by the underlying hardware, called *hardware floats* or *hfloats*. You can create a hardware float by using the hardware float constructor **HFloat**.

> `HFloat( 24375, -3 );`

$$24.3750000000000 \tag{3.80}$$

> `h := HFloat( 24.375 );`

$$h := 24.3750000000000 \tag{3.81}$$

```
> op( h );
```

$$243750000000000000, -16 \qquad (3.82)$$

Note, however, that **hfloats** are binary floating-point numbers, rather than decimal floating-point numbers. That means that unlike the example above, there is often round-off error when decimal numbers are converted into **hfloats**. For more information, see *Hardware Floating-Point Numbers (page 276)*.

```
> op( HFloat(2.3) );
```

$$2299999999999999982, -17 \qquad (3.83)$$

The **SFloatMantissa** and **SFloatExponent** commands also accept hardware floats as input.

```
> SFloatMantissa( h );
```

$$243750000000000000 \qquad (3.84)$$

```
> SFloatExponent( h );
```

$$-16 \qquad (3.85)$$

For more information on floating-point numbers, see *Floating-Point Numbers (page 274)*.

Complex Numbers

Maple supports arithmetic with complex numbers of the form $a + bi$, where $i = \sqrt{-1}$ is the imaginary unit. In Maple, the imaginary unit is normally denoted by **I**; that is, the uppercase letter "I" is used rather than the lowercase "i". Therefore, the complex number with the real part equal to 2 and imaginary part equal to 3 is entered, naturally, as follows.

```
> 2 + 3*I;
```

$$2 + 3I \qquad (3.86)$$

In general, a complex number has the form

```
re + im * I
```

where *re* and *im* are the real and imaginary parts of the complex number, respectively. If the expressions *re* and *im* are of type **extended_numeric**; the resulting complex number will be of type **complex(extended_numeric)**. (It is not necessary that *re* and *im* are reals; they may be arbitrary algebraic expressions. However, in this case, the result of the syntax above will generally be an algebraic expression that will not be a complex numeric constant.)

You can also create complex numbers using the **Complex** constructor. It can be called using either one or two arguments. The single-argument form has the following syntax.

```
Complex( expr )
```

If the argument *expr* is of type **complex**, the **Complex** constructor returns the value of *expr*. Otherwise, if *expr* is of type **extended_numeric**, the **Complex** constructor returns **expr * I**.

```
> Complex( 2 ), Complex( 0 ), Complex( 0.0 );
```
$$2\,\mathrm{I}, 0, 0.\,\mathrm{I} \tag{3.87}$$

```
> Complex( 2 + 3*I ), Complex( infinity ), Complex( undefined );
```
$$2 + 3\,\mathrm{I}, \infty\,\mathrm{I}, \mathit{undefined}\,\mathrm{I} \tag{3.88}$$

The two-argument form has the following syntax.

```
Complex( re, im )
```

The first argument is interpreted as the real part and the second argument is interpreted as the imaginary part, of the complex number constructed.

```
> Complex( 2, 3 ), Complex( 2.1, 3 ), Complex( 0, 0 );
```
$$2 + 3\,\mathrm{I}, 2.1 + 3.\,\mathrm{I}, 0 \tag{3.89}$$

Note that if either of the arguments is a float, the real and imaginary parts of the complex number created are *both* of type float.

A complex zero with floating-point real and imaginary components can have four sign combinations.

```
> z1 := 0.0 + 0.0*I; z2 := 0.0 - 0.0*I;
  z3 := -0.0 - 0.0*I; z4 := -0.0 + 0.0*I;
```
$$z1 := 0. + 0.\,\mathrm{I}$$
$$z2 := 0. - 0.\,\mathrm{I}$$
$$z3 := -0. - 0.\,\mathrm{I}$$
$$z4 := -0. + 0.\,\mathrm{I} \tag{3.90}$$

Similar to **0.0 = -0.0**, numerically, these four complex zeros are numerically equivalent.

```
> evalb( z1 = z2 and z2 = z3 and z3 = z4 );
```
$$\mathit{true} \tag{3.91}$$

If the arguments *re* and *im* are not of type **extended_numeric**, the **Complex** constructor is returned unevaluated.

```
> Complex( u, v );
```

$$Complex(u, v) \qquad (3.92)$$

Except if one of the arguments is complex, in which case, an exception is raised.

```
> Complex( 2 + 3*I, 1 );
Error, invalid arguments for Complex constructor
```

It is important to understand that there is a single complex infinity, which is a point on the Riemann sphere. It can be denoted in different ways:

```
> inf1 := infinity + infinity * I; inf2 := infinity - infinity * I;
  inf3 := -infinity - infinity * I; inf4 := -infinity + infinity *
  I;
```

$$inf1 := \infty + \infty\,I$$
$$inf2 := \infty - \infty\,I$$
$$inf3 := -\infty - \infty\,I$$
$$inf4 := -\infty + \infty\,I \qquad (3.93)$$

However, all of these forms are numerically equivalent.

```
> evalb( inf1 = inf2 and inf2 = inf3 and inf3 = inf4 );
```

$$true \qquad (3.94)$$

They are all treated as distinct from the positive and negative real infinities.

To select the real or imaginary part of a complex number, use the **Re** and **Im** commands, respectively.

```
> Re( 2.3 + sqrt(2)*I );
```

$$2.3 \qquad (3.95)$$

```
> Im( 2.3 + sqrt(2)*I );
```

$$\sqrt{2} \qquad (3.96)$$

Note that, for a symbolic expression of the form **a + b*I**, it is *not* assumed that **a** is the real part and **b** is the imaginary part. Therefore, the **Re** and **Im** commands are not unevaluated on such input.

```
> Re( a + b*I );
```

$$\Re(a + I b) \qquad (3.97)$$

```
> Im( a + b*I );
```

$$\Im(a + Ib) \tag{3.98}$$

However, the **evalc** command uses special rules for processing complex expressions, in which any unknown symbol is assumed to be real. Therefore, when the **evalc** is used, these expressions are returned as follows.

```
> evalc( Re( a + b*I ) );
```

$$a \tag{3.99}$$

```
> evalc( Im( a + b*I ) );
```

$$b \tag{3.100}$$

For more information, refer to the **evalc** help page.

You can change the default name used to input and display the imaginary unit by using the **interface** command.

```
> interface( 'imaginaryunit' = i );
```

$$I \tag{3.101}$$

(The previous value is returned.) After calling the command above, the name **i** is used to represent the imaginary unit.

```
> Complex( 2, 3 );
```

$$2 + 3i \tag{3.102}$$

When this command is used, the name **i** can no longer be used as a program variable. As an example, the following statements display error messages.

```
> i := 2;
Error, illegal use of an object as a name
> add( i^2, i = 1 .. 5 );
Error, illegal use of an object as a name
```

To restore the default imaginary unit, use the following command.

```
> interface( 'imaginaryunit' = I );
```

$$i \tag{3.103}$$

3.6 Indexed Expressions

Indexed expressions represent *selection operations*. The general form of an indexed expression is

```
expr [ index ]
```

where *expr* is an arbitrary expression and *index* represents a sequence of expressions. The following are examples of indexed expressions.

```
> 2[ 3, 4 ];
```

$$2_{3,4} \tag{3.104}$$

```
> a[];
```

$$a_{[\,]} \tag{3.105}$$

```
> a[ 1 ];
```

$$a_1 \tag{3.106}$$

```
> a[ b ];
```

$$a_b \tag{3.107}$$

```
> a[ b, c ];
```

$$a_{b,c} \tag{3.108}$$

```
> map[ 2 ];
```

$$map_2 \tag{3.109}$$

```
> [ 1, 2, 3 ][ 2 ..3 ][ 1 ];
```

$$2 \tag{3.110}$$

Note that the last example above contains a nested (or iterated) indexed expression.

The constructor for indexed expressions is the name **?[]**.

```
> `?[]`( S, [ a, b, c ] );
```

$$S_{a,b,c} \tag{3.111}$$

Note that the indices must be enclosed with square brackets in a list.

All or some of the elements of an index sequence can be extracted by using the **op** command. The **nops** command will tell you how many elements are in the index sequence.

3.6 Indexed Expressions

```
> nops( a[ b, c, d ] );
```
$$3 \qquad (3.112)$$

```
> op( a[ b, c, d] );
```
$$b, c, d \qquad (3.113)$$

```
> op( 2, a[ b, c, d ] );
```
$$c \qquad (3.114)$$

```
> op( 2..3, a[ b, c, d ] );
```
$$c, d \qquad (3.115)$$

Indexed expressions are often used to perform selection operations. The behavior of a selection operation depends on the type of expression, *expr*, and the index sequence given.

If *expr* is itself a sequence of expressions, the index sequence must evaluate to a positive integer, an integral range, or the empty sequence. The following are all examples of valid ways to index a sequence.

```
> expr := (1,2,3,4);
```
$$expr := 1, 2, 3, 4 \qquad (3.116)$$

```
> expr[ 3 ];
```
$$3 \qquad (3.117)$$

```
> expr[ 1 .. 3 ];
```
$$1, 2, 3 \qquad (3.118)$$

```
> expr[];
```
$$1, 2, 3, 4 \qquad (3.119)$$

```
> expr[ 2 .. 1 ];
```

The result of evaluating an indexed sequence is a selection of the components of the sequence. The indexing sequence must represent a valid index or range of indices. Attempting to select an entry beyond the length of the sequence and will raise an error.

```
> expr[ 88 ];
Error, invalid subscript selector
```

Similarly, components of lists, sets, arrays, matrices, and vectors can be selected

```
> L := [1,2,3,4];
```
$$L := [\,1, 2, 3, 4\,] \qquad (3.120)$$

```
> L[ 3 ];
```
$$3 \qquad (3.121)$$

```
> L[ 1 .. 3 ];
```
$$[1, 2, 3] \qquad (3.122)$$

```
> L[];
```
$$1, 2, 3, 4 \qquad (3.123)$$

```
> M := <1,2,3;4,5,6>;
```
$$M := \begin{bmatrix} 1 & 2 & 3 \\ 4 & 5 & 6 \end{bmatrix} \qquad (3.124)$$

```
> M[2,3];
```
$$6 \qquad (3.125)$$

```
> M[1..2,1..2];
```
$$\begin{bmatrix} 1 & 2 \\ 4 & 5 \end{bmatrix} \qquad (3.126)$$

```
> S := { red, blue, green, orange };
```
$$S := \{blue, green, orange, red\} \qquad (3.127)$$

```
> S[ 3 ];
```
$$orange \qquad (3.128)$$

Note that, because sets are sorted data structures, the order at construction time may not match the order stored internally. It is not predictable what color will be returned by the index used to specify the third entry above. (It may not be **green**.)

A negative number may be used as an index, which selects elements starting from the end of the list. Positive and negative indices mixed in a range return an empty selection.

```
> L[ -1 ];
```
$$4 \qquad (3.129)$$

```
> L[ -3 .. -2 ];
```
$$[2, 3] \qquad (3.130)$$

```
> L[ -3 .. 1 ];
```

$$[\,] \tag{3.131}$$

Lists can be used as an index to pick out specific entries, such as the first and third entries of a list, or the four corners of a matrix.

```
> L[ [1,3] ];
```

$$[1, 3] \tag{3.132}$$

```
> M[[1,2],[1,3]];
```

$$\begin{bmatrix} 1 & 3 \\ 4 & 6 \end{bmatrix} \tag{3.133}$$

Indexing on arrays, matrices and vectors is very flexible. In the case of these data structures, round-brackets can also be used to index in a way that is useful to programming. For example, where **M[1]** will return the first row of the matrix, **M(1)** will return the first entry (regardless of the number of dimensions).

```
> M[1];
```

$$\begin{bmatrix} 1 & 2 & 3 \end{bmatrix} \tag{3.134}$$

```
> M(1);
```

$$1 \tag{3.135}$$

This class of data structures are known as rectangular tables, or "rtables" for short. For more information on what ways they can be indexed, refer to the **rtable_indexing** help page.

If *expr* is a name with no assigned value, the result of evaluating the indexed expression is an indexed name. In this case, the index can be any sequence of expressions, and if desired, it is up to your program to define the meaning of the expression.

```
> aName[ x^2 - 3*x, "a string", anotherName[ 2, b ] ];
```

$$aName_{x^2 - 3x,\ \text{"a string"},\ anotherName_{2,\ b}} \tag{3.136}$$

A string may be indexed by a positive integer, a positive integral range, or a general sequence. The indexed string expression evaluates to itself, unless the indexing sequence is an integer or integral range, in which case, the result is a substring of the indexed string.

```
> "abcde"[ 3 ];
```

$$\text{"c"} \tag{3.137}$$

```
> "abcde"[ 2 .. 4 ];
```

$$"bcd" \qquad (3.138)$$

```
> "abcde"[ u, v^2 - s*t ];
```

$$"abcde"_{u,\, v^2 - s\, t} \qquad (3.139)$$

```
> "abcde"[];
```

$$"abcde"_{[\,]} \qquad (3.140)$$

If *expr* evaluates to a table, and if the index given is found in the table the expression evaluates to the corresponding entry. Otherwise, the indexed expression evaluates to itself.

```
> t := table( [ a = 1, b = 2, (c,d) = 3 ] );
```

$$t := table([b = 2, (c, d) = 3, a = 1]) \qquad (3.141)$$

```
> t[ a ];
```

$$1 \qquad (3.142)$$

```
> t[ c, d ];
```

$$3 \qquad (3.143)$$

```
> t[ u, v ];
```

$$t_{u,\, v} \qquad (3.144)$$

If *expr* evaluates to a module, the index must evaluate to the name of an export of the module, and then the entire indexed expression evaluates to the value of **expr:-index**.

```
> m := module() export e, f := 2; end module:
> m[ e ];
```

$$e \qquad (3.145)$$

```
> evalb( e = m[ e ] );
```

$$false \qquad (3.146)$$

```
> m[ f ];
```

$$2 \qquad (3.147)$$

For more information about modules, see *Programming with Modules (page 309)*.

3.7 Member Selection

The member selection operator **:-** is used to select exports of a module, and also to designate a symbol as a global symbol. Member selection expressions have one of the following general forms.

```
modexpr :- expname
:- name
```

The first form above is used to select a member of a module.

```
> m := module() export e, f:= 2; end module:
> m:-e;
```

$$e \qquad (3.148)$$

```
> evalb( e = m:-e );
```

$$false \qquad (3.149)$$

```
> m:-f;
```

$$2 \qquad (3.150)$$

The first operand, *modexpr*, must evaluate to a module. The second operand, *expname*, must be a literal name; it is *not* evaluated. If *expname* is not a name, or is not the name of an export of the module *modexpr*, an exception is raised. The syntax **m:-e** is similar to **m[e]**, in that they both evaluate module **m**'s export **e**. The difference is that the index selection form will evaluate **e** before resolving the export.

In the second form, the operand *name* must be a literal name. The expression **:-name** then evaluates to the *global instance* of the name *name*.

The following example defines, and then immediately calls, a procedure which declares a local variable **t**. Since this local variable is never assigned, it evaluates to itself. The call to the **evalb** command then compares, on the left-hand side of the equation, the local name **t** to the global name **t** resulting from applying the member selection operator to **t**. The result is **false** because the global name **t** and the name **t** local to the procedure are different expressions.

```
> proc() local t; evalb( t = :-t ) end proc();
```

$$false \qquad (3.151)$$

For more information on modules and member selection, see *Programming with Modules (page 309)*.

3.8 Functions

A *function* expression is a Maple expression of the form

```
expr( sequence )
```

that contains zero or more expressions in the sequence within the parentheses. It represents a function call.

```
> F();
```

$$F(\ ) \tag{3.152}$$

```
> F( x );
```

$$F(x) \tag{3.153}$$

```
> F( x, y );
```

$$F(x, y) \tag{3.154}$$

```
> sin( x + y );
```

$$\sin(x + y) \tag{3.155}$$

Typically, **expr** is the name of a procedure or mathematical function. It can be a general expression.

The zeroth operand of a function expression is **expr**.

```
> op( 0, F( x, y, z ) );
```

$$F \tag{3.156}$$

The other operands are the *arguments*,

```
> op( F( x, y, z ) );
```

$$x, y, z \tag{3.157}$$

and the number of operands is the number of arguments.

```
> nops( F( x, y, z ) );
```

$$3 \tag{3.158}$$

```
> nops( F() );
```

$$0 \tag{3.159}$$

Maple supports an algebra of operators, so that complicated expressions such as

```
> (f^2 + g@h - 2)( x );
```

$$f(x)^2 + g(h(x)) - 2 \tag{3.160}$$

can be formed. Note that Maple applies such "operator expressions" to the arguments. @ is the composition operator. For more information on composition of functions, see *Composition (page 108)*.

It is important to know that Maple computes numeric quantities as applicable operators with constant values. Therefore, for example, the expression

```
> 2( x );
```

$$2 \tag{3.161}$$

is computed as an application of the constant operator **2** to the argument **x**, which evaluates to **2**. In fact, numeric "operators" can accept any number of arguments.

```
> 2( x, y, 3 );
```

$$2 \tag{3.162}$$

Note that an expression such as

```
> '2( 3 )';
```

$$2(3) \tag{3.163}$$

(in which unevaluation quotes are used to delay the evaluation process) appears to be a product. However, this expression is, in fact, a function expression. When permitted to evaluate fully, the result is the constant value of the operator.

```
> 2( 3 );
```

$$2 \tag{3.164}$$

Calls to Procedures

The most important kind of function expression to understand is the case in which the zeroth operands is a procedure or, more commonly, an expression (typically, as a name) that evaluates to a procedure.

```
p( arg1, arg2, ..., argN )
```

In this case, *p* is a procedure or an expression, such as a name, that evaluates to a procedure, and *arg1*, *arg2*, ..., *argN* are zero or more argument expressions.

For example, the name **sin** evaluates to a procedure that computes the mathematical **sin** function. A function expression of the form

```
sin( expr )
```

computes the **sin** of its argument **expr**. This is performed as follows: Maple evaluates the name **sin** and finds that it is assigned a procedure. The argument *expr* is evaluated to produce a result. That result is then passed to the procedure assigned to the name **sin** and the result computed by that procedure for the specific input is returned as the overall value of the function call **sin(expr)**.

For information on defining functions and procedures, see *Functional Operators (page 107)* and *Procedures (page 199)*.

3.9 Arithmetic Expressions

Arithmetic Operators

The arithmetic operators in Maple include + (addition), - (subtraction), * (multiplication), / (division), and ^ (exponentiation). These operators are used to create rational expressions, such as polynomials.

```
> x^2 - 3*x + 1;
```

$$x^2 - 3x + 1 \tag{3.165}$$

Addition and Subtraction

The addition operator `+` and the subtraction operator `-` are typically used as binary infix operators, but may also be used as unary prefix operators to indicate a signed expression.

```
> a + b + 3;
```

$$a + b + 3 \tag{3.166}$$

```
> u - v;
```

$$u - v \tag{3.167}$$

```
> +7;
```

$$7 \tag{3.168}$$

```
> -42;
```

$$-42 \tag{3.169}$$

A sum resulting from the evaluation of either an addition or subtraction operation is an expression of type `+`.

```
> type( u - v, '`+`' );
```

$$true \qquad (3.170)$$

The expression **u-v** has the operands **u** and **-v**; that is, it is a sum of the summands **u** and **-v**.

```
> op( u - v );
```

$$u, -v \qquad (3.171)$$

Note that subtraction is not an associative operator.

```
> ( 1 - 2 ) - 3 <> 1 - ( 2 - 3 );
```

$$-4 \neq 2 \qquad (3.172)$$

However, addition is both associative and commutative:

```
> b + a + c = a + b + c;
```

$$b + a + c = b + a + c \qquad (3.173)$$

Although sums are formed by using the binary operator `+`, they are actually expressions of arbitrarily large arity (greater than unity). Since addition is associative, Maple "flattens" all sums of more than two summands during the automatic simplification process. Therefore, an expression of type `+` can have many operands.

```
> nops( a + b + c + d + e );
```

$$5 \qquad (3.174)$$

You can use the name `+` as a constructor to form a sum.

```
> `+`( a, b, c );
```

$$b + a + c \qquad (3.175)$$

Since Maple performs automatic simplification, the number of operands of a sum may not be apparent from the input.

```
> nops( a + 2 + b + 3 + c + 4 );
```

$$4 \qquad (3.176)$$

In this example, Maple combines the integer terms in the sum.

```
> a + 2 + b + 3 + c + 4;
```

$$a + 9 + b + c \qquad (3.177)$$

To see that this occurs during the automatic simplification process, enclose the input in unevaluation quotes to delay evaluation.

```
> 'a + 2 + b + 3 + c + 4';
```

$$a + 9 + b + c \tag{3.178}$$

In a sum such as

```
> '2 + 3';
```

$$5 \tag{3.179}$$

the addition is performed, as indicated, during the automatic simplification process. The same sum can be computed in another way:

```
> u := 3:
> '2 + u';
```

$$2 + u \tag{3.180}$$

In this example, the arithmetic is not performed because the value of the variable **u** does not replace the name **u** during the automatic simplification process. If the unevaluation quotes are removed to allow the full evaluation of the expression, numeric addition is performed.

```
> 2 + u;
```

$$5 \tag{3.181}$$

Since addition is commutative, the order of summands in an expression of type `+` is arbitrary. It is fixed within a Maple session, but may vary from one session to another. Therefore, you must not rely on the operands of a sum occurring in any specific order.

Operands of a sum are automatically simplified, recursively.

```
> '2/3 + sin( 5*Pi/6 - 2*Pi/3 )';
```

$$\frac{2}{3} + \sin\left(\frac{1}{6}\pi\right) \tag{3.182}$$

Since procedures are not called during the automatic simplification process, the example above does not fully simplify to the result

```
> 2/3 + sin( 5*Pi/6 - 2*Pi/3 );
```

$$\frac{7}{6} \tag{3.183}$$

during the automatic simplification process. However, the argument to the **sin** command is computed to the simpler form $\frac{1}{6}\pi$, just as it would if it had been entered by itself.

```
> '5*Pi/6 - 2*Pi/3';
```

$$\frac{1}{6}\pi \tag{3.184}$$

If any numeric literal in a sum is a float, all the numeric operands are converted to floats and their sum is computed as a float. For more information, see *Floating-Point Contagion (page 283)*.

```
> 'a + 2 + b + 3.7 + c + Pi';
```

$$a + 5.7 + b + c + \pi \tag{3.185}$$

Arithmetic computed during the automatic simplification process includes arithmetic with values of infinity, undefined values, and signed (floating-point) zeroes.

```
> '2.3 + undefined';
```

$$Float(undefined) \tag{3.186}$$

```
> '2.3 + infinity';
```

$$Float(\infty) \tag{3.187}$$

```
> '-0.0 + 0';
```

$$-0. \tag{3.188}$$

```
> 'infinity - infinity';
```

$$undefined \tag{3.189}$$

```
> 'infinity - Float(infinity)';
```

$$Float(undefined) \tag{3.190}$$

Sums of non-algebraic summands can be formed. A sum of lists of the same length returns the corresponding list of sums. This occurs during the automatic simplification process.

```
> '[ a, b, c ] + [ x, y, z ]';
```

$$[x + a, y + b, z + c] \tag{3.191}$$

Sums of arrays, matrices, and vectors occur during the regular evaluation process.

```
> <1,2;3,4> + <5,6;7,8>;
```

$$\begin{bmatrix} 6 & 8 \\ 10 & 12 \end{bmatrix} \tag{3.192}$$

Attempting to add lists or matrices of different sizes results in an error.

```
> [ 1, 2 ] + [ 1, 2, 3 ];
Error, adding lists of different length
> <1,2;3,4> + <1,2>;
Error, (in rtable/Sum) invalid arguments
```

Since the addition of sets (which are not ordered) is not well-defined, a sum formed with a set is returned unevaluated.

```
> { 1, 2 } + { 3, 4 };
  { 1, 2 } + [ 3, 4 ];
```

$$\{1,2\} + \{3,4\}$$
$$\{1,2\} + [3,4] \tag{3.193}$$

Multiplication and Division

Products are formed by using the `*` and `/` operators. The result of evaluating either a multiplication or division operation is an expression of type `*`.

```
> type( a * b, '`*`' );
  type( a / b, '`*`' );
```

$$true$$
$$true \tag{3.194}$$

You can use the **dismantle** command to print a representation of the internal structure of any Maple expression.

```
> dismantle( a / b );

PROD(5)
   NAME(4): a
   INTPOS(2): 1
   NAME(4): b
   INTNEG(2): -1
```

The output shows that the quotient is actually stored as a product of two factors: one consisting of the expression **a** with a power of 1 and the other consisting of the expression **b** with a power of −1: $a^{(1)} b^{(-1)}$.

Similar to sums, products are commutative and associative. Also, products are flattened due to associativity, even though the `*` operator is binary. Automatic simplification is applied to products, so as with sums, numeric factors are automatically combined.

```
> '2 * 3 * x * y';
```

$$6xy \qquad (3.195)$$

Also like sums, the order of factors in an expression of type `*` is arbitrary, and may vary between Maple sessions.

```
> 'y * x * 3 * 2';
```

$$6xy \qquad (3.196)$$

The number of operands reflects the number of factors remaining after automatic simplification has taken place.

```
> nops( 2 * 3 * x * y );
```

$$3 \qquad (3.197)$$

```
> op( 2 * 3 * x * y );
```

$$6, x, y \qquad (3.198)$$

The name `*` can be used as a constructor to form products.

```
> `*`( a, b, c );
```

$$abc \qquad (3.199)$$

If any numeric constant in a product is a float, the result of gathering all of the constants into a single factor is a float.

```
> '3.1 * a / 2 / b * 4';
```

$$\frac{6.200000000\, a}{b} \qquad (3.200)$$

```
> '2.3 * ( 5*Pi/6 - 2*Pi/3 )';
```

$$0.3833333333\, \pi \qquad (3.201)$$

This effect does not extend into function calls.

```
> '2.3 * sin( 5*Pi/6 - 2*Pi/3 )';
```

$$2.3 \sin\left(\frac{1}{6}\pi\right) \tag{3.202}$$

You can multiply a list by a number and the product is applied to all of the list elements during the automatic simplification process.

```
> '2 * [ 2, 3 ]';
```

$$[4, 6] \tag{3.203}$$

Matrix multiplication is done with the `.` operator rather than `*`. Division is not defined for matrices.

```
> <1,2;3,4> . <5,6;7,8>;
```

$$\begin{bmatrix} 19 & 22 \\ 43 & 50 \end{bmatrix} \tag{3.204}$$

```
> <1,2;3,4> . LinearAlgebra:-MatrixInverse( <5,6;7,8>);
```

$$\begin{bmatrix} 3 & -2 \\ 2 & -1 \end{bmatrix} \tag{3.205}$$

Multiplying or dividing two arrays of the same size will perform paired element-wise operations on the individual entries. The element-wise operators *~ and /~ can be used on both arrays and matrices to achieve the same result.

```
> Array([[1,2],[3,4]]) * Array([[5,6],[7,8]]);
```

$$\begin{bmatrix} 5 & 12 \\ 21 & 32 \end{bmatrix} \tag{3.206}$$

```
> Array([[1,2],[3,4]]) / Array([[5,6],[7,8]]);
```

$$\begin{bmatrix} \frac{1}{5} & \frac{1}{3} \\ \frac{3}{7} & \frac{1}{2} \end{bmatrix} \tag{3.207}$$

```
> <1,2;3,4> /~ <5,6;7,8>;
```

$$\begin{bmatrix} \frac{1}{5} & \frac{1}{3} \\ \frac{3}{7} & \frac{1}{2} \end{bmatrix} \tag{3.208}$$

```
> <1,2;3,4> *~ <5,6;7,8>;
```

$$\begin{bmatrix} 5 & 12 \\ 21 & 32 \end{bmatrix} \tag{3.209}$$

For more information on element-wise operators, see *Programming-Language Operators (page 19)*.

Exponentiation

Powers are formed by using the `` `^` `` operator.

```
> a^b;
```

$$a^b \tag{3.210}$$

It is strictly a binary operator; nested powers must be written with parentheses.

```
> (a^b)^c;
```

$$\left(a^b\right)^c \tag{3.211}$$

```
> a^(b^c);
```

$$a^{b^c} \tag{3.212}$$

The following input results in a syntax error.

```
> a^b^c;
Error, ambiguous use of `^`, please use parentheses
```

Rational number powers are used to represent roots. Exact roots are left uncomputed, while floating-point roots are computed during the automatic simplification process.

```
> 4^(1/2);
```

$$\sqrt{4} \tag{3.213}$$

```
> '(2.1)^(1/3)';
```

$$1.280579165 \tag{3.214}$$

Expressions to a power of 0 are reduced to unity during the automatic simplification process. The type of the resulting 1 depends on the type of the zero power, unless the base of the expression is a float, in which case the result is a float.

```
> 'a ^ 0';
```

$$1 \qquad (3.215)$$

```
> 'a ^ 0.0';
```

$$1.0 \qquad (3.216)$$

```
> '(x^2 - 1 + 3)^0';
```

$$1 \qquad (3.217)$$

There are some exceptions when infinity and undefined values are raised to a float zero power.

```
> 'Float( undefined ) ^ 0.0';
```

$$Float(undefined) + Float(undefined)\,I \qquad (3.218)$$

```
> 'Float( infinity ) ^ 0.0';
```

$$Float(undefined) \qquad (3.219)$$

```
> 'Float( -infinity ) ^ (-0.0)';
```

$$Float(undefined) - 0.\,I \qquad (3.220)$$

Note the distinction between **Float(-infinity) ^ (-0.0)** and **-Float(infinity) ^ (-0.0)**: the latter is first automatically simplified to **- Float(undefined)** and then to **Float(undefined)**.

In Maple, the indeterminate form **0^0** with an exact base is interpreted as 1.

```
> 0^0;
```

$$1 \qquad (3.221)$$

```
> 0.0 ^ 0;
```

$$1. \qquad (3.222)$$

```
> 0 ^ 0.0;
```

$$Float(undefined) \qquad (3.223)$$

Although a complex floating-point zero does not automatically simplify to a real zero, expressions raised to a complex zero are simplified automatically to an exact or floating-point unity.

```
> a^(0.0 + 0.0*I);
```

$$1 \tag{3.224}$$

Powering of matrices is done in the mathematical sense achieving repeated matrix products. Powering of arrays is done element-wise.

```
> <1,2;3,4> ^3;
```

$$\begin{bmatrix} 37 & 54 \\ 81 & 118 \end{bmatrix} \tag{3.225}$$

```
> Array([[1,2],[3,4]]) ^3;
```

$$\begin{bmatrix} 1 & 8 \\ 27 & 64 \end{bmatrix} \tag{3.226}$$

Rational Expressions

Using sums and products, more complicated expressions can be formed.

```
> expr := ( a + a*b ) / ( a*b - b );
```

$$expr := \frac{a + a\,b}{a\,b - b} \tag{3.227}$$

By using the **dismantle** command, you can see the tree structure of the expression that is formed.

```
> dismantle( expr );

PROD(5)
   SUM(5)
      NAME(4): a
      INTPOS(2): 1
      PROD(5)
         NAME(4): a
         INTPOS(2): 1
         NAME(4): b
         INTPOS(2): 1
      INTPOS(2): 1
   INTPOS(2): 1
   SUM(5)
      PROD(5)
         NAME(4): a
         INTPOS(2): 1
         NAME(4): b
         INTPOS(2): 1
      INTPOS(2): 1
      NAME(4): b
      INTNEG(2): -1
   INTNEG(2): -1
```

Or, as a graph:

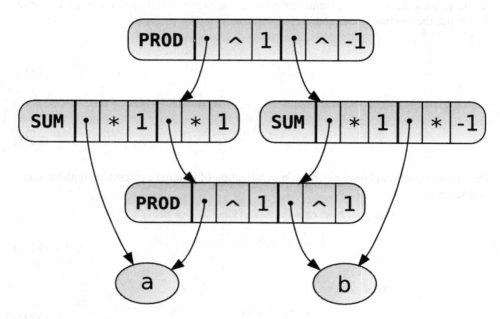

Figure 3.1: expr DAG

Here, *expr* is a product of two operands
```
> nops( expr );
```
$$2 \qquad (3.228)$$
```
> op( expr );
```
$$a + a b, \frac{1}{a b - b} \qquad (3.229)$$

and each operand is itself an expression with two operands.
```
> e1, e2 := op( expr );
```
$$e1, e2 := a + a b, \frac{1}{a b - b} \qquad (3.230)$$
```
> nops( e1 ); nops( e2 );
```
$$2$$
$$2 \qquad (3.231)$$

Maple does *not* automatically simplify the following expression. To perform such simplifications, use the **normal** command.

```
> expr := (x - 1)/(x^2 - 1);
```

$$expr := \frac{x-1}{x^2-1} \qquad (3.232)$$

```
> normal( expr );
```

$$\frac{1}{x+1} \qquad (3.233)$$

The **normal** command only performs normalization of rational expressions with rational coefficients.

```
> expr := ( (sin(t)^2 + cos(t)^2)*(x - 1)/(x^2 - 1));
```

$$expr := \frac{\left(\sin(t)^2 + \cos(t)^2\right)(x-1)}{x^2-1} \qquad (3.234)$$

```
> normal( expr );
```

$$\frac{\sin(t)^2 + \cos(t)^2}{x+1} \qquad (3.235)$$

Note: Use the **simplify** command to apply more powerful simplifications.

Maple also does not automatically expand the products of sums.

```
> (a + b) * (c + d);
```

$$(a+b)(c+d) \qquad (3.236)$$

Use the **expand** command (or the **normal** command, with the **expanded** option) to perform such expansions.

```
> expr := (a + b) * (c + d);
```

$$expr := (a+b)(c+d) \qquad (3.237)$$

```
> expand( expr );
```

$$ac + ad + bc + bd \qquad (3.238)$$

```
> normal( expr, 'expanded' );
```

$$ac + ad + bc + bd \qquad (3.239)$$

Similarly, you must use the **normal** command to simplify the following rational expression.

```
> expr2 := expand( expr ) / (a + b);
```

$$\mathit{expr2} := \frac{ac + ad + bc + bd}{a + b} \qquad (3.240)$$

```
> normal( expr2 );
```

$$c + d \qquad (3.241)$$

Noncommutative Multiplication

Noncommutative multiplication is represented by the dot operator (.), which is used mainly in linear algebra computations for multiplication of matrices and vectors. It may also be used to represent the noncommutative product of other types of mathematical expressions.

```
  A . B;
```

If **A** and **B** are of type **constant**, then **A . B** = **A * B** during the evaluation process (but not during the automatic simplification process). However, if one of **A** and **B** is a Matrix or a Vector, and the other is a Matrix, Vector, or constant, the product is interpreted as a matrix or vector product. If **A** or **B** is an Array (and the other is not a Matrix or Vector), then **A . B** is interpreted as *element-wise* multiplication. For arguments that are not of type Matrix, Vector, or constant, **A . B** remains unevaluated, but more importantly, it is not automatically simplified to or interpreted as being equal to **B . A**.

```
> 7 . 6;
```

$$42 \qquad (3.242)$$

```
> '7 . 6';
```

$$7.6 \qquad (3.243)$$

```
> A.B <> B.A;
```

$$A.B \neq B.A \qquad (3.244)$$

```
> M:=<<1,0,2>|<0,1,2>|<0,0,2>>;
```

$$M := \begin{bmatrix} 1 & 0 & 0 \\ 0 & 1 & 0 \\ 2 & 2 & 2 \end{bmatrix} \qquad (3.245)$$

```
> V:=<10,0,0>;
```

$$V := \begin{bmatrix} 10 \\ 0 \\ 0 \end{bmatrix} \qquad (3.246)$$

```
> M . V;
```

$$\begin{bmatrix} 10 \\ 0 \\ 20 \end{bmatrix} \qquad (3.247)$$

```
> lambda . M . V;
```

$$\lambda \cdot \begin{bmatrix} 10 \\ 0 \\ 20 \end{bmatrix} \qquad (3.248)$$

```
> A := Array([[1,2],[3,4]]);
```

$$A := \begin{bmatrix} 1 & 2 \\ 3 & 4 \end{bmatrix} \qquad (3.249)$$

```
> B := Array([[a,b,c],[d,e,f]]);
```

$$B := \begin{bmatrix} a & b & c \\ d & e & f \end{bmatrix} \qquad (3.250)$$

```
> A . B;
```

$$\begin{bmatrix} a & 2b \\ 3d & 4e \end{bmatrix} \qquad (3.251)$$

```
> 3 . B;
```

$$\begin{bmatrix} 3a & 3b & 3c \\ 3d & 3e & 3f \end{bmatrix} \qquad (3.252)$$

The dot character has three meanings in Maple:

- as a decimal point in a floating-point number (for example, **2.3**),
- as part of a range (for example, **x..y**), or
- as the noncommutative multiplication operator. To distinguish between these three cases, Maple uses the following rule: any dot with spaces before and/or after it that is not part of a number is interpreted as the noncommutative multiplication operator.

For example, **2.3** is a number, **2 . 3** and **2 .3** return **6**, and **2. 3** displays an error.

```
> 2.3, 2 . 3, 2 .3;
```
$$2.3, 6, 6 \qquad (3.253)$$

```
> 2. 3;
Error, unexpected number
```

Factorials

The unary, postfix factorial operator **!** is used to represent the mathematical factorial operation.

```
> 5!;
```
$$120 \qquad (3.254)$$

Maple can compute large factorials quickly.

```
> length( 1000000! );
```
$$5565709 \qquad (3.255)$$

If the argument of the **!** operator is symbolic, it is returned unevaluated.

```
> (a + b)!;
```
$$(a+b)! \qquad (3.256)$$

The argument of the **!** operator is subject to automatic simplification, but factorials are not computed during the automatic simplification process.

```
> '(2+3)!';
```
$$5! \qquad (3.257)$$

If the argument of the **!** operator is a float, the expression is computed using the **GAMMA** function.

```
> 2.3! = GAMMA( 3.3 );
```
$$2.683437382 = 2.683437382 \qquad (3.258)$$

If the argument is a non-negative integer, Maple computes the factorial. If the argument is a negative integer, a numeric event is triggered.

```
> (-3)!;
Error, numeric exception: division by zero
```

However, if the argument is a negative integer float, the complex number **Float(-infinity) - Float(infinity)*I** is returned.

```
> (-3.0)!;
```

$$-Float(\infty) - Float(\infty)\, I \qquad (3.259)$$

For other arguments, the factorial operator is returned unevaluated after first evaluating its argument.

```
> sin( Pi / 6 )!;
```

$$\left(\frac{1}{2}\right)! \qquad (3.260)$$

The command **factorial** is the same as the **!** operator.

```
> factorial( 5 );
```

$$120 \qquad (3.261)$$

Forming Sums and Products

Since creating structures within loops may be inefficient, Maple provides commands for creating sums and products efficiently.

```
add( expression, i=m .. n);
mul( expression, i=m .. n);
```

where **i** is a name, **m** and **n** are numeric values, and **expression** is an expression that depends on **i**.

The **add** command is semantically equivalent to the following loop:

```
> S := 0;
  old := i;
  for i from m to n do
      S := S+expression;
  end do;
  i := old;
  S; # the result
```

The **add** command is more efficient since it does not build each of the many intermediate sums. The semantics of **mul** are similar with the exception that if $n < m$, the result is 1, rather than 0.

```
> mul(a+i, i=1..4);
```

$$(a+1)\,(a+2)\,(a+3)\,(a+4) \qquad (3.262)$$

```
> add(a||i, i=0..3);
```

$$a0 + a1 + a2 + a3 \tag{3.263}$$

In the loop example shown above, each of the expressions $a0$, $a0 + a1$, and $a0 + a1 + a2$ are constructed, stored in memory, and then removed by the garbage collector. That overhead is part of what makes the loop less efficient than the **add** command in this case.

For more information on the **add** and **mul** commands, refer to the **add** help page. For more information on the concatenation operator, ||, see *The Concatenation Operator (page 112)*.

Note: The **add** and **mul** commands differ from **sum** and **product** in that the former are straightforward construction commands while the latter are commands for computing closed forms for symbolic sums and products.

3.10 Boolean and Relational Expressions

Boolean Constants

The Boolean constants in Maple are the names **true**, **false** and **FAIL**. These are otherwise ordinary names, but have a special meaning in a Boolean context.

When you call the Boolean evaluator **evalb**, the expression passed as its argument is interpreted as a Boolean-valued expression if possible, and evaluated as such.

Boolean Operators

Maple supports several operators for the Boolean combination of expressions: **not**, **and**, **or**, **xor**, and **implies**.

The not Operator

The **not** operator represents logical negation. It has the following general syntax.

```
not expr
```

When applied to a Boolean-valued expression, it returns a value according to the following table.

expr	not expr
true	false
false	true
FAIL	FAIL

For example,

```
> not true;
```

$$false \qquad (3.264)$$

```
> not false;
```

$$true \qquad (3.265)$$

```
> not FAIL;
```

$$FAIL \qquad (3.266)$$

The and Operator

The **and** operator represents logical conjunction. It is a binary operator of the form

```
expr1 and expr2
```

If both operands evaluate to a truth value, the entire expression is evaluated according to the following truth table.

expr1	expr2	expr1 and expr2
true	true	true
true	false	false
true	FAIL	FAIL
false	true	false
false	false	false
false	FAIL	false
FAIL	true	FAIL
FAIL	false	false
FAIL	FAIL	FAIL

If a truth value cannot be determined, the expression is returned unevaluated.

```
> x and y;
```

$$x \text{ and } y \qquad (3.267)$$

However, some automatic simplifications are applied to **and** expressions.

```
> true and x;
```

$$x \qquad (3.268)$$

The or Operator

The **or** operator represents logical disjunction. It is a binary operator of the form

```
expr1 or expr2
```

If both operands evaluate to a truth value, the entire expression is evaluated according to the following truth table.

expr1	expr2	expr1 or expr2
true	true	true
true	false	true
true	FAIL	true
false	true	true
false	false	false
false	FAIL	FAIL
FAIL	true	true
FAIL	false	FAIL
FAIL	FAIL	FAIL

If a truth value cannot be determined, the expression is returned unevaluated.

```
> x or y;
```

$$x \text{ or } y \quad (3.269)$$

However, some automatic simplifications are applied to **or** expressions.

```
> false or x;
```

$$x \quad (3.270)$$

The xor Operator

The **xor** operator represents logical exclusive disjunction. It is a binary operator of the form

```
expr1 xor expr2
```

If both of its operands evaluate to truth values, the entire expression is evaluated according to the following truth table.

expr1	expr2	expr1 xor expr2
true	true	false
true	false	true
true	FAIL	FAIL
false	true	true
false	false	false
false	FAIL	FAIL

expr1	expr2	expr1 xor expr2
FAIL	true	FAIL
FAIL	false	FAIL
FAIL	FAIL	FAIL

The implies Operator

The **implies** operator represents logical implication. It is a binary operator of the form

```
expr1 implies expr2
```

If both of its operands evaluate to truth values, the entire expression is evaluated according to the following truth table.

expr1	expr2	expr1 implies expr2
true	true	true
true	false	false
true	FAIL	FAIL
false	true	true
false	false	true
false	FAIL	true
FAIL	true	true
FAIL	false	FAIL
FAIL	FAIL	FAIL

If a truth value cannot be determined, the expression is returned unevaluated.

> `x implies y;`

$$x \Rightarrow y \qquad (3.271)$$

Some automatic simplifications are applied to **implies** expressions.

> `false implies x;`

$$true \qquad (3.272)$$

> `x implies true;`

$$true \qquad (3.273)$$

Relational Operators

Relational operators are used to form comparisons to be evaluated in a Boolean context. The relational operators in Maple are =, <>, <, <=, and **in**. Each is a binary operator that accepts two operands. When evaluated in a Boolean context, each of these operators determines whether its two operands have a certain relationship.

An equation is formed by using the = operator.

> `x = y;`

$$x = y \qquad (3.274)$$

This has the general form

```
expr1 = expr2
```

It represents an equation with **expr1** as the left-hand side and **expr2** as the right-hand side. When evaluated in a Boolean context, it returns a value of **true** if its operands are equal, and returns a value of **false** otherwise.

> `evalb( 1 = 2 );`

$$\textit{false} \qquad (3.275)$$

> `evalb( 2 = 2 );`

$$\textit{true} \qquad (3.276)$$

Note that comparing distinct unassigned names returns a value of **false**.

> `evalb( x = y );`

$$\textit{false} \qquad (3.277)$$

The names **x** and **y** are distinct and unequal names in Maple and, when they are unassigned, they are considered different expressions in a Boolean comparison. If the names **x** and **y** have assigned values, those values are first substituted into the comparison, and the equality computation is performed on the assigned values, rather than the names themselves.

In general, expressions are compared for equality according to their memory address. That is, two expressions are considered equal in a Boolean context if they have the same address in memory. However, for certain expressions, a more mathematical test for equality is used. For example, the floating-point numbers **2.0000** and **2.0** are considered numerically equal, even though they are distinct objects in memory.

> `evalb( 2.0000 = 2.0 );`

$$\textit{true} \qquad (3.278)$$

> `addressof( 2.0000 );`

$$18446884532539008638 \qquad (3.279)$$

```
> addressof( 2.0 );
```
$$18446884532539008670 \qquad (3.280)$$

In fact, when the floating-point number **2.0** is compared to the integer **2**, they are considered equal.

```
> evalb( 2.0 = 2 );
```
$$true \qquad (3.281)$$

Determining whether two procedures are semantically equivalent is an undecidable problem in Computer Science. However, procedures which are detectably equivalent by simple transformations are considered to be equal. For example, it is clear that the name of a procedure parameter is not normally important, so the following two simple procedures are considered equal, although they are distinct expressions in memory.

```
> evalb( proc(x) 2*x end proc = proc(y) 2*y end proc );
```
$$true \qquad (3.282)$$

An inequation can be formed by using the <> operator. The general form is

```
expr1 <> expr2
```

This expression represents non-equality and returns a value of **true** if its operands are unequal, and **false** if its operands are equal.

```
> x <> y;
```
$$x \neq y \qquad (3.283)$$

```
> evalb( 1 <> 2 );
```
$$true \qquad (3.284)$$

```
> evalb( 2 <> 2 );
```
$$false \qquad (3.285)$$

Testing for inequality is performed similarly to testing for equality. Comparing two distinct unassigned names using the <> operator computes the equality of the names. The expression

```
> evalb( x <> y );
```
$$true \qquad (3.286)$$

returns a value of **true** because the names **x** and **y** are distinct as names.

A strict inequality is created by using the < operator. This has the general form

3.10 Boolean and Relational Expressions

```
expr1 < expr2
```

and can also be constructed using the form

```
expr1 > expr2
```

For example,

```
> x < y;
```

$$x < y \qquad (3.287)$$

You can also use the > operator.

```
> y > x;
```

$$x < y \qquad (3.288)$$

Maple automatically converts this to the same expression as results from the first form.

When evaluated in a Boolean context, Maple performs the indicated mathematical comparison, or returns the inequality as unevaluated if the operands do not evaluate to comparable expressions. If the operands are comparable, the inequality evaluates to the value **true** if the first operand is less than, but not equal to, the second operand, and evaluates to **false** otherwise. If the operands are not comparable, the inequality evaluates to itself.

A non-strict inequality is formed using the <= operator. This has the general form

```
expr1 <= expr2
```

It can also be constructed using the form

```
expr1 >= expr2
```

For example,

```
> x <= y;
```

$$x \leq y \qquad (3.289)$$

When evaluated in a Boolean context, and when the operands are comparable, it returns a value of either **true** or **false** according to whether the first operand is less than, or equal to, the second operand.

Membership is represented by the **in** operator. It is used in the general form

```
expr1 in expr2
```

When evaluated in a Boolean context, it evaluates to the value **true** if its first operand **expr1** is a member of its second operand **expr2**. If **expr1** does not belong to **expr2**, the expression evaluates to **false**. Maple can determine a truth value if the second operand **expr2** is a container object; that is, either a set or list, or an unevaluated function call of the form **SetOf(T)**, where **T** is a Maple type. An expression of the form

```
expr in SetOf( T )
```

where **T** is a Maple type is equivalent to the expression **type(expr, T)**.

```
> evalb( 1 in { 1, 2, 3 } );
```
$$true \tag{3.290}$$

```
> evalb( 5 in { 1, 2, 3 } );
```
$$false \tag{3.291}$$

```
> evalb( x in X );
```
$$x \in X \tag{3.292}$$

```
> evalb( 2 in SetOf( integer ) );
```
$$true \tag{3.293}$$

```
> evalb( 2/3 in SetOf( integer ) );
```
$$false \tag{3.294}$$

Note the simplification applied to the statement with the **evalb** command in the following example.

```
> x in A union B;
```
$$x \in A \cup B \tag{3.295}$$

```
> evalb( x in A union B );
```
$$x \in A \text{ or } x \in B \tag{3.296}$$

If the second operand is not an explicit container object, the expression remains an unevaluated **in** expression. However, some automatic simplifications may be applied.

Efficient Boolean Iteration

In the same way the commands **add** and **mul** can be used to efficiently form **+** and ***** expressions, conjunctions and disjunctions can be evaluated efficiently using the **andmap** and **ormap** commands, which are similar to the **map** command described in *Maple Statements (page 173)*.

```
andmap( procedure, expression, ... )
ormap( procedure, expression, ... )
```

The following example considers **type(element,name)** for each element of the list. **ormap** determines whether this statement is true for at least one element of the list. **andmap** determines whether this statement is true for all the elements of the list.

```
> ormap(type, [1, "a", `a`, a()], name);
```
$$true \tag{3.297}$$

```
> andmap(type, [1, "a", `a`, a()], name);
```
$$false \tag{3.298}$$

The main difference between these commands and **map** is that **andmap** and **ormap** have short-circuit ("McCarthy") semantics, which means that an answer is returned as soon as it can be determined.

```
> andmap(proc(x) print(x); x<2 end proc, [1,2,3,4]);
```
$$1$$
$$2$$
$$false \tag{3.299}$$

3.11 Expressions for Data Structures

This section describes basic concepts related to data structure expressions. For more information on programming with data structures, see *Basic Data Structures (page 129)*.

Sequences

The most basic aggregate expression type in Maple is the *sequence*. Sequences are formed by using the `,` (comma) operator.

```
> a, 2/3, sin( x ), 5.1;
```
$$a, \frac{2}{3}, \sin(x), 5.1 \tag{3.300}$$

A sequence consists of zero or more other expressions, called *elements* or *members*. A sequence with exactly one member is automatically simplified to its unique member. The empty sequence, containing zero members, is the value of the name **NULL**, and may be written as ().

```
> evalb( () = NULL );
```
$$true \tag{3.301}$$

Sequences occur in many other data structures as a (principal) component, within which they acquire additional semantics. Some examples include lists, sets, and function calls.

Automatic simplification of sequences is affected by recursively simplifying the component expressions.

> `'2 + 3, 1 - 7, 0^0, sin( Pi / 6 )';`

$$5, -6, 1, \sin\left(\frac{1}{6}\pi\right) \tag{3.302}$$

Nested sequences are also flattened during the automatic simplification process.

> `'( 1, 2 ), 3, ( 4, 5 )';`

$$1, 2, 3, 4, 5 \tag{3.303}$$

Because sequences are used to pass multiple arguments to procedures, it is not normally possible to operate on a sequence *as such* (the **list** type described below is designed for exactly for that reason). For example, you cannot pass a (nontrivial) sequence to the **type** command to check its type. Therefore, there is no Maple type for sequences. However, the **whattype** command returns the name **exprseq** when it is passed either zero or more than one argument.

> `whattype();`

$$exprseq \tag{3.304}$$

> `whattype( 1, 2 );`

$$exprseq \tag{3.305}$$

Note that the name **exprseq** is not the name of any valid type in Maple.

Similarly, you cannot query the zeroth operand of a sequence. For example, the following results in an error.

> `op( 0, ( 1, 2, 3 ) );`

`Error, invalid input: op expects 1 or 2 arguments, but received 4`

This is because the sequence **0, (1, 2, 3)** is flattened to the sequence **0, 1, 2, 3** during automatic simplification of the function call *before* the **op** command is actually called. Therefore, the **op** command is passed four arguments instead of only the two that are apparently intended.

There is no constructor for sequences, but there is a built-in command for creating sequences, called **seq**. The basic syntax of **seq** is below. It accepts many other types of arguments as well.

```
seq(expression, i = integer1..integer2)
```

```
> seq( i^2, i = 1 .. 5 );
```
$$1, 4, 9, 16, 25 \tag{3.306}$$

```
> seq( 2 .. 14 );
```
$$2, 3, 4, 5, 6, 7, 8, 9, 10, 11, 12, 13, 14 \tag{3.307}$$

```
> seq( i, i = 0.4 .. 1.1, 0.3 );
```
$$0.4, 0.7, 1.0 \tag{3.308}$$

For more information on the **seq** command, refer to the **seq** help page.

Another way to create sequences is to use the dollar sign ($) operator.

```
    expression $ i = integer1 .. integer2
> i^2 $ i = 1 .. 5;
```
$$1, 4, 9, 16, 25 \tag{3.309}$$

The dollar sign operator is a binary operator that performs a similar function to the **seq** command, but behaves slightly differently: the $ operator evaluates the expression argument once before any substitutions, while the command does not evaluate until after each substitution of *i*.

```
> cat(a,x) $ x= 1..2;
```
$$ax, ax \tag{3.310}$$

```
> seq(cat(a,x), x= 1..2);
```
$$a1, a2 \tag{3.311}$$

In general, it is recommended that you use the **seq** command instead of the dollar sign operator.

Lists

Lists are created by enclosing a sequence of expressions between square brackets. Lists are essentially sequences, which are designated as a single unit for other operations.

```
    [ sequence ]
> [ 1, 2, 3 ];
```
$$[1, 2, 3] \tag{3.312}$$

Unlike sequences, lists can form properly nested structures.

```
> [ 1, 2, [ 3, 4 ] ];
```

$$[1, 2, [3, 4]] \tag{3.313}$$

Use the **numelems** command to determine the number of members in the enclosed sequence. Note that lists can contain sublists. These are still counted as a single entry.

```
> numelems( [ 1, 2, 3 ] );
```

$$3 \tag{3.314}$$

```
> numelems( [ 1, 2, [ 3, 4 ] ] );
```

$$3 \tag{3.315}$$

To access the i-th operand of a list, use an index to the list expression.

```
> L := [ a, b, c, d ];
```

$$L := [a, b, c, d] \tag{3.316}$$

```
> L[ 3 ];
```

$$c \tag{3.317}$$

To access the sequence of all elements in a list, use the **op** command. Converting back and forth between lists and sequences can be a common operation, and is very efficient.

```
> Lseq := op(L);
```

$$Lseq := a, b, c, d \tag{3.318}$$

```
> L2 := [ op(L), op(L) ];
```

$$L2 := [a, b, c, d, a, b, c, d] \tag{3.319}$$

It is common to create a list by using the **seq** command to create the enclosed sequence.

```
> [ seq( i^2, i = 1 .. 5 ) ];
```

$$[1, 4, 9, 16, 25] \tag{3.320}$$

Lists are ordered; two lists with the same members in a different order are distinct.

```
> evalb( [ 1, 2, 3 ] = [ 2, 1, 3 ] );
```

$$\textit{false} \tag{3.321}$$

Lists are immutable; you cannot change the elements of a list once it has been created. You can, however, create a new list using members of an existing list or lists.

In the next example, we create a new list with second entry **d**.

```
> L := [ a, b, c ];
```
$$L := [a, b, c] \qquad (3.322)$$

```
> L2 := [ L[ 1 ], d, L[ 3 ] ];
```
$$L2 := [a, d, c] \qquad (3.323)$$

You can also use the **subsop** command for this purpose.

```
> L3 := subsop( 2 = d, L );
```
$$L3 := [a, d, c] \qquad (3.324)$$

```
> evalb( L2 = L3 );
```
$$true \qquad (3.325)$$

The example above creates a new list using the original list **L** by substituting its second operand for the expression **d**. If you need to change elements frequently it is usually better to use an array. Arrays can be changed in-place avoiding the need for a copy. For more information on the **subsop** command, refer to the **subsop** help page.

For more information about lists, see *Lists (page 130)*.

Sets

Sets, similar to lists, are created from a sequence of expressions. However, sets use braces ({}) to enclose the sequence.

```
{ sequence }
```

```
> {3, 2, 1};
```
$$\{1, 2, 3\} \qquad (3.326)$$

In addition to the syntactical differences, sets differ from lists in that they are implicitly sorted and do not have duplicate entries. These two properties are enforced during the automatic simplification process.

```
> '{3, -1, 0}';
```
$$\{-1, 0, 3\} \qquad (3.327)$$

```
> '{1, 1, 1, 1}';
```
$$\{1\} \qquad (3.328)$$

In Maple 11 and earlier, the ordering of sets was unpredictable as it was based on the positions of the elements in memory. In Maple 12 and later, set ordering is deterministic, session independent, and based on properties of the contents. This just means that the same set will now appear in the same order even after restarting Maple. For more information on the ordering of sets, refer to the **set** help page.

For more information on how to use sets in programming, see *Sets (page 136)*. More information on Maple expressions related to sets will be described later in this chapter.

Tables

Tables are mutable data structures that associate an index with an entry. Both the index and entry can be arbitrary expressions. The underlying structure is sparse (a hash table), and expands as more entries are inserted.

```
> T := table();
```

$$T := table([\,]) \tag{3.329}$$

```
> T[color] := "red";
```

$$T_{color} := \text{"red"} \tag{3.330}$$

```
> T[color];
```

$$\text{"red"} \tag{3.331}$$

```
> T[1,2,3] := x^2+4;
```

$$T_{1,2,3} := x^2 + 4 \tag{3.332}$$

Assigning values to indexed names is further described in *Indexed Expressions (page 64)*.

Tables can be initially populated by providing a list of equations as an argument to the **table** constructor.

```
> T := table([a=1, b=2, c=3, d=4]);
```

$$T := table([c = 3, d = 4, a = 1, b = 2]) \tag{3.333}$$

```
> T[a] + T[c];
```

$$4 \tag{3.334}$$

For names with tables assigned to them, last name evaluation rules apply. Last name evaluation is explained in more detail in *Evaluation Rules for Tables (page 145)*. The most visible effect of last name evaluation is that the name of the table is displayed by default rather than all of its entries.

```
> T;
```

$$T \tag{3.335}$$

```
> eval(T);
```

$$table([c = 3, d = 4, a = 1, b = 2]) \tag{3.336}$$

Rectangular Tables

Rectangular tables, or *rtables*, are mutable data structures that associate a numeric index sequence with an arbitrary entry. The bounds of the index are predefined and directly correspond to the amount of memory reserved to hold entries.

The same **rtable** data structure is used to implement arrays, matrices, and vectors.

```
> A := Array(0..5,i->2*i);
```

$$A := Array(0..5, \{1 = 2, 2 = 4, 3 = 6, 4 = 8, 5 = 10\}, datatype \\ = anything, storage = rectangular, order = Fortran\_order) \tag{3.337}$$

```
> A[0];
```

$$0 \tag{3.338}$$

```
> A[5];
```

$$10 \tag{3.339}$$

```
> V := Vector([1,2,3]);
```

$$V := \begin{bmatrix} 1 \\ 2 \\ 3 \end{bmatrix} \tag{3.340}$$

```
> V[1];
```

$$1 \tag{3.341}$$

```
> M := Matrix(3,3,shape=identity);
```

$$M := \begin{bmatrix} 1 & 0 & 0 \\ 0 & 1 & 0 \\ 0 & 0 & 1 \end{bmatrix} \tag{3.342}$$

```
> M[2,2];
```

$$1 \tag{3.343}$$

Rectangular tables are very flexible and offer a rich set of features. For a more in-depth discussion of them, see *Arrays (page 148)*.

3.12 Set-Theoretic Expressions

Maple includes a full set of set-theoretic operators for membership relation, set inclusion, and other operations.

Membership

In Maple, the set membership relation is expressed by using the **in** operator. It has the following syntax.

```
a in b
```

where *a* and *b* can be arbitrary expressions.

Normally, a membership expression is returned unevaluated.

```
> a in b;
```
$$a \in b \qquad (3.344)$$

```
> 1 in { 1, 2, 3 };
```
$$1 \in \{1, 2, 3\} \qquad (3.345)$$

However, when evaluated in a Boolean context, one of the values **true** and **false** is returned if the expression *b* evaluates to a set or list and Maple can determine whether the expression *a* belongs to the expression *b*. For more information on Boolean evaluation of membership expressions, see *Boolean and Relational Expressions (page 89)*.

Use the **rhs** and **lhs** commands to extract the right or left hand side of the an **in** operator.

```
> lhs( a in b );
```
$$a \qquad (3.346)$$

```
> rhs( a in b );
```
$$b \qquad (3.347)$$

Set Inclusion

Set inclusion (the subset relation) is represented in Maple by the binary **subset** operator. It has the following syntax.

```
a subset b
```

where *a* and *b* are arbitrary expressions that can evaluate to sets.

```
> a subset b;
```
$$a \subseteq b \qquad (3.348)$$

```
> { 1, 2 } subset {2, 3, 5 };
```
$$false \tag{3.349}$$

```
> {} subset T;
```
$$true \tag{3.350}$$

```
> T subset {};
```
$$T \subseteq \{\,\} \tag{3.351}$$

If Maple can determine whether the expressed relation is true or false, the expression evaluates to **true** or **false**. Otherwise, the expression is returned unevaluated.

An unevaluated set inclusion expression has two operands *a* and *b*.

```
> nops( a subset b );
```
$$2 \tag{3.352}$$

```
> op( a subset b );
```
$$a, b \tag{3.353}$$

The individual operands can be accessed by using the **lhs** and **rhs** commands.

```
> lhs( a subset b );
```
$$a \tag{3.354}$$

```
> rhs( a subset b );
```
$$b \tag{3.355}$$

Other Binary Operators for Sets

You can create new sets from existing sets by using any of the binary set-theoretic operators.

The union of two sets is created by using the **union** operator, which has the following syntax.

```
a union b
```

where *a* and *b* are expressions that can evaluate to a set.

```
> a union b;
```
$$a \cup b \tag{3.356}$$

```
> { 1, 2 } union { 2, 3, 4 };
```
$$\{1, 2, 3, 4\} \tag{3.357}$$

```
> { 1, 2 } union T;
```
$$T \cup \{1, 2\} \tag{3.358}$$

The following expression displays an error message, since the second operand cannot evaluate to a set.

```
> { a, b, c } union "a string";
Error, invalid input: `union` received a string, which is not valid
for its 2nd argument
```

A union expression may be returned unevaluated, and the operands of an unevaluated union expression **a union b** are the expressions **a** and **b**.

```
> nops( a union b );
```
$$2 \tag{3.359}$$

```
> op( a union b );
```
$$a, b \tag{3.360}$$

Note that the union operation is commutative.

```
> a union b;
```
$$a \cup b \tag{3.361}$$

```
> b union a;
```
$$a \cup b \tag{3.362}$$

The union operation is also associative. A union of three or more operands returns an unevaluated function call.

```
> a union b union c;
```
$$union(a, b, c) \tag{3.363}$$

The union operation performs certain normalizations.

```
> a union a;
```
$$a \tag{3.364}$$

```
> {} union a;
```
$$a \tag{3.365}$$

Intersections of sets are represented using the **intersect** operator, which has the general syntax.

```
a intersect b
```

The operands *a* and *b* are expressions that can evaluate to a set.

```
> a intersect b;
```
$$a \cap b \tag{3.366}$$

```
> { 1, 2, 3 } intersect { 3, 4, 5 };
```
$$\{3\} \tag{3.367}$$

```
> {} intersect T;
```
$$\{\} \tag{3.368}$$

Note that although union and intersection are mutually distributive, neither distributes automatically over the other in a symbolic expression. However, the **expand** command can distribute intersections over unions.

```
> expand( a intersect (b union c) );
```
$$a \cap b \cup a \cap c \tag{3.369}$$

Maple takes the canonical form of a set-theoretic expression to be a union of intersections, so the **expand** command does not distribute symbolic unions over intersections.

```
> expand( a union (b intersect c) );
```
$$a \cup b \cap c \tag{3.370}$$

3.13 Other Expressions

Functional Operators

The operator -> (arrow) can be used as a short-hand form to create procedures inline in commands which take procedures as arguments such as Array constructors and the **map** command.

```
( vars ) -> result
```

The following two procedures are identical except in how they are displayed:

```
> x -> x^2;
```
$$x \rightarrow x^2 \tag{3.371}$$

```
> proc(x) x^2 end proc;
```
$$\mathbf{proc}(x) \; x\texttt{\^{}}2 \; \mathbf{end \; proc} \tag{3.372}$$

as are these two:
```
> (x,y,z) -> sqrt(x^2+y^2+z^2);
```
$$(x, y, z) \to \sqrt{x^2 + y^2 + z^2} \qquad (3.373)$$

```
> proc(x,y,z) sqrt(x^2+y^2+z^2) end proc;
```
$$\mathbf{proc}(x, y, z) \text{ sqrt}(x^{\wedge}2 + y^{\wedge}2 + z^{\wedge}2) \textbf{ end proc} \qquad (3.374)$$

For more information on the arrow operator, refer to the **operators,functional** help page. For more information on procedures, see *Procedures (page 199)*.

Composition

Use the operators **@** and **@@** to represent the composition (of functions). The operator **@** denotes the composition of functions and takes the general form

```
f @ g
```

where each of **f** and **g** can be an arbitrary expression.
```
> (f@g)(x);
```
$$f(g(x)) \qquad (3.375)$$

Note that **@** has lower precedence than function application, so that the parentheses surrounding **f@g** above are necessary:
```
> f@g(x);
```
$$f@g(x) \qquad (3.376)$$

The **@** operator performs numerous simplifications and normalizations, and is (left) associative.
```
> (exp @ ln)( s );
```
$$s \qquad (3.377)$$

```
> a @ b @ c @ d;
```
$$a@b@c@d \qquad (3.378)$$

Repeated composition is represented by the operator **@@**. It has the general form

```
f @@ n
```

This denotes the *n*-fold composition of a function *f*.

```
> expand( (f@@3)( x ) );
```

$$f(f(f(x))) \qquad (3.379)$$

Note that the iterated composition is not automatically expanded in the example above. It is necessary to apply the **expand** command.

It is important to distinguish repeated composition of an expression from the arithmetic power. The former is represented in Maple using the **@@** operator, while the latter is represented using the **^** operator.

```
> expand( (f@@2)( x ) );
```

$$f(f(x)) \qquad (3.380)$$

```
> (f^2)( x );
```

$$f(x)^2 \qquad (3.381)$$

The first example above denotes the 2-fold composition of f with itself, while the second denotes the arithmetic square of f. In particular, although the inverses of the circular functions are commonly denoted by a power-like notation in written mathematics, in Maple, for example, **sin^(-1)** denotes the reciprocal of the sin function, while **sin@@(-1)** denotes the arcsine (**arcsin**).

```
> sin@@(-1);
```

$$\text{arcsin} \qquad (3.382)$$

```
> (sin@arcsin)( x );
```

$$x \qquad (3.383)$$

```
> sin^(-1);
```

$$\frac{1}{\sin} \qquad (3.384)$$

```
> (sin^(-1))( x );
```

$$\frac{1}{\sin(x)} \qquad (3.385)$$

Neutral Operators

Neutral operators are constructions that are treated as operators by Maple, but that have no predefined meaning so that they can be customized.

A neutral operator symbol is formed by the ampersand character (&) followed either by a valid Maple name not containing ?, or by a sequence of one or more special characters. For more information, refer to the **neutral** help page.

```
a &name b
```

```
> expr := a &your_operator_name_here b;
```

$$expr := a \ \&your\_operator\_name\_here \ b \qquad (3.386)$$

A commonly used neutral operator is **&*** which is often used for representing a non-commutative multiplication. Unlike dot (.), it does not automatically combine scalar constants.

```
> 1 &* 2;
```

$$1 \ \&* \ 2 \qquad (3.387)$$

```
> 1 . 2;
```

$$2 \qquad (3.388)$$

Ranges

The **..** operator is used to construct ranges, and usually has the following syntax.

```
a .. b
```

in which the endpoints **a** and **b** can be arbitrary expressions.

It is important to distinguish between a range expression, such as **3 .. 7**, with explicit numeric endpoints, and the corresponding sequence **3, 4, 5, 6, 7**. The **seq** command can be used to produce the latter from the former.

Often, a range is used in an expression of the form **i = a .. b**, as an argument to a command (such as **add**), and denotes the range over which an index such as **i** is to vary.

```
> add( i^2, i = 1 .. 5 );
```

$$55 \qquad (3.389)$$

A consecutive sequence of two *or more* dots (.) is parsed as a range operator. For example,

```
> 2 ......... 7;
```

$$2..7 \qquad (3.390)$$

If the left-hand endpoint of a range is a float ending with a decimal point, or if the right-hand endpoint is a float beginning with a decimal point, it is therefore necessary to separate the endpoint from the range operator with one or more space characters.

```
> 2....3;
```

$$2..3 \qquad (3.391)$$

```
> 2. ...3;
```

$$2...0.3 \qquad (3.392)$$

The number of operands of a range expression is equal to 2.

```
> nops( a .. b );
```

$$2 \qquad (3.393)$$

The operands are the left and right-hand endpoints.

```
> op( a .. b );
```

$$a, b \qquad (3.394)$$

Use the **lhs** and **rhs** commands to extract the individual operands of a range expression.

```
> lhs( a .. b );
```

$$a \qquad (3.395)$$

```
> rhs( a .. b );
```

$$b \qquad (3.396)$$

The type of a range expression is **range** or the equivalent form `..`.

```
> type( a .. b, 'range' );
```

$$true \qquad (3.397)$$

```
> type( a .. b, '`..`' );
```

$$true \qquad (3.398)$$

Ranges can be used to index complex data structures as well as strings and sequences.

```
> [ 1, 2, 3, 4, 5 ][ 2 .. 3 ];
```

$$[2, 3] \qquad (3.399)$$

```
> { 1, 2, 3, 4, 5 }[ 2 .. 3 ];
```

$$\{2, 3\} \qquad (3.400)$$

```
> "abcde"[ 2 .. 3 ];
```

$$\text{"bc"} \qquad (3.401)$$

```
> ( 1, 2, 3, 4, 5 )[ 2 .. 3 ];
```
$$2, 3 \tag{3.402}$$

There is a special form of input syntax for ranges in which one or both endpoints is missing.
```
> .. ;
```
$$( ) .. ( ) \tag{3.403}$$

In the example above, each endpoint is the empty sequence () (or **NULL**). It is valid to omit just one of the endpoints.
```
> a .. ;
```
$$a .. ( ) \tag{3.404}$$
```
> .. b;
```
$$( ) .. b \tag{3.405}$$

When used in this way to index a data structure, a missing endpoint denotes the end of the valid range of indices.
```
> [ 1, 2, 3, 4, 5 ][ 3 .. ];
```
$$[3, 4, 5] \tag{3.406}$$
```
> [ 1, 2, 3, 4, 5 ][ .. 4 ];
```
$$[1, 2, 3, 4] \tag{3.407}$$
```
> [ 1, 2, 3, 4, 5 ][ .. ];
```
$$[1, 2, 3, 4, 5] \tag{3.408}$$

Note the distinction between the third example above and the following example
```
> [ 1, 2, 3, 4, 5 ][];
```
$$1, 2, 3, 4, 5 \tag{3.409}$$

in which the index is empty.

The Concatenation Operator

The operator || denotes the concatenation of names and strings. It takes the general form

```
a || b
```

in which the first operand **a** can be either a name or a string, and the second operand **b** can be a name, a string, an integer, an integral range, a character range, or an expression sequence of names, strings, and integers. If the second operand b is another kind of expression, an unevaluated || expression is returned.

```
> "foo" || "bar";
```
$$"foobar" \qquad (3.410)$$

```
> foo || bar;
```
$$foobar \qquad (3.411)$$

```
> foo || "bar";
```
$$foobar \qquad (3.412)$$

```
> "foo" || bar;
```
$$"foobar" \qquad (3.413)$$

```
> x || 1;
```
$$x1 \qquad (3.414)$$

```
> x || (1..3);
```
$$x1, x2, x3 \qquad (3.415)$$

```
> "x" || (1,2,3);
```
$$"x1", "x2", "x3" \qquad (3.416)$$

```
> x || ("a" .. "f");
```
$$xa, xb, xc, xd, xe, xf \qquad (3.417)$$

```
> x || ("s", "t", "w" );
```
$$xs, xt, xw \qquad (3.418)$$

```
> f( y ) || t;
```
$$(f(y)) \| t \qquad (3.419)$$

The type of the result, if not an unevaluated || expression, is determined by the type of the first operand. If the first operand a is a string, the type of the result (or results, in the case of a sequence) is a string. If the first operand is a name, the type of the result, or results, is a name.

The first operand of the || operator is not evaluated, but the second operand is.

```
> u := 2: v := 3:
```

```
> u || v;
```

$$u3 \tag{3.420}$$

The symbol `` `||` ``, which must be enclosed in left single quotes when not used as an infix operator, is a type name.

```
> type( f( y ) || t, `||` );
```

$$true \tag{3.421}$$

If a concatenation expression is returned unevaluated, it has two operands.

```
> nops( f( s ) || t );
```

$$2 \tag{3.422}$$

```
> op( f( s ) || t );
```

$$f(s), t \tag{3.423}$$

For most applications, the **cat** command is more appropriate, as it evaluates all of its arguments. For more information, refer to the **cat** help page.

The Double Colon Operator

The **::** (double colon) operator is used to represent a type test, and takes two operands in the following form.

```
expr :: t
```

where **expr** is an arbitrary expression, and **t** is a type expression. When evaluated in a Boolean context, it is equivalent to **type(expr, t)**.

```
> evalb( [ 1, 2, 3 ] :: list );
```

$$true \tag{3.424}$$

```
> [ 1, 2 ] :: list and 2 > 3;
```

$$false \tag{3.425}$$

In addition to its use as a general Boolean expression, it is used to introduce type annotations on parameters and type assertions for local variables and procedure return types. For more information, see *Procedures (page 199)*.

Outside of a Boolean context, the **::** operator is essentially inert, and returns an expression of type **::** with two operands.

```
> type( a :: b, `::` );
```

$$true \tag{3.426}$$

```
> nops( a :: b );
```
$$2 \tag{3.427}$$

```
> op( a :: b );
```
$$a, b \tag{3.428}$$

You can use the **lhs** and **rhs** commands to access the operands of a :: expression.

```
> lhs( a :: b );
```
$$a \tag{3.429}$$

```
> rhs( a :: b );
```
$$b \tag{3.430}$$

Series

Maple supports generalized power series expansions using a **series** data structure. This is a basic symbolic data structure that is used in many fundamental algorithms, such as the computation of symbolic limits and symbolic integration. There is no syntax for the input of series; a series structure is created by calling the **series** constructor, which has the general forms

```
series( expr, eqn, ord )
series( expr, name, ord )
```

where **expr** is an algebraic expression, **eqn** is an equation of the form

```
name = pt
```

where **name** is a name and **pt** is the point of series expansion. The optional argument *ord* specifies the order of truncation of the series. This is, by default, equal to the value of the environment variable **Order**, whose default value is 6. If the second form using *name* is used, the expansion point is taken to be 0.

```
> series( exp( x ), x );
```
$$1 + x + \frac{1}{2}x^2 + \frac{1}{6}x^3 + \frac{1}{24}x^4 + \frac{1}{120}x^5 + O(x^6) \tag{3.431}$$

```
> series( exp( x ), x, 10 );
```
$$1 + x + \frac{1}{2}x^2 + \frac{1}{6}x^3 + \frac{1}{24}x^4 + \frac{1}{120}x^5 + \frac{1}{720}x^6 + \frac{1}{5040}x^7 + \frac{1}{40320}x^8 + \frac{1}{362880}x^9 + O(x^{10}) \tag{3.432}$$

```
> series( exp( x ), x = 0 );
```

$$1 + x + \frac{1}{2}x^2 + \frac{1}{6}x^3 + \frac{1}{24}x^4 + \frac{1}{120}x^5 + \mathrm{O}(x^6) \qquad (3.433)$$

```
> series( exp( x ), x = 1 );
```

$$e + e(x-1) + \frac{1}{2}e(x-1)^2 + \frac{1}{6}e(x-1)^3 + \frac{1}{24}e(x-1)^4$$
$$+ \frac{1}{120}e(x-1)^5 + \mathrm{O}\big((x-1)^6\big) \qquad (3.434)$$

In general, a truncated power series expansion to order *ord* of *expr*, about the point *pt* is computed. If the expansion point *pt* is infinity, then an asymptotic expansion is computed.

In general, the series expansion is not exact, so there will be an order term of the form

```
O( pt^ord )
```

present as the last term in the series. This is not always present, however. For example, a series expansion of a low-degree polynomial is exact.

```
> series( x^2 + x + 1, x );
```

$$1 + x + x^2 \qquad (3.435)$$

The presence of an order term depends also on the truncation order.

```
> series( x^20 + x + 1, x );
```

$$1 + x + \mathrm{O}(x^{20}) \qquad (3.436)$$

```
> series( x^20 + x + 1, x, 30 );
```

$$1 + x + x^{20} \qquad (3.437)$$

A series data structure prints very much like a polynomial, but it is a distinct data structure. In certain cases, a polynomial (sum of product) data structure is returned. This happens when the generalized series expansion requires fractional exponents.

```
> s := series( sqrt( sin( x ) ), x );
```

$$s := \sqrt{x} - \frac{1}{12}x^{5/2} + \frac{1}{1440}x^{9/2} + \mathrm{O}(x^{13/2}) \qquad (3.438)$$

```
> type( s, 'series' );
```

$$\text{false} \qquad (3.439)$$

The operands of a series expression are as follows.

The 0th operand is an expression of the form $x - a$, where x is the variable of expansion, and a is the expansion point. Odd operands are the coefficients of the series, while positive even operands are the exponents. In general, for a series expression **s**, **op(2*i-1,s)** evaluates to the ith coefficient of **s**, while **op(2*i,s)** evaluates to the ith exponent.

```
> op( 0, series( F( x ), x = a ) );
```

$$x - a \tag{3.440}$$

```
> op( series( exp( x^2 ), x ) );
```

$$1, 0, 1, 2, \frac{1}{2}, 4, O(1), 6 \tag{3.441}$$

Note that the series data structure is sparse in the sense that terms with 0 coefficient are not part of the data structure.

A series structure can be converted to a polynomial by using the **convert** command with the name **polynom** as the second argument.

```
> s := series( exp( x ), x );
```

$$s := 1 + x + \frac{1}{2}x^2 + \frac{1}{6}x^3 + \frac{1}{24}x^4 + \frac{1}{120}x^5 + O(x^6) \tag{3.442}$$

```
> type( s, 'series' );
```

$$true \tag{3.443}$$

```
> p := convert( s, 'polynom' );
```

$$p := 1 + x + \frac{1}{2}x^2 + \frac{1}{6}x^3 + \frac{1}{24}x^4 + \frac{1}{120}x^5 \tag{3.444}$$

```
> type( p, 'polynom' );
```

$$true \tag{3.445}$$

3.14 Attributes

In addition to their operands, certain types of expressions can have other information associated with them in the form of *attributes*. As described earlier in this chapter, protected names are a type of attribute. If an expression has attributes, they can be examined by using the **attributes** command.

```
> attributes(sin);
```

$$protected, \_syslib \tag{3.446}$$

Attributes can be assigned to expressions of the following types: name, string, list, set, Array, Matrix, Vector, equation, procedure, unevaluated function call, or float using the **setattribute** command.

```
setattribute(expression, attributes)
```

The **setattribute** command returns a copy of the expression with the attributes assigned. If the expression is a symbol or string, it is modified in-place. For other data types, the original expression is left unchanged.

```
> x := 1.0;
```
$$x := 1.0 \tag{3.447}$$

```
> setattribute('x', "blue");
```
$$x \tag{3.448}$$

```
> attributes('x');
```
$$\text{"blue"} \tag{3.449}$$

```
> myname := "Johanessphere":
> setattribute(myname, "Great Name", "Not a Real Name");
```
$$\text{"Johanessphere"} \tag{3.450}$$

```
> attributes("Johanessphere");
```
$$\text{"Great Name", "Not a Real Name"} \tag{3.451}$$

```
> y := setattribute('f(z)',"common");
```
$$y := f(z) \tag{3.452}$$

```
> attributes(y);
```
$$\text{"common"} \tag{3.453}$$

```
> attributes('f(z)');
```

All Maple expressions are valid attributes, including expression sequences.

You can check whether an expression has attributes by using the **attributed** type. For more information, refer to the **type,attributed** help page.

```
> type(`just a name`, 'attributed');
```
$$\textit{false} \tag{3.454}$$

```
> type(sin, 'attributed');
```
$$\textit{true} \tag{3.455}$$

3.15 Using Expressions

Evaluating and Simplifying Expressions

Example 1

To understand how Maple evaluates and simplifies expressions, consider the following example.

```
> x := Pi/6:
> sin(x) + 2*cos(x)^2*sin(x) + 3;
```

$$\frac{17}{4} \tag{3.456}$$

Maple first reads and parses the input. As the input is parsed, Maple builds an expression tree to represent the value.

$$\sin(x) + 2\cos(x)^2 \sin(x) + 3$$

Maple simplifies the expression tree and then evaluates the result. The evaluation process substitutes values for variables and invokes any commands or procedures. In this case, **x** evaluates to $\frac{1}{6}\pi$. Therefore, with these substitutions, the expression is

$$\sin\left(\frac{Pi}{6}\right) + 2\cos\left(\frac{Pi}{6}\right)^2 \sin\left(\frac{Pi}{6}\right) + 3$$

When the **sin** and **cos** commands are called, Maple obtains a new "expression tree,"

$$\frac{1}{2} + 2\left(\frac{1}{2}\sqrt{3}\right)^2 \frac{1}{2} + 3$$

Maple simplifies this result to obtain the fraction 17/4.

Example 2

Alternatively, consider the next example: evaluation occurs, but no simplification is possible.

```
> x := 1;
```

$$x := 1 \tag{3.457}$$

```
> sin(x) + 2*cos(x)^2*sin(x) + 3;
```
$$\sin(1) + 2\cos(1)^2 \sin(1) + 3 \tag{3.458}$$

Substituting Subexpressions

The simplest method of substitution in Maple is to use the **subsop** command. This is an operation on the expression tree. It creates a new expression by replacing an operand in the original expression with the given value.

`subsop( n=value, expr);`
`subsop( list=value, expr);`

```
> L := [a, b, [c,d,e]]:
> M := subsop(1=A, L):
> L, M;
```
$$[a, b, [c, d, e]], [A, b, [c, d, e]] \tag{3.459}$$

```
> subsop([3,1]=C, L);
```
$$[a, b, [C, d, e]] \tag{3.460}$$

Note that most operations in Maple do not alter expressions *in-place* but, in fact, create new expressions from old ones. For a list of exceptions, see *Mutable Data Structures (page 141)*.

Also, note that the **subsop** command acts on the expression tree by changing an arrow in the DAG, and not by changing the value of a node which would change all identical instances. That is, in the following example only one instance of **a** is changed, not all. See **Figure 3.2**.

```
> expr := (a+a*b)/(a*b-b);
```
$$expr := \frac{a + ab}{ab - b} \tag{3.461}$$

```
> subsop([1,1]=2*c, expr);
```
$$\frac{2c + ab}{ab - b} \tag{3.462}$$

3.15 Using Expressions • 121

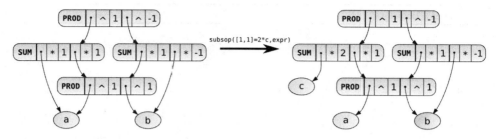

Figure 3.2: subsop Example DAGs

The **subsop** command is powerful, but generally useful only in very specific programming applications. The most generally useful command for substitution is the two-argument version of the **eval** command.

The **eval** command has the following syntax, where **s** is an equation, list, or set of equations.

```
eval( expr, s );
```
> `expr := x^3 + 3*x + 1;`

$$expr := x^3 + 3x + 1 \qquad (3.463)$$

> `eval( expr, x=y );`

$$y^3 + 3y + 1 \qquad (3.464)$$

> `eval( expr, x=2 );`

$$15 \qquad (3.465)$$

> `eval( sin(x) + x^2, x=0 );`

$$0 \qquad (3.466)$$

The **eval** command performs substitution on the expression considered as a DAG rather than a tree, so it can be quite efficient for large expressions with many repeated subexpressions.

An alternative to the **eval** command is the **subs** command, which performs *syntactic* substitution. It computes the expression as a *tree* and replaces subexpressions in an expression with a new value. The subexpressions must be operands, as identified by the **op** command. Using the **subs** command is equivalent to performing a **subsop** operation for each occurrence of the subexpressions to be replaced.

The **subs** command has the following syntax, where *s* is an equation, list, or set of equations.

```
subs( s, expr );
> f := x*y^2;
```
$$f := xy^2 \qquad (3.467)$$
```
> subs( {y=z, x=y, z=w}, f );
```
$$yz^2 \qquad (3.468)$$

The other difference between the **eval** and **subs** commands is demonstrated in the following example.
```
> subs( x=0, cos(x) + x^2 );
```
$$\cos(0) \qquad (3.469)$$
```
> eval( cos(x) + x^2, x=0 );
```
$$1 \qquad (3.470)$$

In the preceding **subs** command, Maple substitutes **0** (zero) for **x** and simplifies the result. Maple simplifies **cos(0) + 0^2** to **cos(0)**. By using the **eval** command, Maple evaluates **cos(0)** to **1** (one).

During the substitution process, operands are compared in the expression tree of **expr** with the left-hand side of an equation.
```
> eval( a*b*c, a*b=d );
```
$$abc \qquad (3.471)$$

The substitution does not result in **d*c** because the operands of the product **a*b*c** are **a**, **b**, **c**. That is, the products **a*b**, **b*c**, and **a*c** do not appear specifically as operands in the expression **a*b*c**. The easiest way to make such substitutions is to solve the equation for one unknown and substitute for that unknown.
```
> eval( a*b*c, a=d/b );
```
$$dc \qquad (3.472)$$

You cannot always use this method; for certain expressions, it may not produce the expected results. The **algsubs** command provides a more powerful substitution facility.
```
> algsubs( a*b=d, a*b*c );
```
$$dc \qquad (3.473)$$

Two more useful substitution commands are **subsindets** and **evalindets**. These commands perform substitution on all subexpressions of a given type; the former uses the **subs** functionality and the latter uses the **eval** functionality.

```
subsindets( expr, atype, transformer, rest )
```
```
evalindets( expr, atype, transformer, rest )
```

```
> evalindets([1,2,3,4,5], prime, x->(x+1)^2);
```
$$[1, 9, 16, 4, 36] \tag{3.474}$$

```
> evalindets((x+1)^2+x^4-1, {`*`,`^`}, expand);
```
$$x^2 + 2x + x^4 \tag{3.475}$$

Structured Types

A simple type check may not always provide sufficient information. For example, the command

```
> type( x^2, `^` );
```
$$true \tag{3.476}$$

verifies that **x^2** is an exponentiation, but does not indicate whether the exponent is, for example, an integer. To do so, you must use *structured* types. Consider the following example.

```
> type( x^2, 'name^integer' );
```
$$true \tag{3.477}$$

Because **x** is a name and **2** is an integer, the command returns a value of **true**.

To learn more about structured types, study the following examples. The square root of **x** does not have the structured type **name^integer**.

```
> type( x^(1/2), 'name^integer' );
```
$$false \tag{3.478}$$

The expression **(x+1)^2** does not have type **name^integer**, because **x+1** is not a name.

```
> type( (x+1)^2, 'name^integer' );
```
$$false \tag{3.479}$$

The type **anything** matches any expression.

```
> type( (x+1)^2, 'anything^integer' );
```
$$true \tag{3.480}$$

An expression matches a *set* of types if the expression matches one of the types in the set.

```
> type( 1, '{integer, name}' );
```
$$true \qquad (3.481)$$

```
> type( x, '{integer, name}' );
```
$$true \qquad (3.482)$$

The type **set(type)** matches a *set* of elements of type **type**.

```
> type( {1,2,3,4}, 'set(integer)' );
```
$$true \qquad (3.483)$$

```
> type( {x,2,3,y}, 'set({integer, name})' );
```
$$true \qquad (3.484)$$

Similarly, the type **list(type)** matches a *list* of elements of type **type**.

```
> type( [ 2..3, 5..7 ], 'list(range)' );
```
$$true \qquad (3.485)$$

Note that e^2 is not of type **anything^2**.

```
> exp(2);
```
$$e^2 \qquad (3.486)$$

```
> type( (3.486), 'anything^2' );
```
$$false \qquad (3.487)$$

Because e^2 is the typeset version of **exp(2)**, it does not match the type **anything^2**.

```
> type( exp(2), 'exp'(integer) );
```
$$true \qquad (3.488)$$

The next example illustrates why you should use unevaluation quotes (') to delay evaluation when including Maple commands in **type** expressions.

```
> type( int(f(x), x), int(anything, anything) );
Error, testing against an invalid type
```

An error occurs because Maple evaluates **int(anything, anything)**.

```
> int(anything, anything);
```
$$\frac{1}{2} \, anything^2 \qquad (3.489)$$

This is not a valid type. If you enclose the **int** command in unevaluation quotes, the type checking works as intended.

```
> type( int(f(x), x), 'int'(anything, anything) );
```

$$true \tag{3.490}$$

The type **specfunc(type, f)** matches the function **f** with zero or more arguments of type **type**.

```
> type( exp(x), 'specfunc(name, exp)' );
```

$$true \tag{3.491}$$

```
> type( f(), 'specfunc(name, f)' );
```

$$true \tag{3.492}$$

The type **function(type)** matches any function with zero or more arguments of type **type**.

```
> type( f(1,2,3), 'function(integer)' );
```

$$true \tag{3.493}$$

```
> type( f(1,x,Pi), 'function( {integer, name} )' );
```

$$true \tag{3.494}$$

In addition to testing the type of arguments, you can test the number of arguments. The type **anyfunc(t1, ..., tn)** matches any function with **n** arguments of the listed types in the correct order.

```
> type( f(1,x), 'anyfunc(integer, name)' );
```

$$true \tag{3.495}$$

```
> type( f(x,1), 'anyfunc(integer, name)' );
```

$$false \tag{3.496}$$

```
> type( f(x), 'anyfunc(integer, name)' );
```

$$false \tag{3.497}$$

Another useful variation is to use the **And**, **Or**, and **Not** type constructors to create Boolean combinations of types. Note that these are different from the **and**, **or**, and **not** logical operators.

```
> type(Pi, 'And( constant, numeric)');
```

$$false \tag{3.498}$$

Pi is of type **symbol**, not of type **numeric**.

```
> type(Pi, 'And( constant, Not(numeric))');
```
$$true \tag{3.499}$$

For more information on structured types, refer to the **type,structured** help page. For more information on how to define your own types, refer to the **type,defn** help page.

The **indets** command is useful for extracting a set of all the subexpressions of a given type.

```
indets( expr, atype)
```

```
> indets(z-exp(x^2-1)+1, 'name');
```
$$\{x, z\} \tag{3.500}$$

```
> indets(Pi+3^(1/2)+4.1, 'integer');
```
$$\{3\} \tag{3.501}$$

```
> indets(Pi+3^(1/2)+4.1, 'numeric');
```
$$\left\{3, \frac{1}{2}, 4.1\right\} \tag{3.502}$$

```
> indets(Pi+3^(1/2)+4.1, 'constant');
```
$$\left\{3, \frac{1}{2}, 4.1, \pi, \sqrt{3}, \pi + \sqrt{3} + 4.1\right\} \tag{3.503}$$

Note that the **indets** command analyzes the entire expression so that the base of the exponent $\sqrt{3}$ is recognized as an integer. If you want to select only subexpressions from the top level, use the command **select** described in *The select, remove, and selectremove Commands (page 187)*.

If you want to test whether that an expression has a subexpression of a given type, use the **hastype** command rather than the **indets** command since it avoids building a potentially large set of expressions.

```
> hastype([1,2,3.,5.,6.,7.], 'float');
```
$$true \tag{3.504}$$

3.16 Exercises

1. Find the numerator and denominator of the irreducible form of **4057114691** divided by **4404825097799**.

2. Construct floating-point numbers using the floating-point number constructor. Construct the number **917.3366** using a positive exponent, and then using a negative exponent. Construct a floating-point approximation of **1/3**.

3. Without using the **Digits** environmental variable, find the difference between π estimated to **20** digits and **10** digits.

4. Calculate the negative complex root of **-1369**, and then sum **3** and the root. Find the inverse of this complex sum. Find the inverse of **(a*b)/c+((a-d)/(b*e))*I)** in standard form, where **a**, **b**, **c**, **d**, and **e** are real.

5. The Fibonacci numbers are a sequence of numbers. The first two numbers in the sequence are zero (**0**) and one (**1**). For n greater than two, the *n*th number in the sequence is the sum of the two preceding numbers. Assign values to indexed names representing the first, second, and general Fibonacci numbers.

6. Using the **time** command, determine the time required to multiply two ten-by-ten matrices.

7. Use Maple to verify de Morgan's laws.

8. Contrast the behavior of functions and expressions by performing the following commands.

    a   Define a function **f** equal to x^3. Define an expression **g** equal to x^3.

    b   Evaluate **f** and **g** at **2**.

    c   Evaluate **f** and **g** at **y**.

    d   Assign the value **2** to **x**. Evaluate **f** and **g**.

9. Swap the values of two variables using one statement.

10. Sum the smallest **100** prime integers.

    Hint: Use the **ithprime** or **nextprime** function.

4 Basic Data Structures

The appropriate use of data structures is an important part of writing efficient programs. Maple provides various data structures that can be used to help make your programs efficient.

4.1 In This Chapter

- Defining and manipulating sets, lists, tables, Arrays, records, stacks, and queues
- Converting between data structures
- Mathematical versus programmer indexing for Arrays
- Performance comparisons of data structures

4.2 Introduction

Maple provides various data structures that you can use for programming and interacting with Maple functions. This chapter focuses on the use of data structures in programming. However, the sections *Lists (page 130)* and *Sets (page 136)* may be useful for users who want to construct arguments for Maple functions.

Maple has many data structures that provide similar functionality, but certain data structures are better suited for certain types of operations. Therefore, when choosing which data structures to use, it is important to select a structure that performs well on the operations used in your code.

Many aspects affect the performance of data structures. However, in Maple, the provided data structures can be divided into two basic classes: *mutable* and *immutable*. The mutable data structures can be modified, that is, the values they store can change. The immutable data structures cannot be changed after they are created. Instead, copies of these structures can be made with different contents. This difference in behavior can have significant impact on the performance of code that uses these structures.

4.3 Immutable Data Structures

Immutable data structures can be useful when storing a fixed collection of elements. Also, because immutable structures are more compact than mutable data structures, especially when storing a small number of elements, they are more memory efficient.

Immutable structures are created with their contents fixed. This means that they cannot be modified in-place. When you change an immutable data structure, a new copy is created with the modified contents and stored as a distinct object in memory. Thus, immutable structures may not be the correct choice if you want to modify the contents of a structure.

In Maple, there are two basic immutable data structures: lists and sets.

Lists

A *list* stores an *ordered* sequence of expressions. The ordering of the elements in a list is fixed when the list is created. Lists, in contrast to sets, will maintain duplicate elements.

Creating Lists

The easiest way to create a list is to enclose a sequence of expressions in square brackets ([]). A sequence of expressions is a series of comma-separated expressions.

```
[ sequence ]
```

This creates a list that contains the elements of **sequence** in the specified order. In the case where **sequence** is empty, **[]** represents an empty list. Compare the results of these examples to those in the *Sets (page 136)* section.

```
> [x, y, y];
```
$$[x, y, y] \qquad (4.1)$$

```
> [a, 1, b, 2];
```
$$[a, 1, b, 2] \qquad (4.2)$$

```
> [y[1], x, x[1], y[1]];
```
$$[y_1, x, x_1, y_1] \qquad (4.3)$$

The elements of a list can be any expressions, even other lists.

```
> L := [[1], [2, a], [X, Y, Z]];
```
$$L := [[1], [2, a], [X, Y, Z]] \qquad (4.4)$$

In Maple, nested lists whose inner lists have the *same* number of elements have a special name, **listlist**.

```
> M := [[a,b], [1,2], [3, 4]];
```
$$M := [[a, b], [1, 2], [3, 4]] \qquad (4.5)$$

```
> type(M, list);
```
$$true \qquad (4.6)$$

```
> type(L, listlist);
```
$$false \qquad (4.7)$$

```
> type(M, listlist);
```
$$true \qquad (4.8)$$

Many Maple functions return sequences. Thus, enclosing a call to one of those functions in square brackets [] creates a list. For example, the **seq** command generates sequences.

> `[ seq( x^j, j=1..3) ];`

$$[x, x^2, x^3] \qquad (4.9)$$

The **op** command can be used to extract the sequence of elements in a list.

> `L := [1,2,3];`

$$L := [1, 2, 3] \qquad (4.10)$$

> `op(L);`

$$1, 2, 3 \qquad (4.11)$$

Thus **op** can be used to create new lists based on existing lists. For example, you can create a new list with an additional element added to the start of the list.

> `L2 := [ 0, op(L) ];`

$$L2 := [0, 1, 2, 3] \qquad (4.12)$$

A list with another element added to the end of the list can be created in a similar way.

> `L3 := [ op(L2), 4 ];`

$$L3 := [0, 1, 2, 3, 4] \qquad (4.13)$$

Multiple lists can also be combined into a single list.

> `L4 := [ op(L), op(L2), op(L3) ];`

$$L4 := [1, 2, 3, 0, 1, 2, 3, 0, 1, 2, 3, 4] \qquad (4.14)$$

Accessing Data Stored in a List

The selection operation, [], can be used to read an element from a list.

> `L := [1,2,3];`

$$L := [1, 2, 3] \qquad (4.15)$$

> `L[1];`

$$1 \qquad (4.16)$$

> `L[2];`

$$2 \qquad (4.17)$$

```
> L[3];
```
$$3 \qquad (4.18)$$

You can also specify a range in the selection operation to extract a sublist containing the elements that are indexed by that range.

```
> L := [ seq( i^2, i=1..10 ) ];
```
$$L := [1, 4, 9, 16, 25, 36, 49, 64, 81, 100] \qquad (4.19)$$

```
> L[3..6];
```
$$[9, 16, 25, 36] \qquad (4.20)$$

```
> L[5..8];
```
$$[25, 36, 49, 64] \qquad (4.21)$$

While it is possible to make an assignment to a list index, this operation can be inefficient since it creates a new list. In fact, assignment to a large list is not permitted in Maple and will produce an error. Assigning a list element is a common error, so if you find yourself wanting to do this, consider using a mutable data structure instead. For more information, see *Mutable Data Structures (page 141)*.

```
> L := [1,2,3]:
> L[1] := 3;
```
$$L_1 := 3 \qquad (4.22)$$

```
> L;
```
$$[3, 2, 3] \qquad (4.23)$$

L is now a new list with a different element at index 1. Thus, assigning to a single element of a list causes the entire list to be copied in the same way as using the **subsop** command. In fact, the previous example is equivalent to the following except in how the result is displayed.

```
> L := [1,2,3]:
> L := subsop(1=3, L);
```
$$L := [3, 2, 3] \qquad (4.24)$$

If you attempt to assign to an index to a large list, an error will occur. Therefore, if you need to make a copy of a list with one changed element, it is recommended that you use the **subsop** command instead.

```
> LL := [ seq( i, i=1..200 ) ]:
```

```
> LL[1] := -1;
```
Error, assigning to a long list, please use Arrays
```
> subsop(1=-1, LL);
```

$[-1, 2, 3, 4, 5, 6, 7, 8, 9, 10, 11, 12, 13, 14, 15, 16, 17, 18, 19, 20,$
$21, 22, 23, 24, 25, 26, 27, 28, 29, 30, 31, 32, 33, 34, 35, 36, 37,$
$38, 39, 40, 41, 42, 43, 44, 45, 46, 47, 48, 49, 50, 51, 52, 53, 54,$
$55, 56, 57, 58, 59, 60, 61, 62, 63, 64, 65, 66, 67, 68, 69, 70, 71,$
$72, 73, 74, 75, 76, 77, 78, 79, 80, 81, 82, 83, 84, 85, 86, 87, 88,$
$89, 90, 91, 92, 93, 94, 95, 96, 97, 98, 99, 100, 101, 102, 103,$
$104, 105, 106, 107, 108, 109, 110, 111, 112, 113, 114, 115,$
$116, 117, 118, 119, 120, 121, 122, 123, 124, 125, 126, 127,$ (4.25)
$128, 129, 130, 131, 132, 133, 134, 135, 136, 137, 138, 139,$
$140, 141, 142, 143, 144, 145, 146, 147, 148, 149, 150, 151,$
$152, 153, 154, 155, 156, 157, 158, 159, 160, 161, 162, 163,$
$164, 165, 166, 167, 168, 169, 170, 171, 172, 173, 174, 175,$
$176, 177, 178, 179, 180, 181, 182, 183, 184, 185, 186, 187,$
$188, 189, 190, 191, 192, 193, 194, 195, 196, 197, 198, 199,$
$200]$

Determining If an Element Is in a List

To test if an expression is contained in a list, use the **member** function.
```
> member( 1, [ 1,2,3 ] );
```
$$true \qquad (4.26)$$
```
> member( 1, [ 2,3,4 ] );
```
$$false \qquad (4.27)$$

You can also use the **in** operator.
```
> evalb( 1 in [1,2,3] );
```
$$true \qquad (4.28)$$
```
> evalb( 1 in [2,3,4] );
```
$$false \qquad (4.29)$$

Getting the Number of Elements in a List

To find the length of a list, use the **numelems** command.

```
> numelems( [ 1,2,3 ] );
```
$$3 \qquad (4.30)$$

```
> numelems( [ 1,2,3,4,5 ] );
```
$$5 \qquad (4.31)$$

```
> numelems( [ seq( i, i=1..127 ) ] );
```
$$127 \qquad (4.32)$$

This can be useful for many tasks, for example, using lists in a loop. For more information on **selectremove**, see *Filtering Data Structure Elements (page 158)*.

```
> L := [seq( i, i=2..100)]:
> divisor := 2:
> while ( numelems( L ) > 0 )
  do
      divisible, L := selectremove( i->(i mod divisor = 0), L ):
      n := numelems( divisible );
      if ( n > 0 ) then
         printf( "%d integer%s whose smallest prime divisor is %d\n",
                n, `if`( n > 1, "s", "" ), divisor ):
      end if;
      divisor := nextprime( divisor );
  end do:
```

```
50 integers whose smallest prime divisor is 2
17 integers whose smallest prime divisor is 3
 7 integers whose smallest prime divisor is 5
 4 integers whose smallest prime divisor is 7
 1 integer  whose smallest prime divisor is 11
 1 integer  whose smallest prime divisor is 13
 1 integer  whose smallest prime divisor is 17
 1 integer  whose smallest prime divisor is 19
 1 integer  whose smallest prime divisor is 23
 1 integer  whose smallest prime divisor is 29
 1 integer  whose smallest prime divisor is 31
 1 integer  whose smallest prime divisor is 37
 1 integer  whose smallest prime divisor is 41
 1 integer  whose smallest prime divisor is 43
 1 integer  whose smallest prime divisor is 47
 1 integer  whose smallest prime divisor is 53
 1 integer  whose smallest prime divisor is 59
 1 integer  whose smallest prime divisor is 61
 1 integer  whose smallest prime divisor is 67
 1 integer  whose smallest prime divisor is 71
 1 integer  whose smallest prime divisor is 73
 1 integer  whose smallest prime divisor is 79
 1 integer  whose smallest prime divisor is 83
 1 integer  whose smallest prime divisor is 89
 1 integer  whose smallest prime divisor is 97
```

Sorting a List

The **sort** command can create a new list with sorted elements from any given list. By default, **sort** arranges elements in *ascending* order.

```
> sort( [ 4,2,3 ] );
```

$$[2, 3, 4] \qquad (4.33)$$

The **sort** command can also accept a second argument that specifies the ordering to use when sorting the elements.

```
> sort( [4,2,3], `>` );
```

$$[4, 3, 2] \qquad (4.34)$$

Applying a Function to the Contents of a List

It is often useful to be able to apply a function to all the elements of a list. The **map** command performs this operation in Maple.

```
> L := [ seq( Pi*i/4, i=0..3 ) ]:
> map( sin, L );
```

$$\left[0, \frac{1}{2}\sqrt{2}, 1, \frac{1}{2}\sqrt{2} \right] \qquad (4.35)$$

```
> map( cos, L );
```

$$\left[1, \frac{1}{2}\sqrt{2}, 0, -\frac{1}{2}\sqrt{2} \right] \qquad (4.36)$$

Maple provides other operations that can work with the members of a list, such as **add** and **mul**.

```
> add( i, i in [ seq( j, j=1..100 ) ] );
```

$$5050 \qquad (4.37)$$

```
> mul( i^2, i in [ 1,2,3,4,5,6,7,8,9,10 ] );
```

$$13168189440000 \qquad (4.38)$$

Finally, a **for** loop can be combined with the **in** operator to loop over the contents of a list.

```
> for i in [1,2,3,4]
  do
      print( i^2 );
  end do;
```

$$1$$
$$4$$
$$9$$
$$16 \qquad (4.39)$$

Sets

A set is an *unordered* sequence of *unique* expressions. When a set is created, Maple reorders the expressions to remove duplicate values and to make certain operations faster.

Creating Sets

The easiest way to create a set is to enclose a sequence of expressions in braces ({}).

```
{ sequence }
```

When Maple creates the set, it performs automatic simplification. This process creates a set that contains the elements of **sequence**; however, during the automatic simplification process, any duplicate elements are removed and the remaining elements are reordered.

Compare the results of these examples to those in the *Lists (page 130)* section.

```
> {x, y, y};
```
$$\{x, y\} \tag{4.40}$$

```
> {a, 1, b, 2};
```
$$\{1, 2, a, b\} \tag{4.41}$$

```
> {y[1],x,x[1],y[1]};
```
$$\{x, x_1, y_1\} \tag{4.42}$$

Similar to lists, sets can be created using functions such as **seq** that return sequences.

```
> { seq( i mod 3, i=1..10 ) };
```
$$\{0, 1, 2\} \tag{4.43}$$

Again, similar to lists, the **op** command can be used to extract the sequence of elements in a set.

```
> S := {1,2,3};
```
$$S := \{1, 2, 3\} \tag{4.44}$$

```
> op(S);
```
$$1, 2, 3 \tag{4.45}$$

However, unlike lists, Maple provides operations for set arithmetic, so for sets **op** is somewhat less important.

Set Arithmetic

Maple provides operators for mathematical set manipulations: **union**, **minus**, **intersect**, and **subset**. These operators allow you to perform set arithmetic in Maple.

```
> s := {x,y,z};
```
$$s := \{x, y, z\} \tag{4.46}$$

```
> t := {y,z,w};
```
$$t := \{w, y, z\} \tag{4.47}$$

```
> s union t;
```
$$\{w, x, y, z\} \tag{4.48}$$

```
> s minus t;
```
$$\{x\} \tag{4.49}$$

```
> s intersect t;
```
$$\{y, z\} \tag{4.50}$$

```
> s subset t;
```
$$false \tag{4.51}$$

```
> s subset {w,x,y,z};
```
$$true \tag{4.52}$$

Accessing Data Stored in a Set

The selection operation, [], can be used to read an element from a set. However, unlike lists, the order in which the elements are specified when creating the set may not correspond to the order they are accessed by indexing.

```
> S := {3,2,1}:
> S[1];
```
$$1 \tag{4.53}$$

```
> S[2];
```
$$2 \tag{4.54}$$

```
> S[3];
```
$$3 \tag{4.55}$$

Unlike lists, you cannot use the selection operation to create new sets.

```
> S[1] := 4;
Error, cannot reassign the entries in a set
```

You can specify a range in the selection operation to extract the elements indexed by the range.

```
> S2 := { seq( i^2, i=1..10 ) };
```
$$S2 := \{1, 4, 9, 16, 25, 36, 49, 64, 81, 100\} \tag{4.56}$$

```
> S2[3..6];
```
$$\{9, 16, 25, 36\} \tag{4.57}$$
```
> S2[5..8];
```
$$\{25, 36, 49, 64\} \tag{4.58}$$

Determining If an Element Is in a Set

To test if an element is contained in a set, use the **member** function.
```
> member( 1, {1,2,3} );
```
$$true \tag{4.59}$$
```
> member( 1, {2,3,4} );
```
$$false \tag{4.60}$$

You can also use the **in** operator.
```
> evalb( 1 in {1,2,3} );
```
$$true \tag{4.61}$$
```
> evalb( 1 in {2,3,4} );
```
$$false \tag{4.62}$$

Getting the Number of Elements in a Set

To find the number of elements in a set, use the **numelems** command.
```
> numelems( {1,2,3} );
```
$$3 \tag{4.63}$$
```
> numelems( {1,2,3,4,5} );
```
$$5 \tag{4.64}$$
```
> numelems( {seq( i, i=1..127 )} );
```
$$127 \tag{4.65}$$

In this example, the features of sets are used to test Collatz's conjecture on the first million integers. Collatz's conjecture states that given any integer, i, if the following function is applied repeatedly, the result will eventually be 1.
```
> collatz := proc( i )
      if ( i = 1 ) then
          1;
```

```
        elif ( type( i, even ) ) then
            i/2;
        else
            3*i+1;
        end if;
    end proc:
```

Begin with a set **S** that consists of the integers from 1 to 1 million. Under repeated application of **collatz**, as numbers converge to 1, the set automatically removes duplicate values, until eventually there is only 1 element left. For more information on the use of **map**, see *Applying a Function to the Contents of a Set (page 140)*.

```
> S := {seq( i, i=1..1000000)}:
> while ( numelems( S ) > 1 )
    do
        S := map( collatz, S ):
    end do:
> S;
```

$$\{1\} \tag{4.66}$$

Applying a Function to the Contents of a Set

As with lists, it can be useful to apply a function to all of the elements of a set. The **map** command works on sets, as it does with lists.

```
> S := { seq( Pi*i/4, i=0..3 ) }:
> map( sin, S );
```

$$\left\{ 0, 1, \frac{1}{2}\sqrt{2} \right\} \tag{4.67}$$

```
> map( cos, S );
```

$$\left\{ 0, 1, -\frac{1}{2}\sqrt{2}, \frac{1}{2}\sqrt{2} \right\} \tag{4.68}$$

Notice that when applying a function to a set, the output is also a set, which means the elements are reordered and duplicate elements are removed.

Maple provides other operations that can work with the members of a list, such as **add** and **mul**.

```
> add( i, i in { seq( j, j=1..100 ) } );
```

$$5050 \tag{4.69}$$

```
> mul( i^2, i in { 1,2,3,4,5,6,7,8,9,10 } );
```
$$13168189440000 \tag{4.70}$$

Finally a **for** loop can be combined with the **in** operator to loop over the contents of a set. Note that the set has been reordered.

```
> for i in {1,4,3,2}
  do
      print( i^2 );
  end do;
```

$$1$$
$$4$$
$$9$$
$$16 \tag{4.71}$$

4.4 Mutable Data Structures

Mutable data structures are structures whose contents can be changed.

The most flexible mutable data structure provided by Maple is the table.

Tables

A *table* stores a collection of index/entry pairs. For a given index, the table contains a particular value, called an entry. Index/entry pairs can be created or removed, or the value associated with an index can be modified.

Creating Tables

A new table can be created by calling the **table** function.

```
> t := table();
```
$$t := table([\,]) \tag{4.72}$$

With no arguments, table creates a new empty table. To create a table that contains certain index/entry pairs, specify the pairs as a list of equations. The left-hand side of an equation is the index and the right-hand side is the entry.

```
> t := table( [ 1=2, a=b, f(x)=y ] );
```
$$t := table([1 = 2, a = b, f(x) = y]) \tag{4.73}$$

If the given list contains one or more expressions that are not equations, the list is treated as a list of entries and the indices are the positions of the entries in the list (1, 2, 3, ...).

```
> t := table( [ a, b, c=d ] );
```

$$t := table([1 = a, 2 = b, 3 = (c = d)]) \qquad (4.74)$$

Note that **c=d** is treated as a entry and not an index/entry pair.

Tables are also created implicitly when you assign to an indexed name.

```
> t2[new] := 10;
```

$$t2_{new} := 10 \qquad (4.75)$$

```
> eval(t2);
```

$$table([new = 10]) \qquad (4.76)$$

Accessing Stored Values

Table indexing is performed using the selection operation, []. To extract data from a table, specify an index in square brackets. The corresponding entry is returned.

```
> t := table( [1=2,a=b,f(x)=y] );
```

$$t := table([1 = 2, a = b, f(x) = y]) \qquad (4.77)$$

```
> t[1];
```

$$2 \qquad (4.78)$$

```
> t[a];
```

$$b \qquad (4.79)$$

```
> t[f(x)];
```

$$y \qquad (4.80)$$

If the table does not contain a entry associated with the index, an unevaluated table reference is returned.

```
> t[2];
```

$$t_2 \qquad (4.81)$$

The selection operation can also be used to add new index/entry pairs to the table.

```
> t[2] := 3;
```

$$t_2 := 3 \qquad (4.82)$$

```
> t[c] := d;
```
$$t_c := d \tag{4.83}$$

```
> t[sin(x)] := 1;
```
$$t_{\sin(x)} := 1 \tag{4.84}$$

```
> t[2];
```
$$3 \tag{4.85}$$

```
> t[c];
```
$$d \tag{4.86}$$

```
> t[sin(x)];
```
$$1 \tag{4.87}$$

Removing an Element

The best way to remove an element from a table is to call the **unassign** function.

```
> t[1] := x;
```
$$t_1 := x \tag{4.88}$$

```
> t[sin(x)] := y;
```
$$t_{\sin(x)} := y \tag{4.89}$$

```
> unassign( 't[1]' );
> t[1];
```
$$t_1 \tag{4.90}$$

```
> unassign( 't[sin(x)]' );
> t[sin(x)];
```
$$t_{\sin(x)} \tag{4.91}$$

The selection operation can also be used to remove an index/entry pair from a table. By assigning the unevaluated table entry to its name, that element is removed from the table. This can be done by using unevaluation quotes (') or the **evaln** command.

```
> t[1] := x;
```
$$t_1 := x \tag{4.92}$$

```
> t[1] := 't[1]';
```

$$t_1 := t_1 \qquad (4.93)$$

```
> t[1];
```

$$t_1 \qquad (4.94)$$

```
> t[sin(x)] := y;
```

$$t_{\sin(x)} := y \qquad (4.95)$$

```
> t[sin(x)] := evaln(t[sin(x)]);
```

$$t_{\sin(x)} := t_{\sin(x)} \qquad (4.96)$$

```
> t[sin(x)];
```

$$t_{\sin(x)} \qquad (4.97)$$

Getting the Number of Elements Stored in a Table

The **numelems** function returns the number of elements stored in a table.

```
> numelems( table( [1] ) );
```

$$1 \qquad (4.98)$$

```
> numelems( table( [1,2,3,4,5] ) );
```

$$5 \qquad (4.99)$$

```
> numelems( table( [seq( i, i=1..127)] ) );
```

$$127 \qquad (4.100)$$

Checking If an Index Is Used

It is often useful to know if a particular index has a value in a table. Use the **assigned** function to check if a table index has an associated entry.

```
> t := table( [1=1] ):
> assigned( t[1] );
```

$$true \qquad (4.101)$$

```
> assigned( t[2] );
```

$$false \qquad (4.102)$$

Evaluation Rules for Tables

Tables, like procedures, use last name evaluation. If a name is assigned a table, the result of evaluating that name is the name and not the table assigned to the name. For more information about last name evaluation, refer to the **last_name_eval** help page.

```
> t := table([1,2,3,4]);
```

$$t := table([1 = 1, 2 = 2, 3 = 3, 4 = 4]) \qquad (4.103)$$

```
> t;
```

$$t \qquad (4.104)$$

To get the assigned value (the table), use the **eval** command.

```
> eval(t);
```

$$table([1 = 1, 2 = 2, 3 = 3, 4 = 4]) \qquad (4.105)$$

Extracting Data

Tables are often used as simple containers for data. Sometimes, it is useful to have a list of the indices used in the table. Maple provides the **indices** function for this purpose.

```
> t := table( [a=1, b=2, c=3, d=4] );
```

$$t := table([c = 3, d = 4, a = 1, b = 2]) \qquad (4.106)$$

```
> indices( t );
```

$$[c], [d], [a], [b] \qquad (4.107)$$

You may not expect to see that **indices** returns a sequence of lists, where each list contains the index. This is because Maple allows sequences to be used as indices in tables.

```
> t2 := table( [ a=1, b=2, (a,b,c)=3 ] );
```

$$t2 := table([a = 1, (a, b, c) = 3, b = 2]) \qquad (4.108)$$

```
> indices( t2 );
```

$$[a], [a, b, c], [b] \qquad (4.109)$$

If the indices were not wrapped in a list, it would be impossible to determine if an index is a single expression or a sequence of expressions. Since using sequences as indices is uncommon, **indices** accepts a **nolist** option, for which **indices** returns a simple sequence and does not wrap each index in a list.

```
> indices( t, 'nolist' );
```

$$c, d, a, b \qquad (4.110)$$

Note that, with the **nolist** option, indices that are sequences are not returned properly.

```
> indices( t2, 'nolist' );
```

$$a, a, b, c, b \tag{4.111}$$

You can also use the **entries** function to get all the values stored in the table.

```
> entries( t );
```

$$[3], [4], [1], [2] \tag{4.112}$$

```
> entries( t, 'nolist' );
```

$$3, 4, 1, 2 \tag{4.113}$$

To extract the index/entry pairs as a sequence of equations, use the **pairs** option to either of the **indices** or **entries** commands.

```
> entries( t, 'pairs' );
```

$$c = 3, d = 4, a = 1, b = 2 \tag{4.114}$$

Copying Tables

If you assign a table to multiple names, all the names reference the same table. Thus, changes to the table using one name are visible from the other names.

```
> t := table( [a=1,b=2,c=3] );
```

$$t := table([c = 3, a = 1, b = 2]) \tag{4.115}$$

```
> t1 := eval( t );
```

$$t1 := table([c = 3, a = 1, b = 2]) \tag{4.116}$$

```
> t[d] := 4;
```

$$t_d := 4 \tag{4.117}$$

```
> eval( t );
```

$$table([c = 3, d = 4, a = 1, b = 2]) \tag{4.118}$$

```
> eval( t1 );
```

$$table([c = 3, d = 4, a = 1, b = 2]) \tag{4.119}$$

If you want to create a copy of a table, use the **copy** function so that the tables can be modified independently.

```
> t1 := copy( t );
```

$$t1 := table([c = 3, d = 4, a = 1, b = 2]) \qquad (4.120)$$

```
> t[e] := 5;
```

$$t_e := 5 \qquad (4.121)$$

```
> eval( t );
```

$$table([c = 3, d = 4, e = 5, a = 1, b = 2]) \qquad (4.122)$$

```
> eval( t1 );
```

$$table([c = 3, d = 4, a = 1, b = 2]) \qquad (4.123)$$

Applying a Function to the Contents of a Table

The **map** function works with tables as it does with lists and sets. When executing a **map** on a table, the mapped function is given the value associated with an index. In the returned table, the result is the entry associated with the index.

```
> t := table( [ x, x^2+2, x^3-x+1, 1/x^2 ] );
```

$$t := table\left(\left[1 = x, 2 = x^2 + 2, 3 = x^3 - x + 1, 4 = \frac{1}{x^2}\right]\right) \qquad (4.124)$$

```
> map( diff, t, x );
```

$$table\left(\left[1 = 1, 2 = 2x, 3 = 3x^2 - 1, 4 = -\frac{2}{x^3}\right]\right) \qquad (4.125)$$

You can use the **indices** and **entries** functions to produce a list that can be mapped over or used in a **for-in** loop. You can also use this technique to modify the original table.

```
> for i in entries(t,'pairs')
  do
      t[lhs(i)] := int( rhs(i), x );
  end do;
```

$$t_1 := \frac{1}{2} x^2$$

$$t_2 := \frac{1}{3} x^3 + 2x$$

$$t_3 := \frac{1}{4} x^4 - \frac{1}{2} x^2 + x$$

$$t_4 := -\frac{1}{x} \qquad (4.126)$$

> `eval(t);`

$$table\left(\left[1 = \frac{1}{2} x^2, 2 = \frac{1}{3} x^3 + 2x, 3 = \frac{1}{4} x^4 - \frac{1}{2} x^2 + x, 4 = -\frac{1}{x}\right]\right) \qquad (4.127)$$

Arrays

In Maple, an Array stores data as an **n**-dimensional rectangular block (*rtable*), that is, an Array has 1 or more dimensions and each dimension has an range of integer indices. By specifying one integer from each range, an element of the Array can be indexed.

Because Arrays are mutable, the values stored in an Array can change.

Creating Arrays

To create an Array in Maple, use the **Array** command and specify the ranges for the dimensions. This creates a new Array with each entry initialized to 0. For Arrays, the ranges do not need to start at 1.

> `Array( 1..3 ); # 1 dimensional Array`

$$\begin{bmatrix} 0 & 0 & 0 \end{bmatrix} \qquad (4.128)$$

> `Array( 1..3, 1..4 ); # 2 dimensional Array`

$$\begin{bmatrix} 0 & 0 & 0 & 0 \\ 0 & 0 & 0 & 0 \\ 0 & 0 & 0 & 0 \end{bmatrix} \qquad (4.129)$$

```
> Array( 1..3, 2..5, -1..1 );  # 3 dimensional Array
```

$$\begin{bmatrix} 1..3 \times 2..5 \times -1..1 \; Array \\ Data \; Type: \; anything \\ Storage: \; rectangular \\ Order: \; Fortran\_order \end{bmatrix} \qquad (4.130)$$

When creating an Array, you can also specify a generator function to populate the Array with data. The generator function takes an index as an argument and returns a value for the corresponding entry.

```
> Array( 1..3, x->x+1 );
```

$$\begin{bmatrix} 2 & 3 & 4 \end{bmatrix} \qquad (4.131)$$

```
> Array( 1..3, 1..4, (x,y)->(x+y) );
```

$$\begin{bmatrix} 2 & 3 & 4 & 5 \\ 3 & 4 & 5 & 6 \\ 4 & 5 & 6 & 7 \end{bmatrix} \qquad (4.132)$$

You can also provide the data for the Array by specifying the data as a list or nested lists.

```
> Array( [1,2,3] );
```

$$\begin{bmatrix} 1 & 2 & 3 \end{bmatrix} \qquad (4.133)$$

```
> Array( [[1,2],[3,4],[5,6]] );
```

$$\begin{bmatrix} 1 & 2 \\ 3 & 4 \\ 5 & 6 \end{bmatrix} \qquad (4.134)$$

Basic Data Access

Arrays are implemented in Maple as a type of **rtable**, a structure also used for **Matrices** and **Vectors**. This means that Arrays have two different indexing mechanisms: mathematical indexing and programmer indexing. Mathematical indexing is intended for use when the Array is viewed as a mathematical object. Programmer indexing provides functionality that is more convenient when using Arrays as a programming tool.

The basic indexing operator, [], provides mathematical indexing. Programmer indexing is accessed by using round brackets, (). For Arrays whose dimension ranges all start at 1, the two indices behave similarly.

```
> A := Array( 1..2, 1..3 ):
> A[1,1] := 1;
```

$$A_{1,1} := 1 \tag{4.135}$$

```
> A(2,1) := 2;
```

$$A := \begin{bmatrix} 1 & 0 & 0 \\ 2 & 0 & 0 \end{bmatrix} \tag{4.136}$$

```
> A(1,1);
```

$$1 \tag{4.137}$$

```
> A[2,1];
```

$$2 \tag{4.138}$$

You may notice that the assignment that uses programmer indexing is displayed differently than the assignment that uses mathematical indexing. This is because the result of an assignment to a programmer indexed Array is the entire array. This can be important when working with large sub-Arrays.

When the ranges do not start at 1, mathematical and programmer indexing are different. Mathematical indexing requires that the indices match the specified ranges, but programming indexing always normalizes the ranges to start at 1.

```
> A := Array( 3..4, 5..6, (x,y)->x+y ):
> A[3,5];
```

$$8 \tag{4.139}$$

```
> A(3,5);
Error, index out of bounds
> A(1,1);
```

$$8 \tag{4.140}$$

This means that programmer indexing can always take advantage of negative indexing, which normally only works when the ranges start at 1. Negative indexing counts backwards from the end of the range.

```
> A[3,-1];
Error, Array index out of range
```

> A[3,6];

$$9 \tag{4.141}$$

> A(1,-1);

$$9 \tag{4.142}$$

Sub-Array Access

A sub-Array of an Array can be accessed by specifying a subrange in place of the indices.

> A := Array(1..5, 1..5, (x,y)->x+y);

$$A := \begin{bmatrix} 2 & 3 & 4 & 5 & 6 \\ 3 & 4 & 5 & 6 & 7 \\ 4 & 5 & 6 & 7 & 8 \\ 5 & 6 & 7 & 8 & 9 \\ 6 & 7 & 8 & 9 & 10 \end{bmatrix} \tag{4.143}$$

> A[1..2,1..3];

$$\begin{bmatrix} 2 & 3 & 4 \\ 3 & 4 & 5 \end{bmatrix} \tag{4.144}$$

> A(2..4,2..3);

$$\begin{bmatrix} 4 & 5 \\ 5 & 6 \\ 6 & 7 \end{bmatrix} \tag{4.145}$$

Sub-Array indexing can also be used to assign to the specified sub-Array.

> A[2..4,2..3] := Array([[a,a],[a,a],[a,a]]);

$$A_{2..4,\,2..3} := \begin{bmatrix} a & a \\ a & a \\ a & a \end{bmatrix} \tag{4.146}$$

```
> A(4..5,4..5) := Array( [[b,b],[b,b]] );
```

$$A := \begin{bmatrix} 2 & 3 & 4 & 5 & 6 \\ 3 & a & a & 6 & 7 \\ 4 & a & a & 7 & 8 \\ 5 & a & a & b & b \\ 6 & 7 & 8 & b & b \end{bmatrix} \tag{4.147}$$

Note that the commands perform the same operation, but display the result differently. This is the consequence of an important difference in how the modification is performed. This can be important when working with large sub-Arrays. Compare the time to perform the assignment in the following examples:

```
> N := 4000:
> A := Array( 1..N, 1..N, (x,y)->rand() ):
> B := Array( 1..N, 1..N ):
> t := time():
> B[1001..4000,1001..4000]:=A[1..3000,1..3000]:
> time()-t;
```

$$0.195 \tag{4.148}$$

```
> t := time():
> B(1001..4000,1001..4000):=A(1..3000,1..3000):
> time()-t;
```

$$0.059 \tag{4.149}$$

The difference in running time of these copies is due to the difference in the result of an assignment to an Array index. For mathematical indexing, a new 3000 by 3000 Array must be created as the result. With programmer indexing, the result is the Array being assigned to in its entirety - an object that already exists.

Automatic Resizing

One of the most important differences between mathematical and programmer indexing is automatic resizing. When reading from or writing to an entry using mathematical indexing, an index that is outside the bounds of the Array will raise an exception.

```
> A := Array( [[1,2,3],[4,5,6]] );
```

$$A := \begin{bmatrix} 1 & 2 & 3 \\ 4 & 5 & 6 \end{bmatrix} \tag{4.150}$$

```
> A[1,4];
Error, Array index out of range
> A[1,4] := a;
Error, Array index out of range
```

However, programmer indexing allows you to write to an entry that is outside the bounds of the current Array. Instead of raising an exception, the Array are automatically resized so that the element can be stored. Reading from an out-of-bounds index will still raise an exception.

```
> A(1,4) := a;
```

$$A := \begin{bmatrix} 1 & 2 & 3 & a \\ 4 & 5 & 6 & 0 \end{bmatrix} \tag{4.151}$$

```
> A(3,5);
Error, index out of bounds
> A(3,5) := b;
```

$$A := \begin{bmatrix} 1 & 2 & 3 & a & 0 \\ 4 & 5 & 6 & 0 & 0 \\ 0 & 0 & 0 & 0 & b \end{bmatrix} \tag{4.152}$$

More Array Indexing

There are more features of, and differences between, mathematical and programmer indexing. For more information on Array indexing, refer to the **rtable_indexing** help page.

Getting the Number of Elements in an Array

The **numelems** function returns the number of elements defined by the bounds of an Array.

```
> numelems( Array( [1,2,3,4,5] ) );
```

$$5 \tag{4.153}$$

```
> numelems( Array( [[1,2,3],[4,5,6]] ) );
```

$$6 \tag{4.154}$$

Getting the Bounds of an Array

As Array bounds may not start at 1, it is important that procedures that accept Arrays be aware of this possibility. The **upperbound** and **lowerbound** functions can be used to get the bounds on the ranges of an Array.

```
> printer := proc( A )
      local lower, upper, i, j;
      lower := lowerbound( A );
      upper := upperbound( A );
      for i from lower[1] to upper[1]
      do
            for j from lower[2] to upper[2]
            do
                  printf( "%a ", A[i,j] );
            end do;
            printf( "\n" );
      end do;
  end proc:
> printer( Array( [[1,2],[3,4]] ) ):
1 2
3 4
> printer( Array( 2..5, 5..7, (x,y)->(x+y) ) ):
7 8 9
8 9 10
9 10 11
10 11 12
```

Copying an Array

As with tables, having multiple variables referencing the same Array does not create new copies of the Array. You can use **copy** to copy the Array.

```
> A := Array( 1..2, 1..2 ):
> B := A;
```

$$B := \begin{bmatrix} 0 & 0 \\ 0 & 0 \end{bmatrix} \tag{4.155}$$

```
> A[1,1] := 1:
```

```
> B;
```

$$\begin{bmatrix} 1 & 0 \\ 0 & 0 \end{bmatrix}$$
(4.156)

```
> B := copy(A):
> A[1,2] := 2:
> A;
```

$$\begin{bmatrix} 1 & 2 \\ 0 & 0 \end{bmatrix}$$
(4.157)

```
> B;
```

$$\begin{bmatrix} 1 & 0 \\ 0 & 0 \end{bmatrix}$$
(4.158)

Testing If Two Arrays Are Equal

For Arrays, there are two notions of equality: do two references point to the same Array, or are they different Arrays that store the same values. To determine if two references refer to the same Array, use = and **evalb**. To test if two Arrays contain the same elements, use the **EqualEntries** command.

```
> CompareArray := proc( A, B )
      if A = B then
          print("two names for one array");
      elif EqualEntries(A,B) then
          print("same elements");
      else
          print("at least one element is different");
      end if;
  end proc:
> A := Array( [[1,2],[3,4]] );
```

$$A := \begin{bmatrix} 1 & 2 \\ 3 & 4 \end{bmatrix}$$
(4.159)

```
> AC := copy(A);
```

$$AC := \begin{bmatrix} 1 & 2 \\ 3 & 4 \end{bmatrix}$$
(4.160)

```
> CompareArray(A,AC);
```
$$\text{"same elements"} \tag{4.161}$$

```
> AR := A;
```
$$AR := \begin{bmatrix} 1 & 2 \\ 3 & 4 \end{bmatrix} \tag{4.162}$$

```
> CompareArray(A,AR);
```
$$\text{"two names for one array"} \tag{4.163}$$

```
> B := Array( [[1,2],[3,5]] );
```
$$B := \begin{bmatrix} 1 & 2 \\ 3 & 5 \end{bmatrix} \tag{4.164}$$

```
> CompareArray(A,B);
```
$$\text{"at least one element is different"} \tag{4.165}$$

There are some other advanced notions of equality such as whether or not arrays with undefined entries should be treated as having equal entries, and whether a Matrix and Array with identical entries should be considered the same. The **IsEqual** command in the **ArrayTools** package allows for different solutions for these two issues compared to **EqualEntries**. The **ArrayTools** package contains a variety of functions for working with Arrays. For more information, refer to the **ArrayTools** help page.

Applying a Function to the Contents of an Array

map can be used with an Array as you would expect

```
> map( x->(x/2), Array( [[1,2,3],[4,5,6]] ) );
```
$$\begin{bmatrix} \frac{1}{2} & 1 & \frac{3}{2} \\ 2 & \frac{5}{2} & 3 \end{bmatrix} \tag{4.166}$$

indices, **entries**, and the **in** operator work with Arrays, so you can use Arrays in **add**, **mul**, and **for** loops. **entries(A,pairs)** can also be used to obtain a list of index/value pairs in the same way that it does for tables.

```
> A := Array( [x,x^3,sin(x)] ):
```

```
> for entry in entries(A,'pairs')
  do
     A[lhs(entry)] := diff( rhs(entry), x ):
  end do:
> A;
```

$$\begin{bmatrix} 1 & 3x^2 & \cos(x) \end{bmatrix} \qquad (4.167)$$

Better Performance with Numeric Arrays

When creating an Array, you can specify a datatype for the Array elements. The given datatype can be either a Maple **type** or a hardware datatype specifier: **integer[n]**, **float[n]**, **complex[n]**. **n** refers to the number of bytes of data for each element. For **integer[n]**, **n** can be 1, 2, 4, or 8. For **float[n]** or **complex[n]**, **n** can be 4 or 8. The datatype **integer[4]** uses 4-bytes, or 32-bits per integer, and **integer[8]** uses 8-bytes, or 64-bits. The 64-bit version has a wider range of signed values, but uses more memory.

When assigning values into the Array, Maple will raise an exception if the given value does not match the specified type.

```
> A := Array( [1,2,3,4], datatype=float[8] );
```

$$A := \begin{bmatrix} 1. & 2. & 3. & 4. \end{bmatrix} \qquad (4.168)$$

```
> A[1];
```

$$1. \qquad (4.169)$$

```
> A[1] := 1.5;
```

$$A_1 := 1.5 \qquad (4.170)$$

```
> A[2] := x^2;
Error, unable to store 'x^2' when datatype=float[8]
```

If you are working with numeric values that can be stored in these hardware types, it can be much faster to use an Array with a hardware type. For more information on numerical programming in Maple, see *Numerical Programming in Maple (page 271)*.

Deprecated: array

The **array** data structure is an older implementation of Arrays. Its use has been deprecated; use Array instead.

4.5 Other Data Structure Operations

Filtering Data Structure Elements

The **select**, **remove**, and **selectremove** functions provide ways to filter the elements of data structures.

`select( f, x )`
`remove( f, x )`
`selectremove( f, x )`

The parameter **f** must be a Boolean-valued function. This function is applied to each of the elements of the data structure **x**. **select** returns the a data structure containing those elements for which **f** returns true. **remove** returns a data structure containing those elements for which **f** returns false. **selectremove** returns two structures, the first consisting of the elements for which **f** returned true and the second consisting of the elements for which **f** returns false.

The type of the return value of these functions matches the type of the argument **x**.

```
> x := [seq(i,i=1..10)];
```
$$x := [1, 2, 3, 4, 5, 6, 7, 8, 9, 10] \tag{4.171}$$

```
> select( isprime, x );
```
$$[2, 3, 5, 7] \tag{4.172}$$

```
> remove( isprime, x );
```
$$[1, 4, 6, 8, 9, 10] \tag{4.173}$$

```
> selectremove( isprime, x );
```
$$[2, 3, 5, 7], [1, 4, 6, 8, 9, 10] \tag{4.174}$$

Calling **selectremove** is more efficient than calling **select** and **remove** separately.

Converting Data Structures

Maple provides the **convert** function, which allows various expressions to be converted from one form to another.

`convert( x, t )`

convert attempts to convert the expression **x** into the form **t**. In particular, Maple supports conversions between the **list**, **set**, **table**, and **Array** types.

```
> x := [1,2,3,4];
```
$$x := [1, 2, 3, 4] \tag{4.175}$$

```
> convert( x, 'set' );
```
$$\{1, 2, 3, 4\} \tag{4.176}$$
```
> convert( x, 'table' );
```
$$table([\,1 = 1, 2 = 2, 3 = 3, 4 = 4\,]) \tag{4.177}$$
```
> convert( x, 'Array' );
```
$$[\,1\ 2\ 3\ 4\,] \tag{4.178}$$

4.6 Other Data Structures

Records

In Maple, a record is a structured data type. It allows you to create a fixed-size structure with user-defined fields. You can use records to create customized structures that can make Maple code easier to read and write.

Create a Record

To create a new record, use the **Record** command. **Record** accepts a sequence of **names** as parameters. Each name becomes a field in the returned record.
```
> r := Record( 'expression', 'variable' );
```
$$r := Record(expression, variable) \tag{4.179}$$
```
> r:-expression := x^2;
```
$$expression := x^2 \tag{4.180}$$
```
> r:-variable := x;
```
$$variable := x \tag{4.181}$$
```
> int( r:-expression, r:-variable );
```
$$\frac{1}{3} x^3 \tag{4.182}$$

If **Record** is passed a single record as an argument, a copy of that record is returned.
```
> r2 := Record( eval(r,1) );
```
$$r2 := Record\bigl(expression = x^2, variable = x\bigr) \tag{4.183}$$

```
> r2:-expression := sin(x^2);
```

$$expression := \sin(x^2) \tag{4.184}$$

```
> int( r2:-expression, r2:-variable );
```

$$\frac{1}{2} \sqrt{2} \sqrt{\pi} \, \text{FresnelS}\left(\frac{\sqrt{2}\, x}{\sqrt{\pi}} \right) \tag{4.185}$$

Note that you must call **eval** on **r** before passing it into **Record**. This is because records use last name evaluation rules, similar to tables.

Record Equality

As with Arrays, two references to Records are considered equal if they reference the same structure. Two different structures that have the same fields and values are not considered equal.

```
> r := Record( 'a'=1, 'b'=2, 'c'=3 ):
> rc := r:
> r2 := Record( 'a'=1, 'b'=2, 'c'=3 ):
> evalb( r = rc );
```

$$true \tag{4.186}$$

```
> evalb( r = r2 );
```

$$false \tag{4.187}$$

To compare two different records, you can use the **verify** command with the **record** argument. **verify/record** returns **true** if the two records have the same set of fields with equal values assigned to them.

```
> r3 := Record( 'a'=1, 'b'=2, 'c'=3, 'd'=4 ):
> r4 := Record( 'a'=1, 'b'=2, 'c'=4 ):
> verify( r, r2, 'record' );
```

$$true \tag{4.188}$$

```
> verify( r, r3, 'record' );
```

$$false \tag{4.189}$$

```
> verify( r, r4, 'record' );
```

$$false \tag{4.190}$$

Packed Records

The **Record** constructor function can also be called with the indexed name **Record[packed]**, to produce a packed record.

Unlike a regular record, a packed record does not create a unique instance of each field name for each record instance. When working with thousands of similar records each with many fields, this can save a significant amount of memory.

Fields of packed records do not exhibit last name evaluation. That is, the expression **r:-a** always produces a value, even if that value is a procedure, table, Matrix, Vector, or another record.

Similarly, it is not possible for a packed record field to *not* have a value. The **assigned** function will always return true, and **unassign**ing a packed record field will set its value to **NULL** instead.

Stacks

A stack is an abstract data type that provides two main operations: push and pop. A push places a new value onto the top of the stack and pushes the existing elements down. A pop removes the element from the top of the stack, moving the elements below up. This creates a element access order referred to as *last in first out* (LIFO).

Stacks are useful for many operations. A typical use of a stack is to turn a recursive algorithm into an iterative one. Instead of recursing on elements, those elements get pushed onto a stack. When the current element has been handled, the element on top of the stack is removed and handled next. By using a stack, the recently discovered elements are handled before elements that were already in the stack, which is similar to how a recursive algorithm works.

Creating a Stack

In Maple, you can create a stack by calling **stack:-new**. If you do not specify any arguments, **stack:-new** creates an empty stack. Maple stacks are implemented on top of tables.

```
> s := stack:-new():
> stack:-push( 1, s );
```
$$1 \qquad (4.191)$$

```
> stack:-push( 2, s );
```
$$2 \qquad (4.192)$$

```
> stack:-pop( s );
```
$$2 \qquad (4.193)$$

```
> stack:-pop( s );
```
$$1 \tag{4.194}$$

You can also pass values into **stack:-new** that populate the stack. These elements are pushed in the order specified.

```
> s := stack:-new(1,2,3,4,5):
> stack:-pop( s );
```
$$5 \tag{4.195}$$

```
> stack:-pop( s );
```
$$4 \tag{4.196}$$

Pushing and Popping

To push and pop elements onto the stack, use the **stack:-push** and **stack:-pop** functions.

```
> s := stack:-new():
> stack:-push( 1, s ):
> stack:-push( 2, s ):
> stack:-pop( s );
```
$$2 \tag{4.197}$$

```
> stack:-push( 3, s ):
> stack:-pop( s );
```
$$3 \tag{4.198}$$

```
> stack:-pop( s );
```
$$1 \tag{4.199}$$

More Stack Functions

To get the number of elements stored in the stack, call **stack:-depth**.

```
> s := stack:-new(a,b,c):
> while stack:-depth( s ) > 0
  do
      print( stack:-pop( s ) );
  end do;
```

$$c$$
$$b$$
$$a \qquad (4.200)$$

To test if a stack is empty, call **stack:-empty**.

```
> s := stack:-new(c,b,a):
> while not stack:-empty( s )
  do
      print( stack:-pop( s ) );
  end do;
```

$$a$$
$$b$$
$$c \qquad (4.201)$$

You can examine the element on the top of a stack, without removing it, by calling **stack:-top**.

```
> s := stack:-new(x,x^2,sin(x)):
> stack:-depth(s);
```

$$3 \qquad (4.202)$$

```
> stack:-top(s);
```

$$\sin(x) \qquad (4.203)$$

```
> stack:-pop(s);
```

$$\sin(x) \qquad (4.204)$$

```
> stack:-depth(s);
```

$$2 \qquad (4.205)$$

```
> stack:-top(s);
```

$$x^2 \qquad (4.206)$$

```
> stack:-pop(s);
```

$$x^2 \qquad (4.207)$$

164 • 4 Basic Data Structures

```
> stack:-depth(s);
```

$$1 \qquad (4.208)$$

```
> stack:-top(s);
```

$$x \qquad (4.209)$$

Queues

The queue is an abstract data type similar to a stack; however, instead of the most recently added element being returned first, the oldest element in the queue is returned first. Elements in a queue are analogous to people waiting in a line. The main operations provided by a queue are **enqueue**, which adds an element to the queue, and **dequeue**, which removes an element from the queue. The access order used by a queue is called *first in first out*, or FIFO.

A queue is used when you want to handle elements in the order that they are discovered. A typical example of using a queue is a breadth-first search of a graph. You dequeue a node and then enqueue any unvisited nodes that are neighbors of the current node. By using a queue, the order in which the nodes are visited is breadth-first.

Create a Queue

To create a queue in Maple, use the **queue:-new** command.

```
> q := queue:-new():
> queue:-enqueue( q, 1 );
```

$$1 \qquad (4.210)$$

```
> queue:-enqueue( q, 2 );
```

$$2 \qquad (4.211)$$

```
> queue:-dequeue( q );
```

$$1 \qquad (4.212)$$

```
> queue:-dequeue( q );
```

$$2 \qquad (4.213)$$

You can also pass values into **queue:-new** to populate the new queue. The elements are enqueued in the order they are specified.

```
> q := queue:-new( 1,2,3 ):
> queue:-dequeue( q );
```

$$1 \qquad (4.214)$$

```
> queue:-dequeue( q );
```

$$2 \tag{4.215}$$

```
> queue:-dequeue( q );
```

$$3 \tag{4.216}$$

Enqueue and Dequeue

You can insert a new element into a queue using **queue:-enqueue** and remove an element from the queue using **queue:-dequeue**.

```
> q := queue:-new():
> queue:-enqueue( q, 1 ):
> queue:-enqueue( q, 2 ):
> queue:-dequeue( q );
```

$$1 \tag{4.217}$$

```
> queue:-enqueue( q, 3 ):
> queue:-dequeue( q );
```

$$2 \tag{4.218}$$

```
> queue:-dequeue( q );
```

$$3 \tag{4.219}$$

More Queue Functions

You can get the number of elements stored in the queue by calling **queue:-length**.

```
> q := queue:-new(a,b,c):
> while queue:-length( q ) > 0
  do
     print( queue:-dequeue( q ) );
  end do;
```

$$\begin{array}{c} a \\ b \\ c \end{array} \tag{4.220}$$

You can test if a queue is empty by calling **queue:-empty**.

```
> q := queue:-new(c,b,a):
> while not queue:-empty( q )
  do
     print( queue:-dequeue( q ) );
  end do;
```

$$c$$
$$b$$
$$a \qquad (4.221)$$

You can examine the front element of a queue, without removing it, by calling **queue:-front**.

```
> q := queue:-new(x,x^2,sin(x)):
> queue:-length(q);
```
$$3 \qquad (4.222)$$

```
> queue:-front(q);
```
$$x \qquad (4.223)$$

```
> queue:-dequeue(q);
```
$$x \qquad (4.224)$$

```
> queue:-length(q);
```
$$2 \qquad (4.225)$$

```
> queue:-front(q);
```
$$x^2 \qquad (4.226)$$

```
> queue:-dequeue(q);
```
$$x^2 \qquad (4.227)$$

```
> queue:-length(q);
```
$$1 \qquad (4.228)$$

```
> queue:-front(q);
```
$$\sin(x) \qquad (4.229)$$

4.7 Data Coercion

Data Coercion refers to the ability to take one data type and automatically convert it into a different data type. This is particularly useful for arguments passed into a procedure, where the expected data type for the procedure is explicitly declared. For more information on data coercion in Maple, see the **coercion** help page.

Maple provides two methods for enabling data coercion. For more information see *The coercion Modifiers (page 211)*.

4.8 Data Structure Performance Comparisons

Maple provides many different data structures, many of which can be used together to perform specific tasks. However, the different performance characteristics of the data structures means that some are better than others in certain situations.

Indexing

The time to perform an indexed look-up into a list, set, table, and Array are all constant time operations. This means that the time needed to find the element does not vary based on the number of elements stored in the structure. Time to perform a look-up into a list or set is relatively similar and is faster than Arrays, which is faster than a table.

Similarly, writing into a table or Array is also a constant time operation, with Array look-ups being slightly faster than table look-ups.

Membership

The **member** function determines if a particular element is stored in a structure. For lists, this requires a linear search of the data in the list. Therefore, the time is proportional to the total length of the list. A set is sorted, so searches of the list can be performed more quickly. Searching within a set takes time proportional to the **log[2]** of the number of elements in the set.

You can use a table for very fast membership testing. Use the table *key* as objects you want to test for, and anything you want for the value. You can then call the **assigned** command to test if the element exists in the table. A table index is a constant time operation, so this membership test is also constant time.

```
> N := 2*10^5:
> memtest := proc( D, N )
      local i;

      for i from 1 to N
      do
```

```
            member( i, D ):
        end do:
    end proc:
> L := [seq( i, i=1..N )]:
> time(memtest(L,N));
```

$$26.625 \tag{4.230}$$

```
> S := {seq( i, i=1..N )}:
> time(memtest(S,N));
```

$$0.352 \tag{4.231}$$

```
> t := table( [seq( i=1, i=1..N ) ] ):
> start := time():
  for i from 1 to N
  do
        assigned( t[i] ):
  end do:
  time()-start;
```

$$0.200 \tag{4.232}$$

Note that to benchmark the **list** and **set** membership functions, the call to **member** is within a function. This is because of the Maple evaluation rules. If the call to the **member** command is at the top level, the list or set is fully evaluated, which requires inspecting each element of the list or set for each call to **member**. The overhead required for these full evaluations would distort the results.

For more information on the Maple evaluation rules, see *Unevaluated Expressions (page 48)*.

Building a Collection of Data

It is often necessary to build a collection of data when you do not know how many elements you are going to have. You should use a table, Array (using programmer indexing), stack, or queue. All of these mutable structures support adding elements in constant time. Using an immutable data structure is slower; the use of a list or a set is not recommended in this situation.

```
> N := 5*10^4:
> A := Array( [] ):
  start := time():
  for i from 1 to N
  do
```

```
        A( i ) := 1:
    end do:
    time()-start;
```

$$0.048 \tag{4.233}$$

```
> t := table():
  start:=time():
  for i from 1 to N
  do
      t[i] := 1:
  end do:
  time()-start;
```

$$0.092 \tag{4.234}$$

```
> l := []: # using a list is quite slow
  start := time():
  for i from 1 to N
  do
      l := [ op(l), i ]:
  end do:
  time()-start;
```

$$47.802 \tag{4.235}$$

4.9 Avoiding Common Problems

When working with data structures, there are a few common problems that you may encounter. This section describes some of these problems to help you avoid making these mistakes yourself.

Passing Sequences into Functions

When a sequence is passed into a procedure, each element of the sequence is treated as a separate argument. This can lead to errors if the procedure is unable to handle the multiple arguments, for example, with the **op** command.

```
> s := a,b,c;
```

$$s := a, b, c \tag{4.236}$$

```
> op( 2, s );
Error, invalid input: op expects 1 or 2 arguments, but received 4
```

Instead, wrap the sequence in a list.

```
> op( 2, [s] );
```

$$b \tag{4.237}$$

Incorrect Index Values

Be careful with the values used for indexing. Specifying values outside valid ranges will raise exceptions. In particular, in Maple, lists and sets start indexing at **1**, not **0**.

```
> L := [1,2,3,4,5,6,7,8];
```

$$L := [1, 2, 3, 4, 5, 6, 7, 8] \tag{4.238}$$

```
> L[0];
Error, invalid subscript selector
> L[9];
Error, invalid subscript selector
```

Further, when specifying the endpoints of a range, make sure that the left-hand side of the range specifies an element before the element specified by the right-hand side.

```
> L[6..3];
Error, invalid subscript selector
> L[6..-5];
Error, invalid subscript selector
```

The only exception to this is if the left-hand side of the range is **n**, then the right-hand side can be **n-1** and the result of this range is an empty structure (list or set).

```
> L[6..5];
```

$$[\,] \tag{4.239}$$

Similar exceptions happen with using [] for selection from Arrays.

```
> A := Array( [5,6,7,8,9,10] );
```

$$A := \begin{bmatrix} 5 & 6 & 7 & 8 & 9 & 10 \end{bmatrix} \tag{4.240}$$

```
> A[7];
Error, Array index out of range
> A[5..3];
Error, inverted range in Array index
```

Array Indices Do Not Always Start at 1

In an Array, the lower bound of the indices may not be 1. If you write a procedure that accepts an Array, you should be prepared to handle Arrays that have been defined for a range of indices that does not start at 1. For more information on how to write procedures that can handle such Arrays, see *Getting the Bounds of an Array (page 154)*.

Do Not Treat Lists and Sets as Mutable

You can use commands such as **op** and **subsop** with lists and sets to create new structures. It is, therefore, possible to treat lists and sets like mutable structures. However, by doing so, you can add a significant amount of processing time to your computations. Make sure that you use actual mutable structures instead.

```
> N := 2*10^4:
> l := [seq( i=i, i=1..N)]:
> t := table( l ):
  start:=time():
  for i from N to 1 by -1
  do
      t[i] := evaln(t[i]):
  end do:
  time()-start;
```

$$0.032 \tag{4.241}$$

```
> start := time():
  for i from N to 1 by -1
  do
      l := subsop( i=NULL, l );
  end do:
  time()-start;
```

$$20.277 \tag{4.242}$$

4.10 Exercises

1. Define a set with elements that are the powers of **13** modulo **100** for exponents ranging from **1** to **1000**. Is **5** a member of the set? Why is it beneficial to use a set instead of a list?

   Hint: You can determine the set by using one statement if you use the **seq** command.

2. Generate the sums of **4** and the first **100** multiples of **3**. Determine the sums that are square-free composite numbers.

Hint: The **numtheory** package has a function that you need to use.

3. Find floating-point approximations for the sum of the square root and cubic root of each of the first **15** powers of 2.

   Hint: Use **map**, **seq**, and **zip**.

4. Write a procedure that implements the sieve of Eratosthenes: Count the number of integers (less than or equal to a given integer) that are prime.

5 Maple Statements

5.1 In This Chapter

- Introduction
- Expression Statements
- Assignments
- Flow Control
- The use Statement
- Other Statements

5.2 Introduction

A *statement* is a single complete piece of code that Maple can execute. There are many types of statements in Maple, including expression statements, assignment statements, selection statements (if ... then), repetition statements (loops), and program instructions (quit, save, read).

A statement differs from an expression in that it is normally evaluated for effect, rather than for its value. Most statements that do *not* consist of a single expression are formed so as to have a side effect.

5.3 Statement Separators

Statements in Maple must be terminated with a semicolon (;) or a colon (:).

Statements can be run in Maple one at a time, or multiple statements can be run on one line. If multiple statements are run on one line, the statements must be separated by a statement separator, either a semicolon (;) or a colon (:).

At the top level, the output of a statement that ends with a colon is hidden.

```
> a:=2: a^2;
```

$$4 \tag{5.1}$$

Note: In the standard interface, for input in 2-D math, the semicolon at the end of a statement can be omitted.

5.4 Expression Statements

The simplest kind of statement in Maple is the expression statement. It consists of an arbitrary expression, whose evaluation constitutes the effect of the statement.

```
> Pi;
```

$$\pi \tag{5.2}$$

```
> sin( Pi - x );
```

$$\sin(x) \tag{5.3}$$

```
> int( sin( Pi - x ), x );
```

$$-\cos(x) \tag{5.4}$$

5.5 Assignments

Assignment statements allow you to associate a value or expression with a name. The assignment statement has the general form

```
lhs := rhs
```

Evaluating the assignment associates the value on the right-hand side of the assignment with the name on the left-hand side. After the assignment has taken effect, the result is the associated value when the assigned name is evaluated.

Here, the name **a** has no assigned value, so it evaluates to itself.

```
> a;
```

$$a \tag{5.5}$$

The following assignment statement associates the value **2 / 3** with the name **a**.

```
> a := 2 / 3;
```

$$a := \frac{2}{3} \tag{5.6}$$

Subsequent evaluation of the name **a** results in the assigned value **2 / 3**.

```
> a;
```

$$\frac{2}{3} \tag{5.7}$$

```
> a + 1 / 3;
```

$$1 \tag{5.8}$$

Associate the symbolic expression **Pi / 2** with the name **b** by executing the following assignment statement.

```
> b := Pi / 2;
```

$$b := \frac{1}{2} \pi \tag{5.9}$$

Subsequently, the assigned value of **b** is used whenever the name **b** appears in an expression.

```
> sin( b );
```

$$1 \tag{5.10}$$

In this expression, the assigned value **Pi / 2** of the name **b** is substituted to yield the expression **sin(Pi / 2)**, and then the value of the procedure **sin** at this expression is computed, resulting in the overall value **1** for the expression.

Multiple Assignment

You can perform several assignments in a single statement, known as a *multiple assignment*. This has the general form

```
(lhs1, lhs2, ..., lhsN) := (rhs1, rhs2, ..., rhsN)
```

The parentheses on the right- and left-hand sides of the assignment are not required, but are considered good practice.

For example, the multiple assignment statement

```
> (x, y, z) := ( sin( t ), cos( t ), tan( t ) );
```

$$x, y, z := \sin(t), \cos(t), \tan(t) \tag{5.11}$$

establishes assigned values for all three names **x**, **y**, and **z**.

```
> x;
```

$$\sin(t) \tag{5.12}$$

```
> y;
```

$$\cos(t) \tag{5.13}$$

```
> z;
```

$$\tan(t) \tag{5.14}$$

The number of components on each side of the assignment operator **:=** must be the same.

```
> (a, b, c) := (2, 3);
Error, ambiguous multiple assignment
```

A common idiom is to use a multiple (double) assignment to swap the values of two variables without introducing an additional temporary variable.

```
> (x, y) := (1, 2):
> x;
```

$$1 \qquad (5.15)$$

```
> y;
```

$$2 \qquad (5.16)$$

```
> (x, y) := (y, x):
> x;
```

$$2 \qquad (5.17)$$

```
> y;
```

$$1 \qquad (5.18)$$

Note that using the swap idiom with unassigned names will lead to an infinite recursion.

```
> (u, v) := (v, u);
```

$$u, v := v, u \qquad (5.19)$$

Evaluating **u** or **v** (full evaluation) produces an error. If you evaluate one level at a time using **eval(u, i)**, you can see what happens.

```
> u;
Error, too many levels of recursion
> v;
Error, too many levels of recursion
> seq( eval( u, i ), i = 1 .. 10 );
```

$$v, u, v, u, v, u, v, u, v, u \qquad (5.20)$$

```
> seq( eval( v, i ), i = 1 .. 10 );
```

$$u, v, u, v, u, v, u, v, u, v \qquad (5.21)$$

5.6 Flow Control

A number of Maple statements are used to direct the flow of control in a program; that is, the sequence in which the various statements of the program are run.

Sequencing

The simplest form of a Maple program is a sequence of zero or more statements, separated either by semicolons or colons. A sequence of statements is run in the order in which they are entered.

For example, running these three statements

```
> a := 2;
```

$$a := 2 \tag{5.22}$$

```
> b := 3;
```

$$b := 3 \tag{5.23}$$

```
> sin( a + b );
```

$$\sin(5) \tag{5.24}$$

executes the assignment to the name **a**, then the assignment to the name **b** is executed and, finally, the value of the expression **sin(a + b)** is computed.

The flow of control in a Maple program consisting of a sequence of statements moves from one statement to the next, in order.

Many Maple statements are *compound* statements that contain statement sequences as constituents.

Branching

The simplest form of flow control is a branching, or **if** statement. Basically, an **if** statement has the syntax

```
if condition then
    statseq
end if
```

in which **condition** is a Boolean-valued expression (that is, one which evaluates to one of the values **true**, **FAIL**, or **false**), and **statseq** is a (possibly empty) sequence of Maple statements, often called the *body* of the **if** statement.

The effect of an **if** statement is to divert the flow of control, under the right conditions, to the body of the statement. If the **condition** expression evaluates to **true**, the flow of control moves into the body of the **if** statement. Otherwise, if the **condition** expression evaluates to **FAIL** or **false**, Maple exits the **if** statement and the flow of control continues at the statement (if any) following the **if** statement.

```
> if 2 < 3 then
      print( "HELLO" )
  end if;
```

$$\text{"HELLO"} \tag{5.25}$$

```
> if 2 > 3 then
      print( "GOODBYE" )
  end if;
```

More generally, an **if** statement has the syntax

```
if condition then
    consequent
else
    alternative
end if
```

Here, **consequent** and **alternative** are statement sequences. If the **condition** expression evaluates to **true**, the **consequent** branch of the **if** statement is executed. Otherwise, the **alternative** branch is executed.

```
> if 2 < 3 then
      print( "CONSEQUENT" )
  else
      print( "ALTERNATIVE" )
  end if;
```

$$\text{"CONSEQUENT"} \tag{5.26}$$

```
> if 2 > 3 then
      print( "CONSEQUENT" )
  else
      print( "ALTERNATIVE" )
  end if;
```

$$\text{"ALTERNATIVE"} \tag{5.27}$$

The most general form of an **if** statement can have several conditions, corresponding consequents, and an optional alternative branch. This general form has the syntax:

```
if condition1 then
    consequent1
elif condition2 then
    consequent2
....
else
    alternative
end if
```

in which there can be any number of branches preceded by **elif**. The effect of this general form of the **if** statement is to divert the flow of control into the *first* branch whose conditional expression evaluates to **true**. This means that the order of the **elif** branches can affect the behavior of the **if** statement.

The branch introduced by **else** is optional. If it is present, and none of the earlier condition expressions evaluates to **true**, then control flows into the **else** branch. If it is not present, and none of the earlier condition expressions evaluates to **true**, then the flow of execution continues with the first statement following the entire **if** statement.

```
> if 2 > 3 then
     print( "CONSEQUENT1" )
  elif 3 > 4 then
     print( "CONSEQUENT2" )
  elif 1 < 5 then
     print( "CONSEQUENT3" )
  elif 2 < 5 then
     print( "CONSEQUENT4" )
  else
     print( "ALTERNATIVE" )
  end if;
```

$$\text{"CONSEQUENT3"} \tag{5.28}$$

```
> if 2 > 3 then
     print( "CONSEQUENT1" )
  elif 3 > 4 then
     print( "CONSEQUENT2" )
  elif 1 > 5 then
     print( "CONSEQUENT3" )
  elif 2 > 5 then
```

```
      print( "CONSEQUENT4" )
   else
      print( "ALTERNATIVE" )
   end if;
```

$$\text{"ALTERNATIVE"} \tag{5.29}$$

The **else** branch, if present, must appear last.

An **if** statement can appear at the top level, as in the examples shown above, but is most commonly used within a procedure or module definition.

A typical use of the **if** statement is to control the flow of execution inside a procedure, depending on information coming from the arguments passed to it.

```
> p := proc( expr )
      if type( expr, 'numeric' ) then
         sin( 2 * expr )
      elif type( expr, { '`+`', '`*`' } ) then
         map( thisproc, _passed )
      else
         'procname'( _passed )
      end if
   end proc:
> p( 2 );
```

$$\sin(4) \tag{5.30}$$

```
> p( x );
```

$$p(x) \tag{5.31}$$

```
> p( x + 1 );
```

$$p(x) + \sin(2) \tag{5.32}$$

In this example, the procedure **p** uses the **type** command to examine its argument **expr**. If the argument is numeric, then it computes the value as **sin(2 * expr)**. Otherwise, if the argument is either a sum or a product, the procedure maps itself over the operands of the expression. Otherwise, the procedure returns unevaluated.

The `if` Command

There is an operator form of branching that can be used within an expression. In this form, **if** is always called with three arguments. The **if** operator has the following syntax:

```
`if`( condition, consequent, alternative )
```

The first argument **condition** is a Boolean-valued expression. The second argument **consequent** is an expression to evaluate if the first argument evaluates to the value **true**. The third argument is an expression to evaluate if the first argument evaluates to either **false** or **FAIL**.

```
> `if`( 1 < 2, a, b );
```

$$a \tag{5.33}$$

```
> `if`( 1 > 2, a, b );
```

$$b \tag{5.34}$$

Note that the name **if** must be enclosed in name (left) quotes in this form.

The **if** command evaluates only one of its second and third arguments, determined based on the value of the first argument. The other argument is not evaluated.

The value of the **if** command (as opposed to the statement form) is that you can embed it within a larger expression.

```
> a := 2/3:
> sin( `if`( a > 0, Pi / 2, -Pi / 2 ) );
```

$$1 \tag{5.35}$$

However, the **if** command is much more limited than the **if** statement. The consequent and alternative must be single expressions, and there is nothing corresponding to the **elif** parts of the statement form.

Loops

To cause a statement, or sequence of statements, to be run more than once, use a loop statement. Maple has a general and flexible loop statement.

The simplest loop has the form **do end do**. This loop does not perform any tasks.

A loop statement has one of the following general forms.

```
for var from start to finish by increment while condition do
    statseq
end do
```

```
for var in container while condition do
    statseq
end do
```

The first line in each of these forms is called the *loop header* or, more formally, the *loop control clause*. The **statseq** part of the loop is a (possibly empty) sequence of statements, referred to as the *body* of the loop.

Each clause that occurs before the keyword **do** in the loop header is optional.

Since most of the examples below are infinite loops; you must interrupt the Maple computation to terminate the loop. For more information, see *Interrupting a Maple Computation (page 11)*.

```
> do end do;
> by -14 do end do;
> for i do end do;
> from 42 do end do;
> to 3 do end do;
> while true do end do;
```

If more than one of the optional clauses appears in the loop header, they may appear in any order.

While Loops

One simple kind of terminating loop is the *while loop*.

```
while condition do
    statseq
end do;
```

The loop header of a **while** loop involves only a single termination condition introduced by the keyword **while**. The loop repeats the statement sequence **statseq** until the Boolean-valued expression **condition** does not hold.

In this example, a loop counts the number of primes whose square is less than 1000.

```
> count := 0:
  p := 2:
  while p^2 < 1000 do
    count := 1 + count;
    p := nextprime( p )
  end do:
  count;
```

(5.36)

This example uses the **nextprime** command, which returns the least prime greater than its argument. The name **count** is given the initial value **0**, and the name **p**, which is used to store the current prime, is initially set to **2**. The loop condition is the expression **p^2 < 1000**, appearing after the keyword **while** and before the keyword **do**. This condition is evaluated at the beginning of each iteration of the loop. If the condition evaluates to **true**, the body of the loop is executed. If the condition evaluates to **false** or **FAIL**, the code continues to execute at the next statement following the loop statement.

If the condition expression evaluates to a value other than **true**, **false** or **FAIL**, an exception is raised.

```
> while 3 do end do;
Error, invalid boolean expression: 3
> while u < v do end do;
Error, cannot determine if this expression is true or false: u < v
```

For more information on Boolean expressions, see *Boolean and Relational Expressions (page 89)*.

Counted Loops

You can use a loop to repeatedly execute a sequence of statements a fixed number of times. These loops use the **from** and **to** clauses.

```
> from 1 to 3 do print( "HELLO" ) end do;
```

$$\text{"HELLO"}$$
$$\text{"HELLO"}$$
$$\text{"HELLO"} \tag{5.37}$$

or equivalently

```
> to 3 do print( "HELLO" ) end do;
```

$$\text{"HELLO"}$$
$$\text{"HELLO"}$$
$$\text{"HELLO"} \tag{5.38}$$

If the **from** clause is omitted, the default value of 1 is used.

Inductive Loops

The most common kind of loop is an inductive loop which is similar to a counted loop, but uses an induction variable whose value changes at each iteration of the loop. This is a particular kind of *for loop* with the general form

```
for var from start to finish by increment do
    statseq
end do;
```

The default value for **start** is **1**, for **finish** is **infinity**, and for **increment** is **1**.

```
> for i to 3 do
    print( i )
  end do;
```

$$1$$
$$2$$
$$3 \qquad (5.39)$$

This loop performs the following tasks:

Maple assigns **i** the (default) value **1** since a starting value was not specified.

Because **1** is less than **3**, Maple executes the statement in the body of the loop, in this case, printing the value of **i**.

Then **i** is incremented by **1** and tested again.

The loop executes until **i>3**. In this case, when the loop terminates, the final value of **i** is **4**.

```
> i;
```

$$4 \qquad (5.40)$$

```
> for i from 7 to 2 by -2 do
    print( i )
  end do;
```

$$7$$
$$5$$
$$3 \qquad (5.41)$$

Loop control parameters (**start**, **finish**, and **increment**) do not need to be integers.

```
> for i from 0.2 to 0.7 by 0.25 do
    print( i )
  end do;
```

$$0.2$$
$$0.45$$
$$0.70 \tag{5.42}$$

In addition to iterating over a numeric range, you can iterate over a range of characters. In this case, you must specify *both* the initial value **start** and the final value **finish** for the induction variable. Furthermore, the value of **increment** must be an integer.

```
> for i from "a" to "g" by 2 do
    print( i )
  end do;
```

$$"a"$$
$$"c"$$
$$"e"$$
$$"g" \tag{5.43}$$

Iterating over a Data Structure

An alternative form of the loop statement allows you to iterate over the operands of an expression (often, a data structure such as a set or list).

```
for var in expr do
    statseq
end do;
```

The induction variable **var** takes on, successively, the operands of the expression **expr**. There are a few exceptions. First, if **expr** is an expression sequence, it does not have operands as such, but the induction variable **var** iterates over the operands of the list **[expr]**. If **expr** is a table, the loop iterates over **[entries](expr)**. (For more information on **entries**, see *Extracting Data (page 145)*.) The order in which these entries are visited is not specified and may vary from one session to another. Finally, if **expr** is an rtable, the loop iterates over the entries of **expr**, but the order of the iteration is not specified.

```
> for i in [ 1, 2, 3 ] do
    print( i )
  end do;
```

$$1$$
$$2$$
$$3 \qquad (5.44)$$

Note that there is a difference between the loop above and the seemingly equivalent loop

```
> for i from 1 to 3 do
    print( i )
  end do;
```

$$1$$
$$2$$
$$3 \qquad (5.45)$$

The difference is the value of the induction variable **i** at the end of the loop. To see this, evaluate the induction variable **i** immediately after running the loop to display its value.

```
> for i in [ 1, 2, 3 ] do end do: i;
```

$$3 \qquad (5.46)$$

```
> for i from 1 to 3 do end do: i;
```

$$4 \qquad (5.47)$$

Looping Commands

Maple provides commands to create some commonly used types of loops. These commands are generally meant to build expressions without creating many intermediate expressions.

The map Command

The **map** command applies a function to every element of an aggregate object. The simplest form of the **map** command is

```
map( f, x )
```

where **f** is a function and **x** is an expression. The **map** command replaces each operand **elem** of the expression **x** with **f(elem)**.

For tables and Arrays (or other rtables), the function is applied to each entry.

```
> map( f, [a,b,c] );
```
$$[f(a), f(b), f(c)] \tag{5.48}$$

Given a list of integers, you can create a list of their absolute values and of their squares by using the **map** command.

```
> L := [ -1, 2, -3, -4, 5 ];
```
$$L := [-1, 2, -3, -4, 5] \tag{5.49}$$

```
> q:=map(abs, L);
```
$$q := [1, 2, 3, 4, 5] \tag{5.50}$$

```
> map(x->x^2, L);
```
$$[1, 4, 9, 16, 25] \tag{5.51}$$

The general syntax of the **map** command is

```
map( f, x, y1, ..., yn )
```

where **f** is a function, **x** is any expression, and **y1**, ..., **yn** are expressions. The action of **map** is to replace each operand of **x** such that the **i**th operand of **x** is replaced by **f(op(i,x), y1, ..., yn)**.

```
> map( f, a+b+c, x, y );
```
$$f(a, x, y) + f(b, x, y) + f(c, x, y) \tag{5.52}$$

```
> map( (x,y) -> x^2+y, L, 1 );
```
$$[2, 5, 10, 17, 26] \tag{5.53}$$

For more information and examples, see *Basic Data Structures (page 129)*.

The select, remove, and selectremove Commands

The **select**, **remove**, and **selectremove** commands also operate on the operands of an expression. The **select** command returns the operands for which the specified Boolean-valued function returns **true**. The **remove** command returns the operands for which the specified Boolean-valued function returns **false**. The **selectremove** command returns two objects: the operands for which the specified Boolean-valued function returns **true** and the operands for which the specified Boolean-valued function returns **false**. The **select**, **remove**, and **selectremove** commands have the same syntax as the **map** command.

```
> X := 2*x*y^2 - 3*y^4*z + 3*z*w + 2*y^3 - z^2*w*y;
```
$$X := 2xy^2 - 3y^4 z + 3zw + 2y^3 - z^2 w y \tag{5.54}$$

```
> select(has, X, z);
```
$$-3y^4z + 3zw - z^2wy \tag{5.55}$$

```
> remove( x -> degree(x)>3, X );
```
$$2xy^2 + 3zw + 2y^3 \tag{5.56}$$

For more information on these commands, see *Other Data Structure Operations (page 158)* or refer to the **select** help page.

The zip Command

The **zip** command merges two lists or Arrays and then applies a binary function. The **zip** command has two forms

| zip(f, u, v) |
| zip(f, u, v, d) |

where **f** is a binary function, **u** and **v** are both lists or rtables, and **d** is any value. The **zip** command takes each pair of operands u[i], v[i], and creates a new list or vector from **f(u[i], v[i])**.

```
> zip( (x,y) -> x || y, [a,b,c,d,e,f], [1,2,3,4,5,6] );
```
$$[a1, b2, c3, d4, e5, f6] \tag{5.57}$$

If the lists or vectors are not the same length, the length of the result depends on whether you provide the argument **d**.

If you do not specify **d**, the length of the result is the same as the length of the smaller list or vector.

```
> zip( (x,y) -> x+y, [a,b,c,d,e,f], [1,2,3] );
```
$$[a + 1, b + 2, c + 3] \tag{5.58}$$

If **d** is specified, the length of the result of the **zip** command is the same as the length of the longer list or vector. Maple replaces the missing value(s) with **d**.

```
> zip( (x,y) -> x+y, [a,b,c,d,e,f], [1,2,3], xi );
```
$$[a + 1, b + 2, c + 3, d + \xi, e + \xi, f + \xi] \tag{5.59}$$

Non-Local Flow Control

There are a couple of statements that are generally used in procedures to control how execution of the procedure ends: **return** and **error**. For more information on these statements, see *Procedures (page 199)*.

The return Statement

The **return** statement causes an immediate return to the point where the current procedure was invoked.

In Command-line Maple, the **return** statement causes an error if it is run at the top level: *Error, return out of context*. In the Standard worksheet interface, **return** can be used at the top level in conjunction with **DocumentTools:-RunWorksheet**.

The error Statement and Exception Handling

The **error** statement raises an exception and interrupts the execution of the current statement. If the exception is not caught (see the following section), a message is printed indicating that an error occurred.

```
error string
```
```
error string, parameter1, parameter2, ...
```

In the first case, an error message is given as a **string**.

```
> error "my error";
```
Error, my error

In the second case, **string** contains several placeholders of the form **%n** or **%-n**, where **n** is a positive integer, to include the provided parameters in the message.

The placeholder **%n** is replaced by the **n**th parameter given. The placeholder **%-n** is replaced by the ordinal form of the **n**th parameter, which should evaluate to an integer. The special placeholder **%0** is replaced with the sequence of all parameters separated by commas and spaces.

```
> x := a+b: n := 10;
```
$$n := 10 \qquad (5.60)$$

```
> error "my error in %1 of the %-2 kind", x, n;
```
Error, my error in a+b of the 10th kind

Trapping Errors

The **try** statement is a mechanism for executing procedure statements in a controlled environment so that if an error occurs, it does not immediately terminate the procedure. The **try** statement has the following syntax

```
try tryStatSeq
    catch catchStrings : catchStatSeq
```

```
    finally finalStatSeq
end try
```

This statement can include several **catch** clauses. The **finally** clause is optional.

If procedure execution enters a **try...catch** block, the **tryStatSeq** is executed. If *no* exceptions occur during the execution of **tryStatSeq**, the **finalStatSeq** in the **finally** clause (if present) is executed. Execution then continues with the statement after **end try**.

If an exception *occurs* during the execution of **tryStatSeq**, execution of **tryStatSeq** terminates immediately. The exception object corresponding to the exception is compared against each **catchString**. Any number of catch clauses can be provided, and each can have any number of **catchStrings** separated by commas. Alternatively, a catch clause does not need to have a catch string. Any given **catchString** (or a catch clause without one) can appear only once in a **try...end try** construct.

If a matching catch clause is found, or the catch clause contains no **catchStrings**, the **catchStatSeq** of that catch clause is executed, and the exception is considered to have been caught. If no matching catch clause is found, the exception is considered *not caught*, and is re-raised outside of the **try** block.

When Maple searches for a matching catch clause, the following definition of "matching" is used.

- Neither the exception object nor the **catchStrings** are evaluated (the exception object has already been evaluated by the error statement that produced it).
- The **catchStrings** are considered to be prefixes of the exception object's **msgString**. If a **catchString** has **n** characters, only the first **n** characters of the **msgString** need to match the **catchString**. This permits the definition of classes of exceptions.
- A catch clause without a **catchString** matches any exception.
- The "result" of a **try** statement (the value that **%** returns if it is evaluated immediately after execution of the **try** statement) is the result of the last statement executed in the **try** statement.

A **catchStatSeq** can contain an **error** statement with no arguments, which also re-raises the exception. When an exception is re-raised, a new exception object is created that records the current procedure name, and the message and parameters from the original exception.

Normally, the **finalStatSeq** of the **finally** clause, if there is one, is always executed before control leaves the **try** statement. This is true in the case that an exception occurs, independent of whether it is caught or whether another exception occurs in the **catch** clause.

This is true even if a **catchStatSeq** re-raises the exception, raises a new one, or executes a **return**, **break**, or **next** statement.

Under certain abnormal circumstances, the **finalStatSeq** is not executed:

- If an exception is caught in an interactive debugger session and you exit the debugger
- If one of the following untrappable exceptions occurs, the exception is not caught, and **finalStatSeq** is not executed:

1. A computation timed out. This exception can only be caught by the **timelimit** command, which raises a "time expired" exception that can be caught. For more information on the **timelimit** command, refer to the **timelimit** help page.
2. A computation has been interrupted. In other words, you pressed **Ctrl+C**, **Break**, or equivalent.
3. Internal system error. This exception indicates a bug in Maple itself.
4. **ASSERT** or local variable type assertion failure. Assertion failures cannot be trapped because they indicate a coding error, not an algorithmic failure.
5. Stack overflow. If a stack overflow occurs, there is generally not enough stack space to perform tasks such as running cleanup code.

If an exception occurs during the execution of a **catchStatSeq** or the **finalStatSeq**, it is treated in the same way as if it occurred outside the **try...end try** statement.

Example 1

A useful application of the **try** and **error** statements is to stop a large computation as quickly and cleanly as possible. For example, suppose that you are trying to compute an integral by using one of several methods, and in the middle of the first method, you determine that it will not succeed. You want to stop that method and try another one. The following code implements this example.

```
> try
      result := MethodA(f,x)
   catch "FAIL":
      result := MethodB(f,x)
   end try:
```

MethodA can stop its computation at any time by executing the statement **error "FAIL"**. The catch clause catches that exception, and proceeds to try **MethodB**. If any other error occurs during the execution of **MethodA**, or if an error occurs during the execution of **MethodB**, it is not caught.

Example 2

Another useful application of the **try** statement is to ensure that certain resources are made available when you are done with them, regardless of whether anything went wrong while you were using them.

Use the following code to access the Maple I/O facilities to read the lines of a file and process them in some way.

```
> f := fopen("myfile",READ,TEXT):
  try
    line := readline(f);
    while line < 0 do
        ProcessContentsOfLine(line);
        line := readline(f)
    end do
  finally
    fclose(f)
  end try:
```

In this example, if any exception occurs while reading or processing the lines of the file, it is not caught because there is no catch clause. However, **fclose(f)** is executed before execution leaves the **try** statement, regardless of whether there was an exception.

The next example uses both **catch** and **finally** clauses to write to a file instead of reading from one.

```
> f := fopen("myfile",WRITE,TEXT):
  try
    for i to 100 do
        fprintf(f,"Result %d is %q\n",i,ComputeSomething(i))
    end do
  catch:
    fprintf(f,"Something went wrong: %q\n",lastexception);
    error
  finally
    fclose(f)
  end try:
```

If an exception occurs, it is caught with the catch clause that has no **catchString**, and the exception object is written into the file. The exception is re-raised by executing the **error** statement with no **msgString**. In all cases, the file is closed by executing **fclose(f)** in the **finally** clause.

5.7 The use Statement

The **use** statement specifies local bindings of names, module exports, and operator overriding. It has the following syntax:

```
use exprseq in
```

```
      stateseq
end use
```

where **stateseq** is a sequence of statements and **exprseq** is a sequence of expressions.

The expressions can be any of the following.

- equation of the form **name = expression**
- module member selection **m:-e**, which is equivalent to the equation **e = m:-e**
- module expression **m**, which is equivalent to the equations **e = m:-e** for all exports **e** of **m**.

For more information about modules and member selection, see *Programming with Modules (page 309)*.

Running a **use** statement executes the body of the statement. Each occurrence of a name that appears on the left side of any of the binding equations is replaced by the right side of the corresponding equation.

For example,

```
> use f = sin, g = cos in
      f( x )^2 + g( x )^2
  end use;
```

$$\sin(x)^2 + \cos(x)^2 \qquad (5.61)$$

The following example establishes local bindings for all of the exports of the **StringTools** package.

```
> use StringTools in
     s := Random( 10, 'lower' );
     Reverse( s )
  end use;
```

$$s := \text{"dzremaidwi"}$$

$$\text{"iwdiamerzd"} \qquad (5.62)$$

Among these are the names **Random** and **Reverse**. Without the **use** statement enclosing them, the two statements would have to be written using fully qualified names.

```
> s := StringTools:-Random( 10, 'lower' );
```

$$s := \text{"qknnyxmuvd"} \qquad (5.63)$$

```
> StringTools:-Reverse( s );
```
$$\text{"dvumxynnkq"} \tag{5.64}$$

You can employ the **use** statement to establish general name bindings.

```
> use a = 2, b = 3, c = 4 in
     a + b + c
  end use;
```
$$9 \tag{5.65}$$

(This is useful when the names bound are used many times within the body of the **use** statement.)

The **use** statement is unique in Maple. It is the only Maple statement that is resolved during the automatic simplification process rather than during the evaluation process. To see this, consider the following simple procedure.

```
> p := proc( x, y )
     use a = x + y, b = x * y in
        a / b
     end use
  end proc;
```
$$p := \mathbf{proc}(x, y) \ (x+y)/(x*y) \ \mathbf{end \ proc} \tag{5.66}$$

Note that there is no **use** statement in the procedure after it has been processed, and **a** and **b** in the body have been replaced by the values on the right-hand side of the binding equations. To see that this processing occurred during automatic simplification (of the procedure definition), enclose the procedure definition in unevaluation quotes.

```
> p := 'proc( x, y )
     use a = x + y, b = x * y in
        a / b
     end use
  end proc';
```
$$p := \mathbf{proc}(x, y) \ (x+y)/(x*y) \ \mathbf{end \ proc} \tag{5.67}$$

use statements can be nested.

```
> use a = 2, b = 4 in
     use x = 3, y = 5 in
        a * x + b * y
     end use
  end use;
```

$$26 \tag{5.68}$$

If a name is bound in **use** statements at two different levels of nesting, the innermost binding visible at the level of an expression is used.

```
> use a = 2 in
    a^2;
    use a = 3 in
        a^2
    end use
  end use;
```

$$4$$
$$9 \tag{5.69}$$

In the following example, the inner binding of the value **3** to the name **a** takes precedence, so the value of the expression **a + b** (and therefore the entire statement) is the number **6**. The inner binding of **3** to **a** has an effect only within the body of the inner **use** statement. Once the execution has exited the inner **use** statement, the binding of **2** to **a** is restored.

```
> use a = 2, b = 3 in
      # here a is bound to 2 and b to 3
      use a = 3 in
          # here, b is still bound to 3, but a is bound to 3
          a + b
      end use;
      # binding of a to 2 is restored
      a + b
  end use;
```

$$6$$
$$5 \tag{5.70}$$

The **use** statement also allows you to rebind Maple operators to override their default behavior. The following is an example in which addition and multiplication are replaced by nonstandard meanings.

```
> use `+` = ((x,y) -> (x+y) mod 3), `*` = ((x,y) -> (x*y) mod 3) in
      1 + 2 * 4
  end use;
```

$$0 \tag{5.71}$$

The following operators can have their default behavior overridden by a **use** statement.

Table 5.1: Operators That Can Be Rebound

@	@@	%	%%	%%%	.
+	*	-	/	mod	^
!	union	minus	intersect	subset	in
$	and	or	not	xor	implies
=	<>	<	<=	assuming	<|>
<,>	[]	{}	?()	?[]	~

Notes:

- The following operators cannot be rebound: concatenation operator (||), member selection operator (:-), type operator (::), range (..), comma (,), functional operator (->), and the assignment operator (:=). The relational operators > and >= can be rebound, but not independently of < and <=, respectively.
- All of the element-wise operators are processed through the element-wise operator (~).
- The operators - and / are treated as *unary* operators (that represent negation and inversion, respectively). Subtraction is represented internally in Maple by forming addition and negation: **a - b = a + (-b)**. Division is formed in a similar way. Therefore, it is not necessary to override the *binary* infix operators - and /.

Note also that an expression such as **a + b + c + d** is treated as though it were parenthesized as **((a + b) + c) + d**, so that each + operator is binary. For example,

```
> use `+` = F in
     a + b + c + d;
     a + ( ( b + c ) + d )
  end use;
```

$$F(F(F(a,b),c),d)$$
$$F(a,F(F(b,c),d)) \tag{5.72}$$

5.8 Other Statements

The quit Statement

The Maple keywords **quit**, **done**, and **stop** perform the same task and, when entered in the command-line interface, cause the Maple process to terminate.

```
> quit
```

```
> done
> stop
```

Note: The **quit** statement cannot be used in the Maple standard interface. In the standard interface, use **File > Close Document** to end your Maple session.

quit, **stop**, and **done** are available as command names if quoted using name quotes. These forms allow you to exit Maple while passing an integer in the range **0 .. 255** as an argument to be returned to the calling process as exit status.

The save Statement

You can save Maple expressions to a file by using the **save** statement. It has the general form

```
save name1, name2, ..., nameN, file
```

The names **namei** are names (that have assigned values) to be saved to the file **file**.

Normally, the file name **file** is a string.

For example, make the following three assignments and run the subsequent **save** statement.

```
> a := proc( x ) sin( x / 2 ) end proc:
> b := 42:
> c := "some text":
> save a, b, c, "myfile.txt";
```

The file **myfile.txt** is created in the current directory (assuming adequate file permissions) containing the following Maple assignment statements.

```
a := proc (x) sin(1/2\*x) end proc;
b := 42;
c := "some text";
```

The read Statement

The **read** statement takes the following form.

```
read filename
```

where **filename** is a string.

```
> read "myfile.txt";
```

$$c := \text{"some text"}$$
$$b := 42$$
$$a := \mathbf{proc}(x) \ \sin(1/2*x) \ \mathbf{end\ proc} \tag{5.73}$$

The file named by **filename** must consist of valid Maple language statements. The statements in the file are executed as they are read, as though they were input into the Maple session in which the **read** statement was entered. Maple displays the results of executing each statement. However, the input statements are *not* echoed to the interface, by default. To change this, set the interface variable **echo** to a value of 2 or higher.

```
> interface( 'echo' = 2 ):
```

5.9 Exercises

1. Find the product of the square root of all prime numbers less than **100**.

   Hint: The function **isprime** determines the primality of an integer.

2. Find the sum of all odd composite numbers less than **150**.

3. Find the sum of the first **30** powers of **2**.

4. Write a looping structure that finds the four substrings (of a string assigned to the name **MyString**) containing only lowercase letters, uppercase letters, decimal digits, and special characters.

   Hint: You can use relational operators to compare characters.

5. Write a procedure, **SPLIT**, that, upon input of a product **f** and a variable **x**, returns a list of two values. The first item in the list should be the product of the factors in **f** that are independent of **x**, and the second item should be the product of the factors that contain an **x**.

   Hint: Use the **has**, **select**, **remove**, and **selectremove** commands.

6 Procedures

A Maple procedure is a sequence of parameter declarations, variable declarations, and statements that encapsulates a computation. Once defined, a procedure can be used to perform the same computation repeatedly for different argument values, from different places in a program, or both. A procedure in Maple corresponds to a function in languages such as C or Java, a procedure or function in Pascal, or a subroutine in FORTRAN and modern versions of BASIC.

Chapter 1 gave a brief introduction to procedures. This chapter describes the syntax and semantics of procedures in detail, and discusses how to best make use of procedures in your programs.

6.1 Terminology

Several terms are used frequently when discussing procedures in Maple and other programming languages. Some of these terms are sometimes used interchangeably, but the distinctions between them are important:

Procedure - In Maple, a procedure is an object that can be invoked by a function call, be passed arguments, perform some operations, and return a result. A procedure definition begins with the keyword **proc**, and ends with **end proc**.

Function Call - A function call, of the form **name(arguments)**, evaluates the **arguments** and then invokes a procedure if **name** has a value that is a procedure. The value of the function call is then the value returned by the procedure. If **name** has no value, then the value of the function call is just **name(evaluatedArguments)**.

Argument - An argument is one of one or more values explicitly included in a function call. Note that a default value is not an argument.

Parameter or *Formal Parameter* - A parameter is a name that is declared in a procedure definition to receive the value of an argument. The parameter name is used to refer to that value within the body of the procedure.

Actual Parameter - An actual parameter is neither an argument nor a (formal) parameter. The term refers to the value that a formal parameter takes during the execution of a procedure. This value can come from an argument or a default value. The term is defined here for completeness; it is not further used in this chapter. Instead we will refer to *the value of the parameter*.

6.2 Defining and Executing Procedures

A Maple procedure definition has the following general syntax:

```
proc( parameterDeclarations ) :: returnType;
    description shortDescription;
    option optionSequence;
    local localVariableDeclarations;
    global globalVariableDeclarations;
    statementSequence
end proc
```

A procedure definition is considered to be an expression in Maple, the evaluation of which produces the procedure itself. The resulting procedure is usually assigned to a name, but it can also be used in other ways such as passing it as an argument to another procedure, or invoking it immediately.

The following is a simple procedure definition. It contains two formal parameters, **x** and **y**, and one statement in the procedure body. There is no description, there are no options, and the procedure does not make use of any local or global variables. In order to be able to use the procedure later, we'll assign it to a name:

```
> SumOfSquares := proc( x, y )
    x^2 + y^2
  end proc;
```

$$SumOfSquares := \mathbf{proc}(x, y) \; x^\wedge 2 + y^\wedge 2 \; \mathbf{end \; proc} \tag{6.1}$$

This procedure computes the sum of the squares of its two arguments. The procedure can be called with any two arguments and Maple will attempt to compute the sum of their squares. Like any computation in Maple, the result can be symbolic. If you want to restrict the types of arguments that are permitted, it is possible to specify the **type** for each argument in the parameter declarations, as described in the next section.

You can invoke (or execute) a procedure by using it in a *function call*:

```
procedureName( argumentSequence )
```

The **procedureName** is usually the name that the procedure was assigned to, although it can also be an actual procedure definition, or another expression that evaluates to a procedure.

The **argumentSequence** is a sequence of expressions that will be evaluated, and then substituted for the corresponding parameters before the execution of the statements comprising the body of the procedure. Note that the arguments are evaluated only once before the execution of the procedure begins. They are *not* evaluated again during execution of the procedure.

The value returned by the procedure is the result of the last statement executed within the procedure. In the following function call, Maple executes the statements in the body of the procedure **SumOfSquares**, replacing the formal parameters **x** and **y** with the arguments **a** and **3**. The result of the last (and in this case, only) statement in the procedure is the returned value:

```
> SumOfSquares(a,3);
```

$$a^2 + 9 \tag{6.2}$$

For more information about return values, see *Returning Values from a Procedure (page 238)*.

6.3 Parameter Declarations

In the procedure definition, **parameterDeclarations** is a sequence of parameter declarations. Procedure parameter declarations can range from very simple to very sophisticated. In its simplest form, a parameter declaration is just the parameter's name. When you call the procedure, you can pass any value as an argument for such a parameter, and if you pass no value at all, the parameter will have no value.

You can extend a parameter declaration by adding a type specification and/or a default value. A type specification ensures that, when the procedure is called, the value of the parameter within the procedure will be of the indicated type, and a default value ensures that a parameter will always have a value even if no corresponding argument was passed.

Maple procedures can also have *keyword parameters*. When invoking a procedure, the corresponding arguments are of the form **keyword=value**, and can appear anywhere in the argument sequence.

When you call a procedure, the arguments are evaluated and then bound to the parameters. In the simplest case, there is a one-to-one correspondence between arguments and parameters; the first argument is bound to the first parameter, the second argument to the second parameter, and so on. The presence of default values and keyword parameters can change this correspondence, as described in this section.

Required Positional Parameters

A required positional parameter is called *required* because a corresponding argument must have been passed in the function call that invoked the procedure if the parameter is used during the execution of the procedure. It is called *positional* because the argument's position within **argumentSequence** must correspond to the position of the parameter in **parameterDeclarations**.

The syntax to declare a required positional parameter is:

```
parameterName :: parameterType
```

The **parameterName** must be a valid symbol, and is used to refer to the parameter within the procedure body. The **:: parameterType** is optional. If it is present and the corresponding argument does not match the specified type, an exception is raised.

In this example, the procedure **Adder** is defined with two parameters, **a** and **b**. The procedure returns the sum of its two arguments. For the parameter **a**, **Adder** expects an argument of type **integer**.

```
> Adder := proc( a::integer, b ) a+b end proc:
> Adder(2,3);
```

$$5 \tag{6.3}$$

The next call to **Adder** raises an exception because the second argument is missing.

```
> Adder(3);
Error, invalid input: Adder uses a 2nd argument, b, which is missing
```

This call raises an exception because the supplied first argument does not match the parameter's specified type.

```
> Adder(2.5,4);
Error, invalid input: Adder expects its 1st argument, a, to be of type
   integer, but received 2.5
```

If a procedure has both required and ordered parameters (described below), all of the required parameters must appear *before* the ordered parameters.

Optional Ordered Parameters

An optional ordered parameter is declared in the same way as a required positional parameter, with the addition of a default value:

```
parameterName :: parameterType := defaultValue
```

The presence of **defaultValue** allows the parameter to be optional. If there are no remaining arguments or the next unused argument does not match the specified **parameterType**, the parameter receives the default value. The non-matching argument, if any, remains available for binding to a later parameter.

As was the case with a required positional parameter, **:: parameterType** can be omitted. The parameter will receive its default value only when there are no more available arguments, since any available argument would have been valid for an untyped parameter.

Usually, **defaultValue** will be of the type specified by **parameterType**, but this need not be the case. The default value can be a *literal* value of any other type, or **NULL**. If the default value is not a literal value, but is an expression that evaluates to something other than itself, then the result of that evaluation must conform to **parameterType**.

This class of parameters is called *ordered* because the arguments are bound to parameters in the order they were passed. If the first unused argument is not bound to the current parameter, it remains as the first available argument for the next parameter.

In this example, the procedure **Adder** is defined with two optional ordered parameters, **a** and **b**, both of type **integer**, and returns their sum:

```
> Adder := proc(a::integer := 10, b::integer := 100.1)
    a + b
  end proc:
> Adder(3,4);
```

$$7 \tag{6.4}$$

```
> Adder(3);
```

$$103.1 \tag{6.5}$$

```
> Adder();
```

$$110.1 \tag{6.6}$$

```
> Adder(3,6.6);
```

$$103.1 \tag{6.7}$$

In the first call to **Adder**, the arguments **3** and **4** were bound to the parameters **a** and **b**, and their sum returned. In the second call, only a single argument was passed, so **b** received its default value. Notice that the default value is not an **integer**, but since it is a literal value, is an acceptable default. In the third call, no arguments were passed and both parameters received their default values.

You may have expected the result of the fourth call to **Adder** to be 9.6, but this is not the case. Why? First, parameter **a** was given the value **3**. Next, **6.6** was considered a candidate for parameter **b**, but was rejected because it is not of type **integer**. Instead, **b** received its default value.

This illustrates an important aspect of calling procedures in Maple, which is that in general, it is acceptable to call a procedure with more arguments than it expects. You will see later how to access these within a procedure, allowing you to write procedures that accept a variable number of arguments, or how to disallow the passing of extra arguments.

Expected Ordered Parameters

An expected ordered parameter is similar to an optional ordered parameter, except that the corresponding argument can be omitted only if all further arguments are also omitted. If there is an argument available, it must match **parameterType** or an exception is raised.

The declaration of an expected ordered parameter declaration differs from that of an optional ordered parameter by enclosing **parameterType** in **expects()**:

```
parameterName :: expects( parameterType ) := defaultValue
```

The procedure below is identical to the one from the previous section, except that parameter **b** has been declared as an expected parameter. When it is called with a second argument of the wrong type, instead of saving that argument for a later parameter, Maple raises an exception:

```
> Adder := proc(a::integer := 10, b::expects(integer) := 100.1)
      a + b
  end proc:
> Adder(3,6.6);
Error, invalid input: Adder expects its 2nd argument, b, to be of type
 integer, but received 6.6
```

Keyword Parameters

Keyword parameters are not positional and not ordered. A keyword parameter is bound to a value when an argument of the form **keyword=value** appears in a procedure invocation. The left-hand side of such an argument specifies the keyword parameter name, and the right-hand side specifies the value it will receive. If **true** is an acceptable value for the parameter, then an argument of the form **keyword** is equivalent to **keyword=true**.

The declaration of a keyword parameter looks very much like that of an optional ordered parameter, except that all keyword parameter declarations are enclosed in braces, much like a **set** is:

```
{ ... parameterName :: parameterType := defaultValue ... }
```

The **:: parameterType** can be omitted, in which case any value can be passed as the right-hand side of the keyword argument. If **parameterType** is specified, then the passed value must be of that type.

As is the case with an ordered parameter, if **defaultValue** is a *literal* value, it need not match **parameterType**.

A procedure can have multiple keyword parameters, which can be declared within a single set of braces, or grouped into multiple sets of braces as desired to improve source code readability. When a procedure is compiled into Maple's internal form, the keyword parameters are consolidated into a single set. If you then display that procedure using Maple's **print** command, the keyword parameters are displayed as a single set, sorted lexicographically.

The simplest and most frequently encountered form of keyword parameter declaration has a single Maple symbol for **parameterName**:

```
> Simple := proc( { simple::integer := 2 } )
      sprintf("simple=%d",simple)
  end proc:
> Simple(simple=3);
```

$$\text{"simple=3"} \tag{6.8}$$

```
> Simple();
```

$$\text{"simple=2"} \tag{6.9}$$

```
> Simple(simple=4.5);
Error, invalid input: Simple expects value for keyword parameter simple
  to be of type integer, but received 4.5
```

It is also possible to declare keyword parameters that can be referred to by indexed names when the procedure is called. If **parameterName** is of the form `` `symbol[symbol]` `` or `` `symbol[integer]` ``, it matches indexed names.

The indexed parameter names are still *symbols* because of the enclosing left single quotes, and are referenced that way within the procedure, but the argument names can be actual indexed names. For more information on indexed keyword arguments, see *Binding of Arguments to Parameters (page 232)*.

As a convenience to the user of a procedure, multiple spellings of the keyword are allowed by specifying a list of the permitted spellings in the declaration:

```
{ ... [ parameterName1, parameterName2, ... ] :: parameterType :=
defaultValue ... }
```

Within the procedure's **statementSequence**, you can refer to the parameter by any of the declared spellings. If you display the procedure using **print**, however, only the first spelling is used.

```
> Spellings := proc( { [color,colour]::symbol := RED } )
     sprintf("color=%a -- colour=%a", color, colour)
  end proc;
```

$$\mathit{Spellings} := \mathbf{proc}(\{[\mathit{color}, \mathit{colour}]{::}\mathit{symbol} := \mathit{RED}\}) \qquad (6.10)$$
$$\qquad \mathit{sprintf}(\text{"color=\%a -- colour=\%a"}, \mathit{color}, \mathit{color})$$
$$\mathbf{end\ proc}$$

```
> Spellings();
```

$$\text{"color=RED -- colour=RED"} \qquad (6.11)$$

```
> Spellings(color=BLUE);
```

$$\text{"color=BLUE -- colour=BLUE"} \qquad (6.12)$$

```
> Spellings(colour=GREEN);
```

$$\text{"color=GREEN -- colour=GREEN"} \qquad (6.13)$$

```
> Spellings(color=ORANGE,colour=PURPLE);
```

$$\text{"color=PURPLE -- colour=PURPLE"} \qquad (6.14)$$

```
> Spellings(colour=YELLOW,color=42);
Error, invalid input: Spellings expects value for keyword parameter
[color, colour] to be of type symbol, but received 42
```

If more than one keyword argument matches a keyword parameter, only the last one takes effect.

Alternate spellings and indexed keywords can be combined by including the indexed keyword symbols in the list of alternate spellings.

The End-of-Parameters Marker

Recall from earlier that Maple usually allows extra arguments to be passed to a procedure. This is useful when implementing procedures that can accept a variable number or type of arguments, but for many procedures, the presence of extra arguments indicates a programming error.

A procedure can be declared to disallow extra arguments (that is, arguments that were not bound to any declared parameter) by ending the sequence **parameterDeclarations** with **$**. If extra arguments remain at the end of argument processing, Maple raises an exception:

```
> TwoSine := proc( x::float := 0.0, $ ) 2 * sin(x) end proc:
> TwoSine(2.3);
```

$$1.491410424 \qquad (6.15)$$

```
> TwoSine();
```
$$0. \tag{6.16}$$
```
> TwoSine(2.3,-4.5);
Error, invalid input: too many and/or wrong type of arguments passed
  to TwoSine; first unused argument is -4.5
> TwoSine(42);
Error, invalid input: too many and/or wrong type of arguments passed
  to TwoSine; first unused argument is 42
```

Default Value Dependencies

You can express the default value **defaultValue** of a parameter in terms of other parameters, as long as the resulting value conforms to the specified type **parameterType**, if any. The parameters on which **defaultValue** depends can appear earlier or later in **parameterDeclarations**. For example, here is a list extraction function that expects a list, a starting index, and an ending index. If the ending index is omitted, the length of the list is used:

```
> SubList := proc( s::list, f::integer := 1, t::integer :=
  numelems(s) )
      s[f..t]
  end proc:
> SubList([a,b,c,d,e],2,3);
```
$$[b, c] \tag{6.17}$$
```
> SubList([a,b,c,d,e],2);
```
$$[b, c, d, e] \tag{6.18}$$

There can be no cyclic dependencies, such as two parameters' default values depending on each other:

```
> NotGood := proc( s := sin(c), c := cos(s) ) s^2 + c^2 end proc;
Error, cyclic dependency detected in parameter s := sin(c) in procedure
  NotGood
```

Usually, Maple evaluates the arguments of a function call from left to right. The use of parameter dependencies in default values will alter this order to ensure that the required values are available by the time they are needed. This is only of consequence if the evaluation of one or more arguments has side effects.

Parameter Modifiers

Parameter modifiers change the way that arguments are evaluated and/or bound to parameters. Modifiers appear as part of the parameter's declaration, in the form of a function call enclosing the parameter type **parameterType**.

You have already seen the **expects** modifier, which changes an optional ordered parameter into an expected ordered parameter.

The seq Modifier

The **seq** modifier allows the parameter to match multiple arguments. When a parameter with a specified type of the form **seq(memberType)** is encountered, it is bound to an expression sequence of all arguments (beginning with the next available one) that are of the type specified by **memberType**.

```
parameterName :: seq(memberType)
```

If *no* arguments match **memberType**, the parameter will receive its default value if one was specified, or **NULL** if there is no default value.

The **seq** modifier cannot be used together with the **expects** modifier, because **seq** is allowed to match zero arguments, whereas **expects** implies that at least one argument must match. The **seq** modifier also cannot be used with a keyword parameter.

You must be careful when working with the value of a **seq** parameter because it might have just one element in it. Such a value is not considered to be a sequence, thus indexing it will not select the element. The safest approach is to enclose the parameter in a list, as in this example:

```
> LargestInteger := proc( x::seq(integer), other::seq(anything) )
    local max, n;
    max := -infinity;
    for n in [x] do
        if n > max then max := n end if
    end do;
    max, [other]
  end proc:
> LargestInteger(4,7,8,2,1);
```
$$8, [\,] \qquad (6.19)$$

```
> LargestInteger(4,7,"not an integer",8,2,1);
```
$$7, [\text{"not an integer"}, 8, 2, 1] \qquad (6.20)$$

The depends Modifier

Usually, a parameter's type is predetermined when the procedure is first written. When arguments are matched to parameters, **parameterType** is not evaluated since this is not expected to yield anything other than what was written. There are cases where this is too restrictive. In that case, use the **depends** modifier to declare that a parameter's type depends on something that could change. Such a dependency is usually on another parameter.

The syntax for a parameter declaration with the **depends** modifier is:

```
parameterName :: depends( parameterTypeExpression )
```

where **parameterTypeExpression** is a type expression that can refer to other parameter names.

For example, you might want to write a procedure like this to find one root of a polynomial:

```
> OneRoot := proc( p::depends(polynom(integer,v)), v::symbol )
      local sols;
      sols := [ solve(p=0,v) ];
      if sols = [] then
          error "no solution"
      else
          sols[1]
      end if
  end proc:
> OneRoot(x^2+3*x+5,x);
```

$$-\frac{3}{2} + \frac{1}{2} \cdot I\sqrt{11} \qquad (6.21)$$

```
> OneRoot(x^2+3*x+5,y);
```

```
Error, invalid input: OneRoot expects its 1st argument, p, to be of
type polynom(integer, y), but received x^2+3*x+5
```

This procedure expects as an argument for its first parameter, **p**, a polynomial in the variable specified by the second parameter, **v**. If the **depends** modifier were omitted, the procedure would only accept polynomials in the global variable **v**.

The **depends** modifier can only be used for required parameters. It cannot be used for optional or expected ordered parameters, nor keyword parameters. If the **depends** modifier is used together with the **seq** modifier, it must appear within it. That is, **parameterType** must be written in the form **seq(depends(memberType))**.

The uneval Modifier

Unlike the other modifiers described so far, the **uneval** modifier takes no arguments. That is, it does *not* enclose another type or modified type. Instead it is used *as* the **parameterType**.

```
parameterName :: uneval
```

A parameter with the **uneval** modifier prevents the corresponding argument from being evaluated when the procedure is called. The effect is the same as if the argument had been enclosed in unevaluation quotes ('...').

The **uneval** modifier can only be used for required positional parameters, and cannot be used in conjunction with any other modifiers. It also cannot be used for any parameter declaration after one that uses the **seq** modifier.

```
> Square := proc( x::uneval ) x^2 end proc:
> (a, b) := (3, 4.5):
> r := Square(a+b);
```

$$r := (a+b)^2 \tag{6.22}$$

```
> eval(r);
```

$$56.25 \tag{6.23}$$

The evaln Modifier

A parameter declared with the **evaln** modifier expects an argument that can be evaluated to a name (that is, an assignable object). This modifier can be used in two different forms, **evaln** or **evaln(valueType)**. In the second form, the resulting name is expected to have a value that matches the type **valueType**.

```
parameterName :: evaln
```

```
parameterName :: evaln(valueType)
```

In effect, declaring a *parameter* with the **evaln** modifier is equivalent to enclosing the *argument* with **evaln** at procedure invocation time, and allows you to write procedures where the user of the procedure does not have to remember to do so.

Like **uneval**, the **evaln** modifier can only be used for required positional parameters, and cannot be used for a parameter declaration after one having a **seq** modifier. The only other modifier that can be used together with **evaln** is the **depends** modifier, in the form **depends(evaln(valueType))**.

```
> SquareName := proc( x::evaln(integer) ) x^2 end proc:
> (a, b) := (3, 4.5):
```

In the first call, the argument **a** is evaluated to **'a'**, which is a name with an integer value.

```
> SquareName(a);
```

$$a^2 \qquad (6.24)$$

In the next call, the argument **b** is evaluated to **'b'**, which is a name, but not with an integer value.

```
> SquareName(b);
Error, invalid input: SquareName expects its 1st argument, x, to be
of type evaln(integer), but received b := 4.5
```

In the next call, the argument does not evaluate to a name.

```
> SquareName(a+b);
Error, illegal use of an object as a name
```

In the next example, the procedure **Accumulate** accumulates all the values of its second argument in the variable passed as its first argument. Notice that the first call fails, because **Accumulate** expects a name with a numeric value, but **total** has not been initialized yet.

```
> Accumulate := proc( r::evaln(numeric), n::numeric )
      r := eval(r) + n
  end proc:
> Accumulate(total,2);
Error, invalid input: Accumulate expects its 1st argument, r, to be
of type evaln(numeric), but received total := total
> total := 0;
```

$$total := 0 \qquad (6.25)$$

```
> Accumulate(total,2);
```

$$2 \qquad (6.26)$$

```
> Accumulate(total,3.5);
```

$$5.5 \qquad (6.27)$$

```
> total;
```

$$5.5 \qquad (6.28)$$

The coercion Modifiers

```
parameterName :: (valueType)
```

```
parameterName :: coerce(valueType, coercion procedure)
```

As stated previously in Chapter 4, coercion refers to the ability to pass one type of data to a procedure and have it receive a different type.

Coercion can be enabled in two ways:

- **Coercion Using ~Type**: You can use a short form notation to invoke Maple built-in coercion functions. This short form notation is a tilde (~) followed by a data type. For example, the command **~Matrix** will accept, among other things, a **listlist** and return a Matrix. This type of ~ function can be used in place of the data type in a procedure declaration. This tells Maple to try testing if the passed parameter is of that type, and if not, call the ~ function to coerce it into that type.

- **Coercion Using coerce()**: You can use long form notation to enable data coercion by using the **coerce()** modifier. The coerce modifier allows you to specify a sequence of types and coercion procedures. A coercion procedure is a procedure that accepts a single typed parameter and converts that parameter into a new expression. When the main procedure is called, the argument is type checked against the parameter types handled by the coercion procedure. The first coercion procedure whose parameter's type matches the type of the argument is called. The return value of the matching coercion procedure is then used as the parameter's value.

```
> p_string :=proc(s::coerce(string, (s::name)->convert(s,string)))
    s;
  end proc;
```

$$p\_string := \mathbf{proc}(s::(coerce(string, s::name \rightarrow convert(s, string))))$$
$$s$$
$$\mathbf{end\ proc} \tag{6.29}$$

```
> p_string("a string");
```

$$\text{"a string"} \tag{6.30}$$

```
> p_string(`a name`);
```

$$\text{"a name"} \tag{6.31}$$

Procedures without Declared Parameters

You can define a procedure without any declared parameters. Some procedures, such as one that generates random numbers, might not depend on any arguments. Other procedures might operate directly on global values, although this is considered poor programming practice.

However, just because a procedure has no declared parameters does not mean that it cannot be passed arguments. Unless a procedure's **parameterDeclarations** ends with $, it is always permissible to pass more arguments than there are declared parameters. All of the arguments are accessible via the special sequence **_passed**, which has one entry corresponding to each argument that was passed. The number of entries is given by **_npassed**. For example, the following procedure produces the sum of all its arguments:

```
> SumOfArgs := proc( )
      add(_passed[i], i=1.._npassed)
  end proc:
> SumOfArgs(42,3.14,sin(-2.5));
```

$$44.54152786 \qquad (6.32)$$

For more information on **_passed** and **_npassed** as well as other special names for working with parameters, see *Special Sequences for Referring to Parameters and Arguments (page 227)*.

6.4 Return Type

The closing parenthesis following a procedure's parameter declarations can be followed by :: and a **returnType** assertion. This is optional. Unlike a **parameterType** specification, **returnType** is only an **assertion**. If **kernelopts(assertlevel)** is set to 2, the type of the value returned by the procedure is checked against the type specified by **returnType**, and if it does not match, an exception is raised:

```
> ReturnInteger := proc( x ) :: integer;
      x^2
  end proc:
> kernelopts(assertlevel=2):
> ReturnInteger(3);
```

$$9 \qquad (6.33)$$

```
> ReturnInteger(Pi);
Error, (in ReturnInteger) assertion failed: ReturnInteger expects its
  return value to be of type integer, but computed Pi^2
```

6.5 The Procedure Body

The body of the procedure is where most of the computation is carried out (although some computation may already have occurred while resolving the **defaultValue** for optional parameters). The procedure body consists of an optional description, option declarations, local and global variable declarations, and executable statements.

The description, option, local variable, and global variable declaration parts are each introduced by their own keyword, and can appear in any order. There can be only one **description** clause and one **option** clause. There can be any number of variable declaration clauses.

Description

Use the description clause to give a procedure a short description that is displayed when the procedure is displayed. The description has no effect on the execution of the procedure. It is only used for documentation purposes.

```
description string, string, ... ;
```

The **description** keyword is followed by one or more string literals, separated by commas.

```
> Average := proc( x::integer, y::integer )
      description "Compute the average of two integers.",
                  "Returns a rational.";
      (x + y) / 2;
  end proc;
```

$$Average := \mathbf{proc}(x::integer, y::integer)$$
$$\quad \mathbf{description} \text{ "Compute the average of two integers.",}$$
$$\quad \text{"Returns a rational.";}$$
$$\quad 1/2*x + 1/2*y$$
$$\mathbf{end\ proc} \tag{6.34}$$

Options

A procedure can be tagged with one or more *options* which alter the behavior or display of the procedure. Options are specified by the keyword **option** or **options**, followed by one or more option names or equations, separated by commas:

```
option optionNameOrEquation, ... ;
options optionNameOrEquation, ... ;
```

Each **optionNameOrEquation** is a symbol or an equation of the form **optionName=value**. Any symbol is allowed as an option name that you can use to tag procedures for your own purposes, but there are several options that are known to Maple.

The arrow and operator Options

The **arrow** option and the **operator** option have meaning when specified together. These options cause Maple to print the procedure using arrow notation:

```
> SumOfSquares := proc( x, y )
      option operator, arrow;
```

```
     x^2 + y^2;
end proc;
```

$$SumOfSquares := (x, y) \rightarrow x^2 + y^2 \qquad (6.35)$$

For information on defining a procedure using arrow notation, see *Functional Operators: Mapping Notation (page 255)*.

The builtin Option

Maple has two classes of procedures: kernel built-in procedures implemented in the C programming language, and library procedures written in the Maple programming language. Because the kernel built-in functions are compiled, you cannot view their procedure definitions. The **builtin** option identifies a kernel procedure.

This option is shown when you display a purely built-in procedure. Instead of displaying the procedure statements, only the **builtin** option is displayed.

For example, the **add** procedure is built into the kernel:

```
> print(add);
```

$$\mathbf{proc}(\ )\ \mathbf{option}\ builtin = add;\ \mathbf{end\ proc} \qquad (6.36)$$

A procedure can have both the **builtin** option and a statement sequence. In that case, invoking the procedure will first invoke the kernel built-in version. If that indicated that it did not compute a result, the statement sequence is executed instead. This mechanism allows the kernel to process common cases very quickly, and defer to library code to handle other cases.

You can use the **type** function to test if an expression is a built-in procedure. An expression is of type **builtin** if it is a procedure with option **builtin**:

```
> type(add, 'builtin');
```

$$true \qquad (6.37)$$

```
> type(int, 'builtin');
```

$$false \qquad (6.38)$$

You cannot create built-in procedures, although there is a mechanism for creating procedures based on externally compiled code. Such procedures have the **call_external** option.

The call_external Option

The **call_external** option appears in procedures generated by the **define_external** procedure. This option indicates that the implementation of the procedure resides in a pre-compiled external library. For more information, see *External Calling: Using Compiled Code in Maple (page 518)*.

The hfloat Option

The **hfloat** option forces all floating-point operations within a procedure to be performed using hardware floating-point values. Depending on the operations performed, this can significantly speed up execution of the procedure at the cost of floating-point accuracy. Procedures that perform many floating-point operations or manipulate the contents of Arrays, Matrices, or Vectors of hardware floating-point values will benefit the most from this option.

The **hfloat** option causes the following differences in the procedure's definition and execution:

Any floating-point constants appearing in the procedure body are converted into hardware floating-point values when the procedure is first created.

Numeric arguments passed to the procedure are converted into hardware floating point values when the procedure is invoked.

Extracting values from hardware floating-point Arrays, Matrices, and Vectors does not incur a conversion to arbitrary precision floating-point form. Instead, the hardware floating-point values are used directly.

Calls to **evalhf** made from within the procedure return a hardware floating point value, and thus do not incur a conversion to arbitrary precision floating-point form.

These differences, together with the rules for contagion of hardware floating-point values in expressions, will usually cause arithmetic operations in the procedure to be performed using hardware floating-point arithmetic.

The use of the **hfloat** option differs from using **evalhf** in a few ways:

When a procedure is executed within the **evalhf** environment, everything is computed using hardware floats, and the operations available are restricted to those that can be done using hardware floats. No other basic data types, such as integers or strings, are available.

The only data structures available within the **evalhf** environment are Arrays.

Performance of a procedure having option **hfloat** is generally better than one operating with arbitrary precision floats, but usually not as good as a procedure operating within **evalhf**. But, a procedure with option **hfloat** has the full power of Maple available to it. All Maple operations, data types (except arbitrary precision software floating point), and data structures can be used in such a procedure.

The **hfloat** option cannot be used in conjunction with the **builtin**, **call_external**, or **inline** options.

Hardware floating-point numbers and computations are discussed in detail in *Numerical Programming in Maple (page 271)*. For more information on hardware floating-point contagion, see *Floating-Point Contagion (page 283)*.

The inline Option

Use the **inline** option to create a procedure that can be expanded inline wherever it is called from. An inline procedure avoids the overhead of a procedure invocation by executing the procedure's statements directly as if it were written in-line instead of in a separate procedure. This can result in improved execution speed and reduced memory usage.

Not all Maple procedures can take advantage of the **inline** option. Only procedures whose body consists of a single *expression* or an expression sequence can be expanded in-line. The body cannot consist of a *statement* or statement sequence. For details on further restrictions that may apply, refer to the **inline** help page.

The overload Option

The presence of option **overload** in a procedure indicates that the procedure will operate only on arguments matching the declared parameters (as is normally the case), and that if the arguments do not match the parameters, the next in a sequence of such procedures is tried.

A sequence of procedures with option **overload** can be combined into a single procedure using the **overload** command. This will produce a new procedure that will, when called, try each **overload** procedure in turn until one is encountered that will accept the arguments, or no procedures remain. In the latter case, an exception will be raised.

The following example uses the **overload** command and procedures with the **overload** option to append an entry to either a **list** (by creating a new list) or a 1-dimensional **Array** (in-place):

```
> Append := overload(
      [
          proc( L::list, x::anything ) option overload;
              [ op(L), x ]
          end proc,
          proc( A::Array(..), x::anything ) option overload;
              A(ArrayNumElems(A)+1) := x
          end proc
      ]
  ):
> Append([1,2],3);
```

$$[1, 2, 3] \tag{6.39}$$

Option **overload** can also be used to specify that a procedure exported by a **package** is only applied to arguments of specific type. If non-matching arguments are passed, the default behavior occurs instead.

For example, you can define a new implementation of `` `+` `` that works only on set arguments. The system default `` `+` `` operator is used for all other cases.

```
> SetOperations := module() option package;
      export `+` := proc( a::set, b::set ) option overload;
          a union b
      end proc;
  end module:
> with(SetOperations);
```
$$[`+`] \qquad (6.40)$$

```
> {1,2,3} + {4,5};
```
$$\{1, 2, 3, 4, 5\} \qquad (6.41)$$

```
> 123 + 45;
```
$$168 \qquad (6.42)$$

For more information on packages, see *Writing Packages (page 383)*.

The procname Option

As you will read later, the special name **procname** used *within* a procedure refers to the name by which the procedure was called. Among other things, this name is used to describe the location that an exception occurred when displaying an error message. It can also be used to return *unevaluated* calls to the procedure, and to make *recursive* calls.

If a procedure has the **procname** option, then the value of the **procname** special name within the procedure is inherited from the procedure that called it. If an error then occurs within the called procedure, the error is reported as having occurred in the calling procedure. This allows you, for example, to break up your procedure into sub-procedures, yet still have any errors reported as if they occurred in your main procedure.

For more information on the uses of **procname**, see *Returning Unevaluated (page 242)* and *Recursion (page 259)*.

The remember, cache, and system Options

The **remember** option activates a procedure's *remember table*. For a procedure with an active remember table, at the end of each invocation of the procedure, an entry that records the computed result for the specified arguments is made in the procedure's remember table.

Subsequent calls to the procedure with the same arguments simply retrieve the result from the remember table instead of invoking the procedure.

The **remember** option allows writing an inherently recursive algorithm in a natural manner without loss of efficiency. For example, the Fibonacci numbers can be computed by the procedure:

```
> Fibonacci := proc( n::nonnegint )
      option remember;
      if n < 2 then
          n
      else
          Fibonacci(n-1) + Fibonacci(n-2)
      end if
  end proc:
```

Without the **remember** option, the time required to compute **Fibonacci(n)** is exponential in **n**. With option remember, the behavior becomes linear. For a comparison of the efficiency of this procedure with and without option remember, see *Profiling a Procedure (page 620)*.

Entries can be explicitly inserted into a procedure's remember table by writing a function call on the left-hand side of an assignment. For example, the Fibonacci procedure can be written:

```
> Fibonacci := proc( n::nonnegint )
      option remember;
      Fibonacci(n-1) + Fibonacci(n-2)
  end proc:
> Fibonacci(0) := 0:
> Fibonacci(1) := 1:
```

A procedure's remember table can grow without bound, and for some procedures, may eventually contain many entries that will never be needed again. Adding the **system** option to a procedure allows Maple's garbage collector to clear out the remember table whenever garbage collection occurs. If a discarded result is needed again later, it will be recomputed.

As an alternative to remember tables, Maple also provides the **cache** option. Unlike a remember table, which can grow without bound, a cache has a maximum number of entries. When the cache becomes full, old entries are removed as new ones are inserted.

The **cache** option can be specified as just the symbol **cache**, or with an optional argument, in the form **cache(N)** where **N** is an integer specifying the size of the cache. If **(N)** is not specified, the cache is sized to hold 512 entries.

You can explicitly insert permanent entries into a procedure's cache using the **Cache:-AddPermanent** function.

When the interface variable **verboseproc** is 3, displaying a procedure also displays the contents of its remember table or cache as comments following the procedure definition:

```
> Fibonacci(7);
```

$$13 \tag{6.43}$$

```
> interface(verboseproc=3):
> print(Fibonacci);
```

$$\begin{aligned}&\mathbf{proc}(n::nonnegint)\\&\quad\mathbf{option}\ remember;\\&\quad Fibonacci(n-1) + Fibonacci(n-2)\\&\mathbf{end\ proc}\#(0) = 0\#(1) = 1\#(2) = 1\#(3) = 2\#(4) = 3\#(5) = 5\#(6) = 8\#\\&(7) = 13\end{aligned} \tag{6.44}$$

The **remember** and **cache** options are mutually exclusive, and the **system** option can only be used in conjunction with the **remember** option.

The trace Option

If a procedure is given the **trace** option, Maple will log each entry to and exit from the procedure, and the result of any assignment made during the execution of the procedure:

```
> Fibonacci := proc( n::nonnegint )
      option remember, trace;
      Fibonacci(n-1) + Fibonacci(n-2)
  end proc:
> Fibonacci(0) := 0:
> Fibonacci(1) := 1:
```

```
> Fibonacci(3);
{--> enter Fibonacci, args = 3
{--> enter Fibonacci, args = 2
value remembered (in Fibonacci): Fibonacci(1) -> 1
value remembered (in Fibonacci): Fibonacci(0) -> 0
```

$$1$$

```
<-- exit Fibonacci (now in Fibonacci) = 1}
value remembered (in Fibonacci): Fibonacci(1) -> 1
```

$$2$$

```
<-- exit Fibonacci (now at top level) = 2}
```

$$2 \tag{6.45}$$

Variables in Procedures

A *variable* is a name representing an item of data, such as a numerical value, character string, or list of polynomials. The value of the variable, that is, *which* data item it represents, can change during the execution of a procedure (or sequence of Maple commands at the top-level, outside of any procedure). There are three different classes of variables that can be used within a procedure: global, local, and lexically scoped.

Global Variables

A *global* variable has meaning within an entire Maple session. Many procedures may access a global variable, and all those procedures will refer to the same instance of that variable. A value assigned to a global variable during one function call will still be there the next time the procedure is called (if it was not changed by another procedure in the meantime).

Global variables are introduced by the **global** keyword, followed by one or more declarations:

```
global variableName := value, ... ;
```

The optional **:= value** part is an assignment that is executed at the beginning of procedure execution. Semantically, it is equivalent to writing a separate assignment statement immediately after all the variable declaration clauses.

A global variable continues to exist and retain its value after the procedure exits, and conceptually, existed (and possibly had a value) before the procedure was executed. Its *lifetime* is thus the duration of the entire Maple session.

Local Variables

A *local* variable has meaning only within a particular procedure. If the same variable name is referenced outside of the procedure or within a different procedure, it refers to a different instance of that name, and is therefore a different variable.

The *lifetime* of a local variable is the time that the procedure is executing. The variable is created when the procedure is first invoked, and is usually discarded when the procedure has finished executing. If the same procedure is later executed again, a new instance of the variable is created. The variable does not retain its value from its previous lifetime.

Local variables are declared using the following syntax:

```
local variableName :: typeAssertion := initialValue, ... ;
```

The only required part of the declaration is **variableName**.

The optional **:: typeAssertion** assertion specifies that the variable is expected to always refer to values of the specified type. Since this is an **assertion**, if **kernelopts(assertlevel)** is set to 2, the type is checked every time a new value is assigned to the variable. If the value is not of the specified type, an exception is raised.

The optional **:= initialValue** ensures that the variable is assigned the specified value before its first use. The **initialValue** can be any Maple expression. If the value is a literal expression sequence, it must be enclosed in parentheses, since otherwise the comma separating the elements of the sequence is interpreted as the comma separating individual variable declarations.

Lexically Scoped Variables

When one procedure is defined within another procedure (or within a **module**), variables in the outer procedure (or module) are visible to the nested procedure. This is called *lexical scoping*. Consider the following procedure, which given a list, produces a new list in which every element has been divided by the element with the largest magnitude, and then raised to a specified integer power:

```
> PowerList := proc( L::list, power::integer )
      local largest := max(abs~(L));
      map( proc(x) (x / largest) ^ power end proc, L )
  end proc:
> PowerList([1,1/2,-3.14],2);
```

$$[0.1014239929, 0.02535599822, 1.000000000] \qquad (6.46)$$

This example uses an *anonymous* nested procedure, declared directly within the expression that uses it. Notice that this inner procedure refers to both of the symbols **power** and **largest**. Because there are no variable or parameter declarations in the inner procedure that declare these symbols, lexical scoping ensures that they are automatically bound to the corresponding symbol in the outer procedure. In other words, **power** in the inner procedure refers to the parameter **power** of the outer procedure, and **largest** in the inner procedure refers to the local variable **largest** of the outer procedure.

Scoping Rules

If you want a variable to be local to a procedure or global, you should declare that variable using a **local** or **global** declaration. Declaring the scope of variables makes it easier to debug your code, and also makes it easier for someone else to understand your procedure.

On the other hand, if a variable is intended to refer to a parameter or local variable declared in an enclosing procedure, you must *not* declare it in the enclosed procedure. Doing so would defeat lexical scoping by making the variable local to the enclosed procedure, and thus a different variable with no connection to the one in the enclosing procedure.

If an undeclared variable does not correspond to a parameter or declared variable in a surrounding procedure, Maple determines its scope, and either automatically declare the variable as local or assume that it is global. When the variable is automatically declared local, such an *implicit declaration* generates a warning:

```
> ImplicitLocal := proc( x, y )
      z := x + y;
      if z < 0 then z^2 else z^3 end if
  end proc:
```
`Warning, `z` is implicitly declared local to procedure `ImplicitLocal``

Whether a variable is implicitly declared local or assumed to be global depends on how it is used:

If the variable appears on the *left-hand* side of an assignment statement or as the controlling variable of a **for** loop, Maple adds the variable to the procedure's **local** declarations. This means that if an enclosed procedure also refers to the variable (without declaration), lexical scoping binds it to the implicitly declared variable of the enclosing procedure. If a procedure in which such an implicit local declaration is displayed using the **print** function, the variable appears within the procedure's **local** declaration clause.

Otherwise, Maple assumes the variable is global. However, the variable is *not* added to the procedure's **global** declaration clause, which means that it is *not* subject to lexical scoping if the same name is used within an enclosed procedure.

Here is a summary of how the scope of a variable is determined:

If the variable is declared as a parameter, local, or global variable in the procedure in which the variable is encountered, the scope is specified by the declaration.

If the variable is not declared and there is a surrounding procedure (or module), the parameter, local (including implicit local), and global declarations of the surrounding procedure are examined. If the variable is found there, that binding is used. If it is not found, the search continues outward through the layers of surrounding procedures.

If the top level (outside of any procedure or module) is reached, the usage of the variable in the original procedure is examined. If it appears on the left-hand side of an assignment or as the controlling variable of a **for** loop, it is added to the procedure's local declarations. Otherwise it is assumed to be a global variable.

Non-Variable Name Bindings

In addition to the binding of names to parameters, local variables, and global variables, you can also explicitly bind other names to objects outside of the procedure with the **uses** clause:

```
uses bindingSpecification, ...
```

The **uses** keyword is followed by one or more bindings, in a form identical to those of the **use** statement, introduced in *The use Statement (page 192)*. These bindings are in effect over the entire body of the procedure, in the same way they would be if the procedure body had been enclosed in a **use** statement.

The **uses** clause must appear at the top of the procedure body, together with the **option**, **description**, and initial **local** and **global** declarations. If you wish to bind names in a subset of the procedure body, use a **use** statement instead.

The Statement Sequence

The **statementSequence** section of the procedure can contain any number of Maple statements, nested arbitrarily deeply. Other than *one level evaluation* and references to parameters, the semantics of statements within a procedure are the same as if those statements were executed outside of any procedure.

Referring to Parameters within the Procedure Body

When referring to parameters in the body of a procedure, there are some things to keep in mind.

Parameters Are Not Variables

Although a parameter declaration has a similar form to a local variable declaration, and parameters are referred to by name the same way that variables are, parameters are *not variables*. In Maple, a parameter *always* represents the argument that was bound to it.

Consider this example, which tries to use a parameter on the left-hand side of an assignment statement:

```
> Add2 := proc( x, y )
    x := x + y
  end proc:
> Add2(3,4);
Error, (in Add2) illegal use of a formal parameter
```

This call to **Add2** results in an error because the statement **x := x + y** is interpreted as **3 := 3 + 4**. This is in contrast to languages such as C or C++, where a parameter is effectively a local variable that has been initialized to the argument value.

A parameter can be used on the left-hand side of an assignment if the *value* of the parameter is a name. The **evaln** parameter modifier can ensure that this is the case. Here is an example you saw earlier:

```
> Accumulate := proc( r::evaln(numeric), n::numeric )
    r := eval(r) + n
  end proc:
> total := 0;
```

$$total := 0 \qquad (6.47)$$

```
> Accumulate(total,2);
```

$$2 \qquad (6.48)$$

```
> Accumulate(total,3.5);
```

$$5.5 \qquad (6.49)$$

```
> total;
```

$$5.5 \qquad (6.50)$$

Here, the parameter **r** evaluates to the name `total`, an assignable object. Although it appears that an assignment to the parameter **r** is being made within the procedure, it is really the *value* of **r**, which in this case is the global variable **total**, that is being assigned to.

Required Parameters

Recall that a *required parameter* is one for which a corresponding argument must have been passed *if the parameter is used during the execution of the procedure*. Failure to pass an argument for a required parameter only raises an exception if an attempt is made to use that parameter during the particular invocation of the procedure.

For example, a procedure may determine, based on the value of its first required parameter, that it does not have to refer to the second required parameter.

```
> Require := proc( x::integer, y::integer )
      if x < 0 then x^2 else x * y end if
  end proc:
> Require(-3);
```

$$9 \tag{6.51}$$

```
> Require(3,4);
```

$$12 \tag{6.52}$$

```
> Require(3);
Error, invalid input: Require uses a 2nd argument, y (of type integer),
 which is missing
```

Parameters with the seq Modifier

If a required (or optional) parameter was declared with the **seq** modifier, then the parameter will *always* have a value. That value will be a sequence of the specified type, a single item of that type, or **NULL** (or the default value for an optional parameter).

To do anything with a **seq** parameter other than pass it on to another procedure, you should convert the parameter value to a list and then work with the list:

```
> AddAndMax := proc( x::seq(numeric) )
      local a := 0, i;
      for i in [x] do
          a := a + i
      end do;
      a, max(x)
  end proc:
```

Without the **[]** brackets around **x**, this procedure would produce unexpected results if called with a single floating-point number. A **for var in expr** loop iterates over the operands of **expr**. If **expr** is a sequence of two or more numbers, it works as expected, but if **expr** were a single float, the loop would iterate over the *float*s operands (the significand and exponent). By enclosing **x** in a list, the loop will always iterate over the arguments bound to **x**.

Parameters with the uneval or evaln Modifiers

Parameters declared with the **uneval** or **evaln** modifiers are used like any other. Because Maple uses one level evaluation rules inside procedures, these parameters do not evaluate any further than they did when the arguments were initially evaluated. The **eval** function can be used to evaluate such parameters further.

Optional and Expected Ordered Parameters

Both *optional* and *expected* ordered parameters are always declared with default values, so using such a parameter within a procedure always yields a value. If an argument was bound to the parameter during procedure invocation, the parameter's value is that argument. Otherwise, the value of the parameter is the declared default value.

Keyword Parameters

Keyword parameters also have declared default values, so using the parameter always yields a value. Unlike ordered parameters, keyword parameters receive their values from arguments of the form **keyword=value**. The value of a keyword parameter is the **value** portion of such an argument, *not* the entire argument.

Special Sequences for Referring to Parameters and Arguments

Maple provides a number of special named expression sequences to make it easy to work with parameters and arguments. These are useful in cases when it would be awkward if they could only be referred to by name.

The special names **_params** and **_nparams** can be used within a procedure to refer to the current values of the positional and ordered parameters. The **_params** symbol represents an expression sequence with **_nparams** members, one corresponding to each declared parameter (excluding keyword parameters). For a given procedure, **_nparams** is constant.

The **_params** symbol can only be used when immediately followed by an index enclosed in square brackets, **_params[indexExpr]**. It cannot be used in any other context. **indexExpr** can evaluate to one of the following:

An integer, **N**, in the range **1** to **_nparams**, or **-_nparams** to **-1**. This is just the selection operation on the sequence **_params**. It yields the value of the Nth parameter when **N > 0**, or the **(_nparams+1+N)**th parameter when **N < 0** (negative integers index **_params** from the end instead of the beginning). If no argument was passed for the requested parameter and no default was declared, the result is **NULL**.

A range of such integers. This yields an expression sequence of values, *with any* **NULL** *values omitted*. A sequence of all the non-**NULL** positional and ordered parameter values can be obtained using **_params[..]**. Note that due to elision of **NULL**s, this could produce fewer than **_nparams** values.

An unevaluated parameter name. The notation **_params['parameterName']** is equivalent to just writing **parameterName**, except when referring to a required positional parameter that was not bound to an argument. In that case **_params['parameterName']** yields **NULL** whereas referring directly to **parameterName** would raise an exception.

The following example multiplies or divides the last three positional parameters by the first, depending on the value of the keyword parameter **multiply**:

```
> MulDiv := proc( a, b, c, d, { multiply := true } )
      if multiply then
          _params[-3..] * a
      else
          _params[-3..] / a
      end if
  end proc:
  MulDiv(100,1,2,3);
  MulDiv(100,1,2,3,multiply=false);
```

$$100, 200, 300$$

$$\frac{1}{100}, \frac{1}{50}, \frac{3}{100} \qquad (6.53)$$

Just as **_params** and **_nparams** can be used to work with positional and ordered parameters in a flexible manner, **_options** and **_noptions** provide similar facilities for working with keyword parameters (often called *keyword options*).

The **_options** symbol represents an expression sequence containing **_noptions** members, one for each declared keyword parameter. Each member of **_options** is an equation of the form **keyword=value**.

If a keyword parameter was declared with multiple spellings, the corresponding member of **_options** uses the first spelling.

Unlike **_params**, **_options** can be used directly, not only through the selection of members of the sequence. Because **_options** returns a sequence of equations, even a member corresponding to an argument with a **NULL** value is non-**NULL**. It is an equation of the form **keyword=NULL**.

When **_options** is used with an index, the index must evaluate to an integer (or a range of integers) in the range **1** to **_noptions** or **-(_noptions)** to **-1**, or the unevaluated name of a keyword parameter.

The order of the equations in **_options** does not necessarily correspond to the order in which the keyword parameters were declared. Instead, the equations are in lexicographic order by keyword (the first spelling for keyword parameters with multiple spellings). This is the same order in which the keyword parameters are printed when the procedure is displayed by the **print** command. As a consequence of this, if a new keyword parameter is added to the procedure definition, the numeric index of the **_options** entry corresponding to a particular keyword parameter could change. Thus, when indexing **_options**, it is safest to use the **_options['parameterName']** form.

The following example uses **_options** to pass all the keyword arguments on to another procedure:

```
> MyRanMat := proc( a::integer, {density::float := 1.0, generator
    := 0..0.5} )
      LinearAlgebra:-RandomMatrix(a, _options)
  end proc:
> MyRanMat(2, density=0.75, generator=1..9);
```

$$\begin{bmatrix} 8 & 0 \\ 4 & 0 \end{bmatrix} \tag{6.54}$$

```
> MyRanMat(3, density=0.88);
```

$$[[0.479746213196451499, 0.400140234444400056, 0.],$$
$$[0., 0., 0.478753417717148799],$$
$$[0.210880641313137496, 0.485296390880307849,$$
$$0.139249109433524199]] \tag{6.55}$$

The next example selects specific keyword arguments to pass to another procedure:

```
> MulRanMat := proc( a::integer, {density::float := 1.0, generator
    := 0..0.5, mult := 1.0} )
      mult * LinearAlgebra:-RandomMatrix(a, _options['density'],
  _options['generator'])
  end proc:
> MulRanMat(4, density=0.75, generator=1..9, mult=x/2);
```

$$\begin{bmatrix} 4x & 0 & x & \frac{9}{2}x \\ \frac{3}{2}x & 0 & \frac{3}{2}x & 0 \\ 0 & \frac{1}{2}x & \frac{9}{2}x & \frac{7}{2}x \\ \frac{7}{2}x & 4x & 2x & \frac{3}{2}x \end{bmatrix} \tag{6.56}$$

When there are more arguments in a function call than needed to match the called procedure's parameters, you can access the remaining arguments inside the procedure by using the special sequence **_rest**. The number of members in this sequence is given by **_nrest**.

Because these extra arguments do not correspond to any declared parameters, it is not possible for such an argument to have a **NULL** value. Recall that the only way for a parameter to be **NULL** is for no argument to have matched a parameter with no declared default value (or a default value of **NULL**). Since there is no declared parameter corresponding to any value in **_rest**, these conditions cannot hold.

This example uses **_rest** and **_nrest** to return the number of entries in a sequence of numbers, together with the maximum, and optionally the mean:

```
> MaxMean := proc( {mean := false})
    if mean then
        _nrest, max(_rest), Statistics:-Mean([_rest])
    else
        _nrest, max(_rest)
    end if
  end proc:
> c := MaxMean(6,200,400, mean=true);
```

$$c := 3, 400, 202. \qquad (6.57)$$

All of the *arguments* that were *passed* to a procedure can be accessed using the special sequence **_passed**, having **_npassed** elements.

Prior to Maple version 10, **_passed** and **_npassed** were known as **args** and **nargs**. These older names are still accepted as synonyms for the newer names for backwards compatibility. Of historical interest, the earliest versions of Maple did not support declared parameters at all; **args** and **nargs** were the only mechanism for processing arguments.

The **_passed** sequence can be used to do explicit argument processing within the body of the procedure, although this is discouraged for two reasons:

Most argument processing requirements can be handled using the mechanisms described so far in this chapter. Doing so is usually significantly faster (in terms of both execution time and development time) than performing the same operations using your own custom argument processing algorithms within the procedure.

When special argument processing requirements do arise, it is often easier to work with **_params**, **_options**, and **_rest**. In many cases, the provided mechanisms can handle most of the processing, and it is only necessary to look at **_rest** to handle additional arguments.

The clearest and most efficient way to write a procedure to find the maximum of an arbitrary sequence of numbers is to use a single parameter with a **seq** modifier, and pass that parameter directly to Maple's built-in **max** function. However, the following example uses **_passed**, **_npassed**, and a **for** loop instead for demonstration purposes:

```
> Maximum := proc( )
      local max := _passed[1], i;
      for i from 2 to _npassed do
          if _passed[i] > max then
              max := _passed[i]
          end if
      end do;
      max
  end proc:
```

Care must be taken when the **_options**, **_rest**, or **_passed** sequences contain only a single entry and that sequence is assigned to a variable (for example, **myOpts := _options**). The variable will receive the value of that single element rather than an expression sequence. The safest way to use these expression sequences is to transform them into lists (for example, **myOpts := [_options]**).

6.6 How Procedures Are Executed

When a procedure definition is entered in Maple or read from a file, Maple does not *execute* the procedure. It does however translate the procedure into an internal representation, process all the parameter and variable declarations, perform lexical scoping and implicit local declaration, and *simplify* the procedure's **statementSequence**.

Automatic simplification of **statementSequence** is similar to simplification of expressions when Maple is used interactively, with a few exceptions. Consider the following procedure:

```
> f := proc(x)
      local t := x + 3 + 0/2;
      if true then
          sqrt(x * 2.0 / 3.0)
      else
          t^2
      end if
  end proc;
```

$$f := \mathbf{proc}(x) \; \mathbf{local} \; t; \; t := x + 3; \; \mathrm{sqrt}(x*2.0/3.0) \; \mathbf{end \; proc} \tag{6.58}$$

During automatic simplification, the division **0/2** has been removed (because it does not contribute to the sum). More significantly, the entire **if...then...else...end if** statement has been replaced by just the body of the first branch, since the **if**-condition is **true**.

Notice that the expression **sqrt(x * 2.0 / 3.0)** has *not* been simplified to **.8164965809*x^(1/2)** as it would have been if entered at the top level, outside of a procedure. If this simplification had been performed, then the result produced by the procedure would depend on the setting of **Digits** (and other aspects of the floating-point environment) both when the procedure was simplified, and a possibly different setting of **Digits** when the procedure is later executed. By not performing any floating-point arithmetic during procedure simplification, the procedure will depend only on the state of the floating-point environment at execution time.

A procedure is *executed* after it has been *invoked* by a *function call*. Generally, the process is:

A function call, of the form **functionName(functionArguments)** is encountered during evaluation of an expression, either at the interactive level or while executing another procedure.

The **functionName** is examined to see if has been assigned a procedure.

The **functionArguments** are evaluated, usually from left to right.

The evaluated arguments are bound to the parameters of the procedure.

All of the procedure's local variables are *instantiated*. That is, for each local variable, a unique instance of the variable's name is created, with no prior value.

Interpretation of the procedure's **statementSequence** begins.

Interpretation continues until the last statement has been executed, an *exception* is raised (either as the result of an operation, or by an explicit **error** statement), or a **return** statement is encountered.

Binding of Arguments to Parameters

Argument processing occurs when a function call results in the invocation of a procedure. First, all the arguments are evaluated (except those corresponding to parameters with the **uneval** or **evaln** modifiers), and then they are matched to the parameters of the procedure.

Binding of Keyword Arguments

Keyword arguments are always matched first unless the procedure has parameters declared with the **uneval** or **evaln** modifiers. Maple makes a pass through the entire sequence of arguments looking for **keyword=value** equations where the **keyword** matches a declared keyword parameter of the procedure.

Whenever a matching keyword parameter is encountered, the right-hand side of the equation becomes the value for that parameter, and the equation is removed from further consideration as an argument. If more than one keyword argument matches a keyword parameter, only the last one takes effect.

6.6 How Procedures Are Executed • 233

Keyword parameter names (the **keyword** part) are Maple symbols like any other. If that symbol is in use as a variable, then using it in a keyword argument may not work as expected since the variable may evaluate to its value. To ensure that this does not happen, it is best to always use unevaluation quotes around the keyword part of a keyword argument:

```
> f := proc( x::integer, { y::integer := 1 }, $ ) x * y end proc:
> y := sin(z):
> f(3,y=2);
Error, invalid input: too many and/or wrong type of arguments passed
 to f; first unused argument is sin(z) = 2
> f(3,'y'=2);
```

$$6 \qquad (6.59)$$

This is a good practice when calling any function, whether it is a procedure you defined or a Maple command. See *Protecting Names and Options (page 49)*.

When calling a procedure that accepts a keyword argument from within another procedure that has a parameter with the same name as the keyword argument, you must use both unevaluation quotes *and* the scope resolution operator, **:-**, to ensure that (the global instance of) the name itself is used instead of the value of the parameter:

```
> f := proc( x::integer, { y::integer := 1 }, $ ) x * y end proc:
> g := proc( y::rational ) f(numer(y), ':-y'=denom(y)) end proc:
> g(3/2);
```

$$6 \qquad (6.60)$$

If a keyword parameter has a declared **parameterType** for which **true** is a valid value (for example, the types **truefalse** or **boolean**), the keyword name alone is interpreted as a synonym for **keyword=true**.

```
> f := proc( x::integer, { square::truefalse := false } )
      if square then x^2 else x end if
  end proc:
> [ f(2), f(3,square=true), f(4,square) ];
```

$$[2, 9, 16] \qquad (6.61)$$

If a keyword parameter's **keyword** is a symbol of the form `` `symbol[symbol]` `` or `` `symbol[integer]` ``, the parameter is treated specially at during argument processing. Although such a **keyword** is still a symbol (because of the enclosing left single quotes), it matches indexed name keyword arguments. Specifically, if an equation whose left-hand side is an indexed name of the form **symbol[symbol]** or **symbol[integer]** is encountered, it matches the keyword parameter whose **keyword** symbol *looks* like the indexed name. For example, the keyword *argument*,

>   axis_label[1] = "time"

matches the keyword *parameter*:

>   `axis_label[1]` :: string := "x"

Keyword arguments with multiple indices are also recognized by attempting to match them using one index at a time. For example, the keyword *argument*,

>   axis_label[1,2] = ""

matches *both* of the keyword *parameters*,

>   `axis_label[1]` :: string := "x", `axis_label[2]` :: string := "y"

and sets them both to the empty string.

The following example illustrates these behaviors:

```
> Indexed := proc( { `name[1]`::string := "hello",
                     `name[2]`::string := "goodbye" } )
      sprintf("name[1]=\"%s\" -- name[2]=\"%s\"", `name[1]`, `name[2]`)
  end proc:
> Indexed(name[1]="hi");
```
$$\text{"name[1]=\"hi\" -- name[2]=\"goodbye\""} \tag{6.62}$$

```
> Indexed(name[1]="bonjour", name[2]="aurevoir");
```
$$\text{"name[1]=\"bonjour\" -- name[2]=\"aurevoir\""} \tag{6.63}$$

```
> Indexed(name[1,2]="good day");
```
$$\text{"name[1]=\"good day\" -- name[2]=\"good day\""} \tag{6.64}$$

```
> Indexed(name[2]=42);
Error, invalid input: Indexed expects value for keyword parameter
`name[2]` to be of type string, but received 42
```

The Special Case of evaln and uneval Modifiers

There is one case in which the first stage of argument processing is not keyword matching. If the procedure was declared with any parameter(s) having an **uneval** or **evaln** modifier, arguments are first assigned to positional parameters from left to right until the rightmost

uneval or **evaln** parameter has been bound to an argument or until all the arguments have been exhausted, whichever happens first. For each argument/parameter pair:

If the parameter has no **parameterType**, the argument matches trivially, and becomes the value for that parameter.

If the parameter has a **parameterType** specification, the argument may or may not match. If it matches, the argument becomes the value for that parameter. If it does not match, an exception is raised.

```
> Accumulate := proc( r::evaln(numeric), n::numeric,
                      { operation::symbol := `+` } )
     r := operation(eval(r),n)
  end proc:
> total := 0:
> Accumulate(total, 2.3);
```
$$2.3 \tag{6.65}$$

```
> Accumulate(total, operation=`*`, 10);
```
$$23.0 \tag{6.66}$$

```
> Accumulate(operation=`*`, total, 100);
Error, illegal use of an object as a name
```

In the last call, an exception is raised because the first argument does not evaluate to a name.

Binding of Arguments to Positional and Ordered Parameters

After all arguments matching keyword parameters have been processed, matching of required positional and optional or expected ordered parameters is carried out. If any parameter had an **uneval** or **evaln** modifier, all parameters up to the rightmost of these will already have received arguments, so further matching begins with the next positional or ordered parameter after that.

Matching is done by traversing the parameter declarations from left to right. As each parameter is examined, an attempt is made to match it to the next unused argument as follows:

If the parameter has no **parameterType**, the argument matches trivially, and becomes the value for that parameter.

If the parameter has **parameterType**, but no **defaultValue**, the argument may or may not match. If it matches, the argument becomes the value for that parameter. If it does not match, an exception is raised.

If the parameter has both **parameterType** and **defaultValue**, the argument may or may not match. If it matches, the argument becomes the value for that parameter. If it does not match, the parameter receives its default value, and the argument remains available for matching a subsequent parameter.

In last two cases above, if the parameter's type uses the **seq** modifier, Maple continues to match additional arguments against the parameter until one is encountered that is not of the correct type. A **seq** parameter never results in an exception, because even if no arguments match, a valid sequence has been produced (the empty sequence).

At the end of this process, if there are any arguments left over, they are either put into the **_rest** sequence, or, if the procedure was declared with the end-of-parameters marker, **$**, an exception is raised.

Conversely, if all the arguments were bound to parameters, but there are parameters remaining to be assigned values, these receive their default values if they have one. Otherwise, they have no value, and attempting to use them (by name) within the procedure raises an exception.

Statement Sequence Interpretation

After all the arguments in a function call have been successfully bound to the procedure's parameters, Maple begins interpreting the procedure's *statement sequence*. Each statement is examined in turn and the necessary actions carried out.

For example, an assignment statement is interpreted by evaluating the right-hand side (the expression to be assigned), and resolving the left-hand side (the target of the assignment). The latter involves evaluating any indices if the left-hand side contains indexed names. Finally, the *value* of the right hand side is assigned to the resolved *variable* on the left-hand side.

When an **if**-statement is encountered, Maple evaluates the condition. If it is **true**, statement sequence interpretation continues with the first statement within the first branch of the **if**-statement. When the statements within that branch have all been executed, interpretation continues with the first statement after the **end if**. If **if**-condition was **false**, Maple looks for an **elif** or **else** branch and continues in a similar manner.

When there are no further statements remaining, Maple behaves as if a **return** statement had been encountered.

Variable Evaluation Rules within Procedures

Maple fully evaluates global variables whenever they are referenced, even within procedures, but local variables are evaluated in a special way. When a local variable is encountered during procedure execution, it is *evaluated only one level*. Consider the following Maple statements, outside of any procedure:

```
> f := x + y;
```

$$f := x + y \tag{6.67}$$

```
> x := z^2 / y;
```

$$x := \frac{z^2}{y} \tag{6.68}$$

```
> z := y^3 + 3;
```

$$z := y^3 + 3 \tag{6.69}$$

Since these statements undergo normal full recursive evaluation, the following result is returned:

```
> f;
```

$$\frac{\left(y^3 + 3\right)^2}{y} + y \tag{6.70}$$

The same sequence of steps within a procedure would yield a different result:

```
> OneLevelEval := proc( )
      local f, x, y, z;
      f := x + y;
      x := z^2 / y;
      z := y^3 + 3;
      f
  end proc:
> OneLevelEval();
```

$$x + y \tag{6.71}$$

The concept of *one-level evaluation* is unique to symbolic languages like Maple, where the *value* of a variable can be, or include, the *name* of another variable. One-level evaluation avoids arbitrarily deep computation at every step of a procedure and is thus important for efficiency. It has very little effect on the behavior of procedures, because most procedures have a sequential structure. When full evaluation of a local variable is required within a procedure, use the **eval** function:

```
> FullEval := proc( )
      local f, x, y, z;
      f := x + y;
      x := z^2 / y;
```

```
    z := y^3 + 3;
    eval(f)
end proc:
> FullEval();
```

$$\frac{\left(y^3+3\right)^2}{y} + y \qquad (6.72)$$

In addition to illustrating one level evaluation, this example also introduces the idea of an *escaped local*. The expression returned by **OneLevelEval** is **x + y** and contains the symbols **x** and **y**. However, these are *not* the global variables of the same names; they are the local **x** and **y** declared in **OneLevelEval**. Because these variables have *escaped*, they continue to exist beyond their normal lifetime even though the procedure has finished executing. Usually, an escaped local indicates a programming error such as forgetting to assign a value to a local variable before using it. There are situations where letting a local escape can be useful, such as generating unique instances of a name that will be guaranteed never to evaluate further.

Returning Values from a Procedure

When a procedure has finished executing, a value is returned. If the procedure was invoked by a function call, possibly within a larger expression, the returned value is used as the value of that function. At the interactive level, the returned value is displayed (unless the input was terminated by a colon instead of a semicolon).

Except when a procedure raises an exception, a value is *always* returned. In the absence of an explicit **return** statement, the returned value is the value of the last statement executed in the procedure. The *value of a statement* means:

The value computed by the right-hand side of an assignment statement.

The value of the expression when the statement is an expression.

The value of the last statement executed within the branches of an **if** statement or within the body of a loop.

Note that **NULL** is a valid expression (and thus a valid statement). A procedure that returns **NULL** is still returning a value, although at the interactive level, nothing is displayed.

You can use an explicit **return** statement to end the execution of the procedure and return a value immediately:

```
return expression;
```

Upon encountering a **return** statement during execution, Maple evaluates the **expression**, and then immediately terminates the execution of the procedure, with the result of the evaluation as the returned value.

This example uses an explicit **return** statement to immediately return the position **i** of a value **x** in a list when the value is found. If the value is not found, the procedure returns 0:

```
> Position := proc( x::anything, L::list )
      local i;
      for i to numelems(L) do
          if x = L[i] then
              return i
          end if
      end do;
      0
  end proc:
> Position(3, [2,3,5,7,1,3,7,9,3,9]);
```
$$2 \tag{6.73}$$

```
> Position(4, [2,3,5,7,1,3,7,9,3,9]);
```
$$0 \tag{6.74}$$

The following procedure computes the greatest common divisor, **g**, of two integers **a** and **b**. It returns the expression sequence **g, a/g, b/g**. The case **a = b = 0** is treated separately because in that case, **g** is zero:

```
> GCD := proc( a::integer, b::integer, $ )
      local g;
      if a = 0 and b = 0 then
          return 0, 0, 0
      end if;
      g := igcd(a,b);
      g, iquo(a,g), iquo(b,g)
  end proc:
> GCD(0,0);
```
$$0, 0, 0 \tag{6.75}$$

```
> div, quo1, quo2 := GCD(12,8);
```
$$div, quo1, quo2 := 4, 3, 2 \tag{6.76}$$

This example illustrates that you can return a sequence of values from a procedure, and that those values can then be assigned to a sequence of names by the caller. Whenever a procedure returns a sequence of values, the result can be assigned to a sequence of the same number of names (a multiple assignment). If you assigned the result to a single name, then the value of that name would be the entire sequence.

Sometimes, it is convenient to write a procedure which will return a different number of values depending on the context in which it was called. A procedure can use the special variable **_nresults** to determine how many results are expected by the caller. Here is a version of the previous procedure that returns only a single result when called from within an arithmetic expression (the tests for the case **a = b = 0** has been omitted for brevity):

```
> GCD := proc( a::integer, b::integer, $ )
      local g := igcd(a,b);
      if _nresults = 1 or _nresults = undefined then
          g
      else
          g, iquo(a,g), iquo(b,g)
      end if
  end proc:
> div := GCD(12,8);
```
$$div := 4 \qquad (6.77)$$

```
> GCD(12,8) ^ 2;
```
$$16 \qquad (6.78)$$

```
> { GCD(12,8) };
```
$$\{4\} \qquad (6.79)$$

```
> div, quo1, quo2 := GCD(12,8);
```
$$div, quo1, quo2 := 4, 3, 2 \qquad (6.80)$$

The **_nresults** variable has the value **undefined** if the procedure was called from within an expression or within the arguments of another function call. It has an integer value if the call was from the top level of an expression appearing on the right-hand side of an assignment. The value of **_nresults** is the number of variables on the left-hand side of the assignment statement.

Do not use **_nresults** in a procedure with the **remember** or **cache** options. Only the first computed result is stored in the remember table or cache. Subsequent calls with the same input but a different number of expected results will not return the expected number of results. (The **Cache** package can be used to manually implement a simulated remember table that works correctly in conjunction with **_nresults**.)

Another alternative for returning more than one value from a procedure is to assign values to *variables* whose names were passed in as *values*. The following procedure determines whether a list **L** contains an expression of type **T**. If found, the procedure returns the index of the (first matching) expression. If the procedure is called with a third argument, then it also assigns the expression to that name.

```
> FindType := proc( T::type, L::list, V::evaln, $ )
      local i;
      for i to numelems(L) do
          if L[i] :: T then
              if _npassed = 3 then
                  V := L[i]
              end if;
              return i
          end if
      end do
  end proc:
> FindType(string, [2,3/4,"Hello",x+y]);
```
$$3 \tag{6.81}$$
```
> FindType(string, [2,3/4,"Hello",x+y], s);
```
$$3 \tag{6.82}$$
```
> s;
```
$$\text{"Hello"} \tag{6.83}$$

When **FindType** was called with two arguments, the procedure just returned the index of the found list element.

When called with three arguments, parameter **V** received the *name, not the value* of global variable **s**. The **evaln** declaration of **V** ensures that **V** will always refer to a name. Just before returning, the procedure assigned the found expression to **s**, as referenced by **V**.

If, during the execution of the procedure, you need to refer to the *value* that has been assigned to a name via an **evaln** parameter, enclose such references to the parameter within a call to **eval**:

```
> Accumulate := proc( r::evaln(numeric), n::numeric )
      r := eval(r) + n
  end proc:
```

Returning Unevaluated

If a procedure cannot perform a requested computation, it can return the unevaluated form of the function call that invoked it. For example, the procedure below computes the larger of two values if it can, or returns unevaluated if it cannot:

```
> Larger := proc( x, y )
      if x :: numeric and y :: numeric then
          if x > y then
              x
          else
              y
          end if
      else
          'Larger'(x,y)
      end if
  end proc:
> Larger(3.2, 2);
```

$$3.2 \tag{6.84}$$

```
> r := Larger(a, 2*b);
```

$$r := Larger(a, 2\,b) \tag{6.85}$$

The unevaluation quotes around **Larger** within the procedure specify that the function call expression will be constructed, but no procedure invocation will take place (therefore this is *not* a recursive call).

The returned unevaluated function call can later be re-evaluated. If **a** and **b** have numeric values at that time, **Larger** will return a number, otherwise it will return unevaluated once again.

```
> a, b := 3, 2;
```

$$a, b := 3, 2 \tag{6.86}$$

```
> r;
```

$$4 \tag{6.87}$$

Because of one level evaluation, the last line in the example above would have to be written as **r := eval(r)** if **r** were a local variable in a procedure.

Rather than using the procedure's name to construct an unevaluated function call to return, you can also use the special name **procname**. The statement, **'Larger'(x,y)** could have been written **'procname'(x,y)**. The advantage to using **procname** is that such unevaluated returns are immediately apparent to anyone reading the source code of your procedure.

Note that if your procedure was called from within another procedure and has the **procname** *option*, then an unevaluated call of the form **'procname'(x,y)** refers to the procedure that invoked your procedure.

By writing procedures to return unevaluated when it is not possible to carry out the computation, you make it easier for the user of the procedure to use it in contexts where otherwise it would produce an error:

```
> plot( Larger(x, 1/x), x = 1/2 .. 2 );
```

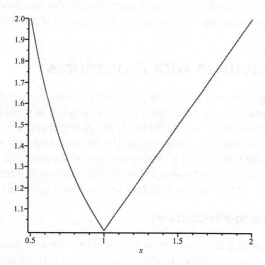

```
> int( Larger(x, 1/x), x = 0.25 .. 2.0 );
```

$$2.886294361 \qquad (6.88)$$

If **Larger** had been implemented without the unevaluated return, both of the above commands would have failed because the first argument to **plot** and **int** could not have been evaluated:

```
> LargerNoUneval := proc( x, y )
      if x > y then
          x
      else
          y
      end if
  end proc:
```

```
> plot( LargerNoUneval(x, 1/x), x = 1/4 .. 2 );
Error, (in LargerNoUneval) cannot determine if this expression is true
or false: 1/x < x
> int( LargerNoUneval(x, 1/x), x = 0.25 .. 2.0 );
Error, (in LargerNoUneval) cannot determine if this expression is true
or false: 1/x < x
```

Many Maple functions use the technique of returning unevaluated. For example, the **sin** and **int** functions return a result when they can, or return unevaluated when it is not yet possible to compute a result.

6.7 Using Data Structures with Procedures

The choice of appropriate data structures to solve a particular problem has already been discussed in *Basic Data Structures (page 129)*, but it is worth keeping in mind how your procedure might be used by you or others in the future. If the problem you are solving involves a small amount of data, you may have been tempted to choose a data structure without regard to efficiency or scalability when writing your procedure. If the procedure is used later to solve a larger problem, it may not be able to handle the problem in a reasonable amount of time or memory if you chose a data structure only suitable for small problems.

Passing Data Structures to Procedures

Traditional procedural programming languages such as Pascal or C usually pass arguments to procedures *by value*. This means that the procedure receives a *copy* of the data passed to it. Such languages also allow values to be passed *by reference*. Pascal does this by prefixing the parameter declaration with the **var** keyword. C requires that the parameter be declared as a *pointer*, using the * prefix, and that the caller explicitly pass the *address* of the argument using the & prefix (except when passing pointers to arrays).

Passing arguments by value ensures that the procedure cannot modify the passed data as a side-effect, but requires making a copy of the data. Passing by reference is more efficient for large data objects, but allows the procedure to (possibly unintentionally) modify the caller's copy of the data.

In Maple, data is always passed by reference, but the immutability of most data types ensures that the procedure cannot modify the caller's copy of the data. The exceptions are Maple's mutable data structures: tables, Arrays, Matrices, Vectors, records, and objects. Modifying these within a procedure will modify the caller's copy. Fortunately, these larger data structures are the ones that you would most often want to pass by reference, since copying such data consumes time and space.

A third argument passing convention seen in some programming languages is passing *by name*. In this case, instead of passing the *value* of a variable, *the variable itself* is passed.

The called procedure can then assign a new value to the variable, which will remain in effect when the procedure returns to the caller. Maple allows passing by name via the **evaln** parameter declaration modifier, or by explicitly quoting the name when calling the procedure. This does not contradict the earlier statement that Maple always passes by reference, because it is now the *variable name* that is being passed by reference.

Returning Data Structures from Procedures

Just as values are always passed by reference, they are *returned* from procedures by reference, too. Thus, the cost in time and space of returning a large structure such as a list is not any more than that of a small piece of data like an integer.

When returning a table or procedure from a procedure, care must be taken to ensure that it is the data structure itself and not the name referring to it that is returned. This is because tables and procedures use last name evaluation.

```
> IncorrectListToTable := proc( L :: list )
      local T := table(), i;
      for i to numelems(L) do
          T[i] := L[i]
      end do;
      T
  end proc:
> IncorrectListToTable(["String",123,Pi]);
```

$$T \tag{6.89}$$

The example above returns the local variable **T** instead of the actual table. Although the returned value can be used as if it were the actual table, every access to it involves an extra level of addressing behind the scenes, thus consuming more time.

```
> ListToTable := proc( L :: list )
      local T := table(), i;
      for i to numelems(L) do
          T[i] := L[i]
      end do;
      eval(T)
  end proc:
> ListToTable(["String",123,Pi]);
```

$$table\left(\left[\,1 = \text{"String"}, 2 = 123, 3 = \pi\,\right]\right) \tag{6.90}$$

Example: Computing an Average

A common problem is to write a procedure that computes the average of **n** data values x_1, x_2, ..., x_n according to the following equation:

$$\mu = \frac{\sum_{i=1}^{n} x_i}{n}$$

Before writing the procedure, think about which data structure and Maple functions to use. You can represent the data for this problem as a list. The **numelems** function returns the total number of entries in a list **X**, while the **i**th entry of the list is obtained by using **X[i]**:

```
> X := [1.3, 5.3, 11.2, 2.1, 2.1];
```
$$X := [1.3, 5.3, 11.2, 2.1, 2.1] \tag{6.91}$$

```
> numelems(X);
```
$$5 \tag{6.92}$$

```
> X[2];
```
$$5.3 \tag{6.93}$$

```
> add( i, i=X );
```
$$22.0 \tag{6.94}$$

Using these ideas, write the procedure **Average** which computes the average of the entries in a list. It handles empty lists as a special case:

```
> Average := proc( L::list, $ )
    local n := numelems(L), i, total;
    if n = 0 then
        error "empty list"
    end if;
    total := add(i,i=L);
    total / n
  end proc:
```

Using this procedure you can find the average of list **X** defined above:

```
> Average(X);
```
$$4.400000000 \tag{6.95}$$

The procedure also works if the list contains symbolic entries:

```
> Average([a, b, c]);
```

$$\frac{1}{3} a + \frac{1}{3} b + \frac{1}{3} c \tag{6.96}$$

Calling **Average** with an empty list raises an exception:

```
> Average([]);
Error, (in Average) empty list
```

A list is a good choice for the data in this example because the data is stored and used in a calculation, but the list itself does not need to be modified.

Example: Binary Search

One of the most basic and well-studied computing problems is that of searching. A typical problem involves searching a list of words (a dictionary, for example) for a specific word **w**. There are many possible methods. One approach is to search the list by comparing each word in the dictionary with **w** until either **w** is found, or the end of the list is reached. Study the code for procedure **LinearSearch** (the first attempt at solving this problem):

```
> LinearSearch := proc( D::list(string), w::string )
      local x;
      for x in D do
          if x = w then
              return true
          end if
      end do;
      false
  end proc:
```

Unfortunately, if the dictionary is large, this approach can take a long time. You can reduce the execution time required by sorting the dictionary before you search it. If you sort the dictionary into ascending order, then you can stop searching as soon as you encounter a word greater than **w**. On average, it is still necessary to search half the dictionary.

Binary searching provides an even better approach. Check the word in the middle of the sorted dictionary. Since the dictionary is already sorted, you can determine whether **w** is in the first or the second half. Repeat the process with the appropriate half of the dictionary until **w** is found, or it is determined not to be in the dictionary.

```
> BinarySearch := proc( D::list(string), w::string )
      local low := 1, high := numelems(D), mid;
      while low <= high do
          mid := trunc((low + high) / 2);
```

```
            if w < D[mid] then
                high := mid - 1
            elif w > D[mid] then
                low := mid + 1
            else
                return true
            end if
        end do;
        false
    end proc:
> Dictionary := [ "induna", "ion", "logarithm", "meld" ];
```

$$\textit{Dictionary} := [\text{"induna"}, \text{"ion"}, \text{"logarithm"}, \text{"meld"}] \tag{6.97}$$

```
> BinarySearch( Dictionary, "hedgehogs" );
```

$$\textit{false} \tag{6.98}$$

```
> BinarySearch( Dictionary, "logarithm" );
```

$$\textit{true} \tag{6.99}$$

```
> BinarySearch( Dictionary, "melody" );
```

$$\textit{false} \tag{6.100}$$

Example: Plotting the Roots of a Polynomial

You can construct lists of any type of object, including other lists. A list that contains two numbers can represent a point in the plane, and a list of such list can represent several such points. The Maple **plot** command uses this structure to generate plots of points and lines.

```
> plot([ [0, 0], [1, 2], [-1, 2] ],
    style=point, symbol=point, color=black);
```

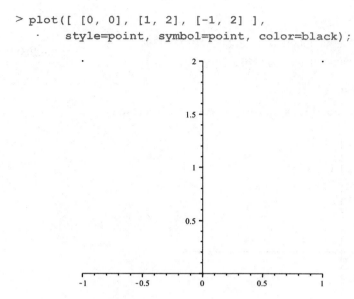

You can make use of this to write a procedure that plots the complex roots of a polynomial. For example, consider the polynomial $x^3 - 1$.

```
> y := x^3-1;
```

$$y := x^3 - 1 \qquad (6.101)$$

First, find the roots of this polynomial. You can find the numeric roots of this polynomial by using **fsolve**. By enclosing the call to **fsolve** in square brackets, you create a list of the roots.

```
> R := [ fsolve(y=0, x, complex) ];
```

$$R := [\, -0.500000000000000 - 0.866025403784439\, I,$$
$$-0.500000000000000 + 0.866025403784439\, I, 1. \,] \qquad (6.102)$$

Next, change this list of complex numbers into a list of points in the plane. The **Re** and **Im** functions return the real and imaginary parts of a complex number respectively. You can use the **map** function and an anonymous procedure to convert the entire list at once.

```
> points := map(z -> [Re(z), Im(z)], R);
```

$$points := [[-0.500000000000000, -0.866025403784439], [$$
$$-0.500000000000000, 0.866025403784439], [1., 0.]] \tag{6.103}$$

Finally, plot the resulting list.

```
> plot(points, style=point, symbol=point, color=black);
```

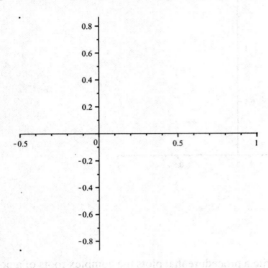

You can automate the process by writing a procedure that follows the same sequence of steps. The input must be a polynomial in **x** with constant coefficients.

```
> RootPlot := proc( p::polynom(constant,x) )
      description "Plots the roots of a polynomial in x";
      local R := [ fsolve(p, x, complex) ];
      local points := map( z -> [Re(z), Im(z)], R );
      plot(points, style=point, symbol=point, color=black)
  end proc:
```

Test the **RootPlot** procedure by plotting the roots of the polynomial $x^6 + 3x^5 + 5x + 10$.

```
> RootPlot( x^6+3*x^5+5*x+10 );
```

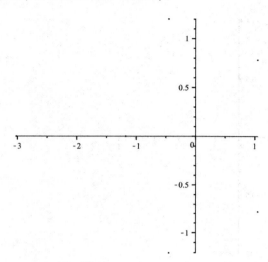

Generate a random polynomial using the **randpoly** function, and then test the **RootPlot** procedure again.

```
> y := randpoly(x, degree=100);
```

$$y := -56x^{95} - 62x^{42} + 97x^8 - 73x^5 - 4x^3 \tag{6.104}$$

```
> RootPlot( y );
```

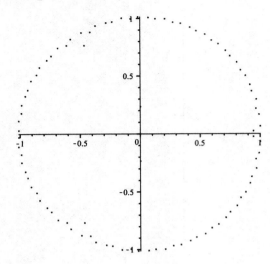

6.8 Writing Usable and Maintainable Procedures

As with any programming language, it is easy to write a Maple procedure that others cannot easily comprehend (or that you, as the author, have trouble understanding when you look at it, or try to modify it, in the future). Maple's syntax provides you with several facilities to alleviate such problems and produce *maintainable code*.

Formatting Procedures for Readability

Although it is possible to enter an entire procedure on a single very long line, this makes it difficult to understand and edit. For example, the binary search procedure shown earlier *could* have been written this way:

```
> BinarySearch := proc( D::list(string), w::string ) local low :=
  1, high := numelems(D), mid; while low <= high do mid := trunc((low
  + high) / 2); if w < D[mid] then high := mid - 1 elif w > D[mid]
  then low := mid + 1 else return true end if end do; false end
  proc:
```

6.8 Writing Usable and Maintainable Procedures

Procedures are more easily readable if written with one statement per line, and with the statements enclosed within the bodies of loops and **if**-statements indented:

```
> BinarySearch := proc( D::list(string), w::string )
      local low := 1, high := numelems(D), mid;
      while low <= high do
          mid := trunc((low + high) / 2);
          if w < D[mid] then
              high := mid - 1
          elif w > D[mid] then
              low := mid + 1
          else
              return true
          end if
      end do;
      false
  end proc:
```

Sometimes, a single statement is too long to fit on a single line. Maple's syntax allows you to insert line breaks and white space between any two syntactic *tokens* such as reserved words, variable names, numbers, and punctuation. Indentation can be used within a statement to clarify the grouping of expressions. For example, the polynomial root plotting procedure could have been written like this:

```
> RootPlot := proc( p::polynom(constant,x) )
      description "Plots the roots of a polynomial in x";
      plot(map(z -> [Re(z), Im(z)],
                [fsolve(p, x, complex)]),
           style=point, symbol=point, color=black)
  end proc:
```

In this version of **RootPlot**, the procedure body consists of a description and a single statement. The indentation makes it clear that **z -> [Re(z), Im(z)]** and **[fsolve(p, x, complex)]** are arguments of the call to **map**, and that the result of this call together with the **style**, **symbol**, and **color** options are the arguments of **plot**.

Commenting Your Code

Comments are one of the most important tools in writing maintainable code. There are two ways of writing comments in Maple procedures:

```
# Comment text until the end of the line.
(* Delimited comment text. *)
```

A # character anywhere within a procedure except inside a **"string"** or **`quoted name`** introduces a comment. Everything following # until the end of the line is considered to be a comment and is ignored by Maple. This form is useful for short comments of one or two lines, or to annotate a line.

```
> Average := proc( )
      # Compute total.
      local total := add(_passed[i],i=1.._npassed);
      # Divide total by number of values.
      total / _npassed;
  end proc;
```

$$\begin{aligned}&Average := \mathbf{proc}(\ ) \\ &\quad \mathbf{local}\ total; \\ &\quad total := add(args[i], i = 1..nargs);\ total/nargs \\ &\mathbf{end\ proc}\end{aligned} \qquad (6.105)$$

Comments enclosed in **(*** and ***)** can begin and end anywhere except within a **"string"** or **`quoted name`**. Everything between the delimiters is ignored by Maple. This form can be used within a line or to write a multiline comment.

```
> BetterAverage := proc( )
      (* This procedure computes the average of its
         arguments. It is an error if no arguments were
         passed. *)
      if _npassed = 0 then
          error "too few values"
      else
          add(_passed[i],i=1.._npassed) (*TOTAL*) / _npassed
      end if
  end proc;
```

$$\begin{aligned}&BetterAverage := \mathbf{proc}(\ ) \\ &\quad \mathbf{if}\ nargs = 0\ \mathbf{then} \\ &\quad\quad \mathbf{error}\ \text{"too few values"} \\ &\quad \mathbf{else} \\ &\quad\quad add(args[i], i = 1..nargs)/nargs \\ &\quad \mathbf{end\ if} \\ &\mathbf{end\ proc}\end{aligned} \qquad (6.106)$$

Notice that comments are discarded by Maple when the procedure is simplified. Comments are purely for the benefit of the programmer(s) who write, read, and maintain the procedure.

As described earlier, a procedure in Maple can also have a **description** section. One or more strings can follow the **description** keyword. Like comments, these have no effect on the execution of the procedure, but they are retained when the procedure is simplified.

```
> AnotherAverage := proc( )
       description "Compute the average of one or more values.",
                   "At least one value must be passed.";
       if _npassed = 0 then
           error "too few values"
       else
           add(_passed[i],i=1.._npassed) / _npassed
       end if
  end proc:
```

You can use Maple's **Describe** command to print a procedure's declared parameters, return type, and description.

```
> Describe(AnotherAverage);

# Compute the average of one or more values.
# At least one value must be passed.
AnotherAverage( )

> Describe(RootPlot);

# Plots the roots of a polynomial in x
RootPlot( p::polynom(constant,x) )
```

6.9 Other Methods for Creating Procedures

Enclosing a sequence of statements in **proc...end proc** is not the only way to create a procedure in Maple. You can also use functional operator notation or the **unapply** function.

Functional Operators: Mapping Notation

Functional operator notation (or *arrow* notation) is a method by which you can create a special form of procedure which represents a mathematical function or mapping. The syntax is:

```
( parameterSequence ) -> expression
```

The **parameterSequence** can be empty, and the **expression** must be a *single* expression or an **if** statement.

```
> F := (x,y) -> x^2 + y^2;
```

$$F := (x, y) \rightarrow x^2 + y^2 \tag{6.107}$$

If the procedure requires only a single parameter, you can omit the parentheses around **parameterSequence**:

```
> G := n -> if n < 0 then 0 else 1 end if;
```

$$G := n \rightarrow \textbf{if } n < 0 \textbf{ then } 0 \textbf{ else } 1 \textbf{ end if} \tag{6.108}$$

Internally, a procedure created using operator notation is the same as any other procedure, except that it will have **options operator, arrow**. You can invoke such a procedure in the usual way:

```
> F(1,2);
```

$$5 \tag{6.109}$$

```
> G(-1);
```

$$0 \tag{6.110}$$

You can use declared parameter types when defining a functional operator:

```
> H := ( n::even ) -> n! * (n/2)!;
```

$$H := n{::}even \rightarrow n! \left(\frac{1}{2} n\right)! \tag{6.111}$$

```
> H(6);
```

$$4320 \tag{6.112}$$

```
> H(5);
Error, invalid input: H expects its 1st argument, n, to be of type
even, but received 5
```

The arrow notation is designed for simple one-line function definitions. It does not provide a mechanism for specifying local or global variables, options, a description, or more than a single statement. If these are required, use the more general **proc...end proc** notation.

The unapply Function

Another way to create a procedure is with the **unapply** function:

```
unapply( expression, parameterSequence )
```

The **expression** must be a *single* expression, and **parameterSequence** a sequence of symbols.

```
> B := x^2 + y^2;
```
$$B := x^2 + y^2 \tag{6.113}$$

```
> F := unapply(B, x, y);
```
$$F := (x, y) \to x^2 + y^2 \tag{6.114}$$

```
> F(3,4);
```
$$25 \tag{6.115}$$

The functional operator notation (or arrow notation) is a *syntax* for writing an operator. The **unapply** function is a *function* mapping expressions to procedures. Use the **unapply** function to create a procedure from an expression that was *computed* instead of one that was *entered*. This works because **unapply** first evaluates the expression and then encloses the result in a procedure. The arrow notation always produces a procedure containing the expression that was entered.

```
> IntExpr := int(1/(x^3+1), x);
```
$$IntExpr := -\frac{1}{6}\ln(x^2 - x + 1) + \frac{1}{3}\sqrt{3}\arctan\left(\frac{1}{3}(2x - 1)\sqrt{3}\right) + \frac{1}{3}\ln(x + 1) \tag{6.116}$$

```
> IntFunc := unapply(evalf(IntExpr), x);
```
$$\begin{aligned}IntFunc := x \to &-0.1666666667\ln(x^2 - 1.x + 1.)\\ &+ 0.5773502693\arctan(1.154700539x - 0.5773502693)\\ &+ 0.3333333333\ln(x + 1.)\end{aligned} \tag{6.117}$$

```
> IntFunc(3.5);
```
$$0.8664586908 \tag{6.118}$$

If you had tried to use operator notation to create the **IntFunc** procedure, you would not get what you expected:

```
> BadIntFunc := x -> evalf(IntExpr);
```
$$BadIntFunc := x \to evalf(IntExpr) \tag{6.119}$$

```
> BadIntFunc(3.5);
```
$$\begin{aligned}&-0.1666666667\ln(x^2 - 1.x + 1.)\\ &+ 0.5773502693\arctan(1.154700539x - 0.5773502693)\\ &+ 0.3333333333\ln(x + 1.)\end{aligned} \tag{6.120}$$

Notice that the result still contains the symbol **x**. This is because the **x** appearing in **IntExpr** is the *global* variable **x**, not the *parameter* **x** of **BadIntFunc**.

Anonymous Procedures

Recall from the beginning of this chapter that a procedure is a valid Maple expression, independent from any name that it may have been assigned to. You can in fact create, manipulate, and invoke a procedure without ever assigning it to name. Such procedures are called *anonymous*.

Consider the following mapping (a procedure in functional operator notation):

```
> x -> x^2;
```

$$x \to x^2 \tag{6.121}$$

You can invoke this anonymous procedure in the following manner:

```
> (x -> x^2) (t);
```

$$t^2 \tag{6.122}$$

Syntactically, this is a Maple function call. Instead of specifying the procedure to call by giving its name, the procedure is given directly. The same method can be used to directly call a procedure defined using the **proc...end proc** notation:

```
> proc( x, y ) x^2 + y^2 end proc (u, v);
```

$$u^2 + v^2 \tag{6.123}$$

Anonymous procedures are often used with the **map** function:

```
> map( x -> x^2, [1,2,3,4] );
```

$$[1, 4, 9, 16] \tag{6.124}$$

They are also used to initialize Arrays in *Arrays (page 148)*. You can find numerous other examples of anonymous procedures in this guide.

Procedures, whether anonymous or not, can be combined in expressions, or processed by operators such as **D**, the differential operator:

```
> D( x -> x^2 );
```

$$x \to 2x \tag{6.125}$$

```
> F := D( exp + 2 * ln );
```

$$F := \exp + 2 \left(z \to \frac{1}{z} \right) \tag{6.126}$$

```
> F(x);
```

$$e^x + \frac{2}{x} \tag{6.127}$$

6.10 Recursion

A procedure is termed *recursive* if it contains a call to itself, either directly, or indirectly through another procedure that it calls. In order for a recursive procedure to produce a result, it must test for some condition under which the recursion terminates. Otherwise, it would go on calling itself forever (until Maple runs out of *stack* space).

You have already seen one example of recursion used to compute Fibonacci numbers in *The remember, cache, and system Options (page 218)*. Another well-known example of recursion is the computation of the factorial of an integer. For any integer $0 < n$, the factorial (denoted by $n!$) is defined by $n! = n(n-1)!$. For $n = 0$, $n!$ is defined to be equal to 1. This definition naturally lends itself to a recursive implementation:

```
> Fact := proc( n::nonnegint, $ )
      if n > 0 then
          n * Fact(n-1)
      else
          1
      end if
  end proc;
```

$$Fact := \mathbf{proc}(n::nonnegint, \$) \\ \mathbf{if}\ 0 < n\ \mathbf{then}\ n*Fact(n-1)\ \mathbf{else}\ 1\ \mathbf{end\ if} \tag{6.128} \\ \mathbf{end\ proc}$$

```
> Fact(0);
```

$$1 \tag{6.129}$$

```
> Fact(4);
```

$$24 \tag{6.130}$$

```
> Fact(-4);
Error, invalid input: Fact expects its 1st argument, n, to be of type
 nonnegint, but received -4
```

The **if**-statement ensures that **Fact** only calls itself when $0 < n$.

Rather than using the name to which the procedure has been assigned to make the recursive call, you can also use **procname** or **thisproc**. This ensures that the recursion continues to work even if the procedure body is later assigned to a different name. The special symbol **procname** refers to the name that the procedure was called with. In the **Fact** example, **procname** would be equivalent to **Fact**. The symbol **thisproc** on the other hand refers to the procedure itself. Calling the procedure recursively using **thisproc** is slightly more efficient, and works within anonymous procedures.

This example uses an anonymous version of the **Fact** procedure above to compute the factorials of a list of numbers:

```
> map( n -> if n > 0 then n * thisproc(n-1) else 1 end if,
       [0, 1, 2, 3, 4] );
```

$$[1, 1, 2, 6, 24] \qquad (6.131)$$

The **BinarySearch** procedure you saw earlier also lends itself to a recursive implementation.

```
> BinarySearch := proc( D::list(string), w::string,
                        low::integer := 1, high ::integer :=
   numelems(D) )
       local mid;
       if low > high then
           # Nothing left to search. Word is not in list.
           false
       else
           mid := trunc((low + high) / 2);
           if w < D[mid] then
               # Search within the left part of the range.
               thisproc(D,w,low,mid-1)
           elif w > D[mid] then
               # Search within the right part of the range.
               thisproc(D,w,mid+1,high)
           else
               # Word was found in middle of current range.
               true
           end if
       end if
   end proc:
```

```
> Dictionary := [ "induna", "ion", "logarithm", "meld" ];
```
$$Dictionary := [\text{"induna"}, \text{"ion"}, \text{"logarithm"}, \text{"meld"}] \tag{6.132}$$
```
> BinarySearch( Dictionary, "hedgehogs" );
```
$$false \tag{6.133}$$
```
> BinarySearch( Dictionary, "logarithm" );
```
$$true \tag{6.134}$$
```
> BinarySearch( Dictionary, "melody" );
```
$$false \tag{6.135}$$

You use this procedure by passing it a sorted list of strings and a word to search for. The two optional parameters, **low** and **high**, specify which range of list elements to search and have default values specifying the entire list. After determining that the word is lexicographically less than or greater than the middle value, this procedure calls itself recursively, passing the list and word, as well as appropriate values for the **low** and **high** parameters to restrict the search. The recursion (and thus the search) ends when the procedure is asked to search a zero-length section of the list (in which case the word was not found), or when the middle element of the specified range contains the word.

If your procedure has the **procname** *option*, any attempt to make a recursive call via **procname** instead of **thisproc** calls the procedure that invoked your procedure.

6.11 Procedures that Return Procedures

Some of the built-in Maple commands return procedures. For example, **rand** returns a procedure which in turn produces randomly chosen integers from a specified range. The **dsolve** function with the **type=numeric** option returns a procedure which supplies a numeric estimate of the solution to a differential equation.

You can write procedures that return procedures too. This section discusses how values are passed from the outer procedure to the inner procedure.

Example: Creating a Newton Iteration

The following example demonstrates how locating the roots of a function by using Newton's method can be implemented in a procedure.

To use Newton's method to find the roots of a function graphically:

Choose a point on the *x*-axis that you think might be close to a root.

Draw the tangent to the curve at that point and observe where the tangent intersects the
x-axis. For most functions, this second point is closer to the real root than the initial guess.
Use the new point as a new guess and repeat this process.

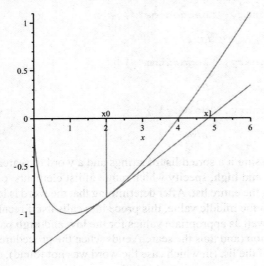

The same process can be expressed numerically as an iteration:

$$x_{k+1} = x_k - \frac{f(x_k)}{f'(x_k)}$$

where x_0 is the initial guess, and x_k is the result of the **k**th iteration.

The following procedure takes a function and creates a new procedure which expects an
initial guess and, for that particular function, generates the next guess. The new procedure
is specific to the function that it was generated for, and does not work for other functions.
To find the roots of a new function, use **MakeIteration** to generate a new iterating procedure.

```
> MakeIteration := proc( expr::algebraic, x::name )
      local iteration := x - expr / diff(expr, x);
      unapply(iteration, x);
  end proc:
```

The procedure returned by the **MakeIteration** procedure maps the name **x** to the expression
assigned to the iteration.

Test the procedure on the expression $x - 2\sqrt{x}$:

```
> expr := x - 2 * sqrt(x);
```

$$expr := x - 2\sqrt{x} \tag{6.136}$$

```
> iter := MakeIteration(expr,x);
```

$$iter := x \to x - \frac{x - 2\sqrt{x}}{1 - \dfrac{1}{\sqrt{x}}} \tag{6.137}$$

The generated procedure, which is assigned to **iter**, returns the solution, $x = 4$ after a few iterations.

```
> x0 := 2.0:
> to 4 do x0 := iter(x0); print(x0) end do:
```

$$4.828427124$$
$$4.032533198$$
$$4.000065353$$
$$4.000000000 \tag{6.138}$$

Observe that the **MakeIteration** procedure above requires its first argument to be an algebraic expression. You can also write a version of **MakeIteration** that works on other procedures (such as functional operators).

```
> MakeIteration := proc( f::procedure )
    (x->x) - eval(f) / D(eval(f));
  end proc:
```

This example uses Maple's ability to treat expressions *containing* procedures *as* procedures. The result of calling this version of **MakeIteration** is an expression with procedures as operands (**x->x** is just a procedure that maps any value to itself).

Because of *last name evaluation*, **MakeIteration** will accept either a procedure or a *name* whose value is a procedure. The calls to **eval** within **MakeIteration** ensure that the result refers to the actual procedure that was passed in, instead of to the name of that procedure.

```
> g := x -> x - cos(x);
```

$$g := x \to x - \cos(x) \tag{6.139}$$

```
> iter := MakeIteration(g);
```

$$iter := (x \to x) - \frac{x \to x - \cos(x)}{x \to 1 + \sin(x)} \tag{6.140}$$

Note that the procedure generated by the call to **MakeIteration** is independent of the name **g** (because of the aforementioned calls to **eval**). Thus, you can later change **g** without breaking **iter**. You can find a good approximate solution to $x - \cos(x) = 0$ in a few iterations.

```
> x0 := 1.0;
```

$$x0 := 1.0 \tag{6.141}$$

```
> to 4 do x0 := iter(x0); print(x0) end do;
```

$$0.7503638679$$

$$0.7391128909$$

$$0.7390851334$$

$$0.7390851332 \tag{6.142}$$

Example: A Shift Operator

Consider the problem of writing a procedure that takes a function, f, as input and returns a function, g, such that $g(x) = f(x + 1)$. You can write such a procedure like this:

```
> ShiftLeft := ( f::procedure ) -> ( x -> f(x+1) ):
```

Try performing a shift on sin(x).

```
> ShiftLeft(sin);
```

$$x \to \sin(x + 1) \tag{6.143}$$

Maple lexical scoping rules declare the **f** within the inner procedure to be the same **f** as the parameter of the outer procedure. Therefore, the **ShiftLeft** procedure works as written.

The previous example of **ShiftLeft** works with univariate functions but it does not work with functions of two or more variables.

```
> h := (x,y) -> x*y;
```

$$h := (x, y) \to xy \tag{6.144}$$

```
> hh := ShiftLeft(h);
```

$$hh := x \to h(x + 1) \tag{6.145}$$

```
> hh(x,y);
Error, (in hh) invalid input: h uses a 2nd argument, y, which is
missing
```

To modify **ShiftLeft** to work with multivariate functions, rewrite it to generate procedures that accept the additional parameters and pass them on to **f**.

```
> ShiftLeft := ( f::procedure ) -> ( x->f(x+1,_rest) ):
> hh := ShiftLeft(h);
```

$$hh := x \rightarrow h(x + 1, \_rest) \tag{6.146}$$

```
> hh(x,y);
```

$$(x + 1) y \tag{6.147}$$

Because the **ShiftLeft** procedure does not call **eval** on parameter **f**, the function **hh** depends on **h**. Changing the value assigned to **h** implicitly changes **hh**:

```
> h := (x,y,z) -> y*z^2/x;
```

$$h := (x, y, z) \rightarrow \frac{y z^2}{x} \tag{6.148}$$

```
> hh(x,y,z);
```

$$\frac{y z^2}{x + 1} \tag{6.149}$$

6.12 The Procedure Object

Recall that a Maple procedure is itself an *expression* in Maple which can be (and usually is) assigned to a name. Like any Maple expression, a procedure has a *type*, and has *operands* (not to be confused with its parameters).

The procedure Type

Maple recognizes all procedures (and names to which a procedure has been assigned) as being of type **procedure**. To verify whether a name or an expression is a procedure, use the **type** function or **::** operator:

```
> F := proc( x ) x^2 end proc:
> type(F, name);
```

$$true \tag{6.150}$$

```
> type(F, procedure);
```
$$true \qquad (6.151)$$

```
> type(F, name(procedure));
```
$$true \qquad (6.152)$$

```
> type(eval(F), name);
```
$$false \qquad (6.153)$$

```
> type(eval(F), procedure);
```
$$true \qquad (6.154)$$

The **procedure** type is a *structured type* (see *Structured Types (page 123)*). Using a structured type allows you to verify that a name refers to a procedure, and additionally verify the specified types of the procedure's parameters.

```
> G := proc( n::integer, s::string )
    print(s);
    2 * n * length(s)
  end proc:
> type(G, procedure(integer,string));
```
$$true \qquad (6.155)$$

Procedure Operands

Every Maple procedure has eight operands, corresponding to sub-parts of the procedure definition. The following table lists each operand and the corresponding **op** call that can be used to access it. In the table, the name **P** represents the name of the procedure, and the **eval** call is necessary so that **op** will be passed the procedure, not the name (because procedures have last name evaluation).

Table 6.1: Procedure Operands

Operand	op Command
Parameters	op(1,eval(P))
All local variables	op(2,eval(P))
Options	op(3,eval(P))
Remember table	op(4,eval(P))
Description	op(5,eval(P))
Declared global variables	op(6,eval(P))
Lexical scoping table	op(7,eval(P))

Operand	op Command
Return type	op(8,eval(P))

The value of any operand can be a single item, an expression sequence if there are two or more items (such as local variables), or **NULL** if there were no items (for example, no options).

The lexical scoping table is an internal structure that records the correspondence between undeclared variables within the procedure and locals (or exports), globals, and parameters of surrounding procedures (or modules). It does not correspond to any part of the procedure as written.

The procedure's statement sequence is *not* one of the operands of the procedure, and thus cannot be extracted by **op**. This is because statements and statement sequences are *not* expressions, and thus cannot be assigned to names or otherwise manipulated.

The following nested procedure illustrates how the parts of the procedure map to the operands. Note that this example refers to the procedure that appears *within*, and is *returned by* procedure **MakeProc** (in order to illustrate lexical scoping). This procedure is not intended to illustrate good programming style, but merely provide an example showing all the possible operands.

```
> MakeProc := proc( offset::integer )
      description "Create and return a procedure";
      proc( n::integer, s::string ) :: integer;
          description "An example to illustrate procedure operands";

          option remember;
          global codes := convert(s,bytes);
          local i;
          total := 0;
          for i to nops(codes) do
              total := total + codes[i]
          end do;
          total * n + offset
      end proc:
  end proc:
Warning, `total` is implicitly declared local to procedure
> P := MakeProc(3):
> P; # The name of the procedure
```

$$P$$

(6.156)

```
> eval(P);  # The procedure
```
    proc(*n*::*integer*, *s*::*string*)::*integer*;
       option *remember*;
       local *i*, *total*;
       global *codes*;
       description "An example to illustrate procedure operands";   (6.157)
       codes := *convert*(*s*, *bytes*);
       total := 0;
       for *i* **to** *nops*(*codes*) **do** *total* := *total* + *codes*[*i*] **end do**;
       total*n + 3
    end proc

```
> op(1,eval(P));  # Parameters
```
$$n\text{::}integer, s\text{::}string \tag{6.158}$$

```
> op(2,eval(P));  # All local variables
```
$$i, total \tag{6.159}$$

```
> op(3,eval(P));  # Options
```
$$remember \tag{6.160}$$

```
> P(3,"nonsense");  # Place an entry in the remember table
```
$$2622 \tag{6.161}$$

```
> op(4,eval(P));  # Show the remember table
```
$$table([\,(3, \text{"nonsense"}) = 2622\,]) \tag{6.162}$$

```
> op(5,eval(P));  # Description
```
$$\text{"An example to illustrate procedure operands"} \tag{6.163}$$

```
> op(6,eval(P));  # Declared global variables
```
$$codes \tag{6.164}$$

```
> op(7,eval(P));  # Lexical table
```
$$offset, 3 \tag{6.165}$$

```
> op(8,eval(P));  # Return type
```
$$integer \tag{6.166}$$

6.13 Exercises

1. Implement the function $f(x) = \left(\sqrt{1-x^2}\right)^3 - 1$, first as a procedure, and then by using the mapping notation. Compute **f(1/2)** and **f(0.5)**, and comment on the different results.

2. You can use $\dfrac{a\,b}{g}$ to compute the least common multiple of two integers, **a** and **b**, where **g** is the greatest common divisor of **a** and **b**. For example, the least common multiple of 4 and 6 is 12. Write a Maple procedure, **LCM**, which takes as input n>0 integers $a_1, a_2, \ldots, a_n$ and and computes their least common multiple. By convention, the least common multiple of zero and any other number is zero.

3. Write a Maple procedure called **Sigma** which, given n>1 data values, $x_1, x_2, \ldots, x_n$, computes their standard deviation. The following equation gives the standard deviation of n>1 numbers, where mu is the average of the data values.

$$\text{sigma} = \sqrt{\dfrac{\sum_{i=1}^{n}(x_i - \text{mu})^2}{n}}$$

4. Write a Maple procedure which, given a list of lists of numerical data, computes the mean of each column of the data.

5. Write a Maple procedure called **Position** which returns the position **i** of an element **x** in a list **L**. That is, **Position(x,L)** should return an integer i>0 such that **L[i]=x**. If **x** is not in list **L**, **0** is returned.

7 Numerical Programming in Maple

An important part of efficient scientific and mathematical programming is numerical computation. Maple provides many tools for computing with floating-point numbers, some for improving efficiency and some for improving accuracy.

7.1 In This Chapter

- An Overview of Numeric Types in Maple
- An Explanation of Floating-Point Numbers in Maple
- Maple Commands for Numerical Computing
- Efficient Numerical Programs

7.2 Numeric Types in Maple

Before discussing numerical computing in Maple, we will first introduce the various numeric data types used in Maple and briefly describe how they are represented. All of the real numbers discussed in this section will pass checks of **type,numeric** or **type,extended_numeric**.

Integers

The most basic numeric type in Maple is the **integer**. Small integers are represented directly as hardware integers (similar to the **int** type in C or **integer** type in Fortran), which allows for maximum efficiency of both CPU time used for arithmetic and memory used for storage. That is, the number can be stored in one machine word and arithmetic operations can be performed with one CPU operation. On 32-bit architectures, integers in the range $-2^{30}-1$ to $2^{30}-1$ are stored in this way, while on 64-bit architectures, integers in the range $-2^{62}-1$ to $2^{62}-1$. Integers stored in this way are referred to as *immediate integers*.

Larger integers are stored in DAGs of type INTPOS or INTNEG, which contain pointers to arrays of digits that can store integers up to magnitude $10^{2^{28}} - 218$ on 32-bit architectures and $10^{2^{35} + 2^{32} - 18}$ on 64-bit architectures.

```
> dismantle(2^80-1);
```

```
INTPOS(6): 1208925819614629174706175
```

```
> dismantle(-2^101+6);
```

INTNEG(6): -2535301200456458802993406410746

The arithmetic for these large integers is computed using the GNU Multiple Precision Arithmetic (GMP) library. This library is quite efficient, but still several orders of magnitude slower than arithmetic on immediate integers since each arithmetic operation will require more than one CPU operation and the larger the integer, the more operations and memory will be needed for arithmetic.

```
> CodeTools:-Usage(add(i,i=-2^15..2^16));
```
memory used=160.50KiB, alloc change=0 bytes, cpu time=14.00ms, real time=13.00ms

$$1610629120 \tag{7.1}$$

```
> CodeTools:-Usage(add(i,i=2^88-2^15..2^88+2^16));
```
memory used=8.92MiB, alloc change=8.00MiB, cpu time=24.00ms, real time=24.00ms

$$30423923890487326980991212339200 \tag{7.2}$$

```
> CodeTools:-Usage(add(i,i=2^4097-2^15..2^4097+2^16));
```
memory used=109.33MiB, alloc change=117.05MiB, cpu time=118.00ms, real time=117.00ms

$$\begin{aligned}&2053372979746399143406655004539955198590467710052061\text{\textbackslash}\\&50613441451484581778462879115910478394945398699[..\\&.1039\text{ digits}...]\\&639539355561974938908606751178417216122109439600358\\&44502548975147538697028344437068066641469725900\tag{7.3}\end{aligned}$$

Any transitions between GMP integers and immediate integers will be completely transparent and it is not possible to tell them apart in general without use low-level tools such as **addressof**. However, you can check if an integer is small enough to fit into a single machine word with types **integer[4]** and **integer[8]** for 4-byte and 8-byte words respectively.

Integers of all types pass a **type,integer** type check.

The **Integer** constructor is guaranteed to return an integer, an extended numeric symbol such as infinity or undefined, a complex number with integer parts, or return unevaluated.

```
> Integer(-2^160);
```

$$-1461501637330902918203684832716283019655932542976 \tag{7.4}$$

```
> Integer(infinity);
```

$$\infty \qquad (7.5)$$

```
> Integer(1/2);
```

$$\text{Integer}\left(\frac{1}{2}\right) \qquad (7.6)$$

The system dependent value for the largest immediate integer can be found with **kernelopts(maximmediate)**, the maximum number of decimal digits in an integer can be found with **kernelopts(maxdigits)**, and the version of the GMP library being used can be found with **kernelopts(gmpversion)**.

Rationals

Exact rational numbers are stored in DAGs of type RATIONAL, which consist of a pair of integers. The first integer is the numerator and can be a POSINT or NEGINT. The second integer is the denominator and is a POSINT. Most low-level programming languages such as C or Fortran do not have an equivalent rational number type.

```
> dismantle(1/2);

RATIONAL(3): 1/2
   INTPOS(2): 1
   INTPOS(2): 2

> dismantle(-10/3);

RATIONAL(3): -10/3
   INTNEG(2): -10
   INTPOS(2): 3
```

Rational numbers can be constructed by using the division operator or the **Fraction** constructor. In either case, automatic simplification will occur to ensure that the denominator is positive and that the fraction is in lowest terms (the numerator and denominator do not have factors in common). This means that the Fraction constructor may return integers in some cases.

```
> dismantle(Fraction(21,7));

INTPOS(2): 3
```

```
> dismantle(Fraction(40,-14));

RATIONAL(3): -20/7
   INTNEG(2): -20
   INTPOS(2): 7
```

Rational number arithmetic is performed in the natural way using integer arithmetic and the **igcd** and **ilcm** operations to reduce to lowest terms.

```
> Fraction(2^20+2^12,2^27-2^13) + Fraction(2^12-1,2^13);
```

$$\frac{68141057}{134209536} \tag{7.7}$$

```
> Fraction(2^20+2^12,2^27-2^13) * Fraction(23,187);
```

$$\frac{5911}{6127242} \tag{7.8}$$

Rational numbers of all types will pass a **type,rational** type check. Only rational numbers that are not also integers will pass a **type,fraction** type check. Additionally, **type,extended_rational** includes all rationals as well as the extended numeric symbols **infinity**, **-infinity**, and **undefined**.

```
> type(1, fraction);
```

$$\textit{false} \tag{7.9}$$

Like the Integer constructor, the Fraction constructor will return unevaluated if it cannot return a value of type extended_rational.

```
> Fraction(x,1);
```

$$\textit{Fraction}(x, 1) \tag{7.10}$$

```
> Fraction(infinity);
```

$$\infty \tag{7.11}$$

Floating-Point Numbers

Floating-point numbers are stored in DAGs of type FLOAT.

In Maple, as in nearly every programming language, floating-point numbers can be constructed using and visually distinguished from integers with a decimal point symbol, '.'. The floating-point number 1. is often treated as equal to the exact integer 1.

```
> evalb(1. = 1);
```
$$true \tag{7.12}$$

Maple floating-point numbers can also be constructed with the **SFloat** constructor (or the equivalent **Float** constructor) and can be checked with the nearly equivalent **type,sfloat** and **type,float** types. We will generally refer to these numbers as *sfloats* to when we need to distinguish them from hardware floating-point numbers (*hfloats*), introduced below.

```
> Float(1);
```
$$1. \tag{7.13}$$

```
> dismantle(SFloat(0.3333));

FLOAT(3): .3333
   INTPOS(2): 3333
   INTNEG(2): -4
```

```
> type(.1, float);
```
$$true \tag{7.14}$$

```
> type(.1, sfloat);
```
$$true \tag{7.15}$$

```
> type(1, float);
```
$$false \tag{7.16}$$

A floating-point number represents a rational number with a fixed precision. That rational number can be recovered with **convert/rational**.

```
> convert(.3333333333, rational, exact);
```
$$\frac{3333333333}{10000000000} \tag{7.17}$$

However, not every rational number can be represented exactly by a floating-point number. For example, the closest floating-point number to $\frac{1}{3}$ is 0.3333333333.

```
> convert(1/3, float);
```
$$0.3333333333 \tag{7.18}$$

Also, unlike numeric types integer and rational, integer and float do not have compatible arithmetic. Floating-point arithmetic has a fixed finite precision, and does round off if the result of arithmetic does not fit into that precision.

```
> 9123456789 + 8123456789 <> convert( 9123456789. + 8123456789.,
    rational, exact);
```

$$17246913578 \neq 17246913580 \tag{7.19}$$

```
> 123456 * 1234567 <> convert( 123456.*1234567., rational, exact);
```

$$152414703552 \neq 152414703600 \tag{7.20}$$

Unlike many other programming languages the precision of sfloat arithmetic can be changed. For this reason, sfloats are known as *arbitrary precision* floating-point numbers.

More information on sfloats and how they differ from the floating-point types in languages such as C and Fortran will be discussed in greater detail in *More about Floating-Point Numbers in Maple (page 279)*.

Hardware Floating-Point Numbers

Floating-point numbers of the type used in languages such as C and Fortran can also be constructed in Maple; they are known as hardware floating-point numbers or *hfloats*. These types are stored as 8-byte double precision IEEE floating-point numbers contained in DAGs of type HFLOAT. Since the . notation is used to construct Maple sfloats, hfloats must be constructed with the **HFloat** constructor. Maple will display sfloats and hfloats the same way, using decimal notation.

```
> HFloat(1);
```

$$1. \tag{7.21}$$

```
> dismantle(HFloat(0.3333));
```

```
HFLOAT(2): .3333
```

The advantage of hfloats over sfloats is that their arithmetic is computed directly using a single CPU operation for each arithmetic operation. Maple sfloats, however, offer much more flexibility and precision. In many ways the difference is analogous to the difference between immediate integers and GMP integers.

Hardware floats can be distinguished from sfloats with the **type,hfloat** type.

```
> type(HFloat(1), float);
```

$$true \tag{7.22}$$

```
> type(HFloat(1), sfloat);
```

$$\textit{false} \qquad (7.23)$$

```
> type(HFloat(1), hfloat);
```

$$\textit{true} \qquad (7.24)$$

```
> type(SFloat(1), hfloat);
```

$$\textit{false} \qquad (7.25)$$

For more information on hardware floats and how they differ from sfloats, see *More about Floating-Point Numbers in Maple (page 279)*.

Extended Numeric Types

The special built-in symbols **infinity** (∞), and **undefined** can be used in numeric arithmetic in Maple. In general, operations involving ∞ simplify automatically to a signed infinity or a complex infinity. For details, refer to the **type,infinity** help page.

```
> -1*infinity;
```

$$-\infty \qquad (7.26)$$

```
> 1/2*infinity;
```

$$\infty \qquad (7.27)$$

```
> 1/infinity;
```

$$0 \qquad (7.28)$$

The **undefined** symbol is usually produced as the result of attempting to carry out an operation that cannot result in a number for the given operands. Almost every arithmetic operation involving **undefined** returns **undefined**. For details, refer to the **type,undefined** help page.

```
> infinity-infinity;
```

$$\textit{undefined} \qquad (7.29)$$

```
> undefined-undefined;
```

$$\textit{undefined} \qquad (7.30)$$

```
> undefined+1;
```

$$\textit{undefined} \qquad (7.31)$$

Integer and rational numbers share exact undefined and infinite symbols while sfloat and hfloat numbers have their own versions of these, which are displayed differently but treated similarly.

```
> Float(infinity);
```

$$\text{Float}(\infty) \tag{7.32}$$

```
> HFloat(undefined);
```

$$\text{HFloat}(undefined) \tag{7.33}$$

Complex Numbers

A complex number in Maple is a DAG of type COMPLEX, which consists of a pair of any of the two numeric types. They can be constructed in the natural way using the symbol I for the imaginary unit, or using the **Complex** constructor.

```
> dismantle(1+I);

COMPLEX(3)
   INTPOS(2): 1
   INTPOS(2): 1

> dismantle(Complex(1/2,1/3));

COMPLEX(3)
   RATIONAL(3): 1/2
      INTPOS(2): 1
      INTPOS(2): 2
   RATIONAL(3): 1/3
      INTPOS(2): 1
      INTPOS(2): 3
```

Automatic simplification will ensure that if one of the parts of a complex number is a float (or hfloat), then other will be made into a float (hfloat).

```
> dismantle(Complex(1., 1/1001));

COMPLEX(3)
   FLOAT(3): 1.
      INTPOS(2): 1
      INTPOS(2): 0
   FLOAT(3): .9990009990e-3
      INTPOS(2): 9990009990
      INTNEG(2): -13
```

```
> dismantle(Complex(HFloat(1.), 1/1001));

COMPLEX(3)
   HFLOAT(2): 1.
   HFLOAT(2): .000999000999


> dismantle(Complex(HFloat(1.), 1.));

COMPLEX(3)
   HFLOAT(2): 1.
   HFLOAT(2): 1.
```

Complex numbers are not of type **type,numeric** but can be checked with type **type,complex** which can also be structured to check for the numeric subtypes of its two components.

```
> type(1+I,numeric);
```
$$\textit{false} \tag{7.34}$$

```
> type(1+I,complex(integer));
```
$$\textit{true} \tag{7.35}$$

Non-numeric Constants

Many Maple expressions represent constants, but are not considered to be of type numeric. This means that arithmetic performed on these constants will be more generic symbolic operations on DAGs of type SUM, PROD, NAME, or FUNCTION. Some examples of non-numeric constants are **Pi** (π), *Catalan*, $\sin(1)$, $\sqrt{5}$, and $\pi + e^2 - \sqrt{1 + 5\,\textit{Catalan}}$.

```
> type(Pi, numeric);
```
$$\textit{false} \tag{7.36}$$

```
> type(sqrt(5)-1, constant);
```
$$\textit{true} \tag{7.37}$$

7.3 More about Floating-Point Numbers in Maple

To take full advantage of floating-point numbers and to avoid many common pitfalls in numerical computing, it is important to understand exactly what floating-point numbers are and how they are represented.

Representation of Floating-Point Numbers in Maple

The dismantle command shows that the two numbers 1 and 1. have different internal representations. 1 is simply stored as an integer while 1. is stored as a pair of integers.

```
> dismantle(1);

INTPOS(2): 1


> dismantle(1.);

FLOAT(3): 1.
   INTPOS(2): 1
   INTPOS(2): 0
```

Similarly, the numbers $\frac{1}{2}$ and 0.5 are also different even though they are both stored as pairs of integers.

```
> dismantle(1/2);

RATIONAL(3): 1/2
   INTPOS(2): 1
   INTPOS(2): 2


> dismantle(0.5);

FLOAT(3): .5
   INTPOS(2): 5
   INTNEG(2): -1
```

In Maple, the FLOAT DAG-type represents a floating-point number in the form **S * 10^E** where both S and E are integers. For 1., the *significand* (or *mantissa*) is $S = 1$ and the *exponent* is $E = 0$. In addition to being specified in decimal notation, floats of this form can be constructed by using scientific notation, or the **Float** constructor.

```
> Float(2,0);
```

$$2. \qquad (7.38)$$

```
> 2*1e0;
```

$$2. \tag{7.39}$$

The advantage of using this significand-exponent representation is that fixed precision approximations of large and small numbers can be stored compactly and their arithmetic can be done efficiently. Storing the integer **10^50** needs at least 167 bits or 3 words on a 64-bit machine. The floating-point number **1e50** can be stored in less than 8 bits but in in practice uses 2 words (one for each integer).

```
> dismantle(10^50);

INTPOS(8): 100000000000000000000000000000000000000000000000000

> dismantle(1e50);

FLOAT(3): .1e51
   INTPOS(2): 1
   INTPOS(2): 50
```

Using two immediate integers, a float can store a much larger range of numbers than a rational number with two immediate integers. The range a rational can represent is about $1.10^{-9}..1.10^{9}$ while a float can represent a range of about $1.10^{-1073741823}..9.10^{1073741823}$. This is a **much** larger range for the same storage cost. Of course, that larger range means that floats of a fixed size can represent fewer numbers in that range. And since floating-point numbers are always of a fixed size, this means that arithmetic will always be of limited precision. That is, each operation will have to round the result to a number that can be represented as another floating-point number.

In Maple, the significand is limited to 10 decimal digits of precision by default but can be changed while the exponent is restricted to being a word-sized integer.

More information on the restrictions on the size of software floats in Maple can be found by using the **Maple_floats** command.

By contrast, hfloats, are represented in base 2, rather than base 10. So they represent numbers using the form $S * 2^E$, where the significand, **S**, is a 52-bit integer and the exponent, **E**, is a 10-bit integer. Thus, the range of numbers representable as hardware floats is $2.225073859 \, 10^{-308}..1.797693135 \, 10^{308}$. Because the largest possible significand of a hardware float has about $\text{floor}\left(\log_{10}(2^{52})\right) = 15$ base-10 digits of precision, hardware floats can be converted to software floats without meaningful loss of precision when Digits is 15. Conversely, so long as their exponent is smaller than 307 and their significand had fewer than 15 digits sfloats can be converted to hfloats without loss of precision.

Precision and Accuracy

By default, 10-digit precision is used for floating-point arithmetic, which means that the arithmetic will be rounded to 10 digits. This means any single floating-point operation will be accurate to 10 digits.

For example, storing **10^50+1** requires 50 decimal digits so it will be rounded in floating-point arithmetic. By contrast, **10^50+10^41** can be stored with 10 digits so it will still be computed accurately.

```
> .1e51 + 1.;
```
$$1.\,10^{50} \tag{7.40}$$

```
> .1e51 + .1e42;
```
$$1.000000001\,10^{50} \tag{7.41}$$

The Digits environment variable can be used to change the working precision used by Maple. Larger values of Digits will allow more accurate computation, but at the cost of slower arithmetic.

```
> Digits := 100:
> .1e51 + 1.;
```
$$1.000000000000000000000000000000000000000000000000001\,10^{50} \tag{7.42}$$

The maximum value for Digits is system dependent and can be found with the **Maple_floats** command.

```
> Maple_floats(MAX_DIGITS);
```
$$38654705646 \tag{7.43}$$

For the default value of Digits, the significand is an immediate integer and so arithmetic will be fast in general. It also means that some numerical function evaluations (such as **sin** in the following example) will be able to use the CPU's native hardware floating-point arithmetic to achieve the needed precision. However, raising Digits about the default value will lead to slower arithmetic and slower function evaluation.

```
> Digits:=10:
> CodeTools:-CPUTime(add(sin(1e-6*i),i=1..100000));
```
$$1.600, 4995.884639 \tag{7.44}$$

```
> Digits:=22:
> CodeTools:-CPUTime(add(sin(1e-6*i),i=1..100000));
```

$$3.676, 4995.884638682140998954 \tag{7.45}$$

Reducing Digits below its default value does not usually lead to large improvements in performance.

```
> Digits:=5:
> CodeTools:-CPUTime(add(sin(1e-6*i),i=1..100000));
```

$$1.073, 4996.0 \tag{7.46}$$

It is also important to note that changing Digits does not necessarily change the accuracy of sequences of multiple floating-point computations; it changes only the precision of the individual operations performed. The following example computes two additions using 10 digits of precision, but *catastrophic cancellation* leads to a mere one digit of accuracy in the final answer.

```
> Digits := 10:
> x := 1234567890.;
```

$$x := 1.234567890 \, 10^9 \tag{7.47}$$

```
> y := -x+1;
```

$$y := -1.234567889 \, 10^9 \tag{7.48}$$

```
> z := 3.141592654;
```

$$z := 3.141592654 \tag{7.49}$$

```
> x+z+y<>z+1;
```

$$4. \neq 4.141592654 \tag{7.50}$$

Ensuring accuracy requires careful study of the problem at hand. In this example, you need 19 digits of precision to get 10 digits of accuracy.

```
> Digits := 19:
> x+z+y=z+1;
```

$$4.141592654 = 4.141592654 \tag{7.51}$$

Floating-Point Contagion

An important property of floating-point numbers in Maple, and nearly every other computing environment, is *contagion*. When numerical expressions are created involving both floating-point numbers and exact numbers, the floating property is *contagious* and causes the answer to become a floating-point number.

```
> 1. * 10;
```

$$10. \tag{7.52}$$

```
> 0. + 10;
```

$$10. \tag{7.53}$$

As you can see, this contagion property can be used as a quick method to convert exact values to floating-point numbers. However, while floating-point contagion extends to all Maple structures of type *numeric* (except, in some cases, hfloats), it does not apply to non-numeric constants.

```
> type(3/4, numeric);
```

$$true \tag{7.54}$$

```
> 4/3 + 0.;
```

$$1.333333333 \tag{7.55}$$

```
> 1.*sqrt(3);
```

$$1.\sqrt{3} \tag{7.56}$$

The **hfloat** type is also contagious, but the precise behavior of the contagion is determined by the **UseHardwareFloats** environment variable. By default, hfloats are contagious for small values of Digits:

```
> type(4/3 + HFloat(0.), hfloat);
```

$$true \tag{7.57}$$

```
> type(1. + HFloat(0.), hfloat);
```

$$true \tag{7.58}$$

```
> HFloat(1.1) * sin(4*Pi/7) -1;
```

$$1.10000000000000 \sin\left(\frac{3}{7}\pi\right) - 1 \tag{7.59}$$

For large values of Digits, hfloats in computations will be converted to sfloats so that the results are sfloats.

```
> Digits := 20;
```

$$Digits := 20 \tag{7.60}$$

7.3 More about Floating-Point Numbers in Maple

```
> type(1 + HFloat(0.), hfloat);
```
$$false \qquad (7.61)$$

```
> type(1 + HFloat(0.), sfloat);
```
$$true \qquad (7.62)$$

If **UseHardwareFloats=true** then hfloats are completely contagious.

```
> UseHardwareFloats := true;
```
$$UseHardwareFloats := true \qquad (7.63)$$

```
> Digits := 20;
```
$$Digits := 20 \qquad (7.64)$$

```
> a := 10.^19+1;
```
$$a := 1.0000000000000000001 \, 10^{19} \qquad (7.65)$$

```
> b := a + HFloat(0.1);
```
$$b := 1.00000000000000 \, 10^{19} \qquad (7.66)$$

```
> type(b, hfloat);
```
$$true \qquad (7.67)$$

If **UseHardwareFloats=false** then hfloats will always be converted to sfloats in computations, regardless of the setting of Digits. The **HFloat** constructor will still create hfloats, however.

```
> UseHardwareFloats := false;
```
$$UseHardwareFloats := false \qquad (7.68)$$

```
> Digits := 10;
```
$$Digits := 10 \qquad (7.69)$$

```
> c := 1 + HFloat(0.1);
```
$$c := 1.100000000 \qquad (7.70)$$

```
> type(c, hfloat);
```
$$false \qquad (7.71)$$

```
> type(HFloat(0.1), hfloat);
```
$$true \qquad (7.72)$$

Table 7.1 summarizes the floating-point contagion rules.

Table 7.1: Floating-Point Contagion Rules

UseHardwareFloats	true	false	deduced	deduced
Digits	any	any	1...15	16...
hfloat + hfloat	hfloat	sfloat	hfloat	sfloat
hfloat + sfloat	hfloat	sfloat	hfloat	sfloat
sfloat + sfloat	sfloat	sfloat	sfloat	sfloat

More on the Floating-Point Model

The software floating-point system is designed as a natural extension of the industry standard for hardware floating-point computation, known as IEEE 754. Thus, there are representations for **infinity** and **undefined** (what IEEE 754 calls a *NaN*, meaning *Not a Number*) as discussed in *Extended Numeric Types (page 277)*.

The IEEE 754 standard defines five rounding algorithms. Two methods called **nearest** and **simple** round to nearest values, and the other three are directed roundings that round up or down (as needed) towards $-\infty$, ∞, or 0. Maple implements all of these rounding modes and the desired mode can be selected by setting the **Rounding** environment variable.

```
> Rounding;
```
$$nearest \qquad (7.73)$$

```
> 1.4^10;
```
$$28.92546550 \qquad (7.74)$$

```
> Rounding := 0;
```
$$Rounding := 0 \qquad (7.75)$$

```
> 1.4^10;
```
$$28.92546549 \qquad (7.76)$$

Another important feature of this system is that the floating-point representation of zero, **0.**, retains its arithmetic sign in computations. That is, Maple distinguishes between **+0.** and **-0.** when necessary. In most situations, this difference is irrelevant, but when dealing with functions that have a discontinuity across the negative real axis, such as $\ln(x)$, preserving the sign of the imaginary part of a number on the negative real axis is important.

For more intricate applications, Maple implements extensions of the IEEE 754 notion of a **numeric event**, and provides facilities for monitoring events and their associated status flags. For more information about this system, refer to the **numerics** help page.

7.4 Maple Commands for Numerical Computing

In this section we will discuss some of the commands available in Maple for floating-point computation.

The evalf Command

The **evalf** command is the primary tool in Maple for performing floating-point calculations in software floating-point mode. You can use **evalf** to compute approximations of non-numeric constants.

```
> evalf(Pi);
```

$$3.141592654 \qquad (7.77)$$

You can alter the number of digits of the approximation by changing the value of the environment variable **Digits**, or by specifying the number as an index to **evalf** (which leaves the value of Digits unchanged).

```
> Digits := 20:
> evalf(Pi);
```

$$3.1415926535897932385 \qquad (7.78)$$

```
> evalf[200](Pi);
```

$$\begin{aligned}3.1415926535897932384626433832795028841971693993751058\backslash\\2097494459230781640628620899862803482534211706798 2\backslash\\1480865132823066470938446095505822317253594081284 8\backslash\\11174502841027019385211055596446229489549303820\end{aligned} \qquad (7.79)$$

```
> evalf(sqrt(2));
```

$$1.4142135623730950488 \qquad (7.80)$$

```
> Digits := 10:
```

Remember that the **Digits** command specifies the precision in decimal digits, unlike hardware floating-point numbers which specify precision in binary digits.

All floating-point computations are performed in *finite precision*, with intermediate results generally being rounded to **Digits** precision. As such, it is possible for round-off errors to accumulate in long computations. Maple ensures that the result of any *single* floating-point arithmetic operation (+, -, *, /, or **sqrt**) is fully accurate. Further, many of the basic functions in Maple, such as the trigonometric functions and their inverses, the exponential and logarithmic functions, and some of the other standard special functions for mathematics, are accurate to within **.6** *units in the last place* (ulps), meaning that if the **Digits + 1st** digit of the true result is a 4, Maple may round it up, or if it is a 6, Maple may round it down. Most mathematical functions in Maple, including numerical integration, achieve this accuracy on nearly all inputs.

It is possible to create software floats with different precisions. Changing the value of **Digits** will not change these numbers; it affects only the precision of subsequent operations on those numbers.

```
> Digits := 50;
```

$$Digits := 50 \tag{7.81}$$

```
> a := evalf(Pi);
```

$$a := 3.1415926535897932384626433832795028841971693993751 \tag{7.82}$$

```
> Digits := 10;
```

$$Digits := 10 \tag{7.83}$$

```
> a;
```

$$3.1415926535897932384626433832795028841971693993751 \tag{7.84}$$

```
> a+1;
```

$$4.141592654 \tag{7.85}$$

```
> evalf(a);
```

$$3.141592654 \tag{7.86}$$

From this example, you can see that **evalf** can be used to create a lower precision float from one of higher precision. This can be used to round a result to a desired number of digits. However, **evalf** will not increase the precision of a low precision float.

```
> evalf[100](1.0);
```

$$1.0 \tag{7.87}$$

```
> evalf[10000](a);
```

$$3.1415926535897932384626433832795028841971693993751 \tag{7.88}$$

The **evalf** command also provides an interface to purely numerical computations of integrals, limits, and sums.

Some definite integrals have no closed-form solution in terms of standard mathematical functions. You can use **evalf** to obtain a numerical answer directly using numerical techniques.

```
> r := Int(exp(x^3), x=0..1);
```

$$r := \int_0^1 e^{x^3}\, dx \qquad (7.89)$$

```
> value(r);
```

$$\int_0^1 e^{x^3}\, dx \qquad (7.90)$$

```
> evalf(r);
```

$$1.341904418 \qquad (7.91)$$

In other cases, Maple can find an exact solution, but the form of the exact solution is almost incomprehensible. The function Beta in the following example is a special function that appears in mathematical literature.

```
> q := Int( x^99 * (1-x)^199 / Beta(100, 200), x=0..1/5 );
```

$$q := \int_0^{\frac{1}{5}} \frac{x^{99}(1-x)^{199}}{\mathrm{B}(100, 200)}\, dx \qquad (7.92)$$

```
> value(q);
```

$$2785229054578052117925524865043430599840384980090969034217041762205271552389776190682816696442051841690247452471818797202945961766386779717574634134906442572750186110143575015735201811298949297254844 9 \big/ \big(21774128091037151646887384971552115934384961767251671031013243122411486103082625144755525240513230831323871784033275024936060378263034137682537367383346083183346165228661133571762601621483528326205933656911850124661471818960066397304198305002716565259568426426994847133755683898925781250000\, \mathrm{B}(100, 200)\big) \qquad (7.93)$$

> evalf(q);

$$3.546007367\,10^{-8} \tag{7.94}$$

The two previous examples use the **Int** command rather than **int** for the integration. If you use **int**, Maple first tries to integrate the expression symbolically. Thus, when evaluating the following commands, Maple determines a symbolic answer and then converts it to a floating-point approximation, rather than performing direct numerical integration. In general, the symbolic computation is more difficult, and thus slower than the numerical computation.

> evalf(int(x^99 * (1-x)^199 / Beta(100, 200), x=0..1/5));

$$3.546007367\,10^{-8} \tag{7.95}$$

Similarly, **evalf** can be used on the inert forms **Limit** and **Sum** to compute using numerical algorithms for computing numeric limits and sums.

> evalf(Limit(sin(erf(1)*x)/(erf(1)^2*x),x=0));

$$1.186660803 \tag{7.96}$$

> evalf(Sum(exp(x), x=RootOf(_Z^5+_Z+1)));

$$4.791792042 + 0.\,I \tag{7.97}$$

When Not to Use evalf

In general the symbolic commands in Maple are able to handle floating-point numbers in their input, but, by their nature floats are not as precise as rationals or symbolic constants. So, even if you want a numerical answer from a command, you should avoid calling evalf on the input.

The following command does not compute the expected answer of 0.1111111111.

> limit(n*(evalf(1/3) - 1/(3+1/n)), n=infinity);

$$-Float(\infty) \tag{7.98}$$

It would have been computed correctly with non-float values in the input.

> evalf(limit(n*(1/3 - 1/(3+1/n)), n=infinity));

$$0.1111111111 \tag{7.99}$$

Numeric Solvers

There are also a number of numerical algorithms available in Maple in commands other than **evalf**. One of the most important is **fsolve** which is short for *floating-point solve*. This command computes numerical solutions to equations or systems of equations. In general, it is much more efficient than calling **evalf** on the result of **solve**, especially if you are interested in only a single solution.

```
> fsolve( exp(x) + 2*sin(x), x);
```

$$-0.3573274113 \tag{7.100}$$

The **fsolve** command is a sophisticated heuristic that chooses among many different algorithms depending on the input. There are several more special purpose solving tools available in the **RootFinding** package.

Several symbolic solvers in Maple also have numeric modes. The **dsolve** and **pdsolve** commands both accept a **numeric** option, which indicates that a numerical answer should be computed using purely numeric methods. For extensive information on these numeric commands, refer to the **dsolve/numeric** and **pdsolve/numeric** help pages.

The evalhf Command

Like **evalf**, **evalhf** computes an numerical approximation of its input. However, **evalhf** uses hardware floats in all intermediate calculations before returning an sfloat.

```
> dismantle( evalhf(1/3) );

FLOAT(3): .333333333333333315
   INTPOS(2): 333333333333333315
   INTNEG(2): -18
```

The **evalhf** command is affected by the value of **Digits**, but since intermediate calculations are done with hfloats, at most 18 digits will be returned.

```
> Digits := 100;
```

$$Digits := 100 \tag{7.101}$$

```
> evalhf(1/3) ;
```

$$0.333333333333333315 \tag{7.102}$$

Notice that in this example the result is only correct to 16 digits. In general, the results from evalhf are guaranteed to 15 digits of accuracy.

To find the number of guaranteed digits for your version of Maple, use **evalhf(Digits)**:

```
> evalhf(Digits);
```

$$15. \tag{7.103}$$

In fact, **evalhf** is, despite superficial similarities, very different from **evalf**. The **evalhf** command uses a completely separate evaluation environment which uses only simple types rather that the Maple DAG types. This means that it can be very fast, but at the cost of being limited in the types of computations it can perform.

```
> Digits := 15;
```

$$Digits := 15 \tag{7.104}$$

```
> c := 10.^14;
```

$$c := 1.00000000000000 \, 10^{14} \tag{7.105}$$

```
> CodeTools:-Usage( evalhf( add( (i+c), i=1..10^6) ) );
memory used=0.86KiB, alloc change=0 bytes, cpu time=27.00ms, real
time=27.00ms
```

$$1.00000000499999867 \, 10^{20} \tag{7.106}$$

```
> CodeTools:-Usage( ( add( (i+c), i=1..10^6) ) );
memory used=126.06MiB, alloc change=119.01MiB, cpu time=718.00ms, real
  time=720.00ms
```

$$1.00000000500000 \, 10^{20} \tag{7.107}$$

```
> c := HFloat(c);
```

$$c := 1.00000000000000 \, 10^{14} \tag{7.108}$$

```
> CodeTools:-Usage( ( add( (i+c), i=1..10^6) ) );
memory used=67.02MiB, alloc change=32.00MiB, cpu time=462.00ms, real
  time=463.00ms
```

$$1.00000000500001 \, 10^{20} \tag{7.109}$$

In particular **evalhf** only handles a specific list of functions. For the list of functions that **evalhf** recognizes, refer to the **evalhf/fcnlist** help page.

```
> evalhf(sin(exp(gamma+2)+ln(cos(Catalan))));
```

$$0.0980197901238379354 \tag{7.110}$$

```
> evalhf( b /3 );
Error, cannot handle unevaluated name `b` in evalhf
```

evalhf works with Arrays of hardware floats. It cannot handle symbols, lists, sets, and most other Maple data structures.

```
> evalhf(map(t->t+1, [1, 2, 3, 4]));
Error, unable to evaluate expression to hardware floats: [1, 2, 3, 4]
```

To create an Array of hardware floats, you can use the option **datatype=float[8]**, which specifies that the elements in the Array are 8-byte hardware floats.

```
> A := Array([1, 2, 3, 4], datatype=float[8]);
```

$$A := \begin{bmatrix} 1. & 2. & 3. & 4. \end{bmatrix} \tag{7.111}$$

```
> evalhf(map(t->t+1, A));
```

$$\begin{bmatrix} 2. & 3. & 4. & 5. \end{bmatrix} \tag{7.112}$$

You can also create an Array that can be used by **evalhf** by using the constructor **hfarray**. Both constructors create an Array of hardware floats. The only difference is that **hfarray** defaults to **C_order** instead of **Fortran_order**.

```
> A := hfarray(1..4, 1..4, (i,j)->ithprime(i)*isqrt(3*(i+j)));
```

$$A := \begin{bmatrix} 4. & 6. & 6. & 8. \\ 9. & 9. & 12. & 12. \\ 15. & 20. & 20. & 25. \\ 28. & 28. & 35. & 35. \end{bmatrix} \tag{7.113}$$

```
> lprint(A);
Array(1 .. 4, 1 .. 4, {(1, 1) = HFloat(4.), (1, 2) = HFloat(6.), (1,
3) = HFloat(6.), (1, 4) = HFloat(8.), (2, 1) = HFloat(9.), (2, 2) =
HFloat(9.), (2, 3) = HFloat(12.), (2, 4) = HFloat(12.), (3, 1) =
HFloat(15.), (3, 2) = HFloat(20.), (3, 3) = HFloat(20.), (3, 4) =
HFloat(25.), (4, 1) = HFloat(28.), (4, 2) = HFloat(28.), (4, 3) =
HFloat(35.), (4, 4) = HFloat(35.)}, datatype = float[8], storage =
rectangular, order = C_order)
```

User-defined Maple procedures can be evaluated in the **evalhf** environment as long as they comply with the restrictions outlined in the **evalhf/procedure** help page.

```
> SlowPower := proc(a,n) local i, s; s:=1; for i to n do s := a*s;
  end do; end proc;
```

$$\begin{aligned} SlowPower := \mathbf{proc}&(a, n) \\ \mathbf{local}\ &i, s; \\ s := 1;\ &\mathbf{for}\ i\ \mathbf{to}\ n\ \mathbf{do}\ s := a*s\ \mathbf{end\ do} \\ \mathbf{end\ proc}& \end{aligned} \tag{7.114}$$

```
> SlowPower(2,10);
```

$$1024 \tag{7.115}$$

```
> evalhf( SlowPower(2,10) );
```
$$1024. \tag{7.116}$$

Numerical Linear Algebra

Maple has access to many libraries for fast numeric computation such as BLAS, CLAPACK, and the NAG® C Library. To take full advantage of the speed provided by these commands, you need to provide them with Matrices and Vectors with the appropriate **datatype**.

For example, floating-point Matrix times Matrix products can been computed very quickly in the BLAS libraries and quickest dispatch to the BLAS commands will happen if the Matrices are created with **datatype=float[8]**.

```
> A := Matrix(5^3,5^3,(i,j)->(i-j+1)/(i+j));
```
$$A := \begin{bmatrix} 125 \times 125 \; Matrix \\ Data \; Type: \; anything \\ Storage: \; rectangular \\ Order: \; Fortran\_order \end{bmatrix} \tag{7.117}$$

```
> CodeTools:-Usage(A^2);
memory used=0.60GiB, alloc change=130.82MiB, cpu time=2.39s, real
time=2.39s
```
$$\begin{bmatrix} 125 \times 125 \; Matrix \\ Data \; Type: \; anything \\ Storage: \; rectangular \\ Order: \; Fortran\_order \end{bmatrix} \tag{7.118}$$

```
> Ahf := Matrix(5^3,5^3,(i,j)->(i-j+1)/(i+j), datatype=float[8]);
```
$$Ahf := \begin{bmatrix} 125 \times 125 \; Matrix \\ Data \; Type: \; float_8 \\ Storage: \; rectangular \\ Order: \; Fortran\_order \end{bmatrix} \tag{7.119}$$

```
> CodeTools:-Usage(Ahf^2);
```
memory used=333.62KiB, alloc change=0 bytes, cpu time=5.00ms, real time=5.00ms

$$\begin{bmatrix} 125 \times 125 \text{ Matrix} \\ \text{Data Type: float}_8 \\ \text{Storage: rectangular} \\ \text{Order: Fortran\_order} \end{bmatrix} \quad (7.120)$$

Of course, many of the linear algebra commands will try to determine if you have a Matrix of low precision floats and will convert to the appropriate datatype automatically. In the next example, Af has **datatype=anything**, but the result of **Af^2** has **datatype=float[8]** and requires only a small, but noticeable, copy and conversion overhead.

```
> Af := Matrix(5^3,5^3,(i,j)->(i-j+1.)/(i+j));
```

$$Af := \begin{bmatrix} 125 \times 125 \text{ Matrix} \\ \text{Data Type: anything} \\ \text{Storage: rectangular} \\ \text{Order: Fortran\_order} \end{bmatrix} \quad (7.121)$$

```
> CodeTools:-Usage(Af^2);
```
memory used=0.54MiB, alloc change=0 bytes, cpu time=7.00ms, real time=6.00ms

$$\begin{bmatrix} 125 \times 125 \text{ Matrix} \\ \text{Data Type: float}_8 \\ \text{Storage: rectangular} \\ \text{Order: Fortran\_order} \end{bmatrix} \quad (7.122)$$

We recommend that you specify **datatype=float[8]** in your constructors explicitly if you intend to perform numeric computations. This makes the numeric nature of the Matrix explicit, and it makes it impossible to accidentally add non-float entries to a Matrix and thus make subsequent computations slower. An exception will be raised if non-numeric entries are assigned into the Matrix.

```
> Ahf[1,1] := sqrt(3);
```
Error, unable to store '3^(1/2)' when datatype=float[8]

Other numeric types will be automatically converted to **float[8]**.

```
> Ahf[1,1] := 45/111;
```

$$Ahf_{1,1} := \frac{15}{37} \tag{7.123}$$

```
> Ahf[1,1];
```

$$0.405405405405405 \tag{7.124}$$

If a Matrix contains only floats, but does not have a **datatype=float[8]** restriction, then addition of symbolic elements results in the more expensive symbolic commands to be used.

```
> Af[1,1] := sqrt(3);
```

$$Af_{1,1} := \sqrt{3} \tag{7.125}$$

```
> CodeTools:-Usage(Af^2);
memory used=406.73MiB, alloc change=198.03MiB, cpu time=2.54s, real
time=2.55s
```

$$\begin{bmatrix} 125 \times 125 \ Matrix \\ Data \ Type: \ anything \\ Storage: \ rectangular \\ Order: \ Fortran\_order \end{bmatrix} \tag{7.126}$$

Another advantage of **float[8]** is that these Matrices are stored in the same way as an **hfarray** which is analogous to an array of floats in the C or Fortran programming languages and different from a Matrix of **datatype=anything** or **datatype=sfloat** which are arrays of Maple DAGs each of which will take more memory than a single 8-byte float. Note the difference in **memory used** in the following two examples.

```
> restart;
> CodeTools:-Usage(Matrix(10^3,3*10^3,(i,j)->10.^4*j+j,
  datatype=sfloat));
memory used=0.80GiB, alloc change=118.32MiB, cpu time=6.62s, real
time=6.64s
```

$$\begin{bmatrix} 1000 \times 3000 \ Matrix \\ Data \ Type: \ sfloat \\ Storage: \ rectangular \\ Order: \ Fortran\_order \end{bmatrix} \tag{7.127}$$

```
> restart;
```

```
> B1:=CodeTools:-Usage(Matrix(10^3,3*10^3,(i,j)->10^4*j+i,
  datatype=float[8]));
```
`memory used=218.62MiB, alloc change=181.98MiB, cpu time=1.86s, real time=1.86s`

$$B1 := \begin{bmatrix} 1000 \times 3000 \text{ Matrix} \\ \text{Data Type: float}_8 \\ \text{Storage: rectangular} \\ \text{Order: Fortran\_order} \end{bmatrix} \quad (7.128)$$

It is also important to note that elements extracted from a **float[8]** rtable will be of type hfloat and so hfloat contagion will apply subject to the current setting of **UseHardwareFloats**.

```
> type(B1[1,1], hfloat);
```

$$true \quad (7.129)$$

There are also many optimized commands for Matrices of complex hfloats. These Matrices can be created using the option **datatype=complex[8]**, and work similarly to those of **datatype=float[8]**.

If you are constructing very large Matrices in your programs, use the **ArrayTools** package to construct and copy Matrices as efficiently as possible.

7.5 Writing Efficient Numerical Programs

Two main points to keep in mind when trying to write efficient numerical programs are:

  Try to use hardware floating-point arithmetic when **Digits** allows

  Try to minimize memory usage where possible

Writing Flexible Numerical Procedures

You can use the **evalhf(Digits)** construct to determine whether hardware floating-point arithmetic provides sufficient precision in a particular application. If **Digits** is less than **evalhf(Digits)**, then you can take advantage of the faster hardware floating-point calculations. Otherwise, you should use software floating-point arithmetic, with sufficient digits, to perform the calculation.

In the following example, the procedure **myevalf** takes an *unevaluated* parameter, **expr**. Without the **uneval** declaration, Maple would evaluate **expr** symbolically before invoking **myevalf**.

```
> myevalf := proc(expr::uneval)
      if Digits < evalhf(Digits) then
          evalf(evalhf(expr));
      else
          evalf(expr);
      end if;
  end proc:
```

The **evalhf** command evaluates many Maple functions, but not all. For example, you cannot evaluate an integral using hardware floating-point arithmetic.

```
> myevalf( Int(exp(x^3), x=0..1) );
Error, (in myevalf) unable to evaluate function `Int` in evalhf
```

You can improve the procedure **myevalf** so that it traps such errors and tries to evaluate the expression using software floating-point numbers instead.

```
> myevalf := proc(expr::uneval)
      if Digits < evalhf(Digits) then
          try
              return evalf(evalhf(expr));
          catch:
          end try;
      end if;
      return evalf(expr);
  end proc:
> myevalf( Int(exp(x^3), x=0..1) );
```

$$1.341904418 \tag{7.130}$$

This procedure provides a model of how to write procedures that use hardware floating-point arithmetic whenever possible.

The **myevalf** procedure returns sfloats. A version that returns hfloats is easiest to write using the hfloat procedure option. This option will cause the procedure to use hfloat arithmetic as much as possible so long as digits less than 15. In particular it convert all floats in the procedure definition into hfloats, and causes **evalhf** to not convert its output to an sfloat.

```
> myevalf := proc(expr::uneval)
      option hfloat;
      if Digits < evalhf(Digits) then
          try
              return evalhf(expr);
          catch:
          end try;
```

```
    end if;
    return evalf(1. * expr);
end proc:
```

The multiplication by 1. was added to the **evalf** return line to induce hfloat contagion causing the output to be an hfloat when possible.

```
> type( myevalf( Int(exp(x^3), x=0..1) ), hfloat);
```
$$true \qquad (7.131)$$

For more information on the **hfloat** option, see *The hfloat Option (page 216)* or refer to the **option_hfloat** help page.

Example: Newton Iteration

This section illustrates how to take advantage of hardware floating-point arithmetic to calculate successive approximations using Newton's method. You can use Newton's method to find numerical solutions to equations. As *Example: Creating a Newton Iteration (page 261)* describes, if x_n is an approximate solution to the equation $f(x) = 0$, then x_{n+1}, given by the following formula, is typically a better approximation.

$$x_{(n+1)} = x_n - \frac{f(x_n)}{f'(x_n)}$$

The procedure **iterate** takes a function, **f**, its derivative, **df**, and an initial approximate solution, **x0**, as input to the equation $f(x) = 0$. The procedure **iterate** calculates at most **N** successive Newton iterations until the difference between the new approximation and the previous one is small. The procedure prints the sequence of approximations to show successive approximations.

```
> iterate := proc( f::procedure, df::procedure,
                   x0::numeric, N::posint, $ )
    local xold, xnew;
    xold := x0;
    xnew := evalf( xold - f(xold)/df(xold) );
    to  N-1 while abs(xnew-xold) > 10^(1-Digits) do
       xold := xnew;
       print(xold);
       xnew := evalf( xold - f(xold)/df(xold) );
    end do;
    return xnew;
end proc:
```

The following procedure calculates the derivative of **f** and passes all the necessary information to **iterate**.

```
> Newton := proc( f::procedure, x0::numeric, N::posint:=15, $ )
    local df;
    df := D(f);
    print(x0);
    return iterate(f, df, x0, N);
  end proc:
```

Use **Newton** to solve the equation $x^2 - 2 = 0$.

```
> f := x -> x^2 - 2;
```

$$f := x \to x^2 - 2 \tag{7.132}$$

```
> Newton(f, 1.5);
```

$$1.5$$
$$1.416666667$$
$$1.414215686$$
$$1.414213562$$
$$1.414213562 \tag{7.133}$$

This version of **Newton** uses sfloats unless the arguments passed in are hfloats. If you add **option hfloat** to the procedure **iterate**, then hfloats are used automatically, provided the value of Digits is small enough.

```
> iterate := proc( f::procedure, df::procedure,
                   x0::numeric, N::posint, $ )
    option hfloat;
    local xold, xnew;
    xold := 1. * x0;
    xnew := 1. * evalf( xold - f(xold)/df(xold) );
    to N-1 while abs(xnew-xold) > 10^(1-Digits) do
       xold := xnew;
       print(xold);
       xnew := evalf( xold - f(xold)/df(xold) );
    end do;
    return xnew;
  end proc:
```

Now the procedure **Newton** will return **hfloats** instead of **sfloats** when Digits is less than 15.

```
> type( Newton(f, 1.5), hfloat);
```

$$1.5$$

$$1.41666666666667$$

$$1.41421568627451$$

$$1.41421356237469$$

$$\textit{true} \tag{7.134}$$

In this case, the procedure is simple enough that we can go beyond **option hfloat** and use the **evalhf** command to achieve best performance. This next version of **Newton** uses evalhf for floating-point arithmetic if possible and reverts to sfloats otherwise. Since **iterate** only tries to find a solution to an accuracy of $10^{\wedge}(1\text{-Digits})$, **Newton** uses **evalf** to round the result of the hardware floating-point computation to an appropriate number of digits.

```
> Newton := proc( f::procedure, x0::numeric, N::posint:=15, $ )
    local df, result;
    df := D(f);
    print(x0);
    if Digits < evalhf(Digits) then
        try
            return evalf( SFloat( evalhf(iterate(f, df, x0, N)) ));
        catch:
        end try;
    end if;
    return evalf( SFloat( iterate(f, df, x0, N) ) );
  end proc:
```

Newton uses hardware floating-point arithmetic for the iterations and rounds the result to software precision. Hardware floating-point numbers have more digits than the software floating-point numbers, given the present setting of **Digits**.

```
> Newton(f, 1.5);
```

$$1.5$$
$$1.416666666666674$$
$$1.41421568627450989$$
$$1.41421356237468987$$
$$1.41421356237309515$$
$$1.414213562 \tag{7.135}$$

Newton must use software floating-point arithmetic to find a root of the following Bessel function.

```
> F := z -> BesselJ(1, z);
```

$$F := z \rightarrow \text{BesselJ}(1, z) \tag{7.136}$$

```
> Newton(F, 4);
```

$$4$$
$$3.82649352308792$$
$$3.83170246715760$$
$$3.83170597020591$$
$$3.831705970 \tag{7.137}$$

Software arithmetic is used because **evalhf** does not recognize **BesselJ** and the symbolic code for **BesselJ** uses the **type** command and remember tables, which **evalhf** does not allow.

```
> evalhf( BesselJ(1, 4) );
Error, unsupported type `('complex')('float')` in evalhf
```

Using a **try-catch** block (as in the previous **Newton** procedure) allows the procedure to work when **evalhf** fails.

The previous **Newton** procedure prints many digits when it is trying to find a ten-digit approximation. The reason is that the **print** command is located inside the **iterate** procedure, which is inside a call to **evalhf**, where all numbers are hardware floating-point numbers, and print as such.

Example: Jacobi Iteration

Jacobi iteration is an iterative method for numerically solving systems of linear equations that are *diagonally dominant* (meaning that the diagonal elements of the matrix representing the system are larger than the sum of all other elements in any given row of the matrix). Given a initial guess of *x0* for the solution to $Ax = b$, the process is: if x_k is an approximation for the solution, then the next approximation is $x_{k+1} = S^{-1} \cdot (b - Rx_k)$ where S is the diagonal of A and $A = S + R$.

The procedure **Jacobi** is a straight forward implementation of Jacobi iteration as it is usually presented in a numerical analysis course.

```
> Jacobi := proc(A::Matrix(numeric), b::Vector(numeric),
  x0::Vector(numeric):=b, MAXIter::posint:=25,
  tolerance::positive:=evalf(LinearAlgebra:-Norm(b,2)*10^(1-Digits)),
  $)
  local i,j,k, x_old, x_new, s, residual, n;
      x_new := evalf(x0);
      n := LinearAlgebra:-Dimension(b);
      x_old := Vector(n, 0, rtable_options(x_new));
      residual := evalf(LinearAlgebra:-Norm(A . x_new-b,2));
      for k to MAXIter while residual > tolerance do
          ArrayTools:-Copy(x_new, x_old);
          for i from 1 to n do
              s := 0;
              for j from 1 to n do
                  if i<>j then
                      s := s + A[i,j] * x_old[j];
                  end if;
              end do;
              x_new[i] := (b[i] - s) / A[i,i];
          end do;

          residual := evalf(LinearAlgebra:-Norm(A . x_new-b,2));
      end do;
      if k < MAXIter then
          return x_new;
      else
          WARNING("Residual %1 greater than tolerance %2 after %3
  iterations", residual, tolerance, k-1);
          return x_new;
```

```
    end if;
end proc:
```

Here we construct a random Matrix that is strongly diagonally dominant to test the procedure. Note that, while in practice Jacobi iteration would not be used on dense Matrices, we use dense Matrices in these examples to illustrate some efficiency principles.

```
> N := 25:
> M := Matrix(N,N,(i,j)->`if`(i<>j,
  RandomTools:-Generate(integer(range=-100..100))/1000.,
  RandomTools:-Generate(integer(range=100..10000))/10.),datatype=float);
```

$$M := \begin{bmatrix} 25 \times 25 \; Matrix \\ Data \; Type: float_8 \\ Storage: rectangular \\ Order: Fortran\_order \end{bmatrix} \quad (7.138)$$

```
> b := LinearAlgebra:-RandomVector(N,datatype=float);
```

$$b := \begin{bmatrix} 1..25 \; Vector_{column} \\ Data \; Type: float_8 \\ Storage: rectangular \\ Order: Fortran\_order \end{bmatrix} \quad (7.139)$$

```
> CodeTools:-Usage( Jacobi(M, b) );
```

memory used=0.64MiB, alloc change=1.00MiB, cpu time=13.00ms, real time=13.00ms

$$\begin{bmatrix} 1..25 \; Vector_{column} \\ Data \; Type: float_8 \\ Storage: rectangular \\ Order: Fortran\_order \end{bmatrix} \quad (7.140)$$

The code is written in such a way that it will automatically work for software floats at higher values of digits.

```
> Digits := 50:
```

7.5 Writing Efficient Numerical Programs • 305

```
> M := Matrix(N,N,(i,j)->`if`(i<>j,
  RandomTools:-Generate(integer(range=-100..100))/1000.,
  RandomTools:-Generate(integer(range=100..10000))/10.),datatype=float);
```

$$M := \begin{bmatrix} 25 \times 25 \ Matrix \\ Data\ Type:\ sfloat \\ Storage:\ rectangular \\ Order:\ Fortran\_order \end{bmatrix} \quad (7.141)$$

```
> b := LinearAlgebra:-RandomVector(N,datatype=float);
```

$$b := \begin{bmatrix} 1..25\ Vector_{column} \\ Data\ Type:\ sfloat \\ Storage:\ rectangular \\ Order:\ Fortran\_order \end{bmatrix} \quad (7.142)$$

```
> CodeTools:-Usage( Jacobi(M, b) );
memory used=14.13MiB, alloc change=13.01MiB, cpu time=81.00ms, real
time=80.00ms
```

$$\begin{bmatrix} 1..25\ Vector_{column} \\ Data\ Type:\ sfloat \\ Storage:\ rectangular \\ Order:\ Fortran\_order \end{bmatrix} \quad (7.143)$$

This implementation works well for small Matrices, but when the dimension becomes large, it becomes very slow.

```
> Digits := 10:
> N := 500:
> M := Matrix(N,N,(i,j)->`if`(i<>j,
  RandomTools:-Generate(integer(range=-100..100))/1000.,
  RandomTools:-Generate(integer(range=100..10000))/10.),datatype=float);
```

$$M := \begin{bmatrix} 500 \times 500\ Matrix \\ Data\ Type:\ float_8 \\ Storage:\ rectangular \\ Order:\ Fortran\_order \end{bmatrix} \quad (7.144)$$

```
> b := LinearAlgebra:-RandomVector(N,datatype=float);
```

$$b := \begin{bmatrix} 1\,..\,500\ Vector_{column} \\ Data\ Type:\ float_8 \\ Storage:\ rectangular \\ Order:\ Fortran\_order \end{bmatrix} \qquad (7.145)$$

```
> CodeTools:-Usage( Jacobi(M, b) );
memory used=177.99MiB, alloc change=48.01MiB, cpu time=1.89s, real
time=1.90s
```

$$\begin{bmatrix} 1\,..\,500\ Vector_{column} \\ Data\ Type:\ float_8 \\ Storage:\ rectangular \\ Order:\ Fortran\_order \end{bmatrix} \qquad (7.146)$$

Adding **option hfloat** to Jacobi is not likely to increase performance, since hfloat contagion from the **float[8]** Matrix elements means that hfloat arithmetic is likely being used everywhere possible already. However, it is possible to rewrite the internal loops as a procedure that can be evaluated with **evalhf**. (It might be possible to rewrite all of **Jacobi** to be evaluatable to **evalhf**, but it would be difficult and potential gains would be modest.)

```
> JacobiHelper := proc(A, b, x_old, x_new, n)
  local s, i, j, l;
  option hfloat;
  # this procedure acts by side effect on x_new
        for i from 1 to n do
            s := 0;
            for j from 1 to n do
                if i<>j then
                    s := s + A[i,j] * x_old[j];
                end if;
            end do;
            x_new[i] := (b[i] - s) / A[i,i];
        end do;
  end proc:
```

And the rest of the procedure with **option hfloat**.

```
> Jacobi := proc(A::Matrix(numeric), b::Vector(numeric),
  x0::Vector(numeric):=b, MAXIter::posint:=25,
```

```
            tolerance::positive:=evalf(LinearAlgebra:-Norm(b,2)*10^(1-Digits)),
     $)
     option hfloat;
     local i,j,k, x_old, x_new, s, residual, n;
        x_new := evalf(x0);
        n := LinearAlgebra:-Dimension(b);
        x_old := Vector(n, 0, rtable_options(x_new));
        residual := evalf(LinearAlgebra:-Norm(A . x_new-b,2));
        for k to MAXIter while residual > tolerance do
            ArrayTools:-Copy(x_new, x_old);
            # JacobiHelper acts by side effect on x_new
            if Digits <= evalhf(Digits) then
                 evalhf( JacobiHelper(A, b, x_old, x_new, n) );
            else
                 ( JacobiHelper(A, b, x_old, x_new, n) );
            end if;
            residual := evalf(LinearAlgebra:-Norm(A . x_new-b,2));
        end do;
        if k < MAXIter then
            return x_new;
        else
            WARNING("Residual %1 greater than tolerance %2 after %3
     iterations", residual, tolerance, k-1);
            return x_new;
        end if;
     end proc:
> CodeTools:-Usage( Jacobi(M, b) );
memory used=3.98MiB, alloc change=0 bytes, cpu time=345.00ms, real
time=345.00ms
```

$$\begin{bmatrix} 1 .. 500\ Vector_{column} \\ Data\ Type:\ float_8 \\ Storage:\ rectangular \\ Order:\ Fortran\_order \end{bmatrix} \qquad (7.147)$$

Using **evalhf** here achieves an impressive speed-up but you can achieve even better speed by taking advantage of the built-in Matrix and Vector operations. In general you code will be faster if you can replace nested loops with calls to external commands for Vectors or Matrices. Those commands will be highly optimized for your platform taking advantage of multiple cores and cache hierarchy where possible.

```
> Jacobi := proc(A::Matrix(numeric), b::Vector(numeric),
  x0::Vector(numeric):=b, MAXIter::posint:=25,
  tolerance::positive:=evalf(LinearAlgebra:-Norm(b,2)*10^(1-Digits)),
  $)
  local k, x_new, S, S_inv, residual;
     x_new := evalf(x0);
     S := LinearAlgebra:-Diagonal(A,datatype=float);
     S_inv := 1 /~ S;
     residual := evalf(LinearAlgebra:-Norm(A.x_new-b,2));
     for k to MAXIter while residual > tolerance do
         # computing R.x as A.x - S.x is probably a bad idea
  numerically
         # but we do it anyway to avoid making the code overly
  complicated
         x_new := S_inv *~ (b - ( A . x_new - S *~ x_new));
         residual := evalf(LinearAlgebra:-Norm(A . x_new-b,2));
     end do;
     if k < MAXIter then
         return x_new;
     else
         WARNING("Achieved tolerance of only %1 after %2 iterations",
  residual, i-1);
         return x_new;
     end if;
  end proc:
> CodeTools:-Usage( Jacobi(M, b) );
memory used=4.13MiB, alloc change=0 bytes, cpu time=42.00ms, real
time=41.00ms
```

$$\begin{bmatrix} 1\,..\,500\ Vector_{column} \\ Data\ Type: float_8 \\ Storage:\ rectangular \\ Order:\ Fortran\_order \end{bmatrix} \qquad (7.148)$$

This sort of speed-up is typical. The built-in numerical linear algebra commands are easily an order of magnitude faster than loops run in Maple, and generally also faster than loops in **evalhf**.

8 Programming with Modules

This chapter describes the structure and flexibility of Maple modules.

Modules allow you to associate related procedures and data in one structure. By creating a module, you can write code that can be reused, transported, and easily maintained. You can also use modules to implement objects in Maple.

This chapter provides several example modules, many of which are available as Maple source code in the **samples** directory of your Maple installation. You can load these examples into the Maple library to modify and extend them, and use them in custom programs.

8.1 In This Chapter

- Syntax and semantics
- Using modules as records or structures
- Modules and **use** statements
- Interfaces and implementations

8.2 Introduction

You may decide to create a module for one of the purposes described below.

Encapsulation

Encapsulation is the act of grouping code together in one structure to separate its interface from its implementation. By doing so, you can create applications that are transportable and reusable and that offer well-defined user interfaces. This makes your code easier to maintain and understand--important properties for large software systems.

Creating a Custom Maple Package

A *package* is a means of bundling a collection of Maple procedures related to a domain. Most of the Maple library functionality is available in packages.

Creating Objects

Objects can be represented using modules. In software engineering or object-oriented programming, an object is defined as an element that has both a state and behavior. Objects are passed the same way as ordinary expressions, but also provide methods which define their properties.

Creating Generic Programs

Generic programs accept objects with specific properties or behaviors. The underlying representation of the object is transparent to generic programs. For example, a generic geometry program can accept any object that exports an **area** method, in addition to other objects. The framework of the program would rely on information in each given object to determine specific behaviors, while the overall program implements a common pattern between the objects.

8.3 A Simple Example

In the following example, a module generates a sequence of numbers.

```
> Counter := module()
      description "number generator";
      export    getNext;
      local     count;
      count := 0;
      getNext := proc()
           count := 1 + count;
      end proc;
  end module:
  Counter:-getNext();
  Counter:-getNext();
  Counter:-getNext();
```

$$1$$
$$2$$
$$3$$
(8.1)

The *module definition* format, which will be described in more detail in the next section, is similar to a procedure definition in that the body is contained within a delimited code block. Also, elements such as local variables, options, and description are declared at the top of the module. Unlike a procedure, the body of the module is evaluated only once when it is declared. The values that are defined during this evaluation process, and the values that are defined in subsequent usage of the module, are stored and can be used again.

In a module definition, you can declare *exported variables*, which are names that will be made available once the module has been run. These exported variables can be accessed by using the member selection operator (:-) or the indexing operation ([]), while *local variables* remain private (that is, they are accessible only by methods within the module). The example above declares and uses one exported local variable called **getNext** and one local variable called **count**.

8.4 Syntax and Semantics

Module definitions have the following general syntax.
```
module()
    local L;
    export E;
    global G;
    options O;
    description D;
    B
end module
```

The Module Definition

All module definitions begin with the keyword **module**, followed by an empty pair of parentheses. This is similar to the parentheses that follow the **proc** keyword in a procedure definition. Following that is an optional declaration section and the module body. The keywords **end module** (or simply **end**) terminate a module definition.

The simplest valid module definition is

```
> module() end;
```

$$\text{module( )} \quad \text{end module} \tag{8.2}$$

which does *not* contain exported variables, local variables, references, global variables, or a body of statements.

The Module Body

The body of a module definition contains the following components:

- Zero or more Maple statements. The body is executed when the module definition is evaluated, producing a module.
- Assignment statements that assign values to the exported names of the module.

Also, the body can optionally contain the following components:

- Assignments to local variables and arbitrary computations.
- A **return** statement, which cannot contain a **break** or **next** statement outside of a loop. Running a **return** statement terminates the execution of the body of the module definition.

Module Parameters

Unlike procedures, module definitions do not have explicit parameters because modules are not called (or invoked) with arguments.

Implicit Parameters

All module definitions have an implicit parameter called **thismodule**. Within the body of a module definition, this special name evaluates to the module in which it occurs. You can, therefore, refer to a module within its own definition before the result of evaluating it has been assigned to a name.

thismodule is similar to **thisproc** in procedures, but is not the same as **procname**. The difference between **thismodule** and **procname** is that **procname** evaluates to a *name*, while **thismodule** evaluates to the module expression itself. There is no concept of a **modulename** implicit variable because the invocation phase of evaluating a module definition is part of its normal evaluation process, and it occurs immediately. Procedures, on the other hand, are not invoked until they are called with arguments. Normally, at least one name for a procedure is known by the time it is called; this is not the case for modules.

Implicit parameters related to passing arguments (for example, **_params**, **_options**, **_passed**, and others) *cannot* be referenced in module definitions. They are only available within the scope of a procedure.

For more information on procedures, see *Procedures (page 199)*.

Named Modules

In a module definition, an optional symbol can be specified after the **module** keyword. Modules created in this way are called *named modules*.

Semantically, named modules are almost identical to normal modules, but the exported variables of named modules are printed differently, allowing the module from which it was exported to be identified visually. In the following example, a normal module is assigned to the name **NormalModule**.

```
> NormalModule := module() export e; end module;
  NormalModule:-e;
```

$$NormalModule := \mathbf{module}(\,)\ \mathbf{export}\ e;\ \mathbf{end\ module}$$

$$e \qquad (8.3)$$

In the following example, the symbol (the name of the module) after the **module** keyword is **NamedModule**.

```
> module NamedModule() export e; end module;
```

$$\mathbf{module}\ NamedModule(\,)\ \mathbf{export}\ e;\ \mathbf{end\ module} \qquad (8.4)$$

```
> NamedModule:-e;
```

$$NamedModule{:}\text{-}e \qquad (8.5)$$

When the definition of a named module is evaluated, the name (which appears immediately after the **module** keyword) is assigned the module as its value and the name is protected (that is, it cannot be modified). Therefore, a named module is usually created only once. For example, an error occurs when the same named module definition above is executed.

```
> module NamedModule() export e; end module;
```

```
Error, (in NamedModule) attempting to assign to `NamedModule` which
is protected
```

Executing the normal module definition again creates a *new* instance of the module and does not result in an error. It simply reassigns the variable **NormalModule** to the new module instance.

```
> NormalModule := module() export e; end module;
```

$$NormalModule := \mathbf{module}(\ )\ \mathbf{export}\ e;\ \mathbf{end\ module} \tag{8.6}$$

If you save a normal module to a Maple library archive, which is a file used to store a collection of internal files, the normal module becomes a named module the next time it is loaded from the library archive. The **savelib** command, which is the command used to save a file to a library archive, takes the name of the variable assigned a module, and saving the file associates this name with the module.

For more information about library archive files, see *Writing Packages (page 383)*.

Important: Do not assign a named module to another variable, for example,

```
> SomeName := eval( NamedModule );
```

$$SomeName := \mathbf{module}\ NamedModule(\ )\ \mathbf{export}\ e;\ \mathbf{end\ module} \tag{8.7}$$

```
> SomeName:-e;
```

$$NamedModule{:}{-}e \tag{8.8}$$

Exports of named modules are printed using the *distinguished* name that was given to the module when it was created, regardless of whether it has been assigned to another name.

Whether a module has a name also affects the reporting of errors that occur during its evaluation. When the second attempt to evaluate the named module definition above generated an error, the error message reported the location of the error by name. In contrast, when an error occurs during the evaluation of a normal module definition, the name **unknown** is used instead.

```
> NormalModule := module() export e; error "oops"; end module;
```

```
Error, (in unknown) oops
```

This process differs from procedure error reporting. Maple cannot report the name of a normal module (that is, the name of the variable to which the module is assigned) because the evaluation of the right-hand side of an assignment occurs before the assignment to the name takes place. Therefore, the error occurs before the association between a variable and the module has occurred.

Declarations

The declarations section of the module must appear immediately after the parentheses. All of the statements in the declarations section are optional, but, at most, one of each kind can be specified. Most module declarations are the same as those for procedures.

For more information, see *Parameter Declarations (page 201)*.

Description Strings

You can provide a brief description to summarize the purpose and function of your modules. Providing a description is valuable to other users who read your code. Include text after the **description** keyword as you would in a procedure definition.

```
> Hello := module()
      description "my first module";
      export say;
      say := proc()
          print( "HELLO WORLD" )
      end proc;
  end module:
```

When the module is printed, its description string is displayed.

```
> eval( Hello );
```

> module( )
> export *say*;
> description "my first module"; (8.9)
>
> **end module**

The **export** declaration is described later in this chapter.

Global Variables

Global variables referenced in a module definition are declared by using the **global** keyword. Following the **global** keyword is a sequence of one or more symbols, which are associated with their global module instances. In certain cases, you must declare a name as a global variable to prevent implicit scoping rules from making it local.

```
> Hello := module()
      export say;
      global message;
      say := proc()
          message := "HELLO WORLD!"
      end proc;
  end module:
> message;
```
$$message \qquad (8.10)$$
```
> Hello:-say();
```
$$\text{"HELLO WORLD!"} \qquad (8.11)$$
```
> message;
```
$$\text{"HELLO WORLD!"} \qquad (8.12)$$

Local Variables

You can define variables that are local to the module definition by using the **local** declaration. Its format is the same as for procedures. The following example is a variant of the previous **Hello** module, which uses a local variable.

```
> Hello := module()
      local loc;
      export say;
      loc := "HELLO WORLD!";
      say := proc()
          print( loc )
      end proc;
  end module:
```

Local variables (or *locals*) cannot be used or changed outside of the module definition in which they occur. In other words, they are private to the module.

A local variable in a module is a distinct object from a global variable with the same name. While local variables in procedures are typically used only for the duration of the execution time of the procedure body, module local variables are stored after the module definition is executed. They can be used to maintain a state. For example, in the Counter example described at the beginning of this chapter, a local **count** variable stores the current value of the counter. The **count** local variable increments each time the **getNext** procedure is invoked. Its new value is stored and can be used the next time the procedure is called. At the same time, because **count** is local, no external programs can change its value and end the sequence defined by the module.

Exported Local Variables

Procedures and modules both support local variables. However, only modules support *exported* local variables, which are often called *exports*.

Module exports are declared by using the **export** declaration. It begins with the keyword **export**, followed by a (nonempty) sequence of symbols. A name is never exported implicitly; exports *must* be declared.

The result of evaluating a module definition is a module. You can view a module as a collection of its exports, which are also referred to as *members* of the module. These are simply names that can (but need not) be assigned values. You can establish initial values for the exports by assigning values to them in the body of the module definition.

The word export is a short form for *exported local variable*. In most cases, a module export is a local variable such as those declared with the **local** declaration. The difference is that you can access the exported local variables of a module after it has been created.

To access an export of a module, use the member selection operator (**:-**). Its general syntax is

```
modexpr :- membername
```

modexpr must be an expression that evaluates to a module and **membername** must be the name of an export of the module to which **modexpr** evaluates. Anything else signals an exception. You cannot access the local variables of an instantiated module by using this syntax.

The **Hello** example above has one export named **say**. In the following example, **say** is assigned a procedure. To call it, enter

```
> Hello:-say();
```

"HELLO WORLD!" (8.13)

The following expression raises an exception because the name **noSuchModule** is not assigned a module expression.

```
> noSuchModule:-e;
Error, `noSuchModule` does not evaluate to a module
```

In the following example, a module expression is assigned to the name **m** and the member selection expression **m:-e** evaluates to the value of the exported variable **e** of **m**.

```
> m := module() export e; e := 2 end module:
  m:-e;
```

2 (8.14)

Since **m** does not export a variable named **noSuchExport**, the following expression raises an exception.

```
> m:-noSuchExport;
Error, module does not export `noSuchExport`
```

In addition to the :- syntax, square brackets can also be used to reference a module export.

```
> m[e];
```

$$2 \qquad (8.15)$$

The square bracket notation has different evaluation rules than member selection. When using the member selection operator (:-), the export name must be known in advance. When using [], the name of the export can be computed. In this example, an exported variables value can be selected from an arbitrary module.

```
> m := module() export a := 1, b := 2, c := 3; end module:
  FirstExport := proc( m::`module` ) local ex := exports(m); return
  m[ex[1]]; end proc;
  FirstExport(m);
```

$FirstExport := \mathbf{proc}(m::module)$
    local ex;
    $ex := exports(m);$ **return** $m[ex[1]]$
end proc

$$1 \qquad (8.16)$$

Important: Exports do not need to have assigned values. The following module exports an unassigned name. This illustrates the importance of distinguishing module exports from global variables.

```
> m := module() export e; end module:
```

References to the exported name **e** in **m** evaluate to the name **e**.

```
> m:-e;
```

$$e \qquad (8.17)$$

Note, however, that this is a *local* name **e** and not the global instance of the name.

```
> evalb( e = m:-e );
```

$$false \qquad (8.18)$$

The first **e** in the previous expression refers to the global **e**, while the expression **m:-e** evaluates to the **e** that is local to the module **m**. This distinction between a global and export of the same name is useful. For example, you can create a module with an export **sin**. Assigning a value to the export **sin** does not affect the protected global name **sin**.

Determining the Export Names

You can determine the names of the exports of a module by using the **exports** procedure.

> `exports( Hello );`

$$say \tag{8.19}$$

> `exports( NormalModule );`

$$e \tag{8.20}$$

This procedure returns the *global* instances of the export names.

> `exports( m );`

$$e \tag{8.21}$$

> `evalb( (8.21) = e );`

$$true \tag{8.22}$$

You can also obtain the local instances of those names by using the option **instance**.

> `exports( m, 'instance' );`

$$e \tag{8.23}$$

> `evalb( (8.23) = e );`

$$true \tag{8.24}$$

> `evalb( (8.23) = m:-e );`

$$false \tag{8.25}$$

You cannot have the same name declared as both a local variable and an exported local variable.

> `module() export e; local e; end module;`
`Error, export and local `e` have the same name`

(The declared exports and locals actually form a partition of the names that are local to a module.)

Testing for Membership in a Module

As described in previous chapters, the **member** command can be used to test whether a value is a member of a set or list.

```
> member( 4, { 1, 2, 3 } );
```

$$false \tag{8.26}$$

This command can also be used for membership tests in modules.

```
> member( say, Hello );
```

$$true \tag{8.27}$$

```
> member( cry, Hello );
```

$$false \tag{8.28}$$

The first argument is a global name whose membership is to be tested, and the second argument is the name of a module. The **member** command returns the value **true** if the module has an export whose name is the same as the first argument.

The **member** command also has a three-argument form that can be used with lists to determine the first position at which an item occurs.

```
> member( b, [ a, b, c ], 'pos' );
```

$$true \tag{8.29}$$

The name **pos** is now assigned the value **2** because **b** occurs at the second position of the list. **[a, b, c]**.

```
> pos;
```

$$2 \tag{8.30}$$

When used with modules, the third argument is assigned the *local instance* of the name whose membership is being tested, provided that the return value is **true**.

```
> member( say, Hello, 'which' );
```

$$true \tag{8.31}$$

```
> which;
```

$$say \tag{8.32}$$

```
> eval( which );
```

$$\mathbf{proc}(\ )\ print(loc)\ \mathbf{end\ proc} \tag{8.33}$$

If the return value from the **member** command is **false**, the name remains unassigned or maintains its previously assigned value.

```
> unassign( 'which' ):
```

```
> member( cry, Hello, 'which' );
```
$$false \tag{8.34}$$
```
> eval( which );
```
$$which \tag{8.35}$$

Module Options

Similar to procedures, a module definition can contain options. The options available for modules are different from those for procedures. Only the options **trace** and **copyright** are common to both procedures and modules. The following four options have a predefined meaning for modules: **load**, **unload**, **package**, and **record**. The **load** and **unload** options cover functionality defined by the **ModuleLoad** and **ModuleUnload** special exports described in the next section.

For more information, refer to the **module,option** help page.

The package Option

A *package* is a collection of procedures and other data that can be treated as a whole. Packages typically gather several procedures that allow you to perform computations in a well-defined problem domain. Packages can contain data other than procedures and can even contain other packages (subpackages).

The **package** option is used to designate a module as a Maple package. The exports of a module created with the **package** option are automatically protected.

For more information, see *Writing Packages (page 383)*.

The record Option

The **record** option is used to identify records, which are fixed-size collections of items. Records are created by using the **Record** constructor and are represented using modules.

For more information, see *Records (page 330)*.

Special Exports

Certain specially named exports, when defined in a module, affect how modules behave in Maple. These special exports are described below. In most cases, they can be declared as either exported local variables or local variables.

The ModuleApply Procedure

When a procedure named **ModuleApply** is declared as an export or local of a module, the module name can be used as if it were a procedure name.

Consider the Counter example described at the beginning of this chapter. Since it only has one method, the calling sequence can be shortened by using the **ModuleApply** function.

```
> Counter := module()
      export ModuleApply;
      local count;
      count := 0;
      ModuleApply := proc()
            count := 1 + count;
      end proc;
  end module:
  Counter();
  Counter();
  Counter();
```

$$1$$
$$2$$
$$3 \tag{8.36}$$

In this example, calls to **Counter:-ModuleApply()** are not needed and the results are the same as those generated by the original Counter example. The **ModuleApply** function can specify and accept any number of parameters.

You can also use the **ModuleApply** function to create module *factories*, a standard object-oriented design pattern described later in this chapter.

The ModuleIterator Procedure

The **ModuleIterator** procedure defines how a module functions when it is used as the **in** clause of a **for** loop.

```
> for e in myModule do
      # Do something with e
  end do;
```

In the example below, the **ModuleIterator** procedure returns two procedures: **hasNext** and **getNext**. These procedures can have any names, and in fact, do not require names. When the **ModuleIterator** procedure is called, an iterator is initialized for the instance, the details of which are kept hidden from the caller. The two returned procedures can then be used to iterate over the instance to perform a specific task. For example, consider a class that implements a form of a set of which **mySet** is an instance. You can iterate over this set as follows:

```
> (hasNext,getNext) := ModuleIterator(mySet);
  while hasNext() do
      e := getNext();
```

```
    # Do something with e.
od;
```

The example above is an explicit use of the **ModuleIterator** procedure. However, this mechanism is also used implicitly by the Maple for-loop construct,

The **hasNext** procedure returns a value of **true** or **false** depending on whether remaining elements need to be processed. Successive calls to **hasNext** with no intervening calls to **getNext** return the same result. The **getNext** procedure returns the next element to process, and increments the iterator. These procedures should be implemented so that it is always safe to call **getNext** after the most recent call to **hasNext** returns a value of **true**. The result of calling **getNext** after **hasNext** has returned a value of **false**, or before **hasNext** has ever been called, is up to the implementer of the class.

The Counter example already contains a **getNext** procedure. A *bounded count* should be added so that the iteration can terminate by using **lower** and **upper** exported values. A statement also needs to be added to determine if any numbers are left in the sequence. The **hasNext** and **getNext** procedures are returned directly by **ModuleIterator**.

```
> Counter := module()
      export getNext, ModuleIterator, lower := 0, upper := 5;
      local hasNext, count := 0;

      hasNext := proc()
          evalb( count < upper );
      end proc;
      getNext := proc()
          count := 1 + count;
          return count;
      end proc;
      ModuleIterator := proc()
          return hasNext, getNext;
      end proc;
  end module;
  for e in Counter do
      e;
  end do;
```

```
    Counter := module( )
        local hasNext, count;
        export getNext, ModuleIterator, lower, upper;

        end module
```

$$
\begin{matrix} 1 \\ 2 \\ 3 \\ 4 \\ 5 \end{matrix} \qquad (8.37)
$$

When the module iterator is used by the **seq**, **add**, or **mul** commands, Maple first checks if the module is an object that exports the **numelems** command. If so, it will call the **numelems** command to determine how large to preallocate the result, and the **hasNext** and **getNext** procedures will return exactly that many elements. If the module does not export a **numelems** method, Maple will increase the result, which will consume more space (as intermediate results are discarded) and time (garbage collection).

The ModuleLoad Procedure

The **ModuleLoad** procedure is executed automatically when a module is loaded from the Maple library archive in which it has been saved. In a normal session, initialization code can be included in the module body. When loading a saved module, extra initialization code is sometimes required to set up run-time properties for the module. For example, a module that loads procedures from a dynamic-link library (.dll) file may need to call the **define_external** function during the initialization process. For more information on the **define_external** function, see *Advanced Connectivity (page 503)*.

Consider the Counter example at the beginning of the chapter. The **count** index can have any value when it is saved. The next time you use it, you might want to reset the count to zero so that it is ready to start a new sequence. This can be done by using the **ModuleLoad** procedure.

```
> Counter := module()
    export getNext, ModuleLoad;
    local count;
    ModuleLoad := proc()
        count := 0;
    end proc;
```

```
    ModuleLoad();
    getNext := proc()
        count := 1 + count;
    end proc;
end module:
Counter:-getNext();
```

$$1 \tag{8.38}$$

Note that the initialization code is contained within the **ModuleLoad** procedure. After that, the **ModuleLoad** procedure is also called. By defining the module in this way, you will get the same results when executing the module definition as you would when loading a saved module from a library archive.

The results of **ModuleLoad** can be duplicated using a procedure with a different name by using the **load**=**pname** option in the option sequence of the module.

ModulePrint

If a module has an export or local named **ModulePrint**, the result of the **ModulePrint** command is displayed instead of the module when a command in that module is executed.

The **ModulePrint** procedure does not display output. Instead, it returns a standard Maple expression that will be displayed. The expression returned can be customized to another object that portrays or summarizes the module.

In the following example, the Counter example will be extended from the **ModuleIterator** example to display a summary of what the module does.

```
> Counter := module()
    export ModuleIterator, getNext, lower := 0, upper := 5;
    local ModulePrint, hasNext, count := 0;

    hasNext := proc()
        evalb( count < upper );
    end proc;
    getNext := proc()
        count := 1 + count;
        return count ;
    end proc;
    ModuleIterator := proc()
        return hasNext, getNext;
    end proc;
    ModulePrint := proc()
        return [[ sprintf("Counter from %d to %d", lower, upper)
```

```
    ]];
      end proc;
end module;
```

$$Counter := [["Counter from 0 to 5"]] \qquad (8.39)$$

ModuleUnload

The **ModuleUnload** procedure is called immediately before a module is discarded. A module is discarded either when it is no longer accessible and is garbage collected, or when you end your Maple session.

```
> M := module()
      export ModuleUnload;
      ModuleUnload := proc() print("I am gone"); end proc;
  end module:
  unassign(M);
  1;2;3;4; gc();
```

$$\begin{aligned} &1\\&2\\&3\\&4 \end{aligned} \qquad (8.40)$$

You may not see the "I am gone" message after executing the code above because several factors determine exactly when memory is free to be garbage collected. At a minimum, no references can be left in the module. It must not be assigned or contained in any other live expression. This includes the ditto operators and the list of display reference handles (that is, the undo/redo buffer of the GUI). Also, it must not be identified as being alive by the garbage collector (i.e. a reference to the module is not found by the collector).

A module can become inaccessible, and therefore subject to garbage collection before the **unload**= procedure is executed, but can then become accessible again when that procedure is executed. In that case, the module is *not* garbage collected. When it eventually is garbage collected, or if you end your Maple session, the **unload**= procedure is *not* executed again.

The behavior of **ModuleUnload** can be duplicated using a procedure with a different name by using the **unload=pname** option in the option sequence of the module.

Implicit Scoping Rules

The bindings of names that appear within a module definition are determined when the module definition is simplified. Module definitions are subject to the same implicit scoping rules that apply to procedure definitions. Under no circumstances is a name ever implicitly determined to be exported by a module; implicitly scoped names can resolve only to exported local variables or global names.

Lexical Scoping Rules

Module definitions, along with procedure definitions, follow standard lexical scoping rules.

Modules can be nested, in the sense that a module can have any of its exports assigned to a module whose definition occurs within the body of the outer module.

Here is a simple example of a submodule.

```
> m := module()
      export s;
      s := module()
          export e;
          e := proc()
              print( "HELLO WORLD!" )
          end proc;
      end module
  end module:
```

The global name **m** is assigned a module that exports the name **s**. Within the body of **m**, the export **s** is assigned a module that exports the name **e**. As such, **s** is a *submodule* of **m**. The **Shapes** package, which is described in *Writing Packages (page 383)*, illustrates the use of submodules.

Modules and procedures can both be nested to an arbitrary depth. The rules for the accessibility of local variables (including exported locals of modules) and procedure parameters are the same as the rules for nested procedures.

Module Factory

The Counter example used up to this point would be more useful if you could have many Counter modules running at the same time, and if they could be specialized according to specified bounds. Modules do not take explicit parameters, but you can write a generic module that could be specialized by using the *factory* design pattern.

To do this, write a *constructor* procedure for the module that accepts the lower and upper bound values as arguments. The following module creates a Counter.

```
> MakeCounter := proc( lower::integer, upper::integer )
      return module()
          export ModuleIterator, getNext;
          local ModulePrint, hasNext, count := lower;
```

```
        hasNext := proc()
            evalb( count < upper );
        end proc;
        getNext := proc()
            count := 1 + count;
            return count ;
        end proc;
        ModuleIterator := proc()
            return hasNext, getNext;
        end proc;
        ModulePrint := proc()
            return [[ sprintf("Counter from %d to %d", lower,
upper) ]];
        end proc;
    end module;
end proc;
c1 := MakeCounter(6,10);
c1:-getNext();
c1:-getNext();
c2 := MakeCounter(2,4);
c2:-getNext();
c1:-getNext();
```

```
MakeCounter := proc(lower::integer, upper::integer)
    return module( )
        local ModulePrint, hasNext, count;
        export ModuleIterator, getNext;
        count := lower;
        hasNext := proc( )  evalb(count < upper)  end proc;
        getNext := proc( )
            count := 1 + count; return count
        end proc;
        ModuleIterator := proc( )
            return hasNext, getNext
        end proc;
        ModulePrint := proc( )
            return [[sprintf("Counter from %d to %d", lower,
                upper)]]
        end proc
    end module
end proc
```

$$c1 := [[\text{"Counter from 6 to 10"}]]$$

$$7$$

$$8$$

$$c2 := [[\text{"Counter from 2 to 4"}]]$$

$$3$$

$$9 \qquad (8.41)$$

In the above example, two specialized Counters operate at the same time with different internal states.

Modules and Types

Two Maple types are associated with modules. First, the name **module** is a type name. Naturally, an expression is of type **module** only if it is a module. When used as a type name, the name **module** must be enclosed in name quotes (`).

```
> type( module() end module, '`module`' );
```

$$\text{true} \tag{8.42}$$

```
> type( LinearAlgebra, '`module`' );
```

$$\text{true} \tag{8.43}$$

Second, a type called **moduledefinition** identifies expressions that are module definitions. In the previous example, the module definition

```
> module() end module:
```

was evaluated before being passed to **type**, so the expression that was tested was not the definition, but the module to which it evaluates. You must use unevaluation quotes (') to delay the evaluation of a module definition.

```
> type( 'module() end module', 'moduledefinition' );
```

$$\text{true} \tag{8.44}$$

Other important type tests satisfied by modules are the types **atomic** and **last_name_eval**.

```
> type( module() end module, 'atomic' );
```

$$\text{true} \tag{8.45}$$

The procedure **map** has no effect on modules; modules passed as an argument to **map** remain unchanged.

```
> map( print, module() export a, b, c; end module );
```

$$\textbf{module}(\ )\ \textbf{export}\ a, b, c;\ \textbf{end module} \tag{8.46}$$

Modules also follow last name evaluation rules. For more information on last name evaluation rules, refer to the **last_name_eval** help page.

```
> m := module() end module:
  m;
  type( m, 'last_name_eval' );
```

$$m$$

$$\text{true} \tag{8.47}$$

Although the type **module** is a surface type, which checks information at the top level of your code, it acts also as a structured type. Parameters passed as arguments to the unevaluated name **module** are interpreted as export names. For example, the module

```
> m := module() export a, b; end module:
```

has the structured module type `` `module`(a, b) ``:

```
> type( m, '`module`( a, b )' );
```

$$true \qquad (8.48)$$

It also has the type `` `module`( a ) ``

```
> type( m, '`module`( a )' );
```

$$true \qquad (8.49)$$

because any module that exports symbols **a** and **b** is a module that exports the symbol **a**.

For more information about structured types, refer to the **type,structure** help page.

8.5 Records

The **Record** command, which was introduced in *Records (page 159)*, is an example of a module factory that can help you to write reusable code. Like an Array, a record is a fixed-size collection of items but, like a table, individual items stored within the record can be referenced by a name, rather than a numeric offset. In Maple, records, which are called structures in C++, are implemented as modules.

Creating Records

To create a record, use the **Record** constructor. In the simplest form, it takes the field names as arguments.

```
> rec := Record( 'a', 'b', 'c' );
```

$$rec := Record(a, b, c) \qquad (8.50)$$

The name **rec** is now assigned a record with fields named **a**, **b**, and **c**. You can access and assign values to these fields by using the expressions **rec:-a**, **rec:-b**, and **rec:-c**.

```
> rec:-a := 2;
```

$$a := 2 \qquad (8.51)$$

```
> rec:-a;
```

$$2 \qquad (8.52)$$

If unassigned, a record field evaluates to the *local* instance of the field name.

```
> rec:-b;
```

$$b \qquad (8.53)$$

> evalb((8.53) = b);

$$true \tag{8.54}$$

This is useful because the entire record can be passed as an *aggregate* data structure.

The record constructor accepts initializers for record fields. That is, you can specify an initial value for any field in a new or unassigned record by passing an equation with the field name on the left side and the initial value on the right.

> r := Record('a' = 2, 'b' = sqrt(3));

$$r := Record\left(a = 2, b = \sqrt{3}\right) \tag{8.55}$$

> r:-b;

$$\sqrt{3} \tag{8.56}$$

In addition, you can associate Maple types with record fields. To associate a type, use the `::` operator with the field name specified as the first operand.

Type assertions can be used in combination with initializers. An incompatible initializer value triggers an assertion failure when the **assertlevel** kernel option is set to 2. For more information, refer to the **kernelopts** help page.

> kernelopts('assertlevel' = 2):

> Record(a::integer = 2.3, b = 2);

$$Record(a::integer = 2.3, b = 2) \tag{8.57}$$

> r := Record('a'::integer = 2, 'b'::numeric);

$$r := Record(a::integer = 2, b::numeric) \tag{8.58}$$

> r:-b := "a string";

Error, assertion failed in assignment, expected numeric, got a string

If the initializer for a record field is a procedure, you can use the reserved name **self** to refer to the record you are creating. This allows records to be self-referential. The name **self** is applicable only to creating records and not to modules in general. For example, you can write a complex number constructor as follows.

> MyComplex := (r, i) ->
      Record('re' = r, 'im' = i, 'abs' = (() -> sqrt(
          self:-re^2 + self:-im^2))):

> c := MyComplex(2, 3):

```
> c:-re, c:-im, c:-abs();
```

$$2, 3, \sqrt{13} \qquad (8.59)$$

Combined with *prototype-based inheritance*, described in *Object Inheritance (page 333)*, this facility makes the **Record** constructor a powerful tool for object-oriented programming.

Record Types

Expressions created with the **Record** constructor are of the type **record**.

```
> type( rec, 'record' );
```

$$true \qquad (8.60)$$

This is a structured type that works the same way as the `module` type, but recognizes records specifically.

```
> r := Record( a = 2, b = "foo" ):
> type( r, 'record( a::integer, b::string )' );
```

$$true \qquad (8.61)$$

Note: In a **record** type, the field types are used to test against the values assigned to the fields (if any), and are not related to type assertions on the field names (if any).

```
> r := Record( a::integer = 2, b::{symbol,string} = "foo" ):
> type( r, 'record( a::numeric, b::string )' );
```

$$true \qquad (8.62)$$

Using Records to Represent Quaternions

Records can be used to implement simple aggregate data structures for which you want named access to slots. For example, four real numbers can be combined to form a quaternion and you can represent this using a record structure as follows.

```
> MakeQuaternion := proc( a, b, c, d )
      Record( 're' = a, 'i' = b, 'j' = c, 'k' = d )
  end proc:
> z := MakeQuaternion( 2, 3, 2, sqrt( 5 ) );
```

$$z := Record\bigl(re = 2, i = 3, j = 2, k = \sqrt{5}\,\bigr) \qquad (8.63)$$

In this example, **z** represents the quaternion **2 + 3i + 2j + sqrt(5)*k** (where i, j, and k are the nonreal quaternion basis units). The quaternion records can now be manipulated as single quantities. The following procedure accepts a quaternion record as its only argument and computes the Euclidean length of the quaternion that the record represents.

```
> qnorm := proc( q )
      use re = q:-re, i = q:-i, j = q:-j, k = q:-k in
          sqrt( re * re + i * i + j * j + k * k )
      end use
  end proc:
> qnorm( z );
```

$$\sqrt{22} \tag{8.64}$$

A Maple type for quaternions can be introduced as a structured record type.

```
> TypeTools:-AddType( 'quaternion', 'record( re, i, j, k )' );
> type( z, 'quaternion' );
```

$$true \tag{8.65}$$

Object Inheritance

The **Record** constructor supports a simple form of *prototype-based inheritance*. An object system based on prototypes does not involve classes; instead, it uses a simpler and more direct form of object-based inheritance. New objects are created from existing objects (called *prototypes*) by *cloning*, that is, by copying and augmenting the data and behavior of the prototype.

The **Record** constructor supports prototype-based inheritance by accepting an index argument, which is the prototype for the new object record.

```
> p := Record( a = 2, b = 3 ); # create a prototype
```

$$p := Record(a = 2, b = 3) \tag{8.66}$$

```
> p:-a, p:-b;
```

$$2, 3 \tag{8.67}$$

```
> r := Record[p]( c = 4 );
```

$$r := Record(a = 2, b = 3, c = 4) \tag{8.68}$$

```
> r:-a, r:-b, r:-c;
```

$$2, 3, 4 \tag{8.69}$$

In this example, the record **p** is the prototype, and the second record **r** inherits the fields **a** and **b**, and their values, from the prototype **p**. It also augments the fields obtained from **p** with a new field **c**. The prototype **p** is not changed.

```
> r:-a := 9;
```

$$a := 9 \qquad (8.70)$$

```
> p:-a;
```

$$2 \qquad (8.71)$$

Behavior, as well as data, can be copied from a prototype. To copy behavior, use a constructor procedure for both the prototype and its clones.

```
> BaseComplex := proc( r, i )
    Record( 're' = r, 'im' = i )
  end proc:
  NewComplex := proc( r, i )
    Record[BaseComplex(r,i)]( 'abs' =
      (() -> sqrt( self:-re^2 + self:-im^2 )) )
  end proc:
> c := NewComplex( 2, 3 ):
> c:-re, c:-im, c:-abs();
```

$$2, 3, \sqrt{13} \qquad (8.72)$$

An object created from a prototype can serve as a prototype for another object.

```
> NewerComplex := proc( r, i )
    Record[NewComplex(r,i)]( 'arg' =
      (() -> arctan(self:-im,self:-re)) )
  end proc:
> c2 := NewerComplex( 2, 3 ):
> c2:-re, c2:-im, c2:-abs(), c2:-arg();
```

$$2, 3, \sqrt{13}, \arctan\left(\frac{3}{2}\right) \qquad (8.73)$$

Note: Prototypes are supertypes of their clones.

```
> subtype( 'record( re, im, abs )', 'record( re, im )' );
```

$$true \qquad (8.74)$$

For example, **NewComplex** creates objects of a type that is a subtype of the objects created by **BaseComplex**.

8.6 Modules and use Statements

The **use** statement is designed to complement models and to make programming with modules easier in some cases.

This section describes how the **use** statement can be used with modules. For more information about the **use** statement, see *The use Statement (page 192)*.

A module **m** can appear in the binding sequence of a **use** statement. The module is regarded as an abbreviation for the sequence of equations **a = m:-a**, **b = m:-b**, ..., where **a, b, ...** are the exports of the module **m**.

For example,
```
> m := module() export a, b; a := 2; b := 3; end module:
  use m in a + b end use;
```

$$5 \qquad (8.75)$$

This is useful for programming with packages.
```
> m := Matrix( 4, 4, [[ 26, 0,   0,   30 ],
                      [ 0,  -41, -90, 0],
                      [ 0,  -7,  -56, 0 ],
                      [ 0,  0,   0,   0]] );
  use LinearAlgebra in
      Determinant( m );
      Rank( m );
      CharacteristicPolynomial( m, 'lambda' )
  end use;
```

$$m := \begin{bmatrix} 26 & 0 & 0 & 30 \\ 0 & -41 & -90 & 0 \\ 0 & -7 & -56 & 0 \\ 0 & 0 & 0 & 0 \end{bmatrix}$$

$$0$$

$$3$$

$$\lambda^4 + 71\lambda^3 - 856\lambda^2 - 43316\lambda \qquad (8.76)$$

Note that a name that appears in a binding list for a **use** statement, which is intended to be a module, must evaluate to a module at the time the **use** statement is simplified. This is necessary because the simplification of the **use** statement must be able to determine the exports of the module. For example, the following attempt to pass a module as a parameter to a procedure does *not* work, and an error occurs when the procedure is simplified.

```
> proc( m, a, b )
      use m in e( a, b ) end use
  end proc;
Error, no bindings were specified or implied
```

The correct way to use a module as a parameter is to specify the names to be bound explicitly, for example,

```
> proc( m, a, b )
      use e = m:-e in e( a, b ) end use
  end proc;
```

$$\mathbf{proc}(m, a, b) \; m\text{:-}e(a, b) \; \mathbf{end \; proc} \tag{8.77}$$

This is necessary because, until the procedure is called with a module expression as first argument, the reference to **e** is ambiguous. The variable **e** could refer to a module export or to another value (such as a global name). To expand the **use** statement, this must be known at the time the procedure is simplified.

Operator Rebinding

The **use** statement also allows most infix and prefix operators in the Maple language to be rebound. This is not operator overloading, which can be performed in some programming languages (such as C++), because the rebinding occurs during the automatic simplification process in Maple.

If an operator name appears on the left side of a binding equation for a **use** statement (consequently, if it is an exported name of a module that is bound with **use**), then the corresponding operator expressions in the body of the **use** statement are transformed into function calls. For example,

```
> use `+` = F in a + b end use;
  m := module()
      export `*`, `+`;
      `+` := ( a, b ) -> a + b - 1;
      `*` := ( a, b ) -> a / b;
  end module:
  s * ( s + t );
  use m in s * ( s + t ) end use;
```

$$F(a, b)$$

$$s(s+t)$$

$$\frac{s}{s+t-1} \qquad (8.78)$$

When a module-based package is loaded by running the **with** command, all of exported operators are rebound at the top level so you do not need to write **use** statements to get the overloaded implementations. If a module, **M**, exports a procedure named +, and you use the command **with(M)**, subsequent sums will be processed through **M:-+**.

In most cases, the new operator procedure should contain the **overload** function. This provides a softer binding where your operator implementation will only be invoked when the arguments passed in match the specified type.

```
> PairMath := module()
    option package;
    export `+`;
    `+` := proc( a::PAIR(integer,integer), b )
        option overload;
        if type(b,PAIR(integer,integer)) then
            PAIR( op(1,a) + op(1,b), op(2,a) + op(2,b) );
        else
            PAIR( op(1,a) + b, op(2,a) + b );
        end if;
    end proc;
end module;
with(PairMath);
PAIR(2,3) + 4;
PAIR(1,1) + PAIR(3,4);
1+1;
```

$PairMath := \mathbf{module}()$
$\quad \mathbf{option}\ package;\ \mathbf{export}\ `+`;$
$\mathbf{end\ module}$

$$[`+`]$$

$$PAIR(6, 7)$$

$$PAIR(4, 5)$$

$$2 \qquad (8.79)$$

In the example above, **PairMath:-+** will only be invoked when the left side of + is a **PAIR** structure. No error occurs when computing 1+1, which is not handled by **PairMath:-+** because **option overload** has been specified for the **PairMath:-+** procedure. When **option overload** is specified, a mismatched type simply moves on to the next + implementation.

Bypassing the current overload occurs on a mismatched parameter type check, or on any **invalid input:** exception raised within the procedure. The module above can be rewritten as follows.

```
> PairMath := module()
      option package;
      export `+`;
      `+` := proc( a, b )
          option overload;
          if type(a,PAIR(integer,integer)) then
              if type(b,PAIR(integer,integer)) then
                  PAIR( op(1,a) + op(1,b), op(2,a) + op(2,b) );
              else
                  PAIR( op(1,a) + b, op(2,a) + b );
              end if;
          elif type(b,PAIR(integer,integer)) then
              PAIR( a + op(1,b), a + op(2,b) );
          else
              error("invalid input: a or b should be a PAIR structure");
          end if;
      end proc;
  end module;
  with(PairMath);
  1 + PAIR(2,3);
  2 + 2;
```

$$PairMath := \mathbf{module}(\,)$$
$$\mathbf{option}\ package;\ \mathbf{export}\ `+`;$$
$$\mathbf{end\ module}$$

$$[`+`]$$

$$PAIR(3, 4)$$

$$4 \tag{8.80}$$

Another option is to use the **overload** function to achieve polymorphism.

```
> PairMath := module()
    option package;
    export `+`;
    local PP, PA, AP;
    PP :=  proc( a::PAIR(integer,integer), b::PAIR(integer,integer)
  )
        option overload;
        print("in PP");
        PAIR( op(1,a) + op(1,b), op(2,a) + op(2,b) );
    end proc;
    PA :=  proc( a::PAIR(integer,integer), b )
        option overload;
        print("in PA");
        PAIR( op(1,a) + b, op(2,a) + b );
    end proc;
    AP :=  proc( a, b::PAIR(integer,integer) )
        option overload;
        print("in AP");
        PAIR( a + op(1,b), a + op(2,b) );
    end proc;
    `+` := overload( [ PP, PA, AP ] );
  end module;
  with(PairMath);
  1 + PAIR(2,3);
  PAIR(2,3) + 4;
  PAIR(1,1) + PAIR(3,4);
  5+5;
```

```
PairMath := module( )
    option package;
    local PP, PA, AP;
    export `+`;

end module
```

$$[`+`]$$
$$\text{"in AP"}$$
$$PAIR(3, 4)$$
$$\text{"in PA"}$$
$$PAIR(6, 7)$$
$$\text{"in PP"}$$
$$PAIR(4, 5)$$
$$10 \tag{8.81}$$

For more information, see the **overload** help page.

8.7 Interfaces and Implementations

Generic programming is a programming style and a software engineering methodology for writing reusable code. Many Maple built-in operations are generic, for example, the addition operator + computes sums of integers, rational numbers, complex numbers, polynomials, special functions, and so on. When using the addition operator +, you do not need to define how an expression is represented-- the automatic simplifier recognizes how Maple expressions are represented. As with any dynamically typed language, Maple allows for generic programming. Most built-in Maple operations (including many standard library commands) are naturally *polymorphic* in that they can perform successfully with many data formats.

Generic Programming as a Good Software Engineering Practice

When working on any large project, it is important to write *reusable* code; that is, code that can perform a well-defined function in a variety of situations. Generic programs do not rely on the details of how their inputs are represented. They can perform their function on *any* inputs that satisfy a specified set of constraints. Normally, these constraints are described in terms of the *behavior* of the inputs rather than on their physical representation or the storage layout of their concrete representation. This behavior is sometimes called a *contract*.

Generic programs rely *only* on the object behavior specified by the contract. They do *not* rely on information of how an object is implemented; therefore, generic programs *separate* interfaces from implementations.

Distinction between Local and Exported Variables

The behavior specified by the contract for a module includes any module exports. Whatever is expressed through its local variables is private to the module, and is not to be relied on, or even known, by clients of the module. (Client access is, in fact, the only technical difference between module locals and exports.)

Before the introduction of the module system, design by contract was enforced in Maple only by convention. Maple commands whose names had to be enclosed in name quotes (`) were considered private, and not for client use. However, this was only a convention. Also, it was necessary to use global variables to communicate information and state among the commands that comprised a subsystem (such as **solve** or **assume**). Now, using modules, it is possible to design software systems that enforce their contracts by a mechanism embedded in the Maple language.

Interfaces

In Maple, contracts are represented by an *interface*, which is a special kind of structured type. It has the form

```
`module`( symseq );
```

where **symseq** is a sequence of symbols or expressions of the form **symbol::type**. For example, an interface for a ring can be written as

```
> `type/ring` := '`module`( `+`, `*`, `-`, zero, one )':
```

while an (additive) abelian group can take the form

```
> `type/abgroup` := '`module`( `+`, `-`, zero )':
```

These symbols are the ones to which clients have access as module exports.

A module is said to *satisfy*, or to *implement*, an interface if it is of the type defined by the interface.

```
> z5 := module()
      description "the integers modulo 5";
      export `+`, `*`, `-`, zero, one;
      `+` := (a,b) -> a+b mod 5;
      `*` := (a,b) -> a*b mod 5;
      `-` := s -> 5-s mod 5;
      zero := 0;
```

```
        one := 1;
    end module:
> type( z5, 'ring' );
```

$$false \tag{8.82}$$

A module can satisfy more than one interface.

```
> type( z5, 'abgroup' );
```

$$false \tag{8.83}$$

Interfaces are an abstraction that form part of the Maple type system. They provide a form of *constrained* polymorphism. Not every Maple type is an interface; only those that have the form described are interfaces. You can define a Maple type (that, as it happens, is not itself an interface) to describe interfaces.

```
> `type/interface` := 'specfunc( {symbol,symbol::type},
                                 `module` )':
```

This is a structured type. It describes expressions that are themselves structured types. They have the form of an unevaluated function call with the operator symbol `module` and all arguments of type **symbol,** or of type **symbol::type**. In the two previous examples in this section, the types **type/ring** and **type/abgroup** are the interface expressions, and the names **ring** and **abgroup** are the respective names of those interfaces.

A Package for Manipulating Interfaces

The following example illustrates a package for manipulating interfaces. The package is small enough that it can be included here, in full, but it is also available in the **samples/ProgrammingGuide** directory of your Maple installation.

```
> Interface := module()
    description "a package for manipulating interfaces";
    global `type/interface`;
    export define,    # define an interface
           extend,    # extend an interface
           extends,   # test for an extension
           equivalent,# test equivalence
           savelib,   # save an interface
           satisfies;   # test whether a module satisfies
                        # an interface
    local  gassign,   # assign to a global variable
           totype,    # convert from interface name to type
           toset,     # convert from interface name to a set
           setup;     # install `type/interface` globally
```

```
option package, load = setup;
# Define a global type for interfaces.
# This assignment takes care of installing the type
# in the Maple session in which this module definition
# is evaluated. Calling `setup()' ensures that this also
# happens when the instantiated module is read from a
# Maple library archive.
`type/interface`
            := 'specfunc( {symbol, `::`}, `module` )';
# Ensure that `type/interface` is defined. This thunk is
# called when the instantiated `Interface' module is read
# from a Maple library archive.
setup := proc()
    global `type/interface`;
    `type/interface`
      := 'specfunc( {symbol, `::`}, `module` )';
    NULL # quiet return
end proc;
# Assign to the global instance of a name
gassign := proc( nom::symbol, val )
    option inline;
    eval( subs( _X = nom,
                proc()
                   global _X;
                   _X := val
                end proc ) )()
end proc;
# Convert an interface name to the corresponding type.
totype := ( ifc::symbol ) -> ( `type/` || ifc );
# Convert an interface name to a set of symbols.
toset := ( ifc::symbol ) -> { op( ( `type/` || ifc ) ) };
# Install a new interface into the type system.
define := proc( ifc )
    description "define an interface";
    if map( type, {args}, 'symbol' ) <> { true } then
        error "arguments must all be symbols"
    end if;
    gassign( `type/` || ifc,
       '`module`'( args[ 2 .. nargs ] ) );
    ifc # return the interface name
end proc;
# Implement subtyping.
```

```
extend := proc( new, old )
    description "extend an existing inteface";
    if map( type, {args}, 'symbol' ) <> { true } then
        error "arguments must all be symbols"
    end if;
    if not type( totype( old ), 'interface' ) then
        error "cannot find an interface named %1", old
    end if;
    define( new, op( totype( old ) ), args[3..nargs] )
end proc;
# Test whether ifc2 is an extension of ifc1.
extends := proc( ifc1, ifc2 )
    description "test whether the second interface "
                "extends the first";
    local t1, t2;
    t1, t2 := op( map( totype, [ ifc1, ifc2 ] ) );
    if not type( [t1,t2], '[interface,interface]' ) then
        if not type( t1, 'interface' ) then
            error "arguments must be interface names, "
                  "but got %1", ifc1
        else
            error "arguments must be interface names, "
                  "but got %1", ifc2
        end if
     end if;
     toset( ifc1 ) subset toset( ifc2 )
end proc;
# Save an interface to the Maple library archive.
savelib := proc()
    description "save a named interface to a "
                "Maple library archive";
    local ifc;
    for ifc in map( totype, [ args ] ) do
        if not type( ifc, 'interface' ) then
            error "arguments must be interfaces, "
                  "but got %1", ifc
        end if;
        :-savelib( totype( ifc ) )
    end do
end proc;
# Test whether a module satisfies an interface.
# This is simply an alternative to a call
```

8.7 Interfaces and Implementations • 345

```
            # to `type()'.
            satisfies := proc( m, ifc )
                description "test whether a module satisfies an interface";

                if not type( totype( ifc ), 'interface' ) then
                    error "second argument must be an interface name, "
                          "but got %1", ifc
                end if;
                type( m, ifc )
            end proc;
            # Test whether two interfaces are equivalent.
            # Since unevaluated function calls compare
            # differently if their arguments are in a
            # different order, we convert them to sets first,
            # and then test for equality.
            equivalent := proc( ifc1, ifc2 )
                description "test whether two interfaces "
                            "are equivalent";
                local t1, t2;
                t1, t2 := totype( ifc1 ), totype( ifc2 );
                if not type( t1, 'interface' ) then
                    error "expecting an interface name, "
                          "but got %1", ifc1
                elif not type( t2, 'interface' ) then
                    error "expecting an interface name, "
                          "but got %1", ifc2
                end if;
                evalb( { op( t1 ) } = { op( t2 ) } )
            end proc;
        end module:
```

This package implements the interface abstraction. It allows you to manipulate interfaces without having to consider how they fit into the Maple type system.

```
> with( Interface );
```

$$[\textit{define, equivalent, extend, extends, satisfies, savelib}] \tag{8.84}$$

```
> define( 'abgroup', '`+`', '`-`', 'zero' );
```

$$\textit{abgroup} \tag{8.85}$$

```
> type( `type/abgroup`, 'interface' );
```

$$\textit{true} \tag{8.86}$$

```
> type( z5, 'abgroup' );
```
$$\textit{false} \tag{8.87}$$
```
> satisfies( z5, 'abgroup' );
```
$$\textit{false} \tag{8.88}$$
```
> extend( 'ring', 'abgroup', '`*`', 'one' );
```
$$\textit{ring} \tag{8.89}$$
```
> type( `type/ring`, 'interface' );
```
$$\textit{true} \tag{8.90}$$
```
> extends( abgroup, ring );
```
$$\textit{false} \tag{8.91}$$
```
> satisfies( z5, 'ring' );
```
$$\textit{false} \tag{8.92}$$
```
> type( z5, 'ring' );
```
$$\textit{false} \tag{8.93}$$

The load Option

This package provides an abstraction of the interface concept in Maple and illustrates a module feature that was not previously demonstrated: the **load=procedure_name** option. In the **Interface** package, this option is used in a typical way. The declaration

```
option load = setup;
```

that appears in the module definition indicates that, when the instantiated module is read from a Maple library archive, the procedure **setup** is to be called. The procedure named must be a local variable or an exported local variable of the module. The local procedure **setup** in this module simply ensures that the global variable **type/interface** is assigned an appropriate value. This assignment is also made in the body of the module so that the assignment is also executed in the session in which the module is instantiated. This is done for illustrative purposes. A better approach would be to invoke **setup** in the body of the module definition.

9 Object Oriented Programming

9.1 In This Chapter

- A brief introduction to Object Oriented Programming will be presented.
- A description of how Object Oriented Programming is implemented in Maple.
- How to override operators and engine routines using Objects.

9.2 Introduction To Object Oriented Programming

Objects are a programming tool that allows data and procedures to be encapsulated together. For example, an object could be created to represent a car. A car object might have variables to track its position, velocity and steering position. The car object might also have procedures to accelerate the car and to adjust the steering. A further procedure could be implemented to update the car's position and velocity based on the current acceleration, velocity and steering. Multiple car objects could be used to represent multiple cars, each with their own positions and velocities, but sharing the same procedures for how the cars move.

Objects can also restrict access to certain variables and procedures. For example the car object would allow other code to call a routine to adjust the steering, but may not allow external code to set the value of the steering variable directly. Although this may seem restrictive, it allows the object to control its internal state. In the car example, it could limit the range of steering.

Terminology

The variables in an object that store the data and procedures are referred to as the object's *members*. Procedures associated with an object are called *methods*. Object members have access controls which limit where the members can be accessed from, similar to modules. Members declared *exported* can be accessed from anywhere. Members declared *local* can only be accessed from within the object's methods. Objects are instances of a *class*. A class describes the exports and locals that each instance of the class (the objects) will have.

Benefits of Object Oriented Programming

Benefits of object oriented programming are:
- The implementation of a class can be changed radically without changing the interface of exported methods. Thus code that uses the objects will not need to change when the internal implementation changes.
- As objects are self contained, they can be reused.
- Objects can define methods that allow them to integrate with existing Maple routines. Thus users can create objects that can be used like built-in types.

- A set of classes can implement a common set of exports. Thus a procedure that uses only the common exports will work with any objects from any of the classes without needing to know which classes the objects belong to.

Good object oriented design can be difficult. In particular, identifying which concepts should be represented as objects can be tricky. A good rule of thumb is that objects should be your "nouns" and methods should be "verbs". Thus you would create an object to represent a car and you call a method to accelerate the car.

9.3 Objects in Maple

Creating a New Class of Objects

To create a new class of objects, use the named module declaration syntax with option object.

```
> module NewObject()
      option object;
      ...
  end module;
```

This will create a new object and assign the new object to the module name (NewObject in the example above). An object created this way will be referred to as a *prototype object*. In Maple, any object (prototype or other) can be used as a representative of the class.

When declaring an object the members must be declared as either local to the object, using a **local** declaration or exported, using an **export** declaration. A member that is declared **local** can only be accessed from the object's methods, or other object's methods of the same class. A member that is exported, can be accessed anywhere.

By default, the values assigned to the object's members are unique to the object. That is, two objects of the same class can have different values assigned to their members. However some members, member procedures in particular, are shared among all objects of a class. Thus members can also be declared as **static**. A **static** member stores only one value that is common to all objects of a class.

Creating More Objects

Once a prototype object exists, it can be used to create new objects using the **Object** routine. The **Object** routine creates a new object of the same class as the object passed into **Object**.

```
> newObj := Object( existingObject );
```

By default, the newly created object will have its members assigned the same values as the object passed to **Object**. However by implementing a **ModuleCopy** routine, the object can perform different actions when new instances are created. A **ModuleCopy** routine can accept additional arguments that are passed into the **Object** routine.

```
> newObj := Object( existingObject, arg1, arg2, ... );
```

Objects and Types

All objects are of **type object**. In addition **type** and **::** can be used to determine if an object is a instance of a particular class by passing an object of the expected class as the type. You can refine this type checking by defining the **ModuleType** method.

9.4 Methods

Methods are procedures assigned to the members of an object. Methods have a few differences from normal procedures.

Methods Can Access Object Locals

A method belonging to a particular class can access both the local and exported members of any object of that class. This allows methods to access and manipulate the internal states of their objects without requiring the objects to export accessor procedures.

Method Names Should Be Declared static

In Maple, most method names should be declared as **static**. In most cases, all objects of the same class use the same procedures for their methods. If the method name is not declared **static**, each object will have a separate copy of the procedure. This can be quite wasteful.

There are some instances where an object will have a non-**static** method. However unless you intend different objects to have different procedures assigned to the method, your method should be **static**.

Methods Are Passed the Objects They Manipulate

Some object oriented languages associate method calls with a particular object. That object is represented via a **self** variable or by allowing direct access to that object's members. Maple does not give a particular object special significance in that way. Instead, all objects that a method needs to manipulate must be passed as parameters.

Calling Methods

To call an object's method, call the method as a standard function call and pass the object in as an argument.

```
> method( ..., object, ... );
```

When a function call is evaluated and an object is passed in as an argument, the object is searched for an exported procedure with a matching name. If one is found, that member procedure is called with the given arguments.

This search proceeds from left to right, so the first object with a matching method is used as the class whose method is invoked.

Objects in Indexed Function Calls

When making an indexed function call (of the form **func[index](args)**) Maple will also check the indices (**index**) for a matching object as well as the arguments. If a matching object is found in the indices, that object will be used before one found in the arguments.

Search an index sequence is also performed from left to right.

Special Methods

There are a set of special methods that a class can define that will automatically be used in various situations. Not all of these methods make sense for all objects. See the method specific help pages for complete details.

ModuleCopy: The **ModuleCopy** method is invoked when a object is copied via the **Object** routine.

ModuleType: The **ModuleType** method is invoked when an object is passed into the **type** routine. It allows a module to have a more precise type check of objects of a particular class.

ModulePrint: The **ModulePrint** method is invoked when an object is pretty-printed.

ModuleDeconstruct: The **ModuleDeconstruct** method is invoked when an object is converted to a 1 dimensional form, usually Maple syntax.

ModuleApply: The **ModuleApply** method is invoked when an object is used as a function in a function call expression.

ModuleLoad: The **ModuleLoad** method is invoked when the object class is read in from a library.

ModuleUnload: The **ModuleUnload** method is invoked when an object is collected.

ModuleIterator: The **ModuleIterator** method creates an interface that can be used to iterate over the contents of the object.

9.5 Overloading Operators

Objects can define methods which allow them to control what happens when those objects are used with various operators. For example, if an object implements a + method, then that method will be invoked if the object appears in a sum expression.

```
> 1 + Obj1 + n;
```

By overloading operators, objects can be used in Maple expressions. This, combined with overloading built-in routines, allows objects to be used naturally in general Maple expressions.

Supported Operators

The following operators can be overloaded by an object:

+	-	*	/	^	!	.	=	<>	<	<=	>	>=
and	or	not	xor	implies	intersect	union	minus	subset	in
[]	{}	?[]	@	@@	&*	&*name*

The following operators, in particular, **cannot** be overridden:

| : | ?() | :- | , | -> | := |

Note: These lists are not the same as the operators that can and cannot be overridden using a **use** statement.

Implementing Operators

In general implementing operators is similar to implementing normal methods. However particular operators have rules that must be followed if they are to be implemented correctly.

The rules for the various operators are documented on the **Object,operators** help page.

9.6 Overloading Built-in Routines

Objects can implement methods to override some built-in routines (like **convert** or **abs**). These methods will be invoked when objects are passed as arguments to the corresponding built-in routines. By overriding built-in routines, user-defined objects can be used in normal Maple expressions. This, combined with overloading operators, allows objects to be used naturally in general Maple expressions.

Any routine implemented in Maple code can be overloaded. However, not all built-in routines (routines implemented in the Maple **kernel**) can be overloaded.

Overridable Built-in Routines

The following built-in routines can be overloaded by object methods:

abs	aname	conjugate	convert	diff	eval	evalhf	evalf
expand	has	hastype	Im	Re	implies	indets	length
map, map2, map[n]	member	normal	numboccur	subs	trunc	type	

Some overloadable built-in routines have a specific interface that must be followed. The interfaces for the overloadable built-ins can be found on the **object,builtins** help page.

9.7 Examples

The following example shows a class for objects representing integers modulo a given base.

```
(* create a new class of objects with a prototype object
       named 'IntMod' *)
module IntMod()
    option object;
    (* These locals maintain the internal state of the ModInt objects.
       base is the modulus, value is the integer.  These members are not
       declared as 'static' so each object has its own values for these
       members. *)

    local base := 1;
    local value := 0;

    (* We implement the 'ModuleApply' and 'ModuleCopy' routines to create a
       nice object factory.  With these defined the prototype object can
       be applied to generate new objects.  These routines are declared
       as 'static', so they are shared between objects of this class. *)
    export ModuleApply::static := proc()
        Object( IntMod, _passed );
    end;

    (* The ModuleCopy routine initializes 'self' using 'proto' and the
       passed arguments. If a value or base is given as a parameter,
       those are used.  Otherwise, these values are copied from 'proto'. *)

    export ModuleCopy::static := proc( self::IntMod, proto::IntMod,
v::integer, b::integer, $ )
        if ( _npassed < 4 ) then
            self:-base := proto:-base;
        else
            self:-base := b;
        end;
        if ( _npassed < 3 ) then
            self:-value := proto:-value;
        else
            self:-value := v mod self:-base;
        end;
    end;
```

```
    (* Implement a 'ModulePrint' routine to allow the objects to
       display nicely *)
    export ModulePrint::static := proc( self::IntMod )
        nprintf( "%d mod %d", self:-value, self:-base );
    end;

    (* We implement a 'ModuleType' routine to allow better type checking.
       This allows a base to be specified in the type check *)
    export ModuleType::static := proc( self, type, b, $ )
        if ( _npassed = 2 ) then
            true;
        else
            evalb( self:-base = b );
        end;
    end;

    (* A getter function to access the value feild *)
    export getValue::static := proc( self::IntMod )
        self:-value;
    end;

    (* Overload the + operator.  This routine accepts any number of
       arguments, it sums any IntMod objects and integers appropriately.
       If there are other terms, a sum expression is returned with one
       IntMod and the remaining terms. *)
    export `+`::static := proc( )
        local ints, imods, total, base, other;
        ( ints, other ) := selectremove( type, [_passed], { 'IntMod',
'integer' } );
        ( imods, ints ) := selectremove( type, ints, 'IntMod' );
        base := imods[1]:-base;
        if ( not andmap( type, imods, 'IntMod'( base ) ) ) then
            error "all IntMods must be of the same base"
        end;
        total := ( `if`( numelems(ints) > 0, ints[1], 0 ) + add( getValue(i),
i in imods ) );
        IntMod( total, base ), op( other );
    end;

    (* Overload the * operator.  Similar to the + operator, we multiply
       out all the IntMod's and integers, and maintian other terms to be
       returned as part of a product expression. *)
    export `*`::static := proc( )
        local ints, imods, total, base, other;
```

```
        ( ints, other ) := selectremove( type, [_passed], { 'IntMod',
'integer' } );

        ( imods, ints ) := selectremove( type, ints, 'IntMod' );

        base := imods[1]:-base;
        if ( not andmap( type, imods, 'IntMod'( base ) ) ) then
            error "all IntMods must be of the same base"
        end;

        total := ( `if`( numelems(ints) > 0, ints[1], 1 ) * mul( getValue(i),
i in imods ) );

        IntMod( total, base ), op( other );
    end;

    (* ^ operator.  We need to handle 3 cases, IntMod as base, IntMod as
       exponent, and both base and exponent are IntMods *)
    export `^`::static := proc( b, e, $ )
        if ( b::IntMod ) then
            if ( e::IntMod ) then
                IntMod( b:-value^e:-value, b:-base );
            elif ( e::integer ) then
                IntMod( b:-value^e, b:-base );
            else
                error( "integer expected for exponent" );
            end;
        else
            b^e:-value;
        end;
    end;
    (* For the comparison operators, handle the cases where there is only
       one argument or one of the arguments is not an IntMod by returning
       false. *)
    export `=`::static := proc( l, r, $ )
        if ( _npassed <> 2 or not l::IntMod or not r::IntMod ) then
            return false;
        end;
        evalb( l:-base = r:-base and l:-value = r:-value )
    end;

    export `<`::static := proc( l, r, $ )
        if ( _npassed <> 2 or not l::IntMod or not r::IntMod ) then
            return false;
        end;
```

```
            evalb( l:-base = r:-base and l:-value < r:-value )
        end;

        export `<=`::static := proc( l, r, $ )
            if ( _npassed <> 2 or not l::IntMod or not r::IntMod ) then
                return false;
            end;
            evalb( l:-base = r:-base and l:-value <= r:-value )
        end;

        export `>`::static := proc( l, r, $ )
            if ( _npassed <> 2 or not l::IntMod or not r::IntMod ) then
                return false;
            end;
            evalb( l:-base = r:-base and l:-value > r:-value )
        end;

        export `>=`::static := proc( l, r, $ )
            if ( _npassed <> 2 or not l::IntMod or not r::IntMod ) then
                return false;
            end;
            evalb( l:-base = r:-base and l:-value >= r:-value )
        end;

        (* override the convert function to allow conversions from IntMods
           to integers. *)
        export convert::static := proc( v, toType, $ )
            if ( v::IntMod ) then
                if ( toType = ':-integer' ) then
                    v:-value;
                else
                    error "cannot convert from IntMod to %1", toType;
                end;
            else
                error "cannot convert into IntMod from %1", v
            end;
        end;
end:
```

> `i0m5 := IntMod( 0, 5 );`

$$i0m5 := 0 \bmod 5 \tag{9.1}$$

> `i1m5 := Object( i0m5, 1 );`

$$i1m5 := 1 \bmod 5 \tag{9.2}$$

```
> type( i1m5, 'IntMod' );
```
$$true \qquad (9.3)$$
```
> type( i1m5, 'IntMod'(3) );
```
$$false \qquad (9.4)$$
```
> type( i1m5, 'IntMod'(5) );
```
$$true \qquad (9.5)$$
```
> i2m5 := i1m5 + 1;
```
$$i2m5 := 2 \bmod 5 \qquad (9.6)$$
```
> i3m5 := i2m5 + 1;
```
$$i3m5 := 3 \bmod 5 \qquad (9.7)$$
```
> i4m5 := i3m5 + 1;
```
$$i4m5 := 4 \bmod 5 \qquad (9.8)$$
```
> i4m5 + 1;
```
$$0 \bmod 5 \qquad (9.9)$$
```
> i3m5+i4m5;
```
$$2 \bmod 5 \qquad (9.10)$$
```
> i1m5 + 9 + i4m5;
```
$$4 \bmod 5 \qquad (9.11)$$
```
> convert( i3m5, 'integer' );
```
$$3 \qquad (9.12)$$
```
> convert( 3, IntMod );
Error, (in IntMod:-convert) cannot convert into IntMod from 3
> i2m5 * i4m5 * y * f(x);
```
$$3 \bmod 5 \, y f(x) \qquad (9.13)$$
```
> i2m5^1;
```
$$2 \bmod 5 \qquad (9.14)$$
```
> i2m5^2;
```
$$4 \bmod 5 \qquad (9.15)$$

```
> i2m5^3;
```

$$3 \bmod 5 \tag{9.16}$$

```
> i2m5^4;
```

$$1 \bmod 5 \tag{9.17}$$

```
> i2m5^5;
```

$$2 \bmod 5 \tag{9.18}$$

```
> evalb(i2m5 < i4m5);
```

$$\textit{true} \tag{9.19}$$

```
> evalb(i3m5 > i2m5);
```

$$\textit{true} \tag{9.20}$$

```
> evalb(i2m5 <= i4m5);
```

$$\textit{true} \tag{9.21}$$

```
> evalb(i3m5 >= i2m5);
```

$$\textit{true} \tag{9.22}$$

```
> evalb(i3m5 = i2m5);
```

$$\textit{false} \tag{9.23}$$

9.8 Avoiding Common Mistakes

Overloaded Operators and Built-in Routines Must Handle All Possibilities

A object's method will be invoked whenever that object appears in a matching function call, regardless of the object's position in the argument sequence. Thus when implementing operators and overloading built-in routines, it is important the handle all the cases where the object could appear.

In the following example it might be easy to assume that when **member** is called the object will be the first argument (the container). However, it is also possible that the object will appear as the second argument (the element being searched for).

```
> module Container()
    option object;
    local t := table();
    export insert::static := proc( c::Container, a, $ )
        c:-t[a] := 1;
```

```
              NULL;
        end;
        export member::static := proc( c, e, $ )
            if ( c::Container ) then
                if ( c:-t[e] = 1 ) then
                    return e;
                else
                    return 0;
                end;
            else
                return ':-member'( c, e );
            end;
        end;
    end:
> container := Object( Container ):
> insert( container, a ):
> member( container, a );
```

$$\text{true} \tag{9.24}$$

```
> member( [container], container );
```

$$\text{true} \tag{9.25}$$

For some possibilities, the correct approach is to simply pass the arguments on to the Maple routine. When doing so, care must be taken to access the correct version of the routine.

Make Sure to Access the Correct Routine

When overloading operators and built-in routines, those overloads will be used within the implementation of the object itself. This means that care should be taken to call the global version of a routine when it is required. In the **member** overload shown earlier, the code invokes the global version of **member**, by using quotes and **:-**. Failing to do so can lead to infinite recursions and other unexpected behavior.

Be Aware of NULL

Be careful when assuming that operators and built-in routines will always be passed a certain number of arguments. Many will accept **NULL** as an argument, and this may lead to fewer arguments then expected.

```
> module Wrapper()
     option object;
     local value := 10;
```

```
        export `=`::static := proc( l, r, $ )
            ( l::Wrapper and r::Wrapper and l:-value = r:-value );
        end;
    end:
> cp := Object( Wrapper ):
> evalb( cp = Wrapper );
```

$$true \qquad (9.26)$$

```
> evalb( cp = 11 );
```

$$false \qquad (9.27)$$

```
> evalb( cp = NULL );
```

"Error, invalid input: Wrapper:-= uses a 2nd argument, r, which is missing" (9.28)

Lexical Scoping Does Not Circumvent local

Members that are declared as local can only be accessed from within the class's methods. This means that methods cannot use lexical scoping to pass values to nested procedures.

```
> module LexicalObj()
      option object;
      local a;
      export b :: static := proc(mm :: m, f, lst :: list, $)
          print(mm:-a);
          return map(x -> f(mm:-a, x), lst);
      end;
  end:
> b(m, `+`, [1,2,3]);
```

$$b(m, `+`, [1,2,3]) \qquad (9.29)$$

In this example, we can print the value of **a** in **b** because **b** is a method. However the **map** fails because the arrow procedure is not a member and thus does not have access to **a**.

10 Input and Output

10.1 In This Chapter

- Introduction
- Input and output in the worksheet
- Input and output with files
- Reading and writing formatted data
- Useful utilities
- 2-D math

10.2 Introduction

This chapter explores the ways in which you can read input and write output programmatically. Here are a few examples of I/O operations in Maple.

- **Example 1:** An integral can be printed in various ways. The two outputs below show the integral in 2-D and 1-D representations, respectively.

```
> y := Int(x^2, x=1..2);
```

$$y := \int_1^2 x^2 \, dx \qquad (10.1)$$

```
> lprint(y);
Int(x^2, x = 1 .. 2)
```

- **Example 2:** The checkfile procedure defined below uses commands in the **FileTools** package to examine the properties of a file.

```
> checkfile := proc(fname :: string)
      return FileTools:-Exists(fname) and
   FileTools:-IsReadable(fname);
   end proc:
```

- **Example 3:** A Matrix is written to a file using the **ExportMatrix** command.

```
> M := LinearAlgebra:-RandomMatrix(5, 4);
```

$$M := \begin{bmatrix} -98 & -76 & -4 & 29 \\ -77 & -72 & 27 & 44 \\ 57 & -2 & 8 & 92 \\ 27 & -32 & 69 & -31 \\ -93 & -74 & 99 & 67 \end{bmatrix} \qquad (10.2)$$

```
> ExportMatrix("testfile", M);
```

$$67 \qquad (10.3)$$

- **Example 4:** The **sscanf** command is used here to read three floating-point numbers from the string given as the first argument.

```
> z := sscanf("X=123.4 Y=-27.9 Z=2.3E-5", "X=%f Y=%f Z=%f");
```

$$z := [\,123.4, -27.9, 0.000023\,] \qquad (10.4)$$

The first example shows the difference between 1-D and 2-D output in Maple. Note that input can also be provided in both forms. In Maple, 1-D math is character-based, is available in all interfaces, and can be controlled by many of the basic I/O commands discussed in this chapter. Typeset or 2-D math is available only with the standard worksheet interface and is generally manipulated interactively using the Maple GUI tools. However, it can be controlled programmatically in a limited way.

Most of this chapter is devoted to the manipulation of files, which is the main way data is shared between Maple and external applications. Many of the file-processing commands also apply to interactive input and output, when 1-D mode is used. For example, the command for formatted writing, **printf**, produces output in a Maple worksheet or document. However, it is essentially identical to the **fprintf** command for printing to a file.

This chapter starts with a discussion of input and output in the worksheet, including some notes on using other interfaces. The next section covers manipulation of files. Tools for importing and exporting general files as well as those specially designed for numerical data are discussed. Later in the chapter, low-level commands for formatted reading and writing, along with other useful utilities, are shown. The chapter concludes with an explanation of 2-D math and how it can be customized programmatically.

10.3 Input and Output in the Worksheet

This section introduces common ways of reading from the keyboard and writing to the screen. In contrast, the following section discusses I/O through the use of files. There is some overlap between the two sections, as the keyboard and screen themselves can be considered files. This is explained further in the "Default and Terminal Files" section of the **file_types** help page.

Interfaces

Maple has several user interfaces, all described on the **versions** help page. In this chapter, it is assumed you are using either the standard worksheet interface or the command-line interface. Most of the I/O operations described here apply to either interface. The major exception is typeset or 2-D math, which is available only with the standard worksheet interface.

You can use the **interface** command to communicate with the user interface. It allows you to query or set certain user interface variables. This is one way of controlling the look of the output. Note that the **interface** command does not affect the actual computation. A few examples are shown below. A complete list of the variables is available on the **interface** help page.

The **version** variable returns the interface version, platform information, build date and build number.

```
> interface(version);
```

$$\textit{Standard Worksheet Interface, Maple 16.00, Linux, January 30 2012 Build ID 725768} \tag{10.5}$$

The **prettyprint** variable controls how Maple expressions are rendered as output.

```
> interface(prettyprint=1):
  Diff(f(x), x);
```

$$\frac{d}{dx} f(x) \tag{10.6}$$

```
> interface(prettyprint=3):
  Diff(f(x), x);
```

$$\frac{d}{dx} f(x) \tag{10.7}$$

The **rtablesize** variable specifies the largest-sized **rtable** that will be displayed inline. If an **rtable** has a dimension that is larger than this integer, then it is displayed as a placeholder.

```
> interface(rtablesize);
```

$$10 \tag{10.8}$$

```
> Matrix(5, 5, (i,j)->i+j);
```

$$\begin{bmatrix} 2 & 3 & 4 & 5 & 6 \\ 3 & 4 & 5 & 6 & 7 \\ 4 & 5 & 6 & 7 & 8 \\ 5 & 6 & 7 & 8 & 9 \\ 6 & 7 & 8 & 9 & 10 \end{bmatrix} \qquad (10.9)$$

```
> Matrix(15, 15, (i,j)->i+j);
```

$$\begin{bmatrix} 15 \times 15 \; Matrix \\ Data\; Type:\; anything \\ Storage:\; rectangular \\ Order:\; Fortran\_order \end{bmatrix} \qquad (10.10)$$

Interactive Output

By default, the output from a statement entered in the worksheet is automatically printed to the screen, unless the statement is terminated by a colon. In the previous section, you saw how to use the **interface** command to customize certain aspects of the output. Another way to adjust the output is to set the **printlevel** environment variable. The default value of **printlevel** is 1. When it is set to a higher value, additional information pertaining to procedure calls is printed. This is one way of tracing a procedure for debugging purposes. For more information about debugging programs, see *Testing, Debugging, and Efficiency (page 581)*.

The **print** command prints Maple expressions using the current setting of the **prettyprint interface** variable. In the worksheet, the default output is 2-D math and in the command-line version, the default is a simulated math notation using text characters. Note that the **print** command returns **NULL** and thus the output cannot be regenerated with the **ditto** commands.

The **print** command is particularly useful in two situations. First, it can be used to print intermediate results calculated within a procedure. Normally, only the returned value of a procedure is printed when it is called.

```
> p := proc(n)
        local i;
        for i to n do
            i^2;
        end do;
    end proc:
```

```
> p(5);
```

$$25 \tag{10.11}$$

```
> q := proc(n)
        local i;
        for i to n do
            print(i^2);
        end do;
    end proc:
> q(5);
```

$$1$$
$$4$$
$$9$$
$$16$$
$$25 \tag{10.12}$$

The **print** command can also be used to print procedures and other expressions that follow last name evaluation rules. For more information, refer to the **last_name_eval** help page.

```
> print(q);
```

$$\mathbf{proc}(n) \ \mathbf{local} \ i; \ \mathbf{for} \ i \ \mathbf{to} \ n \ \mathbf{do} \ print(i^2) \ \mathbf{end} \ \mathbf{do} \ \mathbf{end} \ \mathbf{proc} \tag{10.13}$$

The **lprint** command prints Maple expressions in a character-based notation that is similar to the format used for 1-D input. Like the **print** command, the value returned by a call to **lprint** is **NULL**, and the output cannot be recalled using the **ditto** operator. When the **prettyprint interface** variable is set to 0, Maple uses **lprint** to print all expressions to the interface.

```
> lprint(expand(x+y)^5);
(x+y)^5
```

Another commonly used command is **printf**, which produces formatted output. This command will be discussed in *Reading and Writing Formatted Data (page 375)*.

If you want to redirect all output that normally goes to the screen to a file, use the **writeto** and **appendto** commands. This is an easy way to log the input and output of a Maple session, particularly if you are using the command-line interface. In the standard worksheet interface, you can simply save the current worksheet or document. For more information on writing to files, see *Input and Output with Files (page 366)*.

Interactive Input

Normally, input is passed to Maple procedures directly through the procedure's parameters. In the standard worksheet interface, input can also be provided through Maplets and components. For more information about these topics, see *Programming Interactive Elements (page 487)*.

The **readline** and **readstat** commands are also available for interactive input, though these are less commonly used. The **readline** command reads the next line from the terminal or a file and returns it as a string, while the **readstat** command reads the next statement from the terminal and returns the value of that statement.

Customization

You can customize the prettyprinting of a function **fnc** in a limited way by defining a **print/fnc** procedure. In the following example, expressions of the form **g(x)** should be printed so that the argument is repeated three times in a list.

```
> `print/g` := proc(x) [x, x, x] end proc:
> g(b^2);
```

$$[b^2, b^2, b^2] \tag{10.14}$$

```
> g(5.8);
```

$$[5.8, 5.8, 5.8] \tag{10.15}$$

There is a similar facility for prettyprinting a module. If a module has an export or local named **ModulePrint**, then the result of the **ModulePrint** command is displayed instead of the module when a command in the module is executed. For more information, see *Programming with Modules (page 309)*.

10.4 Input and Output with Files

Introduction

This section covers input and output using files, which is recommended when you have a large amount of data to process. This also provides a way for Maple to share data with external applications. In this chapter, the term "file" is not limited to a disk file, but can include the default output stream to a terminal or worksheet output region. Below is a brief introduction to a few concepts related to files. For more detailed information, refer to the **file** and **file_types** help pages.

- **Text and binary files:** The Maple I/O library works with both text files (streams of characters) and binary files (streams of bytes). The I/O commands allow you to specify the type of file and generally assume a text file if no information is given.

- **Read and write modes:** At any given time, a file may be open either for reading or for writing. If you attempt to write to a file which is open for reading, Maple closes and reopens the file for writing. If you do not have permission to write to the file, then an error occurs.
- **The default and terminal files:** The Maple I/O library treats the user interface as a file. The identifier **default** refers to the current input stream, the one from which Maple reads and processes commands. The identifier **terminal** refers to the top-level input stream, the current input stream when you started Maple. When Maple is run interactively, **default** and **terminal** are equivalent.
- **File names and descriptors:** Maple I/O commands refer to files in one of two ways: by name (given as a string) or by descriptor. A file descriptor identifies a file after you have opened it using its name and offers slight advantages in terms of efficiency and flexibility. The commands described in this section accept either a name or a descriptor as the file identifier.
- **Current directory:** If you create files using the examples in this chapter, the files are saved in the current directory. To query or set the current working directory, use the **currentdir** command.

Working with General Files

This section covers the manipulation of general files. If you are working with files of numerical data, it is recommended that you use the commands described in *ImportMatrix and ExportMatrix (page 372)*.

There are two sets of commands that you can use. The first subsection below describes the basic top-level commands for file manipulation. Alternatively, you can use the **FileTools** package, which provides a simpler interface to the other commands and offers additional functionality. For most file operations, the **FileTools** package is recommended, but the two sets of commands are generally compatible and can be used interchangeably on a file.

The Maple I/O Library

Below is a description of commonly used commands in the Maple I/O library.

- **Opening and closing files**

  Before you can read from or write to a file, you must open it. When referring to files by name, this happens automatically with the first file operation. When you use descriptors, however, you must explicitly open the file first to create the descriptor. The **fopen** command takes as arguments the filename, a mode (**READ**, **WRITE** or **APPEND**) and optionally, the file type (**TEXT** or **BINARY**).

  ```
  > f := fopen("testfile", 'WRITE', 'TEXT');
  ```

When you are finished with a file, you can close it with the **fclose** command, which takes the file identifier as its argument. This operation ensures that all information is written to the disk. When you exit Maple or use the **restart** command, Maple automatically closes any open files, whether they were opened explicitly with **fopen** or implicitly through one of the other I/O commands.

- **Reading and writing lines of text**

The **readline** command reads one newline-terminated line from a file and returns a string containing that line. The **writeline** command writes one or more strings to a file, separated with newline characters, and returns a count of the characters. If the file is not already open with type **TEXT**, then the **readline** or **writeline** command will open the file automatically.

```
> writeline("testfile", "The first line", "The second line");
```

- **Reading and writing bytes**

The **readbytes** command reads one or more or bytes from a file and returns a list of integers. Optionally, you can specify that the file is to be opened in text rather than binary mode, and in this case, a string is returned. You can also provide a previously created **rtable** to the **readbytes** command and it will return the data in the **rtable**. Similarly, the **writebytes** command writes bytes from a string or list to a file. More information about both commands can be found on their help pages.

- **Reading and writing formatted input and output**

The **fscanf** command parses expressions from a file based on a format string. Similarly, the **fprintf** command prints expressions to a file based on a format string. Both commands are similar to the C standard library commands of the same names. Both **fscanf** and **fprintf** are described in greater detail in *Reading and Writing Formatted Data (page 375)*.

- **Other file utilities**

There are a number of other useful file utilities, including **iostatus** (obtain the status of an open file), **fremove** (remove a file), **fflush** (flush output), **filepos** (sets or returns the position), and **feof** (check if the current position is at the end). For more information about these commands, refer to their help pages.

Below is a simple example that uses a few of the commands introduced here. The file generated will be placed in your current working directory, which you can set with the **currentdir** command.

First, define a **Vector** of floating-point values.

```
> V := Vector([1.20, 4.85, 6.23, 2.45, 7.99]):
> n := LinearAlgebra:-Dimension(V):
```

Next, create a new file called prices1.txt and write a number of lines, one for each **Vector** entry.

```
> fid := fopen("prices1.txt", 'WRITE', 'TEXT'):
> writeline(fid, "List of Prices"):
  for i to n do
      fprintf(fid, "Item %d costs %.2f\n", i, V[i]):
  end do:
> fclose(fid):
```

Now open the file again and read the values from each line, adding them up as they are read.

```
> fid := fopen("prices1.txt", 'READ', 'TEXT'):
> readline(fid):
> pricesum := 0.:
  while not feof(fid) do
      t := fscanf(fid, "Item %d costs %f\n"):
      pricesum := pricesum + t[2]:
  end do:
> fclose(fid):
```

Finally, reopen the file to append a line showing the sum of the prices.

```
> fid := fopen("prices1.txt", 'APPEND', 'TEXT'):
> fprintf(fid, "\nThe sum of the prices is: %.2f\n", pricesum):
> fclose(fid):
```

If you encounter an error while using any of the I/O commands listed in this section, refer to the **IO_errors** help page for more information about the source of the error. Common mistakes include reading from a file that does not exist and writing to a file for which you do not have permission to alter.

The FileTools Package

The **FileTools** package is a collection of file manipulation utilities. It covers most of the functionality described in the previous section and provides an easy-to-use interface. It also contains a large number of additional commands that are useful when working with files.

The **FileTools** package contains two subpackages: **FileTools:-Text** and **FileTools:-Binary**. These subpackages contain commands to work with text files and binary files, respectively.

Some of the commonly used commands are listed below. A full list of commands is available in the **FileTools** help page.

- **Opening and closing files**

    The **FileTools:-Text:-Open** command allows a file to be opened, with options to indicate whether Maple can create the file if it does not already exist, overwrite it, or append to it. It returns a file descriptor. As with the situation described in the previous section, it is not always necessary to open a file before using it, as a file is automatically opened when you use a **FileTools** command to access it. The **FileTools:-Text:-Close** command closes a file and ensures all data is written to disk. When you exit Maple, all open files are automatically closed. The **FileTools:-Text:-OpenTemporaryFile** command causes a temporary file to be opened. Corresponding commands are available in the **Binary** sub-package: **FileTools:-Binary:-Open**, **FileTools:-BinaryClose**, and **FileTools:-Binary:-OpenTemporaryFile**.

- **Reading from and writing to binary files**

    The **FileTools:-Binary:-Read** and **FileTools:-Binary:-Write** commands are available for reading and writing binary data. Unlike the **readbytes** and **writebytes** commands, the **FileTools** commands support a number of hardware data types and allows the byte order to be specified. There is also a **FileTools:-Binary:-CountBytes** command for returning the total number of bytes left in a file.

- **Reading from and writing to text files**

    The **FileTools:-Text** subpackage has a large number of commands for reading and writing text. The **FileTools:-Text:-Readline** and **FileTools:-Text:-Writeline** commands read and write a line at a time. The **FileTools:-Text:-ReadFile** command reads all lines in a file at once.

    The **FileTools:-Text:-ReadFloat** and **FileTools:-Text:-WriteFloat** commands offer simple ways to read and write a single float. The **FileTools:-Text:-ReadNextFloat** command is useful if you want to read the next float while ignoring all characters preceding it. The **FileTools:-Text:-CountFloats** command counts the number of floating-point numbers remaining in the file. Similar commands are available for integers, characters, and strings as well.

- **Checking and modifying properties of files**

    The **FileTools** package has commands that allow you to examine the properties of a file, such as **FileTools:-Status**, **FileTools:-Exist**, and **FileTools:-AtEndOfFile**. There are a number of additional commands that check if a file is open, readable, writable, lockable, or executable. The package also includes commands that return a file's size and position.

    It is possible to modify files, by using, for example, the **FileTools:-Rename** and **FileTools:-Remove** commands. There are also commands for copying, locking, and unlocking files.

- **Performing directory operations**

10.4 Input and Output with Files

The **FileTools** package also includes commands to work with directories and file paths, such as **FileTools:-ListDirectory**, **FileTools:-MakeDirectory** and **FileTools:-AbsolutePath**.

The following example is similar to the one shown in the previous section using the basic I/O commands, but this time, you will use the **FileTools** package.

First, create a new file prices2.txt containing a title and a line for each of the values in **V**. Here, you can use the commands for writing strings, integers and floats, without worrying about specifying the formatting precisely.

```
> with(FileTools:-Text):
> V := Vector([1.20, 4.85, 6.23, 2.45, 7.99]):
> fid := Open("prices2.txt", 'overwrite'):
> WriteLine(fid, "List of Prices"):
  for i to n do
      WriteString(fid, "Item");
      WriteInteger(fid, i, 'delim'=" ");
      WriteString(fid, "costs");
      WriteFloat(fid, V[i], 'leftdelim'=" "):
      WriteLine(fid, ".");
  end do:
> Close(fid);
```

Now, open the file again and read the floating-point values from each line. The **CountLines** and **ReadNextFloat** commands make this task easier, as you do not have to check for the end of file or explicitly read other characters in each line.

```
> fid := Open("prices2.txt"):
> ReadLine(fid):
> pricesum := 0.:
  numlines := CountLines(fid):
  for i to numlines do
      ReadNextInteger(fid):
      pricesum := pricesum + ReadNextFloat(fid):
  end do:
> Close(fid):
```

Finally, open the file again to append a line showing the sum of the prices.

```
> fid := Open("prices2.txt", 'append'):
> WriteLine(fid, "", "The sum of the prices is:"):
```

```
> WriteFloat(fid, pricesum):
> Close(fid):
```

Importing and Exporting Numerical Data

The basic I/O commands and the **FileTools** package can be used to read from and write to any text or binary file. However, if the file that you want to read or write consists exclusively of numeric data, then it is much easier to use one of the commands designed for this type of file.

ImportMatrix and ExportMatrix

The **ImportMatrix** and **ExportMatrix** commands read and write data that can be stored in a **Matrix** or **Vector**.

These commands support different types of files, including some that are generated or recognized by other software applications. The formats supported are: MATLAB®, Matrix Market, comma-separated values (.csv), and generic delimited files. The **source** and **target** options are used to indicate the desired format.

Files created with MATLAB versions 5, 6 or 7 can be imported. By default, the **ExportMatrix** command generates a MATLAB Version 7 binary file, using data compression as described on the **StringTools:-Compress** help page, when the **target=Matlab** option is provided. However, it is possible to generate a Version 6 file without compression by adding the **mode=v6** option. You can also read and write MATLAB ASCII files using the **mode=ascii** option. Import and export of both dense and sparse Matrices are supported with MATLAB format.

Matrix Market files are imported and exported using the **MatrixMarket** value for the **source** and **target** options. The Matrix Market coordinate and array formats are supported; the pattern format is not supported.

For .csv and general delimited files, the **format** option can be used to indicate whether the storage is dense or sparse. In the latter case, only the nonzero entries are present in the imported or exported file.

Below is a small example showing how **ImportMatrix** and **ExportMatrix** work with MATLAB arrays. The file will be placed in your current working directory.

Generate two random Matrices and export them to a MATLAB Version 6 file. The number of bytes written is returned by the **ExportMatrix** command.

> `A := LinearAlgebra:-RandomMatrix(3, 4, 'datatype'=float[8]);`

$$A := \begin{bmatrix} -70. & -94. & -53. & 40. \\ 13. & -7. & 21. & 97. \\ -58. & 12. & -25. & 43. \end{bmatrix} \qquad (10.16)$$

> `B := LinearAlgebra:-RandomMatrix(2, 5, 'datatype'=float[8]);`

$$B := \begin{bmatrix} 96. & -80. & -29. & 89. & -67. \\ 93. & -92. & 96. & -55. & 77. \end{bmatrix} \qquad (10.17)$$

> `ExportMatrix("testfile.mat", [A, B], 'target'='Matlab', 'mode'='v6');`

$$432 \qquad (10.18)$$

Now, read the MATLAB arrays back into Maple using the **ImportMatrix** command. It is not necessary to use the **source** and **mode** options in this case. The **ImportMatrix** command can automatically recognize MATLAB binary files. With most text files (MATLAB or otherwise), you will have to specify the source type.

> `M := ImportMatrix("testfile.mat");`

$$M := \left["mat1", \begin{bmatrix} -70. & -94. & -53. & 40. \\ 13. & -7. & 21. & 97. \\ -58. & 12. & -25. & 43. \end{bmatrix}\right], \left["mat2", \begin{bmatrix} 96. & -80. & -29. & 89. & -67. \\ 93. & -92. & 96. & -55. & 77. \end{bmatrix}\right] \qquad (10.19)$$

A sequence of two lists is returned, with each list containing a string and a Matrix. The string shows the name stored with each matrix in the MATLAB file. The names are automatically assigned by the **ExportMatrix** command, but you can specify your own names with the **arraynames** option.

Now, export the Matrix **A** to a text file with values delimited by spaces.

> `ExportMatrix("anotherfile.txt", A, 'target'='delimited', 'delimiter'=" ");`

$$282 \qquad (10.20)$$

Import the contents of the file back into Maple. In this case, it is necessary to specify the source and the character used as delimiter.

```
> ImportMatrix("anotherfile.txt", 'source'='delimited', 'delimiter'="
    ");
```

$$\begin{bmatrix} [-70.000000000000000, -94.000000000000000, \\ -53.000000000000000, 40.000000000000000], \\ [13.000000000000000, -7.000000000000000, \\ 21.000000000000000, 97.000000000000000], \\ [-58.000000000000000, 12.000000000000000, \\ -25.000000000000000, 43.000000000000000]] \end{bmatrix} \qquad (10.21)$$

Notice that only a single Matrix is returned. Multiple Matrices can be exported to MATLAB, but with other formats, only a single Matrix can be saved in a file. Also, only MATLAB arrays have names associated with them.

Other Commands

The **readdata** command reads numeric data from a text file into Maple. The data in the file must consist of integers or floating-point values arranged in columns, separated by white space, and it is returned in a list or list of lists.

The **writedata** command writes numeric data from a Maple vector, matrix, list or list of lists into a text file. This command accepts an optional argument in the form of a procedure that allows you to control the formatting of the output.

Files Used by Maple

In additional to the general files that can be manipulated by the I/O commands described earlier in this section, several other files are used implicitly by Maple. A few are described briefly below. For more information, refer to the **file** help page.

- **Maple language files**

  A Maple language file contains statements conforming to the syntax of the Maple language. These are the same as statements that can be entered interactively. Any filename can be used for a Maple language file, but the name cannot end with ".m". The standard file extension for Maple language files is ".mpl".

  Maple language files can be created using a text editor or the **save** statement. Maple procedures and complex scripts of commands are usually written in a text editor, while the **save** statement is used to save results or procedures that were entered into Maple interactively.

  Maple language files may be read using the **read** statement. The statements within the file are read as if they were being entered into Maple interactively, except that they are not echoed to the screen unless the **echo interface** variable has been set to 2 or higher.

Maple includes a **preprocessor** modeled on the C preprocessor and Maple language files may include preprocessor directives such as **$include** and **$define**.

- **Internal format files**

  Maple internal format files are used to store expressions compactly. Expressions stored in this format can be read by Maple faster than those stored in the Maple language format. These files are identified by filenames ending with the two characters ".m" (or ".M" on platforms where filenames are not case-sensitive).

  Like Maple language files, Maple internal format files are read and written using the **read** and **save** statements. The presence of the ".m" ending in the filename specifies that the file is an internal format file, and not a language file.

- **Library archives**

  Maple uses library archive files to store collections of internal format files. These files end with the extension ".mla" (or, for older library archive files, with extension ".lib"). For more information about creating Maple libraries, see *Writing Packages (page 383)*.

- **Help databases**

  A Maple help database is a file that stores a collection of files representing help pages in the Maple help system. It contains the information required to index, navigate, and search the help system, and its filename has the extension ".hdb". For more information, refer to the **worksheet/reference/maplehdb** help page.

- **Worksheet files**

  If you are using Maple with a graphical user interface, you can save your worksheet. In the standard worksheet interface, files are identified by names ending with ".mw". In the classic worksheet interface, files end in ".mws". Both types of files are portable between the graphical user interfaces on different platforms.

- **Maplet Files**

  Maple worksheets can be saved as ".maplet" files. The **MapletViewer** runs such files independent of the Maple worksheet environment.

10.5 Reading and Writing Formatted Data

The scanf and printf Commands

The **scanf** and **printf** commands allow you to read from and write to the terminal using a specified format. The formatting information is provided by a format string. Below is an example showing how the **printf** command is used to display floating-point values.

Enter the following Vector of values:

```
> V := Vector([.8427007929, .9953222650, .9999779095, .9999999846,
    1.000000000]);
```

$$V := \begin{bmatrix} 0.8427007929 \\ 0.9953222650 \\ 0.9999779095 \\ 0.9999999846 \\ 1.000000000 \end{bmatrix} \quad (10.22)$$

Print each value on a single line, preceded by an integer indicating its position. The format string is the first argument to the **printf** command. This string consists of two conversion specifications, "%d" and "%.2e", along with other characters to be printed, including the newline character "\n". The first conversion specification indicates that the first argument following the format string should be printed as an integer. The second conversion specification indicates that the second argument following the format string should be printed in scientific notation, with two digits after the decimal point.

```
> for i to LinearAlgebra:-Dimension(V) do
      printf("%d%12.2e\n", i, V[i]);
  end do;
1     8.43e-01
2     9.95e-01
3     1.00e+00
4     1.00e+00
5     1.00e+00
```

The **scanf** and **printf** commands belong to a family of related commands that provide formatted I/O capabilities. The other commands will be discussed later in this chapter. These commands are based on similarly named functions from the C programming language library.

For example, the **sscanf** command below reads an integer, a space, a character, and a floating-point value from the string given as the first argument. The conversion specifications, "%d", "%c" and "%f", will be explained in the next section.

```
> sscanf("892 123.456E7","%d %c%f");
```

$$\begin{bmatrix} 892, \text{"1"}, 2.3456\, 10^8 \end{bmatrix} \quad (10.23)$$

Format Strings

As you saw in the previous examples, the format string passed to **scanf** or **printf** specifies exactly how Maple is to parse the input or write the output. It consists of a sequence of conversion specifications that may be separated by other characters.

First, consider the specification for the **scanf** command, which has the format shown below. What follows is a brief explanation of the specification. For more information, refer to the **scanf** help page.

%[*][*width*][*modifiers*]*code*

- The character "%" begins each conversion specification.

- The optional character "*" indicates that the item scanned is to be discarded and not returned as part of the result.

- The optional *width* indicates the maximum number of characters to be scanned for this object. You can use this to scan one larger object as two smaller objects.

- The optional *modifier* affects the type of value to be returned. The most common of these is "Z", which, when preceding any of the numeric format codes, indicates that a complex value is to be scanned.

- Several format codes are available for use with **scanf**. A few of the more commonly used ones are mentioned here.

    "d" -- integer

    "f" -- floating-point number

    "c" -- character

    "s" -- string

    "a" -- Maple expression

The specification for the **printf** command is similar to that for **scanf**. The differences are summarized here. For more information, refer to the **printf** help page. The specification has the following format.

%[*flags*][*width*][.*precision*][*modifiers*]*code*

- As with **scanf**, the conversion specification for **printf** begins with "%". The optional *width* and *modifiers* are similar to those described earlier. The *width* value indicates the minimum number of characters to output for the field.

- The optional *flag* can be one of several characters affecting how numeric values are displayed. For example, the flag "+" indicates that signed numeric values are output with a leading "+" or "-" sign.

- The format codes for **printf** are similar to those for **scanf**. One notable difference is that, while "e" and "g" are equivalent to "f" for **scanf**, they produce different output in **printf**. The code "e" causes a numeric value to be printed in scientific notation, while output using the code "g" uses one of integer, fixed-point or scientific notation, depending on the numeric value.

The **scanf** and **printf** commands can also be used to print **rtables**. For more information about the flags used for this purpose, refer to the **rtable_printf** help page.

Related Commands

Several commands are related to **scanf** and **printf**:

- **fscanf** and **fprintf**

  These commands read from and write to a file instead of the terminal. They take a filename or descriptor as an additional argument, but otherwise use the same calling sequence as **scanf** and **printf**.

- **sscanf** and **sprintf**

  These commands read from and write to a string (which is then returned) instead of the terminal. The **sscanf** command takes a string as an additional argument, but otherwise these commands use the same calling sequence as **scanf** and **printf**.

- **nprintf**

  This command is the same as **sprintf** except that it returns a Maple symbol instead of a string.

All these commands are described fully on the **scanf** and **printf** help pages.

10.6 Useful Utilities

This section describes other tools that are useful for input and output.

The StringTools Package

The **StringTools** package is a collection of utilities for manipulating strings. These commands are frequently used in conjunction with the basic input and output commands, for analyzing or converting data that is read or written. The **StringTools** package includes numerous commands; for brevity, we will describe only a few commands that may be of interest to users performing input/output operations in Maple. These include commands for

- converting the case of characters (*e.g.*, **StringTools:-LowerCase**)
- performing character class tests (*e.g.*, **StringTools:-HasDigit**)
- comparing strings (*e.g.*, **StringTools:-IsPrefix**)

- doing pattern-matching and text searching (*e.g.*, **StringTools:-Substitute**)
- handling whitespace (*e.g.*, **StringTools:-TrimRight**)

Two commands that are relevant to file I/O are **StringTools:-Compress** and **StringTools:-Uncompress**. The first command uses an algorithm from the zlib library to compress the input into a lossless and more compact format, while the second reverses the process. These commands are compatible with the commands for reading and writing bytes described in *Input and Output with Files (page 366)*.

For more information about the zlib library, visit **http://www.zlib.net**.

Conversion Commands

Some additional commands may be useful when you are performing input and output operations in Maple.

- The **convert/bytes** help page shows how to transform strings into bytes using the **convert** command.
- The **parse** command allows you to parse a string as a Maple statement. For example, the following command parses the given string, evaluates it, and returns the expression **4*x^2**.

```
> parse("x^2+3*x^2");
```

$$4x^2 \qquad (10.24)$$

10.7 2-D Math

Introduction

Typeset or 2-D math is available with the standard worksheet interface. Normally, input and output of 2-D math is done interactively using the Maple GUI tools. However, certain aspects of the input and output can be controlled programmatically in a limited way.

There are two available modes for typesetting: standard and extended. The mode can be changed by using the **interface** command. The following command shows the current setting in your worksheet or document:

```
> interface(typesetting);
```

$$standard \qquad (10.25)$$

Standard typesetting uses default rules for displaying expressions. With extended typesetting, the rules can be customized using the Typesetting Rule Assistant (**TypesettingRuleAssist**) or exports from the **Typesetting** package. The Typesetting Rules Assistant and the **Typesetting** package exports can also be used to adjust how 2-D input is parsed, regardless of the typesetting mode used for output.

The Typesetting Package

The **Typesetting** package provides commands for programmatically customizing extended typesetting output in certain situations and for controlling how particular 2-D expressions are parsed. It also includes internal-use commands that are not intended for general use. Additionally, the package exports a number of names that act as Maple typesetting tags similar to MathML tags.

The commands available to users are described on the **Typesetting** help page. A subset of the commands are listed below:

- **Typesetting:-Settings**: adjust general extended typesetting settings, such as whether dot notation for derivatives is used and whether functions such as $2(x)$ should be interpreted as implicit multiplication.

- **Typesetting:-Suppress**: suppress dependencies of functions (so that f can be interpreted as $f(x)$, for example).

- **Typesetting:-EnableTypesetRule**, **Typesetting:-EnableParseRule** and **Typesetting:-EnableCompletionRule**: control specific typesetting, parsing and command-completion rules.

- **Typesetting:-UseSymbolForTypeset**: control the display of operator symbols.

Extended typesetting output is produced by the **Typeset** command When this command is called, an unevaluated function is returned. This output, which is recognized by the Maple GUI, is not intended to be altered by users. Because the structure is meant for internal use, the tag names and format of the structure may change from one Maple release to another.

```
> lprint(Typesetting:-Typeset(BesselJ(v, x)));
Typesetting:-mrow(Typesetting:-msub(Typesetting:-mi("J", fontstyle =
 "normal"), Typesetting:-msemantics = "BesselJ"), Typesetting:-mi("v")),
 Typesetting:-mo("&ApplyFunction;"), Typesetting:-mfenced(Typesetting:-
mi("x")))
```

Additional Tips

- Users are discouraged from manipulating the typesetting structures created for internal use. However, in rare circumstances, it may be useful to call the **Typesetting:-Typeset** command. For example, standard typesetting mode is generally used for typeset text in plots. Extended typesetting output produced by the **Typeset** command may be passed to plays inside the **typeset** structure. For more information, see *Typesetting (page 461)*.

- Occasionally, you may find it necessary to manipulate a typeset expression programmatically without having the expression evaluate. For example, you want to print $\frac{1}{2} + \frac{1}{3}$

without having it evaluate to $\frac{5}{6}$, or you want to use $x+$, which gives an error when evaluated in Maple. In theses situations, it is useful to create an atomic identifier. To do this, you must be working in the standard worksheet interface. Enter the expression in the input line, select it and then use the 2-D math context menu to convert to an atomic identifier. If you **lprint** the result, you will see a name (such as `` `#mrow(mi("x"),mo("&plus;"))` ``, for $x+$) that can now be used within a Maple program written in 1-D math.

10.8 Exercises

1. Write a loop (with a single statement in its body) that prints strings listing the cubes of the integers **1** to **10**.

2. Create a file in a text editor that contains the following lines.

    ```
    x := 1;           # valid input line
    if := 2;}         # invalid assignment
    y := 3;           # valid input line
    two words := 4;   # invalid assignment
    ```

    Save the file. In a Maple session, open the file by using the **read** statement. Observe how Maple reacts to invalid statements.

3. Create a data file in a text editor that contains the following information.

    ```
    1  2  3
    4  5  6
    ```

    Save the file. Read this file into a Maple session, convert the data to a list, and reverse its order. Write the reversed data in the same format to a different file.

11 Writing Packages

This section describes how to collect a large software project in Maple into a *package* that is easy to maintain. Packages can be configured to load automatically when you start Maple and distributed to other users as a library rather than as Maple source code.

11.1 In This Chapter

- What is a package
- Writing Maple packages by using modules
- Examples of custom packages

11.2 What Is a Package

A *package* is a collection of procedures and other data that can be treated as a whole. Packages typically gather a number of procedures that enable you to perform computations in a well-defined problem domain. Packages may contain data other than procedures, and may even contain other packages (subpackages).

Packages in the Standard Library

A number of packages are shipped with the standard Maple library. For example, the **group**, **numtheory**, **CodeGeneration**, and **LinearAlgebra** packages are all provided with Maple, along with several dozen others. The **group** package provides procedures for computing with groups that have a finite representation in terms of permutations, or of generators and defining relations. The **LinearAlgebra** package provides numerous procedures for computational linear algebra.

Packages Are Modules

Modules are the implementation vehicle for packages. A module represents a package by its exported names. The exported names can be assigned arbitrary Maple expressions, typically procedures, and these names form the package.

For more information about modules, see *Programming with Modules (page 309)*.

Some older and deprecated Maple packages such as **simplex** and **networks** are not implemented using modules; they are implemented using tables. In table-based packages, the name of a package command is used as the index into a table of procedures. It is not recommended to write new packages using tables since modules allow much more flexibility.

Package Exports

Some of the data in a package is normally made accessible to the user as an export of the package. For packages implemented as modules, the package exports are the same as the exports of the underlying module. For packages implemented as tables, the package exports are the names used to index the underlying table.

Accessing the exports of a package is a fundamental operation that is supported by all packages. If **P** is a Maple package, and **e** is one of its exports, you can access **e** by using the fully qualified reference **P[e]**. If **P** is a module, you can also use the syntax **P:-e**. These methods of accessing the exports of a module are normally used when programming with a package.

Note that the member selection operator (:-) is left-associative. If **S** is a submodule of a module **P**, and the name **e** is exported by **S**, then the notation **P:-S:-e** is parsed as **(P:-S):-e**, and so it refers to the instance of **e**, which is local to **S**. This concept is important for referencing members of subpackages. For example,

```
> CodeTools:-Profiling:-Coverage:-Print();
```

calls the procedure **Print** in the subpackage **Coverage** in the subpackage **Profiling**, which is part of the **CodeTools** package. You can use indexed notation for this.

```
> CodeTools[Profiling][Coverage][Print]();
```

Using Packages Interactively

For interactive use, it is inconvenient to enter fully qualified references to all of the exports of a package. To facilitate the process of entering package command names, the Maple procedure **with** is provided for the interactive management of package namespaces. By using **with**, you can globally impose the exported names of a package. This allows you to access the package exports, without typing the package prefix, by making the names of the exports accessible at the top level of the Maple session. For example, to use the **numtheory** package, enter the command

> with(numtheory);

$$[\textit{GIgcd, bigomega, cfrac, cfracpol, cyclotomic, divisors, factorEQ,}$$
$$\textit{factorset, fermat, imagunit, index, integral\_basis, invcfrac,}$$
$$\textit{invphi, iscyclotomic, issqrfree, ithrational, jacobi, kronecker,}$$
$$\lambda, \textit{legendre, mcombine, mersenne, migcdex, minkowski,}$$
$$\textit{mipolys, mlog, mobius, mroot, msqrt, nearestp, nthconver,}$$
$$\textit{nthdenom, nthnumer, nthpow, order, pdexpand, } \phi, \pi,$$
$$\textit{pprimroot, primroot, quadres, rootsunity, safeprime, } \sigma,$$
$$\textit{sq2factor, sum2sqr, } \tau, \textit{thue}] \qquad (11.1)$$

This command makes the names exported by the **numtheory** package (a list of which is returned by the call to **with**) available temporarily as top-level Maple commands.

> cfrac((1 + x)^k, x, 5, 'subdiagonal', 'simregular');

$$\cfrac{1}{1 - \cfrac{kx}{1 + \cfrac{1}{2} \cfrac{(1+k)x}{1 - \cfrac{1}{6} \cfrac{(k-1)x}{1 + \cfrac{1}{6} \cfrac{(k+2)x}{1 + \ldots}}}}} \qquad (11.2)$$

11.3 Writing Maple Packages By Using Modules

A Simple Example

The simplest type of package is a collection of related procedures that are bundled together for convenience, for example, **PolynomialTools** or **ArrayTools** are packages which are both included with Maple. The following is an example of a custom package.

```
> SomeTools := module()
  description "Some useful tools";
  option package;
  export axpy, sqrm1, identity;
      axpy := proc(a::algebraic, x::algebraic, y::algebraic, $)
      description "compute a times x plus y";
          return a*x + y;
      end proc; # axpy
      identity := proc()
      description "return the arguments";
          return _passed;
```

```
        end proc; # axpy
        sqrm1 := proc(x::algebraic, $)
        description "square minus one";
            return x^2 - 1;
        end proc;
    end module; # Some Tools
```

$$SomeTools := \mathbf{module}(\,)$$
$$\quad \mathbf{option}\ package;$$
$$\quad \mathbf{export}\ axpy, sqrm1, identity;$$
$$\quad \text{description "Some useful tools";} \tag{11.3}$$

end module

This example is simply a module that consists of a few exported members that are procedures and an option called **package**. As with all modules, its members can be accessed by using the **:-** and **[]** operators.

```
> SomeTools:-axpy(1,1,1);
```
$$2 \tag{11.4}$$

```
> SomeTools[sqrm1](2);
```
$$3 \tag{11.5}$$

The **package** option also allows you to call the package by using the **with** command to access the package exports.

```
> with(SomeTools);
```
$$[axpy, identity, sqrm1] \tag{11.6}$$

```
> identity("nothing");
```
$$\text{"nothing"} \tag{11.7}$$

If the **with** command is used to call a module that does not include the **package** option, an exception will occur:

```
> SomeOtherTools := module() export Nothing; Nothing := x->x; end
  module;
```

$$SomeOtherTools := \mathbf{module}(\,)\ \mathbf{export}\ Nothing;\ \mathbf{end\ module} \tag{11.8}$$

```
> with(SomeOtherTools);
```
Warning, SomeOtherTools is not a correctly formed package - option
`package' is missing

$$[\textit{Nothing}] \tag{11.9}$$

Packages generally include many lines of Maple code, so you will probably want to create and modify them in a specialized editor designed for programming such as *vim* or *emacs*. In the example above, the definition of the module **SomeTools** have been put in a file called **SomeTools.mpl** in the **samples/ProgrammingGuide/** directory of your Maple installation). If you copy this file into the current directory, it can then be loaded in Maple by using the **read** command.

```
> read("SomeTools.mpl");
```

This allows you to access the **SomeTools** package commands in a Maple worksheet or document. You can include a **read** statement as the first executed command or in the startup code of a Maple worksheet or document.

Custom Libraries

If you prefer not to call the **read** command to load your custom package, you can save your package as a Maple library archive (.mla) file. This allows your package to be available whenever Maple is started; however, it is loaded into memory only if it is required. In contrast, the **read** method automatically loads the package into memory.

Before a package can be saved to a library archive, it must be loaded into Maple, either directly in a worksheet or by using the **read** command. Then, the simplest method for saving it to a library archive is to call the **savelib** command.

Before calling the **savelib** command, you may want to set up a directory to store your custom library. For example, you can create a directory called **maple** in your home directory and use the **LibraryTools** commands to create an empty .mla file in which to store your library.

```
> mylibdir := cat(kernelopts(homedir), kernelopts(dirsep), "maple",
    kernelopts(dirsep), "toolbox", kernelopts(dirsep), "personal",
    kernelopts(dirsep), "lib");
```

$$\text{"C:\textbackslash Documents and Settings\textbackslash juser\textbackslash maple\textbackslash toolbox\textbackslash personal\textbackslash lib"} \tag{11.10}$$

```
> FileTools:-MakeDirectory(mylibdir, 'recurse');
> LibraryTools:-Create(cat(mylibdir, kernelopts(dirsep),
    "packages.mla"));
```

```
> libname := mylibdir, libname;
```

$$libname :=$$
$$\text{"C:\textbackslash Documents and Settings\textbackslash juser\textbackslash maple\textbackslash toolbox\textbackslash personal\textbackslash lib",}$$
$$\text{"C:\textbackslash Program Files\textbackslash Maple 15\textbackslash lib"} \qquad (11.11)$$

To save a new value for **libname** (a predefined variable, which specifies the location of the main Maple library, and package and user libraries), and to make sure that this directory is the default location for saving in the future after you use the **restart** command, add the line above to your Maple initialization file, which specifies initialization settings for Maple.

For more information on initialization files, see the **worksheet/reference/initialization** help page.

Note: Maple automatically adds **lib** subdirectories of directories in **HOMEDIR/maple/toolbox** to the predefined variable **libname**. Therefore, modifying the **.mapleinit** or **maple.ini** file is only necessary if you want to designate this directory as the default location in which the **savelib** command will save your library files.

You can modify the Maple initialization file manually in a text editor or by using the **FileTools** commands in Maple:

```
> mapleinitfile := cat(kernelopts(homedir), kernelopts(dirsep),
    `if`(kernelopts(platform)="unix", ".mapleinit", "maple.ini"));
```

$$\text{"C:\textbackslash Documents and Settings\textbackslash juser\textbackslash maple.ini"} \qquad (11.12)$$

```
> FileTools:-Copy(mapleinitfile, cat(mapleinitfile, ".mpl.bak"));
> FileTools:-Text:-Open( mapleinitfile, 'append');
> FileTools:-Text:-WriteLine(mapleinitfile, cat("libname :=
    \"",mylibdir,"\", libname:"));
> FileTools:-Text:-Close( mapleinitfile );
```

Restart, and verify that your **libname** is set now correctly.

```
> restart;
> libname;
```

Finally, save the package to the library archive by calling the **savelib** command.

```
> savelib( 'SomeTools' );
```

Enter the **restart** command, followed by the **ShowContents** command in **LibraryTools** to verify that the package has been added to the library archive. If everything has worked correctly, you can now use the **with** command to access the package commands.

```
> restart;
> LibraryTools:-ShowContents(libname[1]);
> with(SomeTools);
```

Running the **savelib** command saves the module to the first library archive found in the path specified by the global variable **libname** or the library archive in the path specified by the global variable **savelibname**, if it is defined. (At least one of these values must be defined.) You can save your package to a different library archive by using the **LibraryTools:-Save** command or by providing a file name as a second argument to the **savelib** command.

You will want to remove this example package from your library when you are done. This can be done using the **Delete** command in the **LibraryTools** package.

```
> LibraryTools:-Delete('SomeTools', libname[1]);
```

You can confirm that it has been deleted.

```
> LibraryTools:-ShowContents(libname[1]);
```

> **Important**: Always make sure that the standard Maple library directory is write-protected to avoid saving expressions in it. If you accidentally save a file to the standard Maple library, you may need to reinstall Maple to restore the main library archive.

11.4 A Larger Example

Several additional techniques are useful for writing larger packages. Some of these techniques will be described in the context of an example package called **RandomnessTests** whose full source can be found in the **samples/ProgrammingGuide/RandomnessTests** directory, which is located in the directory where Maple is installed. It is a package containing procedures to analyze the randomness of a sequence of bits.

ModuleLoad

Often, a package needs to initialize the internal or global state when it is loaded. For example, many packages define new types for the type system. Generally, these types are not needed unless the package is loaded, and so they are created by the **ModuleLoad** local member of the package. In this example, we will define a type **BinarySequence** that is a linear data type containing only zeros and ones.

```
> ModuleLoad := proc()
        TypeTools:-AddType
            (
                ':-BinarySequence',
                proc(L)
```

```
                type(L, list({identical(0),identical(1)}))
                or type(L, 'Vector'({identical(0),identical(1)}))
                or ( type(L, 'Array'({identical(0),identical(1)}))
                    and nops([rtable_dims(L)])=1
                    and op([1,1], [rtable_dims(L)])=1 );
            end proc
        );
    end proc;
```

The local named **ModuleLoad** will automatically run when a module is loaded from a library. If you are using the **read** command to load the definition of the module into Maple or if you enter it in a worksheet, this procedure will not run automatically.

You can also define the local **ModuleUnload**, which will run if the module is removed from memory because it is not being used. In this case, the custom type definition **BinarySequence** is removed.

```
> ModuleUnload := proc()
        TypeTools:-RemoveType(':-BinarySequence');
    end proc;
```

It is also possible to use the **load=proc** and **unload=proc** options in the module definition to specify different procedures to be invoked when a package is loaded and unloaded respectively. However, the use of the **ModuleLoad** and **ModuleUnload** procedures is recommended.

The Preprocessor and Structured Source Files

If a package has many exports, it often useful to put each export into its own source file. The Maple **preprocessor** is similar to the preprocessor of a C compiler. It allows you to specify the names of source files and macro definitions to include in a master .mpl file, which defines the contents of your package.

To include the file name of an export in an .mpl file, you can use the **$include** directive.

To define macros, you can use the **$define** directive.

In our example, we have a file called RandomnessTests.mpl, which has several exports stored in the same directory in the files: WaldWolfowitz.mm, BitFrequency.mm, Compressibility.mm, BinaryRank.mm. The following example shows the contents of the RandomnessTests.mpl file.

Table 11.1: RandomnessTests

```
##MODULE RandomnessTests
##
##DESCRIPTION
```

11.4 A Larger Example

```
##- A package containing commands for testing the randomness of
## binary sequences.
$define RANDINFO ':-RandomnessTests'
$define MAINLEVEL 2
RandomnessTests := module()
option package;
export
    WaldWolfowitz,
    BitFrequency,
    Compressibility,
    BinaryRank;
local
    Runs,
    ModuleLoad,
    ModuleUnload;
    ModuleLoad := proc()
        TypeTools:-AddType
        (
            ':-BinarySequence',
            proc(L)
                type(L, list({identical(0),identical(1)}))
                or type(L, 'Vector'({identical(0),identical(1)}))
                or ( type(L, 'Array'({identical(0),identical(1)}))
                    and nops([rtable_dims(L)])=1
                    and op([1,1], [rtable_dims(L)])=1 );
            end proc
        );
    end proc;
    ModuleUnload := proc()
        TypeTools:-RemoveType(':-BinarySequence');
    end proc;
$include "WaldWolfowitz.mm"
$include "BitFrequency.mm"
$include "Compressibility.mm"
$include "BinaryRank.mm"
end module; # RandomnessTests
```

When this file is loaded into Maple from the command-line interface or by using the **read** command in a Maple worksheet or document, Maple automatically replaces each **$include** directive with the contents of the file specified.

The file also includes two **$define** directives which are macros that are not used in this file, but will be used in the included files. Including them in the top-level source file allows us to make package-wide changes by editing the macros in one place. In our example, these macros will be used to control the **userinfo** definitions throughout the package. The following line appears in the WaldWolfowitz.mm file:

```
userinfo(MAINLEVEL, RANDINFO, nprintf("sequence has %d runs", runs));
```

When loaded, the preprocessor will transform this line into the following:

```
> userinfo(2, ':-RandomnessTests', nprintf("sequence has %d runs",
    runs));
```

Macros can also have parameters such as the following macro in the BinaryRank.mm file:

```
$define GF2RankProbability(m,n,r)
2^(r*(n+m-r)-m*n)*mul(((1-2^(l-n))*(1-2^(l-m)))/(1-2^(l-r)),l=0..(r-1))
```

which allows **GF2RankProbability** to be used as if it were a procedure. However, it will be replaced inline by the preprocessor. This is similar to how procedures with option **inline** function, but with more restrictions.

Subpackages

When creating large packages, it is useful to organize commands into smaller subpackages. Our package does this with a **Visualization** subpackage and a **Data** submodule to store sample random inputs.

Achieving this is as simple as including the definition for these other modules and packages within the top-level package.

11.5 Example: A Shapes Package

In this section, a sample package is presented to illustrate concepts that may be helpful when working with modules and submodules, and putting them together into a package.

Modules allow you to create packages with a hierarchical structure; this cannot be done with table-based implementations of packages. This section covers the following topics:

- Organizing the source code for a large package that has a nontrivial substructure.
- A description of the **Shapes** package, including details of its design and implementation
- Hints related to source code organization.

The package presented in this section provides the means to compute areas and circumferences of various planar figures, which are called shapes.

> **Note:** Only portions of the source code for this package are shown. The fully commented source code can be found in the **samples/ProgrammingGuide/shapes** directory of your Maple installation.

Source Code Organization

The **Shapes** package is organized into several source files:

- shapes.mpl
- point.mm
- segment.mm
- circle.mm
- square.mm
- triangle.mm

To avoid platform-specific differences, all of the source files are located in the same directory or folder.

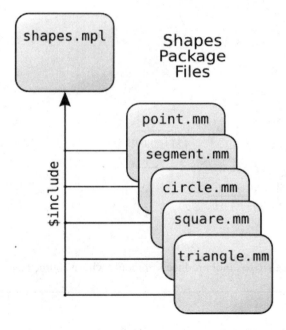

Figure 11.1: Organization of Package Source Files

To define the module that implements this package, use the Maple preprocessor to include the remaining source files at the appropriate point in the master source file shapes.mpl. A number of **$include** directives are included in shapes.mpl, such as

```
$include         "point.mm"
$include         "segment.mm"
```

Splitting a large project into several source files makes it easier to manage and allows several developers to work on a project at the same time. The source file is divided into shape-specific functionality. Most of the functionality for points, for instance, is implemented by the source code stored in the point.mm file.

Package Architecture

The **Shapes** package is structured as a module with several exported procedures. Individual submodules provide specific functionality for each shape type supported by the package. Each of these shape-specific submodules is stored in its own source file; these files are included into the main package source file, shapes.mpl.

The package module **Shapes** has a submodule, which is also called **Shapes**. The submodule **Shapes:-Shapes** contains one submodule for each shape supported. The submodule hierarchy is illustrated in **Figure 11.2**.

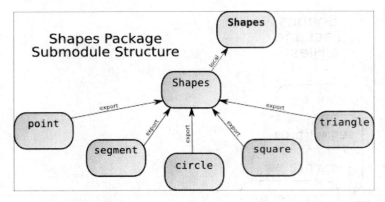

Figure 11.2: Design of Package

The result of preprocessing the main file shapes.mpl produces a module whose source has the following general form.

```
Shapes := module()
    option package;
    export make, area, circumference;
    local Shapes, circum_table;
    Shapes := module()
        export point, segment, circle, square, triangle;
        point := module() ... end module;
        segment := module() ... end module;
        .....
    end module;
```

```
       make := proc() ... end proc;
       area := proc() ... end proc;
       circum_table := table(); ...
       circumference := proc() ... end proc;
end module:
```

The Package API

The **Shapes** package exports the following procedures:

- **make**
- **area**
- **circumference**

The make Procedure

The exported procedure **make** creates shapes. It is used to create a shape expression from the input data. For example, points are derived from their x and y coordinates.

```
> org := make( 'point', 0, 0 );
```

$$org := make(point, 0, 0) \qquad (11.13)$$

A circle is created from its center and radius.

```
> circ := make( 'circle', org, 2 );
```

$$circ := make(circle, make(point, 0, 0), 2) \qquad (11.14)$$

In each case, the name of the shape is passed as the first argument to specify which kind of shape to return.

The area Procedure

To compute the area of a shape, call the exported procedure **area** with the shape as its argument.

```
> area( circ );
```

$$area(make(circle, make(point, 0, 0), 2)) \qquad (11.15)$$

The circumference Procedure

The exported procedure **circumference** computes the circumference of a given shape.

```
> circumference( circ );
```

$$circumference(make(circle, make(point, 0, 0), 2)) \qquad (11.16)$$

Shape Representation

Shapes are represented as unevaluated function calls. The arguments to the call are the instance-specific data for the shape. For example, a point with coordinates (2,3) is represented by the unevaluated function call **POINT(2, 3)**. Some instance data are shapes themselves. For example, a segment is represented, using its endpoints, as an unevaluated function call of the form **SEGMENT(start_point, end_point)**. The start and end points of the segment can be obtained by calling the point constructor.

Procedure Dispatching

The **Shapes** package illustrates three types of procedure dispatching.

- Dispatching on submodule exports
- Conditional dispatching
- Table-based dispatching

Dispatching on Submodule Exports

The **make** procedure, which is exported from the **Shapes** package, uses the **Shapes:-Shapes** submodule for procedure dispatching.

To test whether a method for a given shape is available, the **make** procedure tests whether there is a submodule by that name in the **Shapes:-Shapes** submodule. If no such submodule is found, an exception is raised. Otherwise, the **make** export from the submodule is passed the arguments that were given to the top-level **Shapes:-make** procedure. The **make** source code is as follows.

```
> make := proc( what::symbol )
        description "constructor for shapes";
        local    ctor,       # the shape constructor,
                              # if found
                 theShape;   # the submodule for the
                              # kind of shape requested
        if not member( what, Shapes, 'theShape' ) then
              error "shape `%1' not available", what
        end if;
        if member( ':-make', theShape, 'ctor' ) then
              ctor( args[ 2 .. nargs ] )
        else
              error "no constructor provided for "
                    "shape %1", what
        end if
  end proc:
```

The first argument to **make** is a symbol that specifies the shape to create (**point**, **circle**, **triangle**). This symbol is used as an index in the **Shapes:-Shapes** submodule. The first statement uses the **member** command to test whether the symbol passed in the **what** parameter is exported by the **Shapes:-Shapes** submodule. If it is not found, an appropriate diagnostic is issued and an exception raised. If **member** returns the value **true**, then its third argument, the local variable **theShape**, is assigned the export found in the submodule.

For example, if **what** is the symbol **circle**, then the local variable **theShape** is assigned the submodule **Shapes:-Shapes:-circle** that implements operations on circles. The same idea is used to select the shape-specific constructor; it is the value assigned to the local variable **ctor** when the value **true** is returned from the second call to the **member** command. Any remaining arguments are used as data to construct the shape. These are passed to the **make** export in a shape-specific submodule, if found, and are not checked further at this level. This design localizes the shapes to the corresponding submodule.

Conditional Dispatching

The procedure **area** uses a simple conditional dispatching mechanism. The tag of the input shape is extracted and is used in direct comparisons with hard-coded values to determine which shape-specific **area** subcommand to call to perform the area computation.

```
> area := proc( shape )
      description "compute the area of a shape";
      local   tag;
      if not type( shape, 'function' ) then
          error "expecting a shape expression, "
                "but got %1", shape
      end if;
      # Extract the "tag" information from the shape
      tag := op( 0, shape );
      # Dispatch on the "tag" value
      if tag = ':-POINT' then
          Shapes:-point:-area( shape )
      elif tag = ':-SEGMENT' then
          Shapes:-segment:-area( shape )
      elif tag = ':-CIRCLE' then
          Shapes:-circle:-area( shape )
      elif tag = ':-SQUARE' then
          Shapes:-square:-area( shape )
      elif tag = ':-TRIANGLE' then
          Shapes:-triangle:-area( shape )
      else
          error "not a recognized shape: %1", tag
```

```
        end if
    end proc:
```

Table-based Dispatching

The third dispatch method illustrated in the **Shapes** package is table-based. This technique is used by the exported procedure **circumference**, which references the table **circum_table** to look up the appropriate procedure to call. This table is built by assigning its entries in the body of the **Shapes** package.

```
> circum_table := table();
> circum_table[ 'POINT' ]    := Shapes:-point:-circumference;
> circum_table[ 'SEGMENT' ]  := Shapes:-segment:-circumference;
> circum_table[ 'CIRCLE' ]   := Shapes:-circle:-circumference;
> circum_table[ 'SQUARE' ]   := Shapes:-square:-circumference;
> circum_table[ 'TRIANGLE' ] := Shapes:-triangle:-circumference;
```

The source code for the procedure **circumference** is as follows.

```
> circumference := proc( shape )
        description "compute the circumference of a "
                    "shape expression";
    if not type( shape, 'function' ) then
        error "expecting a shape, but got %1", shape
    end if;
    if assigned( circum_table[ op( 0, shape ) ] ) then
        circum_table[ op( 0, shape ) ]( shape )
    else
        error "no circumference method available "
              "for shape %1. Supported shapes "
              "are: %2", tag,
                sprintf( "%q", op( ALL_SHAPES ) )
    end if
    end proc:
```

Minimal checking is done to ensure that the input has the right structure. If an entry is found in the table **circum_table** for the shape tag (as with the **area** procedure), the corresponding procedure is called with the given shape as an argument. (The shape must be passed as an argument, so that the shape-specific submodule can extract the instance data from it.) Otherwise, a diagnostic is issued and an exception is raised.

Shape-specific Submodules

As already noted, each shape is implemented in a shape-specific submodule. The set of exports of each module varies, but each supports the required exports **make**, **area**, and **circumference** in the top-level **Shapes** module. Certain shapes support other operations. Only two submodules are described here. You can see the source for the other submodules in the sample source code.

The point Submodule

The submodule that implements points is fairly simple. In fact, it makes no reference to any lexically scoped variables in its parent modules (**Shapes** and **Shapes:-Shapes**).

```
> point := module()
      description "support commands for points";
      export make, area, circumference, xcoord, ycoord;
      option package;
      make := ( x, y ) -> 'POINT'( x, y );
      area := () -> 0;
      circumference := () -> 0;
      xcoord := p -> op( 1, p );
      ycoord := p -> op( 2, p );
  end module:
```

Since the area and circumference of a point are both 0, these procedures are easy to implement. In addition to the required exports, the **point** submodule also exports two utility procedures, **xcoord** and **ycoord**, for retrieving the x and y coordinates of a point. Providing these values makes it possible for clients of this submodule to use it without requiring information about the concrete representation of points. This makes it easier to change the representation later, if required.

Within this submodule, the names **make**, **area**, and **circumference** are the same as the names with the same external representation at the top-level **Shapes** module.

The circle Submodule

This submodule provides the circle-specific commands for the **Shapes** package.

```
> circle := module()
      export  make, center, radius, diameter,
              area, circumference;
      option package;
      make := proc( cntrPt, radius )
              'CIRCLE'( cntrPt, radius )
      end proc;
```

```
        center := circ -> op( 1, circ );
        radius := circ -> op( 2, circ );
        diameter := circ -> 2 * radius( circ );
        circumference := circ ->  Pi * diameter( circ );
        area := circ -> Pi * radius( circ )^2;
     end module:
```

Again, some extra commands are provided in addition to those required at the top level of the **Shapes** package. The exported procedure **radius** is used to define other commands. It can be made local to this submodule.

12 Graphics

Maple offers a variety of ways to generate 2-D and 3-D plots. This chapter shows you how to create and manipulate such plots programmatically. You will learn about the Maple plotting library, the plot data structure, and how to write your own graphics procedures.

12.1 In This Chapter

- Introduction
- The Plot Library
- Programming with Plots
- Data Structures
- Customizing Plots
- Animations
- Miscellaneous Topics
- Avoiding Common Problems

12.2 Introduction

Plots in Maple

A plot in Maple is a 2-D or 3-D graphical representation of a mathematical object, such as a function or a set of statistical data. In most of this chapter, we will be assuming a Cartesian coordinate system. We will generally refer to the horizontal and vertical axes in 2-D plots as the x and y axes, respectively, while the axes in 3-D plots will be called the x, y, and z axes.

The following command generates a 2-D plot of the function $x^3 - x^2 + 3$ over the range -2 to 2.

```
> plot(x^3-x^2+3, x=-2..2, 'title'="A First Plot");
```

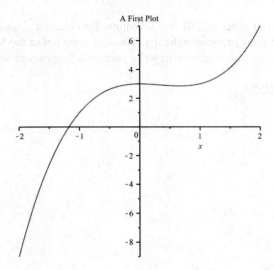

The **plot** command is commonly used to create 2-D plots and it is described in more detail in *Generating 2-D and 3-D Plots (page 404)*. There is a corresponding **plot3d** command for creating 3-D plots. In the previous statement, the three arguments to the **plot** command are the Maple expression **x^3-x^2+3** representing the function to be plotted, an equation specifying the plotting variable and range, and an option indicating that a title be added.

If you are using Maple's Standard Interface, executing the previous statement produces a plot in the current document. You can also create plotting output for other interfaces (for example, plots that open in a different window) and plots that are saved as a graphics file. For more information, see *Interfaces and Devices (page 479)*.

Generating a Plot

The **plot** and **plot3d** commands are not the only ways to generate plots. Maple has an extensive library of commands for plotting and related tasks. These are described in *The Plot Library (page 403)*. A plot that is generated with a library command is returned as a plot data structure. This is described in the section *Data Structures (page 441)*.

Maple also provides interactive ways to create and modify plots, including:

- the Interactive Plot Builder,
- dragging and dropping, and

- context menus.

More information about these topics can be found in the **Maple User Manual**. If you are interested in simply creating a plot to be displayed in a Maple worksheet, then these easy-to-use, interactive methods are recommended. However, if you want to write programs that build and manipulate plots, then it is necessary to be familiar with Maple's plotting library commands.

Plots can also be used as embedded components, which means they are created as graphical interface components that can be manipulated through various actions. For more information, see *Programming Interactive Elements (page 487)*

12.3 The Plot Library

This section provides an overview of the most commonly used plotting commands in the library. Refer to the Maple Plotting Guide (**Help > Manuals, Resources, and more > Plotting Guide**) for a pictorial listing of the kinds of plots that can be generated in Maple. The commands described here can be entered in the worksheet to generate individual plots, or they can be used in combination within procedures.

Many of the commands introduced in this section are from the **plots** package, so we will make the short form of the names available.

```
> with(plots);
```

$$[\textit{animate, animate3d, animatecurve, arrow, changecoords,}\\
\textit{complexplot, complexplot3d, conformal, conformal3d,}\\
\textit{contourplot, contourplot3d, coordplot, coordplot3d,}\\
\textit{densityplot, display, dualaxisplot, fieldplot, fieldplot3d,}\\
\textit{gradplot, gradplot3d, implicitplot, implicitplot3d, inequal,}\\
\textit{interactive, interactiveparams, intersectplot, listcontplot,}\\
\textit{listcontplot3d, listdensityplot, listplot, listplot3d, loglogplot,}\\
\textit{logplot, matrixplot, multiple, odeplot, pareto, plotcompare,}\\
\textit{pointplot, pointplot3d, polarplot, polygonplot, polygonplot3d,}\\
\textit{polyhedra\_supported, polyhedraplot, rootlocus, semilogplot,}\\
\textit{setcolors, setoptions, setoptions3d, spacecurve,}\\
\textit{sparsematrixplot, surfdata, textplot, textplot3d, tubeplot}]$$

(12.1)

Most plotting commands accept optional arguments that change the default look of the plots. These options are summarized on the **plot/option** and **plot3d/option** help pages, and the most commonly used ones are described in *Customizing Plots (page 449)*. We will refer to options that apply to the entire plot, such as **title** or **gridlines**, as **global** options. Options that apply to individual elements, such as **color**, are called **local** options.

Generating 2-D and 3-D Plots

Introduction

There are two basic plotting commands in Maple: **plot** and **plot3d**. The **plot** command produces 2-D curves from representations of mathematical functions in one independent variable, and the **plot3d** command generates 3-D surfaces from representations of functions in two variables.

The following command generates a 2-D plot of the function $e^{\frac{1}{2}x} - 5x + x^2$ over the range 1 to 5.

```
> plot(exp(x/2)-5*x+x^2, x=1..5, 'color'="NavyBlue", 'thickness'=2);
```

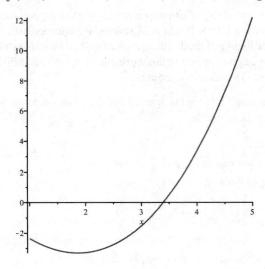

The following command generates a 3-D plot of the function $\sin(x)\sin(y)$ over x and y ranges of $-\pi$ to π.

```
> plot3d(sin(x)*sin(y), x=-Pi..Pi, y=-Pi..Pi, 'transparency'=0.2);
```

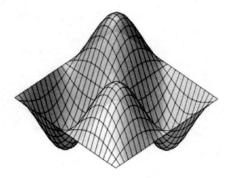

In both these statements, the first argument is an expression representing the curve or surface to be plotted. This is followed by ranges for the independent variables. Finally, optional arguments may be added.

Expression and Operator Forms

The two plotting statements in the previous section use the expression form of the **plot** and **plot3d** commands. These plots can also be generated using the operator form of the calling sequence.

```
> plot(proc(x) exp(x/2)-5*x+x^2 end proc, 1..5, 'color'="NavyBlue",
    'thickness'=2);
```

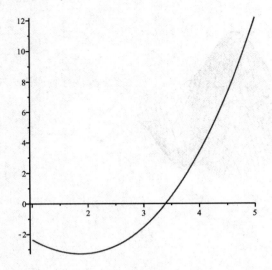

```
> plot3d((x, y)->sin(x)*sin(y), -Pi..Pi, -Pi..Pi,
  'transparency'=0.2);
```

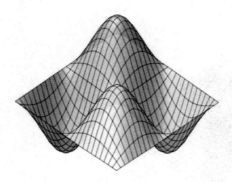

In the operator form of the calling sequence, the first argument must be a **procedure**. It can be written using **proc ... end proc**, as in the call to **plot** or with arrow notation, as in the call to **plot3d**. It can be the name of any predefined procedure, including ones from the Maple library, as in the following example.

```
> plot3d(binomial, 0..5, 0..5);
```

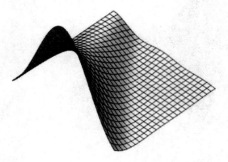

The procedure must accept one floating-point input argument in the 2-D case and two such arguments in the 3-D case, and it must return a floating-point value. For the operator form of the calling sequence, the range arguments are simple ranges rather than equations, as with the expression form of the calling sequence.

The operator form is primarily used when the function to be plotted is not easily written as a Maple expression in the plotting variables.

```
> p := proc(x)
      if abs(x)<0.1 then
          100*x
      elif abs(x)>0.5 then
          4*x
      else
          1/x
      end if;
  end proc:
```

```
> plot(p, -1..1);
```

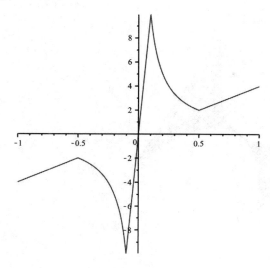

Normally, ranges given to a plotting command must have endpoints that evaluate to floating-point numbers. However, you can get an infinity plot by including **infinity** as one of the endpoints. For more information, refer to the **plot/infinity** help page. With 3-D plots, you can also use, in the range for one variable, an expression that depends on the other variable.

```
> plot3d(x*y, x=-1..1, y=-x^2..x^2);
```

To display multiple curves or surfaces in a single plot, provide a list of expressions or procedures to the **plot** or **plot3d** command. With the **plot** command, the options that affect the look of an individual curve, such as **color** or **thickness**, also accept lists of values.

```
> plot([sin(x), cos(x)], x=-Pi..Pi, 'color'=["Niagara BlueGreen",
  "Niagara DarkOrchid"]);
```

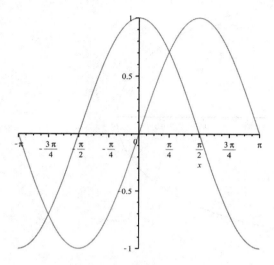

If you want to generate a 3-D plot containing three surfaces, you must add the option **plotlist=true** to distinguish this plot from a parametric plot, which is described in the next section.

Occasionally, users get unexpected results by mixing the two calling sequences. Common errors are described in *Mixing Expression and Operator Forms (page 479)*

Parametric Form

In the previous examples, the first argument is used to calculate the value of the dependent variable as a function of the independent variable or variables. A parametric curve, where the x and y values are functions of a single parameter t, can also be plotted by the **plot** command. Similarly, a parametric surface, where the x, y, and z values are functions of two parameters s and t, can be plotted by the **plot3d** command.

To generate a 2-D parametric plot, provide as the first argument a list containing three items: an expression for the x value, an expression for the y value, and an equation containing the parameter and its range.

```
> plot([sin(t), cos(t), t=0..Pi]);
```

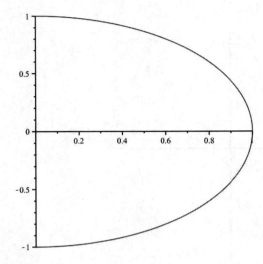

To generate a 3-D parametric plot, provide as the first argument a list containing three expressions, for the *x*, *y*, and *z* values respectively. Two additional arguments are required, each in the form of an equation containing one of the parameters and its range.

```
> plot3d([s^2, cos(s), t*cos(t)], s=0..2*Pi, t=0..Pi);
```

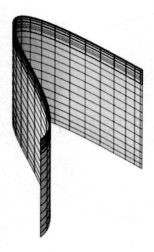

Operator form can also be used with parametric plots. The two previous examples are written using operator form as follows. As with non-parametric plots, options may be added.

```
> plot([sin, cos, 0..Pi], thickness=3, linestyle=dash);
```

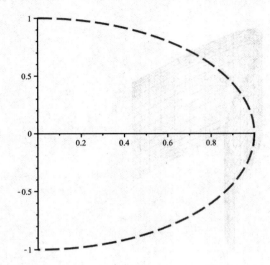

```
> plot3d([(s,t)->s^2, (s,t)->t*cos(s), (s,t)->cos(t)], 0..2*Pi,
    0..Pi, 'axes'='boxed');
```

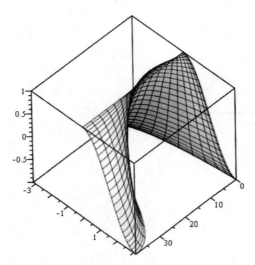

The calling sequences for parametric plots are explained in detail on the **plot/details** and **plot3d** help pages.

Plotting Points, Polygons, and Text

Points

The **plots:-pointplot** and **plots:-pointplot3d** commands are used to plot collections of 2-D or 3-D points. These points can be provided as lists of two-element or three-element lists. Alternatively, they can be provided as two or three **Vectors**. The options **symbol** and **symbolsize**, described on the **plot/options** help page, can be used to change the look of each point.

```
> pointplot([[0, 1], [1, -1], [3, 0], [4, -3]], 'color'= ["Red",
  "Green", "Black", "Blue"], 'symbol'='asterisk', 'symbolsize'=15,
  'view'=[-1..5, -4..2]);
```

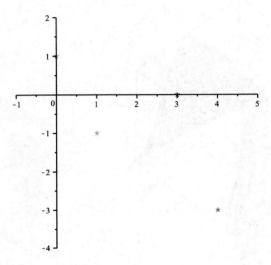

```
> xvector := <1, 2, 3, 4, 6>:
  yvector := <1, 3, 5, 8, 9>:
  zvector := <0, 1, 0, 1, 0.5>:
  pointplot3d(xvector, yvector, zvector, 'color'="Niagara Burgundy",
   'axes'='boxed', 'symbol'='solidsphere', 'symbolsize'=20);
```

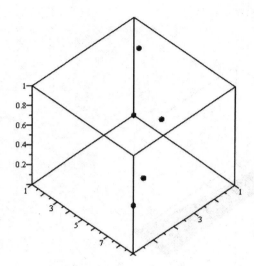

The **plot** command also offers a calling sequence in which a collection of points is provided. The **plot** command differs from the **pointplot** command in that a connecting line is drawn by default. To draw discrete points with the **plot** command, use the **style=point** option.

If you have a large data set, it is highly recommended that you create the data set as a **Matrix** with the **datatype** option set to **float**. You can import data sets created by applications other than Maple by using the **ImportMatrix** command or the **ImportData** assistant.

Polygons and Polyhedra

The **plots:-polygonplot** and **plots:-polygonplot3d** commands plot polygons in 2-D or 3-D space. The vertices of the polygons are specified in a way similar to the way points are specified for the **pointplot** and **pointplot3d** commands.

```
> polygonplot3d(Matrix([[0, 1, 1], [1, -1, 2], [3, 0, 5], [1, 1,
  1]], 'datatype'='float'), 'color'="Niagara BluishPurple",
  'axes'='boxed');
```

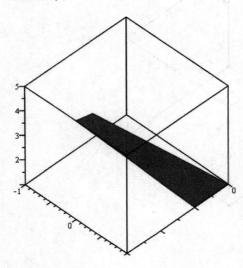

The **plots:-polyhedraplot** command can be used to display any of the polyhedra described on the **plots/polyhedra_supported** help page.

```
> polyhedraplot([0, 0, 0], 'polytype' = 'dodecahedron', 'scaling'
    = 'constrained', 'orientation'=[76, 40]);
```

The **polyhedraplot** command makes use of the **geometry** and **geom3d** packages. Use these packages if you want to do more computations with geometric objects. These objects can be plotted with the **geometry:-draw** and **geom3d:-draw** commands.

The **plottools** package also offers commands to create geometric objects. The result of these commands is a plot data structure. For more information about this package, see *Creating Plot Structures (page 446)*.

Text on Plots

Text can be added to plots with the **title** and **caption** options. Axis and tickmark labels can also be specified with the **labels** and **tickmarks** options. For details on specifying tickmarks, refer to the **plot/tickmarks** help page. The text can be a string, a Maple expression, or an unevaluated **typeset** call, which allows you to combine mathematical expressions and strings. The mathematical expressions are typeset as described in *Typesetting (page 461)*.

```
> plot(x^2, x=-2..2, 'title'='typeset'("A plot of the function ",
x^2));
```

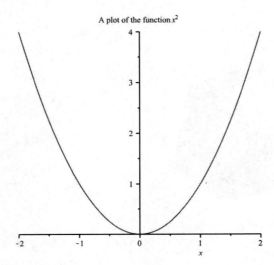

The **plots:-textplot** and **plots:-textplot3d** allow you to create plots containing text objects at arbitrary locations. The first argument is a list consisting of the coordinate values followed by the text to be placed at the location defined by the coordinates. Common options used with the **textplot** and **textplot3d** commands include the **font** option, to change the font type and size, and the **align** option, to position the text relative to the coordinate values.

```
> textplot([1, 2, f(x)], 'font'=['times', 20], 'align'='above');
```

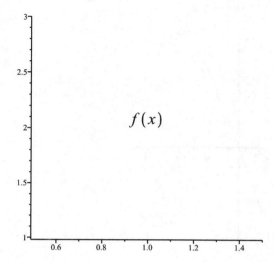

Usually, text objects are displayed in combination with other plot elements. In the next section, you will learn how to merge plots created with the commands introduced so far.

Combining Plots

This section describes how to use the **plots:-display** command to combine plots, or more specifically, plot data structures. Two or more plots can be merged into a single plot or they can be placed side-by-side in a tabular arrangement.

When a plot is generated using any library command, a plot data structure is created. This structure can be assigned to a variable to be reused or modified. A detailed explanation of how the structures are formed is available in *Data Structures (page 441)*, but it is not necessary to understand the details in order to manipulate the structures as described here.

Merging Plots

To combine the elements of two or more plots into a single plot, use the **plots:-display** command, with the plots contained in a list as the first argument.

```
> sinecurve := plot(sin(x), x=-Pi..Pi):
> maxtext := textplot([Pi/2, 1, "maximum"], 'align'='above'):
```

```
> display([sinecurve, maxtext], 'caption'="This plot shows a local
  maximum of the sin function.");
```

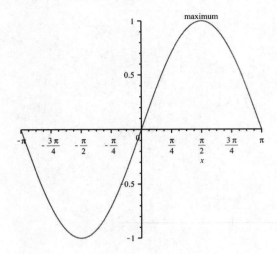

This plot shows a local maximum of the sin function.

Any combination of plot structures created from arbitrary Maple plotting commands can be combined using the **display** command, with a some restrictions. Usually, different types of plots (2-D, 3-D, arrays of plots, and animations) cannot be mixed.

When plots are merged, their options are also merged if possible. If there is a conflict, the **display** command will try to resolve it. For example, if two plots with different titles are merged, the **display** command will arbitrarily choose one for the merged plot.

The **display** command allows additional options to be provided. In the case of global options (ones that apply to the entire plot such as **caption**), these additional options will override those given for the individual plots. However, local options specified within the plots are generally not overridden.

The **display** command accepts the option **insequence=true**, which causes the plots to be displayed sequentially in an animation rather than merged. This use of the **display** command is discussed in *Animations (page 470)*.

Generating an Array of Plots

The **display** command can be used to generate a tabular display of plots by providing a one-dimensional or two-dimensional **Array** of plot structures as the first argument. An animation plot structure can also be given, in which case the frames of the animation are displayed in tabular form.

Unlike the situation where plots are merged, you can mix different types of plots in an array of plots. For example, you can create an array containing both 2-D and 3-D plots.

A limited number of options can be passed to this command. Most global plot options are accepted and are applied to each plot in the Array individually.

For more information about this feature, including the **aligncolumns** option that allows you to align the *x*-axes of plots within a column, refer to the **plot/arrayplot** help page.

Specialty Plots

In this section, a few commonly used commands for specialty plots are introduced. Refer to the **Maple Plotting Guide** for a complete list of commands available.

The **plots:-implicitplot** and **plots:-implicitplot3d** commands generate plots of implicitly defined curves and surfaces.

```
> implicitplot(x^2-y^2 = 1, x = -Pi .. Pi, y = -Pi .. Pi,
    'color'="Niagara BluishPurple", 'thickness'=2, 'gridrefine'=2);
```

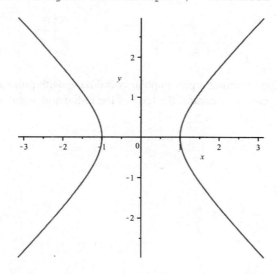

The **plots:-contourplot** command generates a contour plot for an expression in two variables. The **plots:-contourplot3d** command does the same but generates a 3-D display.

```
> contourplot3d(-5*x/(x^2+y^2+1), x=-3..3, y=-3..3,
  'filledregions'=true, 'coloring'=["Niagara Burgundy", "Niagara
  Navy"]);
```

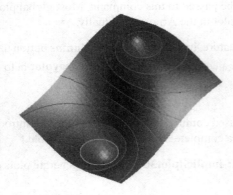

The **plots:-polarplot** command generates a plot in polar coordinates with polar axes. This command offers a number of options to control the look of the radial and angular axes.

```
> polarplot(theta, theta = 0..2*Pi,
  'axis'['radial']=['color'="Niagara DeepBlue"]);
```

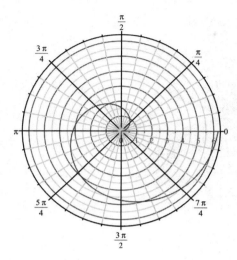

To plot in other coordinate systems, you can use the **coords** option. However, unlike with the **polarplot** command, these plots are drawn with Cartesian axes. For a complete list of supported coordinate systems, refer to the **coords** help page,

```
> plot3d(z, theta=0..2*Pi, z=-1..1, 'coords'='cylindrical');
```

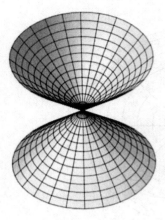

The **plots:-dualaxisplot** command creates a plot with two *y*-axes located at the left and right sides of the plot. You can provide either two expressions or two plot data structures.

```
> dualaxisplot(plot(x^2, x=0..10, 'labels'=[x, x^2], 'legend'=x^2),
    plot(x^3, x =0..10, 'color'="Niagara Navy", 'labels'=[x, x^3],
    'legend'=x^3), 'title'="A Comparison");
```

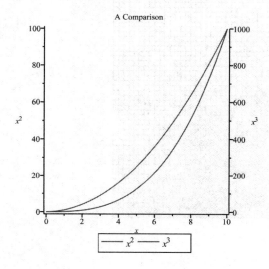

The **plots:-densityplot** command creates a plot of a function of two variables colored by the function value. You can create a grayscale or RGB-colored plot.

```
> densityplot(sin(x+y), x=-1..1, y=-1..1);
```

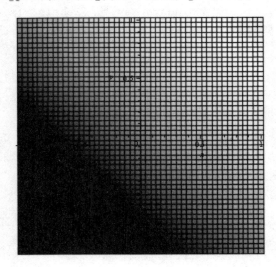

The **plots:-fieldplot** and **plots:-fieldplot3d** commands generate plots of 2-D or 3-D vector fields.

```
> fieldplot3d([(x, y, z)->2*x, (x, y, z)->2*y, (x, y, z)->1], -1..1,
     -1..1, -1..1);
```

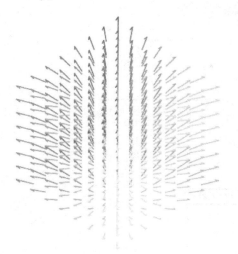

Other Packages

Many of the plotting commands introduced so far are part of the **plots** package. Several other packages in Maple also contain visualization commands.

The **plottools** package includes commands for generating and transforming graphical objects. This package is described in *Creating Plot Structures (page 446)*.

The **Student** package consists of several subpackages designed to assist with the teaching and learning of mathematics. Each Student package has a collection of visualization commands. For example, for Calculus, refer to the **Student/Calculus1/VisualizationOverview** help page.

```
> Student:-Calculus1:-RollesTheorem(sin(x), x=1..3*Pi-1);
```

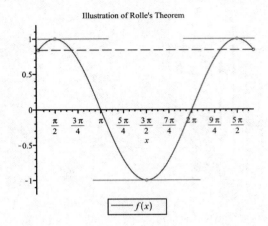

For the function $f(x) = \sin(x)$ on the interval $[1, 3\pi - 1]$, a graph showing $f(x)$, the line connecting $(1, f(1))$ and $(3\pi - 1, f(3\pi - 1))$, tangents parallel to the line connecting $(1, f(1))$ and $(3\pi - 1, f(3\pi - 1))$.

The **Statistics** package contains a large number of commands for visualizing univariate and multivariate data. These are listed in the **Statistics/Visualization** help page.

```
> chartvalues := [seq(i=sqrt(i), i=1..15)]:
  Statistics:-PieChart(chartvalues, sector=0..180);
```

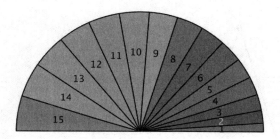

As mentioned in *Polygons and Polyhedra (page 417)*, geometric objects can be created and displayed with the **geometry** and **geom3d** packages.

In the **GraphTheory** package, directed and undirected graphs can be drawn with the **GraphTheory:-DrawGraph** command. In addition, the package provides many predefined graphs as well as visualizations of some algorithms.

```
> with(GraphTheory):
  with(SpecialGraphs):
  DrawGraph(PetersenGraph());
```

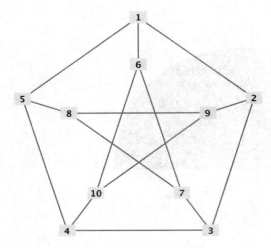

12.4 Programming with Plots

Now that you are familiar with the wide range of commands available in the Maple plotting library, you can combine them to create custom graphics procedures. In this section, you will examine two simple examples: one in 2-D and one in 3-D. In later sections, additional programming examples will be provided as new concepts are introduced.

A 2-D Example

This first example shows how plotting commands can be combined to create a single plot.

```
> f := x*sin(x):
  fderiv := diff(f, x):
  fplot := plot(f, x=-2*Pi..2*Pi, 'color'="Niagara Burgundy",
  'legend'=f, 'thickness'=2):
  fdplot := plot(fderiv, x=-2*Pi..2*Pi, 'color'="Niagara Navy",
  'legend'=fderiv):
```

```
> plots:-display([fplot, fdplot], 'title'="A function and its
  derivative", 'titlefont'=["Helvetica", 16]);
```

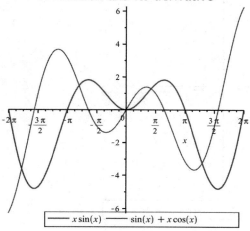

You can make this code more general and reusable by defining a procedure to produce a similar plot given an expression as the first argument, and an equation involving the plotting variable and range as the second argument.

```
> derivativeplot := proc(f, r :: name=range)
      local fderiv, v, fplot, fdplot;

      # Extract the plotting variable and compute derivative.
      v := lhs(r);
      fderiv := diff(f, v);
      # Create both curves.
      fplot := plot(f, r, 'color'="Niagara Burgundy", 'legend'=f,
  'thickness'=2):
      fdplot := plot(fderiv, r, 'color'="Niagara Navy",
  'legend'=fderiv):
      # Combine into final plot.
      plots:-display([fplot, fdplot], 'title'="A function and its
  derivative",
          'titlefont'=["Helvetica", 16]);
  end proc:
```

```
> derivativeplot(t^3-4*t^2+2*t, t=-3..3);
```

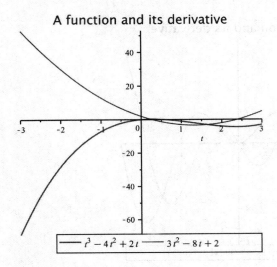

There are a few modifications that can be made to improve **derivativeplot**, such as error-checking and processing of additional plotting options.

In the **derivativeplot** procedure, the **name=range** type is specified for the **r** parameter, and the type-checking of this argument is done automatically by the built-in parameter processing facilities in Maple. However, it is useful to check for correctness of the first expression. Specifically, **derivativeplot** should check that the first argument is an expression in one variable and that variable matches the one given in the second argument. For example, the following incorrect call would produce an empty plot.

```
> derivativeplot(x^3-4*x^2+2*x, t=-3..3);
```
Warning, expecting only range variable t in expression x^3-4*x^2+2*x
to be plotted but found name x

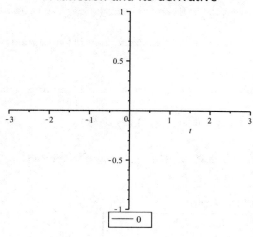

Many visualization commands in the Maple library that use the basic plotting procedures **plot**, **plot3d**, and **plots:-display** assume that additional arguments are global plot options to be passed along for processing by these commands. In the modified **derivativeplot** procedure below, the unprocessed arguments in **_rest** are passed to the **display** command. For more information on **_rest**, see *Special Sequences for Referring to Parameters and Arguments (page 227)*.

Here is the new **derivativeplot** procedure.

```
> derivativeplot := proc(f, r :: name=range)
      local fderiv, vnames, v, p1, p2, pfinal;

      # Extract the plotting variable, check that it matches the
      # indeterminate names in f, and then compute derivative.
      v := lhs(r);
      vnames := select(type, indets(f), 'name');
      if nops(vnames)>1 then
          error "too many variables in expression %1", f;
      elif nops(vnames)=1 and vnames[1]<>v then
```

```
        error "variable in expression %1 does not match %2", f,
v;
      end if;
      fderiv := diff(f, v);
      # Create both curves.
      p1 := plot(f, r, 'color'="Niagara Burgundy", 'legend'=f,
'thickness'=2):
      p2 := plot(fderiv, r, 'color'="Niagara Navy", 'legend'=fderiv):

      # Combine into final plot.
      plots:-display([p1, p2], 'title'="A function and its
derivative",
           'titlefont'=["Helvetica", 16], _rest);
end proc:
> derivativeplot(x^3-4*x^2+2*x, x=-3..3, 'axes'='boxed', 'title' =
  "My latest plot");
```

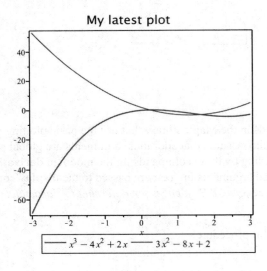

Notice that the **title** option in the last **derivativeplot** call replaces the default title specified within the procedure. The convention followed by many Maple commands is that, when there are duplicate option names in the calling sequence, the last value given is the one that is applied. However, if you added the option **color="Green"**, that would not change the default colors of the two curves. That is because the **color="DarkRed"** and **color="Navy"**

options have been saved in the plot data structures **p1** and **p2** as local options, and they will not be overridden by plot options passed to the **display** command.

A 3-D Example

The next example defines a procedure that accepts a list of expressions in one variable and displays these as "ribbons" in a 3-D plot.

The following **ribbonplot** procedure accepts a list of expressions in one variable, an equation containing the variable name and range, and an optional keyword parameter, **numberpoints**. The **numberpoints** option specifies the number of points along the ribbon and is set to 25 by default. For brevity, this procedure does not include the error-checking of the list of expressions as for the **derivativeplot** example.

```
> ribbonplot := proc(f::list, r::name=range, {numberpoints::posint
    := 25})
     local i, p, y, n;
     n := nops(f);
     p := Vector(n);
     # Generate a 3-D plot for each expression and combine with
     # plots:-display.
     for i to n do
         p[i] := plot3d(f[i], r, y=i-0.75..i, 'grid'=[numberpoints,
  2]);
     end do;
     plots[display](convert(p, 'list'), _rest);
  end proc:
```

In the procedure **ribbonplot**, a **Vector** is used to store the **n** plot structures generated by the **plot3d** command. The **grid** option is passed to **plot3d** to specify the number of sample points in each plot direction. As with the previous example, additional global plot options are passed directly to the **plots:-display** command.

Call **ribbonplot** with four expressions as the input and using the default options. Then, call it again with more sample points and constrained scaling.

> ribbonplot([cos(x), cos(2*x), sin(x), sin(2*x)], x=-Pi..Pi);

```
> ribbonplot([cos(x), cos(2*x), sin(x), sin(2*x)], x=-Pi..Pi,
  'numberpoints'=40, 'scaling'='constrained');
```

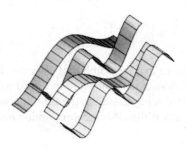

Now, change the **ribbonplot** procedure so that it accepts input in operator form instead of expression form. Following the convention of the **plot** and **plot3d** command, in the modified procedure, the second argument is the plotting range, with no plotting variable specified. In addition, this version of **ribbonplot** allows a **ribboncolors** option that lets the user specify the color of each ribbon. If no such option is provided, the ribbons are colored with the default surface shading for 3-D plots.

```
> ribbonplot := proc(f::list, r::range, {numberpoints::posint :=
  25,
          ribboncolors::list({name,string}):=[]})
      local i, p, y, n, nr;
      n := nops(f);
      p := Vector(n);
      # Check that the number of ribbon colors matches the number
  of
      # procedures.
      nr := nops(ribboncolors);
      if nr>0 and nr<>n then
          error "%1 ribbon colors needed", nr;
      end if;
```

```
        # Generate a 3-D plot for each procedure and combine with
        # plots:-display. Include a ribbon color if provided.
        for i to n do
            p[i] := plot3d((u,v)->f[i](u), r, i-0.75..i,
    'grid'=[numberpoints, 2],
                    `if`(nr=0, NULL, 'color'=ribboncolors[i]));
        end do;
        plots[display](convert(p, 'list'), _rest);
    end proc:
```

This procedure contains a check to ensure that the number of ribbon colors is the same as the number of procedures in the list **f**. Also, each procedure in **f** must be turned into a procedure with two input parameters before being passed to the **plot3d** command. In the call to **plot3d**, the **color** option is passed only if the **ribboncolors** option had originally been provided.

```
> g := proc(x) if x < 0 then cos(x) else cos(2*x); end if; end proc:
  ribbonplot([g, sin, cos+sin], -Pi..Pi, 'transparency'=0.5,
       'ribboncolors'=["DarkBlue", "DarkRed", "DarkGreen"]);
```

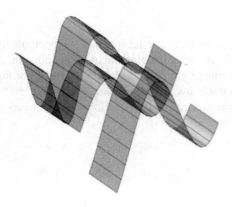

12.5 Data Structures

When you generate a plot in Maple, a plot data structure is created. The data structure is in the form of an unevaluated **PLOT**, **PLOT3D**, or **_PLOTARRAY** function call. The function arguments specify the objects to be plotted, as well as properties such as color or line thickness.

```
> PLOT(POINTS([0., 0.], [1., 1.]), SYMBOL(_SOLIDBOX, 20));
```

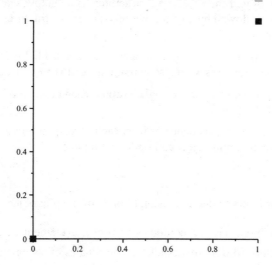

These structures are Maple expressions; therefore, they can be assigned to variables and used in the same way as other expressions. When you enter a plotting command, the plot data structure is generated. Then, the output displayed depends on the current interface or plotting device requested. If you are using the standard worksheet interface and the plot output has not been redirected to a non-default device, you will see the plots rendered as they are shown in this guide.

In this section, you will learn about the components of the plot data structure and the tools available to manipulate them. An understanding of the internal data structure is useful when writing programs that create and transform plots. However, it is strongly recommended that you use the available Maple library commands to generate plots and plot components whenever possible, rather than building the structures directly. Because these structures are part of the internal representation of plots, new graphics features offered in future Maple releases may necessitate minor updates to the format.

Types of Data Structures

This section provides an overview of the major components in plot data structures. Full details are available in the **plot/structure** help page. Note that some data structure names, those introduced in Maple 10 or later versions, are prefixed with underscores.

Basic Structures

- **PLOT** -- 2-D plot. Contains any of the object data structures listed below, except for **MESH** and **ISOSURFACE**, followed by any number of 2-D option structures. Can also contain an **ANIMATE** structure.
- **PLOT3D** -- 3-D plot. Contains any of the object data structures listed below, followed by any number of 3-D option structures. Can also contain an **ANIMATE** structure.
- **_PLOTARRAY** -- Array of plots. Contains a single **Matrix**, each element of which is a **PLOT** or **PLOT3D** structure.
- **ANIMATE** -- Animation. Contains a sequence of lists, each corresponding to a single frame in the animation and containing object and option structures.

Object Structures

In the following description, d refers to the dimension (2 or 3) of the plot object.

A collection of n points in d dimensions is specified as a list of n d-element sublists or as an n by d **Matrix**. Each sublist or **Matrix** row holds the coordinates of a single point.

- **CURVES** -- 2-D or 3-D curve(s). Contains one or more collections of points in list or **Matrix** format as described above. Each collection of points defines a single curve.
- **POLYGONS** -- 2-D or 3-D polygon(s). Contains one or more collections of points in list or **Matrix** format, each defining the vertices of a single polygon.
- **POINTS** -- 2-D or 3-D points. Contains a collection of points in list or **Matrix** format.
- **TEXT** -- 2-D or 3-D text object. Contains a point in list format followed by the string or expression to be displayed.
- **GRID** -- 3-D surface over a regular grid. Contains ranges in the x and y directions, followed by a two-dimensional **Array** or list of lists containing the grid data.
- **MESH** -- 3-D surface over an arbitrary grid. Contains the x, y, and z coordinates corresponding to points over an m by n grid. This data is contained in a three-dimensional **Array** or in nested lists.
- **ISOSURFACE** -- 3-D volume of data, which consists of function values over a regular grid. This results in a rendering of a 3-D surface approximating the zero surface of the

function. Contains x, y, z, and $f(x, y, z)$ values over an m by n by k grid. The data is contained in a four-dimensional **Array** or in nested lists.

Each object structure may contain one or more local option structures following the required data. For example, the following structure produces two polygons, one blue and one purple.

```
> PLOT(POLYGONS([[0., 0.], [0., 1.], [1., 1.], [1., 0.]], COLOR(RGB,
    0., 0., 1.)), POLYGONS([[1., 1.], [1., 2.], [2., 2.], [2., 1.]],
    COLOR(RGB, .5, 0., .5)));
```

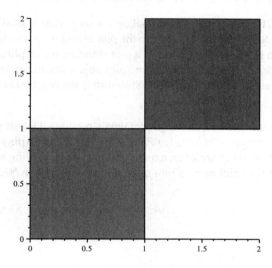

Option Structures

There are a large number of option structures, some used for either 2-D plots or 3-D plots only, and some that apply to both. Most of the option structures have a direct correspondence to plot options described on the **plot/options** and **plot3d/option** help pages. (Note that the converse is not necessarily true. Several plot options do not have associated option structures.) Here are a few examples.

- The **symbol=asterisk** option is translated to **SYMBOL(_ASTERISK)** in the plot data structure.

- The **color="Turquoise"** option is translated to **COLOUR(RGB, 0.25098039, 0.87843137, 0.81568627)**.

- The **title="Another Plot"** and **titlefont=["Helvetica", 30]** options together translate to **TITLE("Another plot", FONT("Helvetica", 30))**.

In *The Plot Library (page 403)*, the concept of global options (options that apply to the entire plot) and local options (ones that apply to a particular plot object) was introduced. This concept applies in a similar way to plot structures. Local option structures, such as **STYLE** or **TRANSPARENCY** can appear inside one or more plot object structures (**CURVES**, **TEXT**, etc.). Global option structures, such as **TITLE**, appear outside the plot object structures and usually there is only one instance of each kind of structure.

Some options, such as **COLOR**, can appear as a global option as well as a local option. In this situation, the value of the local option is applied to the plot object with which it is associated, and it is not overridden by the global option. If a plot structure has duplicate options at the same level (all global, or all local within the same plot object structure), such as two **CAPTION** entries, then the last one appearing in the structure is the one that is applied when the plot is rendered.

The **plots:-display** command can be used to merge plot data structures. Details on how option structures are combined are given in *Merging Plots (page 421)*. The **display** command can also be used to add an option structure to an existing plot. In the following example, the **display** command accepts the **thickness=3** plot option and adds **THICKNESS(3)** to the data structure.

```
> p := plot(x^2-2*x+1, x=-4..4, 'color'="Niagara DarkOrchid"):
```

> p;

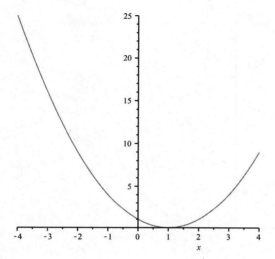

```
> plots:-display(p, 'thickness'=3);
```

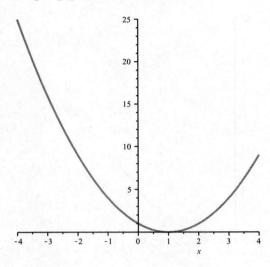

Creating Plot Structures

Complete plot structures are normally created with commands such as the ones in the **plots** package. If you want to generate data structures for individual plot objects, it is recommended that you use the commands in the **plottools** package rather than build them yourself.

- Frequently used commands include ones for generating the basic plot objects, such as **plottools:-curve**, **plottools:-point**, and **plottools:-polygon**. Note that the **plots:-surfdata** command can be used to generate 3-D surfaces. Other commands include ones for generating common geometric shapes, such as **plottools:-ellipse**, **plottools:-sphere**, and **plottools:-tetrahedron**.

The **plottools** commands do not produce complete plots, so the output will consist of the data structure in text form rather than a rendered image. To view the result of a **plottools** command, you must pass it to the **plots:-display** command.

```
> with(plottools):
> t := torus([1, 1, 1], 1, 2, 'color'="LightBlue",
  'transparency'=.5):
> s := sphere([5, 2, 3], 2, 'color'="LightGreen", 'transparency'=.7):
```

```
> plots:-display([t, s], 'scaling'='constrained');
```

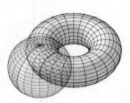

As shown in this example, options may be passed to the **plottools** commands. These must be local options that are applicable to the type of structure that is produced. The **color** option applies to any plot object, while the **transparency** option is used only with plot objects that are rendered as surfaces. The **scaling** option is a global option that applies to an entire plot; thus, it is included in the call to **display** instead of the calls to **torus** and **sphere**.

Altering Plot Structures

In addition to the commands for building plot structures, the **plottools** package also contains commands for altering structures. These commands, which accept 2-D or 3-D plots as input, include ones for translation, scaling, and rotation of a plot.

```
> p := plots:-arrow([0,1], 'color'="Orange"):
> pr := rotate(p, Pi/2):
```

> plots[display]([p, pr], 'scaling'='constrained', 'axes'='boxed');

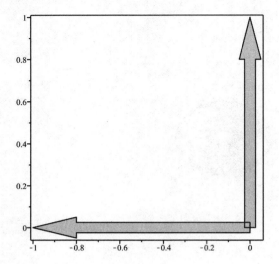

You can apply an arbitrary transformation to a 2-D or 3-D plot using the **plottools:-transform** command. To do this, define a procedure **f** that represents a mapping f from R^m to R^n, where m and n can take values 2 or 3. The procedure must take as input m arguments and return a list of n components. If you pass **f** to the **transform** command, it returns a procedure that takes a 2-D or 3-D plot data structure as its argument and returns a transformed plot.

> p := plots:-contourplot(2*x^2+y^2, x=-3..3, y=-3..3, 'filled',
  'coloring'=["Purple", "Teal"]):
> f := (x, y)->[x, y, 0]:
> tf := transform(f):

```
> plots:-display(tf(p), 'axes'='boxed', 'view'=['default', 'default',
    -2..2], 'scaling'='constrained');
```

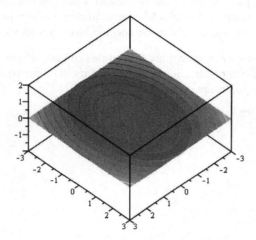

12.6 Customizing Plots

In this section, you will look at different ways of customizing plots by providing options to the Maple plotting commands. The complete list of options is available in the **plot/options** and **plot3d/option** help pages. Here, a few of the more commonly used ones are described.

In the descriptions in this section, it is assumed that you are using the **plot** and **plot3d** commands. However, many other plotting commands in Maple accept these options as well.

Controlling the Sampling

The commands for plotting curves and surfaces generate points by sampling the function to be plotted over the specified range or ranges. Several options are available to control how the sampling is done. All these options must be provided when the curve or surface is first created. They cannot be used with the **plots:-display** command or with the **plottools** commands that alter existing plot structures.

Number of Points

The **numpoints** option sets the minimum number of sampling points used by the **plot** and **plot3d** commands. Because the **plot** command uses an adaptive plotting scheme, it usually generates more points than this number. The **plot3d** command does not use an adaptive scheme and generates a number of points close to the specified **numpoints** value.

The **grid** option is an alternative way of specifying the number of sample points in 3-D plots. This option takes a list of two positive integers that specify the dimensions of the rectangular grid over which the points are generated.

```
> p1 := plot3d(.5*sin(x+y), x = -Pi .. Pi, y = -Pi .. Pi, grid =
    [10, 10]):
> p2 := plot3d(.5*sin(x+y)+1, x = -Pi .. Pi, y = -Pi .. Pi):
> p3 := plot3d(.5*sin(x+y)+2, x = -Pi .. Pi, y = -Pi .. Pi, grid=[40,
    40]):
> plots:-display([p1, p2, p3]);
```

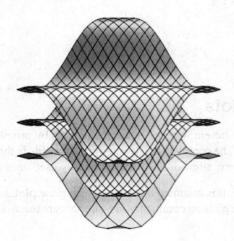

Adaptive Plotting

In 2-D plotting, the **numpoints** value is used to set the initial sample points. When the **adaptive** option value is set to **true** (the default value), the intervals defined by the initial sample points are further subdivided in an attempt to get a better representation of the function. The attempts at subdivision are based on the current sample values, and intervals are subdivided a maximum of six times. The **adaptive** option can also take a positive integer value that controls the maximum times intervals are subdivided.

If the **adaptive** option is set to **false**, the number of points generated is the same as the **numpoints** value (or the default value, if it is not provided).

The **sample** option allows you to provide a set of points at which the function is to be sampled. If adaptive plotting is allowed, the final set of sample points includes those in the provided list but normally consists of many more. To use exactly the list of points given by the **sample** option, specify **adaptive=false**.

```
> plot(x^2, x=0..4, 'adaptive'='false', 'sample'=[seq(0.1*i,
  i=0..40)], style=point);
```

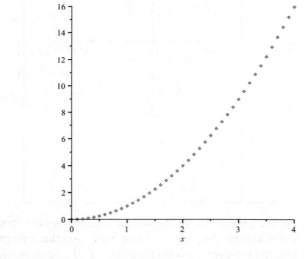

The **adaptive** and **sample** options are not available for 3-D plotting.

Discontinuities

If a function with a discontinuity is being plotted, then evaluation at the point of discontinuity will lead to an undefined value, which results in a gap in the plotted curve or surface. It is more likely that the function is evaluated at points very close to the discontinuity, and this can lead to a distorted view of the plot when the values are extremely large or small and an inappropriate connecting of the points over the discontinuity.

In the 2-D case, the **discont** option can be used with the **plot** command when you suspect a discontinuity. The **plot** command uses the **discont** and **fdiscont** commands to detect discontinuities and divides the plotting range into subranges over which the plot is continuous. In the following example, the plot on the left contains extraneous vertical lines. These are avoided in the right-hand-side plot generated with the **discont** option.

```
> plots:-display(Array([plot(tan(x), x=-Pi..Pi, y=-4..4),
    plot(tan(x), x=-Pi..Pi, y=-4..4, 'discont'=true)]));
```

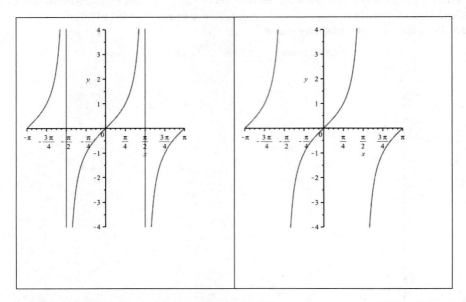

Usually, removable discontinuities are ignored. However, you can use the **showremovable** suboption to draw a circle on the plot to mark the point of discontinuity. Another suboption is **usefdiscont**, which controls how the **fdiscont** command is used to find discontinuities numerically. For more information about all the suboptions available for the **discont** option, refer to the **plot/discont** help page.

Colors

The **color** option is used to specify the color of plot objects in 2-D and 3-D plots, and its value can take several forms. A few of these are described in this section. For more details, refer to the **plot/color** help page. Default colors are chosen by Maple when none are specified.

Specifying a Single Color

The easiest way to apply a color to a plot object is to provide the name of a color known to the Maple plotting commands. The list of all such color names and their associated RGB values is available on the **plot/colornames** help page. These names correspond to commonly used HTML color names.

```
> plot3d(binomial, 0..5, 0..5, 'color'="Niagara GreenishBlue");
```

Alternatively, a plot color structure can be used as the value for the **color** option. This takes one of the following forms: **COLOR(RGB, v1, v2, v3)**, **COLOR(HSV, v1, v2, v3)**, or **COLOR(HUE, v1)**. More information about the **COLOR** structure is available in the **plot/structure** help page.

Using Multiple Colors

The **color** option can be applied to individual objects that are then combined using the **plots:-display** command. Some commands, such as **plot**, allow you to provide a list of objects to be plotted as well as a list of colors to be applied in order.

```
> plot([seq(i+sin(x), i = 1 .. 4)], x = 0 .. 4*Pi, 'color'= ["Niagara
    Navy", "Niagara Burgundy", "Niagara Olive", "Niagara PaleRed"]);
```

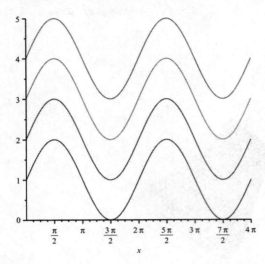

If no colors are provided, the **plot** command uses a default list of colors. To see the default list used by **plot** and several other 2-D plotting commands, use the **plots:-setcolors** command.

```
> plots:-setcolors();
```

$$\begin{aligned}&\text{["\#78000E", "\#000E78", "\#4A7800", "\#3E578A", "\#780072",}\\&\text{"\#00786A", "\#604191", "\#004A78", "\#784C00", "\#91414A",}\\&\text{"\#3E738A", "\#78003B", "\#00783F", "\#914186", "\#510078",}\\&\text{"\#777800"]}\end{aligned}$$
(12.3)

```
> plot([seq(i+sin(x), i = 1 .. 4)], x = 0 .. 4*Pi);
```

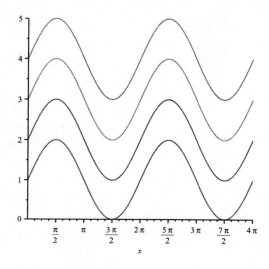

The **plots:-setcolors** command also allows you to set new default colors. If there are fewer colors than curves, the colors are repeated in order.

```
> plots:-setcolors(["Indigo", "ForestGreen"]):
```

```
> plot([seq(i+sin(x), i = 1 .. 4)], x = 0 .. 4*Pi);
```

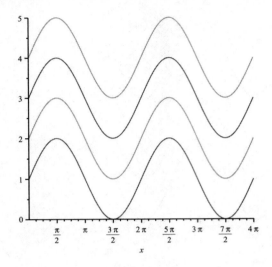

The following command resets the colors to the original default colors.

```
> plots:-setcolors('default'):
```

The ColorTools Package

The **ColorTools** package contains commands for working with colors and color palettes, as well as converting between supported color formats. For a complete list of ColorTools commands and supported color formats, see the **ColorTools** help page.

Coloring 3-D Surfaces

When you plot a 3-D surface, the surface is shaded using a default shading scheme based on the coordinates of the points that define the surface. As with 2-D plots, a single color can be provided through the **color** option. Alternatively, a different shading may be specified with the **shading** option.

```
> plot3d(x^2*y, x=-1..1, y=-1..1, 'shading'='zgreyscale');
```

You can obtain a customized shading parametrized by the plot variables. To do this, provide an expression or a list of three expressions in terms of the plot variables. If a single expression is given, it is taken to be a hue value; if a list of three expressions is given, the triplet is taken to be RGB values.

```
> plot3d(x^2*y, x = -Pi/2 .. Pi/2, y = -1 .. 1, color = y^2*cos(x));
```

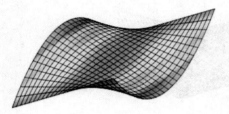

Similarly, if the input is given as procedures instead of expressions in two plotting variables, the color can be specified by a procedure or a list of three procedures that take two input parameters and return a single value. More details are provided in the **plot3d/colorfunc** help page.

View

The **view** option determines the extent of the axes in the rendered plot. In the next example, the plot data structure produced by the **plot** command contains all the points generated from the given range, **-2..4**. However, the view is restricted to the portion of the plot in the box defined by x values in the range **-1..3** and y values in the range **-3..0**.

```
> plot(-x^2+2*x-1, x=-2..4, 'axes'='boxed', 'thickness'=3,
    'view'=[-1..3,-3..0]);
```

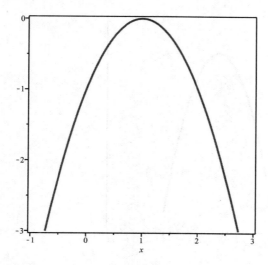

In the next example, the specified *x*-axis view is much larger than the range. Since the computed points are based on the range $x = -2..4$, the displayed curve is only shown for this range. To generate the curve for the entire *x* range from -5 to 7, you must re-execute the plot with **x=-5..7** as the second argument.

```
> plot(-x^2+2*x-1, x=-2..4, axes=boxed, thickness=3, view=[-5..7,
  -10..2]);
```

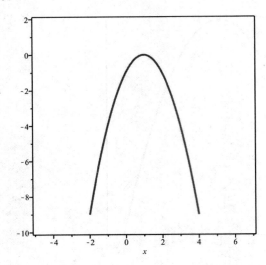

In certain cases, the plotting command automatically sets the view option based on the provided ranges. Otherwise, the default view is determined by the minimum and maximum values of the data points generated.

smartview option

The **plot** command generates data based on the range provided by the user or on a default range, if the user does not provide range data. When the **smartview=true** option is provided, the view is restricted to the most important regions of the plot.

To prevent such a restriction use the **smartview=false** option.

For example:

```
> plot(1/(x-1));
```

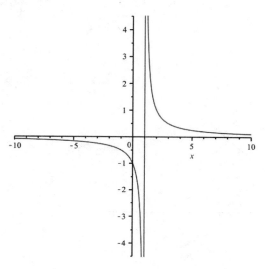

```
> plot(1/(x-1),view=alldata);
Error, (in plot) expecting option view to be of type {"default",
list({"default", range(realcons)}), range(realcons)} but received
alldata
```

Typesetting

Typeset text and mathematics can appear anywhere in a 2-D or 3-D plot where text is allowed. This includes text provided by the **plots:-textplot** command and the following options: **caption, labels, legend, tickmarks**, and **title**.

You can provide arbitrary expressions to the **textplot** command or as values for the options to the command. These expressions are displayed on the plot as typeset output whenever possible. Strings are displayed as plain text without the quotation marks, but names such as **x, y**, and **Pi** are typeset. To concatenate several expressions, wrap them inside a typeset structure.

```
> plot(x^2/(x+5), x=1..5, 'caption'='typeset'("A plot of ",
  x^2/(x+5), "."));
```

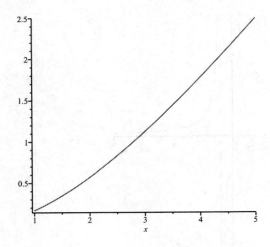

A plot of $\frac{x^2}{x+5}$.

The **plot/typesetting** help page provides more details about using typeset mathematics in plots. It includes tips on using 2-D math input to generate typeset expressions that are not easily expressed in 1-D math input. These expressions can then be made into atomic identifiers through the context menu and then converted to 1-D math to be used programmatically. For more information about 1-D and 2-D math input modes, see *2-D Math (page 379)*.

Axes and Gridlines

Several options are available for customizing the look of axes and gridlines, including:

- **axes** and **axesfont** for specifying the style of axes and the font for tickmark labels
- **labels** and **labelfont** for adding labels to axes and specifying the font for the labels
- **gridlines** for adding gridlines to 2-D plots.
- **tickmarks** for controlling the number of tickmarks or for specifying custom tickmarks and labels

```
> plots:-implicitplot([x^2-y^2 = 1, y = exp(x)], x = -Pi .. Pi, y
  = -Pi .. Pi, 'color' = ["Blue", "DarkGreen"], 'axes' = 'boxed',
  'tickmarks' = [3, 3], 'labelfont' = ["Times", 16]);
```

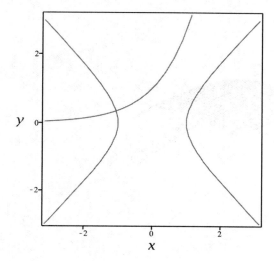

You can obtain greater control over the look of each axis by using the **axis** or **axis[dir]** option and providing a list of suboptions. To apply suboptions to one axis, use the indexed **axis[dir]** option, where the direction **dir** is 1, 2, or 3, with 3 applicable to 3-D plots only. To apply the suboptions to all axes, use the **axis** option without the index.

The suboptions include **gridlines** and **tickmarks** options, which are similar to the regular options of these names but offer more flexibility. Other suboptions are **color** (to change the color of an axis), **location** (to move an axis to the lowest or highest value of the view range or to the origin), and **mode**. This last suboption allows you to use logarithmic scaling for an axis. (Note that you can also create log plots with the **plots:-logplot**, **plots:-semilogplot**, and **plots:-loglogplot** commands.)

```
> plot3d(x*y, x = 1 .. 10, y = 1 .. 10, 'axes' = 'normal', 'axis'[3]
    = ['mode' = 'log', 'color' = "Crimson"]);
```

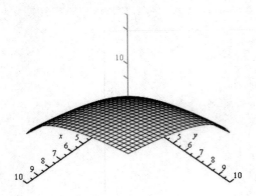

Coordinate Systems

Plots are normally plotted in the Cartesian coordinate system, but you can use the **coords** option to plot in a different system. The 2-D and 3-D coordinate systems recognized by Maple and the transformations that they represent are listed in the **coords** help page.

```
> plot3d(y, x=-Pi..Pi, y=0..2*Pi, 'coords'='cylindrical');
```

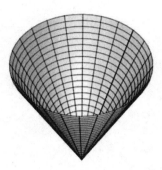

The **coords** option must be used at the time the plot is generated. However, the **plots:-changecoords** command can be used to transform a plot structure that has already been created to one that uses a different coordinate system.

When working with alternate coordinate systems, two useful commands are **plots:-coordplot** and **plots:-coordplot3d**, which provide graphical representations of coordinate systems using lines or surfaces of constant value.

> `plots:-coordplot('rose', 'color'=["Blue", "Magenta"]);`

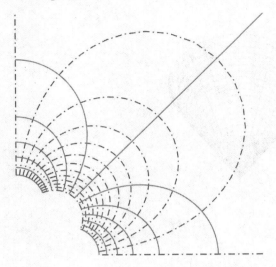

Because the polar coordinate system is commonly used, Maple has a **plots:-polarplot** command for plotting in this system. Polar axes are displayed by default, and special options are available for customizing the look of these axes. In particular, the **coordinateview** option can be used to restrict the view in the polar coordinate system.

```
> plots:-polarplot([[t, t, t = -Pi .. Pi], [2*cos(t), sin(t), t =
  -Pi .. Pi]], 'color' = ["DarkRed", "Brown"], 'axis'['angular'] =
  ['color' = "Navy"], 'coordinateview'=[0..4, 0..Pi]);
```

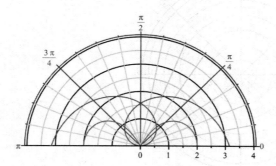

The style of the coordinate axes (either **polar** or **cartesian**) can be changed with the **axiscoordinates** option. This option is available for 2-D plots in general and is not restricted to the **polarplot** command.

```
> plot([s*sin(s), s*cos(s), s = 0 .. 4*Pi], 'axiscoordinates' =
  'polar');
```

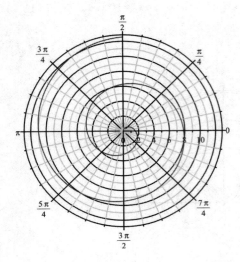

Setting Options

The section *Colors (page 452)* describes the use of the **plots:-setcolors** commands to set the default curve colors for 2-D plots. More general commands for setting options for all 2-D and 3-D plotting commands are **plots:-setoptions** and **plots:-setoptions3d**.

The **plots:-setoptions** command allows you to specify options that are applied to all 2-D plots created in the same Maple session. The **plots:-setoptions3d** command performs a similar function for 3-D plots. These settings are recognized by the **plot**, **plot3d**, and **plots:-display** commands, as well as a number of other plotting commands in Maple.

In the following example, the default symbol for point plots is set to **solidcircle** with a symbol size of 20.

```
> plots:-setoptions('symbol'='solidcircle','symbolsize'=20);
```

> `plots:-pointplot([seq([i, i^2], i=0..10)]);`

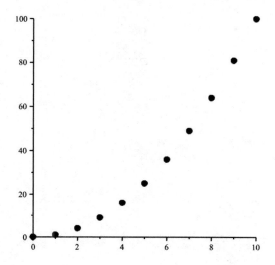

The default value is overridden in the following example, which provides the **symbol** option explicitly in a command.

```
> plots:-pointplot([seq([i, i^2], i=0..10)], 'symbol'='box');
```

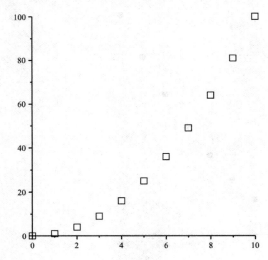

12.7 Animations

Building an Animation with plots:-display

The **plots:-display** command can be used to build an animation. The calling sequence is

```
plots:-display(L, insequence=true)
```

where **L** is a list of plot structures, all 2-D or all 3-D. An animation will be created in which the plots in **L** appear in sequence, one in each frame.

```
> for i to 10 do
      plotframe[i] := plot(0.75*x^i, x=0..1):
  end do:
  plots:-display([seq(plotframe[i], i=1..10)], insequence=true,
  scaling=constrained);
```

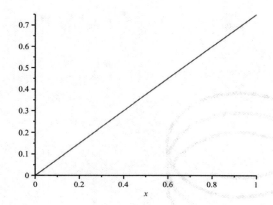

The plots:-animate command

The **plots:-animate** command can be used to create an animation from a single command with one varying parameter. Any Maple plotting command that produces a 2-D or 3-D plot, including ones in packages not primarily intended for plotting, can be used.

The following example shows how to create an animation with the **plots:-spacecurve** command. The first argument to **animate** is the procedure name. The second argument is the list of arguments to be passed the the given procedure. This list contains a parameter whose range, over which the animation will vary, is given in the final argument to **animate**.

472 • 12 Graphics

```
> plots:-animate(plots:-spacecurve, [[cos(t), sin(t), (2+sin(a))*t],
    t=0..20, 'thickness'=5, 'numpoints'=100, 'color'="Black"],
    a=0..2*Pi);
```

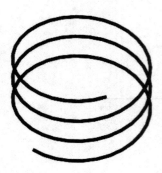

a = 0.

You can animate a custom procedure instead of a Maple library command.

```
> p := proc (s, t) plots:-display([plottools:-disk([s*cos(s),
    s*sin(s)], 1, 'color' = "Orange"), plottools:-disk([t*cos(t),
    t*sin(t)], 2, 'color' = "Blue")], 'scaling' = 'constrained') end
    proc:
```

```
> plots:-animate(p, [a, a+3*Pi], a=0..4*Pi);
```

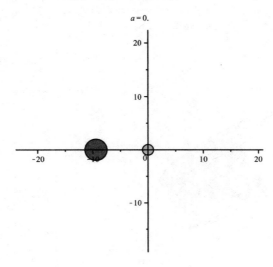

3-D Animations with the viewpoint Option

An animation can be generated from any static 3-D plot with the **viewpoint** option. This option allows you to create the animation by varying the viewpoint through the plot, as if a camera were flying through the space. The position, direction, and orientation of the camera can be varied.

There are several ways to create the animation, which are all described on the **plot3d/viewpoint** help page. The simplest way is to use one of the standard viewpoint paths, such as **circleleft**.

```
> plots:-polyhedraplot([0, 0, 0], 'polytype'='OctagonalPrism',
  'scaling'='constrained', 'viewpoint'='circleleft',
  'lightmodel'='light3', 'glossiness'=1);
```

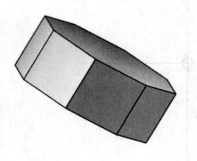

Another way is to provide a parametrically defined path.

```
> plot3d(1, x = 0..2*Pi, y = 0..Pi, 'coords'='spherical',
   'viewpoint'=['path'=[[50*t, 80*cos(t), 100*sin(t)], t=-3*Pi..Pi]]);
```

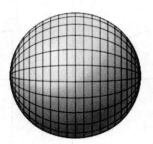

Other Animation Commands

There are a number of other commands in Maple for creating animations, such as **plots:-animatecurve** (for visualizing the drawing of a curve) and ones for specific applications such as those in the **Student** package.

Displaying an Animation as an Array of Plots

Animations, like other plots, can be combined using the **plots:-display** command and put into arrays of plots. You can display an entire animation, frame by frame, in a table by passing it directly to the **plots:-display** command.

```
> anim := plots:-animatecurve([sin(t), cos(t), t=0..2*Pi],
   'thickness'=3, 'color'="Indigo", 'frames'=9):
```

```
> plots:-display(anim, 'view'=[-1..1, -1..1],
    'scaling'='constrained');
```

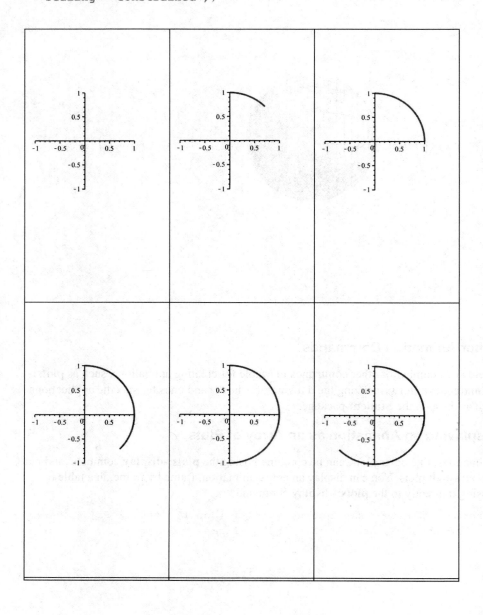

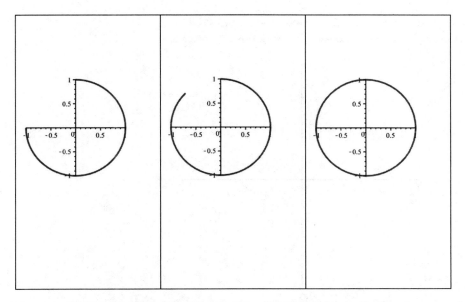

If you specify the **insequence** option to **plots:-display**, then it is displayed as a regular animation.

```
> plots:-display(anim, 'view'=[-1..1, -1..1],
   'scaling'='constrained', 'insequence'=true);
```

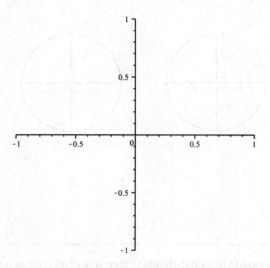

12.8 Miscellaneous Topics

Efficiency in Plotting

The Floating-Point Environment

The plotting commands attempt to evaluate the input expressions or procedures using the floating-point hardware of the underlying system whenever possible. This is done through calls to the **evalhf** command. If the environment variable **Digits** is greater than the value of **evalhf(Digits)**, or if an initial attempt using **evalhf** fails, then the slower **evalf** command is used for numerical evaluation. For an introduction to the **evalhf** and **evalf** commands, see *Maple Commands for Numerical Computing (page 287)*.

To maximize efficiency, expressions and procedures passed to plotting commands should be written so that they can be evaluated by **evalhf** if possible. For more information on the functions and constructs supported by **evalhf**, refer to the **evalhf/procedure** and **evalhf/fcnlist** help pages.

Lists and rtables

Plotting large datasets of points is much more efficient when you use **rtables** rather than lists. For instance, for efficiency, when using the **plots:-pointplot** and **plots:-pointplot3d** commands, provide the input as a **Matrix** of datatype **float[8]**. If your data is in an external file, it can be imported directly into a **Matrix** with the **ImportMatrix** command.

It is recommended that you build plot structures by using the commands in the plotting library. However, if you want to build the plot structures directly, similar guidelines apply. Most plot data structures (described in *Data Structures (page 441)*) allow the data to be stored in either a list or an **rtable**. **rtables** should be used for those structures that support them, and they should be created with the **datatype=float[8]** and **order=C_order** options.

Interfaces and Devices

The Maple standard worksheet interface provides all of the functionality for plotting described in this chapter. If you are using another interface, then some of the plotting features will not be available. For more details about the differences, refer to the **plot/interface** help page.

With any of these interfaces, you can redirect plotting output to an alternative device. The devices available are listed in the **plot/device** help page and include common graphics formats such as JPEG and PostScript®.

Plot output is controlled by a number of interface variables such as **plotdevice** (the name of the plotting device) and **plotoutput** (the name of an output file). These are described in the **interface** help page. The **plotsetup** command provides a simpler way to set up these interface variables, without having to use the **interface** command directly.

For example, the following command specifies that all subsequent plot output be in PostScript format and be saved in a file called **plot.ps**. Furthermore, the PostScript driver will use a portrait orientation with no border. The **plotsetup(default)** command restores the default output options.

```
> plotsetup('ps', 'plotoutput'="plot.ps", 'plotoptions' =
  "portrait,noborder");
> plotsetup('default');
```

12.9 Avoiding Common Problems

Mixing Expression and Operator Forms

If the first argument to a plotting command is an expression in the plotting variable, these same plotting variables must appear in the range arguments. A common mistake is to omit the plotting variable in the ranges or to use a different variable name accidentally. It is also a mistake to provide a procedure as the first argument but then to use variable names in the subsequent range arguments. The first example below generates an error, while the next one produces an empty plot with a warning that the plotting function could not be evaluated to numeric values.

```
> plot(sin, x=0..Pi);
```
Error, (in plot) expected a range but received x = 0 .. Pi
```
> plot(sin(x), 0..Pi);
```
Error, (in plot) procedure expected, as range contains no plotting variable

Another common mistake is to use the expression form when you mean to provide an operator. A typical example is the following:

```
> p := proc(x) if type(x, 'positive') then sqrt(x) else 0 end if;
  end proc;
```

$$p := \mathbf{proc}(x) \\ \quad \mathbf{if}\ type(x, 'positive')\ \mathbf{then}\ \mathrm{sqrt}(x)\ \mathbf{else}\ 0\ \mathbf{end\ if} \\ \mathbf{end\ proc} \tag{12.4}$$

The correct way to plot this procedure over the range -1 to 1 is the use operator form.

```
> plot(p, -1..1, 'axes'='boxed');
```

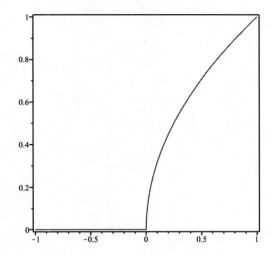

If you attempt to use expression form, then **p(x)** is evaluated immediately, the value 0 is passed to the **plot** command as the first argument, and the resulting plot is a horizontal line.

```
> plot(p(x), x=-1..1, 'axes'='boxed');
```

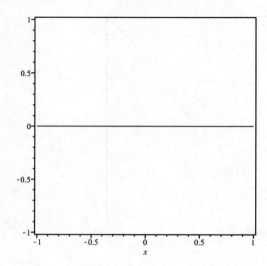

Generating Non-numeric Data

Most of the Maple plotting commands are meant to work with real-valued functions, though specialized commands such as **plots[complexplot]** are available for plotting complex-valued functions. Generally, when evaluation of the input expression or procedure results in a complex value, the value is replaced by an undefined value. Many plotting commands check for numbers with very small imaginary parts and will convert these numbers to real numbers, with the criteria for dropping an imaginary part depending on the **Digits** environment variable and on its relative size compared to the real part. This procedure helps to avoid problems caused by round-off errors during the computation. However, it is advisable to ensure that the input expression or procedure always evaluates to a numeric value.

In the first example below, the ragged edge is caused by the fact that some of the values are undefined. The second example, which has the range of **t** going from 0 to **s** instead of 0 to 1, produces a more accurate plot.

```
> plot3d(sqrt(s^2-t^2), s=0..1, t=0..1);
```

```
> plot3d(sqrt(s^2-t^2), s=0..1, t=0..s);
```

Non-numeric data can also be produced as the result of mistyping a variable name. In the example below, the second argument mistakenly contains the variable **z** instead of **x**. Consequently, when a numeric value in the range **0..Pi** is substituted for the variable **z** in the expression **sin(x)**, the result remains the algebraic expression **sin(x)**, which is non-numeric. This leads to a warning from Maple and an empty plot.

12.9 Avoiding Common Problems

```
> plot(sin(x), z=0..Pi);
```
Warning, expecting only range variable z in expression sin(x) to be plotted but found name x

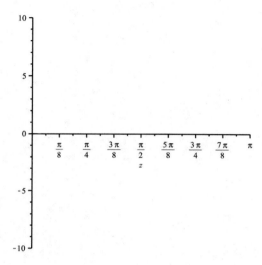

13 Programming Interactive Elements

The Maple standard interface provides several tools for building interactive mathematical content. It includes a set of *embedded components*, which are configurable graphical controls, buttons, meters, and other interactive components that you can insert in a Maple document to analyze, manipulate, and visualize equations and Maple commands. For example, several task templates in Maple use embedded components to demonstrate mathematical concepts.

The Maple library also includes a package called *Maplets* for building custom user interfaces to allow users to perform analysis tasks related to your mathematics. Several Maple commands, such as the tutors in the **Student** package, use Maplets that allow users to perform various tasks.

13.1 In This Chapter

- Programming embedded components
- Programming Maplets

13.2 Programming Embedded Components

In the Maple standard interface, embedded components are available in the **Components** palette. These components include boxes, lists, gauges, and dials.

Adding Embedded Components to a Document

When you click an icon in the **Components** palette, the corresponding embedded component is inserted in your document at the current cursor location. For example, you can insert a button Button within a paragraph, or you can include a series of plot components, sliders, and check boxes that function together.

You can use a table to lay out the components in your document. To insert a table, from the **Insert** menu, select **Table**. You can then insert buttons, plots, gauges, math, text, and so on in each table cell.

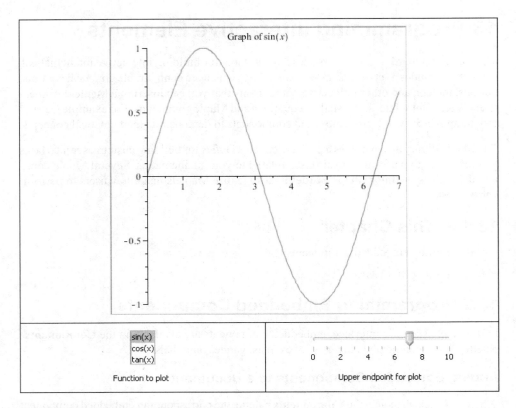

Editing Component Properties

Embedded components can be programmed to accomplish specific tasks when mouse actions are performed. For example, button components and sliders can be programmed to display information when they are clicked or dragged, and a plot component can be programmed to display points when it is clicked. To program an embedded component to perform a task, you must edit the properties of the embedded component and, in most cases, provide the code needed to accomplish the task.

For example, if you want to provide code for a button component, you would right-click (**Control**-click for Macintosh) the button component that you inserted in your document and select **Properties**. You would then click the **Edit** button beside **Action When Clicked** to display a window in which you can enter the code (see **Figure 13.1**). By default, this window contains sample code that you can start with.

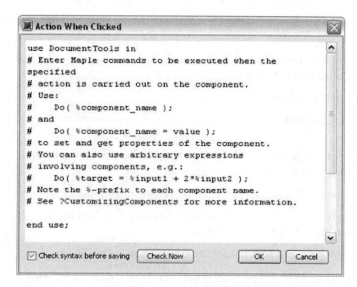

Figure 13.1: Code Region for an Embedded Component

Each embedded component has different properties that you can edit. For more information about the properties for a specific component, refer to the **EmbeddedComponents** help page and browse to the page of the component that you want to use.

Tip: If you are working with multiple components in a document, you may find it easier to include the code for all of the component actions in one area, for example, the startup code region of your document. For more information, see the **worksheet,documenting,startup-code** help page.

Example: Creating a Tic-Tac-Toe Game

In the following example, a tic-tac-toe game will be created using embedded components in Maple. This example contains nine list boxes that are organized in a 3 by 3 table.

It is possible to associate code with each of the list boxes individually. However, if you want to change this code in the future, you would need to change it in nine places. A simpler approach is to write a Maple module that contains the code to perform the action and call that code from each list box.

1. Open a new Maple document.
2. To insert a table, from the **Insert** menu, select **Table...**

3. In the **Rows** and **Columns** fields, enter **3**, and click **OK**.

4. Place your cursor in the top-left cell of your table.

5. On the left side of the Maple window, open the **Components** palette and click the list box component icon.

6. In your document, right-click (**Control**-click for Macintosh) the list box component that you inserted and select **Component Properties...**

7. Click the **Edit** button beside **Item List**.

8. In the item list, double-click **ListBox**, replace this value with a hyphen character (-), and press **Enter**.

9. Click the **Add** button, double-click the new field, enter **X** in this field, and press **Enter**. Repeat this step to add a list item for **O**.

10. To close the dialog box, click **OK**.

11. Click the **Edit** button beside **Action When Selection Changes** and replace the default code with **TicTacToe:-Select(%this);**, and click **OK**.

12. In the **Name** field, specify the name **ListBox0** for the component.

Tip: Make sure that all of the embedded components in your document have unique names.

13. To close the **Properties** dialog box, click **OK**.

14. In the document, select the list box, and then copy and paste it into all of the remaining cells.

Note: You can copy and paste embedded components within a document or from one document to another. A unique name is assigned to each pasted component - the number in the component name is incremented. Other details associated with the component, for example, properties and actions, are copied in their original form.

15. Below the table, enter the following module to perform the action.

```
> TicTacToe := module()
      uses DT = DocumentTools;
      export Select;
      Select := proc( what )
          if DT:-GetProperty( what, 'value' ) <> "-" then
              DT:-SetProperty( what, 'enabled', false );
          end if;
      end proc;
  end module;
```

The **%this** argument, which is passed as the value of the **what** parameter to the **TicTacToe:-Select** procedure, is set to the name of the component that generates the action. Therefore, the result is that if you select either the "X" or the "O" list element, the list box is dimmed and the user's selection cannot be changed.

For more information about modules, see *Programming with Modules (page 309)*.

Alternatively, you can save this module in a Maple library archive, which is a separate file in which you can store Maple procedures, modules, and other data. For more information, refer to the **repository** help page.

Retrieving and Updating Component Properties

The examples above use commands from the **DocumentTools** package to retrieve information from components and update component properties. This package includes the following commands.

- **GetProperty**: Retrieve information from a component.
- **SetProperty**: Update a component.
- **Do**: An alternate interface to both **GetProperty** and **SetProperty**. This command can be used to retrieve and update components.

For more information about the properties that can be retrieved and set for each component, refer to the **EmbeddedComponents** help page and browse to the help page of the component that you want to use.

Using the GetProperty Command to Retrieve Properties

You can specify two arguments for the **DocumentTools:-GetProperty** command: the name of the component and the property (or option) to be retrieved. **Note:** The value returned by the **GetProperty** command will either be a number or a string. For example, the command **DocumentTools:-GetProperty(component_name, 'visible')** returns a value of "true" or "false". To retrieve the corresponding Boolean value, the result must be processed by the **parse** command: **parse(DocumentTools:-GetProperty(component_name, 'visible'))** returns a value of **true** or **false**. However, in many cases, this extra step is not necessary. For example, the comparison

```
> if DocumentTools:-GetProperty( component_name, 'visible' ) = "true"
    then
```

will be faster than

```
> if parse( DocumentTools:-GetProperty( component_name, 'visible'
    ) ) then
```

Using the SetProperty Command to Update Properties

You can specify the following arguments for the **DocumentTools:-SetProperty** command: the name of the component to update, the property to update, the new value for that property, and an optional parameter to indicate whether the update occurs immediately.

Code associated with a component can perform many different tasks. In particular, it can update other components. For example, you can create a plot component that returns certain values displayed in **TextArea** components or makes changes to other plots when the plot component is clicked.

When code is run as a result of a mouse event that updates other components, those updates occur after that code runs successfully. While this process is efficient, in some cases, you might want these updates to occur immediately. In such cases, you can use the optional **refresh = true** parameter, or simply **refresh**.

Using the Do Command to Retrieve and Update Component Properties

The **DocumentTools:-Do** command is a convenient interface to both the **DocumentTools:-GetProperty** and **DocumentTools:-SetProperty** commands. Components can be referenced as variables in expressions. For example, suppose that you have a math container component, two text area components, a button, and a plot component. You can enter a math expression in the variable **x** in the math container, numbers in each of the text areas and click the button, causing the expression to be plotted over the range specified by the numbers. Assuming the components that you inserted in your document are named **MathContainer0**, **TextArea0**, **TextArea1**, **Button0**, and **Plot0**, respectively, you can accomplish this task by using the single command **DocumentTools:-Do(%Plot0 = plot(%MathContainer0, 'x' = %TextArea0 .. %TextArea1))**.

Consider the following points when deciding whether to use the **DocumentTools:-Do** command to retrieve or update components.

- The embedded component type determines the default property retrieved or set by the **Do** command. For most components, the **value** property is the default property that is retrieved or set. This means that the **Do** command must query the GUI to determine which information to retrieve. The **GetProperty** and **SetProperty** commands avoid this step by requiring you to specify which property to retrieve. However, if you are working with a small number of components, this extra step will usually be insignificant.

- The names of components appearing in the first argument to **Do** must be literal names prefixed by **%**. That is, you cannot use the **Do** command to access or update a component with a name that is determined programmatically.

13.3 Programming Maplets

You can use Maplet technology to build custom interfaces for any Maple functionality. Maplets can be run in the Maple standard interface. In Windows, you can also run Maplets in the Maplet Viewer, which is an application that you can run outside of the Maple standard interface. For more information about the Maplet Viewer, refer to the **MapletViewer** help page.

Maplets support standard UI elements including buttons, drop lists, text fields, and sliders. Some of the available UI elements are specific to Maple, for example, math fields and plot regions. For more information about these elements, refer to the **Maplets,Elements** help page.

Before creating a Maplet, familiarize yourself with the features of the various **layout managers**, which define how the elements of your Maplets are positioned and laid out.

This section describes basic information related to laying out elements in Maplets. For advanced information, refer to the **examples,AdvancedMapletsLayout** worksheet.

Layout Managers

A *layout manager* defines the locations and positions of the UI elements in a Maplet window. Three layout managers are available.

- Box layout (**BoxLayout**): this layout manager can be used to create boxes that contain elements positioned horizontally or vertically relative to other elements.
- Grid layout (**GridLayout**): this layout manager positions elements in a specific cells in a grid, similar to a spreadsheet.
- Border layout (**BorderLayout**): this layout manager allows you to lay out elements in specific regions, according to compass directions.

For simple Maplets, using a layout manager is often sufficient; however, for more complex Maplets, you may need to use multiple layout managers or nest layout managers one inside the other.

Note: For clarity, the full command for each layout control is used in this chapter.

The three layout managers are available in the **Maplets,Elements** subpackage of the **Maplets** package. In this chapter, assume that the following command has been run.

```
> with(Maplets:-Elements):
```

This command allows the **Maplets:-Elements** package commands to be used without prefixing them with **Maplets:-Elements:-....**

Box Layout

The **box layout** is the most commonly used layout manager. It is a nested construct of containers where elements can be displayed either horizontally or vertically in the Maplet window. For example,

```
> mlet := Maplet(BoxLayout(border=true, caption="outer",
      BoxColumn(border=true, caption="inner1",
          Button("OK1", onclick=Shutdown()),
          Button("OK2", onclick=Shutdown())
      ),
      BoxColumn(border=true, caption="inner2",
          TextBox("Misc. Text", height=5)
      )
  )):
  Maplets:-Display(mlet);
```

As shown in the example above, you can use a **BoxColumn** element to specify a column in a box layout. You can also use a **BoxRow** element to specify a row in a box layout.

For detailed information about box layouts, refer to the **Maplets,Elements,BoxLayout** help page.

Controlling the Spacing in a Box Layout

In a box layout, box row, or box column you can use the **inset** option to specify the amount of spacing between the border of the box element and its contents.

In a row or column of a box layout, you can also use the **spacing** option to specify the amount of spacing that separates individual elements in that row or column.

The following examples demonstrate the use of these options.(**Note:** In both cases, the outer **BoxLayout** element has the **inset** option set to 0 so that the formatting of the **BoxColumn** element can be displayed more easily):

Example 1: Using the inset Option

In this example, the **spacing** option is set to 0, so the buttons are positioned close to each other in the generated Maplet window. The buttons are positioned in the center of the Maplet because the **inset** value displays space between the buttons and the border of the box element.

```
> mlet := Maplet(BoxLayout(inset=0,
      BoxColumn(inset=10, spacing=0,
          Button("OK1", onclick=Shutdown()),
          Button("OK2", onclick=Shutdown())
      )
```

```
     )):
 Maplets:-Display(mlet);
```

Example 2: Using the spacing Option

In this example, the **spacing** option displays space between the buttons in the generated Maplet window. Also, since the **inset** option is set to 0, no spacing is displayed between the border of the box element and the buttons. As a result, the buttons are closely aligned with the top and bottom borders of the box element.

```
> mlet := Maplet(BoxLayout(inset=0,
      BoxColumn(inset=0, spacing=10,
          Button("OK1", onclick=Shutdown()),
          Button("OK2", onclick=Shutdown())
          )
      )):
 Maplets:-Display(mlet);
```

Displaying Elements Vertically and Horizontally in a Box Layout

The **vertical** option can be specified for box layouts only. When the **vertical** option is set to **false**, elements are displayed horizontally in the Maplet window; when the **vertical** option is set to **true**, elements are displayed vertically. For more control over the spacing of the elements in a box layout, use the box layout with either a **BoxRow** element (when the **vertical** option is set to **false**) or a **BoxColumn** element (when the **vertical** option is set to **true**).

The following example shows two buttons that are positioned vertically and closely spaced.

```
> mlet := Maplet(BoxLayout(inset=0, vertical=true,
      Button("OK1", onclick=Shutdown()),
      Button("OK2", onclick=Shutdown())
      )):
 Maplets:-Display(mlet);
```

In the following example, the spacing has been removed by nesting the buttons in a **BoxColumn** element.

```
> mlet := Maplet(BoxLayout(inset=0,
      BoxColumn(inset=0, spacing=0,
          Button("OK1", onclick=Shutdown()),
          Button("OK2", onclick=Shutdown())
          )
      )):
 Maplets:-Display(mlet);
```

Grid Layout

In a **grid layout**, all of the elements are displayed in a rectangular grid.

Each grid layout must contain one or more **GridRow** elements which must, in turn, contain one or more **GridCell** elements.

Note: Each row or column of the grid is sized according to the maximum height or width of all the elements in that row or column. By default, no spacing is displayed between the largest elements in a grid layout.

The following is a simple example of a grid layout.

```
> mlet := Maplet(GridLayout(border=true, caption="grid",
      GridRow(
          GridCell(Label("Button1:")),
          GridCell(Button("OK1", onclick=Shutdown()))
      ),
      GridRow(
          GridCell(Label("Button2:")),
          GridCell(Button("OK2", onclick=Shutdown()))
      )
   )):
  Maplets:-Display(mlet);
```

For detailed information about grid layouts, refer to the **Maplets,Elements,GridLayout** help page.

Specifying the Width and Height of Grid Cells

You can specify the width and height of a **GridCell** element. The **GridCell** element must be added in the top-left cell in the grid. For example, if you want to create a **GridCell** element with a height of two grid cells, the element must appear in the first **GridRow** that contains it, and the **GridRow** element that follows it will be adjusted to allow it to fit.

```
> mlet := Maplet(GridLayout(
      GridRow(
          GridCell(height=2,
              Button("2h", width=52, height=2*25,
                  onclick=Shutdown())
          ),
          GridCell(
              Button("1a", width=52, height=25,
                  onclick=Shutdown())
          ),
          GridCell(
```

```
                Button("1b", width=52, height=25,
                    onclick=Shutdown()
                )
            ),
            GridRow(
                # This is where the button above extends into
                GridCell(
                    Button("1c", width=52, height=25,
                        onclick=Shutdown()
                    )
                ),
                GridCell(
                    Button("1d", width=52, height=25,
                        onclick=Shutdown()
                    )
                ),
            GridRow(
                GridCell(
                    Button("1e", width=52, height=25,
                        onclick=Shutdown()
                    )
                ),
                GridCell(width=2,
                    Button("2w", width=2*52, height=25,
                        onclick=Shutdown()
                    )
                )
            )
    )):
    Maplets:-Display(mlet);
```

In the following example, the **full** alignment option is used, so it is not necessary to specify a size for each button.

```
> mlet := Maplet(GridLayout(halign=full, valign=full,
        GridRow(
            GridCell(height=2,
                Button("2h", onclick=Shutdown()
                )
            ),
            GridCell(
                Button("1a", onclick=Shutdown()
                )
            ),
            GridCell(
                Button("1b", onclick=Shutdown()
                )
            ),
```

```
        GridRow(
            # This is where the button above extends into
            GridCell(
                Button("1c", onclick=Shutdown())
                ),
            GridCell(
                Button("1d", onclick=Shutdown())
                )
            ),
        GridRow(
            GridCell(
                Button("1e", onclick=Shutdown())
                ),
            GridCell(width=2,
                Button("2w", onclick=Shutdown())
                )
            )
        )):
Maplets:-Display(mlet);
```

Border Layout

Unlike the other layout managers, the **border layout** is a container element for other layout managers, though, it can be used for simple Maplets.

Five positions in the layout can be filled: **north**, **south**, **west**, **east**, and **center**, each of which has its own layout rules. See **Figure 13.2**.

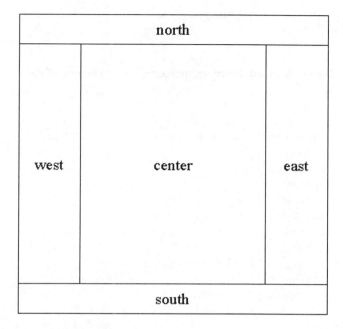

Figure 13.2: Border Layout Diagram

In terms of resizing, **north** and **south** extend horizontally, **east** and **west** extend vertically, and **center** extends in both directions.

Positioning Elements in a Border Layout

The **constraint** option can be used in **GridCell** elements to indicate where its elements should be placed in the Maplet window. Valid options are **north**, **south**, **west**, **east**, and **center**.

The following is a simple example of a border layout.

```
> mlet := Maplet(BorderLayout(
    GridCell2(constraint=north,
        Label("This is a long title")),
    GridCell2(constraint=south,
        Label("This could be a status bar")),
    GridCell2(constraint=east,
        Button("East", onclick=Shutdown())),
    GridCell2(constraint=west,
        Button("West", onclick=Shutdown())),
    GridCell2(constraint=center,
```

```
            Button("Center", onclick=Shutdown()))
    )):
Maplets:-Display(mlet);
```

Not all constraint options need to be specified; however, including more than one of the same constraint returns an error.

Example:

```
> mlet := Maplet(BorderLayout(border=true, caption="borderlayout",
    GridCell2(constraint=north,
        Label("This is a long title")),
    GridCell2(constraint=south,
        Label("This could be a status bar")),
    GridCell2(constraint=east,
        Button("East", onclick=Shutdown())),
    GridCell2(constraint=west,
        Button("West", onclick=Shutdown())),
    GridCell2(constraint=center,
        Button("Center", onclick=Shutdown()))
    )):
Maplets:-Display(mlet);
```

For detailed information about border layouts, refer to the **Maplets,Elements,BorderLayout** help page.

Aligning Elements in a Border Layout

In a **BorderLayout** the north, south, and center cells can extend horizontally, and the east, west, and center cells can extend vertically. As a result, the elements in the border layout can be stretched. Unlike the other layout managers, the elements are stretched to fit within the layout, so alignment must occur in the elements themselves. Note that horizontal alignment options (**halign**) can only be specified for the elements in the north, south, and center **GridCell2** elements, and vertical alignment options (**valign**) can only be specified for the elements in the east, west, and center **GridCell2** elements.

Examples

The following example is the same as the example above, except that the **halign** option has been specified for the north and south labels (note the alignment is specified in the **Label** elements):

```
> mlet := Maplet(BorderLayout(
    GridCell2(constraint=north,
        Label("This is a long title", halign=left)),
    GridCell2(constraint=south,
```

```
            Label("This could be a status bar", halign=left)),
        GridCell2(constraint=east,
            Button("East", onclick=Shutdown())),
        GridCell2(constraint=west,
            Button("West", onclick=Shutdown())),
        GridCell2(constraint=center,
            Button("Center", onclick=Shutdown()))
        )):
    Maplets:-Display(mlet);
```

In the following example, the element in the center cell stretches to fit a larger layout.

```
> mlet := Maplet(BorderLayout(
      GridCell2(constraint=north,
          Label("This is a very long title which causes "
              "the center to stretch")
          ),
      GridCell2(constraint=east, Button("East", onclick=Shutdown())),

      GridCell2(constraint=west, Button("West", onclick=Shutdown())),

       GridCell2(constraint=center, Button("Center",
  onclick=Shutdown()))
      )):
  Maplets:-Display(mlet);
```

14 Advanced Connectivity

This chapter describes how to connect Maple to other applications. Maple can be connected as the main interface (for example, to a database), as a hidden engine (for example, as part of a Microsoft® Excel® plug-in), or side-by-side with another application (for example, a CAD application). You can also use Maple to generate code.

14.1 In This Chapter

- Connecting to the Maple engine
- Embedding external libraries in Maple
- Connecting Maple to another program
- Code generation

Connecting to the Maple Engine

There are several ways to use the Maple computation engine in other applications. For example, you can create a financial application that runs calculations using the MapleNet web service API; create a plug-in for Microsoft Excel in both Visual Basic and C++ to perform Maple computations in a spreadsheet; and create an engineering process to generate and batch process scripts using the Maple command-line interface. These are examples of real situations where you can use Maple as a calculation engine embedded in an external interface.

For more information, see *MapleNet (page 504)*, *OpenMaple (page 506)*, and *The Maple Command-line Interface (page 516)*.

Using External Libraries in Maple

Most dynamic link-libraries (.dlls) that contain mathematical functions written in another programming language can be linked directly in Maple. Using the commands in these libraries usually requires you to translate the Maple data into a format that the external library can interpret. Maple provides an extensive API for data conversions, evaluation, and process control. You can, therefore, use a custom library of functions in Maple as if it were a regular Maple package. You can also use the Maple external API to connect Maple to a hardware device for data acquisition, link with an open source suite of utilities, or to avoid rewriting legacy code.

For more information, see *External Calling: Using Compiled Code in Maple (page 518)*.

Connecting Maple to Another Program

You can set up Maple to communicate with another program by using the Maple external API. For example, by using the **CAD** package, you can set up Maple to communicate with

CAD applications. Other methods are available, such as setting up a communication channel to the other program using the **Sockets** package.

For more information, see *CAD Connectivity (page 541)*, *Maple Plug-in for Excel (page 542)*, *Connecting MATLAB and Maple (page 543)*, and *Accessing Data over a Network with TCP/IP Sockets (page 530)*.

Code Generation

The Maple programming language and the worksheet environment are ideal for creating prototypes. They are also ideal for error-free algebraic manipulations and long calculations. When you create a prototype that includes various formulas, you can easily write that program in the native language that is used by your application. The generated code can then be compiled and embedded directly in your application.

The **CodeGeneration** package provides commands for translating Maple code into other programming languages such as C, Visual C#, Fortran, Java, MATLAB®, and Visual Basic. The resulting code can be compiled and used in applications other than Maple.

For more information, see *Code Generation (page 531)*.

14.2 MapleNet

You can use MapleNet to publish your Maple applications on the web. Two key features are provided by MapleNet: in-browser interfaces and the ability to connect to a Maple computation engine over the Internet or an intranet.

MapleNet is a Maple add-on product. For more information, visit **http://www.maplesoft.com/products/maplenet/index.aspx**.

Computation on Demand

A *web service* is software on a web server that listens for requests and waits to perform a specific job. The MapleNet web service, in particular, waits to run Maple commands.

A desktop application that has a network connection can communicate with the MapleNet web service to perform computations. The client computer that runs the desktop application does not require Maple, a Maple license, or specific software to communicate with the web service.

The server-side infrastructure for Maple web services is provided by the MapleNet API. You can build client applications to use the MapleNet web service by using tools such as the Microsoft C# toolkit, Apache™ Axis plug-in for Eclipse, IBM® WebSphere®, and the NetBeans IDE.

Web services are defined by using a file containing the Web Services Description Language (WSDL). Before creating a client application, download the definition of the MapleService by using the WSDL file located at the following URL.

http://yourserver.com:port/maplenet/services/MapleService?wsdl

This URL points to a link on your server where MapleNet is installed. **yourserver.com** is the name or IP address of your MapleNet server and **port** is the HTTP port on which your server listens for requests (for example, 80 or 8080).

This URL can be used in your web services toolkit so that you can create the code to connect to the MapleService web service.

The following language-independent APIs are the most commonly used methods in the web service.
```
String    result  = evaluate(String expression);
String[]  results = callMaple(String[] expressions);
```

The **evaluate** method accepts a string that is a valid Maple expression and returns a string corresponding to the results generated by Maple after evaluating that expression.

The **callMaple** method accepts an array of strings of valid Maple expressions and returns an equivalent number of strings corresponding to the results generated by Maple after each expression is evaluated.

When a call to the web service is complete, the Maple kernel is released. In other words, the state (for example, variable assignments) is not preserved.

Results are returned from the web service call as text. The text can either be a 1-D Maple output expression or a Base64-encoded plot. Plot results take the following form.
```
"_Base64GIF(width,height,data)"
```

In this example, **_Base64GIF** is a literal text string, which indicates that the result is an encoded plot. Following this string are two integers indicating the width and height of the output plot. Finally, **data** is the binary plot data, which is a Base64-encoded .gif image. A Base64 decoder must be used to translate the data into binary data that can either be rendered by your client application or written out to form the bytes of a .gif file.

For more information and examples, refer to the **MapleNet Publisher's Guide**.

Embedding a Maple Application in a Web Application

Embedding a Maple application is easy: save your Maple document on a MapleNet server, open a web browser, and point to the saved .mw file. Your worksheet is not only visible, but also interactive if you included buttons, plots, or other embedded components in the .mw file.

Maplet applications are also easy to publish over the web.

Maple can also be embedded in larger web applications and used as the underlying computation engine for your application. For example, by using MapleNet functionality, you can use Maple as the graphics engine for scientific or business plots; you can also create an equation editor to read formula input or display formatted equations.

You can also use two other technologies to include Maple as part of your web applications: Java applets and JavaServer Pages (JSP).

Java applets, in conjunction with the MapleNet Java API, extend the browser capabilities beyond those provided by HTML alone. For example, the Maple equation editor is an applet that you can use to capture input using natural math notation. Another applet allows you to embed 3-D plots with controls for rotation, zooming, and changing properties such as constrained access and color shading. By using the Java API, you can create custom applets, for example, an applet that plots points in-place where you click, and uses Maple to compute a smooth curve that interpolates the points. To run applets, you require a Java-enabled browser.

JSP provides an alternate technology. Unlike applets, JSP pages are resolved on the server; the client computer only processes HTML code. Therefore, no special requirements are needed for the browser or computer running the browser to display the JSP results.

JSP is an extension to HTML. An HTML file can be extended by adding <maple> tags. When the web server displays one of these pages, it replaces the <maple> tags with the result of the specified computation. The result is an embedded image, text, or any other element that you want to include.

MapleNet comes with complete documentation and detailed examples. For more information on the Java applet and JSP APIs, refer to the **MapleNet Publisher's Guide**.

14.3 OpenMaple

OpenMaple is an interface that lets you access the Maple computation engine by referencing its dynamic-link library (.dll) file.

> **Note:** The **OpenMaple** interface is available on all platforms supported by Maple. The convention in this guide is to use the terminology related to **.dll** files, in place of **.so** or **.dylib** on other systems.

You can use this interface to embed calls to Maple in other applications.

Interfaces to access the OpenMaple API are provided for use with C, C++, Java, Fortran, C#, and Visual Basic. All of these interfaces are built on the C API, so they all reference the primary library, **maplec.dll**, which is located in your Maple binary directory. This library can be accessed from other languages by following the protocol established in the **maplec.dll** file.

Complete example programs are available in the **samples/OpenMaple** subdirectory of your Maple installation. In conjunction with reading this section, you may want to try extending one or more of those examples before creating your own programs.

Application-specific header files can be found in the **extern/include** subdirectory of your Maple installation. If you are developing a Java application, you can find the **jopenmaple.jar** file in the **java** subdirectory of your Maple installation.

Runtime Environment Prerequisites

To run your application, two paths must be set up in your local environment.

- the path to the **maplec.dll** file
- the path to the top-level directory in which Maple is installed

In Windows, depending on the source programming language, calls to initialize the **OpenMaple** interface will locate these paths automatically so that the Maple commands will work without additional configuration steps.

Note: If your application does not initialize, set your Windows **%PATH%** environment variable to include the Maple **bin.win** or **bin.X86_64_WINDOWS** directory. To find out which path to use, run the **kernelopts(bindir)** command in Maple.

In UNIX, Linux, Solaris, and Macintosh, the **MAPLE**, and **LD_LIBRARY_PATH** or **DYLD_LIBRARY_PATH** environment variables must be set before starting your application. To set these environment variables, add the following lines to the start-up script of your calling application, where **$MAPLE** is your Maple installation directory.

```
#!/bin/sh
export MAPLE="/usr/local/maple"
. $MAPLE/bin/maple -norun
myapp $*
```

These commands run the **maple** launch script to configure your environment without starting Maple. The period (.) prefix in a Bourne shell causes the commands to be *sourced*, thus, applying the settings to future sessions. Starting the application would be done via the above script rather than calling the executable directly.

Interface Overview

Each **OpenMaple** application contains the following components:

- a *text callback* to display or hide the output generated by Maple when an expression is evaluated

- commands to initialize the Maple engine
- calls to API commands to compute with Maple

The examples in this section show how to run a Maple computation using the **OpenMaple** API. Each example evaluates an expression and then exits. The examples in this section are intended to help you get started using the API. For detailed examples and descriptions, refer to the **OpenMaple** help page.

Text Callbacks

In each example, a text callback is defined. Output that would normally be displayed after an expression is evaluated in a Maple session is routed through *callbacks*. This output includes the following:

- results from evaluated commands that are terminated with a semicolon
- output from the **print** command, the **printf** command, and other display-related commands
- **userinfo** and warning messages
- diagnostic output from the debugger, high settings from **printlevel**, and trace output
- error messages if no error callback is defined
- resource status messages if no status callback is defined
- displayed help pages

The text callback is not the only way to control output in your **OpenMaple** application. For more control, individual results can be converted to strings, which can be displayed in text boxes or directed in any way you want. When using this method of controlling output, the text callback can be defined as a procedure that does not perform any operations (that is, does not direct the output anywhere). Note that the Java example below uses the predefined **EngineCallBacksDefault** class, which configures a method to print output using the **System.out** method. In general, if the text callback is left undefined by setting it to 0 or **null**, the output is directed to the console.

Initializing the Maple Engine

You can initialize the Maple engine by calling the *StartMaple* function in most versions of the API, or by creating an *Engine* class in the Java version of the API. In all cases, the initialization process loads the **maplec.dll** file and sets up the initial state so that the **OpenMaple** interface can evaluate commands. Despite the name *StartMaple*, this is only an initialization step; no separate Maple process is started.

The initialization process follows standard Maple start-up steps, including reading and running initialization files, setting library paths, and setting default security options. The startup state can be controlled by using the first parameter passed to the **StartMaple** function.

14.3 OpenMaple

This parameter is an array of strings that specify options accepted by the command-line interface. For more information about these options, refer to the **maple** help page.

Calling API Commands to Compute with Maple

When the **OpenMaple** interface is initialized, a *kernel vector handle* (or *engine class*), can be used to access all of the other methods in the API. The most common method lets you parse and evaluate arbitrary Maple commands. If a command is terminated with a semicolon, the display output is directed to your defined callbacks. This command also returns the result as a Maple data structure. The return value can be passed to other API commands for further analysis.

The **OpenMaple** interface manages Maple internal data structures and performs garbage collection. The data structures that are returned by an API function are automatically protected from garbage collection. The Maple command **unprotect:-gc** must be called to clean the memory reserved for these tasks. The **OpenMaple** Java interface is the only exception to this rule. Because the **OpenMaple** Java interface implements Maple structures as native objects, it manages object references by using a weak hash map, and therefore Maple data does not need to be unprotected.

Maple data structures are all declared as a single black box *ALGEB*, *IntPtr*, or similar type. Methods for inspecting and manipulating these data structures are provided. The API methods should be used, rather than dereferencing them directly in the data.

C/C++ Example

```
#include <stdio.h>
#include <stdlib.h>
#include "maplec.h"
/* callback used for directing result output */
static void M_DECL textCallBack( void *data, int tag, char *output )
{
   printf("%s\n",output);
}
int main( int argc, char *argv[] )
{
   char err[2048];  /* command input and error string buffers */
   MKernelVector kv;  /* Maple kernel handle */
   MCallBackVectorDesc cb = { textCallBack,
                        0,   /* errorCallBack not used */
                        0,   /* statusCallBack not used */
                        0,   /* readLineCallBack not used */
                        0,   /* redirectCallBack not used */
                        0,   /* streamCallBack not used */
                        0,   /* queryInterrupt not used */
                        0    /* callBackCallBack not used */
```

```
                };
    ALGEB r;   /* Maple data-structures */
    /* initialize Maple */
    if( (kv=StartMaple(argc,argv,&cb,NULL,NULL,err)) == NULL ) {
        printf("Fatal error, %s\n",err);
        return( 1 );
    }
    r = EvalMapleStatement(kv,"int(x,x);");
    StopMaple(kv);
    return( 0 );
}
```

This example can be entered in a file called "test.c".

Additional examples are available in the **samples/OpenMaple** directory of your Maple installation.

The method used to build this program depends on which compiler you are using. The following command is specific to the GCC compiler on a 64-bit version of Linux; it is useful as a reference for other platforms.

```
gcc -I $MAPLE/extern/include test.c -L $MAPLE/bin.X86_64_LINUX -lmaplec
-lmaple -lhf -lprocessor64
```

In this example, **$MAPLE** is your Maple installation directory. Note that the C header files can be found in the **$MAPLE/extern/include** directory and the library files can be found in the **$MAPLE/bin.$SYS** directory. In this case, $SYS is **X86_64_LINUX**; check the library path you need to specify by running the **kernelopts(bindir)** command in Maple. The remaining -*l* options specify which libraries need to be linked. In Windows, you only need to link to the **maplec.lib** library. Other platforms may require several libraries to be linked, including **libmaplec.so**, **libmaple.so**, and **libhf.so**. If you do not specify a library as required, the compiler returns a message indicating that undefined references to functions exist, or a dependent library cannot be found.

When this example is built, a file called **test.exe** is created. **Note:** The file might be called **a.out** or another name, depending on your compiler. Before this executable file can be run, you must specify the path of the Maple dynamic libraries. For more information, see *Runtime Environment Prerequisites (page 507)*.

After setting up your environment, run the binary file as you would run any other executable file. For example, create a shortcut icon and double-click it, or enter the file name at a command prompt.

```
test.exe
```

The following output is displayed.

```
1/2*x^2
```

C# Example

```
using System;
using System.Text;
using System.Runtime.InteropServices;
class MainApp {
  // When evaluating an expression, Maple sends all of the displayed
  // output through this function.
  public static void cbText( IntPtr data, int tag, String output )
  {
      Console.WriteLine(output);
  }
  public static void Main(string[] args) {
     MapleEngine.MapleCallbacks cb;
     byte[] err = new byte[2048];
     IntPtr kv;
     // pass -A2 which sets kernelopts(assertlevel=2) just to show
     // how in this example. The corresponding argc parameter
     // (the first argument to StartMaple) should then be 2
     // argv[0] should always be filled in with a value.
     String[] argv = new String[2];
     argv[0] = "maple";
     argv[1] = "-A2";
     // assign callbacks
     cb.textCallBack = cbText;
     cb.errorCallBack = null;
     cb.statusCallBack = null;
     cb.readlineCallBack = null;
     cb.redirectCallBack = null;
     cb.streamCallBack = null;
     cb.queryInterrupt = null;
     cb.callbackCallBack = null;
     try {
         kv = MapleEngine.StartMaple(2,argv,ref
cb,IntPtr.Zero,IntPtr.Zero,err);
     }
     catch(DllNotFoundException e) {
         Console.WriteLine(e.ToString());
         return;
     }
     catch(EntryPointNotFoundException e) {
         Console.WriteLine(e.ToString());
         return;
     }
     // make sure we have a good kernel vector handle back
```

```
      if( kv.ToInt64() == 0 ) {
         // If Maple does not start properly, the "err" parameter will be
filled
         // in with the reason why (usually a license error).
         // Note that since we passed in a byte[] array, we need to remove
         // the characters past \0 during conversion to string
         Console.WriteLine("Fatal Error, could not start Maple: "
            +
System.Text.Encoding.ASCII.GetString(err,0,Array.IndexOf(err,(byte)0))
         );
         return;
      }
      MapleEngine.EvalMapleStatement(kv,"int(x,x);");
      MapleEngine.StopMaple(kv);
   }
}
```

This example can be entered in a file called "test.cs".

To build this example, you can open a Microsoft .NET Framework SDK Command Prompt. Browse to the directory that contains the **test.cs** file and enter the following command.

```
csc test.cs $MAPLE\\extern\\include\\maple.cs
```

$MAPLE is the directory in which Maple is installed. The **maple.cs** file contains the **MapleEngine** class definition. and defines an interface to the **maplec.dll** file.

When this example is built, a file called **test.exe** is created. This file can usually be run without additional environment settings. For more information, see *Runtime Environment Prerequisites (page 507)*.

Run the binary file as you would run any other executable file. For example, create a shortcut icon and double-click it, or enter the file name at a command prompt.

```
test.exe
```

The following output is displayed.

```
1/2*x^2
```

Java Example

```
import com.maplesoft.openmaple.*;
import com.maplesoft.externalcall.MapleException;
class test
{
   public static void main( String args[] )
   {
      String a[];
```

```
        Engine t;
        int i;
        a = new String[1];
        a[0] = "java";
        try
        {
            t = new Engine( a, new EngineCallBacksDefault(), null, null );
            t.evaluate( "int( x,x );" );
        }
        catch ( MapleException e )
        {
            System.out.println( "An exception occurred" );
            return;
        }
        System.out.println( "Done" );
    }
}
```

This example can be entered in a file called **test.java**.

This example and others are available in the **samples/OpenMaple/Java/simple** subdirectory of your Maple installation.

To build this program, enter the following at a command prompt, where **$JDKBINDIR** is the directory in which your Java development tools are installed, and **$MAPLE** is the directory in which Maple is installed.

```
$JDKBINDIR/javac -classpath
"$MAPLE/java/externalcall.jar;$MAPLE/java/jopenmaple.jar" test.java
```

> **Note:** The same command can be used to build the example in UNIX and Macintosh; however, use a colon (:) to separate the directories in the classpath instead of a semicolon.

When this example is built, a **test.class** file is created in the current directory. Before this file can be run, the path of the Java OpenMaple native library must be specified for your Java Virtual Machine. For more information, see *Runtime Environment Prerequisites (page 507)*. In Windows, Java OpenMaple applications also require the **%PATH%** environment variable to be set.

You can use the Java Virtual Machine to run the generated class file by entering the following command. Note that the third entry in the classpath is a period (.) indicating the current directory.

```
$JDKBINDIR/java -classpath
"$MAPLE/java/externalcall.jar;$MAPLE/java/jopenmaple.jar;." test
```

Note: The same command can be used to build the example in UNIX and Macintosh; however, use a colon (:) to separate the directories in the classpath instead of a semicolon.

The following output is displayed.

```
1/2*x^2
Done
```

Visual Basic 6 Example

```
Public kv As Long
Public cb As MapleCallBack
Public Sub TextCallBack(data As Long, ByVal tag As Integer, ByVal output As
 Long)
    Dim OutputString As String
    OutputString = MaplePointerToString(output)
    MainForm.OutputText.Text = MainForm.OutputText.Text + vbCrLf +
OutputString
End Sub
Private Sub Form_Load()
    Dim error As String
    Dim args(0 To 1) As String
    'init callbacks
    cb.lpTextCallBack = GetProc(AddressOf TextCallBack)
    cb.lpErrorCallBack = 0
    cb.lpStatusCallBack = 0
    cb.lpReadLineCallBack = 0
    cb.lpRedirectCallBack = 0
    cb.lpQueryInterrupt = 0
    cb.lpCallBackCallBack = 0
    ' start Maple
    kv = StartMaple(0, args, cb, 0, error)
    If kv = 0 Then
        MsgBox "Error starting Maple: " + StrConv(error, vbUnicode),
vbCritical, ""
        Unload Me
        End
    End If
    dim result as Long = EvalMapleStatement(kv, "int(x,x);" )
End Sub
```

This example can be entered in a file called "test.bas".

Other examples are available in the **samples/OpenMaple/msvb** directory of your Maple installation.

To build this example, create a new project, and add both the **test.bas** and **$MAPLE/extern/include/maple.bas** files to your project. **$MAPLE** is the directory in which Maple is installed. Create a form called "MainForm" and add a text box named "OutputText" to the form.

Build and run this example by pressing F5. When this example is built, a form that shows a text box filled with the value **1/2*x^2** is displayed.

Visual Basic .NET Example

```
Friend Class MainForm
    Inherits System.Windows.Forms.Form
    Public kv As IntPtr
    Public cb As MapleCallBack
    Public Sub MyTextCallBack(ByRef data As Integer, ByVal tag As Short,
ByVal output As String)
        tbOutput.Text = tbOutput.Text & vbCrLf & " (" & tag & ") " & output
    End Sub
    Public Sub MyErrorCallBack(ByRef data As Integer, ByVal Offset As Short,
 ByVal output As String)
        MsgBox(" at offset " & Str(Offset) & " " & output,
MsgBoxStyle.Information, "")
    End Sub
    Private Sub MainForm_Load(ByVal eventSender As System.Object, ByVal
eventArgs As System.EventArgs) Handles MyBase.Load
        Dim args(1) As String
        'init callbacks
        cb.lpTextCallBack = AddressOf MyTextCallBack
        cb.lpErrorCallBack = AddressOf MyErrorCallBack
        cb.lpStatusCallBack = 0
        cb.lpReadLineCallBack = 0
        cb.lpRedirectCallBack = 0
        cb.lpQueryInterrupt = 0
        cb.lpCallBackCallBack = 0
        ' start Maple
        Try
            args(1) = "-A2"
            kv = StartMaple(1, args, cb, 0)
        Catch e As StartMapleException
            MsgBox("Error starting Maple: " & e.Message, "")
            Me.Close()
        End Try
        Dim result As IntPtr
        result = EvalMapleStatement(kv, "int( x,x );" )
        If result = 0 Then
            tbOutput.Text = "invalid expression"
```

```
        Else
            tbOutput.Text = MapleToString(kv, MapleALGEB_SPrintf1(kv, "%a",
result))
        End If
    End Sub
End Class
```

This example can be entered in a file called "test.bas".

To build this example, create a new project, and add both the **test.bas** and **$MAPLE/extern/include/maple.vb** files to your project. **$MAPLE** is the directory in which Maple is installed. Create a form called "MainForm" and add a text box named "tbOutput" to the form.

Build and run the example by pressing F5. When this example is built, a form that shows a text box filled with the value **1/2*x^2** is displayed.

Memory Usage

Maple allocates memory from the operating system in large portions. On most platforms, this process is performed by the C **malloc** function; 64KB of memory is allocated during a Maple session. This memory is not returned to the operating system (that is, by **free**) until the Maple session ends.

When Maple no longer requires a block of memory, that memory block is added to an internal list of free storage. Maple has several storage lists for different sizes of memory blocks so that it can quickly find blocks of the required size. For example, Maple uses three-word blocks, so it maintains a list of blocks of that size that are free. Maple allocates additional memory from the operating system only when it cannot respond to a request using its storage lists.

The more memory Maple is allocated by the operating system, the less it is allocated in the future because it reuses memory. For most applications, 4MB of memory must be available for allocation.

14.4 The Maple Command-line Interface

When considering how to use the Maple engine as part of another application, interface, or automatic process, several options are available. One of the simplest options is to use the Maple command-line interface.

The command-line version of Maple is a simple interface that, when used interactively, displays an input prompt (>), runs commands, and displays the output as text-based results. You can use this interface in batch mode to direct input to an application, specify a text file to run, or evaluate a command using the **-c** option.

In Windows, the command-line interface is called **cmaple.exe**. You can run this file from either the **bin.win** or **bin.X86_64_WINDOW** directory of your Maple installation, depending on your platform. On other platforms, you can start the command-line interface by running the **maple** script located in the **bin** directory of your Maple installation.

Starting the Maple command-line interface, automatically executing a command file, and stopping the Maple session can take about one tenth of a second, depending on which commands are run and the speed of your system. The quick start-up time and the minimal amount of processing required make the Maple command-line interface suitable to be called from other applications, even for quick calculations.

Batch Files

A batch file is a Maple script that can run in the Maple command-line interface, run statements, and exit. The results can be displayed or directed to a file.

One method of using the command-line interface to solve a problem is to create an **.mpl** script, which includes the input data. If this script is called **solve.mpl**, you could run the script as follows.

```
cmaple solve.mpl > solve.output
```

In this example, the output is redirected to a file named **solve.output**. You can configure an application to read this output file to capture the result.

Note: .mpl is the standard file extension for a Maple language file, which is a text file that can contain Maple statements. For more information, refer to the **file** help page.

You can use the **-q** option to hide extra output that interferes with parsing results automatically. For more options on the Maple command-line interface, refer to the **maple** help page.

Directing Input to a Pipeline

To avoid using the file system, input to the command-line interface can be directed to a pipeline. The following example shows how to perform this task at a command prompt.

```
echo "int(x,x);" | cmaple
```

Specifying Start-up Commands

You can use the **-c** option to specify start-up commands to be run by the Maple command-line interface. Although the **-c** option can be followed by any valid Maple statement, the syntax must be carefully quoted to avoid being interpreted by the shell of the calling system. For example, the following syntax can be entered at a Windows command prompt.

```
cmaple -c "datafile := `c:/temp/12345.data`" -c N:=5;
```

The equivalent command in a UNIX shell requires different quoting.

```
/usr/local/maple/bin/maple -c 'datafile:="/tmp/12345.data";' -c N:=1;
```

Statements that do not use characters that are special to the system interpreter can be left unquoted, as with the case of **-c N:=1;** above. This statement does not use spaces, pipe characters, redirect symbols, quotes, or other characters that have meaning to the interpreter.

14.5 External Calling: Using Compiled Code in Maple

In Maple, you can load a dynamic-link library (.dll) file that contains functions written in a programming language other than Maple, and then use those functions in Maple as you would use any other commands.

External functions that accept and return basic types (for example, integers and floats) can be called directly in Maple after defining the calling sequence of the external function. Alternatively, if you want to call functions that use complicated types, or if you require more control over the conversion of data structures you want to access, you can use the Maple *external function interface* to create and compile a *wrapper* file.

Calling a Function in a Dynamic-link Library

Most external functions that are compiled in a .dll file use standard hardware types such as integers, floating-point numbers, strings, pointers (to strings, integers, and floating-point numbers), matrices, and vectors. Maple can translate the hardware representation of these external functions so that the external functions are recognized in Maple. This method is efficient and easy to use because it does not require the use of a compiler. This method of *directly calling* the external code allows you to use an external library without modifying the Maple library.

To understand the Maple external calling facility, consider the following C code, which adds two numbers and returns the result.

```
int add( int num1, int num2 )
{
    return num1+num2;
}
```

Three basic steps are required to call a function in a .dll library.

- Create or obtain a .dll file
- Create a function specification in Maple
- Call the external function from within Maple

Create or Obtain a .dll file

The external functions that you want to call from Maple must be compiled in a .dll file. You can either create the code and compile the .dll file yourself or obtain an existing .dll file that contains the functions you want to use in Maple.

The external library functions in a .dll file must have been compiled using the **_stdcall** calling convention, which is the default convention used by most compilers in UNIX, Macintosh, and 64-bit Windows, but must be specified when using most 32-bit Windows compilers. Options are also available for calling .dll files created by Fortran compilers and classes created in Java.

Create a Function Specification

Before using an external function in Maple, you must provide a description (or *function specification*), which includes the following information.

- Name of the function in the .dll file. In the example above, the name is **add**.
- Type of parameters the function passes and returns. In the example above, all of the parameters are of type **int**.
- Name of the .dll file that contains the function. In the example above, assume that the C code has been compiled into a .dll file called **mylib.dll**.

A function specification translates the external function into a form that can be recognized and interpreted by Maple.

At a Maple prompt, you can define the function specification by calling **define_external** as follows.

```
> myAdd := define_external(
        'add',
        'num1'::integer[4],
        'num2'::integer[4],
        'RETURN'::integer[4],
        'LIB'="mylib.dll"
    );
```

Examine this function and note the following characteristics.

- The first argument of the **define_external** function (in this example, **add**) is the name of the external function as exported by the .dll file. In the C code, the function is called **add**. However, because the **define_external** function is assigned to the name **myAdd** above, the Maple procedure that will be generated after you define the function specification will be called **myAdd**. This is the command that you will use to call the external function within Maple.

- If Java or Fortran was used to create the external function, you must specify **JAVA** or **FORTRAN** as the second argument to indicate the programming language. The default language is C, so this parameter does not need to be specified in the example above since the **add** function was written in C.

- The parameters **num1** and **num2**, which are both of type *int*, describe the arguments of the function to be called. These values should be specified in the order in which they appear in your documentation or source code for the external function, regardless of issues such as the passing order (left to right versus right to left). By doing so, the Maple procedure returned by the **define_external** function has the same calling sequence as the external function when it is used in the language for which it was written. The only exception is that one argument can be assigned the name **RETURN**. This argument specifies the type returned by the function rather than a parameter passed to the function. In the example above, the return type does not have a name, so the keyword **RETURN** is used.

For information on specifying parameter types, see *Specifying Parameter Types for Function Specifications (page 521)*.

- Specifying the parameter types is independent of the compiler. The specification is always defined in the same way, regardless of the method used to compile the .dll file. The example above uses the C type **int**, which is specified as *integer[4]* in Maple. The **4** in the square brackets indicates the number of bytes used to represent the integer. Some C compilers use 4-byte (32-bit) *long* data types, but other compilers use 8-bytes (64-bit) for the same data structure. If you are using the *long* data type, the specification in Maple will need to be either *integer[4]* or *integer[8]*, depending on the way your .dll file was built. For more information about common type relations, see **Table 14.2**.

- The name of the .dll file containing the external function is specified by defining the **LIB** parameter. In the example above, **mylib.dll** specifies the file name of the library in which the function is located. The format of this name is system-dependent and certain systems require a full path to the file. In general, the name should be in the same format as you would specify for a compiler on the same system. If you are calling a Java method, **dll-Name** is the name of the class containing the method.

Important: Specify the function exactly and make sure that the arguments are in the correct order. Failure to do this will not cause any problems when you are defining the specification; however, unexpected results may be produced or your program may stop responding when the external function is called within Maple.

Calling the External Function

Calling the **define_external** function for **myAdd** returns a Maple procedure that translates the Maple types to hardware types that can work with an external function. This procedure can be used in the same way as other Maple commands.

> myAdd(1,2);

$$3 \tag{14.1}$$

> a := 33:
> b := 22:
> myAdd(a,b);

$$55 \tag{14.2}$$

> r:= myAdd(a,11);

$$r := 44 \tag{14.3}$$

Specifying Parameter Types for Function Specifications

Maple uses its own notation to provide a generic well-defined interface for calling compiled code in any language. The format of each type descriptor parameter is as follows.

```
argumentIdentifier :: dataDescriptor
```

The return value description is also defined by using a data descriptor, with the name **RETURN** as the *argumentIdentifier*. If the function returns no value, no **RETURN** parameter is specified. Also, if no parameters are passed, no argument identifiers are required.

Scalar Data Formats

External libraries generally handle scalar data formats that are supported by your platform. All array, string, and structured formats are created from these. The data descriptors used to represent scalar formats usually contain a type name and size. The size represents the number of bytes needed to represent the given hardware type. **Table 14.1** lists the basic type translations for standard C, Fortran, and Java compilers.

Table 14.1: Basic Data Types

Maple Data Descriptor	C Type	Fortran Type	Java Type
integer[1]	char	BYTE	byte
integer[2]	short	INTEGER2	short
integer[4]	int or long^1	INTEGER or INTEGER4	int
integer[8]	long^1 or long long	INTEGER8	long

Maple Data Descriptor	C Type	Fortran Type	Java Type
float[4]	float	REAL or REAL4	float
float[8]	double	DOUBLE PRECISION or REAL8	double
char[1]	char	CHARACTER	char
boolean[1]	char	LOGICAL1	boolean
boolean[2]	short	LOGICAL2	
boolean[4]	int or long^1	LOGICAL or LOGICAL4	
boolean[8]	long^1 or long long	LOGICAL8	

Note: The C type *long* is typically 4 bytes on 32-bit systems and 4 or 8 bytes on 64-bit systems. Use the *sizeof* operator or consult your compiler documentation to verify *sizeof(long)*.

Structured Data Formats

In addition to the basic types listed in **Table 14.1**, Maple also recognizes certain compound types that can be derived from the basic types, such as arrays and pointers. These compound types are listed in **Table 14.2**. For a complete list and a detailed specification, refer to the **define_external,types** help page.

Table 14.2: Compound Data Types

Maple Data Descriptor	C Type	Fortran Type	Java Type
ARRAY(datatype = float[8], ...)	type A	type A	type[] A
string[n]	char x[n]	CHARACTER2	string
complex[4]	struct{ float re, im; }	COMPLEX or COMPLEX8	NA

Maple Data Descriptor	C Type	Fortran Type	Java Type
complex[8]	struct{ double re, im; }	DOUBLE COMPLEX or COMPLEX16	NA
REF(typename)	TYPENAME	NA	NA

External Function Interface

Alternatively, you may want to call call a .dll file that directly manipulates Maple data structures, rather than converting them automatically to standard data types. By doing so, you can either write custom applications that are integrated with Maple or provide custom conversions for data passed to prebuilt .dll files. Maple provides an API for directly managing Maple data structures and operations performed on them.

This API, or *external function interface*, is a subset of the API provided by the **OpenMaple** interface. Unlike the **OpenMaple** interface, you do not need to define stream callbacks because Maple is the primary interface. Also, the kernel-vector handle returned from a call to the **StartMaple** function in the **OpenMaple** API is, instead, passed as an argument to the external function defined in your .dll file.

Currently, the API is defined for C/C++ and Fortran, and certain portions of the API can be used for external functions written in Java. Other languages such as Visual C# and Visual Basic can interface through a small C++ layer.

The API function prototypes for manipulating Maple data structures are located in the **$MAPLE/extern/include** directory where **$MAPLE** is the directory in which Maple is installed. The header file **maplec.h** must be included when writing custom C wrappers. One of the header files, **maplefortran.hf** or **maplefortran64bit.hf**, must be included when writing custom Fortran wrappers. Other header files, **mplshlib.h**, and **mpltable.h** contain macros, types, and data structures that are needed for direct manipulation of Maple data structures.

In your C code, Maple uses the following lines as an entry point to call the external function directly with no argument conversion.

```
ALGEB myExternalFunction(
   MKernelVector kv,
   ALGEB args
);
```

Two parameters are in the external function declaration. The first is a handle that will be required to call any Maple API function. The second is a Maple *expression sequence* of all the arguments passed when the external function is called. The API function *MapleNumArgs* can be used to determine the number of elements in the expression sequence. This variable can be treated as an array of DAGs starting at index **1** (not **0**). Therefore, **args[1]** is the first parameter passed to the external function.

```
> myFunc := define_external('myExternalFunction', 'MAPLE', 'LIB'=
  "myStuff.dll"):
```

When using the **define_external** function to declare an interface to an external function that directly manipulates Maple structures, you do not need to provide a description of the arguments and their types. Instead, add the keyword option, **MAPLE**.

Again, consider the simple example that adds two numbers passed by Maple. This time, with explicit data type conversions using the API, and defining the external function prototype, as described above, the C function appears as follows.

```
/* Program to add two numbers from Maple */
#include <stdio.h>
#include <stdlib.h>
#include <maplec.h>
ALGEB myAdd( MKernelVector kv, ALGEB args )
{
    int a1, a2, r;
    if( MapleNumArgs(kv,args) != 2 )
        MapleRaiseError(kv,"Incorrect number of arguments");
    a1 = MapleToInteger32(kv,((ALGEB*)args)[1]);
    a2 = MapleToInteger32(kv,((ALGEB*)args)[2]);
    r = a1 + a2;
    return( ToMapleInteger(kv,(M_INT) r) );
}
```

This program first checks if the Maple function call passes exactly two arguments. It then converts the two arguments to hardware integers and adds them. The result is converted to a Maple integer and returned.

This program can be compiled into a .dll file using a C compiler of your choice. Ensure that you link with the Maple API .dll file. The .dll file can be placed in the Maple binary directory, as given by **kernelopts(bindir)**, or a subdirectory within the directory specified by the **PATH** environment variable. If you are using .dll files outside of the Maple binary directory, you may need to specify the full path to the .dll file in the **LIB** argument to the **define_external** function. UNIX developers may also need to set their load-library path.

To complete the example, the *myAdd* function can be linked in Maple and used as any other Maple procedure.

```
> myAdd := define_external('myAdd', 'MAPLE', 'LIB'= "myAdd.dll"):
> myAdd(2,3);
                                5                              (14.4)
```

```
> myAdd(2.2,1);
Error, (in myAdd) integer expected for integer[4] parameter
> myAdd(2^80,2^70);
Error, (in myAdd) integer too large in context
```

The equivalent Fortran wrapper is as follows.

```
Program to add two numbers from Maple
INTEGER FUNCTION myAdd(kv, args)
INCLUDE "maplefortran.hf"
INTEGER kv
INTEGER args
INTEGER arg
INTEGER a1, a2, r
CHARACTER ERRMSG*20
INTEGER ERRMSGLEN
ERRMSGLEN = 20
IF ( maple_num_args(kv, args) .NE. 2 ) THEN
    ERRMSG = 'Incorrect number of arguments'
    CALL maple_raise_error( kv, ERRMSG, ERRMSGLEN )
    myAdd = to_maple_null( kv )
    RETURN
ENDIF
arg = maple_extract_arg( kv, args, 1 )
a1 = maple_to_integer32(kv, arg)
arg = maple_extract_arg( kv, args, 2 )
a2 = maple_to_integer32(kv, arg)
r = a1 + a2
myAdd = to_maple_integer( kv, r )
END
```

Once compiled into a .dll file, the same syntax can be used in Maple to access the function. The only difference is the additional keyword **'FORTRAN'** in the **define_external** call.

```
> myAdd := define_external('myAdd','MAPLE','FORTRAN','LIB'=
                           "myAdd.dll"):
> myAdd(2,3);
```

$$5 \qquad (14.5)$$

For more examples, refer to the **define_external,CustomWrapper** help page.

Specifying Parameter Passing Conventions

Each programming language uses a specific convention for parameter passing. For example, C uses the *pass-by-value* convention; passing parameters *by reference* must be performed explicitly by passing an address. Fortran uses the pass-by-reference convention. Pascal uses either, depending on how the parameter was declared.

The Maple external calling mechanism supports C, Fortran, and Java calling conventions. There is an external API for writing custom wrappers for C and Fortran, but not for Java. The default convention used is C. To use Fortran calling conventions, specify the name **FORTRAN** as a parameter to the **define_external** function.

```
> f := define_external(`my_func`,`FORTRAN`, ...);
```

To use Java calling conventions, specify the name **JAVA** as a parameter to the **define_external** command. Also, specify the **CLASSPATH**= option to point to the classes used.

```
> f := define_external(`my_func`,`JAVA`, CLASSPATH="...", ...);
```

Some other compiler implementations, such as Pascal and C++, can work with C external calling by using the correct definitions and order of passed parameters.

Generating Wrappers Automatically

When you specify the keyword **WRAPPER** in the call to the **define_external** function, Maple generates code for data translations. Maple compiles this code into a .dll file and dynamically links to the new library. Subsequently invoking the procedure that is returned by the **define_external** function calls the newly generated conversion command before calling the external function in the library you provided.

The C code generated by Maple wraps the Maple data structures by translating them to hardware equivalent types. Therefore, the code file is called the *wrapper*, and the library generated by this code is called the *wrapper library*.

Generating wrappers can provide an easy way to start writing custom code that references the Maple external function interface. The term *wrapper* also refers to the code you write to communicate with existing .dll files, as it does for the code Maple generates for the same reason. Your code is sometimes called a *custom wrapper*.

Consider the original **add** function that was introduced at the beginning of this chapter. In the following example, the **WRAPPER** option is used to generate a wrapper using the **define_external** function. As shown, you can also use the **NO_COMPILE** option to prevent the generated wrapper from compiling. The name of the generated file is returned instead.

```
> myAdd := define_external(
        'add',
        'WRAPPER',
```

14.5 External Calling: Using Compiled Code in Maple

```
            'NO_COMPILE',
            'num1'::integer[4],
            'num2'::integer[4],
            'RETURN'::integer[4]
    );
```

```
myAdd := "mwrap_add.c"
```

The file **mwrap_add.c** resembles the following.

```
/* MWRAP_add Wrapper
   Generated automatically by Maple
   Do not edit this file. */
#include <stdio.h>
#include <stdlib.h>
#include <string.h>
#include <mplshlib.h>
#include <maplec.h>
MKernelVector mapleKernelVec;
typedef void *MaplePointer;
ALGEB *args;
/* main - MWRAP_add */
ALGEB MWRAP_add( MKernelVector kv,
        INTEGER32 (*fn) ( INTEGER32 a1, INTEGER32 a2 ),
        ALGEB fn_args )
{
    INTEGER32 a1;
    INTEGER32 a2;
    INTEGER32 r;
    ALGEB mr;
    int i;
    mapleKernelVec = kv;
    args = (ALGEB*) fn_args;
    if( MapleNumArgs(mapleKernelVec,(ALGEB)args) != 2 )
        MapleRaiseError(mapleKernelVec,"Incorrect number
        of arguments");
    /* integer[4] */
    a1 = MapleToInteger32(mapleKernelVec,args[1]);
    /* integer[4] */
    a2 = MapleToInteger32(mapleKernelVec,args[2]);
    r = (*fn)(a1, a2);
    mr = ToMapleInteger(mapleKernelVec,(long) r);
    return( mr );
}
```

The generated wrapper is a good starting point for writing your own code. Some extra variables and declarations may be used because the wrapper generation is generic. For example, the use of **args** rather than **fn_args** avoids the need for a cast with **args[1]**, but it is also a static global variable which is useful when working with callbacks that need access to the argument sequence outside the main entry point.

Passing Arguments by Reference

External functions follow normal Maple evaluation rules in that the arguments are evaluated during a function call. It therefore may be necessary to enclose assigned names in right single quotes (unevaluation quotes) when passing arguments by reference. For example, consider the following function that multiplies a number by two in-place.

```
void double\_it( int *i )
{
    if( i == NULL ) return;
    *i *= 2;
}
```

In Maple, the definition of this function could appear as follows.

```
> double_it := define_external('double_it', i::REF(integer[4]),
                               LIB="libtest.dll");
```

When running this function, the argument **'i'** is converted from the Maple internal representation of an integer to a 4-byte hardware integer. A pointer to the hardware integer is then passed to the external function, **'double_it'**. Although **'i'** is declared as a pointer to an integer, you can call **'double_it'** with non-pointer input.

```
> double_it(3);
```

In this case, a pointer to the hardware integer **3** is sent to **'double_it'**. The modified value is not accessible from Maple. To access the modified value, the parameter must be assigned to a name. The name must be enclosed in unevaluation quotes to prevent evaluation.

```
> n:=3;
> double_it(n);   # n is evaluated first, so 3 is passed
> n;
```

$$3 \tag{14.6}$$

```
> double_it('n');  # use unevaluation quotes to pass 'n'
> n;
```

$$6 \tag{14.7}$$

For numeric data, the string **"NULL"** can be passed as a parameter to represent the address **0** (the C NULL). For strings, because **"NULL"** is a valid string, the integer **0** represents the address **0**.

```
> double_it("NULL");
  concat := define_external('concat',
      RETURN::string, a::string, b::string,
      LIB="libtest.dll"):
  concat("NULL","x");
```

$$\text{"NULLx"} \tag{14.8}$$

```
> concat(0,0);
```

$$0 \tag{14.9}$$

In the **concat** example, the C code might look like the following. Note that this function does not clean the memory as it should.

```
char * concat( char* a, char *b )
{
    char *r;
    if( !a \\ !b ) return( NULL );
    r = (char*)malloc((strlen(a)+strlen(b)+1)*sizeof(char));
    strcpy(r,a);
    strcat(r,b);
    return( r );
}
```

External API

An external API is provided if you want to expand existing wrappers or write custom wrappers. Because this API is the same as that of **OpenMaple**, most of the internal documentation is referenced in the **OpenMaple** help pages. In particular, refer to the **OpenMaple,C,API** and **OpenMaple,VB,API** help pages and related pages.

Additional examples can be found in the **examples,ExternalCalling** page. Sample code is provided in the **samples/ExternalCall** directory of your Maple installation. In particular, all of the external calling sample code provided in the individual help pages in **OpenMaple,C,API** can be found in the **samples/ExternalCall/HelpExamples** directory. This code is precompiled in the **HelpExamples.dll** file provided with Maple so that you can run the examples in your Maple session.

System Integrity

The Maple kernel cannot control the quality or reliability of external functions. If an external function performs an illegal operation, such as accessing memory outside of its address space, that operation may result in a segmentation fault or system error. The external function may stop responding and cause Maple to stop responding as well.

If an external function accesses memory outside of its address space but within the Maple address space, the external function will likely *not* stop responding, but certain parts of Maple may not function correctly, resulting in unexpected behavior or a crash later in the Maple session. Similarly, an external function that directly manipulates Maple data structures can produce unexpected results by misusing the data structure manipulation facilities.

Therefore, use external calling at your own risk. Whether an external function is one that you have written, or supplied by a third party to which you have declared an interface (that is, by using the **define_external** function), Maple must rely on the integrity of the external function when it is called.

14.6 Accessing Data over a Network with TCP/IP Sockets

The **Sockets** package allows Maple to communicate with data sources over the Internet, such as web sites and remote Maple sessions running on a network.

You can create a Maple server in a Maple session and configure the server to send a message to that session.

Socket Server

A *socket server* can be a public web service such as a stock quote service. The following example shows how to create a Maple procedure that acts as a service that listens for a socket connection and sends a message when a connection is found.

The server action is defined in the following procedure.

```
> myServer := proc( sid )
        uses Sockets;
        Write( sid, sprintf( "Hello %s on port %d, from %s\r\n",
               GetPeerHost( sid ), GetPeerPort( sid ),
  GetHostName() ) )
  end proc:
```

The following commands cause the Maple session in which they are called to start the servicing requests. This call is not returned. To run the code, enter the procedure definition above and the **Serve** command below in a Maple worksheet. (Remove the comment character (#) before running the code.)

```
> #Sockets:-Serve( 2525, myServer );
```

Socket Client

To write a simple client, the socket must first be opened. To do so, specify the name of the host and the port number of the host to which you want to connect.

```
> sid := Sockets:- Open ( "localhost", 2525 );
```

To get information from the server, the socket must be read.

```
> Sockets:-Read(sid);
```

When you are finished, close the socket.

```
> Sockets:-Close(sid);
```

14.7 Code Generation

In Maple, code generation is one of several powerful tools for deploying results to other systems. Maple can translate formulas, numerical procedures, data sets, and matrices to compiled languages. Maple supports translation to C, Visual C#, MATLAB, Java, Visual Basic, and Fortran.

```
> with( CodeGeneration );
```

$$[C, CSharp, Fortran, IntermediateCode, Java, LanguageDefinition, Matlab, Names, Save, Translate, VisualBasic] \qquad (14.10)$$

Calling CodeGeneration Commands

You can call the **CodeGeneration** commands using the following syntax, where L is one of the supported languages, for example, **C**.

```
CodeGeneration[*L*]( *expression*, *options* )
```

The *expression* can take one of the following forms.

- A single algebraic expression: Maple generates a statement in the target language assigning this expression to a variable.

- A list of equations of the form *name*=*expression*: Maple interprets this list as a sequence of assignment statements and generates the equivalent sequence of assignment statements in the target language.

- A list, array, or rtable: Maple generates a statement or sequence of statements assigning the elements to an array in the target language.

- A Maple procedure or module: Maple generates an equivalent structure in the target language. For example, to translate a procedure to C, Maple generates a function along with any necessary directives for library inclusion. To translate a module to Java, Maple generates a Java class declaration with exports translated to public static methods and module locals translated to private static methods. For more information on translating code to a specific language, refer to the **CodeGeneration** help page and browse to the help page for the target programming language that you want to use.

You can use many options with the **CodeGeneration** commands. For more information, refer to the **CodeGenerationOptions** help page. Some of the commonly used options are listed below.

- **optimize**=**value**: This option specifies whether the Maple code is optimized before it is translated. The default value is **false**. When this option is set to **true**, the **codegen[optimize]** function is used to optimize the Maple code before it is translated.

- **output**=**value**: This option specifies the form of the output. By default, the formatted output is printed to the console. If a name (different from the name **string**) or a string is specified as the value, the result is appended to a file of that name. If the value is the name **string**, a string containing the result is returned. This string can then be assigned and manipulated.

- **declare**=**[declaration(s)]**: This option specifies the types of variables. Each declaration has the form **varname::vartype** where **varname** is a variable name and **vartype** is one of the Maple type names recognized by the **CodeGeneration** package, as described in the **TranslationDetails** help page. Declarations specified using this option override any other type declarations in the input code.

Notes on Code Translation

Because the Maple programming language differs from the target languages supported by the **CodeGeneration** package, the generated output may not be completely equivalent to the input code. The **CodeGeneration/Details** help page provides more information on the translation process and hints on how to take full advantage of the facilities. In addition, some help pages contain notes that are relevant to specific languages. For more information, refer to the help pages for the corresponding target language, for example, **CodeGeneration/General/CDetails**.

Translation Process

The **CodeGeneration** commands recognize a subset of the Maple types, which are listed in the **CodeGeneration/Details** help page. The Maple types are translated to appropriate types in the target language. Compatibility of types is checked before operations are translated, and type coercions are performed if necessary. The **CodeGeneration** commands attempt to determine the type of any untyped variables. You can control type analysis and deduction by using the **coercetypes**, **declare**, **deducetypes**, and **defaulttype** options. For more information, refer to the **CodeGenerationOptions** help page.

The **CodeGeneration** commands can translate a subset of the Maple commands, which are listed on the **CodeGeneration/Details** help page. Some commands are translated only to certain target languages. For more information about a specific language, refer to its detailed help page, for example, **CodeGeneration/General/CDetails**.

The return type of a procedure is determined automatically if you do not declare it. If more than one return statement is specified, the types of all objects returned must be compatible in the target language. If a return statement contains a sequence of objects, the sequence is translated into an array. Implicit returns are recognized in some cases, but translations to explicit returns can be suppressed by using the **deducereturn=false** option. When necessary, an automatically generated return variable is used to store a return value.

Lists, Maple data structures of the type **array**, and rtables are translated to arrays in the target language. It is recommended that you declare the type and ranges for all arrays. In some target languages, arrays are reindexed to begin at index 0.

Example 1: Translating a Procedure to Java

```
> f := proc(x)
    local y;
    y := ln(x)*exp(-x);
    printf("The result is %f", y);
  end proc:
> CodeGeneration[Java](f);
import java.lang.Math;

class CodeGenerationClass {
  public static void f (double x)
  {
    double y;
    y = Math.log(x) * Math.exp(-x);
    System.out.print("The result is " + y);
  }
}
```

Example 2: Translating a Procedure to C

In this example, the **defaulttype** option sets the default type to **integer** and the **output** option specifies that a string is returned. In this case, the output is assigned to the variable **s**.

```
> g := proc(x, y, z)
    return x*y-y*z+x*z;
  end proc:
```

```
> s := CodeGeneration[`C`](g, defaulttype=integer, output=string);
```
$$s := \text{"int g (int x, int y, int z)}$$
$$\{$$
$$\text{return}(x * y - y * z + x * z);$$
$$\}$$
$$\text{"}$$
(14.11)

Example 3: Translating a Procedure to Fortran

In this example, because Fortran 77 is not case-sensitive, the variable **X** is renamed to avoid a conflict with the variable **x**.

```
> h := proc(X::numeric, x::Array(numeric, 5..7))
    return X+x[5]+x[6]+x[7];
  end proc:
> CodeGeneration[Fortran](h);
Warning, the following variable name replacements were made: ["cg"]
 = ["x"]
      doubleprecision function h (X, cg)
        doubleprecision X
        doubleprecision cg(5:7)
        h = X + cg(5) + cg(6) + cg(7)
        return
      end
```

Example 4: Translating an Expression to MATLAB

In this example, the **optimize** option is used to minimize the number of arithmetic operations called in the exported code. The default exported code would have recomputed a value for **(3 - c * b + a * b)**, which appears many times. To avoid recomputing the value, common subexpressions are evaluated once and stored in variables so that other expressions can refer to the value.

```
> M := 1 / < a,3,c; 1,b,2; -1,0,-1 >;
```

$$M := \begin{bmatrix} -\dfrac{22}{-729+22c} & \dfrac{3}{-729+22c} & -\dfrac{2(-3+11c)}{-729+22c} \\ -\dfrac{1}{-729+22c} & \dfrac{-33+c}{-729+22c} & \dfrac{-66+c}{-729+22c} \\ \dfrac{22}{-729+22c} & -\dfrac{3}{-729+22c} & \dfrac{723}{-729+22c} \end{bmatrix}$$
(14.13)

```
> CodeGeneration:-Matlab(M, optimize = true);
t1 = -729 + 22 * c;
t1 = 1 / t1;
t2 = 22 * t1;
t3 = 3 * t1;
cg = [-t2 t3 (6 - 22 * c) * t1; -t1 (-33 + c) * t1 (-66 + c) * t1; t2
 -t3 723 * t1;];
```

Example 5: Translating a Procedure to Visual Basic

In the following example, all of the parameters are assigned a floating-point type by default. The **defaulttype** option determines how to interpret variables that do not have a type.

```
> f := proc(x, y, z) return x*y-y*z+x*z; end proc:
> CodeGeneration:-VisualBasic(f,defaulttype=integer);
Public Module CodeGenerationModule

  Public Function f( _
    ByVal x As Integer, _
    ByVal y As Integer, _
    ByVal z As Integer) As Integer
    Return x * y - y * z + x * z
  End Function
End Module
```

Example 6: Using the defaulttype and deducetypes Options

Maple attempts to determine the types of variables that do not have a type automatically. The default type is assigned only to those variables that do not have a type after the automatic type deduction process. In the following example, the parameters *y* and *z* are assigned a floating-point type because they are in an expression involving the float variable x. Therefore, the default type, **integer**, is not assigned.

```
> f := proc(x::float, y, z) x*y-y*z+x*z; end proc:
> CodeGeneration:-C( f, defaulttype=integer );
double f (double x, double y, double z)
{
  return(x * y - y * z + x * z);
}
```

You can turn off the automatic type deduction process by setting the **deducetypes** option to **false**. In the following example, the parameters *y* and *z* are now assigned the default type.

```
> CodeGeneration:-C(f, defaulttype=integer, deducetypes=false);
double f (double x, int y, int z)
{
  return(x * (double) y - (double) (y * z) + x * (double) z);
}
```

You can turn off the explicit type coercion process by setting the **coercetypes** option to **false**.

```
> CodeGeneration:-C(f, defaulttype=integer, deducetypes=false,
  coercetypes=false);
double f (double x, int y, int z)
{
  return(x * y - y * z + x * z);
}
```

Example 7: Using the declare Option

You can control how types are assigned by specifying the parameter, local variable, and return types explicitly in procedures or by using the **declare** option with expressions.

```
> CodeGeneration:-C(1+x+y, declare=[x::float, y::integer]);
cg0 = 0.1e1 + x + (double) y;
```

The Intermediate Code

All Maple input to the **CodeGeneration** translators is processed and converted to an inert intermediate form called *intermediate code*. The intermediate code is the basic object on which all **CodeGeneration** translators operate. For information about the intermediate code, refer to the **CodeGeneration/General/IntermediateCodeStructure** help page.

The names that appear in intermediate code expressions are part of the **CodeGeneration:-Names** subpackage.

Error and warning messages displayed from **CodeGeneration** package commands sometimes refer to the intermediate form of the Maple expression that triggered the message.

When determining the cause of an error message or writing and debugging custom language definitions, it is recommended that you determine the intermediate form of a Maple expression input. In general, you can determine the intermediate form by using the **CodeGeneration:-IntermediateCode** translator. However, because some aspects of the intermediate code are specific to the language to which you are translating, it may help to see the intermediate code for a specific translator. This can be done by setting the command **infolevel[CodeGeneration]** to a value greater than 3 and performing a translation.

The following example shows the intermediate code for the expression **2x^2-1**. The first argument of the **Scope** structure is the name of a type table used internally during the translation process.

```
> CodeGeneration[IntermediateCode](2*x^2-1);
Scope( nametab,
  StatementSequence(
    Assignment(GeneratedName("cg1"), Sum(Product(Integer(2),
Power(Name("x"), Integer(2))), Negation(Integer(1))))
  )
)
```

Extending the CodeGeneration Translation Facilities

The **CodeGeneration** package is distributed with translators for several programming languages. In addition, you can define new translators to enable the **CodeGeneration** package to generate code for other languages. Tools for this task are available in the **LanguageDefinition** subpackage of **CodeGeneration**.

Custom translators can define a complete language, extend existing language definitions, overriding and extending only those language components that need to be changed.

To view a list of languages that are currently supported by the **CodeGeneration** package, and thus available for extending, use the **CodeGeneration:-LanguageDefinition:-ListLanguages** command.

The Printing Phase

As described previously, the **CodeGeneration** package first processes the Maple input and translates it to an intermediate form. This step is followed by the *printing* phase, which translates the intermediate form to a Maple string according to transformation rules specific to the target language.

For each name used in the intermediate form, there is a *print handler* procedure. During the printing phase, Maple traverses the intermediate form recursively. For each subexpression of the intermediate form, Maple invokes the print handler associated with that class of expressions.

Defining a Custom Translator

This section explains the process of defining a translator for a target language.

Using a Printer Module

For each **CodeGeneration** language definition, there is an associated Maple module called a **Printer** module, which contains language-specific print handlers and data. A **Printer** module has several functions, which set and reference language-specific printing data.

There are two ways to obtain a **Printer** module: the **LanguageDefinition:-GenericPrinter()** returns a generic **Printer** module containing no language-specific data, and the **LanguageDefinition:-Get(language_name):-Printer** command returns a copy of the **Printer** module used for a previously defined language **language_name**.

The most frequently used **Printer** package command is **Print**. When it is given a string, the **Print** command prints the string to a buffer. When given an intermediate-form expression, the **Print** command invokes the print handler appropriate for the expression. In this manner, **Print** recurses through the intermediate form until it is printed in its entirety to the buffer. At this point, the translation process is complete.

Table 14.3 lists the important **Printer** commands. For a complete list and more detailed information, refer to the **CodeGeneration/LanguageDefinition/Printer** help page.

Table 14.3: Printer Commands

AddFunction	Define a translation for a command name and type signature
AddOperator	Define a translation for a unary or binary operator
AddPrintHandler	Set a procedure to be the *print handler* for an intermediate form name
GetFunction	Get a translation for a command name and type signature
GetOperator	Get a translation for a unary or binary operator
GetPrintHandler	Get the current print handler' procedure for an intermediate form name
Indent	Indent a printed line when supplied as an argument to **Print**
Print	Print arguments to buffer
PrintTarget	Initiate printing of an intermediate form

The following commands illustrate how data is stored and retrieved from a **Printer** module.

```
> with(CodeGeneration:-LanguageDefinition):
```

```
> Printer := GenericPrinter():
> Printer:-AddOperator( Addition = "+" );
```
$$\text{"+"} \tag{14.14}$$
```
> Printer:-AddFunction( "sin", [numeric]::numeric, "sine" );
```
$$[\text{"sine"}, \{\,\}] \tag{14.15}$$
```
> Printer:-GetOperator( Addition );
```
$$\text{"+"} \tag{14.16}$$
```
> Printer:-GetFunction( "sin", [numeric]::numeric );
```
$$[\text{"sine"}, \{\,\}] \tag{14.17}$$

Within a language definition, the **Printer** module associated with the language definition can be referenced by the name **Printer**. **Note:** This applies to both of the language definition methods described in the next section.

Language Translator Definition

There are two distinct methods of defining a language translator for use by the **CodeGeneration** package: using the **LanguageDefinition:-Define** command and creating a language definition module.

For simple languages or small extensions of existing languages, use the **LanguageDefinition:-Define** command. To create a translator that preprocesses or postprocesses the generated output, or makes frequent use of a utility function in translations, create a language definition module. The language definition module approach is used for all translators supplied with the **CodeGeneration** package.

Using the Define Command

The **Define** command takes a series of function call arguments **f1**, **f2**, ... where the command names are, for example, **AddFunction**, **AddFunctions**, **AddOperator**, **AddPrintHandler**, **AddType**, and **SetLanguageAttribute**.

These function calls accept identical syntax and perform the same actions as the **Printer** commands of the same name. That is, they define print handlers and other data specific to the language translation you are defining. For more information on these commands, refer to the **CodeGeneration/LanguageDefinition/Printer** help page.

The **Define** command automatically creates a **Printer** module for the language. You do not need to create one using the **LanguageDefinition:-GenericPrinter** or **LanguageDefinition:-Get** commands.

This example illustrates a C translator, in which the translated code uses a specialized library function **mymult** for multiplication instead of the built-in ***** operator.

```
> CodeGeneration:-LanguageDefinition:-Define("MyNewLanguage",
    extend="C",
    AddPrintHandler(
        CodeGeneration:-Names:-Product = proc(x,y)
            Printer:-Print("mymult(", args[1], ", ", args[2],
                ")");
        end proc
    )
):
```

Note that in the previous example, one of the arguments of the **LanguageDefinition:-Define** command is the function call **AddPrintHandler**, which takes a name and a procedure as arguments. The supplied procedure therefore *prints* any **Product** subexpression of the intermediate form. The call to **Printer:-Print** specifies that the translator uses the automatically generated **Printer** module.

Creating a Language Definition Module

A *language definition module* is a Maple module with the exports **PrintTarget** and **Printer**. The module exports must satisfy the following criteria.

- **Printer**: A **Printer** module, that is, either a generic **Printer** module returned by the **CodeGeneration:-LanguageDefinition:-GenericPrinter** command or a **Printer** module obtained from another language definition module using the **LanguageDefinition:-Get("language_name"):-Printer** command.

- **PrintTarget**: Returns the translated output as a string. In most cases, the **PrintTarget** command calls the **Printer:-PrintTarget** command.

The body of the module definition must contain a sequence of calls to **Printer** commands that define language-specific data and utility procedures.

Once defined, a language definition module can be added to to the set of languages recognized by the **CodeGeneration** package by using the **CodeGeneration:-LanguageDefinition:-Add** command.

When creating your language definition module, you must delay the evaluation of the module by using unevaluation quotes before adding it using the **LanguageDefinition:-Add** command. That is, the language definition module must be added as a module definition and not as a module.

The following example adds a definition module. Note the use of unevaluation quotes around the module definition to delay its evaluation.

```
> UppercaseFortran77 := 'module()
    export Printer, PrintTarget;
    Printer := eval(CodeGeneration:-LanguageDefinition:-Get(
        "Fortran")):-Printer;
    PrintTarget := proc(ic, digits, prec, func_prec, namelist)
        Printer:-SetLanguageAttribute("Precision" = prec);
        StringTools:-UpperCase(Printer:-PrintTarget(args));
    end proc:
  end module':

> CodeGeneration:-LanguageDefinition:-Add("UppercaseFortran",
    UppercaseFortran77);
```

Using a New Translator

After creating the language definition using either the **LanguageDefinition:-Define** or **LanguageDefinition:-Add** commands, translate your code to the new language using the **CodeGeneration:-Translate** command.

The following example demonstrates the use of a new translator. Compare the output of the **Fortran** command with that of the new translator.

```
> p1 := proc() sin(x+y*z)+trunc(x); end proc:

> CodeGeneration:-Fortran(p1);
        doubleprecision function p1 ()
          p1 = sin(x + y * z) + dble(int(aint(x)))
          return
        end

> CodeGeneration:-Translate(p1, language="UppercaseFortran");
        DOUBLEPRECISION FUNCTION P1 ()
          P1 = DSIN(X + Y * Z) + DBLE(INT(DINT(X)))
          RETURN
        END
```

14.8 CAD Connectivity

If Autodesk Inventor®, NX®, or SolidWorks® software is installed on your computer, you can set up Maple to communicate with your computer aided design (CAD) application. By connecting your CAD application to Maple, you can retrieve parameters from a CAD drawing, work with those values in Maple, and send the new values to the CAD application to incorporate them in your drawing.

The commands available to the interface depends on the CAD application that you are using. Each application uses a different naming convention for parts and hierarchies of parts in a CAD drawing. In Maple, you can use the **CAD Link Assistant** as a starting point to find out about the information available from your CAD application and how to reference it. For more information, refer to the **CADLink** help page.

The Maple **CAD** package contains subpackages that are specific to individual CAD applications. After selecting the relevant subpackage to use, the first step is to establish a connection to the CAD system. The **OpenConnection** command opens the CAD application, or connects to a session that is already running on your computer. Both Maple and the CAD application can run side-by-side; updates in either system are automatically reflected in the other system.

The next step is to connect to a particular part or assembly within the CAD application. The **GetActiveDocument**, **OpenPart**, or another related command will establish this connection.

When a connection is established with the CAD application and part of the CAD drawing is opened, Maple can extract parameter values, properties, and in some cases the geometry of the part. Maple can then be used to analyze these values to optimize the configuration or test aspects of the design (for example, whether the part can withstand applied force or heat). If necessary, modified parameters can be saved in the CAD application.

14.9 Maple Plug-in for Excel

Maple is available as an add-in to Microsoft Excel for Windows. The Maple Excel link allows you to use Maple commands, including commands that generate Maple plots, as formulas in Microsoft Excel spreadsheets.

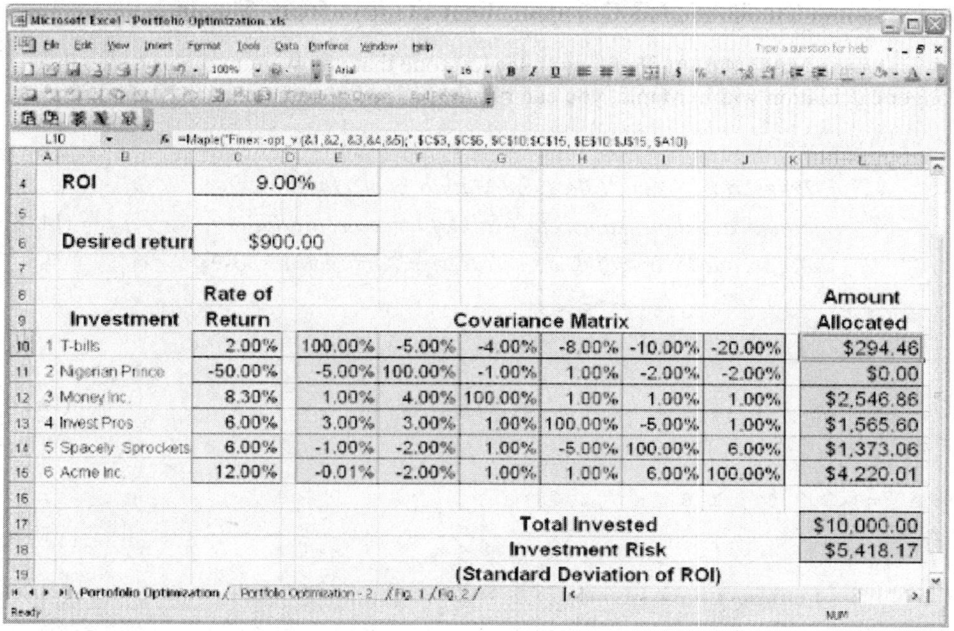

ROI	9.00%						
Desired return	$900.00						
Investment	Rate of Return	Covariance Matrix					Amount Allocated
1 T-bills	2.00%	100.00%	-5.00%	-4.00%	-8.00%	-10.00%	-20.00%	$294.46
2 Nigerian Prince	-50.00%	-5.00%	100.00%	-1.00%	1.00%	-2.00%	-2.00%	$0.00
3 Money Inc.	8.30%	1.00%	4.00%	100.00%	1.00%	1.00%	1.00%	$2,546.86
4 Invest Pros	6.00%	3.00%	3.00%	1.00%	100.00%	-5.00%	1.00%	$1,565.60
5 Spacely Sprockets	6.00%	-1.00%	-2.00%	1.00%	-5.00%	100.00%	6.00%	$1,373.06
6 Acme Inc.	12.00%	-0.01%	-2.00%	1.00%	1.00%	6.00%	100.00%	$4,220.01
					Total Invested			$10,000.00
					Investment Risk (Standard Deviation of ROI)			$5,418.17

Figure 14.1: Maple in Excel

In the following example, an Excel formula forms a quadratic polynomial from the coefficients in cells C1, D3, and B6. You can enter this formula in cell A1 of the Excel spreadsheet.

```
=Maple( "&1*x^2 + &2*x + &3;", $C$1, $D$3, $B$6 )
```

In the Excel spreadsheet, enter a string containing the Maple code that you want to return, substituting any parameters contained in spreadsheet cells using an ampersand character (&) followed by a number. Include a semicolon (;) after the Maple command. After the string, list the cell references that should be substituted into the string in the order of the numbers you entered.

For more examples, refer to the **Excel** help page.

14.10 Connecting MATLAB and Maple

If MATLAB is installed on your computer, you can access the MATLAB computation engine to perform computations in Maple and you can access the Maple computation engine to perform computations in MATLAB.

You must first configure Maple to communicate with MATLAB. For more information, refer to the **Matlab,setup** help page.

Accessing the MATLAB Computation Engine from Maple

If you have a MATLAB .m file file with legacy code that you want to run as a step in a longer calculation within Maple, you can run the following commands in Maple.

> with(Matlab);

$$[AddTranslator, FromMFile, FromMatlab, chol, closelink,$$
$$defined, det, dimensions, eig, evalM, fft, getvar, inv, lu, \qquad (14.18)$$
$$ode15s, ode45, openlink, qr, setvar, size, square, transpose]$$

> a := <1,2,3 ; 4,5,6; 7,8,9>;

$$a := \begin{bmatrix} 1 & 2 & 3 \\ 4 & 5 & 6 \\ 7 & 8 & 9 \end{bmatrix} \qquad (14.19)$$

> b := <3,2,5 ; 1,8,2; 7,3,4>;

$$b := \begin{bmatrix} 3 & 2 & 5 \\ 1 & 8 & 2 \\ 7 & 3 & 4 \end{bmatrix} \qquad (14.20)$$

> setvar("ma",a)
> setvar("mb",b)
> evalM("result = yourmfile(ma,mb)")
> getvar("result")

The example above illustrates how Maple and MATLAB maintain separate name spaces, and the specific commands for transferring data between both applications. The matrices a and b are initially defined as Maple variables. By using the *setvar* command, they are copied into MATLAB data structures and assigned to the MATLAB variables *ma* and *mb*. By using the *evalM* command, you specify a command for MATLAB to parse and run. The result can be copied into a Maple data structure by using the *getvar* command.

For more information, refer to the **Matlab** help page.

Accessing the Maple Computational Engine from MATLAB

Maple provides the Maple Toolbox, which contains hundreds of MATLAB commands to communicate directly with the Maple engine. To perform a computation, you enter Maple Toolbox commands in MATLAB, for example,

```
>>    syms x y
>>    f = x^2+3*y^2-5*x*y+2*x-7*y-12
```

```
f =
                    2       2
           x  + 3 y  - 5 y x + 2 x - 7 y - 12
>> P = solve( diff(f,x), diff(f,y) )
P =
        x: -23/13
        y: -4/13
```

In MATLAB, the variables *x* and *y* are declared as *symbolic* by using the **syms** command. These variables can then be used with normal MATLAB operators to create larger symbolic expressions. The Maple Toolbox provides commands, such as *solve* and *diff*, to manipulate the Maple expressions you created. In addition to these commands you can use a generic *maple* command to evaluate arbitrary Maple commands.

15 Parallel Programming

Computers with multicore processors are now commonplace. To take advantage of the power of multicore computers, Maple provides tools for parallel programming. This chapter provides a basic introduction to parallel programming in Maple.

15.1 In This Chapter

- The two forms of parallel programming available in Maple, shared memory and multiple process.
- An introduction to shared memory programming using the Task Programming Model.
- An introduction to multiple process programming using the Grid Programming Model

15.2 Introduction

Maple provides tools for two different types of parallel programming. The Task Programming Model enables parallelism by executing multiple tasks within a single process. The second type of parallelism comes from the Grid package, which enables parallelism by starting multiple processes.

Each type of parallelism has advantages and disadvantages. The Task Programming Model is a high level programming tool that simplifies many aspects of parallel programming. In the Task Programming Model, tasks share memory thus they can work closely together, sharing data with low overhead. However because they share memory, code running one task must be careful not to interfere with code running in other tasks. As the Task Programming Model is very new to Maple, much of the Maple library has not been verified to work correctly with tasks. This means that much of Maple's core functionality cannot be used in task-based code.

As Grid uses multiple process parallelism it does not suffer from this problem, each process has its own independent memory. Thus you can use all of Maple's library routines in multiple process execution. Further, with the addition of the Grid Computing Toolbox, you can execute multiple process parallelism across multiple computers which can allow you to access far more computing power. However because the processes are independent the cost of communication between processes can be quite high. As well, balancing the computation evenly across all the available processors, especially those on remote computers, can be difficult.

15.3 Introduction to Parallel Programming with Tasks

Parallel Execution

Consider two procedures, **f** and **g**. **f** contains a sequence of statements, $f_1, f_2, ..., f_n$, and **g** contains the sequence, $g_1, g_2, ..., g_m$. If these two procedures are run in serial, they can be run in two possible orders: **f** followed by **g**, or **g** followed by **f**. In other words, the order in which the statements are run can be either $f_1, f_2, ..., f_n, g_1, g_2, ..., g_m$ or $g_1, g_2, ..., g_m, f_1, f_2, ..., f_n$. The programmer defines the order in which the statements are run. For example, if f_i must run before g_j for the code to execute correctly, the programmer can call **f** before **g** to make sure that the statements run in the correct order.

```
> f := proc()
      local i;
      for i from 1 to 5
      do
          print( procname[i] );
      end do;
  end proc:
```

```
> g := eval(f):
  f();
  g();
```

$$f_1$$
$$f_2$$
$$f_3$$
$$f_4$$
$$f_5$$
$$g_1$$
$$g_2$$
$$g_3$$
$$g_4$$
$$g_5 \qquad (15.1)$$

If **f** and **g** are called in parallel (that is, at the same time), different sequences can be generated. Although f_2 will run before f_3, the order in which f_2 runs relative to g_2 cannot be controlled. Therefore, the order could be g_1, g_2, f_1, g_3, f_2, f_3, ... or it could be f_1, g_1, f_2, f_3, g_2, g_3, ... or any other valid order. Also, the statements can be ordered differently each time these procedures are run; every possible order will eventually happen, given enough iterations.

The following example uses functions from the **Task Programming Model**. These functions are described in the *Task Programming Model (page 556)* section of this chapter. For now, consider these functions as a way to start *tasks*, which are functions that can run in parallel.

```
> Threads:-Task:-Start( null, Task=[f], Task=[g] );
```

$$g_1$$
$$f_1$$
$$g_2$$
$$f_2$$
$$g_3$$
$$f_3$$
$$g_4$$
$$f_4$$
$$g_5$$
$$f_5 \tag{15.2}$$

Running the statement above multiple times generates different sequences.

If the code requires f_i to execute before g_j to run correctly, running these functions in parallel may produce errors, even if f_i is the first statement of **f** and g_j is the last statement of **g**. Every possible order will eventually occur; therefore, to write correct parallel code, you must guarantee that every possible order of execution leads to a correct result.

```
> f := proc( n )
    local i, tmp;
    global shared;

    for i from 1 to n
    do
        tmp := shared;
        shared := tmp+1;
    end do;
    NULL;
  end proc:
> g := eval(f):
```

```
> shared := 0:
> Threads:-Task:-Start( null, Task=[f,1000], Task=[g,1000] ):
> shared;
```

$$1110 \tag{15.3}$$

In the example above, **f** and **g** increment the global variable **shared** 1000 times. You might expect the final value of **shared** to be 2000; however, this is not the case. The for loop contains two statements:

- 1 : $tmp := shared$
- 2 : $shared := tmp + 1$

When **f** and **g** are running in parallel, these statements could run in the following order:

- $f_1 : tmp_f := shared$
- $g_1 : tmp_g := shared$
- $g_2 : shared := tmp_g + 1$
- $f_2 : shared := tmp_f + 1$

and the increment performed by **g** is lost.

In some orders, the total will be 2000 and, in fact, every value from 1000 to 2000 could occur. Therefore, even for this simple example, there are 1001 different possible outcomes and even more possible orders.

In sequential programs, the order in which statements are run are defined by the programmer. In parallel code, the order in which statements run is not defined exclusively by the code. In other words, a programmer who writes parallel code must consider all of the different possible orders to determine if the code is correct.

Functions that work correctly when run in parallel with other code are called *safe*. Functions that do not work correctly when run in parallel with other code are called *unsafe*.

How the Ordering Is Determined

The operating system can interrupt and pause a task that is running for many reasons. If the task tries to access a memory location, the operating system may need to transfer the value into a register. This process could take hundreds, thousands, or even millions of cycles. If the task tries to access a system resource (for example, by reading or writing data, allocating memory, and so on), the operating system may need to pause the task while it waits for the resource to become available. Also, the operating system may move a task from a core to allow another process to run.

Therefore, many factors may cause a task to pause for a brief or long time period. In some cases, the task may pause as a result of the action that is being performed; however, other factors are beyond the task's control.

Issues Caused by Multiple Orders

These multiple potential orders may cause other issues when developing parallel code. For example, parallel code can be difficult to test because orders that cause issues may not occur during testing. This is particularly true if you are developing code on a single-core computer. Many orders that are possible on multiple-core computers may never occur on a single-core computer.

Controlling Parallel Execution

The previous section provided a simple example of parallel code with 1001 possible outcomes. Each outcome can result from multiple statement orders and there are numerous potential statement orders for even simple code. The only way to write correct parallel programs is to get a handle on all of these orders.

Execution Orders That Do Not Matter

Many of the possible orders will not cause problems. Consider the following example, which is similar to the previous one.

```
> f := proc( n )
    local i, tmp;
    global shared;

    shared[procname] := 0;
    for i from 1 to n
    do
        tmp := shared[procname];
        shared[procname] := tmp+1;
    end do;
    NULL;
  end proc:
> g := eval(f):
> shared := table():
> Threads:-Task:-Start( null, Task=[f,1000], Task=[g,1000] ):
```

```
> shared[f]+shared[g];
```

$$2000 \tag{15.4}$$

In this case, the result is 2000 each time you run the code. The difference between this example and the example above is that although there are just as many statement orders, the orders do not cause conflicts. In this example the two tasks are not writing to the same location in memory. In general, statements that cause issues are statements that access shared data. In the first example, the two tasks share the value stored by the variable, **shared**. As the two tasks modify **shared**, conflicts occur. In this example, both threads write to different variables, so no conflicts occur. The regions of code that contain statements that cause conflicts are called *critical sections*.

By understanding this concept, you can limit yourself to worrying about the orderings that involve critical sections. This also implies that if you have fewer critical sections in your parallel code, it will be easier to make the code work properly.

Shared Data in Maple

Since sharing data may cause issues in parallel programming, it is useful to consider how data can be shared in Maple. A piece of data is *shared* if it is accessible from multiple tasks that are running in parallel. Also, data that can be accessed from a shared value is also shared. In particular, if a shared variable is assigned a module, all of the data in the module is also shared, including the module locals. Similarly, remember tables of shared procedures are also shared.

The most common way data is shared is using global variables. A global variable can be accessed from anywhere in the code, so whenever a procedure uses a global variable, it could conflict with another procedure running in parallel. In a similar way, lexically scoped variables that are used in tasks that run in parallel are also shared. Another way to share data is to pass the same value into multiple tasks as an argument.

For more information, see *Variables in Procedures (page 221)*.

Sharing Data Safely

It is often necessary to share data to implement a parallel algorithm, so you must consider how to share data safely.

The simplest method for sharing data safely is to treat the shared data as read-only. If the tasks do not modify the shared data, no conflicts will occur. However, if even one task modifies the shared data, all of the tasks (even the ones that simply read data) must access shared data carefully.

Another method is to share a data structure, such as an Array, but limit which elements of the structure are accessible by certain tasks. For example, two tasks can share an Array if each task only accesses one half of the Array. In such an example, the tasks share a structure, but not the data within the structure.

In the following example, an Array is shared between two tasks.

```
> task := proc( A, lo, hi )
      local i, x;

      for i from lo to hi
      do
          x := A[i];
          A[i] := x^4+4*x^3+6*x^2+4*x+1;
      end do;
  end proc:
> N := 10^5:
> N2 := floor(N/2):
> A := Array( 1..N, x->(Float(x)/N) ):
  Threads:-Task:-Start( null, Task=[task,A,1,N2],
  Task=[task,A,N2+1,N] ):
```

Protecting Critical Sections

If you can't avoid creating critical sections using techniques like the ones described in the previous section, you will need to protect them by creating *mutual exclusion* sections of your code. These sections guarantee that at most one task can execute code in the protected sections at a time.

To create a mutual exclusion zone, use a **Mutex**. A mutex can be in one of two states: *locked* or *unlocked*. If a mutex is unlocked, any task can lock it. If a mutex is locked and a task attempts to lock it, the task waits until the mutex is unlocked, and then it attempts to lock the mutex again. This means that only one task can lock the mutex.

If all of the tasks only access the critical section while holding the lock, there will never be more than one task accessing the shared data at a time. Therefore, by using a mutex, multiple tasks can run in parallel and share data without conflicting with other tasks.

The following example takes the unsafe code from the first example and adds a mutex to make it safe.

```
> task := proc(m, n)
      local i, tmp;
      global common_variable;

      for i to n do
```

15.3 Introduction to Parallel Programming with Tasks • 555

```
            Threads:-Mutex:-Lock(m);
            tmp := common_variable;
            common_variable := tmp + 1;
            Threads:-Mutex:-Unlock(m)
        end do;
        NULL
    end proc:
> common_variable := 0:
> m := Threads:-Mutex:-Create():
> Threads:-Task:-Start( null, Task=[task,m,1000], Task=[task,m,1000]
    ):
> common_variable;
```

$$2000 \tag{15.5}$$

Note: The excessive use of mutexes may cause performance issues. First, simply having to lock and unlock a mutex will add processing time to your code. However, more significantly, if a thread tries to lock a mutex that is already locked, it must wait. This waiting period reduces the parallelism of the algorithm.

The mutex example shown above falls into this category. The body of the task runs while holding a lock, which means that, at most, one task can run that code at a time. To fix this, limit the access to the global variable. For this example, a local variable can be used and the local results can be combined once at the end of the execution.

```
> task := proc(m, n)
      local i, local_sum;
      global common_variable;

      local_sum := 0;
      for i to n do
          local_sum := local_sum + 1;
      end do;
      Threads:-Mutex:-Lock(m);
      common_variable := common_variable + local_sum;
      Threads:-Mutex:-Unlock(m)
  end proc:
> common_variable := 0:
> m := Threads:-Mutex:-Create():
```

```
> Threads:-Task:-Start( null, Task=[task,m,1000], Task=[task,m,1000]
    ):
> common_variable;
```

$$2000 \tag{15.6}$$

15.4 Task Programming Model

The **Task Programming Model** is a high-level parallel programming interface. It is designed to make parallel programming easier.

Tasks

Consider the following Maple procedure.

```
> f := proc() fc( f1(args1), f2(args2), ..., fn(argsn) ); end proc;
```

To evaluate f, the fi values are evaluated and their return values are computed. These return values are then passed to fc as arguments. When fc completes, its return value is passed as the return value of f. The Task Programming Model takes this pattern, but creates *tasks* for the fi values and fc. A *task* is a piece of executable code. In Maple, a task is a procedure combined with a set of arguments to that procedure. Once a task is created, the Maple kernel can run it. By allowing the kernel to schedule tasks, Maple can automatically distribute them to available processors of your computer.

In the example above, a function call, fi, can be replaced by a task, ti, in a straightforward way: the procedure is fi and the arguments are $argsi$. However, the task, tc, corresponding to the function call fc is more complex. The function call fc will not run until all the fi calls have completed, thus supplying their return values to fc as arguments. Similarly, the task tc must wait for values from ti before it can run. The procedure of tc is fc, and its arguments are the values returned by the other tasks. These other tasks are called the *child* tasks of tc. Similarly, tc is called the *parent* of the ti tasks. The task tc is called the *continuation* task.

In the example code above, the value returned by f is the return value of fc. Similarly, when a task, t, creates a continuation task, the value returned by the continuation task is given to the parent of t. When this happens, any value returned by the task t is discarded. t is effectively replaced by tc. This occurs because, in the Task Programming Model, tasks always run until they are complete. A task t, does not need to stop in the middle of its execution to wait for child tasks to complete; instead it can finish and the continuation task will handle the return values of the child tasks. If t does not create any tasks, its return value is given to its parent.

The Task Tree

In the Task Programming Model, any task can replace itself with child tasks and a continuation task. Therefore, these newly created tasks can also create additional tasks. This process creates a tree of tasks. *Leaf nodes* are the tasks that do not have child tasks and *internal nodes* are the tasks that have child tasks. A leaf task does not have child tasks, so it can run at any time. As leaf tasks complete, their parent tasks may become leaf tasks, allowing them to run.

Starting Tasks

To create the first task, call the **Threads:-Task:-Start** function.

```
> Start( task, arg1, arg2, ..., argn ):
```

task is the procedure to run as the first task and **arg1**, **arg2**, ..., **argn** are the arguments to **task**.

```
> task := proc( )
      `+`( _passed );
  end proc:
> Threads:-Task:-Start( task, 1,x^3,q/3 );
```

$$1 + x^3 + \frac{1}{3} q \tag{15.7}$$

This procedure creates one task. After the task runs and returns a value (or a continuation function returns a value), that value is the returned by the **Start** function. Starting a task by itself is not as useful as starting multiple tasks that run in parallel.

To start child tasks and a continuation function, call the **Threads:-Task:-Continue** function.

```
> Continue( cont, arg1, arg2, ..., argn ):
```

cont is the procedure to use for the continuation task. **arg1**, **arg2**, ..., **argn** are either arguments to **cont** or child task specifiers of the form

```
Task=[task, targ1, targ2, ..., targn ]
Tasks=[task, [targs1], [targs2], ..., [targsm] ]
```

The first task specifier creates one task with the procedure **task** and arguments **targ1**, **targ2**, ..., **targn**. The second task specifier creates **m** tasks, each using **task** as the procedure and the sequence of expressions **targsi** as arguments to task **i**.

As **Continue** replaces a running task with child tasks and a continuation task, it can only be called from within a running task. In addition, it can only be called once per task. However **Continue** can be called from any running task, including a continuation task.

When a child task completes, its return value is passed to its parent as a parameter. The position of the parameter corresponds to the position the task was specified in the call to the **Continue** function. The following example illustrates how this passing works.

```
> task := proc(i)
      cat( t, i );
  end proc:

> start := proc( )
      Threads:-Task:-Continue( print, 1, Task=[task,2], 3,
  Tasks=[task,[4],[5]], 6 );
  end proc:

> Threads:-Task:-Start( start );
```

$$1, t2, 3, t4, t5, 6 \tag{15.8}$$

The simple example shown earlier can be modified to use the Task Programming Model.

```
> task := proc(n)
      local sum, i;

      sum := 0;
      for i from 1 to n
      do
          sum := sum+1;
      end do;

      sum;
  end proc:

> start := proc( )
      Threads:-Task:-Continue( `+`, Task=[task,1000],
  Task=[task,1000] );
  end proc:

> Threads:-Task:-Start( start );
```

$$2000 \tag{15.9}$$

By using the value passing behavior of the Task Programming Model, this problem can be solved without using global variables or a mutex. The return values of the two child tasks are passed to the continuation function, +. It adds them together and returns the computed value. This value is then returned by the **Start** function.

Task Management

Now that you have the functions to create tasks, you must determine how many tasks to start. To understand this, a few parallel programming concepts must be considered. Parallel algorithms are said to *scale* if they get faster when they run on more cores. A good parallel algorithm will scale linearly with the number of available processors.

To achieve linear scaling, a parallel algorithm must consider *load balancing*. Load balancing refers to techniques used to distribute the work evenly over all the cores of your computer. If you want to use **n** cores, you would want to divide the work into **n** even parts. However, you may not be able to determine how to divide the *work* evenly. Dividing the *input* into **n** evenly sized parts may not divide the work evenly. It is possible that one task will require more time to evaluate than the others. Once the other tasks complete, their cores will be idle while the remaining task runs.

One way to solve this problem is to create a large number of small tasks. This way, each task is relatively small. However, even if one task requires more time to run, the other cores can run many other tasks while one core is running the long task. Another advantage is that you can create the tasks without considering the number of cores. Thus your code does not need to know about the underlying hardware.

One limitation is that creating tasks requires resources. If the tasks are too small, the resources required to create the tasks may dominate the running time. Consider the following example, which is run on a computer with four cores.

```
> add_range := proc(lo, hi)
      local i;
      add( i, i = lo..hi );
  end proc:
```

The **add_range** function adds the numbers from **lo** to **hi**.

```
> N := 3*10^7:
> start := time[real]():
  add_range( 1, N );
  time[real]()-start;
```

$$3.281$$

$$450000015000000 \tag{15.10}$$

```
> parallel_add_range := proc( lo, hi, n )
      local i,step,d;

      d := hi-lo+1;
      step := floor( d/n );
```

```
        Threads:-Task:-Continue( `+`, Tasks=[ add_range,
                seq( [i*step+lo,(i+1)*step], i=0..n-2 ),
                [ (n-1)*step+lo,hi ] ] );
end proc:
```

The **parallel_add_range** function also adds the numbers from **lo** to **hi**, but it distributes the work over **n** tasks.

```
> start := time[real]():
  Threads:-Task:-Start( parallel_add_range, 1, N, 2 );
  time[real]()-start;
```

$$1.646$$

$$450000015000000 \tag{15.11}$$

```
> start := time[real]():
  Threads:-Task:-Start( parallel_add_range, 1, N, 4 );
  time[real]()-start;
```

$$1.353$$

$$450000015000000 \tag{15.12}$$

```
> start := time[real]():
  Threads:-Task:-Start( parallel_add_range, 1, N, 100 );
  time[real]()-start;
```

$$1.045$$

$$450000015000000 \tag{15.13}$$

Increasing the number of tasks from 2 to 4 increases the performance, as you would expect on a 4 core computer. However further increasing the number of cores from 4 to 100 also increases the performance. By using a larger number of tasks, Maple is better able to schedule the work onto available cores.

```
> start := time[real]():
  Threads:-Task:-Start( parallel_add_range, 1, N, 10000 );
  time[real]()-start;
```

$$2.131$$

$$450000015000000 \tag{15.14}$$

However, running 10000 tasks introduces a slowdown. The overhead of managing the tasks begins to become significant. The Task Programming Model is a relatively new feature in Maple, so this overhead will be reduced in future versions of Maple.

Coarse-grained Versus Fine-grained Parallelism

Consider the following example.

```
> work := proc(n) # do O(n) "work"
      local i;
      for i from 1 to n
      do
      end do;
      n;
  end proc:
> N := 100000000: # the total amount of work
  M := 100:
  n := N/M:
  A := [ seq( M, i=1..n ) ]: # evenly distributed work
> t:=time[real]():
  add( work( A[i] ), i=1..nops(A) );
  time[real]()-t;
```

$$16.764$$

$$100000000 \qquad (15.15)$$

In this example, the time taken by the **work** function depends on the input value **n**. This process can be parallelized at a high level by subdividing over the input Array until a base case is reached.

```
> task := proc( A, low, high )
      local i, count, mid;
      mid := high-low;
      if ( mid > 10000 ) then
          mid := floor(mid/2) + low;
          Threads:-Task:-Continue( `+`,
                  Task=[ task, A, low, mid ],
                  Task=[ task, A, mid+1, high ] );
      else
          count := 0;
          for i from low to high
          do
              count := count + work(A[i]);
          end do;
          count;
      end if;
  end proc:
```

```
> t:=time[real]():
  Threads:-Task:-Start( task, A, 1, nops(A) );
  time[real]()-t;
```

$$5.820$$

$$100000000 \tag{15.16}$$

You can see that this provides a reasonable speedup. High-level parallelism, as shown in the example above, is called *coarse-grained* parallelism. Generally, coarse-grained parallelism refers to dividing a problem into subproblems at a high level, and then running the subproblems in parallel with each other.

However, if a different input is specified, the weakness of coarse-grained parallelism can be seen. For example, if work is distributed unevenly, the speedup is not as significant.

```
> N2 := N/2:
  n := N2/M:
  A2 := [ N2, seq( M, i=1..n ) ]:
> t:=time[real]():
  Threads:-Task:-Start( task, A2, 1, nops(A2) );
  time[real]()-t;
```

$$11.170$$

$$100000000 \tag{15.17}$$

This happens because subdividing over the range does not take into account the actual amount of work necessary to compute the subranges. In the example above, the first subrange contains over half the work. Therefore, it may be difficult to divide the work into equal subsections, by only looking at the input.

Another approach to parallelizing a problem like this is to parallelize the **work** function.

```
> workTask := proc(n)
     local i, m;
     if ( n > 10000 ) then
         m := floor( n/2 );
         Threads:-Task:-Continue( `+`,
                 Task=[ workTask, m ],
                 Task=[workTask, n-m ] );
     else
         for i from 1 to n
         do
         end do;
```

```
            n;
        end if;
    end proc:
> work := proc(n) # do O(n) "work"
       local i;
       if ( n > 10000 ) then
           Threads:-Task:-Start( workTask, n );
       else
           for i from 1 to n
           do
           end do;
           n;
       end if;
   end proc:
> t:=time[real]():
  add( work( A2[i] ), i=1..nops(A2) );
  time[real]()-t;
```

$$11.909$$

$$100000000 \tag{15.18}$$

Low-level parallelism, as shown in the example above, is called *fine-grained* parallelism. Simply using the parallel **work** function gives a speedup in this case. However, fine-grained parallelism also has flaws. In particular, although the **work** function is faster for large inputs, it is not faster than the sequential version for small inputs. Thus, when you have an even distribution of work, there is no advantage to using this approach.

```
> t:=time[real]():
  add( work( A[i] ), i=1..nops(A) );
  time[real]()-t;
```

$$19.405$$

$$100000000 \tag{15.19}$$

The best solution is to use both coarse and fine-grained parallelism. **Note:** The **work** function has been redefined, so **task** will now use the new definition.

```
> t:=time[real]():
  Threads:-Task:-Start( task, A2, 1, nops(A2) );
  time[real]()-t;
```

$$4.914$$

$$100000000 \qquad (15.20)$$

Using both coarse and fine-grained parallelism combines the best of both of these approaches.

15.5 Examples

The N Queens Problem

On an **N** by **N** chess board, find the positions for **N** queens such that no two queens can capture each other. A queen can capture other chess pieces in the row and column in which it is positioned, and along the two diagonals that pass through the queen's position.

We will represent the board position by an Array of length **N**. Each element of the Array is an integer in the range **1..N**, and each integer only appears once. The combination of the Array index and the element stored at that index specify the position of a queen.

This representation is sufficient because only one queen can be in each row and column at a time. These restrictions can be specified while creating the positions, so when the chess board layouts are checked for valid solutions, we only need to look for conflicts along the diagonals.

```
nQueens := module()
    local checkBoard,
          completeBoardAndCheck,
          searchTask,
          continuation,
          subInit;
    export ModuleApply;

    (* Check a board layout to see if it is a valid solution. Row
       and column conflicts have already been filtered out based on
       how the board was constructed, so we only need to look for
       conflicts along the diagonals. *)

    checkBoard := proc( n, board::Array )
        local i, j, index;
        for i from 1 to n-1
        do
            index := board[i]+1;
```

```
            for j from i+1 to n while index <= n
            do
                if ( index = board[j] ) then
                    return NULL;
                end if;
                index := index + 1;
            end do;

            index := board[i] - 1;
            for j from i+1 to n while index >= 0
            do
                if ( index = board[j] ) then
                    return NULL;
                end if;
                index := index - 1;
            end do;
        end do;

        return Array(board); # return a copy with this instance
    end proc;

    (* Given an incomplete board, fill in all the remaining possibilities and
       then test them. This is the main sequential part of the algorithm. *)

    completeBoardAndCheck := proc( n, board, i, unused )
        local j;

        if ( i < n ) then
            return op( map( proc( j )
                                board[i] := j;
                                completeBoardAndCheck( n, board, i+1,
                                    unused minus {j} )
                            end proc, unused ) );
        else
            board[n] := unused[1];
            return checkBoard( n, board );
        end if;
    end proc;

    (* This is the high-level search. We create partial layouts
       and either create tasks to create additional layouts or perform
       the deep searches. *)
```

```
        searchTask := proc( i::posint, n::posint, m::nonnegint, board::list )
            local j, k, boards, a, used, unused;

            unused := { $1..n } minus convert( board[1..i-1], set );

            if ( i <= m ) then
                Threads:-Task:-Continue( passed,
                    Tasks = [ searchTask,
                        seq( [i+1, n, m, [ op(board), j] ], j in unused ) ]
);
            else
                # Turn lists into Arrays because we work in-place to save memory

                return completeBoardAndCheck( n,
                    Array( 1..n, board, datatype=integer[8]), i, unused );
            end if;

            return NULL;
        end proc;

        (* The main entry point.  n is the size of the board and m is
           how deep to create new tasks *)

        ModuleApply := proc( n::posint, m::nonnegint )
            local board;

            Threads:-Task:-Start( searchTask, 1, n, m, [] );
        end proc;
end module:
```

By passing 0 as the second argument, child tasks are not actually created. The following is the running time for sequential execution.

> `time[real]( nQueens( 9, 0 ) );`

$$10.867 \tag{15.21}$$

New tasks are created for all of the permutations for the first two rows of the chess board.

> `time[real]( nQueens( 9, 2 ) );`

$$4.651 \tag{15.22}$$

15.6 Limitations of Parallel Programming

Parallel programming in Maple is a relatively new feature. Maple has some limitations that affect the performance of parallel code. As new versions of Maple are released, these limitations will change. For more details about the following limitations, refer to the **multithreaded** help page.

Library Code

Only certain Maple library commands are thread-safe. If a Maple command is thread-safe, a note is included in its help page. If a Maple command that is not thread-safe is used in parallel code, may not work correctly.

A list of all the thread safe functions is available in the Maple help system on the **index/threadsafe** help page.

Maple Interpreter

The Maple interpreter executes all the code written in Maple. It is able to execute most Maple statements in parallel, however there are some internal systems that can reduce parallelism.

For a description of the performance issues in your version of Maple, see the **multithreaded/performancelimitations** help page.

15.7 Avoiding Common Problems

This section provides a list of hints and common mistakes that will help you understand and avoid common errors made in parallel programming.

Every Execution Order Will Happen

In parallel code, all possible execution orders will eventually occur. Therefore, never assume that a statement of one task will complete before another statement in another task, no matter how unlikely it seems that the other statement could run first. Always use the parallel programming tools in Maple (that is, the task dependencies in the Task Programming Model or mutexes) to enforce the order of execution.

Lock around All Accesses

It is common to think that if you have shared data, you only need to lock when modifying the data, but not when reading from the data. In general, this is not correct. If one task is reading data and another task starts writing data, the task that writes data can interfere with the parallel task that reads data. (Do not forget that tasks can pause at any time.) The only way to keep the task that writes data from interfering with the task that reads data is by having the task that reads data acquire the lock.

Debugging Parallel Code

Debugging parallel code can be difficult in many ways. The multiple possible orders can make bugs difficult to find. In particular, running your parallel code on a single-core machine may not produce orders that occur on a multicore machine.

Sometimes, the best way to debug parallel code is to do careful code inspections (that is, reading over the code) with the implications of parallel execution in mind. In the most extreme case, you can consider the shared data as the state in a state machine and the critical sections as transitions. This can allow you to see potential states and transitions that you did not consider.

15.8 Introduction to Grid Programming

The Grid package allows the user to launch multiple copies of Maple's computation engine. Each copy of the engine is independent, thus they do not share memory as in the Task Programming Model. This means if the engines need to share data they must communicate by sending messages back and forth.

Starting a Grid-Based Computation

To start a new computation using the Grid package, use the **Grid:-Launch** command. This starts new copies of computation engine, called *Nodes*, and passes a command to each node.

```
> hello := proc()
        printf("I'm node %d of %d\n",Grid:-MyNode(),Grid:-NumNodes());
        Grid:-Barrier();
  end:
> Grid:-Launch(hello);
I'm node 2 of 8
I'm node 3 of 8
I'm node 1 of 8
I'm node 4 of 8
I'm node 5 of 8
I'm node 6 of 8
I'm node 7 of 8
I'm node 0 of 8
```

This example creates a number of nodes, and executes the **hello** function on each node. The **Grid:-NumNodes** command returns the number of nodes that were started by **Launch**.

Grid:-MyNode returns an integer in the range **0** to **NumNodes()-1** which can be used to identify the executing node. The **Grid:-Barrier** command creates a synchronization point. All the nodes must execute the **Barrier** command before any of them can proceed past it.

Node 0 is given special significance in Grid programming. The value returned by the function executing in node 0 is returned by the **Launch** command. Thus when node 0 returns a value, the whole Grid computation is considered complete. Nodes that are still running are terminated. This is why the call to **Barrier** is necessary in the previous example, without it node 0 could exit before the other threads have completed executing their commands.

Communicating between Nodes

As nodes are independent processes, to share data you need to explicitly send data from one node to another.

Launch

Launch allows you to specify data that will be passed to the given functions as arguments. Additionally, **Launch** can automatically import global names to each node when nodes are started. As well, **Launch** can export global names from node 0 when it exits. In the following example, we pass two arguments into **func**, **arg1** and **arg2**, and import the global variable **data1** into each node using the **imports** argument. We also set the value of **data2** in node 0 and use the **exports** argument to update the value in the main context.

```
> func := proc(arg1, arg2)
    global data1, data2;
    printf( "%d: %a %a %a\n", Grid:-MyNode(), arg1, arg2, data1 );

    Grid:-Barrier();

    if ( Grid:-MyNode() = 0 ) then
        data2 := 1;
    end;
end:
```

```
> Grid:-Launch( func, 10, 20, imports=[ 'data1'=30 ], exports=[
    'data2' ] ):
4: 10 20 30
5: 10 20 30
6: 10 20 30
2: 10 20 30
3: 10 20 30
1: 10 20 30
0: 10 20 30
7: 10 20 30
> data2;
```

$$data2 \tag{15.23}$$

One important use of the **imports** option is the ability to pass user defined functions that are needed on the nodes. These functions will not be available on the nodes if they are not explicitly imported to the nodes.

The Grid package also contains two commands for explicitly sending data from one node to another, **Grid:-Send** and **Grid:-Receive**.

Send

Send allows one node to send a Maple expression to another node. **Send** accepts two arguments, an integer that identifies the destination node and the expression to send. **Send** does not wait for the target node to receive the message before returning.

Receive

Receive receives an expression that was sent from another node. **Receive** has one optional argument, an integer, that identifies the sender from whom an expression should be read. Without the argument **Receive** will return an expression from any sender. If there is no expression available, a call to **Receive** will wait until an expression is received. Some care should be taken as it is possible to cause a deadlock if all nodes are waiting to receive a message and no one is sending.

An Example Using Send and Receive

```
> circ := proc()
    local r, me := Grid:-MyNode(), n := Grid:-NumNodes();
    if me = 0 then
        Grid:-Send(1,0);
        r := Grid:-Receive(n-1);
    else
        r := Grid:-Receive(me-1);
```

```
            Grid:-Send(me+1 mod n, r, me);
        end if;
    end:
> [ Grid:-Launch( circ ) ];
```

$$[0, 1, 2, 3, 4, 5, 6, 7] \tag{15.24}$$

The next section includes a more complex example using **Send** and **Receive**.

15.9 Grid Examples

Computing a Mandelbrot Set

Here is a simple function for computing the Mandelbrot set. It creates a 2 dimensional Array that stores the computed values.

```
Mandelbrot := module()
    local MandelLoop,
          ModuleApply;

    MandelLoop := proc( X, Y, imageArray, i_low, i_high, j_low, j_high,
iter, bailout )
        local i, j, Xc, Yc, Xtemp, Ytemp, Xold, Yold, k, t;
        option hfloat;

        for i from i_low to i_high do
            for j from j_low to j_high do
                Xtemp := X[i];
                Ytemp := Y[j];
                Xc := Xtemp;
                Yc := Ytemp;
                k := 0;
                while k < iter do
                    Xold := Xtemp;
                    Yold := Ytemp;
                    Xtemp := Xold^2-Yold^2+Xc;
                    Ytemp := 2*Xold*Yold+Yc;
                    t := Xtemp^2+Ytemp^2;
                    if Xtemp^2+Ytemp^2 >= bailout then
                        imageArray[i, j, 1] := k - ln( ln( t ) )/ln(2.);
                        imageArray[i, j, 2] := imageArray[i, j, 1];
                        imageArray[i, j, 3] := imageArray[i, j, 1];
                        break;
                    end if;
                    k := k+1;
```

```
                end do
              end do;
          end do;
     end proc:

     ModuleApply := proc ( ptsY, ptsX, iter, X1, X2, Y1, Y2, bailout )
         local X, Y, imageArray, i:

         X := Vector(ptsX, i->X1+(X2-X1)*(i-1)/(ptsX-1) , datatype =
float[8]);
         Y := Vector(ptsY, i->Y1+(Y2-Y1)*(i-1)/(ptsY-1) , datatype =
float[8]);
         imageArray := Array(1 .. ptsY, 1 .. ptsX, 1 .. 3, datatype =
float[8]);

         MandelLoop( X, Y, imageArray, 1, ptsX, 1, ptsY, iter, bailout );

         return imageArray;
     end proc:
end:
```

```
> N := 500:
  s := time[real]():
  points := Mandelbrot( N, N, 100, -2.0, .7, -1.35, 1.35, 10.0 ):
  time[real]()-s;
```

$$68.913 \tag{15.25}$$

We can implement a Grid-based implementation by dividing the input range into evenly sized chunks. In the following example a node uses its node identifier to determine which chuck of the final Array it should use. Once a node has completed its computation, it sends the computed Array to node 0. Node 0 collects all the results and returns them. These results are then combined into a single output Array.

```
Mandelbrot := module()
   local MandelLoop,
         MandelGrid,
         ModuleApply;

   MandelLoop := proc( X, Y, imageArray, i_low, i_high, j_low, j_high,
iter, bailout )
       local i, j, Xc, Yc, Xtemp, Ytemp, Xold, Yold, k, t;
       option hfloat;

       for i from i_low to i_high do
           for j from j_low to j_high do
```

```
            Xtemp := X[i];
            Ytemp := Y[j];
            Xc := Xtemp;
            Yc := Ytemp;
            k := 0;
            while k < iter do
                Xold := Xtemp;
                Yold := Ytemp;
                Xtemp := Xold^2-Yold^2+Xc;
                Ytemp := 2*Xold*Yold+Yc;
                t := Xtemp^2+Ytemp^2;
                if t >= bailout then
                    imageArray[i, j, 1] := k - ln( ln( t ) )/ln(2.);
                    imageArray[i, j, 2] := imageArray[i, j, 1];
                    imageArray[i, j, 3] := imageArray[i, j, 1];
                    break;
                end if;
                k := k+1;
            end do
        end do;
    end do;
end proc:

MandelGrid := proc( X, Y, iter, bailout )
    local i, n, step, imageData, start, endp;

    n := Grid:-NumNodes();
    i := Grid:-MyNode();
    step := floor( numelems( X )/n );

    if ( i = 0 ) then
        start := 1;
        endp := step;
    elif ( i = n-1 ) then
        start := step*(n-1)+1;
        endp := numelems(X);
    else
        start := step*i+1;
        endp := step*(i+1);
    end;

    imageData := Array( start..endp, 1..numelems(Y), 1..3,
datatype=float[8] );
    MandelLoop( X, Y, imageData, start, endp, 1, numelems(Y), iter,
bailout );
```

```
            if ( i > 0 ) then
                Grid:-Send(0,imageData);
            else
                [ imageData, seq( Grid:-Receive(i), i = 1..n-1 ) ];
            end;
        end proc:

        ModuleApply := proc ( ptsX, ptsY, iter, X1, X2, Y1, Y2, bailout )
            local X, Y, imageData, ret, i, l, u:

            X := Vector(ptsX, i->X1+(X2-X1)*(i-1)/(ptsX-1) , datatype =
float[8]);
            Y := Vector(ptsY, i->Y1+(Y2-Y1)*(i-1)/(ptsY-1) , datatype =
float[8]);

            ret := Grid:-Launch( MandelGrid, X, Y, iter, bailout,
                                imports=[ ':-MandelLoop'=eval(MandelLoop)
] );
            imageData := Array( 1..ptsX, 1..ptsY, 1..3, datatype=float[8] );

            for i in ret
            do
                l := lowerbound( i );
                u := upperbound( i );
                imageData[l[1]..u[1], l[2]..u[2], 1..3] := i;
            end;

            imageData;
        end proc:
end:
```

For this example we are executing on a four core machine.

```
> Grid:-NumNodes();
```

$$4 \qquad (15.26)$$

```
> s := time[real]():
  points := Mandelbrot( N, N, 100, -2.0, .7, -1.35, 1.35, 10.0 ):
  time[real]()-s;
```

$$30.189 \qquad (15.27)$$

Although we do see a speed up, it is not a good as we'd expect. If you execute this example and watch the CPU utilization, you'll notice that some nodes complete quite quickly, while others run for longer. This indicates that the distribution of work is uneven between nodes.

We can improve this by using a Client/Server model for work distribution. In this model, one node (node 0 in our case) acts as a server handing out work to clients as they request it. As long as work is available the clients can continue computing. In the following example the server passes row indexes to the clients. The client then computes the entire row. The computed row is sent back to the server, which collects all the rows and reconstructs them into the final Array.

It is important to notice that the following example starts an extra node. The server node does relatively little work, compared to the other nodes. Thus we create one client for each processor. The server node does not need a complete processor for itself.

```
Mandelbrot := module()
    local
            ComputeLine,
            GridFunction,
            Server,
            Client,
            ModuleApply;

    ComputeLine := proc( X, Y, imageArray, j_low, j_high, iter, bailout )
        local j, Xc, Yc, Xtemp, Ytemp, Xold, Yold, k, t;
        option hfloat;

    for j from j_low to j_high do
        Xtemp := X;
        Ytemp := Y[j];
        Xc := Xtemp;
        Yc := Ytemp;
        k := 0;

        imageArray[j, 1] := 0.0;
        imageArray[j, 2] := 0.0;
        imageArray[j, 3] := 0.0;

        while k < iter do
            Xold := Xtemp;
            Yold := Ytemp;
            Xtemp := Xold^2-Yold^2+Xc;
            Ytemp := 2*Xold*Yold+Yc;
            t := Xtemp^2+Ytemp^2;
            if t >= bailout then
                imageArray[j, 1] := k - ln( ln( t ) )/ln(2.);
                imageArray[j, 2] := imageArray[j, 1];
                imageArray[j, 3] := imageArray[j, 1];
                break;
            end if;
```

```
            k := k+1;
        end do;
    end do;
end proc:

Server := proc( X, Y, iter, bailout )
    local i, msg, imageData;

    imageData := Array( 1..numelems(X), 1..numelems(Y), 1..3,
datatype=float[8] );

    for i from 1 to numelems(X)
    do
        # get a request for work
        msg := Grid:-Receive();
        # send out work
        Grid:-Send( msg[1], i );

        if ( numelems( msg ) > 1 ) then
            # if the request included a result, store it
            imageData[ msg[2], 1..numelems(Y), 1..3 ] := msg[3];
        end;
    end;

    # we've sent out all the data, receive the last results
    for i from 1 to Grid:-NumNodes()-1
    do
        msg := Grid:-Receive();
        imageData[ msg[2], 1..numelems(Y), 1..3 ] := msg[3];
    end;

    # send terminate messages out to the nodes.
    for i from 1 to Grid:-NumNodes()-1
    do
        Grid:-Send( i, -1 );
    end;

    imageData;
end;

Client := proc( i, X, Y, iter, bailout )
    local msg, imageData;

    imageData := Array( 1..numelems(Y), 1..3, datatype=float[8] );
```

```
        # send the initial request for data
        Grid:-Send( 0, [i] );

        do
            # wait for a reply
            msg := Grid:-Receive( 0 );

            # if it is a terminate message break out of the loop
            if ( msg = -1 ) then
                break;
            end;

            # calculate the row, send it back to the master
            ComputeLine( X[msg], Y, imageData, 1, numelems(Y), iter, bailout );
            Grid:-Send( 0, [i,msg,imageData] );
        end;

        NULL;
    end;

    GridFunction := proc( X, Y, iter, bailout )
        local i;

        i := Grid:-MyNode();
        if ( i = 0 ) then
            Server( X, Y , iter, bailout );
        else
            Client( i, X, Y , iter, bailout );
        end;
    end proc:

    ModuleApply := proc ( ptsX, ptsY, iter, X1, X2, Y1, Y2, bailout )
        local X, Y, ret:

        X := Vector(ptsX, i->X1+(X2-X1)*(i-1)/(ptsX-1) , datatype = float[8]);
        Y := Vector(ptsY, i->Y1+(Y2-Y1)*(i-1)/(ptsY-1) , datatype = float[8]);

        Grid:-Launch( GridFunction, X, Y, iter, bailout,
                        numnodes=Grid:-NumNodes()+1,
                        imports=[
                            ':-ComputeLine'=eval(ComputeLine),
                            ':-Server'=eval(Server),
```

```
                        ':-Client'=eval(Client)
                        ] );
    end proc:
end:
> s := time[real]():
  points := Mandelbrot( N, N, 100, -2.0, .7, -1.35, 1.35, 10.0 ):
  time[real]()-s;
```

$$15.033 \tag{15.28}$$

Using the client/server model to better distribute the work over the nodes, we get speed ups that match our expectations, four processors leads to a four times speed up.

15.10 The Grid Computing Toolbox

In addition to the Grid package included in Maple, the **Grid Computing Toolbox** is available as an add-on for Maple. The Grid Computing Toolbox enables nodes to run on remote Grid servers. These remote servers can support a much larger number of nodes distributed over multiple computers.

An algorithm implemented on top of the Grid package that ships with Maple should work on top of the Grid Computing Toolbox. The Grid Computing Toolbox does introduce new functions, however these functions are mostly dedicated to managing remote servers.

There are a few differences between local and remote execution. First, local nodes may start with local Maple libraries available. These libraries will generally not be available to remote nodes. Instead of relying on sharing the libraries via **libname**, explicitly pass the routines you need using the **Launch** command's **imports** parameter.

15.11 Limitations

There are a few situations where it may be difficult to effectively take advantage of the Grid package.

Memory Usage

With the Grid package, multiple processes run on the local machine. If the original computation requires a significant amount of memory, then each Grid node may still require a significant amount of memory, effectively multiplying the amount of memory needed by the number of nodes. This could consume all the memory resources on the machine, which can make the entire computation slower in the long run.

Cost of Communication

Passing data between nodes can be slow. Algorithms where each node needs to have access to a large amount of data may be difficult to speed up using the Grid package. Minimizing the amount of data passed between nodes can be an effective way to optimize a Grid-based computation.

Load Balancing

The Grid package currently does not have any built in load balancing. Therefore the programmer is responsible for making sure that all the nodes are kept busy. This can be difficult. You need to balance the need to have work available for nodes to compute with the overhead of excessive communication.

15.12 Troubleshooting

Deadlocking

Some care must be taken when using **Send** and **Receive**. A call to **Receive** will wait until a message is received, so if all nodes call **Receive** when there are no messages to be read, the execution will deadlock. In addition there are a few limitations on what types of expressions can be used for messages. See the **Grid:-Send** help page for more information.

When an unhandled exception is raised on a node this will cause the node to exit prematurely. This may cause a **Send** or **Receive** to be missed, leading to a deadlock.

'libname' and Other Engine Variables

The nodes started by the Grid package are independent from the main engine. Thus changes in the state of the main engine will not be reflected in the other nodes. In particular the value of **libname** on the nodes may not be the same as the value of **libname** in the main engine. When running local grid, the local nodes will use the same **libname** as used in the main engine when the first Grid computation is started. Later changes to **libname** will not effect the nodes. In general, it is better to use the **Launch** command's **imports** argument to pass values to the nodes instead of relying on **libname**.

With remote servers and the Grid Computing Toolbox, the value of **libname** in the main engine will have no effect on the value of **libname** set in the remote nodes.

Missing Functions

Forgetting to send all the necessary functions to the nodes may lead to nodes exiting without properly executing the work they have been given. This may occur without any exceptions being raised.

16 Testing, Debugging, and Efficiency

New programs, whether developed in Maple or any other language, sometimes work incorrectly. Problems that occur when a program is run can be caused by syntax errors introduced during implementation, logic errors in the design of the algorithm, or errors in the translation of an algorithm's description into code. Many errors can be subtle and hard to find by visually inspecting your program. Maple provides error detection commands and a debugger to help you find these errors.

Maple has several commands to help you find errors in procedures. Among these are commands to trace procedure execution, check assertions, raise exceptions and trap errors, and verify procedure semantics and syntax.

Additionally, the Maple debugger lets you stop in an executing Maple procedure, inspect and modify the values of local and global variables, and continue the execution process, either to completion, or one statement or block at a time. You can stop the execution process when Maple reaches a particular statement, when it assigns a value to a specified local or global variable, or when a specified error occurs. This facility lets you investigate the inner workings of a program.

Even when a program is working correctly, you may want to analyze its performance to try to improve its efficiency. Maple commands are available to analyze the time and memory consumption involved in running a program.

16.1 In This Chapter

- Using the Maple debugger
- Detailed debugger information
- Additional commands for error detection
- Measuring and improving program efficiency

16.2 The Maple Debugger: A Tutorial Example

The Maple debugger is a tool that you can use to detect errors in your procedures. Using this facility, you can follow the step-by-step execution of your code to determine why it is not returning the results that you expect.

This section illustrates how to use the Maple debugger as a tool for debugging a Maple procedure. The debugger commands are introduced and described as they are applied. For more information about the debugger commands, see *Maple Debugger Commands (page 593)*.

You can use the command-line Maple debugger or you can use the interactive Maple debugger available in the standard interface.

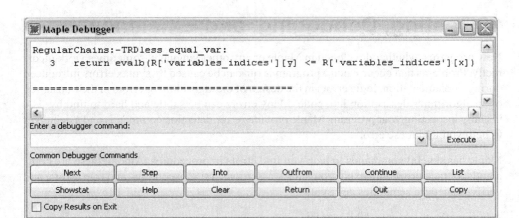

Figure 16.1: The Maple Debugger in the Standard Interface

In the standard interface, the interactive Maple debugger is opened automatically by Maple when a breakpoint or watchpoint is encountered during the execution of a program. An interactive debugger window is displayed, which contains the following components:

- a main text box that displays a procedure name and the debugger output
- a field for entering commands and an associated **Execute** button
- buttons that perform common debugging functions

While the interactive debugger has a different user interface, it otherwise functions identically to the command-line Maple debugger. For more information, refer to the **InteractiveDebugger** help page.

This section introduces various debugger commands. To present and describe all of the options available for these commands, the command-line debugger will be used instead of the interactive debugger. Note that the **Common Debugger Commands** buttons in the interactive debugger always implement the corresponding commands with their *default* options. To run a debugger command with non-default options in the interactive debugger, enter the command and options in the **Enter a debugger command:** field and click the **Execute** button.

Example

Consider the following procedure, **sieve**, which is used as a case study. It implements the *Sieve of Eratosthenes*: given a parameter **n**, return a count of the prime numbers less than or equal to **n**. To debug the **sieve** procedure, breakpoints and watchpoints will be used to stop the the execution of the procedure at selected points or on selected events.

```
> sieve := proc(n::integer)
       local i, k, flags, count,twicei;
       count := 0;
       for i from 2 to n do
          flags[i] := true;
       end do;
       for i from 2 to n do
          if flags[i] then
             twicei := 2*i;
             for k from twicei by i to n do
                flags[k] = false;
             end do;
             count := count+1;
          end if;
       end do;
       count;
   end proc:
```

Numbering the Procedure Statements I

To use the Maple debugger, you can enter several debugger commands. Many of these debugger commands refer to statements in the procedures that you are debugging. *Statement numbers* allow such references. The **showstat** command displays a Maple procedure along with numbers preceding each line that begins a new statement.

```
> showstat(sieve);

sieve := proc(n::integer)
local i, k, flags, count, twicei;
   1   count := 0;
   2   for i from 2 to n do
   3     flags[i] := true
       end do;
   4   for i from 2 to n do
   5     if flags[i] then
   6       twicei := 2*i;
   7       for k from twicei by i to n do
   8         flags[k] = false
           end do;
   9       count := count+1
       end if
     end do;
  10   count
end proc
```

Note: The numbers preceding each line differ from line numbers that may be displayed in a text editor. For example, keywords that end a statement (such as **end do** and **end if**) are not considered separate Maple commands and are therefore not numbered.

Invoking the Debugger I

To invoke the Maple debugger, execute a procedure and then stop the execution process within the procedure. To execute a Maple procedure, call it by using a Maple command at the top level or call it from another procedure. The simplest way to stop the execution process is to set a *breakpoint* in the procedure.

Setting a Breakpoint

Use the **stopat** command to set a breakpoint in the **sieve** procedure.

```
> stopat(sieve);
```

$$[sieve] \qquad (16.1)$$

This command sets a breakpoint before the first statement in the procedure **sieve**. When you subsequently execute the **sieve** procedure, Maple stops before executing the first statement and waits for you to provide instructions on what to do next. When the execution process stops, the debugger prompt is displayed (**DBG>**).

Note: If a procedure has a remember table or a **cache** table, you may have to run the **restart** command before running a second or subsequent **stopat** command. For more information about remember tables and cache tables, see *The remember, cache, and system Options (page 218)* or refer to the **remember** or **CacheCommand** help pages.

In the following example, the **sieve** procedure is called.

```
> sieve(10);
sieve:
   1*   count := 0;

DBG>
```

Several pieces of information are displayed after the debugger prompt.

- The previously computed result. This particular execution process stopped at the first statement before making any computations, so no result appears.
- The name of the procedure in which the execution process has stopped (**sieve**).
- The execution process stopped before statement number **1**. An asterisk (*) follows this statement number to indicate that a breakpoint was set before the statement.

At the debugger prompt, you can evaluate Maple expressions and call debugger commands. Maple evaluates expressions in the context of the stopped procedure. You have access to the same procedure parameters, and local, global, and environment variables as the stopped procedure. For example, since the **sieve** procedure was called with parameter value **10**, the formal parameter **n** has the value **10**.

```
DBG> n
10
sieve:
   1*   count := 0;
```

For each expression that Maple evaluates,

- the result of the expression is displayed; if there is no result, the most recent previous result is displayed (this output can be suppressed by using a colon to terminate the command entered at the **DBG>** prompt)
- the name of the stopped procedure
- the statement number where the procedure stopped followed by the statement, and
- a new debugger prompt.

Note: To remove a breakpoint from a procedure, use the **unstopat** command.

Controlling the Execution of a Procedure during Debugging I

Debugger commands control how the procedure is executed once the debugger is started. Some commonly used debugger commands are **next**, **step**, **into**, **list**, **outfrom**, and **cont**.

The **next** command runs the next statement at the current nesting level. After the statement is run, control is returned to the debugger. If the statement is a control structure (for example, an **if** statement or a loop), the debugger runs any statements within the control structure that it would normally run. It stops the execution process before the next statement *after* the control structure. Similarly, if the statement contains calls to procedures, the debugger executes these procedure calls in their entirety before the execution process stops.

```
DBG> next
0
sieve:
   2     for i from 2 to n do
           ...
         end do;
DBG>
```

The **0** in the first line of the output represents the result of the statement that was run--that is, the result of **count := 0**. A "*" does not appear next to the statement number because there is no breakpoint set immediately before statement **2**. The debugger does not show the body of the **for** loop, which itself consists of statements with their own statement numbers, unless the execution process actually stops within its body. Maple represents the body of compound statements by ellipses (**...**).

Running the **next** command again results in the following output.

```
DBG> next
true
sieve:
   4     for i from 2 to n do
           ...
         end do;
DBG>
```

The execution process now stops before statement **4**. Statement **3** (the body of the previous **for** loop) is at a deeper nesting level. The loop is executed **n-1** times. The debugger displays the last result computed in the loop (the assignment of the value **true** to **flags[10]**).

> **Tip:** If you want to repeat the previous debugger command, as shown in the second **next** command above, you can press *Enter* at the **DBG>** prompt. You can also view your recent command history using the up and down arrow keys on your keyboard.

To step into a nested control structure (such as an **if** statement or **for** loop) or a procedure call, use the **step** debugger command.

```
DBG> step
true
sieve:
   5        if flags[i] then
```

```
          ...
          end if
DBG> step
true
sieve:
   6            twicei := 2*i;

DBG>
```

If you use the **step** debugger command when the next statement to run is *not* a deeper structured statement or procedure call, it has the same effect as the **next** debugger command.

```
DBG> step
4
sieve:
   7            for k from twicei by i to n do
                   ...
                end do;

DBG>
```

At any time during the debugging process, you can use the **showstat** debugger command to display the current status of the debugging process.

```
DBG> showstat

sieve := proc(n::integer)
local i, k, flags, count, twicei;
   1*    count := 0;
   2     for i from 2 to n do
   3        flags[i] := true
          end do;
   4     for i from 2 to n do
   5        if flags[i] then
   6           twicei := 2*i;
   7 !         for k from twicei by i to n do
   8              flags[k] = false
              end do;
   9           count := count+1
          end if
        end do;
  10     count
end proc

DBG>
```

Maple displays a debugger prompt to indicate that you are still working within the Maple debugger. The asterisk (*) indicates the *unconditional* breakpoint. An exclamation point (!) that follows a statement number (see line 7) indicates the statement at which the procedure is stopped.

To continue the debugging process, run another debugger command. For example, you can use **into** or **step** to enter the innermost loop.

The behavior of the **into** debugger command is between that of the **next** and **step** commands. The execution process stops at the next statement in the current procedure independent of whether it is at the current nesting level or in the body of a control structure (an **if** statement or a loop). That is, the **into** command steps into nested statements, but not procedure calls. It executes called procedures completely and then stops.

```
DBG> into
4
sieve:
   8          flags[k] = false

DBG>
```

A debugger command that is related to **showstat** is the **list** command. It displays the previous five statements, the current statement, and the next statement to indicate where the procedure has stopped.

```
DBG> list

sieve := proc(n::integer)
local i, k, flags, count, twicei;
      ...
   3       flags[i] := true
         end do;
   4     for i from 2 to n do
   5       if flags[i] then
   6         twicei := 2*i;
   7         for k from twicei by i to n do
   8 !         flags[k] = false
             end do;
   9         count := count+1
           end if
         end do;
      ...
end proc

DBG>
```

You can use the **outfrom** debugger command to finish the execution process at the current nesting level or at a deeper level. Execution of the procedure is stopped once a statement at a shallower nesting level is reached, that is, after a loop terminates, a branch of an **if** statement executes, or the current procedure call returns.

```
DBG> outfrom
true = false
sieve:
    9          count := count+1

DBG> outfrom
1
sieve:
    5          if flags[i] then
                  ...
               end if

DBG>
```

The **cont** debugger command continues the execution process until either the procedure stops normally or encounters another breakpoint.

```
DBG> cont
```

$$9 \qquad (16.2)$$

The procedure does not give the expected output. Although you may find the reason obvious from the previous debugger command examples, in other cases, it may not be easy to find procedure errors. Therefore, continue to use the debugger. First, use the **unstopat** command to remove the breakpoint from the **sieve** procedure.

```
> unstopat(sieve);
```

$$[\,] \qquad (16.3)$$

Invoking the Debugger II

The procedure **sieve** maintains the changing result in the variable **count**. Therefore, a logical place to look during debugging is wherever Maple modifies **count**. The easiest way to do this is by using a *watchpoint*, which starts the debugger whenever Maple modifies a variable that you identify.

Setting a Watchpoint

Use the **stopwhen** command to set watchpoints. In this case, the execution process will stop whenever Maple modifies the variable **count** in the procedure **sieve**.

```
> stopwhen([sieve,count]);
```

$$[[\textit{sieve}, \textit{count}]] \tag{16.4}$$

The **stopwhen** command returns a list of all the currently *watched* variables (that is, the variables that you provided to the **stopwhen** command).

Execute the **sieve** procedure again.

```
> sieve(10);
```

```
count := 0
sieve:
   2     for i from 2 to n do
            ...
         end do;

DBG>
```

The execution process stops because Maple modified **count** and the debugger displays the assignment statement **count := 0**. Similar to breakpoints, the debugger then displays the name of the procedure and the next statement to be run in the procedure. Note that the execution process stops *after* Maple assigns a value to **count**.

This first assignment to **count** is correct. Use the **cont** debugger command to continue the execution process.

```
DBG> cont
count := 1
sieve:
   5     if flags[i] then
            ...
         end if

DBG>
```

At first glance, this may look correct. Assume that the output is correct and continue the execution process.

```
DBG> cont
count := 2*1
sieve:
   5     if flags[i] then
            ...
         end if

DBG>
```

This output appears to be incorrect because Maple should have simplified **2*1**. Note that it printed **2*l** (two times the letter l) instead. By examining the source text for the procedure, you can see that the letter "**l**" was entered instead of the number "**1**". Since the source of the error has been discovered, you can stop the procedure. Use the **quit** debugger command to stop the debugger, and then use the **unstopwhen** command to remove the watchpoint from the procedure.

```
DBG> quit
Interrupted
```

> unstopwhen();

$$[\,] \tag{16.5}$$

After correcting the source code for **sieve**, run the **restart** command, re-execute that source code (for example, read it into your command-line session or re-execute that code region in your worksheet), and execute the procedure again.

> restart;

> sieve := proc(n::integer)
            local i, k, flags, count,twicei;
            count := 0;
            for i from 2 to n do
                flags[i] := true;
            end do;
            for i from 2 to n do
                if flags[i] then
                    twicei := 2*i;
                    for k from twicei by i to n do
                        flags[k] = false;
                    end do;
                    count := count+1;
                end if;
            end do;
            count;
    end proc:

> sieve(10);

$$9 \tag{16.6}$$

This result is still incorrect. There are four primes less than 10, namely 2, 3, 5, and 7. Therefore, start the debugger once more, stepping into the innermost parts of the procedure to investigate. Since you do not want to start executing the procedure from the start, set the breakpoint at statement **6**.

```
> stopat(sieve,6);
```
$$[sieve] \qquad (16.7)$$
```
> sieve(10);
```
```
true
sieve:
   6*       twicei := 2*i;

DBG> step
4
sieve:
   7         for k from twicei by i to n do
             ...
             end do;

DBG> step
4
sieve:
   8             flags[k] = false

DBG> step
true = false
sieve:
   8             flags[k] = false

DBG>
```

The last step reveals the error. The previously computed result should have been **false** (from the assignment of **flags[k]** to the value **false**), but instead the value **true = false** was returned. An equation was used instead of an assignment. Therefore, Maple did not set **flags[k]** to **false**.

Once again, stop the debugger and correct the source text.

```
DBG> quit
Interrupted
```

The following code represents the corrected procedure.

```
> sieve := proc(n::integer)
          local i, k, flags, count,twicei;
          count := 0;
          for i from 2 to n do
              flags[i] := true
          end do;
```

```
          for i from 2 to n do
             if flags[i] then
                twicei := 2*i;
                for k from twicei by i to n do
                   flags[k] := false;
                end do;
                count := count+1;
             end if;
          end do;
          count;
    end proc:
```

Execute the **sieve** procedure again to test the corrections.

> `sieve(10);`

$$4 \tag{16.8}$$

The **sieve** procedure returns the correct result.

16.3 Maple Debugger Commands

This section provides additional details about the commands used in *The Maple Debugger: A Tutorial Example (page 581)* and a description of other debugger commands.

Numbering the Procedure Statements II

The **showstat** command has the following syntax. The **procedureName** parameter is optional.

```
showstat( procedureName );
```

If **showstat** is called with no arguments, all procedures that contain breakpoints are displayed.

You can also use the **showstat** command to display a single statement or a range of statements by using the following syntax.

```
showstat( procedureName, number );
showstat( procedureName, range );
```

In these cases, the statements that are not displayed are represented by ellipses (...). The procedure name, its parameters, and its local and global variables are always displayed.

```
> f := proc(x)
          if x <= 2 then
             print(x);
          end if;
```

```
            print(-x);
    end proc:
> showstat(f, 2..3);

f := proc(x)
        ...
    2     print(x)
        end if;
    3   print(-x)
end proc
```

Invoking the Debugger III

This section provides additional information about breakpoints and watchpoints.

Setting Breakpoints

The **stopat** command has the following syntax, where **procedureName** is the name of the procedure in which to set the breakpoint, **statementNumber** is the line number of the statement in the procedure *before* which the breakpoint is set, and **condition** is a Boolean expression which must be *true* to stop the execution process. The **statementNumber** and **condition** arguments are optional.

```
stopat( procedureName, statementNumber, condition );
```

The **condition** argument can refer to any global variable, local variable, or parameter of the procedure. These *conditional* breakpoints are indicated by a question mark (**?**) if the **showstat** command is used to display the procedure.

Since the **stopat** command sets the breakpoint before the specified statement, when Maple encounters a breakpoint, the execution process stops and Maple starts the debugger *before* the statement.

> **Note:** This means that you *cannot* set a breakpoint after the last statement in a statement sequence--that is, at the end of a loop body, an if statement body, or a procedure.

If two identical procedures exist, depending on how you created them, they may share breakpoints. If you entered the procedures individually, with identical procedure bodies, they do not share breakpoints. If you created a procedure by assigning it to the body of another procedure, their breakpoints are shared.

```
> f := proc(x) x^2 end proc:
  g := proc(x) x^2 end proc:
  h := op(g):
  stopat(g);
```

$$[g, h] \tag{16.9}$$

```
> showstat();

g := proc(x)
   1*   x^2
end proc


h := proc(x)
   1*   x^2
end proc
```

Removing Breakpoints

The **unstopat** command has the following syntax, where **procedureName** is the name of the procedure that contains the breakpoint, and **statementNumber** is the line number of the statement where the breakpoint is set. The **statementNumber** parameter is optional.

```
unstopat( procedureName, statementNumber );
```

If **statementNumber** is omitted in the call to **unstopat**, *all* breakpoints in the procedure **procedureName** are cleared.

Setting Explicit Breakpoints

You can set an explicit breakpoint by inserting a call to the **DEBUG** command in the source text of a procedure. The **DEBUG** command has the following syntax. The **argument** parameter is optional.

```
DEBUG( argument );
```

If no argument is included in the **DEBUG** command, execution in the procedure stops at the statement *following* the location of the **DEBUG** command, and then the debugger is started.

Note: The **showstat** command does not mark explicit breakpoints with an "*" or a "?".

```
> f := proc(x,y) local a;
        a:=x^2;
        DEBUG();
        a:=y^2;
  end proc:
```

```
> showstat(f);

f := proc(x, y)
local a;
   1   a := x^2;
   2   DEBUG();
   3   a := y^2
end proc

> f(2,3);
```
```
4
f:
   3   a := y^2
DBG> quit
Interrupted
```

If the argument of the **DEBUG** command is a Boolean expression, the execution process stops only if the Boolean expression evaluates to **true**. If the Boolean expression evaluates to **false** or **FAIL**, the **DEBUG** command is ignored.

```
> f := proc(x,y) local a;
           a:=x^2;
           DEBUG(a<1);
           a:=y^2;
           DEBUG(a>1);
           print(a);
  end proc:
> f(2,3);
```
```
9
f:
   5   print(a)
DBG> quit
Interrupted
```

If the argument of the **DEBUG** command is a value other than a Boolean expression, the debugger prints the value of the argument (instead of the last result) when the execution process stops at the following statement.

```
> f := proc(x)
           x^2;
           DEBUG("This is my breakpoint. The current value of x is:",
   x);
```

```
            x^3;
    end proc:
> f(2);
```

```
"This is my breakpoint. The current value of x is:",
2
f:
   3    x^3

DBG>
```

Removing Explicit Breakpoints

The **unstopat** command cannot remove explicit breakpoints. You must remove breakpoints that were set by using **DEBUG** by editing the source text for the procedure.

```
DBG> unstopat
[f]
f:
   3    x^3

DBG> showstat

f := proc(x)
   1    x^2;
   2    DEBUG("This is my breakpoint. The current value of x is:", x);
   3  !  x^3
end proc

DBG> quit
Interrupted
```

Note: If you display the contents of a procedure by using the **print** command (or **lprint**) and the procedure contains a breakpoint that was set by using **stopat**, the breakpoint appears as a call to **DEBUG**.

```
> f := proc(x) x^2 end proc:
> stopat(f);
```

$$[f, g, h] \qquad (16.10)$$

```
> print(f);
```

$$\textbf{proc}(x) \; DEBUG(\;); \; x^2 \; \textbf{end proc} \qquad (16.11)$$

Setting Watchpoints

The **stopwhen** command can take the following forms.

```
stopwhen( globalVariableName );
stopwhen( [procedureName, variableName] );
```

The first form specifies that the debugger should be started when the global variable **globalVariableName** is changed. Maple environment variables, such as **Digits**, can also be monitored by using this method.

```
> stopwhen(Digits);
```

$$[Digits] \qquad (16.12)$$

The second form starts the debugger when the (local or global) variable **variableName** is changed in the procedure **procedureName**.

When any form of **stopwhen** is called, Maple returns a list of the current watchpoints.

The execution process stops *after* Maple assigns a value to the watched variable. The debugger displays an assignment statement instead of the last computed result (which would otherwise be the right-hand side of the assignment statement).

Clearing Watchpoints

The syntax to call **unstopwhen** is the same as that for **stopwhen**. Similar to the **stopwhen** command, the **unstopwhen** command returns a list of all (remaining) watchpoints.

If no arguments are included in the call to **unstopwhen**, then *all* watchpoints are cleared.

Setting Watchpoints on Specified Errors

You can use an error watchpoint to start the debugger when Maple returns a specified error message. When a watched error occurs, the procedure stops executing and the debugger displays the statement in which the error occurred.

Error watchpoints are set by using the **stoperror** command. The **stoperror** command has the following syntax

```
stoperror( "errorMessage" );
```

where **errorMessage** is a *string* or a *symbol* that represents the error message returned from the evaluation of a Maple expression. If the argument is a string, the debugger will be started when an error for which the given string is a prefix is encountered. A list of the current error watchpoints is returned.

If no argument is entered in the call to **stoperror**, the list of current (error) watchpoints is returned.

```
> stoperror();
```
$$[\,] \tag{16.13}$$

```
> stoperror( "numeric exception: division by zero" );
```
$$[\text{"numeric exception: division by zero"}] \tag{16.14}$$

```
> stoperror();
```
$$[\text{"numeric exception: division by zero"}] \tag{16.15}$$

If the special name `all` is used instead of a specific error message as the parameter to the **stoperror** command, a procedure stops executing when *any* error that would not be trapped occurs.

Errors trapped by an error trapping construct (**try...catch** statement) do not generate an error message. Therefore, the **stoperror** command cannot be used to catch them. For more information about the **try...catch** structure, see *Trapping Errors (page 189)*. If the special name `traperror` is used instead of a specific error message as the parameter to the **stoperror** command, a procedure stops executing when any error that is trapped occurs. If the **errorMessage** parameter is entered in the form **traperror["message"]** to **stoperror**, the debugger starts only if the error specified by **"message"** is trapped.

When a procedure stops executing because of an error which causes an exception, continued execution is not possible. Any of the execution control commands, such as **next** or **step** (see *Controlling the Execution of a Procedure during Debugging I (page 585)* and *Controlling the Execution of a Procedure during Debugging II (page 601)*), process the error as if the debugger had not intervened. For example, consider the following two procedures. The first procedure, **f**, calculates **1/x**. The other procedure, **g**, calls **f** but traps the **"division by zero"** error that occurs when **x = 0**.

```
> f := proc(x) 1/x end proc:
  g := proc(x) local r;
          try
            f(x);
          catch:
            infinity;
          end try;
  end proc:
```

If procedure **g** is executed at **x=9**, the reciprocal is returned.

```
> g(9);
```

$$\frac{1}{9} \tag{16.16}$$

At **x=0**, as expected, a value of infinity is returned.

> `g(0);`

$$\infty \tag{16.17}$$

The **stoperror** command stops the execution process when you call **f** directly.

> `stoperror("numeric exception: division by zero");`

$$[\text{"numeric exception: division by zero"}] \tag{16.18}$$

> `f(0);`

```
Error, numeric exception: division by zero
f:
   1   1/x
DBG> cont
Error, (in f) numeric exception: division by zero
```

The call to **f** from **g** is within a **try...catch** statement, so the **"division by zero"** error does not start the debugger.

> `g(0);`

$$\infty \tag{16.19}$$

Instead, try using the **stoperror(traperror)** command.

> `unstoperror( "numeric exception: division by zero" );`

$$[\,] \tag{16.20}$$

> `stoperror( `traperror` );`

$$[\mathit{traperror}] \tag{16.21}$$

This time, Maple does not stop at the error in **f**.

> `f(0);`

`Error, (in f) numeric exception: division by zero`

However, Maple starts the debugger when the trapped error occurs.

> `g(0);`

```
Error, numeric exception: division by zero
f:
   1   1/x

DBG> step
Error, numeric exception: division by zero
```

```
g:
   3         infinity
DBG> step
```

$$\infty \tag{16.22}$$

In the case that a particular error message is specified in the form **traperror["message"]**, the debugger is started only if the error specified by **"message"** *is* trapped.

Clearing Watchpoints on Specified Errors

Error watchpoints are cleared by using the top-level **unstoperror** command. The syntax to call the **unstoperror** command is the same as for the **stoperror** command. Like the **stoperror** command, the **unstoperror** command returns a list of all (remaining) error watchpoints.

If no argument is included in the call to **unstoperror**, *all* error watchpoints are cleared.

```
> unstoperror();
```

$$[\ ] \tag{16.23}$$

Controlling the Execution of a Procedure during Debugging II

After stopping the execution of a procedure and starting the debugger, you can examine the values of variables or perform other experiments (see the following section, **Changing the State of a Procedure during Debugging**). After you have examined the state of the procedure, you can continue the execution process by using several different debugger commands.

The most commonly used debugger commands are **into**, **next**, **step**, **cont**, **outfrom**, **return**, and **quit**.

The **return** debugger command causes execution of the currently active procedure call to complete. The execution process stops at the first statement after the current procedure.

The other commands are described in the tutorial in *The Maple Debugger: A Tutorial Example (page 581)*. For more information on these and other debugger commands, refer to the **debugger** help page.

Changing the State of a Procedure during Debugging

When a breakpoint or watchpoint stops the execution of a procedure, the Maple debugger is started. In the debugger mode, you can examine the state of the global variables, local variables, and parameters of the stopped procedure. You can also determine where the execution process stopped, evaluate expressions, and examine procedures.

While in the debugger mode, you can evaluate any Maple expression and perform assignments to local and global variables. To evaluate an expression, enter the expression at the debugger prompt. To perform assignments to variables, use the standard Maple assignment statement.

```
> f := proc(x) x^2 end proc:
> stopat(f);
```

$$[f] \qquad (16.24)$$

```
> f(10);
```

```
f:
   1*   x^2
DBG> sin(3.0);
.1411200081
f:
   1*   x^2
DBG> cont
```

$$100 \qquad (16.25)$$

The debugger evaluates any variable names that you use in the expression in the context of the stopped procedure. Names of parameters or local variables evaluate to their current values in the procedure. Names of global variables evaluate to their current values. Environment variables, such as **Digits**, evaluate to their values in the stopped procedure's environment.

If an expression corresponds to a debugger command (for example, your procedure has a local variable named **step**), you can still evaluate it by enclosing it in parentheses.

```
> f := proc(step) local i;
           for i to 10 by step do
               i^2
           end do;
       end proc:
> stopat(f,2);
```

$$[f] \qquad (16.26)$$

```
> f(3);
```

```
f:
   2*   i^2
DBG> step
```

16.3 Maple Debugger Commands • 603

```
1
f:
    2*     i^2

DBG> (step)
3
f:
    2*     i^2

DBG> quit
Interrupted
```

When the execution process is stopped, you can modify local and global variables by using the assignment operator (:=). The following example sets a breakpoint in the loop only when the index variable is equal to **5**.

```
> sumn := proc(n) local i, sum;
            sum := 0;
            for i to n do
                sum := sum + i
            end do;
    end proc:
> showstat(sumn);

sumn := proc(n)
local i, sum;
   1   sum := 0;
   2   for i to n do
   3       sum := sum+i
       end do
end proc

> stopat(sumn,3,i=5);
```

$$[sumn] \qquad (16.27)$$

```
> sumn(10);
```

```
10
sumn:
   3?    sum := sum+i
```

Reset the index to **3** so that the breakpoint is encountered again.

```
DBG> i := 3
sumn:
   3?    sum := sum+i
```

```
DBG> cont
17
sumn:
   3?      sum := sum+i

DBG> cont
```

$$62 \tag{16.28}$$

Maple has added the numbers **1**, **2**, **3**, **4**, **3**, and **4** and returned **17** as the result. By continuing the execution of the procedure, the numbers **5**, **6**, **7**, **8**, **9**, and **10** are added and **62** is returned as the result.

Examining the State of a Procedure during Debugging

You can use two debugger commands to return information about the state of the procedure execution. The **list** debugger command shows you the location where the execution process stopped within the procedure and the **where** debugger command shows you the stack of procedure activations.

The **list** debugger command has the following syntax.

```
list procedureName statementNumber[..statNumber]
```

The **list** debugger command is similar to the **showstat** command, except that you do not need to specify arguments. If no arguments are included in the call to **list**, only the five previous statements, the current statement, and the next statement to be executed are displayed. This provides some context in the stopped procedure. In other words, it indicates the *static* position where the execution process stopped.

The **where** debugger command shows you the stack of procedure activations. Starting from the top level, it shows you the statement that is executing and the parameters it passed to the called procedure. The **where** debugger command repeats this for each level of procedure call until it reaches the current statement in the current procedure. In other words, it indicates the *dynamic* position where execution stopped. The **where** command has the following syntax.

```
where numLevels
```

To illustrate these commands, consider the following example. The procedure **check** calls the **sumn** procedure from the previous example.

```
> check := proc(i) local p, a, b;
           p := ithprime(i);
           a := sumn(p);
           b := p*(p+1)/2;
```

```
            evalb( a=b );
end proc:
```

There is a (conditional) breakpoint in **sumn**.

```
> showstat(sumn);

sumn := proc(n)
local i, sum;
   1   sum := 0;
   2   for i to n do
   3?     sum := sum+i
       end do
end proc
```

When **check** calls **sumn**, the breakpoint starts the debugger.

```
> check(9);
```

```
10
sumn:
   3?      sum := sum+i
```

The **where** debugger command shows that

- **check** was called from the top level with argument **9**,
- **check** called **sumn** with argument **23**, and
- the execution process stopped at statement number **3** in **sumn**.

```
DBG> where
TopLevel: check(9)
        [9]
check: a := sumn(p)
        [23]
sumn:
   3?     sum := sum+i

DBG> cont
```

$$true \tag{16.29}$$

The next example illustrates the use of **where** in a recursive function.

```
> fact := proc(x)
          if x <= 1 then
             1
          else
```

```
           x * fact(x-1)
        end if;
end proc:
> showstat(fact);

fact := proc(x)
   1   if x <= 1 then
   2      1
        else
   3      x*fact(x-1)
        end if
end proc
> stopat(fact,2);
```

$$[\,fact\,] \tag{16.30}$$

```
> fact(5);
```

```
fact:
   2*      1

DBG> where
TopLevel: fact(5)
          [5]
fact: x*fact(x-1)
          [4]
fact: x*fact(x-1)
          [3]
fact: x*fact(x-1)
          [2]
fact: x*fact(x-1)
          [1]
fact:
   2*      1

DBG>
```

If you do not want to view the entire history of the nested procedure calls, use the **numLevels** parameter in the call to the **where** debugger command to print a specified number of levels.

```
DBG> where 3
fact: x*fact(x-1)
          [2]
fact: x*fact(x-1)
          [1]
fact:
```

```
       2*       1
DBG> quit
Interrupted
```

The **showstop** command (and the **showstop** debugger command) displays a report of all the currently set breakpoints, watchpoints, and error watchpoints. Outside the debugger at the top level, the **showstop** command has the following syntax.

```
showstop();
```

The next example illustrates the use of the **showstop** command.

```
> f := proc(x) local y;
        if x < 2 then
            y := x;
            print(y^2);
        end if;
        print(-x);
        x^3;
   end proc:
```

In the following example, breakpoints are set.

```
> stopat(f):
> stopat(f,2):
> stopat(int);
```

$$[f, int] \tag{16.31}$$

In the following example, watchpoints are set.

```
> stopwhen(f,y):
> stopwhen(Digits);
```

$$[Digits, [f, y]] \tag{16.32}$$

In the following example, an error watchpoint is set.

```
> stoperror( "numeric exception: division by zero" );
```

$$["numeric exception: division by zero"] \tag{16.33}$$

The **showstop** command reports all the breakpoints and watchpoints.

```
> showstop();

Breakpoints in:
   f
   int

Watched variables:
   Digits
   y in procedure f

Watched errors:
   "numeric exception: division by zero"
```

Using Top-Level Commands at the Debugger Prompt

The **showstat**, **stopat**, **unstopat**, **stopwhen**, **unstopwhen**, **stoperror**, and **showstop** commands can be used at the debugger prompt. The following list describes the syntax rules for top-level commands used at the debugger prompt.

- Do not enclose the arguments of the command in parentheses.

- Do not separate the arguments of the command with a comma. The arguments must be separated by a space character.

- Do not use colons or semicolons to end statements.

- The procedure name is not required by any command. Commands that use a procedure name assume the currently stopped procedure if one is not specified.

- For the **stoperror** command, double quotes are not required.

Except for these rules, the debugger prompt call for each command is of the same form and takes the same arguments as the corresponding top-level command call.

Restrictions

At the debugger prompt, the only permissible Maple statements are debugger commands, expressions, and assignments. The debugger does not permit statements such as **if**, **while**, **for**, **read**, and **save**. However, you can use `if` to simulate an **if** statement and **seq** to simulate a loop.

The debugger cannot set breakpoints in, or step into, built-in commands, such as **diff** and **has**. These commands are implemented in **C** and compiled into the Maple kernel. Debugging information about these commands is not accessible to Maple. However, if a built-in command calls a library command, for example, the **diff** command calling `diff/sin`, you can use a breakpoint to stop in the latter.

If a procedure contains two identical statements that are expressions, the debugger cannot always determine the statement at which the execution process stopped. If this situation occurs, you can still use the debugger and the execution process can continue. The debugger issues a warning that the displayed statement number may be incorrect.

Note: This issue occurs because Maple stores all identical expressions as a single occurrence of the expression. The debugger cannot determine at which invocation the execution process stopped.

16.4 Detecting Errors

This section describes some simple commands that you can use for detecting errors in procedures that are written in Maple. If you are not successful in finding the error by using these commands, you can use the Maple debugger, which is discussed in *The Maple Debugger: A Tutorial Example (page 581)* and *Maple Debugger Commands (page 593)*, to display the stepwise execution of a procedure.

Tracing a Procedure

The simplest tools available for error detection in Maple are the **printlevel** environment variable, and the **trace** and **tracelast** commands. You can use these facilities to trace the execution of both user-defined and Maple library procedures. However, they differ in the type of information that is returned about a procedure.

The **printlevel** variable is used to control how much information is displayed when a program is executed. By assigning a large integer value to **printlevel**, you can monitor the execution of statements to selected levels of nesting within procedures. The default value of **printlevel** is **1**. Larger, positive integer values cause the display of more intermediate steps in a computation. Negative integer values suppress the display of information.

The **printlevel** environment variable is set by using the following syntax, where **n** is the level to which Maple commands are evaluated.

```
printlevel := n;
```

To determine what value of **n** to use, note that statements within a particular procedure are recognized in levels that are determined by the nesting of conditional or repetition statements, and by the nesting of procedures. Each loop or **if** condition increases the evaluation level by 1, and each procedure call increases the evaluation level by 5. Alternatively, you can use a sufficiently large value of **n** to ensure that all levels are traced. For example, **printlevel := 1000** displays information in procedures up to 200 levels deep.

```
> f := proc(x) local y; y := x^2; g(y) / 4; end proc:
  g := proc(x) local z; z := x^2; z * 2; end proc:
```

```
> f(3);
```

$$\frac{81}{2} \qquad (16.34)$$

```
> printlevel := 5;
> f(3);
```

```
{--> enter f, args = 3
                                           y := 9
                                             81/2
<-- exit f (now at top level) = 81/2}
                                             81/2
```

```
> printlevel := 10;
> f(3);
```

```
{--> enter f, args = 3
                                           y := 9
{--> enter g, args = 9
                                           z := 81
                                              162
<-- exit g (now in f) = 162}
                                             81/2
<-- exit f (now at top level) = 81/2}
                                             81/2
```

The amount of information that is displayed depends on whether the call to the procedure was terminated with a colon or a semicolon. If a colon is used, only the entry and exit points of the procedure are printed. If a semicolon is used, the results of the statements are also printed.

To reset the value of the **printlevel** variable, reassign its value to **1**.

```
> printlevel := 1;
```

By assigning a large value to **printlevel**, the trace of *all* subsequent Maple procedure calls is displayed. To display the trace of *specific* procedures, you can use the **trace** command. The **trace** command has the following syntax, where **arguments** is one or more procedure names.

```
trace(arguments);
```

The **trace** command returns an expression sequence containing the names of the traced procedures. To begin tracing, call the procedure.

```
> trace(f, g);
```

$$f, g \tag{16.35}$$

```
> f(3):
```

```
{--> enter f, args = 3
{--> enter g, args = 9
<-- exit g (now in f) = 162}
<-- exit f (now at top level) = 81/2}
```

Similar to **printlevel**, the amount of information that is displayed during tracing when **trace** is used depends on whether the call to the procedure was terminated with a colon or a semicolon. If a colon is used, only entry and exit points of the procedure are printed. If a semicolon is used, the results of the statements are also printed.

To turn off the tracing of specific procedures, use the **untrace** command.

```
> untrace(f, g);
```

$$f, g \tag{16.36}$$

```
> f(3);
```

$$\frac{81}{2} \tag{16.37}$$

Note: You can use **debug** and **undebug** as alternate names for **trace** and **untrace**.

If running a procedure results in the display of an error message, you can use the **tracelast** command to determine the last statement executed and the values of variables at the time of the error. The **tracelast** command has the following syntax.

```
tracelast;
```

After an error message is displayed, the following information is returned from a call to **tracelast**.

- The first line displays which procedure was called and what values were used for the parameters.
- The second line displays the # symbol, the procedure name with the line number of the statement that was executed, and the statement that was executed.
- Finally, if there are any local variables in the procedure, they are displayed with their corresponding values.

```
> f := proc(x) local i, j, k;
          i := x;
          j = x^2;
          seq(k, k=i..j);
  end proc:
> f(2, 3);
Error, (in f) unable to execute seq
> tracelast;
```
```
f called with arguments: 2, 3
 #(f,3): seq(k,k = i .. j)
Error, (in f) unable to execute seq
 locals defined as: i = 2, j = j, k = k
```

You can find the error in this procedure by studying the results of the **tracelast** command--the assignment to the local variable **j** incorrectly uses an equal sign (=) instead of an assignment operator (:=).

The information provided by **tracelast** can become unavailable whenever Maple does a garbage collection. Therefore, it is advisable to use **tracelast** immediately after an error occurs. For more information about garbage collection in Maple, see *Garbage Collection (page 626)*.

Using Assertions

An *assertion* is a verification of the state of Maple at the time the assertion is made. You can include assertions in your procedure to guarantee pre- and post-conditions, and loop invariants during execution by using the **ASSERT** command. You can also use assertions to guarantee the value returned by a procedure or the value of local variables inside a procedure. The **ASSERT** command has the following syntax.

```
ASSERT( condition, message );
```

If **condition** evaluates to **false**, an error is generated and **message** is printed. If the first argument evaluates to **true**, **ASSERT** returns **NULL**.

To check assertions, turn on assertion checking before executing a procedure that contains an **ASSERT** command. To query the current state of assertion checking, or turn assertion checking on or off, use the **kernelopts** command.

The default state for assertion checking is no assertion checking (**assertlevel=0**).

Programming note: You should use assertions to verify that your program is working as intended. You should not use assertions to validate computations or values which are not completely in the control of your program, such as user input.

Turn assertion checking on:

```
> kernelopts(assertlevel=1);
```

$$0 \tag{16.38}$$

Note that when you set a kernelopts variable, such as when you turn assertion checking on or off, **kernelopts** returns its *previous* value.

At any time during the Maple session, you can check the setting for assertion checking by entering the following command.

```
> kernelopts(assertlevel);
```

$$1 \tag{16.39}$$

If assertion checking is on and a procedure that contains an **ASSERT** statement is executed, the condition represented by the **ASSERT** statement is checked.

```
> f := proc(x, y) local i, j;
        i := 0;
        j := 0;
        while (i <> x) do
          ASSERT(i > 0, "invalid index");
          j := j + y;
          i := i + 1;
        end do;
        j;
  end proc;
```

$$
\begin{aligned}
&f := \mathbf{proc}(x, y) \\
&\quad \mathbf{local}\ i, j; \\
&\quad i := 0; \\
&\quad j := 0; \\
&\quad \mathbf{while}\ i <> x\ \mathbf{do} \\
&\quad\quad \mathit{ASSERT}(0 < i, \text{"invalid index"});\ j := j + y;\ i := i + 1 \\
&\quad \mathbf{end\ do}; \\
&\quad j \\
&\mathbf{end\ proc}
\end{aligned}
\tag{16.40}
$$

```
> f(2, 3);
Error, (in f) assertion failed, invalid index
```

Use the **kernelopts** command again to turn assertion checking off. (Again, **kernelopts** returns its *previous* value.) When assertion checking is off, the overhead of processing an **ASSERT** statement in a procedure is minimal.

```
> kernelopts(assertlevel=0);
```

$$1 \tag{16.41}$$

For information on assertion checking and procedures, see *Return Type (page 213)*) and *Variables in Procedures (page 221)*.

Related to assertions are Maple warning messages. The **WARNING** command causes a specified warning message to display. The warning is preceded by the string "'Warning, '". The **WARNING** command has the following syntax.

```
WARNING( msgString, msgParam1, msgParam2, ... );
```

The **msgString** parameter is the text of the warning message and **msgParam***i* are optional parameters to substitute into **msgString**, if any. For more information on message parameters, see *Handling Exceptions (page 615)*.

```
> f := proc(x)
       if x < 0 then
           WARNING("sqrt(%1) is complex", x);
       end if;
       sqrt(x);
  end proc;
```

$$f := \mathbf{proc}(x)$$
$$\quad \mathbf{if}\ x < 0\ \mathbf{then}\ \textit{WARNING}(\text{"sqrt(\%1) is complex"}, x)\ \mathbf{end\ if};$$
$$\quad \text{sqrt}(x)$$
$$\mathbf{end\ proc} \tag{16.42}$$

```
> f(-2);
```

```
Warning, sqrt(-2) is complex
```

$$I\sqrt{2} \tag{16.43}$$

By default, warning messages are displayed. You can hide warning messages by using the **interface(warnlevel=0)** command. In this case, the warning is not displayed and the call to **WARNING** has no effect.

```
> interface(warnlevel=0);
```

$$3 \tag{16.44}$$

```
> f(-2);
```

$$I\sqrt{2} \qquad (16.45)$$

Handling Exceptions

An *exception* is an event that occurs during the execution of a procedure that disrupts the normal flow of instructions. Many kinds of actions can cause exceptions, for example, attempting to read from a file that does not exist. Maple has two mechanisms available when such situations occur:

- the **error** statement to raise an exception, and
- the **try...catch...finally** block to handle exceptions.

Raising Exceptions

The **error** statement raises an exception. Execution of the current statement sequence is interrupted, and the block and procedure call stack is popped until either an exception handler is encountered, or execution returns to the top level (in which case the exception becomes an error). The **error** statement has the following syntax.

```
error msgString, msgParam1, msgParam2, ...
```

The **msgString** parameter is a string that gives the text of the error message. It can contain numbered parameters of the form **%n** or **%-n**, where **n** is an integer. These numbered parameters are used as placeholders for actual values. In the event that the exception is printed as an error message, the actual values are specified by the **msgParam** values.

For example,

```
> error "%1 has a %-2 argument, %3, which is missing", f, 4, x;
Error, f has a 4th argument, x, which is missing
```

A numbered parameter of the form **%n** displays the **n**th **msgParam** in line-printed notation (that is, as **lprint** would display it). A numbered parameter of the form **%-n** displays the **n**th **msgParam**, assumed to be an integer, in ordinal form. For example, the **%-2** in the previous error statement is displayed as "**4th**". The special parameter **%0** displays all the **msgParams**, separated by a comma and a space.

The **error** statement evaluates its arguments and then creates an exception object which is an expression sequence with the following elements.

- The name of the procedure in which the exception was raised. If the exception occurred in a procedure local to a module, then the name of the innermost visible (non-local) calling procedure is used. If the exception occurred at the top level (not within a procedure), then the first element of the exception object will be the constant **0**.

- The **msgString**.
- The **msgParams**, if any.

The created exception object is assigned to the global variable **lastexception** as an expression sequence. For more information on **lastexception**, refer to the **error** help page.

> **Note:** The actual arguments to the **error** statement are also assigned to **lasterror** for compatibility with older versions of Maple.

> **Note:** To view the value of the **lastexception** variable within the debugger, use the **showexception** debugger command.

The **error** statement normally causes an immediate exit from the current procedure to the Maple session. Maple prints an error message of the following form.

```
Error, (in procName) msgText
```

In this case, **msgText** is the text of the error message (which is constructed from the **msgString** and optional **msgParams** of the **error** statement), and **procName** is the name of the procedure in which the error occurred, or the name of the innermost non-local procedure in the current call stack if the procedure is a module local. If the procedure does not have a name, **procName** is displayed as **unknown**. If the error occurs at the top level, outside any procedure, the **(in procName)** part of the message is omitted.

The **error** statement is commonly used when parameter declarations are not sufficient to check that the actual parameters to a procedure are of the correct type. The following **pairup** procedure takes a list **L** of the form [x_1, y_1, x_2, y_2, ..., x_n, y_n] as input, and creates from it a list of the form [[x_1, y_1], [x_2, y_2], ..., [x_n, y_n]]. A simple type check cannot determine if list **L** has an even number of elements, so you must check this explicitly by using an **error** statement.

```
> pairup := proc(L::list)
       local i, n;
       n := nops(L);
       if irem(n, 2) = 1 then
           error "list must have an even number of "
                 "entries, but had %1", n;
       end if;
       [seq( [L[2*i-1], L[2*i]], i=1..n/2 )];
   end proc:
> pairup([1, 2, 3, 4, 5]);
Error, (in pairup) list must have an even number of entries, but had 5
```

```
> pairup([1, 2, 3, 4, 5, 6]);
```

$$[[1,2],[3,4],[5,6]] \tag{16.46}$$

For information on trapping errors using a **try...catch** statement, see *Trapping Errors (page 189)*.

Checking Syntax

The Maple **maplemint** command generates a list of semantic errors for a specified procedure, if any. The semantic errors for which **maplemint** checks include parameter name conflicts, local and global variable name conflicts, unused variable declarations, and unreachable code. The **maplemint** command has the following syntax.

```
maplemint( procedureName );
```

In the case where the specified procedure is free of semantic errors, **maplemint** returns **NULL**.

```
> f := proc() local a, i; global c;
        for i from 1 to 10 do
            print(i);
            for i from 1 to 5 do
                if a = 5 then
                    a := 6;
                    return true;
                    print(`test`);
                end if;
            end do;
        end do;
    end proc:

> maplemint(f);
    This code is unreachable:
       print(test)
    These global variables were declared, but never used:
       c
    These local variables were used before they were assigned a value:
       a
    These variables were used as the same loop variable for nested loops:
       i
```

Similar to **maplemint**, Maple also has an external program utility called **mint**. The **mint** program is called from outside Maple; it is used to check both semantic and syntax errors in an external Maple source file.

16.5 Creating Efficient Programs

After a Maple procedure is debugged, you would normally want to improve the performance of the code. Maple commands are available to analyze the time and memory consumption involved in executing individual statements. Maple also provides commands to monitor the efficiency of procedures.

During the performance improvement phase, note that Maple is based on a small kernel written in **C** and on large libraries of Maple code which are interpreted. Therefore, whenever performance is critical, it is generally most efficient to perform computations by using the built-in commands in the kernel. The phrase **option** *builtin* is used to identify the built-in commands. For example, the **add** command is a built-in command in Maple. To determine if a command is built-in, use the **print** command with the command name as its argument.

```
> print(add);
```

$$\text{proc( ) option } \textit{builtin} = \textit{add}; \quad \text{end proc} \tag{16.47}$$

The **option** *builtin* phrase identifies **add** as a built-in command, and the identifier following *builtin* is either a name or number that identifies this particular command in the kernel.

For more information about efficiency in Maple programming, refer to the **efficiency** help page.

Displaying Time and Memory Statistics

A simple way to measure the time requirements of an executed command at the interactive level is to use the **time** command. The **time** command has the following syntax.

```
time( expr )
```

The following statements all return the sum of the same sequence of numbers. However, by using the **time** command, it is clear that the second expression, which uses the **add** command, is the most efficient method with respect to time consumption.

```
> time( `+`(seq(2^i, i=1..10^5) ) );
```

$$1.686 \tag{16.48}$$

```
> time( add(2^i, i=1..10^5) );
```

$$0.507 \tag{16.49}$$

Two options are available to compare these expression with the equivalent **for...do** statement. The first is to wrap the statement in an anonymous function call:

```
> time( proc() local S, i; S:=0: for i from 1 to 10^5 do S := S +
  2^i end do: end proc() );
```

$$1.119 \tag{16.50}$$

Another solution is to use the other form of the **time** command with no arguments, which returns the total CPU time used since the start of the Maple session. The time is reported in seconds and the value returned is a floating-point number.

```
time()
```

To find the time used to execute a particular statement or group of statements, use the following statements.

```
st := time():
... statements to be timed ...
time() - st;
```

Therefore, you could use the following set of statements to calculate the amount of time (in seconds) required to add the first 10,000 powers of 2 by using the **add** command.

```
> st:=time(): S:=0: for i from 1 to 10^5 do S := S + 2^i end do:
  time()-st;
```

$$1.124 \tag{16.51}$$

CPU time is not the only important measure of efficiency. For most code, the amount of memory used is equally important. This can be measured with the command

```
kernelopts(':-bytesused')
```

For parallel code, the *real* or *wall clock* time is also important. The **time** command with the index **real** measures real time used:

```
time[':-real']()
```
```
time[':-real']( expr )
```

A uniform interface to all of these metrics is available in the **CodeTools** package.

```
CodeTools:-Usage(expression, options)
```

By default, **CodeTools:-Usage** prints the time and memory usage in evaluating the expression. If you want to save the results, you can specify an output option, which ensures that values that can be saved are returned.

```
> CodeTools:-Usage( `+`(seq(sign(i)*2^abs(i), i=-10^4..10^4)),
  'output'='all');
```
$$Record(realtime = 0.098, cputime = 0.099, bytesused = 53131816,$$
$$bytesalloc = 79679488, output = 1) \qquad (16.52)$$

```
> CodeTools:-Usage( `+`(Threads:-Seq(sign(i)*2^abs(i),
  i=-10^4..10^4)), 'output'='all');
```
$$Record(realtime = 0.062, cputime = 0.205, bytesused = 52158448,$$
$$bytesalloc = 43388928, output = 1) \qquad (16.53)$$

```
> CodeTools:-Usage( add(sign(i)*2^abs(i), i=-10^4..10^4),
  'output'='all');
```
$$Record(realtime = 0.113, cputime = 0.102, bytesused = 39139224,$$
$$bytesalloc = 0, output = 1) \qquad (16.54)$$

```
> CodeTools:-Usage( Threads:-Add(sign(i)*2^abs(i), i=-10^4..10^4),
  'output'='all');
```
$$Record(realtime = 0.019, cputime = 0.142, bytesused = 39167840,$$
$$bytesalloc = 0, output = 1) \qquad (16.55)$$

```
> CodeTools:-Usage( proc() local S, i; S:=0: for i from -10^4 to
  10^4 do S := S + sign(i)*2^abs(i) end do: end proc(),
  'output'='all');
```
$$Record(realtime = 0.183, cputime = 0.142, bytesused = 51605728,$$
$$bytesalloc = 0, output = 1) \qquad (16.56)$$

For most computers, the third expression above will have the lowest **cputime** and **bytesused** values. Depending on the parallelism available, the fourth expression, which uses **Threads:-Add**, may have the lowest **realtime** value. The first two expressions will have the highest **bytesused** values since they both create large sequences of $2*10^4$ numbers before adding them to **1**.

Profiling a Procedure

The **Profiling** subpackage of **CodeTools** can be used to display run-time information about a procedure (or procedures). The run-time information is displayed in tabular form and it contains the number of calls to the procedures, the CPU time used, and the number of bytes used by each call. To turn on profiling, use the **Profile** command.

```
CodeTools:-Profiling:-Profile( procedureNames )
```

16.5 Creating Efficient Programs

Then, to display the run-time information collected for the profiled procedures use the **SortBy** command.

```
CodeTools:-Profiling:-SortBy( )
```

To display the line-by-line profiling information for the specified procedure, use the **PrintProfiles** command. If no argument is given to **PrintProfiles**, the run-time information for all profiled procedures is displayed.

```
CodeTools:-Profiling:-PrintProfiles( procedureName )
```

To illustrate the use of profiling in Maple, consider the following procedures that compute the **n**th Fibonacci number. Both procedures contain the same code except that **Fibonacci1** uses **option remember**.

For more information about **option remember**, see *The remember, cache, and system Options (page 218)*.

```
> Fibonacci1:=proc(n)
       option remember;
       if n<2 then
          n
       else
          Fibonacci1(n-1)+Fibonacci1(n-2)
       end if;
  end proc:
> Fibonacci2:=proc(n)
       if n<2 then
          n
       else
          Fibonacci2(n-1)+Fibonacci2(n-2)
       end if;
  end proc:
```

Turn on profiling for both procedures.

```
> with(CodeTools:-Profiling):
> Profile(Fibonacci1);
> Profile(Fibonacci2);
```

Execute the procedures.

```
> Fibonacci1(25);
```

(16.57)

```
> Fibonacci2(25);
```

$$75025 \tag{16.58}$$

Use the **SortBy** command to display the run-time information about **Fibonacci1** and **Fibonacci2**.

```
> SortBy();

function              calls      time      time%       words   words%
------------------------------------------------------------------------
Fibonacci1              26       0.001      0.17         478    0.04
Fibonacci2          242785       0.605     99.83     1213923   99.96
------------------------------------------------------------------------
total:              242811       0.606    100.00     1214401  100.00
```

Use **PrintProfiles** to display the line-by-line run-time information.

```
> PrintProfiles(Fibonacci1);

Fibonacci1

Fibonacci1 := proc(n)
       |Calls  Seconds  Words|
PROC   |  26    0.001    478|
   1   |  26    0.000     78|   if n < 2 then
   2   |   2    0.000      0|       n
                                 else
   3   |  24    0.001    400|       Fibonacci1(n-1)+Fibonacci1(n-2)
                                 end if
end proc
```

```
> PrintProfiles(Fibonacci2);
Fibonacci2

Fibonacci2 := proc(n)
        |Calls  Seconds   Words|
   PROC |242785   0.605 1213923|
      1 |242785   0.266  728355|   if n < 2 then
      2 |121393   0.054       0|      n
                                   else
      3 |121392   0.285  485568|      Fibonacci2(n-1)+Fibonacci2(n-2)
                                   end if
end proc
```

By studying the run-time information, particularly the number of calls to each procedure, you can see that it is more efficient to use **option remember** in a recursive procedure.

To turn off profiling, use the **UnProfile** command. If no argument is given to **UnProfile**, all procedures currently profiled are returned to their original state.

```
UnProfile( procedureName )
```

When a procedure is unprofiled, all run-time information for that procedure is lost.

```
> UnProfile();

> SortBy();
Warning, total execution time is 0
Warning, total words used is 0

function                    calls      time     time%           words   words%
-----------------------------------------------------------------------------
-----------------------------------------------------------------------------
total:                          0     0.000    100.00               0   100.00
```

The **CodeTools:-Profiling** package has several other useful commands, including **LoadProfiles** and **SaveProfiles**, which can be used to save and load profile information to and from a file. By using these commands, you can collect profiling information from commands run with **restart** commands in between. In the following code, both calls to **myproc** will be profiled and the data collected as if they had been executed right after each other.

```
> CodeTools:-Profiling:-Profile(myproc);

> myproc( input1 );
```

```
> CodeTools:-Profiling:-SaveProfiles( "myproc.profile", 'overwrite'
    );
> restart;
> CodeTools:-Profiling:-LoadProfiles( "myproc.profile" );
> myproc( input2 );
```

The older **profile** facility is also still available but it is slower and does not provide line-by-line profiling information. It is still useful for profiling the use of built-in procedures, which are not supported by **CodeTools:-Profiling**. For more information, refer to the **profile** help page.

In some cases, it is useful to collect profiling information on every procedure which is invoked during the evaluation of a Maple expression. In this situation, use the **exprofile** command with the **profile** kernel option. The output of **exprofile** can be verbose for moderately complicated code.

```
> a:=proc(); b(100); end proc:
> b:=proc(n);
    if n>0 then c(n-2); end if;
  end proc:
> c:=proc(n);
    if n>0 then b(n+1); end if;
  end proc:
> kernelopts(profile=true):
> writeto('output');
> a();
> kernelopts(profile=false);
> writeto(terminal);
> exprofile('output',alpha);
```

16.6 Managing Resources

Maple provides several commands for managing computer resources during computation. In particular, the **timelimit** command controls the maximum amount of time available for a computation, **gc** starts the garbage collection process, and **kernelopts** provides communication with the Maple kernel.

Setting a Time Limit on Computations

The **timelimit** command is used to limit the amount of CPU time for a computation. The **timelimit** command has the following syntax, where **time** is the time limit (in seconds) to evaluate **expression**.

```
timelimit( time, expression )
```

If the expression is successfully evaluated within the specified time, **timelimit** returns the value of the expression. If the time limit is reached before the expression is evaluated, **timelimit** raises an exception.

```
> f := proc()
       local i;
       for i to 100000 do
           2^i
       end do
   end proc:
> timelimit(0.25, f());
```

The exception raised by timelimit can be caught with a **try...catch** construct.

```
> try
     timelimit(0.25, f());
  catch "time expired":
    NULL;
  end try;
```

Multiple calls to **timelimit** can be nested, causing both limits to be active at once.

```
> g := proc(t)
      try
          timelimit(t, f());
      catch "time expired":
          error "time expired in g";
      end try;
  end proc:
> timelimit(10, g(0.25) );
> timelimit(0.25, g(10) );
```

Note that in the second of these examples, the inner call, **g(10)** would normally have finished without triggering the time limit exception. The outer time limit of 0.25 cpu seconds prevented the inner call from completing. Thus, the time-out event did not occur *inside* **g** and so is not trapped by the **catch** clause in **g**. This illustrates that a **try-catch** construct cannot capture a time limit exception event generated by a **timelimit** call in a surrounding scope.

For more information on catching **time expired** exceptions and nested time limits, refer to the **timelimit** help page.

Garbage Collection

Garbage collection deletes all objects that are no longer in use by the program and are occupying space in memory. In Maple, garbage collection will also recover storage from the remember tables of procedures that use an **option system** or **option builtin** by removing entries that have no other references to them.

For more information about procedure options, see *Options (page 214)*.

Garbage collection is also used to clear cache tables that have temporary entries when a memory usage threshold is reached.

The Maple garbage collection command is **gc**. It has the following syntax.

```
gc()
```

Garbage collection occurs automatically when the memory management system determines that memory resources are low. Alternatively, the **gc** command explicitly schedules a garbage collection cycle and returns a value of **NULL**. However, the use of **gc** is discourage since the underlying memory management system attempts to balance memory usage and performance by tracking the memory behavior of the program. The decision of when to initiate a garbage collection can be skewed by directly calling **gc**.

The **kernelopts** command is used to query garbage collection information such as the number of bytes returned after the last garbage collection and the number of times the garbage collection process has run.

```
> kernelopts( gcbytesavail );
> kernelopts( gcbytesreturned );
> kernelopts( gctimes );
```

Other Kernel Options for Managing Resources

The **kernelopts** command is provided as a mechanism of communication between the user and the Maple kernel. You have already seen several uses of kernelopts in this guide, including how to use **kernelopts** to check assertions in procedures. Specifically, this command is used to set and query variables that affect kernel computations in Maple.

The following **kernelopts** options can be used to limit Maple's use of system resources.

The **cpulimit**, **datalimit**, and **stacklimit** options can be used to set limits on the resources available to Maple and must be used carefully. Unlike the **timelimit** command, once one of these limits is reached, Maple may shut down without warning without prompting you to save your work. This makes these limit options most useful for running in non-interactive sessions.

On some platforms, including all Windows platforms, the detection of limit violations is tied to garbage collection and therefore the detection of limit violations will be inaccurate for code that rarely starts the garbage collection process. If the garbage collection process does not occur, Maple does not detect limit violations.

These options can also be set using the **-T** command-line option. For more information, refer to the **maple** help page.

The **filelimit** and **processlimit** limit options can similarly be used to limit the number of open files and external processes that Maple can use at one time. Some internal Maple commands open files or run processes and thus will fail if these limits are too low.

If the option **limitjvmheap** is set to **true** then the Java external calling virtual machine is limited to the amount of memory given in the limit option **jvmheaplimit**.

The option **cacheclearlimit** is used to set a threshold at which Maple is allowed to clear temporary elements from cache tables during garbage collection.

An informational kernelopts option is **memusage** which will display how much memory is currently in use, listed by DAG type.

```
> kernelopts( memusage );
```

Note: There is a Maplet application that provides a graphical user interface to a subset of the kernel options. This Maplet can be opened by calling **Maplets:-Examples:-KernelOpts()**.

16.7 Testing Your Code

Occasionally, code may be incorrect after it is first written or changed. For that reason, it is very important that code is tested. In Maple, you can create tests for code in many ways. This section introduces some useful Maple commands for testing and provides suggestions on how to create useful tests.

Verifying Results with verify

One common difficulty in producing good tests is verifying that the computed results match the expected result. Maple provides the general and powerful command **verify** to make this possible in many cases.

The default mode of the **verify** command is simple **evalb** equality checking.

```
> verify(10, 20);
> verify(10, 10.00);
```

More complicated objects require more complicated tests.

```
> verify(10+x, 10.00+x);
> verify(Array(1..3,[1,2,3]), Array([1,2,3],'readonly'));
```

The **verify** command called with a third argument provides numerous different structured verifiers, many of which are similar to the structured type of the expressions being compared. For full details, refer to the **verify** and **verify/structured** help pages.

```
> verify(10+x, 10.00+x, 'float(10)' );
> verify(Array(1..3,[1,2,3]), Array([1,2,3],readonly), 'Array');
> verify({0.32}, {0.320002, 0.319996},'set(float(1e5))');
```

A Simple Test Harness

An easy way to test code is to write a series of **verify** statements into a text file which can then be read directly by the command-line interface or the **read** command.

For the **sieve** example introduced in *The Maple Debugger: A Tutorial Example (page 581)*, the following statements can be saved in a file called **sieveTest.mpl**:

Table 16.1: sieveTest.mpl

```
verify(sieve(1), 0);
verify(sieve(2), 1);
verify(sieve(10), 4);
verify(sieve(100), 25);
verify(sieve(1223), 200);
verify(sieve(-1), 0);
verify(sieve(-1000), 0);
```

If the **sieve** function works properly, reading or running this file from the command line

```
maple -s -q < sieveTest.mpl
```

should produce output that contains **true** values.

```
true
true
true
true
true
true
true
```

This output is easy to inspect visually for correctness. If the number of tests in one file is large, you may want to produce errors for failures, and let successful tests proceed without further action. The command **CodeTools:-Test** is a front-end to **verify** that provides this functionality as well as allowing you to test expected errors and customize verifications. The output format is quite flexible. In the following example, we use the **quiet** option to suppress output for passed tests, and the **label** option to give each test a unique identifier, so we can easily identify failures. Here is the new version of the test harness:

Table 16.2: sieveTest2.mpl

```
with(CodeTools):
Test(sieve(1), 0, quiet, label=10);
Test(sieve(2), 1, quiet, label=20);
Test(sieve(10), 4, quiet, label=30);
Test(sieve(100), 25, quiet, label=40);
Test(sieve(1223), 200, quiet, label=50);
Test(sieve(-1), 0, quiet, label=60);
Test(sieve(-1000), 0, quiet, label=70);
Test(sieve(sqrt(2)), "invalid input", testerror, quiet, label=80);
Test(sieve(1), -1, quiet, label=90);
```

which should produce just one line of output:

```
Error, (in CodeTools:-Test) TEST FAILED: 90
```

This new test harness has the advantage that failures are highlighted as errors, so they stand out visually. If you remove the **quiet** option, you will also get a short message for each test that passes. That can be useful to ensure that false positive results are less likely to occur due to tests being skipped.

Writing Good Tests

Much has been written on the subject of writing good sets of tests. In general, it is best to test as many of the corner cases as possible in addition to a few typical cases.

For example, if a procedure takes a list as input, there should be a test case for the empty list.

For more comprehensive references on testing software, see for example:

- B. Beizer. **Software Testing Techniques**. Van Nostrand Reinhold, second edition, 1990.

- C. Kaner, J. Falk, H.Q. Nguyen. **Testing Computer Software**. Wiley, second edition, 1999.

- G.J. Myers. **The Art of Software Testing**. Wiley, second edition, 2004.

Test Coverage

Good suites of tests exercise every statement in the code that is being tested. Maple provides a package to measure the coverage of a suite of tests in **CodeTools:-Profiling:-Coverage**.

To use this code, activate profiling of the procedure (or procedures) you want to test as described in *Profiling a Procedure (page 620)*. Then run your test suite and use the command **CodeTools:-Profiling:-Coverage:-Print** to get a report on which lines in your procedures were not run while running the test suite.

For example, we could add the following to the test file for sieve in the previous section:
Table 16.3: Modified sieveTest2.mpl

```
with(CodeTools):
Profiling:-Profile(sieve);
...
Profiling:-Coverage:-Print();
```

When run, in addition to the test output, this produces the message:

```
sieve (8): all statements covered
```

which informs us that the procedure was called 8 times and every statement in the procedure was executed at least once. If statements had been missed, those missed statements would be printed.

The command **CodeTools:-Profiling:-Coverage:-Percent** provides much more compact output, and in this case would produce:

```
sieve 100.00%
```

16.8 Exercises

1. The following procedure tries to compute $1 - x^{|a|}$.

   ```
   > f := proc(a::integer, x::anything)
           if a<0 then
               a := -a
           end if;
           1-x^a;
       end proc:
   ```

   Determine what is wrong with this procedure.

   Hint: Use the Maple debugger described in *The Maple Debugger: A Tutorial Example (page 581)* and *Maple Debugger Commands (page 593)* to isolate the error.

2. The following recurrence relation defines the Chebyshev polynomials of the first kind, $T_n(x)$.

$$T_0(x) = 1, \ T_1(x) = x, \ T_n(x) = 2x\,T_{n-1}(x) - T_{n-2}(x)$$

The following procedure computes $T_n(x)$ in a loop for any given integer n.

```
> T := proc(n::integer, x) local t1, tn, t;
       t1 := 1; tn := x;
       for i from 2 to n do
           t := expand(2*x*tn - t1);
           t1 := tn; tn := t;
       end do;
       tn;
  end proc:
```

This procedure has several errors. Which variables must be declared local? What happens if n is zero or negative? Identify and correct all errors, using the Maple debugger where appropriate. Modify the procedure so that it returns unevaluated if n is a symbolic value.

Appendix A Internal Representation

The table below lists the structures that are currently implemented in Maple.

Each structure, along with the constraints on its length and contents, is described in the sections that follow.

Table A.1: Maple Structures

AND	ASSIGN	BINARY	BREAK	CATENATE
COMPLEX	CONTROL	DCOLON	DEBUG	EQUATION
ERROR	EXPSEQ	FLOAT	FOR	FOREIGN
FUNCTION	GARBAGE	HASH	HASHTAB	HFLOAT
IF	IMPLIES	INEQUAT	INTNEG	INTPOS
LESSEQ	LESSTHAN	LEXICAL	LIST	LOCAL
MEMBER	MODDEF	MODULE	NAME	NEXT
NOT	OR	PARAM	POLY	POWER
PROC	PROD	RANGE	RATIONAL	READ
RETURN	RTABLE	SAVE	SERIES	SET
SDPOLY	STATSEQ	STOP	STRING	SUM
TABLE	TABLEREF	TRY	UNEVAL	USE
XOR	ZPPOLY			

A.1 Internal Functions

The internal functions in Maple are divided into five groups:

Evaluators

The evaluators are the main functions responsible for evaluation. There are six types of evaluations: statements, algebraic expressions, Boolean expressions, name forming, arbitrary precision floating-point arithmetic, and hardware floating-point arithmetic. The user interface calls only the statement evaluator, but thereafter there are many interactions between evaluators. For example, the statement

```
if a > 0 then b||i := 3.14/a end if;
```

is first analyzed by the statement evaluator, which calls the Boolean evaluator to resolve the **if** condition. Once completed (for example, a **true** result is returned), the statement evaluator is invoked again to perform the assignment, for which the name-forming evaluator is invoked with the left-hand side of the assignment, and the expression evaluator with the right-hand side. Since the right-hand side involves floating-point values, the expression evaluator calls the arbitrary precision floating-point evaluator.

Normally, you do not specifically call any of the evaluators. However, in some circumstances, when a nondefault type of evaluation is needed, you can directly call **evalb** (the Boolean evaluator), **evaln** (the name-forming evaluator), **evalf** (the arbitrary precision floating-point evaluator), or **evalhf** (the hardware floating-point evaluator).

Algebraic Functions

Algebraic functions are commonly called *basic functions*. Some examples are taking derivatives (**diff**), dividing polynomials (**divide**), finding coefficients of polynomials (**coeff**), computing series (**series**), mapping a function (**map**), expanding expressions (**expand**), and finding indeterminates (**indets**).

Algebraic Service Functions

These functions are algebraic in nature, but serve as subordinates of the functions in the previous group. In most cases, these functions cannot be explicitly called. Examples of such functions are the internal arithmetic packages, the basic simplifier, and retrieval of library functions.

Data Structure Manipulation Functions

These are similar to the algebraic functions, but instead of working on mathematical objects, such as polynomials or sets, they work on data structures, such as expression sequences, sums, products, or lists. Examples of such functions are operand selection (**op**), operand substitution (**subsop**), searching (**has**), and length determination (**length**).

General Service Functions

Functions in this group are at the lowest hierarchical level. That is, they can be called by any other function in the system. They are general purpose functions, and not necessarily specific to symbolic or numeric computation. Some examples are storage allocation and garbage collection, table manipulation, internal I/O, and exception handling.

A.2 Flow of Control

The flow of control does not need to remain internal to the Maple kernel. In many cases, where appropriate, a decision is made to call functions that are written in Maple and are a part of the Maple library. For example, many uses of the **expand** function are handled in the kernel. However, if an expansion of a sum to a large power is required, the internal **expand** function calls the external Maple library function **'expand/bigpow'** to resolve it. Functions such as **diff**, **evalf**, **series**, and **type** make extensive use of this feature.

Therefore, for example, the basic function **diff** cannot differentiate any function. All of that functionality is included in the Maple library in procedures named **'diff/function-Name'**. This is a fundamental feature of Maple since it permits:

- Flexibility (the ability to change the Maple library)
- Customization (by defining your refined handling functions)
- Readability (much of the Maple functionality is visible at the user level)

Maple allows the kernel to remain small by offloading nonessential functions to the library.

A.3 Internal Representations of Data Types

The parser and some internal functions build all of the data structures used internally by Maple. All of the internal data structures have the same general format:

Header	$Data_1$	...	$Data_n$

The header field, stored in one or more machine words, encodes the length of the structure and its type. Additional bits are used to record simplification status, garbage collection information, persistent store status, and various information about specific data structures (for example, whether a **for** loop contains a **break** or **next** statement).

The length is encoded in 26 bits on 32-bit architectures, resulting in a maximum single object size of 67,108,863 words (268,435,452 bytes, or 256 megabytes). On 64-bit architectures, the length is stored in 32 bits, for a maximum object size of 4,294,967,295 words (34,359,738,360 bytes or 32 gigabytes).

Every structure is created with its own length, and that length does not change during the existence of the structure. Furthermore, the contents of most (but not all) data structures are never changed during execution because it is unpredictable how many other data structures are referring to them and relying on them not to change. The normal process for modifying a structure is to copy it and then to modify the copy. Structures that are no longer used are eventually reclaimed by the garbage collector.

The following sections describe each of the structures currently implemented in Maple, along with the constraints on their lengths and contents. The 6-bit numeric value identifying the type of structure is of little interest, so symbolic names will be used.

The notation ^**something** in the data structure depictions indicates that the value stored in that field of the structure is a pointer to the value (**something**), rather than being the **something** itself.

AND: Logical AND

AND	^expr1	^expr2

Maple syntax: **expr1 and expr2**

Length: 3

ASSIGN: Assignment Statement

ASSIGN	^name-seq	^expr-seq

Maple syntax: **name1, name2, ... := expr1, expr2, ...**

Length: 3

The left-hand side *name* entries must evaluate to assignable objects: **NAME, FUNCTION, MEMBER** or **TABLEREF** structures, or a sequence thereof. If the left-hand side is a sequence, the right-hand side must be a sequence of the same length.

BINARY: Binary Object

BINARY	data	...

Maple syntax: none

Length: arbitrary

The **BINARY** structure can hold any arbitrary data. It is not used directly as a Maple object, but is used as storage for large blocks of data within other Maple objects (currently only **RTABLE** structures). It is also sometimes used as temporary storage space during various kernel operations.

BREAK: Break Statement

BREAK

Maple syntax: **break**

Length: 1

CATENATE: Name Concatenation

CATENATE	^name	^expr

Maple syntax: **name || expr**

Length: 3

- If the *name* entry is one of **NAME, CATENATE, LOCAL,** or **PARAM**, and if the *expr* entry evaluates to an integer, **NAME,** or **STRING,** the result is a **NAME**.
- If the *name* entry is a **STRING** or **CATENATE** that resolves to a **STRING**, and if the *expr* entry evaluates to an integer, **NAME,** or **STRING,** the result is a **STRING**.

- If *expr* is a **RANGE**, the result is to generate an **EXPSEQ** of the **NAME** or **STRING** structures.

COMPLEX: Complex Value

COMPLEX	^re	^im
COMPLEX	^im	

Maple syntax: **Complex(re,im)**, **Complex(im)**, **re + im * I** or **im * I**

Length: 2 or 3

The *re* and *im* fields must point to **INTPOS**, **INTNEG**, **RATIONAL**, or **FLOAT** structures, one of the **NAME**s **infinity** or **undefined**, or a **SUM** structure representing **-infinity**. In the length 3 case, if either **re** or **im** is a **FLOAT**, the other must be a **FLOAT** as well.

CONTROL: Communications Control Structure

CONTROL	^integer

Maple syntax: none

Length: 2

This is an internal structure used for communication between the kernel and user interface. Such a structure never reaches the user level, or even the mathematical parts of the kernel.

DCOLON: Type Specification or Test

DCOLON	^expr	^type-expr

Maple syntax: **expr :: typeExpr**

Length: 3

This structure has three interpretations depending on the context in which it is used. When it appears in the header of a procedure definition, it is a parameter declaration that has a type. When it appears in the **local** section of a procedure or on the left-hand side of an assignment, it is a type assertion. When it appears elsewhere (specifically, in a conditional expression), it is a type test.

DEBUG: Debug

DEBUG	^expr1	^expr2	...

Maple syntax: none

Length: 2 or more

This is another structure that is only used internally. It is used by the kernel when printing error traceback information to transmit that information up the call stack.

EQUATION: Equation or Test for Equality

EQUATION	^expr1	^expr2

Maple syntax: **expr1 = expr2**

Length: 3

This structure has two interpretations depending on the context in which it is used. It can be either a test for equality, or a statement of equality (not to be confused with an assignment).

ERROR: Error Statement

ERROR	^expr

Maple syntax: **error "msg", arg, ... arg**

Length: 2

This structure represents the Maple **error** statement. The *expr* is either a single expression (if only a message is specified in the **error** statement), or an expression sequence (if arguments are also specified). The actual internal tag used for the **ERROR** structure is **MERROR** to prevent a conflict with a macro defined by some C compilers.

EXPSEQ: Expression Sequence

EXPSEQ	^expr1	^expr2	...

Maple syntax: **expr1, expr2, ...**

Length: 1 or more

An expression sequence is an ordered sequence of expressions. It is most commonly used to construct lists, sets, and function calls. Extracting an expression sequence from a list or set **L** can be done by using the command **op(L)**. This operation is very efficient as it does not involve creation of a new structure. Similarly, if **E** is an expression sequence, then constructing a list using **[E]** involves almost no work and is also very efficient. Constructing a set using **{E}** requires **E** to be sorted. A function call data structure is made up of the function name plus the expression sequence of arguments. During evaluation of a function call, the argument sequence gets flattened into one expression sequence. That is, **f(E1,E2)** is turned into **f(e11,e12,...e1n,e21,e22,...e2m)** where **e1i** constitutes the members of the expression sequence **E1**, and **e2i** constitutes the members of the expression sequence **E2**. Thus it is not possible to pass raw expression sequences as arguments to functions. Typically sequences are wrapped in lists, as **f([E1],[E2])** in order to keep the element groupings intact. The special value **NULL** is represented by an empty expression sequence. Thus, **[NULL]** is equivalent to **[]**, and **f(NULL)** is equivalent to **f()**.

FLOAT: Software Floating-Point Number

FLOAT	^integer1	^integer2	^attrib-expr

Maple syntax: **1.2**, **1.2e3**, **Float(12,34)**, **Float(infinity)**

Length: 2 (or 3 with attributes)

A floating-point number is interpreted as **integer1 * 10^integer2**. A floating-point number can optionally have attributes, in which case, the length of the structure is 3 and the third word points to a Maple expression. This means that several floating-point numbers with the same value but different attributes can exist simultaneously.

The *integer2* field can optionally be one of the names, **undefined** or **infinity**, in which case the **FLOAT** structure represents an undefined floating-point value (not-a-number, or NaN, in IEEE terminology), or a floating-point infinity. When *integer2* is **undefined**, *integer1* can accept different small integer values, allowing different NaN values to exist. When *integer2* is **infinity**, *integer1* must be 1 or -1.

FOR: For/While Loop Statement

FOR	^name	^from-expr	^by-expr	^to-expr	^cond-expr	^stat-seq
FOR	^name	^in-expr		^cond-expr	^stat-seq	

Maple syntax:
```
for name from fromExpr by byExpr to toExpr
    while condExpr do
        statSeq
end do
```

Maple syntax:
```
for name in inExpr
    while condExpr do
        statSeq
end do
```

Length: 7 or 5

The *name* follows the same rules as the *name* field of the **ASSIGN** structure, except that it can also be the empty expression sequence (**NULL**), indicating that there is no controlling variable for the loop.

The *from-expr*, *by-expr*, *to-expr*, and *cond-expr* entries are general expressions. All are optional in the syntax of **for** loops and can therefore be replaced with default values (1, 1, **NULL**, and **true** respectively) by the parser.

The *stat-seq* entry can be a single Maple statement or expression, a **STATSEQ** structure, or **NULL** indicating an empty loop body. An additional bit in the header of the **FOR** structure is used to indicate whether the *stat-seq* entry contains any **break** or **next** statements.

FOREIGN: Foreign Data

FOREIGN	...

Maple syntax: none

Length: 1 or more

This structure is similar to the **BINARY** structure, except that it is for use by Maple components outside the kernel, such as the user interface. A **FOREIGN** structure is exempt from garbage collection, and the external component is responsible for freeing this structure when it is finished using it.

FOREIGN data structures can be created and managed in external code by using the **MaplePointer** API functions. For more information, refer to the **OpenMaple,C,MaplePointer** help page.

FUNCTION: Function Call

FUNCTION	^name	^expr-seq	^attrib-expr

Maple syntax: **name(exprSeq)**

Length: 2 (or 3 with attributes)

This structure represents a function invocation (as distinct from a procedure definition that is represented by the **PROC** structure). The *name* entry follows the same rules as in **ASSIGN**, or it can be a **PROC** structure. The *expr-seq* entry gives the list of actual parameters; this entry is always an expression sequence (possibly of length 1, which indicates that no parameters are present).

GARBAGE: Garbage

GARBAGE	...

Maple syntax: none

Length: 1 or more

This structure is used internally by the Maple garbage collector as a temporary object type for free space.

HFLOAT: Hardware Float

HFLOAT	floatword	
HFLOAT	floatword	floatword

Maple syntax: none

Length: 2 on 64-bit architectures; 3 on 32-bit architectures

This structure is used to store a hardware floating-point value. The one or two words (always 8 bytes) after the header store the actual double-precision floating-point value. **HFLOAT** objects can appear as the result of floating-point computations, I/O operations, or by extracting elements from hardware floating-point **RTABLE** structures. They look like and are treated as indistinguishable from software **FLOAT** objects.

IF: If Statement

IF	^cond-expr1	^stat-seq1	^cond-expr2	^stat-seq2	...	...	^stat-seqN

Maple syntax:
```
if condExpr1 then
   statSeq1
elif condExpr2 then
   statSeq2
...
else statSeqN
end if
```

Length: 3 or more

This structure represents the **if** ... **then** ... **elif** ... **else** ... **end if** statements in Maple. If the length is even, the last entry is the body of an **else** clause. The remaining entries are interpreted in pairs, where each pair is a condition of the **if** or **elif** clause, followed by the associated body.

IMPLIES: Logical IMPLIES

IMPLIES	^expr1	^expr2

Maple syntax: **expr1 implies expr2**

Length: 3

INEQUAT: Not Equal or Test for Inequality

INEQUAT	^expr1	^expr2

Maple syntax: **expr1 < > expr2**

Length: 3

This structure has two interpretations, depending on the context in which it is used. It can be either a test for inequality or an inequality statement.

INTNEG: Negative Integer

INTNEG	GMP-integer

Maple syntax: -123

Length: 2 or more

This data structure represents a negative integer of arbitrary precision. For a complete description of the integer representation, including positive integers, see the following section.

INTPOS: Positive Integer

INTPOS	GMP-integer

Maple syntax: 123

Length: 2 or more

This data structure represents a positive integer of arbitrary precision. Integers are represented internally in a base equal to the full word size of the host machine. On 32-bit architectures, this base is 4294967296. On 64-bit architectures, the base is 2^{64}. Integers in this range use the GNU Multiple Precision Arithmetic (GMP) library for integer arithmetic.

Small integers are not represented by data structures. Instead of a pointer to an **INTPOS** or **INTNEG** structure, a small integer is represented by the bits of what would normally be a pointer. The least significant bit is 1, which makes the value an invalid pointer (since pointers must be word-aligned). Such an integer is called an *immediate integer*.

The range of integers that can be represented in this way is -1,073,741,823 to 1,073,741,823 (that is, about $+-10^9$) on 32-bit architectures, and -4,611,686,018,427,387,903 to 4,611,686,018,427,387,903 (that is, about $+-410^{18}$) on 64-bit architectures. (Note that the maximum (non-immediate) integer magnitude in Maple is about **$2^{2,147,483,488}$** on 32-bit architectures and **$2^{274,877,906,688}$** on 64-bit architectures.)

LESSEQ: Less Than or Equal

| LESSEQ | ^expr1 | ^expr2 |

Maple syntax: **expr1 <= expr2**, **expr2 >= expr1**

Length: 3

This structure has two interpretations, depending on the context. It can be interpreted as a relation (that is, an inequation) or as a comparison (for example, in the condition of an **if** statement, or the argument to a call to **evalb**). Maple does not have a greater-than-or-equal structure. Any input of that form is stored as a **LESSEQ** structure.

LESSTHAN: Less Than

| LESSTHAN | ^expr1 | ^expr2 |

Maple syntax: **expr1 < expr2**, **expr2 > expr1**

Length: 3

Similar to the **LESSEQ** structure above, this structure has two interpretations, depending on the context. It can be interpreted as a relation (that is, an inequation), or as a comparison (for example, in the condition of an **if** statement, or the argument to a call to **evalb**).

Maple does not have a greater-than structure. Any input of that form is stored as a **LESS** structure.

LEXICAL: Lexically Scoped Variable within an Expression

| LEXICAL | integer |

Maple syntax: **name**

Length: 2

This represents an identifier within an expression in a procedure or module that is not local to that procedure, but is instead declared in a surrounding procedure or module scope. The *integer* field identifies which lexically scoped variable of the current procedure is being referred to. The *integer*, multiplied by 2, is an index into the *lexical-seq* structure referred to by the **PROC** DAG of the procedure. Specifically, |**integer**| * 2 - 1 is the index to the **NAME** of the identifier, and |**integer**| * 2 is the index to a description (**LOCAL**, **PARAM**, or **LEXICAL**) relative to the surrounding scope. The value of *integer* can be positive or negative. If *integer* is a positive value, the original identifier is a local variable of a surrounding procedure; if *integer* is a negative value, it is a parameter of a surrounding procedure.

LIST: List

LIST	^expr-seq	^attrib-expr

Maple syntax: **[expr, expr, ...]**

Length: 2 (or 3 with attributes)

The elements of the *expr-seq* are the elements of the list. The list can optionally have attributes.

LOCAL: Local Variable within an Expression

LOCAL	integer

Maple syntax: **name**

Length: 2

This structure indicates a local variable when it appears within an expression in a procedure or module. The *integer* is an index into the procedure *local-seq*. At procedure execution time, it is also an index into the internal data structure storing the active locals on the procedure activation stack, and stores private copies of the **NAME**s of the local variables (private copies in the sense that these **NAME**s are not the same as the global **NAME**s of the same name).

MEMBER: Module Member

MEMBER	^module	^name

Maple syntax: **module:-name**

Length: 3

This structure represents a module member access in an expression. **MEMBER** objects typically do not persist when a statement is simplified. Instead, they are replaced by the actual member that they refer to (an instance of a **NAME**).

MODDEF: Module Definition

MODDEF	param-seq	local-seq	option-seq	export-seq	stat-seq	desc-seq
global-seq	lexical-seq	mod-seq	static local-seq	static export-seq	static name-seq	

Maple syntax:
```
module modName ( )
    description d1, d2, ...;
    local l1, l2, ...;
    local sl1::static, sl2::static, ...;
    export e1, e2, ...;
```

```
    export se1::static, se2::static, ...;
    global g1, g2, ...;
    option o1, o2, ...;
    statSeq
end module
```

Length: 13

The parameter sequence (*param-seq*), which occurs between the parentheses after **mod-Name**, points to an expression sequence describing the formal parameters of the module. Currently, Maple does not support parameterized modules, so this field always points to the sequence containing only an instance of the name **thismodule**.

The local sequence (*local-seq*) points to an expression sequence listing the explicitly and implicitly declared local variables. Each entry is a **NAME**. The explicitly declared variables appear first. Within the module, locals are referred to by **LOCAL** structures, the local variable number being the index into the local sequence. The instances of these names appear in the **MODULE** structure.

The export sequence (*export-seq*) points to an expression sequence listing the exported module members. Each entry is a **NAME**. Within the module, exports are referred to by **LOCAL** structures, the local variable number being the number of elements in the local sequence, plus the index into the export sequence. The instances of these names appear in the **MODULE** structure.

The option sequence (*option-seq*) points to an expression sequence of options to the module (for modules, options are the same as attributes). Each entry is a **NAME** or **EQUATION** specifying an option. Typical options are **package**, **load=**... and **unload=**...

The statement sequence (*stat-seq*) field points to a single statement or a statement sequence (**STATSEQ**). If the module has an empty body, this is a pointer to **NULL** instead.

The description sequence (*desc-seq*) field points to an expression sequence of **NAME**s or **STRING**s. These sequences are meant to provide a brief description of what the module does and are displayed even when the value of **interface(verboseproc)** is less than 2.

The global sequence (*global-seq*) field points to a list of the explicitly declared global variables in the module (those that appeared in the **global** statement). This information is never used at run time, but is used when simplifying nested modules and procedures to determine the binding of lexically scoped identifiers (for example, an identifier on the left-hand side of an assignment in a nested procedure can be global if it appears in the **global** statement of a surrounding context). This information is also used at printing time, so that the **global** statement contains exactly the global identifiers that were declared originally.

The lexical sequence (*lexical-seq*) field points to an expression sequence of links to identifiers in the surrounding scope, if any. The sequence consists of pairs of pointers. The first pointer of each pair is to the globally unique **NAME** of the identifier; this is needed at simplification and printing time. The second pointer is a pointer to a **LOCAL**, **PARAM**, or **LEXICAL** structure which is understood to be relative to the surrounding scope. When a module definition is evaluated, the lexical sequence is updated by replacing each of the second pointers with a pointer to the actual object represented. The name pointers are not modified, so that the actual identifier names are still available. The *lexical-seq* for a module contains entries for any surrounding-scope identifiers used by that module or by any procedures or modules contained within it.

The module name (*mod-name*) field points to the optional name of the module. If a module name is specified when the module is declared, the name appears there. If no module name is specified, this field will contain a value of **NULL**.

The *static local-seq* points to an expression sequence listing the local variables that were explicitly declared as :static. Each entry is a **NAME**. Within the module, static locals are referred to by **LOCAL** structures, the local variable number being the index into the *static local-seq* minus the number of nonstatic locals and exports. A static local shares its value among all instances of a class.

The *static export-seq* points to an expression sequence listing the exported module members declared as static. Each entry is a **NAME**. Within the module, exports are referred to by **LOCAL** structures, the local variable number being the number of elements in the *local-seq*, *static local-seq*, and *export-seq*, plus the index into the *static export-seq*.

The *static name-seq* stores the instances of the static locals and exports. It appears in the **MODDEF** structure as these static variables are shared among all modules with the same definition.

MODULE: Module Instance

MODULE	^export-seq	^mod-def	^local-seq

Maple syntax: none

Length: 4

Executing a module definition (**MODDEF**) results in a module instance. Each local or exported member of the module is instantiated and belongs to that instance of the module. The *export-seq* field points to an expression sequence of names of the instantiated exports (as opposed to the global names, as stored in the module definition). The *mod-def* field points back to the original module definition. The *local-seq* field points to an expression sequence of names of the instantiated local variables of the module.

NAME: Identifier

NAME	^assigned-expr	^attrib-expr	characters	characters	...

Maple syntax: name

Length: 4 or more

The *assigned-expr* field points to the assigned value of the name. If the name has no assigned value, this field is a null pointer (not a pointer to **NULL**). The next field points to an expression sequence of attributes of the name. If there are no attributes, this field points to the empty expression sequence (**NULL**). The remaining fields contain the characters that form the name, stored 4 or 8 for each machine word (for 32-bit and 64-bit architectures respectively). The last character is followed by a zero-byte. Any unused bytes in the last machine word are also zero. The maximum length of a name is 268,435,447 characters on 32-bit architectures and 34,359,738,351 characters on 64-bit architectures.

NEXT: Next Statement

NEXT

Maple syntax: **next**

Length: 1

NOT: Logical NOT

NOT	^expr

Maple syntax: **not expr**

Length: 2

OR: Logical OR

OR	^expr1	^expr2

Maple syntax: **expr1 or expr2**

Length: 3

PARAM: Procedure Parameter in an Expression

PARAM	integer

Maple syntax: **name**

Length: 2

This structure indicates a parameter when it appears in a procedure. The *integer* is an index into the procedure *param-seq*. Several special **PARAM** structures exist:

PARAM	0

This structure represents the Maple symbol **_npassed** (formerly **nargs**), the number of arguments passed when the procedure was called.

PARAM	-1

This structure represents the Maple symbol **_passed** (formerly **args**), the entire sequence of arguments passed when the procedure was called.

PARAM	-2

This structure represents the Maple symbol **procname**, referring to the currently active procedure.

PARAM	-3

This structure represents the Maple symbol **_nresults**, the number of results expected to be returned from the procedure.

PARAM	-4

This structure represents the Maple symbol **_params**, the sequence of declared positional arguments passed when the procedure was called.

PARAM	-5

This structure represents the Maple symbol **_nparams**, the number of declared positional arguments passed when the procedure was called.

PARAM	-6

This structure represents the Maple symbol **_rest**, the sequence of undeclared arguments passed when the procedure was called.

PARAM	-7

This structure represents the Maple symbol **_nrest**, the number of undeclared arguments passed when the procedure was called.

PARAM	-8

This structure represents the Maple symbol **_options**, the sequence of options in the procedure.

PARAM	-9

This structure represents the Maple symbol **_noptions**, the number of options in the procedure.

PARAM	-10

This structure represents the Maple symbol **thisproc**, referring to the instance of the currently active procedure.

At procedure execution time, the *integer* (if positive) is used as an index into the internal data structure **Actvparams**, which is part of the Maple procedure activation stack, and stores pointers to the values (which are also Maple structures) of the actual parameters passed to the procedure.

POLY: Multivariate Polynomials with Integer Coefficients

POLY	^indet_seq	m[i] degrees	m[i] coeff	m[i+1] degrees	m[i+1] coeff	...

Maple syntax:
```
newpoly := proc(a) proc()
 option builtin=sdmpoly;
 end proc("create",a) end proc;
newpoly(2*y^3+4*x*y+4);
```

Length: **2*(number of monomials) + 2**

This is an internal representation for multivariate polynomials of limited degree and integer coefficients.

Each degree word stores the total degree of the monomial and each individual degree. For example, **5*x^2*y^3** is a two-variable polynomial with total degree 5 and degree 2 on the x term, and degree 3 on the y term. The numbers 5, 2, and 3 are packed into a single *degree* word. The packing depends on the number of variables in the polynomial. Because the packing must fit in one word of memory, not all polynomials can be represented in this way. The most common polynomials can be stored in this data structure, which can be operated on efficiently.

Each coefficient word must be an integer data structure.

The *indet_seq* is the sequence of indeterminates that occur in the polynomial. The indeterminates must be simple **NAME**s.

The polynomial is always stored in one of three sorted orders.

- **PLEX**: Monomials are compared first by their degree in vars[1], with ties broken by degree in vars[2], and so on.
- **GRLEX**: Monomials are compared first by their total degree, with ties broken by degree of vars[i].
- **TDEG**: Monomials are compared first by their total degree, with ties broken by reverse lexicographic order, that is, by smallest degree in x[n], x[n-1], and so on.

POWER: Power

| POWER | ^expr1 | ^expr2 |

Maple syntax: expr1 ^expr2

Length: 3

This structure is used to represent a power when the exponent is not an integer, rational, or floating-point value. When the exponent is numeric, the **POWER** structure is converted to a length 3 **PROD** structure.

PROC: Procedure Definition

| PROC | ^param-seq | ^local-seq | ^option-seq | ^rem-table | ^stat-seq | ^desc-seq |
| ^global-seq | | ^lexical-seq | | ^eop | | ^return-type |

Maple syntax:
```
proc ( paramSeq ) :: returnType;
      description descSeq;
   local localSeq;
   export exportSeq;
   global globalSeq;
   option optionSeq;
   statSeq
end proc
```

Length: 10 or 11 (the return type is optional)

The *param-seq* points to an expression sequence describing the formal parameters of the procedure. Each entry is either a **NAME** or a **DCOLON** (which, in turn, contains a **NAME** and an expression specifying a type). Within the procedure, parameters are referred to by **PARAM** structures, the parameter number being the index into the *param-seq*.

The *local-seq* points to an expression sequence listing the explicitly and implicitly declared local variables. Each entry is a **NAME**. The explicitly declared variables appear first. Within the procedure, locals are referred to by **LOCAL** structures, the local variable number being the index into the *local-seq*.

The *option-seq* field points to an expression sequence of options to the procedure (for procedures, options are the same as attributes). Each entry is a **NAME** or **EQUATION** specifying an option. Commonly used options are **cache**, **operator**, and `Copyright ...`.

The *rem-table* field points to a hash table containing remembered values of the procedure. Entries in the table are indexed by the procedure arguments, and contain the resulting value. If there is no remember table, this field contains a pointer to **NULL**, which is the empty expression sequence.

The *stat-seq* field points to a single statement or a statement sequence (**STATSEQ**). If the procedure has an empty body, this is a pointer to **NULL** instead. For each procedure that is built into the kernel, there is a wrapper **PROC** that has the option **builtin** in its *option-seq*, and a single Maple integer pointed to by its *stat-seq*. The integer gives the built-in function number.

The *desc-seq* field points to an expression sequence of **NAME**s or **STRING**s. These are meant to provide a brief description of what the procedure does, and are displayed even when the **interface(verboseproc)** command is less than 2.

The *global-seq* field points to a list of the explicitly declared global variables in the procedure (those that appeared in the global statement). This information is never used at run time, but it is used when simplifying nested procedures to determine the binding of lexically scoped identifiers. For example, an identifier on the left-hand side of an assignment in a nested procedure can be global if it appears in the global statement of a surrounding procedure. This information is also used at procedure printing time, so that the **global** statement will contain exactly the same global identifiers that were declared in the first place.

The *lexical-seq* field points to an expression sequence of links to identifiers in the surrounding scope, if any. The sequence consists of pairs of pointers. The first pointer of each pair is to the globally unique **NAME** of the identifier; this is needed at simplification and printing time. The second pointer is a pointer to a **LOCAL**, **PARAM**, or **LEXICAL** structure which is understood to be relative to the surrounding scope. When a procedure is evaluated (not necessarily called), the *lexical-seq* is updated by replacing each of the second pointers with a pointer to the actual object represented. The name pointers are not modified, so that the actual identifier names are still available. The *lexical-seq* for a procedure contains entries for any surrounding-scope identifiers used by that procedure or by any procedures contained within it.

The *eop* field is **BINARY**. The first entry specifies the number of positional parameters of the procedure. The remaining entries, if any, specify the evaluation order permutation for the procedure (that is, an evaluation order for the arguments that is consistent with any dependencies among the parameter specifications).

The *return-type* field is present only if a return type has been specified for the procedure. A return type is an assertion about the type of the value returned by the procedure; if **kernelopts(assertlevel)** is set to 2, then this type is checked as the procedure returns.

PROD: Product, Quotient, Power

PROD	^expr1	^expon1	^expr2	^expon2	...	...

Maple syntax: **expr1 ^ expon1 * expr2 ^ expon2 ...**

Length: 2n + 1

This structure is interpreted as pairs of factors and their numeric exponents. Rational or integer expressions to an integer power are expanded. If a rational constant is in the product, this constant is moved to the first entry by the simplifier. A simple power, such as a^2, is represented as a **PROD** structure. More complex powers involving non-numeric exponents are represented as **POWER** structures.

RANGE: Range

RANGE	^expr1	^expr2

Maple syntax: **expr1 .. expr2**

Length: 3

RATIONAL: Rational

RATIONAL	^integer	^pos-integer

Maple syntax: **1/2**

Length: 3

This structure is one of the basic numeric objects in Maple. Note that this is not a division operation, but only a representation for rational numbers. Both fields must be integers (**INTPOS**, **INTNEG**, or an immediate integer) and the second must be positive.

READ: Read Statement

READ	^expr

Maple syntax: **read expr**

Length: 2

The Maple **read** statement. The expression must evaluate to either a string or symbol (**STRING** or **NAME** structure), and specifies the name of the file to read.

RETURN: Return Statement

RETURN	^expr-seq

Maple syntax: **return expr1, expr2, ...**

Length: 2

The Maple **return** statement. The expression sequence is evaluated, giving the value(s) to return.

RTABLE: Rectangular Table

RTABLE	^data	^maple-type	^index-func	^attrib	flags	num-elems
L_1	U_1	...	...	L_N	U_N	P_1	P_2	

Maple syntax: **rtable(...)**

Length: **2n + p** where **n** is the number of dimensions (0 to 63), and **p** is 0, 1, or 2, depending on the number of P_i parameters.

The *data* field points to either a block of memory (for dense and NAG-sparse **RTABLE**s), or to a **HASHTAB** structure (for Maple-sparse **RTABLE**s). The data block is either an object of type **BINARY**, or memory allocated directly from the storage manager of the operating system when the block is too large to be allocated as a Maple data structure. If the data block is a **BINARY** object, the *data* pointer points to the first data word, not to the object header.

The *maple-type* field points to a Maple structure specifying the data type of the elements of an **RTABLE** of Maple objects. If the **RTABLE** contains hardware objects, the *maple-type* field points to the Maple **NAME** anything.

The *index-func* field points to either an empty expression sequence (**NULL**), or an expression sequence containing at least one indexing function and a pointer to a copy of the **RTABLE** structure. The copy of the **RTABLE** is identical to the original structure, except that its *index-func* field refers to one less indexing function (either **NULL**, or another expression sequence containing at least one indexing function and a pointer to another copy of the **RTABLE** with one less indexing function again).

The *attrib* field points to an expression sequence of zero or more arbitrary attributes, which can be set by the **setattribute** command and queried by using the **attributes** command.

The *flags* field is a bit field containing the following subfields.

- data type - 5 bits - indicates that one of several hardware data types or a Maple data type (as specified by *maple-type*) is being used.
- subtype - 2 bits - indicates if the **RTABLE** is an Array, Matrix, or Vector.
- storage - 4 bits - describes the storage layout (for example, sparse, upper triangular, and so on)
- order - 1 bit - indicates C or Fortran ordering of **RTABLE** elements.
- read only - 1 bit - indicates that the **RTABLE** is to be read-only once created.
- foreign - 1 bit - indicates that the space pointed to by the *data* field does not belong to Maple, so Maple should not garbage collect it.

- eval - 1 bit - indicates if full evaluation should occur on lookup. For more information, refer to the **rtable_eval** help page.
- literal - 1 bit - optimization for internal type checking of data contained in an **RTABLE**.
- number of dimensions - 6 bits - the number of dimensions of the **RTABLE**, from 0 to 63.

The *num-elems* field indicates the total number of elements of storage allocated for the data. For a Maple-sparse **RTABLE**, *num-elems* is not used. For a NAG-sparse **RTABLE**, and for other formats that grown in size since initial allocation, *num-elems* specifies the number of elements currently allocated, some of which might not be in use.

The $L_i..U_i$ fields specify the upper and lower bounds of each dimension; they are stored directly as signed machine integers. The limits on bounds are -2,147,483,648 to 2,147,483,647 for 32-bit architectures and -9,223,372,036,854,775,808 to 9,223,372,036,854,775,807 for 64-bit architectures. The total number of elements cannot exceed the upper limit numbers either. Space is always reserved for at least 4 dimensions in case the rtable is redimensioned.

The remaining P_i fields refer to storage specific properties such as the number of bands above and below the diagonal and the number of elements that are sorted in NAG-sparse storage.

SAVE: Save Statement

SAVE	^expr-seq

Maple syntax: **save expr, expr, ...**

Length: 2

The Maple **save** statement. The expression sequence gives a list of names of objects to save, and either a file name or Maple library archive name (.mla) in which to save them. The file or library archive name can be specified as a **NAME** or **STRING**.

SDPOLY: Sparse Distributed Multivariate Polynomial

SDPOLY	^expr	^term_ordering	^coeff_domain	^coeff_1	exp_1	...	exp_n
...	...		^coeff_m	exp_1	...	exp_n	

Maple syntax: none

Length: For a polynomial of m terms with n variables, the length is $4 + m(n + 1)$

The *expr* entry stores the indeterminates of the polynomial (symbol for univariate cases or expression sequence of symbols for multivariate cases).

The *term_ordering* is either null or a pointer to a Maple procedure that is used to compare the *exponent_vector* to sort the polynomial terms. When *term_ordering* is null, lexicographic order is used to sort the polynomial terms.

The *coeff_domain* is either null or a pointer to a Maple module that is used to perform coefficient arithmetic (addition and multiplication). When *coeff_domain* is null, ordinary arithmetic is used. Each of the following **m** terms consists of a coefficient coeff_i (i=1..m) followed by an exponent_vector [exp_j] (j=1..n). Coefficient coeff_i is a non-zero Maple expression. Exponent_vector [exp_j] is an array of **n** hardware integers. Each integer stores the exponent of the corresponding indeterminate. By default, the polynomial terms are sorted by lexicographic order (that is, sorted by descending powers of indeterminate).

SERIES: Series

SERIES	^expr1	^expr2	integer	^expr3	integer	...	...

Maple syntax: none

Length: **2n + 2**

This is the internal representation of a series in Maple. There is no input syntax for a series; one can only be generated from a computation. The first expression has the general form **x-a**, where **x** denotes the variable of the series used to perform that expansion, and **a** denotes the point of expansion. The remaining entries are interpreted as pairs of coefficients and exponents. The exponents are integers, *not* pointers to integers or immediate integers. The exponents appear in increasing order. A coefficient **O(1)** (a function call to the function **O**, with parameter 1) is interpreted specially by Maple as an order term.

SET: Set

SET	^expr-seq	^attrib-expr

Maple syntax: { expr, expr, ... }

Length: 2 (or 3 with attributes)

The entries in the expression sequence of the set are sorted in a deterministic order. For details, see the **set** help page.

STATSEQ: Statement Sequence

STATSEQ	^stat1	^stat2	...

Maple syntax: **stat1; stat2; ...**

Length: 3 or more

This structure represents a sequence of two or more statements, and can be used wherever a single statement (for example, **ASSIGN**, **IF**, **FOR**) can appear. A statement sequence, containing only a single statement, is replaced by that statement. A statement sequence containing no statements is replaced by the empty expression sequence (**NULL**). Nested **STATSEQ** structures are flattened. All of the above transformations are made by the simplifier.

STOP: Quit Statement

STOP

Maple syntax: **quit**, **done**, or **stop**

Length: 1

STRING: Character String

STRING	reserved	^attrib-expr	characters	characters	...

Maple syntax: "This is a string"

Length: 4 or more

A Maple string is structurally similar to a **NAME**, except that it has no *assigned-value* field. The *attrib-expr* field points to an expression sequence of attributes of the string. If there are no attributes, this field points to the empty expression sequence (**NULL**). The remaining fields contain the characters that form the string, stored 4 or 8 per machine word (for 32-bit and 64-bit architectures respectively). The last character is followed by a zero-byte. Any unused bytes in the last machine word are also zero.

The maximum length of a string is 268,435,447 characters on 32-bit architectures and 34,359,738,351 characters on 64-bit architectures.

SUM: Sum, Difference

SUM	^expr1	^factor1	^expr2	^factor2	...	...

Maple syntax: **expr1 * factor1 + expr2 * factor2 ...**

Length: 2n + 1

This structure is interpreted as pairs of expressions and their numeric factors. Rational or integer expressions with an integer factor are expanded and the factor replaced with 1. If there is a rational constant in the sum, this constant is moved to the first entry by the simplifier. Simple products, such as **a*2**, are represented as **SUM** structures. More complex products involving non-numeric factors are represented as **PROD** structures.

TABLE: Table

| TABLE | ^index-func | ^array-bounds | ^hash-tab |

Maple syntax: N/A

Length: 4

This is a general table type, as created by the **table** and **array** commands in Maple. The *index-func* points to either a **NAME** or a **PROC**. For general tables, the *array-bounds* field points to the empty expression sequence (**NULL**). For **array**s (not to be confused with **Array**s, which are implemented as **RTABLE**s), the *array-bounds* field refers to an expression sequence of **RANGE**s of integers. The *hash-tab* field points to a **HASHTAB** structure containing the elements.

TABLEREF: Table Reference

| TABLEREF | ^name | ^expr-seq | ^attrib-expr |

Maple syntax: **name [expr]**

Length: 3 (or 4 with attributes)

This data structure represents a table reference, or indexed name. The *name* entry follows the same rules as for **ASSIGN**, or it may be a **TABLE** or **MODULE** structure. (The parser will not generate a **TABLEREF** with a **TABLE** structure for the *name* entry, but this can occur internally.) The expression sequence contains the indices.

TRY: Try Statement

| TRY | ^try-stat-seq | ^catch-str | ^catch-stat-seq | ... | ... | ^final-stat-seq |

Maple syntax:
```
try tryStat
    catch "catchStr": catchStat
    ...
    finally finalStat;
end try
```

Length: 3 or more

This structure represents a **try** statement, and can have an arbitrary length, depending on how many **catch** blocks are contained within it, and whether it has a **finally** block. The *catch-strs* point to the catch string of the corresponding **catch** block. If no catch string is specified, the *catch-str* points to **NULL**. Empty *catch-stat-seqs* are also represented by pointers to **NULL**, as is an empty (but present) **finally** block.

The actual internal tag used for the **TRY** structure is **MTRY** to prevent collision with a macro defined by some C exception handling libraries.

UNEVAL: Unevaluated Expression

UNEVAL	^expr

Maple syntax: **'expr'**

Length: 2

USE: Use Statement

USE	^bindings	^statseq

Maple Syntax:

```
use bindings in
 statseq
end use
```

Length: 3

The *bindings* component points to an expression sequence of equations whose left-hand sides are symbols, and the *statseq* component points to a sequence of statements that form the body of the **use** statement. The right-hand sides of the binding equations can be arbitrary expressions.

The **use** statement introduces a new binding contour and binds the names that appear on the left-hand side of the equations in *bindings*. For convenience, on input, a module **'m'** can appear among the *bindings*, and is treated as if it were the sequence $e1 = m\text{:-}e1, e2 = m\text{:-}e2, \ldots$, where the ei are the exports of **'m'**. Within the sequence *statseq* of statements, the symbols appearing on the left-hand side of the equations in *bindings* are bound to the corresponding right-hand sides. The previous bindings of those symbols are restored upon exit from the **use** statement. Bindings are resolved during automatic simplification.

XOR: Logical Exclusive-Or

XOR	^expr1	^expr2

Maple syntax: **expr1 xor expr2**

Length: 3

ZPPOLY: Polynomials with Integer Coefficients modulo n

ZPPOLY	^indet	mod	coef0	coef1	...
ZPPOLY	^indet_seq	mod	^zppoly0	^zppoly1	...

Maple syntax: **modp1(ConvertIn(expr, indet), n);**

Maple syntax: **modp2(ConvertIn(expr, indet1, indet2), n);**

Length: **degree(zppoly) + 2** (for the zero polynomial)

Length: **degree(zppoly) + 3** (otherwise)

This is the internal representation of univariate and bivariate polynomials modulo some integer. The **modp1()** and **modp2()** front ends provide a suite of functions to work on this data structure operating in the domain of polynomials in one or two variables with integer coefficients modulo n, written Z_n_x or $Z\_\_n[x,y]$, respectively. *indet_seq* is an expression sequence of the indeterminates of the polynomial: (x), or (x,y). *mod* is the integer modulus of the integer domain. In a univariate polynomial, the coefficients are stored in the following order.

(coef0*indet^0 + coef1*indet^1 + ... + coefi*indet^i) mod n

A bivariate polynomial contains pointers to univariate ZPPOLY structures representing the coefficients of the first indeterminate.

(coef0(indet2)*indet1^0 + coef1(indet2)*indet1^1 + ...) mod n

where each **coefi** is a univariate polynomial in **indet1** mod n.

All coefficients are stored, including zero coefficients. The leading coefficient is always non-zero.

A.4 Hashing in Maple

An important factor in achieving the overall efficient performance of Maple is the use of hash table-based algorithms for critical functions. Tables are used in both simplification and evaluation, as well as for less critical functions. For simplification, Maple keeps a single copy of each expression, or subexpression, during a session. This is done by keeping all objects in a table. In procedures, the **cache** and **remember** options specify that the result of each computation of the procedure is to be stored in a *remember table* associated with the procedure. Finally, tables are available to the user as one of the Maple data types.

All table searching is done by hashing. Three types of hash tables are available: basic, dynamic, and cache. Basic hash tables are used for most Maple hashing. They are automatically promoted to dynamic hash tables when they are filled with a large number of elements. Dynamic hash tables are designed to work with a large number of elements. Cache tables are a type of hash table that store only *recently* inserted items.

Basic Hash Tables

The algorithm used for the basic hash tables is direct chaining, except that the chains are dynamic vectors instead of the typical linked lists. The two data structures used to implement hash tables are **HASHTAB** and **HASH**.

Hash Table

HASHTAB	^hash-chain1	^hash-chain2	...

Maple syntax: none

Length: $2^n + 1$

This is an internal data structure with no Maple syntax equivalent. It is used in the representation of tables within Maple. Each entry points to a hash chain (a **HASH** structure), or is a null pointer if no entry has been created in that hash chain yet (that is, with that entry location as its hash value). The size of a **HASHTAB** structure depends on the type of table and the platform, but is always a power of 2 plus one.

Hash Chain

HASH	key	^expr1	key	^expr2	...	...

Maple syntax: none

Length: $2n + 1$

Each table element is stored as a pair of consecutive entries in a hash bucket vector. The first entry of this pair is the hash key, and the second is a pointer to a stored value. In some cases (for example, procedure remember tables and user-defined tables), the key is also a pointer. In other cases, the key is a hashed value (for example, the simplification table, the symbol table). The key cannot have the value zero (or the null pointer) since this is used to indicate the bottom of the bucket.

Dynamic Hash Tables

The Maple dynamic hash table is a complicated data structure. a brief overview is presented here.

Instead of using a flat, fixed-length directory, Maple dynamic hash tables use a tree structure with contiguous bits from the hash key to select a child. A child of a directory can be a subdirectory or a hash chain. For example, a top-level directory may use the first 10 bits to index 1024 children. One of its children may be a directory that uses, for example, the next 8 bits of the key to index 256 children.

A hash chain in a dynamic table stores elements using key value pairs (in the same way that a hash chain does in a basic hash table). The first n bits of the keys in a hash chain are identical, where n is the number of bits required to locate the hash chain. The remaining bits are arbitrary. Using the example in the previous paragraph, the elements of a hash chain that is a child of the directory with 256 children have hash keys that are identical in the first 18 bits.

When a hash chain with unused bits overflows, it is split into two. This may require creating a subdirectory with two children or doubling the size of the hash chain's parent directory. In either case, another bit from the hash key is introduced for indexing. This bit is used to divide the elements of the old chain into the two new chains. If the hash chain has no unused bits for indexing, the chain grows as needed. This growth occurs only if many elements are inserted with identical hash keys.

Cache Hash Tables

Cache tables have two classes of entries: permanent and temporary. Each bucket in the table has 4 entries reserved as temporary, followed by a pointer to a variable-sized chain.

Permanent entries, as designated by the way they are inserted, are stored exclusively in the variable-sized chain, which can grow as needed.

Temporary entries are inserted in the normal way you would include a value in a basic hash table or remember table. These are hashed to identify the bucket in which they are to be stored. The existing entries in that bucket are pushed right by one, and the new entry is put in the leading, "most-recent" spot. Reinserting an expression will cause it to be promoted to the "most-recent" spot. Inserting a fifth element that hashes to the same bucket will cause the least recently inserted temporary element to be removed from the table.

The maximum size of the cache table can be specified at creation time. Because cache tables have a maximum size, and because as new elements are added old ones may be removed, the cache table does not grow continuously as values are added. When used as a remember table, they are useful for temporarily storing elements that were recently computed, and likely to be needed again. Over time, as more elements are inserted, the old elements will be discarded.

Cache tables can be created by using the **Cache** command, or as a remember table in a procedure with the **cache** option specified. The advantage of using a cache table over standard remember tables is that a cache table has a maximum size. This means that a cache table does not act as a memory trap, storing a large number of values that cannot be reclaimed by the garbage collector. As cache tables allow permanent elements to be added, they can be used in procedures that cannot use option system remember tables.

The Simplification Table

The most important table maintained by the Maple kernel is the *simplification table*. All simplified expressions and subexpressions are stored in the simplification table. The main purpose of this table is to ensure that simplified expressions have a unique instance in memory. Every expression which is entered into Maple or generated internally is checked against the simplification table. If it is found in the simplification table, the new expression is discarded and the old one (the one in the simplification table) is used. This task is done by the simplifier, which recursively simplifies (applies all the basic simplification rules) and checks against the table. The garbage collector deletes the entries in the simplification table that cannot be reached from a global name or from a live local variable.

The task of checking for equivalent expressions within thousands of subexpressions would not be feasible if it were not done with the aid of hashing. Every expression is entered in the simplification table using its signature as a key. The signature of an expression is a hashing function itself, with one important attribute: signatures of trivially equivalent expressions are equal. For example, the signatures of the expressions **a+b+c** and **c+a+b** are identical; the signatures of **a*b** and **b*a** are also identical. If the signatures of two expressions disagree, the expressions cannot be equal at the basic level of simplification.

In Maple 13, the use of the basic and dynamic hash tables as the data structure behind the simplification table was phased out in favor of a new structure that worked better in a multithreaded environment. In particular, the new table guarantees atomic inserts. This removed the need for locking, and, because the simplification table is used so often, greatly improved performance when running many threads.

Searching for an expression in the simplification table is done by:

- Simplifying recursively all of its components
- Applying the basic simplification rules
- Computing its signature and searching for this signature in the table

If the signature is found, then a full comparison is performed (taking into account that additions and multiplications are commutative) to verify that it is the same expression. If the expression is found, the one in the table is used and the searched one is discarded. A full comparison of expressions has to be performed only when there is a collision of signatures.

Since simplified expressions are guaranteed to have a unique occurrence, it is possible to test for equality of simplified expressions using a single pointer comparison. Unique representation of identical expressions is significant for the efficiency of tables, and therefore the **remember** option. Also, since the relative order of objects is preserved during garbage collection, sequences of objects can be ordered by machine address. For example, sets containing mutable objects are represented this way. The set operations, such as union or intersection, can be done in linear time by merging sorted sequences. Sorting by machine address is also available by using the **sort** command.

The Name Table

The simplest use of hashing in the Maple kernel is the *name table*. This is a symbol table for all of the global names. Each key is computed from the character string of the name and the entry is a pointer to the data structure for the name. The name table is used to locate global names formed by the lexical scanner or by name concatenation. It is also used by functions that perform operations on all global names. These operations include:

- Marking for garbage collection
- Saving a Maple session environment in a file
- The Maple commands **anames** and **unames**, which return all assigned and unassigned global names, respectively

Remember Tables

A remember table is a hash table in which the argument(s) to a procedure call are stored as the table index, and the result of the procedure call is stored as the table value. Because a simplified expression in Maple has a unique instance in memory, the address of the arguments can be used as the hash function. Therefore, searching a remember table is very fast.

Several kernel functions use remember tables including **evalf**, **series**, **divide**, **normal**, **expand**, **diff**, **readlib**, and **frontend**. The functions **evalf**, **series**, and **divide** are handled internally in a special way for the following reasons:

- **evalf** and **series** need to store some additional environment information (**'Digits'** for evalf and **'Order'** for series). Consequently, the entries for these are extended with the precision information. If a result is requested with the same or less precision than what is stored in the table, the table value is retrieved and rounded. If a result is produced with more precision than what is stored, it is stored in the table, replacing the lower precision value.

- **evalf** remembers only function calls (this includes named constants); it does not remember the results of arithmetic operations.

- If a division operation succeeds and the divisor is a nontrivial polynomial, the **divide** function stores the quotient in its remember table. Otherwise, no value is stored in the remember table.

If **option remember** is specified together with **option system**, at garbage collection time, the remember table entries which refer to expressions no longer in use elsewhere in the system are removed. This provides a relatively efficient use of remembering that does not waste storage for expressions that have disappeared from the expression space. As garbage collection time can be unpredictable, cache remember tables provide an alternate approach similar to option system, by remembering only the most recently computed results.

Maple Language Arrays and Tables

Tables and arrays are provided as data types in the Maple language through the **table** and **array** commands.

Note: Unlike the **array** command, the **Array** command creates a rectangular table, which is described in the following subsection. An array is a table for which the component indices must be integers within specified bounds. Tables and arrays are implemented using the Maple internal hash tables. Because of this, sparse arrays are equally as efficient as dense arrays. A table object consists of the following.

- Index bounds (for arrays only)
- A hash table of components
- An indexing function

The components of a table **T** are accessed using a subscript syntax (for example, **T[a,b*cos(x)]**). Since a simplified expression is guaranteed to have a unique instance in memory, the address of the simplified index is used as the hash key for a component. If no component exists for a given index, then the indexed expression is returned.

The semantics of indexing into a table are described by its indexing function. Aside from the default, general indexing, some indexing functions are provided by the Maple kernel. Other indexing functions are loaded from the library or are supplied by the user.

Maple Language Rectangular Tables

Rectangular tables (as implemented by the **RTABLE** structure) can use a variety of storage formats. One format, Maple-sparse, is identical to that used in tables and arrays, namely a hash table. For Matrices, there is another sparse format, NAG-sparse, which uses one vector for each dimension to record indices, and one more vector to record the values of the entries. Most **RTABLE** storage formats are dense, the simplest being the rectangular format. Other dense formats include upper-triangular and band, where storage is allocated only for the upper triangle or a band of elements respectively. To the user, rectangular tables appear as objects of type **Array**, **Matrix**, **Vector[row]**, and **Vector[column]**. Note that an **Array** is not the same as an **array**. For more information, refer to the **Array** and **array(deprecated)** help pages.

Portability

The Maple kernel and the command-line interface are not associated with any one operating system or hardware architecture. The Maple kernel is designed to be portable to any system which supports a C compiler, a flat address space, and a 32-bit or 64-bit word size. Refer to the **Install.html** file on your product installation disc for a list of currently supported operating system versions.

Most of the source code comprising the kernel is the same across all platforms. Extensive use of macros and conditional compilation take care of platform dependencies, such as word size, byte ordering, storage alignment requirements, differences in hardware floating point support, and sometimes, C compiler bugs.

The Maple library is interpreted by the Maple kernel. Therefore, other than issues such as maximum object size, it is completely independent of the underlying architecture.

The Standard worksheet graphical user interface is implemented in Java, which is platform-independent. This includes custom GUI features such as embedded components and Maplets.

Index

Symbols
!, 33
#, 33
& operator, 110
.. operator, 110
1-D output, 361
2-D math, 379
2-D output, 361
:, 331
:-, 69, 316
:: operator, 114
:= operator, 3
?, 33
?[], 64
@ operator, 108
@@ operator, 108
[], 32
{}, 32
~, 19

A
altering plot structures, 447
animations
    3-D with viewpoint options, 473
    plots:-animate command, 471
anyfunc type, 125
argument
    definition, 199
Arrays
    applying a function to contents, 156
    automatic resizing, 152
    copying, 154
    creating, 148
    getting bounds, 154
    getting number of elements, 153
    numeric, 157
    testing for equality, 155
arrow notation, 255
assignment operator, 3, 45
automatic resizing
    Arrays, 152
automatic simplification, 51

B
backslash, 26, 29, 33
braces
    forming sets, 32
breakpoints, 584
    explicit, 595
        removing, 597
    removing, 595
built-in commands, 8

C
case-sensitivity in Maple, 22
code generation
    defining new translators, 537
    intermediate code, 536
    printing phase, 537
    translation process, 532
CodeTools:-Profiling:-LoadProfiles, 623
CodeTools:-Profiling:-PrintProfiles, 621
CodeTools:-Profiling:-Profile, 620
CodeTools:-Profiling:-SaveProfiles, 623
CodeTools:-Profiling:-SortBy, 621
colon, 2, 30, 173
comma
    forming expression sequence, 32
command-line interface, 517
comments, 7
Complex constructor, 60
complex numbers, 278
    evalc command, 63
    Re and Im commands, 62
concatenation
    names, 25
    strings, 25
connectivity
    CAD applications, 541
    Excel, 542
    TCP/IP sockets, 530

constants
    special, 46
    symbolic, 46, 279
copying Arrays, 154
copying tables, 146
creating
    Arrays, 148
    efficient programs, 623
        displaying time and memory statistics, 618
        profiling a procedure, 620
    lists, 130
    queues, 164
    records, 159
    sets, 136
    tables, 141
creating plot structures, 446
customizing plots
    axes and gridlines, 462
    colors, 452
    controlling sampling, 449
    coordinate systems, 464
    setting options, 468
    typesetting, 461
    view option, 458

D

DAG, 33
data structures
    Arrays, 148
    converting, 158
    filtering elements, 158
    immutable, 139
    lists, 130
    mutable, 157
    queues, 164
    records, 159
    sets, 136
    tables, 141
    types, 442
data types, 37
    internal representation, 635
debugging

breakpoints, 584, 594
    explicit breakpoints, 595
    numbering statements, 583
    removing watchpoints, 591
    viewing the debugging process status, 587
    watchpoints, 589, 598
definition
    argument, 199
    function call, 199
delaying evaluation, 31, 48
detecting errors, 591
    checking syntax, 617
    handling exceptions, 615
        raising exceptions, 615
    tracing a procedure, 609
    using assertions, 612
dismantle command, 38
DLL, 515, 529
DocumentTools:-Do command, 492
DocumentTools:-GetProperty command, 491
DocumentTools:-SetProperty command, 492
dot character, 86
double colon operator, 114
double quotes
    displaying a text string, 2, 27

E

embedded components
    adding to document, 487
    DocumentTools:-Do command, 492
    DocumentTools:-GetProperty command, 491
    DocumentTools:-SetProperty command, 492
    editing component properties, 488
    programming, 491
    retrieving and updating component properties, 491
equality
    records, 160
error statement handling, 189
escape characters, 33
eval command, 9, 121

difference between eval and subs, 121
evalc command, 63
evalf command, 287
evalhf command, 291
evalindets command, 122
evaluating expressions, 119
evaluation
    delaying, 31, 48
evaluation rules, 9, 34, 159, 168, 317, 528
    tables, 145
exception handling, 189
expand command, 107
expression sequence, 32
expression statements, 174
expressions
    converting to strings, 28
    evaluating and simplifying, 119
    grouping terms, 31
    rational, 81
    set-theoretic, 104
    tree form, 38
    union, 106
exprofile command, 624
extended numeric, 277
external functions, 529
    calling, 518
    calling mechanism, 526
    specifying parameter types, 520
    translating, 518
    wrappers, 526
extracting data from tables, 145

F

file input and output
    files used by Maple, 374
    general files, 367
        FileTools package, 369
        Maple I/O library, 367
    importing and exporting numerical data, 372
    introductory concepts, 366
floating-point numbers
    catastrophic cancellation, 283
    Digits, 282
    hardware, 276
    IEEE 754, 286
    precision, 282
    representation, 280
    software, 274
floats
    exponent, 57
    hardware, 57
    Maple_floats command, 57
    significand, 57
    software, 57
flow of control, 634
for loop, 136, 230
    debugging
        next command, 586
        step command, 586
    ModuleIterator procedure, 321
    scoping rules, 223
format strings, 377
fprintf command, 378
fractions
    denom command, 56
    Fraction constructor, 56
    numer command, 56
fscanf command, 378
full evaluation, 9
function call, 70, 200
    definition, 199
function type, 125

G

garbage collection, 325, 626
global variables
    modules, 314
    procedures, 200
Grid computing toolbox, 578
Grid programming
    communicating between nodes, 569
        Launch command, 569
        Receive command, 570
        Send command, 570
Grid-based computation

670 • Index

starting, 568

H

hash tables, 660
hashing in Maple, 659
    Arrays and Tables, 664
    basic hash tables, 660
    cache hash tables, 661
    dynamic hash tables, 660
    name table, 663
    portability, 664
    rectangular Tables, 664
    remember tables, 663
    simplification table, 662
help databases, 375
HFloat
    constructor, 59
hfloat
    option, 298

I

Im command, 62
imaginary unit
    changing default, 63
in operator, 104
indets command, 126
indexed expression
    extracting individual elements, 64
indexed expressions constructor, 64
indexing
    mathematical, 149
    negative, 150
    programmer, 149
indices function, 145
    nolist option, 145
infinity, 277
input and output
    interactive input, 366
    interactive output, 364
    with files
        files used by Maple, 374

files used by Maple,help databases, 375
files used by Maple,internal format files, 375
files used by Maple,library archives, 375
files used by Maple,Maple language files, 374
files used by Maple,Maplet files, 375
files used by Maple,worksheet files, 375
general files, 367
general files,FileTools package, 369
general files,Maple I/O library, 367
importing and exporting numerical data, 372
introductory concepts, 366
worksheet
    interfaces, 363
integers
    determining length, 55
    GMP, 272
    immediate, 271
    signed, 55
interactive input
    worksheet, 366
interactive output
    worksheet, 364
interface command, 363
    variables
        echo, 198
        imaginaryunit, 63
        prettyprint, 363
        rtablesize, 363
        typesetting, 379
        verboseproc, 10
        version, 363
interfaces
    worksheet input and output, 363
internal format files, 375
internal representation
    data types, 635
        assignment statement, 636

Index • 671

binary object, 636
break statement, 636
character string, 656
communications control structure, 637
complex value, 637
debug, 637
difference, 656
equation, 638
error statement, 638
expression sequence, 638
for loop statement, 639
foreign data, 640
function call, 640
garbage, 640
hardware float, 641
identifier, 647
if statement, 641
less than, 643
less than or equal, 643
lexically scoped variables, 643
list, 644
local variables, 644
logical AND, 635
logical IMPLIES, 641
logical NOT, 647
logical OR, 647
logical XOR, 658
module definition, 644
module instance, 646
module member, 644
multivariate polynomials with integer coefficients, 649
name concatenation, 636
negative integer, 642
Next statement, 647
not equal, 642
polynomials with integer coefficients modulo n, 658
positive integer, 642
Power, 650
procedure definition, 650
procedure parameters, 647
product, 651

quit statement, 656
quotient, 651
range, 652
read statement, 652
rectangular table, 653
return statement, 652
save statement, 654
series, 655
set, 655
software float, 639
sparse distributed multivariate polynomial, 654
statement sequence, 655
sum, 656
table, 657
table reference, 657
test for equality, 638
test for inequality, 642
try statement, 657
type specification, 637
unevaluated expressions, 658
use statement, 658
while loop statement, 639
interrupt a Maple computation, 11
   command-line, 12
   hard interrupt, 12
   worksheet
      interrupt icon, 12
      stop icon, 12
intersect operator, 106

K

kernel, 1
kernelopts
   maxdigits, 55

L

last name evaluation, 9, 102, 145, 245, 263
left single quotes
   forming names, 22
library archives, 375
line continuation character, 29

lists, 130
    accessing data stored in, 131
    creating, 130
    nested, 130
local variables, 6
    modules, 315
loops
    commands, 186

M

macro definitions, 390
map command, 135
Maple character set, 17
Maple debugger, 591
    command-line, 582
    debugger commands, 585
    debugger prompt, 584
    interactive, 582
    starting, 584
    stopping, 591
    syntax rules, 608
Maple internal functions
    algebraic functions, 634
    algebraic service functions, 634
    data structure manipulation functions, 634
    evaluators, 633
    general service functions, 634
Maple keywords, 18
Maple language files, 374
Maple library, 1
Maple library archive, 387
Maple library commands
    printing, 10
Maple preprocessor, 390
Maple types, 37
Maple User Interface, 1
MapleNet, 505
    Java API, 506
    JSP API, 506
Maplet files, 375
Matrix
    creating, 32
maximum number of digits, 55

member function, 133
member selection, 69, 316
members
    exported, 347
    local, 347
memory
    clearing, 12
methods, 349
module definitions
    body, 311
    declaring statements, 314
    implicit scoping rules, 325
    lexical scoping rules, 326
    named modules, 312
    parameters, 311
    syntax, 311
ModuleIterator procedure, 321
modules
    exports, 316
    members, 316
    options, 320

N

name tables, 663
names, 3, 22
    equality of, 44
    multiple assignment, 175
    unassigning, 51
    with blank spaces, 22
    with international characters, 22
nested lists, 130
nolist option
    indices function, 145
nprintf command, 378
numelems command, 134
numeric types, 271

O

object oriented programming
    class
        creating new, 348
        introduction, 347

members
    definition, 347
methods, 349
    calling, 349
    static vs non-static, 349
modules
    definition, 347
objects, 348
    definition, 347
    indexed function calls, 350
    special methods, 350
op command, 36, 131, 137
OpenMaple, 515
operators
    &, 110
    .., 110
    :-, 69
    ::, 114
    @, 108
    @@, 108
    addition, 72
    arithmetic, 3
    binary, 19
    division, 76
    element-wise, 19
    if, 180
    in, 104
    intersect, 106
    member selection, 69
    multiplication, 76
    set-theoretic, 104
    subtraction, 72
    unary, 19
    union, 105

P

packages, 320, 383
    exports, 384
    organizing, 392
    saving, 387
packed records, 161
parallel programming
    mutex, 554
    sharing data, 553
parameter
    definition, 199
plot library, 431
    combining plots, 421
        generating plot array, 422
        merging plots, 421
    generating plots, 404
        expression and operator forms, 405
        parametric form, 411
    other packages, 429
    plotting points, 415
    plotting polygons, 417
    specialty plots, 423
    text on plots, 419
plot structures
    altering, 447
    creating, 446
plots
    animate command, 471
    generating, 402
    programming with, 439
plots:-animate command, 471
prettyprinting, 366
print
    defining custom printing, 366
printf command, 375
procedure call, 8
procedure definition, 4
procedures
    adding comments, 7
    declaring parameters
        parameter modifiers, 208
    defining, 4
    invocation, 8
    maintainable code, 252
        adding comments, 253
        formatting procedures for readability, 252
    options
        cache, 219
    syntax, 6
profiling a procedure, 620

programming
    with plots, 439
protected names, 47

Q

queues
    creating, 164
    dequeue, 165
    enqueue, 165
quit statement, 196
quotes
    double, 2, 27
    left single, 22
    right single, 31

R

rational numbers, 273
Re command, 62
read statement, 197
records, 333
    creating, 159
    equality, 160
remember tables, 663
restart command, 12
return statement, 189
right single quotes
    delaying evaluation, 31
rtables, 148

S

save statement, 197
scanf command, 375
selection operation, 131, 142, 317
semicolon, 2, 30, 173
separating statements, 30
sequence, 32
setattribute command, 118
sets, 32, 136
    accessing data stored in, 138
    arithmetic, 137
setting time limit on computations, 625
SFloat

constructor, 58
simplifying expressions, 119
sort command, 135
specfunc type, 125
special characters, 17
special methods, 350
    ModuleApply, 350
    ModuleCopy, 350
    ModuleDeconstruct, 350
    ModuleIterator, 350
    ModuleLoad, 350
    ModulePrint, 350
    ModuleType, 350
    ModuleUnload, 350
sprintf command, 378
square brackets, 32
    and braces, 32
sscanf command, 378
stacks
    creating, 161
    popping, 162
    pushing, 162
strings, 2, 27
    concatenation, 25
    length, 24
    mutability, 26
    parsing, 27
    searching, 25
StringTools package, 378
StringTools:-StringBuffer command, 26
structured types, 34, 123
sub-Array access, 151
subexpressions
    substituting, 120
subs command, 121
    difference between eval and subs, 121
subsindets command, 122
subsop command, 120
substituting subexpressions, 120
substrings
    extracting, 24

T

table indexing, 142
tables
    applying a function to contents, 147
    checking index, 144
    copying, 146
    creating, 141
    evaluation rules, 145
    extracting data, 145
    getting number of elements, 144
    removing an element from, 143
testing code
    test coverage, 629
    verifying results, 627
    writing good tests, 629
timelimit command, 625
tracing a procedure, 609
try statement, 189
type checking, 34
type command, 47
typeset math, 379
typesetting package, 380

interactive output, 364
interfaces, 363

U

undefined, 277
unevaluation quotes, 31, 48
union operator, 105
UnProfile command, 623
use statement, 339

V

Vector
    creating, 32
verify command, 627
viewing help pages, 2

W

web services, 504
white space characters, 28
worksheet files, 375
worksheet input and output
    interactive input, 366